TEXTBOOK

Obligations:
CONTRACT LAW

FOURTH EDITION

D G CRACKNELL
LLB, of the Middle Temple, Barrister

OLD BAILEY PRESS

OLD BAILEY PRESS
at Holborn College, Woolwich Road,
Charlton, London SE7 8LN

First published 1997
Fourth edition 2003
Reprinted 2004

ISBN 1 85836 502 3

British Library Cataloguing-in-Publication.
A CIP Catalogue record for this book is
available from the British Library.

Acknowledgement
The publishers and author would
like to thank the Incorporated
Council of Law Reporting for
England and Wales for kind
permission to reproduce extracts
from the Weekly Law Reports, and
Butterworths for their kind
permission to reproduce extracts
from the All England Law Reports.

Printed and bound in Great Britain

Contents

9 Capacity *157*

Introduction – Minors – Necessaries – Voidable contracts – The Minors' Contracts Act 1987 – Liability of a party contracting with a minor – Liability of a minor in tort – Restitution – Mentally disordered persons – Persons who are drunk – Partnerships – Corporations

10 Mistake *170*

Introduction – Types of mistake – Mutual mistake – Unilateral mistake – Non est factum – Mistake in equity – Common law and equity considered

11 Duress and Undue Influence *217*

Introduction – The common law doctrine of duress – The equitable rules of undue influence – The limited, and now suspect, principle of inequality of bargaining power – The protection afforded by certain statutory provisions

12 Privity of Contract *236*

Introduction – Privity and consideration – Circumstances falling outside the rule – Attempts to impose liabilities on third parties (prior to the Contracts (Rights of Third Parties) Act 1999) – Attempts to impose benefits on third parties (prior to the Contracts (Rights of Third Parties) Act 1999) – Creation of a benefit by equity – Section 56 Law of Property Act 1925 – Remedies of the contracting party – Statutory exceptions – The Contracts (Rights of Third Parties) Act 1999

13 Illegality *251*

Introduction – Contracts which break the law – Contracts contrary to public policy – Covenants in restraint of trade – Enforcement of illegal contracts – Severance – Recovery of money or property paid or transferred under an illegal contract – Collateral agreements

14 Frustration *284*

Introduction – Initial development of the doctrine – Tests for frustration – Examples of frustration – Scope of the doctrine – Effects of frustration

15 Discharge of the Contract – Performance, Agreement and Breach *297*

Introduction – Performance: the general rule – Modification of the general rule – Stipulations as to time of performance – Agreements – Bilateral discharge – Unilateral discharge – Breach

16 Remedies for Breach of Contract – Damages *315*

Introduction – Damages – Remoteness of damage – Causation – Measure of damages – Type of damage recoverable – Mitigation of damages – Liquidated damages clauses – Deposit and part payment – Action for an agreed sum

17 Remedies for Breach of Contract – Equitable Remedies *353*

Specific performance: introduction – When damages are an inadequate remedy – Factors considered in awarding specific performance – Particular contracts – Specific performance and third parties – Injunction: introduction – Types of injunction – Damages in lieu of specific performance or injunction

Preface

Old Bailey Press textbooks are written specifically for students. Whatever their course they will find our books clear and concise, providing comprehensive and up-to-date coverage. Written by specialists in their field, our textbooks are reviewed and updated on a regular basis. A companion 150 Leading Cases, Revision WorkBook and Cracknell's Statutes are also published.

The *Obligations: Contract Law* textbook is designed for use by any undergraduates who have Contract Law within their syllabus. It will be equally useful for all CPE/LLDip students who must study Contract Law as one of their 'core' subjects.

Knowledge of recent cases is extremely important for those studying for their examinations. It demonstrates not only an active interest in the law as it develops, but also the dynamic nature of the law which is constantly adapting to changing social and economic trends.

This edition covers many recent cases, including decisions of the House of Lords in *Bank of Credit and Commerce International SA* v *Ali* [2001] 1 All ER 961 (construction of release), *Royal Bank of Scotland* v *Etridge (No 2)* [2001] 4 All ER 449 (lender's duty to surety wife) and *Farley* v *Skinner* [2001] 4 All ER 801 (damages for loss of peace and quiet). Court of Appeal decisions noted include *Great Peace Shipping Ltd* v *Tsavliris Salvage (International) Ltd, The Great Peace* [2002] 4 All ER 689 (common mistake) and *Sandeman Coprimar SA* v *Transitos y Transportes Integrales SL* (2003) The Times 13 February (collateral contracts).

Attention is also drawn to the Sale and Supply of Goods to Consumers Regulations 2002 which make signigicant amendments to the law in this field and create new rights in relation to consumer guarantees.

Account has been taken of developments up to 28 February 2003.

Table of Cases

Table of Statutes and Other Materials

1

Introduction

1.1 The problems of studying the law of contract

1.2 Definitions

1.3 Historical development and the theories underlying contract

1.4 Overlap with other legal topics

1.5 Methods of studying the law of contract

1.1 The problems of studying the law of contract

A number of problems arise in the study of any legal topic. In the case of contract law there are four basic problems in particular.

1. Concepts and terminology are specific. It is often not so much that terms used are strange or highly technical, but that there are ordinary everyday words or phrases which may have some specific definition in a contractual context.
2. There are large numbers of cases. The general principles of contract law are still, to a large extent, judge made. That is to say, the rules were formulated by the courts over a lengthy period of time. Even now, there are comparatively few statutes governing contractual law.
3. Contract law tends to overlap with other areas, in particular, with tort and property law.
4. The twentieth century has seen the development of a number of 'specialist' areas, such as contracts of employment and shipping or insurance contracts. Often these subjects are really not much affected at all by ordinary contractual rules and, instead, are governed by legislation specially enacted for the purpose. Normally, a student will never really need to come into contact with these topics at all, but it can be quite confusing if he or she stumbles on, say, a contract of employment case which he reads about in the paper and tries to fit it into what he knows of ordinary common law rules of contract. While it is important to recognise that such specialised fields of contract exist, with one or two exceptions, they really have no great importance or relevance for a student embarking on a study of the law of contract.

(As to those exceptions, see, for example, Chapter 20.)

Items 1–3 will be examined more closely in the following paragraphs.

1.2 Definitions

It is notoriously difficult to define very generalised concepts like 'a contract'. It is perhaps an oversimplification to say that it is a 'legally enforceable agreement', but if we look at some standard definitions, we see that this is a common theme.

Thus, in Treitel:

> 'A contract is an agreement giving rise to obligations which are enforced or recognised by the law. The factor which distinguishes contractual from other legal obligations is that they are based on the agreement of the contracting parties.'

And Anson:

> 'We may provisionally describe the law of contract as that branch of the law which determines the circumstances in which a promise shall be legally binding on the person making it.'

Pollock described a contract as 'a promise or set of promises which the law will enforce'.

American Restatement (Second) of the Law of Contract, 1978:

> 'A contract is a promise or a set of promises for the breach of which the law gives a remedy or the performance of which the law in some way recognises as a duty.'

From these definitions it would appear that the law of contract is about promises and agreements; however, the scope and operation of the subject – and the meaning of 'agreement – cannot be adequately explained without a consideration of:

1. the historical development of the law of obligations and the emergence of contractual remedies;
2. the theories underlying the purpose of the law of contract which necessarily involve a consideration of prevailing economic and philosophical attitudes.

1.3 Historical development and the theories underlying contract

By the fourteenth century the common law courts had established jurisdiction over certain civil wrongs which were known as trespasses. Flexible forms of action came to be developed which allowed litigants to adapt these forms to the particular circumstances of the case. These actions included a form in which the plaintiff alleged that the defendant had undertaken (in Latin: assumpsit) a certain obligation and then by negligent misconduct had caused him damage. This was an important development because earlier the only form of obligation that could be enforced was a debt for a specific sum. Even more important was the fact that while the old debt actions were tried by jury, the new assumpsit action could be heard after the ritual of swearing an oath.

By 1602 (*Slade's Case* (1602) 4 Co Rep 92a) the writ of assumpsit had become the general remedy for informal contracts and it was the concept of assumpsit that became the basis for the modern law of contract and quasi contract.

This foundation of contract in assumpsit (and the earlier debt) is reflected, in broad terms, in two kinds of situations in which a contractual remedy might be sought.

1. When the plaintiff complains of an invasion of his rights by the defendant's breach of undertaking.
2. When the plaintiff seeks a contractual remedy to recover a sum of money owed to him by the defendant, often for goods sold or services supplied.

It could be said that the first situation reflects the assumpsit origin of contract and the second the origin in debt.

The other particularly important time, historically, for the law of contract was the nineteenth century. The philosophy of laissez faire which prevailed in the nineteenth century involved the belief that the law should interfere with people's activities as little as possible. In the area of the law of contract this belief found expression in the words of Sir George Jessel in *Printing and Numerical Registering Co v Sampson* (1875) LR 19 Eq 462:

> 'If there is one thing more than another which public policy requires, it is that men of full age and competent understanding, shall have the utmost liberty in contracting and that their contracts, when entered into freely and voluntarily, shall be held sacred and shall be enforced by the Courts of Justice.'

This robust view did not recognise that people are seldom free to choose whether or not to contract, or to choose the other contracting party, or to determine the terms of their contracts. In particular, when one party enjoys a monopoly or is otherwise economically dominant, the other party may be especially at a disadvantage.

However, not all nineteenth-century judges shared the vigorous opinions expressed above. In recognition of this, statutes – particularly towards the end of the nineteenth century and during this century – have sought to impose terms and limit the power of economically dominant parties. We shall be examining the scope and effect of this legislation in later sections.

Theories of contract

The main question here is: Why should promises be enforced? Several answers to this question can be isolated: each of which has gained prominence according to the prevalent economic/social/political theory of the period.

1. *Natural law: honour theory* When the church had considerable influence on the mores of society, it was thought that promises ought to be kept and the law should reflect this fact.
2. *Laissez faire: bargain theory* This idea, perhaps, represents the basis of 'classical' contract: the law should enforce bargains, supported by adequate quid pro quo moving from both sides, made by free men of full age and capacity. Such a theory was less acceptable when people realised that the market economy did not make all men free: accordingly, contract became the means of social control by the state, for example, Hire Purchase Act, food and drugs legislation etc.
3. *Welfare state: reliance theory* This theory is based on the notion that where one person has altered his position to his detriment on the basis of another's promise, the other should make good the detriment, or give compensation if he goes back on his promise.

1.4 Overlap with other legal topics

Contract and property

The main difference between the law of property and the law of contract is that the former is said to create rights 'in rem' while the latter creates rights 'in personam'.

Thus contracts and conveyances were always kept separate. In English law, however, a contract can act as a conveyance of property or rights and property (except for land), and this can lead to problems when a contract turns out to be defective for, say, mistake or illegality. Thus property problems can arise under the guise of contract, and some of the rules reflect historical attitudes to property, rather than principles that might be more appropriate to a consumer society.

This was recognised by Lord Denning, in particular, who was always concerned for the rights of the bona fide purchaser. See, for example, *Lewis* v *Averay* [1972] 1 QB 198.

Contract and tort

We have already seen that contract, quasi-contract and tort all have a common origin.

There is nowadays an increasing recognition by the judiciary that the traditional and long-accepted rigid division of the law of obligations into contract and tort is without historic foundation and unrealistic. See, for example, *Brooks Wharf and Bull Wharf* v *Goodman Bros* [1937] 1 KB 534; [1936] 3 All ER 695, *Hedley Byrne & Co Ltd* v *Heller and Partners Ltd* [1964] AC 465; [1963] 2 All ER 575, *The Albazero* [1977] AC 774; [1976] 3 All ER 129 and *Tennant Radiant Heat Ltd* v *Warrington Development Corp* [1988] 11 EG 71.

Contract and equity

Equity has contributed a wider view of the reasons for enforcing contracts than the narrow, consideration-based approach articulated at common law in cases such as *Eastwood* v *Kenyon* (1840) 11 Ad & El 438 and *Currie* v *Misa* (1875) LR 10 Exch 153.

In particular, courts of equity have shown greater concern to enforce promises than to uphold bargains; the focus of attention is the promisor and the need for him to keep substantive faith.

This approach is easily confused with the common law approach and the confusion was compounded once equity ceased to be administered by a separate court. The reason for the confusion is that equity is only applied at the court's discretion. And this discretion – to enforce promises – will only be exercised, inter alia, where not to do so would cause more harm to the plaintiff than to the defendant. In other words, the plaintiff must satisfy the court that, in the circumstances which exist *at the time of the hearing* (not, as in common law, those which existed at the time of the alleged breach), he will lose more if the court does not act than the defendant will if the court does act. See, for example: *Foster* v *Robinson* [1951] 1 KB 149 and *Binions* v *Evans* [1972] Ch 359. These cases are quite consistent with equity's general approach, but completely inconsistent and inexplicable, in terms of common law considerations.

The other major difference between law and equity relates to its remedies. Equity will enforce the promise directly through specific performance or injunction: when this is not appropriate, damages may be awarded but calculated not, as at common law, at the date of the breach of contract, but at the date when the court decides to act against the defendant for breaking his promise or undertaking.

1.5 Methods of studying the law of contract

Contract is one of the few areas of law with which almost everyone comes into day-to-day contact. Whilst, superficially at least, that might be regarded as advantageous to the student embarking on a study of contract law, it is in reality often a hindrance rather than a help.

To the extent that everyone makes contracts in their daily lives – a week's supply of groceries, a newspaper, a car or even a house – everyone tends to regard themselves an expert in a rather 'do-it-yourself' area of law. Familiarity with the basic concept of a contract breeds, if not contempt, then perhaps a rather deceptive feeling of over-confidence.

The general body of contract law is immense, and this fact creates one of the student's greatest problems. The sheer volume of information facing a student may seem, at least initially, a daunting if not downright impossible task to grasp.

Nowhere is this more true than as to case law. The general principles of contract law are still, as noted earlier, of a judge-made origin. That is to say, most of the major principles are contained in judicial decisions rather than statute. Cases are still the most important source of contract law and it is important that the student becomes used, from a very early stage, to reading and researching his or her own case reports. While it *is* possible to go through an entire contract course without ever going near a law library, it is not a course of action to be recommended!

Students who depend on textbook resumés of cases and who never read a case report themselves are at a considerable disadvantage.

From reading as many cases as possible, right from the word go, it is possible to gain an insight into how the courts reach their decisions, how judges interpret facts and how they apply legal principles to those facts.

No casebook or textbook will give the student the sort of information to be found in a report. Although, in a textbook, the student may find some basic facts and the decision neatly documented, what he or she will *not* find, unless he or she reads the full report for him or herself, is whether the court was reluctant to reach its decision, or whether a dissenting judgment was of particular interest or importance, or what other cases the court considered or rejected.

Strictly speaking, it does not even matter what cases the student reads, though obviously the majority of students will seek out the 'classics' – the cases of major importance in a particular area. But *any* cases are useful reading; in working out what the courts took into account (or what they perhaps *should* have taken into account), will help to fix the topic in the memory and sharpen the student's own perceptions of the subject.

It does no good to learn a few (or even a lot) of cases off by heart – this will only give a static view of contract. Nor is it wise to think that each case establishes one rule or law.

Rather it is the relationship between whole groups of cases which may be of importance. It is only by careful study of a series of cases at a time that the student begins to pick out patterns of conduct and can begin to predict how the courts might react in future similar cases and how the law on the topic might progress.

The law of contract should never be studied in self-contained sections. Unfortunately it often is!

None of the rules relating to contract exists in a vacuum, and the student who is constantly revising and updating his or her notes, in the light of what he or she learns as the course progresses, will have a higher level of understanding of the topic as a whole.

It is also helpful to note that aspects of contract can be approached at differing levels of complexity. Offer and acceptance, for example, because it is dealt with at the beginning of the course, is often treated in a very simplistic way. Areas of contractual law which are traditionally dealt with towards the end of the course are often dealt with by lecturers in greater detail and, because of this, some areas seem deceptively simple and others gain a needless reputation for being complicated.

In order for the student to have some idea of the rules of contract law before he or she starts to study the individual topics in details, it is strongly recommended that an elementary book should be read.

2

Offer and Acceptance

2.1 General principles

2.2 The offer

2.3 Duration and termination of offer

2.4 Acceptance

2.5 Communication of acceptance

2.1 General principles

There are three basic essentials to the creation of a contract which will be recognised and enforced by the courts. These are contractual intention, agreement and consideration. Contractual intention will be dealt with in Chapter 4 and consideration will be examined in Chapter 3.

This chapter is concerned with the means by which the courts ascertain that the parties have, in fact, reached agreement. The method traditionally adopted is to analyse the dealings between the parties in terms of offer and acceptance. As we have already seen, this is an objective test, and the question asked is whether there has been a definite offer by one party and an unqualified acceptance by the other.

Note that often today, in a complex commercial transaction, it may be difficult to determine the precise stages of offer and acceptance. See *New Zealand Shipping Co Ltd* v *AM Satterthwaite & Co Ltd (The Eurymedon)* [1975] AC 154.

Opinions seem equally divided among the judiciary as to whether the old traditional approach of analysing 'stages' of offer and acceptance is still a viable approach, or whether it is unduly constrictive in modern commercial contracts and produces a false and unrealistic result. On balance it seems to be Lord Diplock's view that it is only 'exceptional cases' which cannot be analysed in this way that holds sway. Certainly other more flexible approaches have been suggested (eg Lord Denning's test in *Butler Machine Tool* v *Ex-cell-o Corporation (England) Ltd* [1979] 1 WLR 401) but these have, so far, not found favour.

Although the courts have expressed from time to time a certain unease regarding the rigidity of the orthodox matching of offer and acceptance, there is no real sign of any concerted move towards a more flexible, free-ranging approach. The judiciary would still appear to favour an approach which, with all its manifest disadvantages, nevertheless gives some appearance of producing a clear and unambiguous picture of agreement (or lack of it).

2.2 The offer

Definition

The offer is an expression of willingness to contract made with the intention (actual or apparent) that it shall become binding on the offeror as soon as it is accepted by the person to whom it is addressed.

An offer can be made to one person or a group of persons, or to the world at large. The offeror is bound to fulfil the terms of his offer once it is accepted.

The issue of whether there would be a valid offer to the world at large was considered in *Carlill* v *Carbolic Smoke Ball Co Ltd* [1893] 1 QB 256.

The offer was contained in a newspaper advertisement. Bowen LJ said:

> 'It was also said that the contract was made with all the world – that is with everybody, and you cannot contract with everybody. It is not a contract made with all the world. It is an offer made to all the world and why should an offer not be made to all the world which is to ripen into a contract with anybody who comes forward and performs the conditions?'

The offer may be made in writing, by words or conduct. All that is necessary is that the terms of the offer are clear and that the offer was made with the intention that it should be binding if accepted.

In ascertaining whether there has, in fact, been an offer capable of acceptance, the courts have applied the principles set out below.

Types of offer: unilateral

Some offers are purely one sided. They are made without the offeror's having any idea whether they will ever be taken up and accepted, and thereby be transformed into a contract.

Such an offer is said to be unilateral. An example has already been noted in *Carlill* v *Carbolic Smoke Ball Co Ltd* (the facts of which are set out below).

This offer, also classified as an offer to the world at large, was typical of the type in which manufacturers offer to pay compensation to users of their product, if the product does not live up to expectations. Often, such offers are part of a general publicity campaign popularising the product.

Similarly, other publicity offers, such as those occasionally mounted by newspapers, offering a reward for the first person to swim the Irish Sea, or find the Loch Ness monster, are unilateral offers.

On a more homely note, the 'lost and found' columns of any newspaper will carry offers of rewards for lost items or pets. A person making such an offer has no idea whether it will ever be accepted, hence it is unilateral.

Types of offer: bilateral

The majority of offers are bilateral. Most contracts are negotiated on a promise for a promise basis. While it is not always true, most people make an offer to one named offeree or, at most, a small group of potentially interested parties. Again it is not always the case, but many contracts are made with both parties present on a face-to-face basis.

Thus an offer to sell a house involves a promise by the offeror to sell, in return for the offeree's promise to pay. Similarly, an offer to build a house involves the builder's offer to construct the house in return for the customer's promise to pay for it. These are both examples of bilateral offers.

Invitation to treat

An invitation to treat made by one party to another is not an offer. An invitation to treat is made at a preliminary stage in the making of an agreement, where one party seeks to ascertain whether the other would be willing to enter into a contract and, if so, upon what terms. It is an invitation extended by one party to the other to enter into negotiations, or to make an offer. An invitation to treat cannot be accepted so as to form a binding contract, since it is nearly always the invitee who is being asked to make the offer.

To distinguish between an offer and an invitation to treat it is necessary to look at the intention of the person making it, as revealed by his words or actions, and at the surrounding circumstances. It is not an offer unless it was made with the intention that it should be binding as soon as the person to whom it was addressed communicates his assent.

The words used by the parties are not themselves conclusive. An 'offer' may, in fact, be 'an invitation to treat' or vice versa. The court looks at both the words used and the surrounding circumstances to determine the real intention of the parties.

See, for example, the forms of wording used in the following cases: *Spencer* v *Harding* (1870) LR 5 CP 561:

> 'We are instructed to offer ... for sale by tender'

which was held to be an invitation to treat (see below), and *Clifton* v *Palumbo* [1944] 2 All ER 497:

> 'I am prepared to offer you ... my ... estate for £600,000.'

The land in question was a large scattered estate. The Court of Appeal held that this was not a definite offer to sell, but a preliminary statement as to price, which was just one of the questions to be settled between the parties.

Lord Greene MR said:

> 'There is nothing in the world to prevent an owner of an estate of this kind contracting to sell it to a purchaser, who is prepared to spend so large a sum of money, on terms written out upon a half sheet of note paper of the most informal description and even, if he likes,

on unfavourable conditions. But I think it is legitimate, in approaching the construction of a document of this kind, containing phrases and expressions of doubtful significance, to bear in mind that the probability of parties entering into so large a transaction and finally binding themselves to a contract of this description couched in such terms, is remote. If they have done it, they have done it, however unwise and however unbusinesslike it may be. The question is, Have they done it?'

A statement which expresses itself as an 'acceptance' may, in fact, be an offer: *Bigg* v *Boyd Gibbons Ltd* [1971] 1 WLR 913, [1971] 2 All ER 183. The relevant statement was 'for a quick sale I would accept £26,000'. This was held to be, in fact, an offer capable of acceptance so as to create a binding agreement. See also *Harvey* v *Facey* (below).

However, a statement is not an offer if the person making it states clearly that he is *not* to be bound by the acceptance of the other party, but only where he himself signifies his acceptance. See *Financings Ltd* v *Stimson* [1962] 1 WLR 1184. See also *Butler Machine Tool Co Ltd* v *Ex-cell-o Corporation (England) Ltd*.

The following are examples of statements that have been held to be invitations to treat: *Harvey* v *Facey* [1893] AC 552. The plaintiffs telegraphed the defendants in relation to a piece of land:

'Will you sell us Bumper Hall Pen? Telegraph lowest cash price.'

The defendants replied:

'Lowest cash price for Bumper Hall Pen, £900.'

The plaintiffs then telegraphed:

'We agree to buy Bumper Hall Pen for £900 asked by you.'

The Judicial Committee of the Privy Council held that the defendants' telegram was not an offer, but an invitation to treat, telling the plaintiffs the lowest price that they would accept for the land. The plaintiffs' second telegram was an offer, but there was no contract because it had not been accepted.

In *Gibson* v *Manchester City Council* [1978] 2 All ER 583 CA; [1979] 1 All ER 972 HL Manchester City Council (Conservative) adopted, in 1970, a policy of selling council houses to their tenants. The respondent, a tenant of a council house, wrote to the Council asking for a form giving details of the purchase and mortgage terms available. On 10 February 1971, the City Treasurer wrote to the respondent that the Council 'may be prepared to sell the house to you at a purchase price of £2,725 less 20% = £2,180 freehold'. The letter also gave details of mortgages that might be available, and went on 'if you would like to make formal application to buy your council house please complete the enclosed application form and return it to me as soon as possible'. The application was headed, 'Application to buy a council house' and concluded: 'I ... now wish to buy my council house. The above answers are correct and I agree that they shall be the basis of the arrangements regarding the purchase'. The respondent completed the form except for the purchase price and returned it to the Council on 5 March 1971.

On 18 March he wrote again to the Council: 'I would be obliged if you will carry on with my purchase as per my application already in your possession.'

Before formal written contracts had been prepared and exchanged by the parties, Council policy changed and they decided only to sell houses where the contracts had already been exchanged.

The respondent brought an action seeking specific performance of the contract of sale, which he claimed to be constituted by the letter of 10 March from the City Treasurer and his application of 5 March.

The County Court judge and the Court of Appeal considered that there was an enforceable agreement. The House of Lords took a contrary view and adopted the dissenting judgment of Geoffrey Lane LJ in the Court of Appeal.

He said:

> 'It is said that the letter of 10th March 1971 constitutes a firm offer to sell.
>
> It is largely a matter of impression, but although to Lord Denning MR and Ormrod LJ it appears perfectly plain that that was a firm offer, to me it appears equally plain that it was not. First of all, the words used "may be" in the first paragraph and "may grant a mortgage" and finally the words "if you would like to make an application to buy your council house" are strange words to use if this was indeed a formal offer on behalf of the Council. It is in my judgment no more than one would expect of a letter coming from a City Treasurer. It is a letter setting out the financial terms on which it may be that the Council will be prepared to consider the sale and purchase in due course.'

Further grounds upon which Geoffrey Lane LJ held that there was no firm offer capable of acceptance were (1) that the letter was from the City Treasurer rather than the Town Clerk from whom a firm offer would have come; and (2) that the formal contract would have contained a number of provisions, such as restrictive covenants, to which the alleged agreement made no reference.

One interesting point arising from this case (*Gibson*) was originated by Lord Denning MR in the Court of Appeal [1978] 2 All ER at p586:

> 'To my mind it is a mistake to think that all contracts can be analysed into the form of offer and acceptance. I know in some of the textbooks it has been the custom to do so; but as I understand the law there is no need to look for strict offer and acceptance. You should look at the correspondence as a whole and at the conduct of the parties and see therefrom whether the parties have come to an agreement on everything that is material. If by their correspondence and their conduct you can see an agreement on all material terms, which was intended thenceforward to be binding, then there is a binding contract in law even though all the formalities have not been gone through. For that proposition I would refer to *Brogden* v *Metropolitan Railway Co* (1877) 2 App Cas 666.'

In the hearing in the Lords a year later, Lord Diplock seems to have accepted that Lord Denning MR's statement of the law in this matter could be valid, though not in the instant case:

> 'My Lords, there may be certain types of contract, though I think they are exceptional, which do not fit easily into the normal analysis of a contract as being constituted by offer and acceptance; but a contract alleged to have been made by exchange of correspondence

between the parties in which successive communications other than the first are in reply to one another is not one of these ... I venture to think that it was by departing from ... (the) ... conventional approach that the majority of the Court of Appeal was led into error. ([1979] 1 All ER 972 at p974.)

(One such exceptional case is, perhaps, illustrated by *New Zealand Shipping* v *Satterthwaite & Co Ltd* [1974] 1 All ER 1015.)

The distinction between offers and invitations to treat is often hard to draw as it depends upon the intention of the person making the statement. Surrounding circumstances and the normal pattern of dealing (eg, what is usual in a particular trade or industry) may give valuable clues as to the parties' intentions. For example, in *Metal Scrap Trade Corporation* v *Kate Shipping Co Ltd (The Gladys) (No 2)* [1994] 2 Lloyd's Rep 402 the question arose as to the exact point at which an invitation to treat was converted into an offer. In this case, the plaintiff (MSTC) was a state funded scrap metal firm, operating in India, which specialised in breaking up old ships. Its mode of operation was, essentially, to invite offers from the international market, channelled through Indian brokers, for suitable ships. Owners were requested to provide particulars of the ship on a standard MSTC questionnaire form. MSTC would then indicate verbally to the broker in question, that they were prepared to make either 'a firm offer' or an offer 'sub recon' (which was not firm unless or until confirmed by MSTC). Once the brokers indicated acceptance of a 'firm offer' or an offer 'sub recon' had been confirmed and accepted, then and only then, was a standard (Norwegian) form or Memorandum of Agreement sent to the broker to complete as appropriate, pending final signature by MSTC and the ship's owner. In the present case, having made an offer 'sub recon', but prior to the formal Memorandum of Agreement being agreed and signed, MSTC withdrew from the negotiations. The defendants argued that a contract of sale had come into existence, and that, since it contained an arbitration clause, any further dispute should be decided by arbitration.

The defendant and the plaintiff had had previous dealings and the general pattern of preliminary negotiations was always the same. The court decided that the parties still had so many issues to negotiate, it could not be the case that, at the point MSTC withdrew from the preliminaries, there was any intention on the part of either party to make a binding contract They had never progressed to formal offer and acceptance. (See section 2.1 as to 'stages' of offer and acceptance.) However, in some cases the distinction is settled, presumptively, at least, by authority or by statute. These cases are dealt with below.

Display of goods in shops

The issue is whether the display of goods in shops, on shelves or in the window with a price tag attached is an offer or an invitation to treat. If it is an offer, then the customer can accept it by indicating his desire to buy the item and the shopkeeper must then sell it to him at the stated price. If, on the other hand, it is an invitation to treat, the offer is made by the customer in seeking to buy the item, and the shopkeeper can accept or refuse the offer as he wishes.

The leading case is *Pharmaceutical Society of Great Britain* v *Boots Cash Chemists (Southern) Ltd* [1952] 2 All ER 456; [1953] 1 All ER 482. The defendants adapted their shop, or one of them, to a self-service system. A customer, on entering, was given a basket and, having selected from the shelves the articles he required, put them in the basket and took them to the cash desk. Near the desk was a registered pharmacist who was authorised, if necessary, to stop a customer removing any drug from the shop. The court had to decide whether the defendants had broken the provisions of s18 Pharmacy and Poisons Act 1933, which made it unlawful to sell any listed poison 'unless the sale is effected under the supervision of a registered pharmacist'. The vital and obvious question is where the 'sale' in fact took place, and at what time, and this depended upon whether the display of goods was an offer or an invitation to treat. The plaintiffs contended that it was an offer which was accepted when the customer put an article into his basket, and if this article was a 'poison' it was therefore 'sold' before the pharmacist could intervene. According to the defendants, the display was only an invitation to treat. An offer to buy was made when the customer put an article in the basket, and this offer the defendants were free to accept or reject. If they accepted, they did so only when the transaction was approved by the pharmacist near the cash desk. Lord Goddard at first instance, had no hesitation in deciding that the display was only an invitation to treat so that the law had not been broken, and the Court of Appeal upheld his reasoning and adopted his decision. He said:

> 'The transaction is in no way different from the normal transaction in a shop in which there is no self-service scheme. I am quite satisfied it would be wrong to say that the shopkeeper is making an offer to sell every article in the shop to any person who might come in and that that person can insist on buying any article by saying "I accept your offer". I agree with the illustration put forward during the case of a person who might go into a shop where books are displayed. In most bookshops customers are invited to go in and pick up books and look at them even if they do not buy them. There is no contract by the shopkeeper to sell until the customer has taken the book to the shopkeeper or his assistant and said "I want to buy this book" and the shopkeeper says "yes". That would not prevent the shopkeeper, seeing the book picked up, saying, "I am sorry I cannot let you have that book; it is the only copy I have got and I have already promised it to another customer". Therefore, in my opinion, the mere fact that a customer picks up a bottle of medicine from the shelves in this case does not amount to an acceptance of an offer to sell. It is an offer by the customer to buy, and there is no sale effected until the buyer's offer to buy is accepted by the acceptance of the price.'

In *Fisher* v *Bell* [1961] 1 QB 394 a flick knife was displayed in a shop window with a price tag attached. The issue was whether the law prohibiting the display of such items for sale had been breached. Lord Parker stated:

> 'It is clear according to the ordinary law of contract that the display of an article with a price on it in a shop window is merely an invitation to treat. It is in no sense an offer for sale, the acceptance of which constitutes a contract.'

On the other hand, in *Chapleton* v *Barry Urban District Council* [1940] 1 KB 532, a display of deck chairs under a 'For Hire' sign was held to be an offer (see below).

Advertisements

Whether or not advertisements can amount to offers depends to a large extent on whether they are bilateral or unilateral, that is, capable of acceptance by one or a limited number of persons, or open to all the world to accept.

Advertisements of bilateral transactions

Such advertisements are usually held not to amount to offers. Two reasons are given. First, such advertisements may lead to further bargaining, as in the case of an advertisement of land for sale. Second, the vendor may wish to assure himself that the prospective purchaser will be able to pay for the goods before entering into a binding agreement.

The following have been held to be invitations to treat.

Advertisement in a newspaper of goods for sale – *Partridge* v *Crittenden* [1968] 2 All ER 421. Here the appellants inserted in a periodical entitled 'Cage and Aviary Birds' an advertisement, 'Bramblefinch cocks and hens, 25s.'. The words 'offer for sale' were not used, but the advertisement was placed under the heading, 'classified advertisements'. The appellants were charged with unlawfully offering for sale a wild live bird.

The Divisional Court quashed the conviction. Lord Parker said:

> 'I think that when one is dealing with advertisements and circulars, unless they come from manufacturers, there is business sense in their being construed as invitations to treat and not offers for sale.'

Circulation of a catalogue by a wine merchant – *Grainger & Son* v *Gough* [1896] AC 325. This was held to be an attempt to induce offers from recipients, not an offer itself.

Lord Herschell pointed out the inconvenience of a contrary interpretation:

> 'The transmission of such a price list does not amount to an offer to supply an unlimited quantity of the wine described at the price named, so that as soon as an order is received there is a binding contract to supply that quantity. If that were so the merchant might find himself involved in any number of contractual obligations to supply wine of a particular description which he would be quite unable to carry out, his stock of wine of that description being necessarily limited.'

Advertisement that a scholarship examination will be held. In *Rooke* v *Dawson* [1895] 1 Ch 480, this was held not to amount to an offer to a candidate that the examination would be held.

Advertisements of unilateral contracts

Such advertisements are commonly held to amount to offers. The leading case is *Carlill* v *Carbolic Smoke Ball Co Ltd* [1893] 1 QB 256.

The defendants issued an advertisement promising to pay £100 to any person who used, as prescribed, carbolic smoke balls made by them, and then caught influenza. They stated that they had deposited £1,000 with their bankers 'shewing our sincerity in this matter'. The plaintiff used the smoke balls, caught influenza and claimed her £100. The defendants claimed, inter alia, that she was not entitled to payment because their advertisement had not amounted to an offer.

It was held that this advertisement did constitute an offer and the defendants had indicated their intention to be bound by the deposit with their bankers.

Bowen LJ said:

> 'It is not like cases in which you offer to negotiate or you issue advertisements that you have got a stock of books to sell, or houses to let, in which cases there is no offer to be bound by any contract. Such advertisements are offers to negotiate – offers to receive offers – offers to chaffer'.

Note that there is a strong presumption that advertisements in trade journals and the like are offers, not invitations to treat. For example, Lord Parker's comment in *Partridge* v *Crittenden* (above) clearly considers manufacturers' advertisements and circulars to be true offers. Advertisements promising rewards for the recovery of lost property or for information leading to the capture or conviction of a criminal are commonly regarded as offers. See *Gibbons* v *Proctor* (1891) 64 LT 594 and *Williams* v *Carwardine* (1833) 5 Car & P 566.

Ticket cases

An area which has caused difficulty, and is still far from clear, involves contracts where a ticket is given by one party to the other. The question usually arises in the context of whether the ticket is a contractual document, and hence whether the parties are bound by any conditions printed on that ticket, or referred to on the ticket, and further details may be sought in Chapter 8 on exclusion clauses.

Whether or not a ticket is a contractual document and its role in the formation of the contract depends upon: (1) whether that ticket was intended to be a contractual document; and (2) the mode and timing of its issue.

In *Chapleton* v *Barry Urban District Council* (above), deck chairs were offered for hire under a sign setting out the price per hour and which requested the public to obtain tickets from the attendant and retain them for inspection. The plaintiff took two chairs and obtained two tickets from the attendant, which he did not read. He sat on a chair which collapsed. He sued the Council who relied upon a clause printed upon the ticket excluding liability.

The Court of Appeal held the Council liable. The sign constituted the offer which the plaintiff accepted when he took two deck chairs. The tickets amounted to no more than receipts, and hence any terms on those tickets were not part of the contract, which had been concluded prior to their issue.

In some cases, it is clear that the ticket is a contractual document and that the request for a ticket is an offer and the issue of that ticket an acceptance. This would appear to be the case with cinema, raffle and cloakroom tickets.

In other cases, the proffering of the ticket has been held to be an offer and the taking of that ticket, an acceptance. See *Thompson* v *London Midland & Scottish Railway Co* [1930] 1 KB 41 where a contract of carriage is booked by telephone the contract is not complete until the ticket has been received, whether or not paid for beforehand.

In *Cockerton* v *Naviera Aznar SA* [1960] 2 Lloyd's Rep 450, the question was discussed in relation to automatic ticket-issuing machines in *Thornton* v *Shoe Lane Parking Ltd* [1971] 2 QB 163.

The plaintiff had parked his car in the defendant's automatic car park. At the entrance there was a sign setting out the charges and stating: 'All cars parked at customer's risk'. As the defendant drove in, a light changed from red to green and a ticket was pushed at him by a machine. The transaction was analysed in terms of offer and acceptance by Lord Denning:

> 'The customer pays his money and gets a ticket. He cannot refuse it. He cannot get his money back. He may protest to the machine, even swear at it; but it will remain unmoved. He is committed beyond recall. He was committed at the very moment when he put his money in the machine; the contract was concluded at that time. It can be translated into offer and acceptance in this way. The offer is made when the proprietor of the machine holds out as being ready to receive the money. The acceptance takes place when the customer puts money in the slot. The terms of the offer are contained in the notice placed on or near the machine, stating what is offered for the money. He (the customer) is not bound by the terms printed on the ticket because the ticket comes too late. The contract had already been made.'

A case that is hard to reconcile with the above, or indeed with common sense, is *Wilkie* v *London Passenger Transport Board* [1947] 1 All ER 258.

There the issue was the process of formation of a contract of carriage on a public transport bus. This part of the decision was obiter as the Court of Appeal found that the plaintiff was, in fact, a bare licensee, not a party to a contract at all. Lord Greene MR thought that a contract was made when an intending passenger 'puts himself either on the platform or inside the bus'. Hence the offer must be made by the transport authority in running the bus and that offer is accepted by a passenger when he gets on the bus. If this is the case, then there is a complete contract before any payment is made or a ticket issued, and that process results in the formation of a second contract.

The difficulty with Lord Greene's analysis is that the passenger gives no consideration when he gets on the bus, so that it could be argued that a passenger could not enforce the contract of carriage. A more realistic analysis of the formation of the contract is that the running of the bus or the advertisement of bus services is an invitation to treat. The offer is made by the passenger when he gets on the bus and it is accepted by the transport authority when they take his money. This leaves open the question of whether the ticket is a mere receipt or a contractual document.

Auction sales

The question of whether an auctioneer's call for bids was an offer or an invitation to treat was considered in *Payne* v *Cave* (1789) 3 Term Rep 148.

It was there decided that the call for bids is an invitation to treat, a request for offers. The bids made by persons at the auction are offers which the auctioneer can accept or reject as he chooses.

This principle now has statutory form in s57(2) Sale of Goods Act 1979, which provides that a sale by auction is completed by the fall of the hammer and, up until then, a lot can be withdrawn. Likewise, an auctioneer can generally withdraw lots before he accepts the bid.

Goods put in for sale by auction are sold either with a reserve price or without. If the former is the case, then there is no contract if the auctioneer mistakenly accepts a bid lower than the reserve price and the item can be withdrawn even after the hammer has fallen. See *McManus* v *Fortescue* [1907] 2 KB 1.

Where the auction is advertised as being held without reserve, there is no contract of sale between the owner of the property and the highest bidder if the auctioneer refuses to accept the highest bid. But in *Warlow* v *Harrison* (1859) 1 E & E 309, it was held (obiter) that the auctioneer is liable in such a case on a separate contract between himself and the highest bidder that the sale be without reserve. The request for bids at the auction is an offer by the auctioneer that he will, on the owner's behalf, accept the highest bid, and this offer is accepted by bidding. Hence if the auctioneer refuses to sell an item to the highest bidder, that bidder can sue the auctioneer for breach of contract.

The *Warlow* v *Harrison* approach was adopted and confirmed by the Court of Appeal in *Barry* v *Heathcote Ball & Co (Commercial Auctions) Ltd* [2001] 1 All ER 944. The defendant auctioneers were instructed to sell two engine analysers, specialist equipment used in the motor trade. The claimant had been told the sale would be 'without reserve'. New machines had a list price of £14,000 each. The auctioneer attempted to start the bidding at £5,000, then £3,000, but the claimant, the only person interested, bid just £200 for each machine. The auctioneer refused to accept that bid and withdrew the machines from sale. The claimant sought damages for breach of contract and he was awarded £27,600. The defendants' appeal against this decision was dismissed.

As Sir Murray Stuart-Smith explained, although there was no contract between the purchaser and vendor, that did not prevent there being a collateral agreement between the auctioneer and bidder. As to damages, where a seller wrongfully refused to deliver goods to the buyer, the measure of damages where there was a market in the goods was prima facie to be ascertained by the difference between the contract price and the market or current price of the goods at the time when they ought to have been delivered: s51(3) Sale of Goods Act 1979. The same approach was appropriate here.

An advertisement that an auction is to be held does not constitute an offer to hold it capable of acceptance. In *Harris* v *Nickerson* (1873) LR 8 QB 286, the plaintiff was held not to be entitled to recover the money expended on travelling to attend an auction that had been advertised and which was then cancelled.

Tenders

Where goods are advertised for sale by tender, the statement is not an offer, but an invitation to treat; that is, it is a request by the owner of the goods for offers to purchase them. It is not an offer to sell to the person making the highest tender. See *Spencer* v *Harding* (1870) LR 5 CP 561.

Likewise, where a building contract is put out for tender, this is a request for offers by contractors which can then be accepted or rejected.

In *Harvela* v *Royal Trust of Canada* [1985] 1 All ER 261, the Court of Appeal had to consider the proper construction of an invitation to submit tenders. The telex, inviting the tenders, contained the term that:

'We bind ourselves to accept (the highest offer) provided such offer complies with the terms of this telex.'

In his judgment Waller LJ said:

'If it were not for the words "We bind ourselves to accept", this would have been a mere invitation to treat; but those words in my opinion make it an offer which the bidder being highest accepted' (at p265).

(Note: the decision of the Court of Appeal in *Harvela* was reversed by the House of Lords, but not on these grounds: [1985] 2 All ER 966.) See also acceptance of tenders (below).

Subject to contract

The words 'subject to contract' are used by parties who are negotiating as to the terms of a contract to indicate that documents passing from one to the other are not intended to be offers capable of acceptance so as to form a binding contract. This topic is dealt with more fully in Chapter 5.

2.3 Duration and termination of offer

An offer continues in existence, capable of acceptance until it is brought to an end. There are six ways in which this can occur.

Revocation

The offer may be revoked by the offeror at any time up until it is accepted. See *Payne* v *Cave* (above). This is the case even where the offeror has stated that the offer will remain open for a certain period, unless the offeree can establish the existence of a separate and distinct contract to keep the offer open. In *Routledge* v *Grant* (1828) 4 Bing 653 the offeror stated that the offer would remains open for six weeks. He was held entitled to revoke the offer prior to the end of six weeks. The offeree could only insist on the offer remaining in existence for that period if he could show that he had bought the option to purchase by a separate agreement, and for separate consideration.

An offer to settle an action made under Part 36 of the Civil Procedure Rules is an offer to enter into a contract with the offeree and, as such, it may be withdrawn at any time prior to acceptance: *Scammell* v *Dicker* (2001) The Times 14 February.

Communication of revocation

The only requirement imposed on the offeror is that the revocation of the offer must be communicated to the offeree(s). Unless and until the revocation is so communicated, it is ineffective. There must be actual communication of the revocation. Deemed communication as in the case of the postal rule in acceptance (see 'Occurrence of a terminating condition', below) is not enough. It must be shown that the offeree was actually aware of the revocation.

In *Byrne* v *Van Tienhoven* (1880) 5 CPD 344, the defendants posted a letter on 1 October offering to sell to the plaintiffs 1,000 boxes of tinplates. They posted a letter revoking that offer on 8 October, which reached the plaintiffs on 20 October. Meanwhile, the plaintiffs had posted a letter accepting the offer on 15 October. Under the postal rule of acceptance, the offer was accepted when the plaintiffs posted their letter of acceptance. The revocation was not effective until it actually reached the plaintiffs, on 20 October, by which time the contract had been formed.

There is no requirement that the revocation be directly communicated to the offeree. It is sufficient that it can be shown that he was aware of the revocation prior to his acceptance.

In *Dickinson* v *Dodds* (1876) 2 Ch D 463, on 10 June the defendant gave the plaintiff a written offer of sale of a house for £800, which stated that the offer would remain open until 9 am on 12 June. On 11 June the defendant sold the house to a third party, and the plaintiff was told of this sale by a fourth party on the evening of 11 June. Before 9 am on 12 June, the plaintiff handed the defendant a letter purporting to accept the offer. It was held that the plaintiff was fully aware of the revocation before he 'accepted' the offer and that the revocation was effective.

Revocation of unilateral offers

The cases set out above are all examples of bilateral offers, that is, the offer to be bound by a promise in exchange for a promise by the offeree. Where the offer is unilateral, the basic principle is the same, but a little more difficult to apply.

A unilateral offer is accepted by the offeree performing an act. Acceptance will not be complete until the act itself is complete. The question that then arises is whether the offer can be withdrawn at any time before complete acceptance, or whether it must be withdrawn before the offeree commences performance of the act that constitutes acceptance. The former position is in accordance with the general rules on the revocation of offers, but it could lead to injustice.

If, for instance, a man offers a reward of £1,000 to the first person to swim the English Channel, acceptance is not complete until a swimmer actually reaches the shore. An application of the conventional rules would allow the offeror to revoke his offer as the swimmer comes in sight of land.

The question of the revocability of unilateral offers once performance has commenced was considered in two Court of Appeal decisions.

In *Errington* v *Errington and Woods* [1952] 1 KB 290, a father bought a house for his son and daughter-in-law to live in. He paid one-third of the purchase price in cash and borrowed the remainder from a building society on mortgage. He told the son and daughter-in-law that if they paid the mortgage instalments, he would convey the house to them when the payments were complete. They duly paid the instalments. The father purported to revoke his offer to convey the house before the whole mortgage had been repaid. It was held that there must be a term implied into the offer that it would be irrevocable once performance had commenced.

In *Daulia* v *Four Millbank Nominees Ltd* [1978] 2 All ER 557, the defendants were the owners of land. They agreed in a telephone conversation with the plaintiffs that if the plaintiffs produced a banker's order for the amount of the deposit, and attended at the defendants' solicitors the next morning to sign and exchange contracts, then the defendants would enter into a binding contract to sell the land to the plaintiffs.

The plaintiffs duly fulfilled these conditions. The defendants, having had a higher offer, refused to enter into the contract of sale. The plaintiffs sued for damages for breach by the defendants of their unilateral contract.

The effect of this decision is that unilateral contracts go through two stages. Once the offeree has commenced performance of the act that constitutes acceptance, the offer can no longer be revoked. But until that act has been completely performed, the offer has not been accepted so as to form a binding contract.

Hence, while the man who offered the £1,000 for swimming the English Channel cannot revoke his offer once someone has started the swim, the swimmer cannot claim the reward unless he completes the crossing.

Rejection by the offeree

An offer that is rejected by the offeree cannot be subsequently accepted by him, once the rejection has been communicated to the offeror. There must be a specific rejection of the offer, not merely an enquiry as to some of the details of the offer. This topic is dealt with in more detail below, in 'Acceptance' and 'Counter-offers'.

Lapse of time

Where an offer is stated to be open for a specific length of time, then the offer automatically terminates when that time limit expires. Where there is no express time limit, an offer is normally open only for a reasonable time.

What constitutes 'reasonable' will depend largely on the subject matter of the proposed contract. Thus an offer to sell perishable goods will remain open for far less long than an offer involving land or shares. In *Ramsgate Victoria Hotel Co* v *Montefiore* (1866) LR 1 Ex Ch 109, the defendant offered to buy the plaintiffs' shares in June. He heard nothing more until the end of November when he was told that his offer had been accepted and he was required to pay the purchase price. On his refusal, he was sued for that price. It was held that he was entitled to refuse as his offer had not been accepted within a reasonable time and had therefore lapsed.

Occurrence of a terminating condition

An offer may be made subject to a condition. If that condition is not satisfied, the offer is not capable of acceptance. Examples of such conditions are that the offer must be accepted within a stated time or, in an offer to sell goods, that the goods are in a saleable condition or that an applicant for life insurance is in the same state of health as he was when he made his application.

In *Financings Ltd* v *Stimson* [1962] 3 All ER 386, the Court of Appeal considered the case of a man who had offered to purchase a car. Between the making of the offer and its acceptance, the car was badly damaged when a stranger crashed into it outside the garage.

Donovan LJ said:

> 'The county court judge held that there must be implied a term that, until acceptance, the goods would remain in substantially the same state as at the date of the offer; and I think that this is both good sense and good law.'

Death

The effect of the death of the offeror depends upon the nature of the offer. If it involved the performance of a promise which was personal to the offeror, such as writing a book or singing at a concert, then the offer cannot be accepted once news of the death has been communicated to the offeree. There must be actual communication. Where the offer was not dependent upon the offeror personally, then his death has no effect, and the offer remains capable of acceptance, and if accepted, is binding upon the estate of the offeror.

In *Bradbury* v *Morgan* (1862) 1 H & C 249, there is no clear English authority on the effect of the death of the offeree. In *Reynolds* v *Atherton* (1921) 125 LT 690, the question was considered obiter by Warrington LJ, who considered that the death of the offeree operates as a revocation of an offer. This view was not endorsed by the House of Lords.

In *Re Irvine* (1928) 3 DLR 268, a Canadian decision, a letter of acceptance was handed by a man to his son for posting. The man died before the letter was posted and it was held that the acceptance was ineffective as the offer had lapsed on the offeree's death.

Insanity, incapacity, insolvency or impossibility

The power to make an offer may be inhibited by, or the power to accept an offer terminated by, the occurrence of any of the following events either before the making of the offer or before its acceptance: the insanity or drunkenness of either party; intervening incapacity in the case of a corporation; the intended contract becoming illegal; and the performance of the contract becoming impossible. These topics are dealt with in more detail in Chapters 9, 13 and 14.

2.4 Acceptance

Definition

An acceptance is a final and unqualified acceptance of the terms of an offer. Unless it can be shown that there was such an acceptance, then there is no contract. In some cases, it is obvious that there has been an unqualified acceptance of the exact terms of an offer. Where the offeror sets out his offer and requests an answer of 'yes or no' from the offeree, it is not difficult to determine whether or not there has been acceptance. Frequently, however, progress towards agreement involves long and arduous bargaining by the parties. In those circumstances, the courts must look carefully at the dealings between the parties to decide whether there has, in fact, been an agreement and upon which terms.

Where an offer is made in the alternative, the acceptance must stipulate which alternative has been accepted. In *Peter Lind & Co Ltd* v *Mersey Docks and Harbour Board* [1972] 2 Lloyd's Rep 234, an offer to build a terminal was made by a tender quoting two alternative prices, fixed and 'cost-plus'. The offeree purported to accept 'your tender', without stating which price. It was held that there was no acceptance and hence no contract.

In addition to being a firm and unqualified acceptance of all the terms of the offer, the fact of acceptance must normally be communicated to the offeror before there is a concluded contract. The rules as to communication are dealt with below (see 2.5).

Acceptance by conduct

Acceptance of a bilateral offer normally takes the form of words, either spoken or written. But in the case of unilateral offers, that is, the offer of a promise in return for the performance of some act by the offeree, the offeree's performance of that act is the acceptance of the offer.

In *Carlill* v *Carbolic Smoke Ball Co Ltd* (above), the offer was contained in the advertisement by the company. Mrs Carlill accepted the offer by inhaling the smoke balls in accordance with the instructions. Acceptance was complete without the need to communicate the fact of acceptance to the company, an exception to the usual rule which requires communication before acceptance is complete. In practical terms, there will normally be communication of the fact that the act has been performed in order to collect the reward that has been offered, but there is a complete contract in existence once the act of acceptance has been completely performed, whether or not the offeror is aware that this is the case.

Acceptance is not complete until the act of acceptance has been completely performed. Where the offer is of a reward for the return of a lost cat, the offer is accepted when someone looks for, finds and returns the cat. The offeree will not be entitled to enforce the contract and claim his reward until he returns the cat. Starting to look for the cat is not enough.

The requirement that there be complete performance of the act of acceptance before there is a concluded contract was emphasised in the case of *Daulia* v *Four Millbank Nominees Ltd* (above), where Goff LJ said:

' ... the true view of the unilateral contract must in general be that the offeror is entitled to require full performance of the condition that he has imposed and short of that he is not bound'.

See also *Errington* v *Errington and Woods* (above) for a discussion of the acceptance by conduct of a unilateral offer.

In addition to the act of acceptance being completely performed, it must have been performed by the offeree with the intention of accepting the offer in order to amount to an acceptance, as was the case in *Taylor* v *Allon* [1966] 1 QB 304.

Occasionally, both offer and acceptance are alleged to have been made by conduct. In such cases, it is difficult to ascertain the terms of the agreement or, indeed, if there was in fact agreement at all. In such cases, the courts may apply the standard of reasonableness, that is, imply a term that a reasonable price was to be paid for goods sent by A to B and used by B. Or the court might look at previous dealings between the parties.

In *Brogden* v *Metropolitan Railway Co* (1877) 2 App Cas 666, the existence and terms of an agreement between the parties were established by reference to a draft agreement which had not been formally agreed by either party. The railway company had submitted a draft agreement to the plaintiff (a coal merchant) for the supply of coal by the plaintiff to the railway company. The plaintiff had amended the draft, written 'approved' upon it and returned it to the railway company, who did not expressly approve the amendments, but put it away in a drawer. The coal merchant commenced deliveries of coal to the railway company, who accepted those deliveries for two years. The supply and payment were upon the terms of the draft agreement, as amended. When a dispute arose, the plaintiff refused to continue supplying coal, and when sued for non-delivery, claimed that there was not and never had been a binding agreement between the parties. The House of Lords held that a contract came into existence either when the railway company ordered the first load of coal from Brogden upon the new terms, or when the first delivery of coal was made by Brogden and accepted by the railway company.

The point to note from this decision is that if two parties act as though there is a contract between them, then the courts will try to spell out the terms of a contract by reference either to previous dealings between the parties, or to customary terms. Conduct of itself cannot, however, be construed as an acceptance of an order if the offer prescribes the form of acceptance, and the conduct alone does not fulfil the requirements.

In *Wettern Electric Ltd* v *Welsh Development Agency* [1983] 2 All ER 629, the defendants offered the plaintiffs a licence to occupy a factory in a letter which stated: 'If you accept this licence on the above terms, will you please complete the acknowledgement and acceptance at the foot of the enclosed copy and return it to us at your earliest convenience.' The plaintiff did not complete the acknowledgement, but went into occupation of the factory. It was held that the act of going into occupation of the factory by the plaintiffs was not an acceptance of the defendants' offer, since that offer had required acceptance in another manner.

Counter-offers

In order to create a binding agreement, the offer and acceptance must match. The offeree must accept all the terms of the offer. If in his reply to an offer, the offeree introduces a new term or terms, or varies the terms of the offer, then that reply cannot amount to an acceptance. Instead, the reply is treated as an offer itself, a counter-offer, which the original offeror is free to accept or reject.

In *Tinn* v *Hoffman & Co* (1873) 29 LT 271, the offeree responded to an offer to sell 1,200 tons of steel with a request to purchase 800 tons. He was told that there had been no acceptance of the offer of sale. Instead, there had been a counter-offer to purchase 800 tons, which the sellers were free to accept or reject.

A counter-offer not only fails as an acceptance, it also generally amounts to a rejection of the original offer, which cannot then be subsequently accepted. This is illustrated in *Hyde* v *Wrench* (1840) 3 Beav 334. The defendant offered to sell the plaintiff a farm for £1,000. The plaintiff offered £950, which the defendant refused. The plaintiff then purported to accept the offer of £1,000 and sought specific performance of a contract for the sale of land. It was held that no contract existed. The plaintiff had rejected the defendant's original offer with his counter-offer, and that original offer no longer existed so as to be capable of later acceptance.

In order to amount to a counter-offer, the offeree's reply must itself be capable of acceptance. That is, it must contain either expressly or impliedly all the essential terms.

Counter-offers may be compared with offers of a lesser amount in full settlement of a debt. In *Inland Revenue Commissioners* v *Fry* (2001) The Times 10 December the Revenue claimed tax amounting to £113,082 from Mrs Fry. Following negotiations, Mrs Fry wrote to the Revenue enclosing a cheque for £10,000. In her letter she said should the Revenue accept her offer, it should present the cheque for payment and she would take this as acceptance of her offer in settlement of her tax liability. The Revenue cashed the cheque but subsequently informed Mrs Fry that her offer was unacceptable. Jacob J held that the Revenue was entitled to the full amount of tax which it had claimed. He explained that it was fundamental to the existence of a binding contract that there was a meeting of minds. A unilateral offer prescribing the manner of acceptance could be accepted by an offeree acting in accordance with that manner. However, the Revenue doubtless received thousands of cheques each day. Obviously they should be banked as soon as possible. The cashing of the cheque gave rise to no more than a rebuttable presumption of acceptance. In all the circumstances, that presumption had been fully rebutted and the taxpayer had failed to establish the existence of any contract whereby her tax liability had been extinguished.

Request for information

It is necessary to distinguish between a reply that amounts to a new offer and a reply which is merely a request for further information as to the terms of the offer. If the offeree is merely seeking further information before deciding whether to accept an offer, or enquiring as to whether the offeror will modify his terms, then he is not necessarily making a counter-offer. Whether a reply does or does not amount to a counter-offer is a matter of construction for the court. If the reply does not amount to a counter-offer, then the original offer remains in existence and is still capable of acceptance.

In *Stevenson* v *McLean* (1880) 5 QBD 346, the defendant offered on Saturday to sell the plaintiffs 3,800 tons of iron 'at 40s. nett cash per ton, open until Monday'. On Monday, the plaintiffs telegraphed 'Please wire whether you would accept 40s. for delivery over two months, or if not, longest limit you would give.' No reply was received, so by a telegram sent at 1.34 pm the plaintiffs accepted the offer to buy at 40s. cash. Meanwhile, the defendant sold the iron to a third party and informed the plaintiffs of this by a telegram sent at 1.25 pm, which crossed with the plaintiffs' telegram. When the plaintiffs sued for non-delivery, it was held that there was a valid contract of sale between the plaintiffs and defendant. The plaintiffs' first telegram was not a counter-offer which destroyed the defendant's offer, but 'a mere inquiry, which should have been answered and not treated as a rejection of the offer'.

Clarification of implied terms

Where the reply to an offer contains terms that are not expressly set out in the offer, the reply will not amount to a counter-offer if those terms would, in any case, be implied into the offer. This is because the offeree is not in fact introducing new terms into the offer.

An example of the above would occur if, in response to an offer to sell goods, the prospective purchaser stated in his reply that the goods must be suitable for the purpose for which he was purchasing them. In any case, such a term would be implied into the contract for sale by the Sale of Goods Act 1979. Hence no new terms have been included.

The test to determine whether a reply by an offeree amounts to a counter-offer or not is whether a reasonable person in the position of the offeror would regard the purported acceptance 'as introducing a new term into the bargain and not as a clear acceptance of the offer'. See *Global Tankers Inc* v *Amercoat Europa NV* [1975] 1 Lloyd's Rep 666.

The 'battle of forms'

The rule that offer and acceptance must correspond with each other gives rise to problems where each party wants to contract on the basis of standard terms and these terms differ. This would occur where neither of the contracting parties are private individuals. For instance, company A offers to sell goods to company B, stating that the sale will be subject to company A's standard terms, as printed on the back of the document containing the offer. Company B reply stating that they want to buy the goods, at the price offered, but that the sale should be subject to B's standard terms as printed on the back of B's order form, which differ materially from A's.

This problem, and the methods by which the courts should approach it, was considered by the Court of Appeal in *Butler Machine Tool Co Ltd* v *Ex-cell-o Corporation (England) Ltd* (above). The facts were as follows.

23 May 1969: The sellers offered to sell a machine to the buyers for £75,535 to be delivered in 10 months. The offer included certain terms, including a clause for variation of the price to the price ruling at the date of delivery. The offer was subject to an overriding clause that the seller's terms and conditions, as stated in the offer, 'shall prevail over any terms and conditions in the Buyer's order'.

27 May 1969: The buyers placed an order subject to their own, materially different, terms and conditions including, in particular, a term for a fixed price. At the foot of the order was a tear-off acknowledgement slip stating 'We accept your order on the Terms and Conditions stated thereon.'

5 June 1969: The sellers completed and returned the buyers' acknowledgement slip with a letter stating that the order was accepted on the basis of their quotation of 23 May.

At the date of delivery, the sellers claimed an increase in price for the machine of about £3,000. The buyers refused liability to pay the extra price on the grounds that the contract was made under their terms and conditions at a fixed price. The sellers contended that it was their terms and conditions which prevailed and they were, therefore, entitled to the increased price.

It was held (at first instance) that since in their opening offer the sellers had said that their terms should prevail over any sought to be imposed by the buyers, the subsequent dealings were subject to that condition and, therefore, all the other original conditions imposed by the seller. The Buyers appealed. The Court of Appeal upheld the appeal.

Note the principles of law which emerge from this case.

1. Where the contracting parties form a contract which purports to be on the terms and conditions of both parties and those terms and conditions are at variance then:

   a) if the variation is insignificant, the offeree can impose the variation without drawing the offeror's attention specifically to it. The offeree, despite imposition of minor amendments to the offeror's conditions, nonetheless accepts the original offer.

   b) Where there is a difference which is so significant as would affect the price, the offeree cannot take advantage of it unless he clearly draws it to the attention of the offeror. In this case, the original offeree is now offering to enter into a different contract. The offer is made by him and is a counter-offer, which may or may not be accepted by the original offeror, such counter-offer may act as non-acceptance or refusal of the original offer (or it may simply be an enquiry as to whether the offeror will accept the new terms, whilst leaving open the possibility of acceptance under the original terms).

2. Where a counter-offer is accepted on its terms, then the original offer becomes totally eradicated. This must be so for, in the instant case, the major factor in the letter of 23 May was the term that the conditions thereof would be paramount. If the reference by the sellers to this letter referred only to the price and identity of the machine, then the letter must be seen by the court as a nullity in that the price was, under the terms of that letter, subject to change and, therefore, the 'price' identified could only be the price from the buyer's point of view.

3. It is difficult to reconcile the concept of a 'battle of forms' with the fundamental idea that contracting parties should be ad idem. Both parties in this type obviously consider that their terms and conditions prevail, and are replying on those terms and conditions.

Note, however, that the case of *Hartog* v *Colin and Shields* [1939] 3 All ER 566 (see Chapter 10) would appear to suggest that the seller in such cases might rely on mistake.

Acceptance of tenders

A tender is an offer (see 'Tenders' above). Normally, the acceptance of a tender leads to the formation of a contract by which the person tendering is bound to perform that which he has offered, at the price stated in the tender. This would be the case, for instance, where tenders were invited by a town council for the building of a new town hall; various builders submit tenders and, mindful of their duty to the ratepayers, the council accept the lowest priced. That acceptance creates a single contract under which the builders are bound to erect the town hall and the council to pay for it.

Difficulties arise, however, where tenders are invited for the periodical supply of goods. In such circumstances, it is a matter of construction of the original invitation to tender as to whether or not 'acceptance' of that tender leads to the formation of a contract.

Such invitations to tender can be divided into two broad types. First, an advertisement by A Ltd for offers to supply a specified quantity of goods, to be supplied during a specified time. In response to this invitation, B Ltd offers to supply the required quantity at a stated price. Acceptance of B Ltd's tender creates a contract, under which B Ltd are bound to supply the goods and the buyers A Ltd, are bound to accept them and pay for them. The only matter which is not settled is the timing of the deliveries, but the fact that these are to be by instalments as and when demanded, does not prevent a concluded agreement coming into existence on the acceptance of the tender.

Secondly, an advertisement by A Ltd for offers to supply goods up to a stated maximum, during a certain period, the goods to be supplied as and when demanded. Acceptance by A Ltd of a tender received from B Ltd in response to this invitation does not create a contract under which A Ltd is bound to accept delivery of the goods up to the stated maximum. Instead, A's acceptance converts B's tender into a *standing offer* to supply the goods up to the stated maximum at the stated price as and when requested to do so by A. The standing offer is accepted each time A places an order, so that there are a series of separate contracts for the supply of goods. A will not be in breach of contract if no orders are placed at all. Likewise, B's standing offer may be revoked, providing that it is not revoked at a time when it has been accepted by the placing of a specific order by A Ltd.

This second type of tender is illustrated in *Great Northern Railway* v *Witham* (1873) LR 9 CP 16. The plaintiffs advertised for tenders for the supply of stores. The defendant replied: 'I undertake to supply the company for 12 months with such quantities of (specified items) as the company may order from time to time.' The company accepted the tender, and for some months gave various orders which were filled by the defendant. Later, the company ordered some of the specified items, within the 12 months, and the defendant refused to supply them. It was held that his non-delivery was a breach of contract, as the placing of the order for the goods by the company was an acceptance of the defendant's standing order, which created a contract binding on the defendant to supply the goods ordered. The defendant could revoke his offer, but not in respect of goods that had already been ordered.

The question of acceptance of tenders was also considered in *Blackpool & Fylde Aero Club Ltd* v *Blackpool BC* [1990] 1 WLR 1195.

The defendant local authority owned the local airport for which it granted concessions for the operation of scenic and pleasure flights. On the expiry date of the current concessions, it invited the plaintiffs and seven other companies to tender for the new concession. The plaintiffs currently held the existing pleasure flight concession. The invitation to submit tenders was accompanied by a condition that no tender received after a certain date/time would be considered. The plaintiff's tender was posted by hand in the town hall letterbox, before the expiry date but, unfortunately, the box was not cleared regularly and the town clerk received the tender, which was higher than any of the others submitted, after the deadline. The local authority announced that they were not considering it because it was too late.

The Court of Appeal held that where invitations are issued to specified parties to submit tenders, and the submission procedure is clearly laid down, along with a fixed date for submission, then if an invitee complied with the submission procedure and submitted his tender within the deadline, he had not just a moral but a contractual right to be considered.

The Court of Appeal held that, though an invitation to tender was normally no more than an offer to consider bids, circumstances could exist whereby it gave rise to binding contractual obligations. Although the invitation did not specifically state this, a careful examination of what the parties said, and did, established a clear intention on the part of the defendants to be bound to examine, and give equal consideration to, all tenders submitted within the deadline. Since the plaintiffs had submitted on time, they were entitled to expect their tender to be considered in conjunction with all the other tenders.

Conditional acceptance

A conditional assent to an offer is not an acceptance of that offer. Conditional assents occur most often in the case of negotiation for the sale of land. The use of the phrase 'subject to contract' in a response to an offer is a conditional assent, which means that the offeree is stating that his assent to the terms of the offer is conditional upon a formal contract being drawn up. Until there is an acceptance which is not stated to be 'subject to contract', there is no contract.

Whether or not an assent is conditional is a matter of construction. The cases discussed above in relation to 'Subject to contract' dealt with the interrelationship between the use of the phrase and the requirements of s40(1) LPA 1925 (now repealed). It has never been suggested that an assent marked 'subject to contract' can amount to an effective acceptance of an offer, unless it has been agreed that the condition is to be waived. Where words other than 'conditional' or 'subject to contract' are used, the position is less clear.

In *Branca* v *Cobarro* [1947] 2 All ER 101, a vendor agreed to sell his mushroom farm for £5,000. He had stated in writing: 'this is a provisional agreement until a fully legalised agreement, drawn up by a solicitor, and embodying the conditions herewith stated is signed.' Branca paid a deposit of £500, which he subsequently sought to recover, arguing that there was no concluded contract.

At first instance, the plaintiff, Branca, obtained judgment. On appeal, Lord Greene MR said:

'A provisional agreement is going to have efficacy until a certain event happens, ie the efficacy of the agreement is not made conditional on the happening of that event.'

Asquith LJ said:

'The word "until" seems to me plainly to imply that the agreement is to be immediately fully binding unless and until superseded by a subsequent agreement.'

The appeal was allowed.

The test to be applied is whether the parties have made the operation of their agreement conditional upon the coming into existence, at some later date, of a further document. If that is the case, then there is no contract unless and until that further document is executed.

If, on the other hand, the parties have agreed that their existing agreement will subsequently be replaced by a more formal written agreement, they are bound by the existing informal agreement.

Acceptance in ignorance of an offer

The question that arises is whether an offeree who performs the act that constitutes acceptance while ignorant of the existence of the offer thereby validly accepts that offer. There is little authority on this point, but it would seem illogical to consider such an acceptance to be valid, as it ignores the requirement of intention on the part of the offeree. In *Upton-on-Severn RDC* v *Powell* [1942] 1 All ER 220 the defendant, whose house was on fire, telephoned the police station and asked for the fire brigade. He was entitled to the services of the Pershore Fire Brigade free of charge as he lived in its district, but the police officer called the Upton Fire Bridge in the mistaken belief that the defendant lived in their district. At the time they put out the fire, the Upton Fire Bridge shared this view. Later the defendant was sued for payment by the Upton Fire Brigade. He was held contractually bound to pay for those services.

The decision is difficult to reconcile with principle as, at the time they performed the services, the fire brigade had no thought of reward of those services, so how could that amount to an acceptance?

Motive for the acceptance

An offeree may perform the act that constitutes acceptance of an offer, with knowledge of that offer, but for a motive other than accepting the offer. The question that then arises, is whether his act amounts to a valid acceptance.

In *Williams* v *Carwardine* (1833) 5 Car & P 566, the defendant offered a reward of £20 to anyone who gave information leading to the conviction of the murderers of Walter Carwardine. The plaintiff was aware of the offer, and thinking that she had not much longer to live, signed 'a voluntary statement to ease my conscience, and in the hopes of forgiveness hereafter'.

As a result of the statement, the murderer was convicted. The plaintiff was held entitled to enforce the agreement and obtain her reward. Patterson J said: 'We cannot go into the plaintiff's motives.'

A similar conclusion was reached in *Carlill* v *Carbolic Smoke Ball Co Ltd* (above), where the plaintiff's motive in doing the act of acceptance (taking the smoke balls) was to avoid catching influenza, not to accept the defendant's offer. The plaintiff was held entitled to recover.

In the Australian case of *R* v *Clarke* (1927) 40 CLR 227, a different conclusion was reached. The Government of Western Australia offered a reward of £1,000 'for such information as shall lead to the arrest and conviction of' the murderers of two police officers, and added that, 'if the information should be given by an accomplice, not being himself the murderer, he should receive a free pardon'. Clarke saw the offer, and he was an accomplice. Some time later he gave the necessary information. He claimed the reward from the Crown by Petition of Right. He admitted not only that he had acted solely to save his own skin, but that, at the time when he gave the information, the question of the reward had passed out of his mind.

The High Court of Australia held that his claim must fail. He was, in their opinion, in the same position as if he had never heard of the reward. Higgin J said:

> 'Clarke had seen the offer, indeed, but it was not present to his mind – he had forgotten it and gave no consideration to it in his intense excitement as to his own danger. There cannot be assent without knowledge of the offer; and ignorance of the offer is the same thing, whether it is due to never hearing of it or forgetting it after hearing.'

The position therefore seems to be that an acceptance which is wholly motivated by factors other than the existence of the offer has no effect. Where, however, the existence of the offer plays some part, however small, in inducing a person to do the required act, there is a valid acceptance of the offer.

Cross-offers

The third situation where ignorance might appear to be no bar to a completed contract is in the area of cross-offers. However, it seems that there is generally no contract if two persons make identical cross-offers, neither knowing of the other's offer when he made his own; for example, if X writes to Y offering to sell Y his car for £500 and Y simultaneously writes to X offering to buy his car for £500. The natural reaction would be for one or both parties to seek to confirm that they are in agreement, and that extra communication would be an acceptance. Without it there can be no contract implied. Certainty is thus guaranteed, and conventional practice promoted. Blackburn J, in *Tinn* v *Hoffman & Co* (1873) 29 LT 271, said:

> 'When a contract is made between two parties, there is a promise by one in consideration of the promise made by the other; there are two assenting minds, the parties agreeing in opinion and one having promised in consideration of the promise made by the other – there is an exchange of promises. But I do not think exchanging offers would, upon principle, be at all the same thing. The promise or offer being made on each side in ignorance of the promise or offer made on the other side, neither of them can be construed as an acceptance of the other.'

2.5 Communication of acceptance

The general rule

The general rule is that an acceptance must be communicated to the offeror. Until and unless the acceptance is so communicated, no contract comes into existence. Hence where, as in *Brogden* v *Metropolitan Railway Co*, the offeree fails to inform the offeror whether or not the offer has been accepted, there is no acceptance. If the offeree decides to accept the offer and writes a letter of acceptance which he then forgets to post, again there is no effective acceptance of the offer. The same result would follow if the offeree communicated his acceptance only to his own agent.

In order for an acceptance to be accepted, it must be *brought to the attention of the offeror*. Hence, there is no contract if, as Lord Denning MR said in *Entores* v *Miles Far East Corporation* [1955] 2 QB 327 at p332:

> ' ... the words of acceptance are drowned by an aircraft flying overhead; or if they are spoken into a telephone after the line has gone dead or become so indistinct that the offeror does not hear them.'

Exceptions to the general rule

The general rule as to acceptance does not apply, or is modified in the following cases.

1. Where the offeror expressly or impliedly waives the requirement that acceptance be communicated. This is generally the case with unilateral contracts and may sometimes be the case with bilateral agreements. The topic is dealt with in more detail below (see 'Silence').
2. Where the offeror is estopped from denying that the acceptance was communicated. This will be the case if it was in fact sent or spoken by the offeree, but was not received or heard by the offeror as a result of his own fault

or omission. This would be the case in the example given by Lord Denning MR in *Entores* v *Miles Far East Corporation* (above):

> '... if the listener on the telephone does not catch the words of acceptance but nevertheless does not ask for them to be repeated.'

A similar result would follow if the acceptance was sent by telex to the offeror's office during office hours, but is simply not read by anyone there after it has been transcribed on to the offeror's machine.

3. Where the acceptance is communicated to the offeror's agent and that agent has authority to receive that acceptance on behalf of his principal. See *Henthorn* v *Fraser* [1892] 2 Ch 27.
4. Where the postal rule applies, in which case the acceptance can be effective before it is in fact received by the offeror. This is dealt with in detail below, in 'The postal rule'.

There is no requirement that the acceptance must be communicated specifically by the offeree. All that is required is that the offeror knows of the acceptance and hence there can be a valid contract, even though the acceptance was not brought to his attention by the offeree. See *Bloxham's Case* (1864) 33 Beav 529.

But where the acceptance is communicated to the offeror by a person other than the offeree, there will be no contract if that third party had no authority to so act on behalf of the offeree, and the circumstances indicate that the offeree's decision to accept was not yet regarded by him as irrevocable. See *Powell* v *Lee* (1908) 99 LT 284.

What constitutes communication of acceptance?

An acceptance is communicated when and where it is brought to the attention of the offeror, unless the postal rule applies, in which case the acceptance is communicated when the letter of acceptance is posted by the offeree.

Methods of communication are divided into those where communication is more or less instantaneous: face-to-face conversation, telephone, telex and fax; and into those where there is a time lag between the dispatch and receipt: letters and telegrams. The postal rule applies only to letters and telegrams.

Where the method of communication is instantaneous, then the offer is accepted when the offeror actually hears the acceptance. If the offeree speaks his acceptance but it is not heard by the offeror, then it has not been effectively communicated.

In *Entores* v *Miles Far East Corporation* (above), the issue was where a contract had been made. The plaintiffs were a London company and the defendants an American corporation with agents in Amsterdam. Both the plaintiffs and the Amsterdam agents used telex machines. The plaintiffs made an offer to the Amsterdam agents by telex, to buy goods from them. This offer was accepted, also by telex. The defendants were alleged to have broken this contract and the plaintiffs wished to show that the agreement had been made in England, so that legal proceedings could be commenced in England for breach of contract. The defendants contended that the postal rule applied, so that the offer was accepted when the telex was dispatched, in Holland.

Parker LJ said:

> 'Where ... the parties are in each other's presence, or, though separated by space, communication between them is instantaneous, there is no need for such a rule of convenience (the postal rule). To hold otherwise would leave no room for the operation of the general rule that notification of the acceptance must be received. An acceptor could say: "I spoke the words in your presence, albeit softly, and it matters not that you did not hear me"; or "I telephoned you and accepted, and it matters not that the telephone went dead and you did not get my message" ... So far as telex messages are concerned, although the despatch and receipt of a message is not completely instantaneous, the parties are to all intents and purposes in each other's presence just as if they were in telephonic communication, and I can see no reason for departing from the general rule that there is no binding contract until notice of the acceptance is received by the offeror. That being so, and since the offer was made by the plaintiffs in London and notification of the acceptance was received by them in London, the contract resulting therefrom was made in London.'

The Court of Appeal decision in *Entores* was approved by the House of Lords in the case of *Brinkibon Ltd* v *Stahag Stahl* [1982] 1 All ER 293.

The plaintiffs were an English company and the defendants an Austrian company, based in Vienna. After negotiations, the defendants offered to sell steel bars to the plaintiffs. The plaintiffs accepted this offer by a telex sent to the defendants in Vienna. The contract was not performed and the plaintiffs commenced proceedings for breach of contract, in England. The defendants claimed that the contract was made in Austria, so that the English courts did not have jurisdiction.

The House of Lords held that where there was instantaneous communication between the offeror and the offeree, the formation of a contract was governed by the general rule that a contract was concluded where and when acceptance of the offer was received by the offeror. Since the telex communication from the buyers in London to the sellers in Austria was instantaneous, the contract was made in Austria. The House of Lords considered the possibility that there might be circumstances in which, although telex was used, communication was not in fact instantaneous. This could occur where a telex was sent at night or when the offeror's office was closed.

Lord Wilberforce said, in relation to such circumstances:

> 'No universal rule can cover all such cases; they must be resolved by references to the intentions of the parties, by sound business practice and in some cases by a judgment where the risk should lie.'

Recently the court in *Manatee Towing Co* v *Oceanbulk Maritime SA (The Bay Ridge)* [1999] 2 All ER (Comm) 306 found that where no conclusive agreement had been reached and the parties were still in the midst of negotiating, a fax sent by the offeree confirming the main agreed terms could not be deemed as proper acceptance as it would not be construed as an intention to create legal relations.

Conversely, the Court of Appeal in *Society of Lloyd's* v *Twinn and Another* (2000) The Times 4 April held that there was no conceptual reason why an offeree should not validly accept an offer even though he indicated doubt in his ability to perform his part of the contract and asked the offeror for some indulgence. An acceptance which sought an indulgence would be effective if it was clear that the offeree was unconditionally accepting the offer.

The postal rule

The postal rule applies where there is a lag between despatch of an acceptance and receipt of that acceptance by the offeror. That is, where acceptance is by letter or telegram. In such a case, acceptance is communicated when the offeree posts the letter or telegram. This is an exception to the general rule, under which acceptance is complete once it is brought to the attention of the offeror.

Attempts have been made to justify the rules of postal offer and acceptance. It is best explained as a (somewhat arbitrary) rule of convenience. Essentially, the main problem in negotiating a contract by post is that letters get delayed or lost. Probably the most telling argument is that if an offeror indicates he is willing to negotiate by post, he is indicating his willingness to bear the risks involved.

Where acceptance is by post, there are three possible moments when that acceptance could be complete:

1. when the letter is posted by the offeree;
2. when the letter is delivered to the offeror;
3. when the letter is actually brought to the attention of the offeror.

It is easier to keep accurate records of the date and time at which a letter was posted, than the moment when it was delivered or the time when the offeror actually became aware of its existence. Hence it can be argued that in the interests of certainty as to the time when the contract was formed, the time of acceptance should be the time of posting.

A second ground upon which this departure from the general rule can be supported is that of the allocation of risk. Where postal acceptance has been expressly or impliedly stipulated by the offeror (see below), then the offeree may reply by that method. Postal communication bears the risk of letters being lost or delayed in the post. If acceptance was only complete when a letter was received by the offeror, then the offeree would not know whether or not he was a party to a binding agreement until the letter was received, and if, in fact, the letter never does arrive, the offeree could find himself acting on the assumption that he was a party to a contract when this does not turn out to be the case.

The risk borne by the offeror where acceptance is complete upon the posting of the letter of acceptance is that he is then bound by the agreement before he actually is aware of the acceptance. If the letter of acceptance is delayed or lost, then the offeror may assume that his offer was not accepted and enter into a contract for the disposal of the same goods. This would be a breach of the original contract. However, it was the offeror who stipulated acceptance by post, and hence it can be argued that he should bear the risk.

Development of the postal rule

The present rule was first laid down in *Adams* v *Lindsell* (1818) B & Ald 681.

On 2 September the defendants wrote to the plaintiffs offering to sell them a quantity of wool and requiring acceptance in the course of post. On 5 September the letter arrived, having been misdirected in the post by the defendants. On receipt of the letter, the plaintiffs immediately posted an acceptance. On 9 September the letter arrived, but meanwhile the defendants had sold the fleeces elsewhere, not having received a reply as expected on 7 September. The court held that the contract was completed on 5 September.

Application of the postal rule

A letter is 'posted' when it is put into the control of the Post Office (for example, by placing it in a letter box) or one of its employees authorised to receive letters. Giving a letter to an unauthorised person will not amount to acceptance of an offer. See *Re London and Northern Bank* [1900] 1 Ch 220.

Jones wrote to a company applying for shares and the company's servant took a letter of acceptance to the post at 7 am. Outside the Post Office the servant handed the letter to a postman. On the same day, a letter withdrawing Jones' offer arrived at the company's office at 8.30 am and was opened at 9.30 am.

The question was whether there had been acceptance before communication of the withdrawal of the offer.

Cozens-Hardy J said:

'The postman was not an agent of the Post Office to receive letters. The Postal Guide at page 47 expressly stated that town postmen are not allowed to take charge of letters from the post ... The mere fact of handing the letter to the postman outside St Martin le Grand Post Office was not a posting of the letter.'

The rule is best explained as one for the convenience of an offeree, assuming that the offeror will take responsibility for loss or delay in the post since he chose to open negotiations by this method. This may be misguided if the offeror is in fact a counter-offeror.

Thesiger J, in *Household Fire Insurance* v *Grant* (1879) 4 Ex D 216, said:

'As soon as the letter of acceptance is delivered to the Post Office the contract is made as complete and final and absolutely binding as if the acceptor had put his letter in the hands of a messenger sent by the offeror himself as his agent.'

This was a case turning upon loss of the letter, but was decided by a majority, overruling a previous decision. It would seem, therefore, that the arguments of convenience for and against applying the postal rule to such a situation are finely balanced. On the one hand, it may be harsh to hold an offeror liable on an acceptance which through no fault of his own, was never received by him; on the other, it may be equally hard to deprive the offeree of the benefit of an acceptance if he had taken all reasonable steps to communicate it. English law favours the offeree on the grounds that it is the offeror who 'trusts to the post' and that the offeror can always safeguard himself by stipulating in the offer that the acceptance must be actually communicated to him, and that postal rules will not apply.

In *Holwell Securities v Hughes* [1974] 1 WLR 155, the defendants granted the plaintiffs a six-month option to purchase property; the option was to be exercised by notice in writing to the defendants. The plaintiffs' solicitors sent a written acceptance exercising the option, but the letter was never delivered. The plaintiffs sought specific performance of the contract. At first instance, Templeman J dismissed the action.

On appeal, the plaintiffs argued that the postal rule applied and the option was properly exercised when the letter was put in the post.

Lawton LJ said:

'The plaintiffs were unable to do what the agreement said they were to do, namely fix the defendant with knowledge that they had decided to buy his property. If this construction of the option clause is correct there is no room for the application of any rule of law relating to the acceptance of offers by posting letters ... It becomes clear that the parties cannot have intended that the posting of a letter should constitute the exercise of the option.'

In *Yates Building Co Ltd v R J Pulleyn & Sons (York) Ltd* [1975] 237 EG 183, the facts of this case were that an offer was made, stipulating that acceptance should be by recorded delivery or registered post. The acceptance was actually made by ordinary post. The offerors therefore returned the acceptance, which it was never disputed arrived within the stipulated time limit, saying that they were not bound by it since it did not accord with the prescribed mode. By that time it was too late for the offerees to accept by the prescribed means.

Lord Denning MR with Lord Scarman concurring said that one has to look at the overall purpose for stipulating a particular mode of acceptance. Though their terminology differed, both judges drew a distinguishing line between mandatory requirements, and those which were purely optional or permissive. In the instant case, the purpose for stipulating recorded delivery or registered mail was to protect the offeree. Since the acceptance had indubitably arrived, no one, least of all the offerors, had been prejudiced.

Telegrams and telexes

The 'postal rule' also applies to acceptance by telegram. See *Bruner v Moore* [1904] 1 Ch 305. It does not apply to acceptance by telex or, presumably, to fax. The problem in relation to acceptance by telex and fax is not *when* the offer has been accepted because communication is nearly instantaneous, but *where* it has been accepted. This is significant for determining whether English law governs the contract, or whether the English court has jurisdiction to hear a case or to order service of notice of a writ outside the jurisdiction. (Students interested in this aspect should refer to a textbook on conflict of laws.) It is axiomatic that the contract is complete on acceptance. If A in Belgium accepts an offer by telex made by B in England, the contract could be capable of being made in Belgium or England. It will, however, be very rare that the contract will be deemed to have been made in Belgium. This question was first discussed in *Entores Ltd* v *Miles Far East Corporation* (1955) (above), and has been upheld in the *Brinkibon* case. (See 'What constitutes communication of acceptance?', above.)

Silence

An offeree who does nothing in respect to an offer is not bound by the terms of that offer. The offeror cannot, in other words, impose silence as acceptance by the offeree.

In *Felthouse* v *Bindley* (1862) 11 CBNS 869, the plaintiff and his nephew had been negotiating about the sale of the nephew's horse. Having apparently reached agreement, the plaintiff wrote to his nephew to clarify whether the amount was in pounds and shillings or guineas. He concluded his letter by saying: 'If I hear no more about him I consider the horse is mine at £3 15s.' The nephew did not reply, but had decided to accept the offer. He instructed the auctioneer who was selling his farming stock not to sell the horse as it had already been sold. The auctioneer mistakenly sold the horse and was sued by the plaintiff in conversion. The Common Pleas held that at the time of the auction, no contract had been concluded for the sale of the horse between the plaintiff and his nephew.

In view of the fact that the nephew had decided to accept the offer and had informed the auctioneer accordingly, this decision is perhaps difficult to understand. The Exchequer Chamber, in affirming the decision on appeal, appears to have emphasised the alternative ground for the decision that the then requirements of the Statute of Frauds had not been complied with because there had been no delivery, part payment or memorandum in writing to vest the property in the plaintiff.

Though the decision at first instance in *Felthouse* v *Bindley* has been criticised on the facts, the general principle laid down in that case, that an offeror cannot impose silence as acceptance, has not been challenged.

What has not been fully resolved in England is the extent to which an offeror may, expressly or impliedly, waive communication of acceptance by the offeree. If the principle in *Felthouse* v *Bindley* is for the protection of the offeree, it does not seem satisfactory for the offeror who has waived the necessity of communication to be able to deny the validity of the contract. This is recognised in unilateral contracts, but the extent of this recognition in bilateral contracts is uncertain.

Although silence cannot of itself amount to acceptance, inaction on the part of the offeree may justifiably entitle the offeror to infer that his offer has been accepted.

In *Rust* v *Abbey Life Insurance Co* [1979] 2 Lloyd's Rep 355, the plaintiff applied and paid for a 'property bond' which was allocated to her on the terms of the defendant's usual policy of insurance. After a period of some seven months, the plaintiff sought recovery of the payment she had made on the basis that there had been no concluded contract. Her claim was rejected on the grounds that her application had been an offer and the issue of the policy an acceptance. It was further held, however, that, even if the issue of the policy had been a counter-offer, that counter-offer had been accepted by the plaintiff by her conduct in taking no action for the period in question.

Note that the Unsolicited Goods and Services Act 1971 now gives further protection to offerees in respect of 'imposed silent acceptance'.

Revocation of posted acceptance

Can an offeree withdraw his acceptance, after it has been posted, by a later communication, which reaches the offeror before the acceptance? There is no clear authority in English law. A strict application of the postal rule would not permit such withdrawal. This view is supported by decisions in New Zealand in *Wenkheim* v *Arndt* (NZ) 1JR (1873) and South Africa in *A-Z Bazaars* v *Minister of Agriculture* [1974] (4) SA 392 (c).

3

Consideration

3.1 Introduction

3.2 Definitions

3.3 Four principles

3.4 Promissory estoppel

3.1 Introduction

To speak of a doctrine of consideration is something of a misnomer. There is no one doctrine with a coherent rationale, but rather a body of rules evolved by the courts, the function of which is to put some limit on the enforceability of agreements in law.

It is a general principle of the English law of contract that an informal gratuitous promise is not enforceable as a contract. Either the promise must be formalised by being made under seal, or it must be supported by consideration. This does not mean that a promise for which there is no consideration is devoid of legal effect. (See section 3.4 below.)

The problem discussed in this chapter is what, in law, constitutes consideration so as to make the promise it supports enforceable as a contract.

3.2 Definitions

Consideration is defined by Lush J in *Currie* v *Misa* (1875) LR 10 Ex 153 at p162:

> '... a valuable consideration in the sense of the law may consist either in some right, interest, profit or benefit accruing to the one party, or some forbearance, detriment, loss or responsibility given suffered or undertaken by the other.'

Despite criticisms, it is the traditional definition which the courts have consistently applied, and it is that traditional approach to which we shall largely confine ourselves.

The courts have always looked on consideration in terms of a dichotomy of benefit to the promisor (the person making the promise), or detriment to the promisee (the person to whom the promise is made). These requirements are alternative. For instance, where A guarantees B's bank overdraft, the promisee bank suffers detriment by advancing money to B but no benefit to A, the promisor, need be shown.

The benefit/detriment dichotomy can bear two separate meanings. First, it may be used in the sense of any act, forbearance or promise that has economic value ('factual' benefit/detriment). Secondly, it is used in the sense of an act, forbearance or promise the performance of which is not already legally due ('legal' benefit/detriment). The courts have never consistently drawn the above distinction but, as will be seen, there are a number of cases where there was undoubted actual benefit/detriment, but there has been held to be no legal consideration.

A further division of the types of consideration is that distinguishing executed consideration (an act or forbearance in return for a promise) and executory consideration (mutual promises).

3.3 Four principles

Generally, it can be said that there are four principles governing the sufficiency and nature of consideration. These principles are hedged about with exceptions. The principles are:

1. consideration must move from the promisee;
2. consideration need not move to the promisor;
3. past consideration is not good consideration;
4. consideration must be sufficient but need not be adequate.

The effect of the last principle is ameliorated by the operation of equity by what is now known as 'promissory estoppel'. The position at common law will be examined first. Each principle and the exceptions to it will be dealt with in turn.

Consideration must move from the promisee

As has been indicated above, a person may provide consideration either by conferring a benefit upon another, or by undertaking to suffer a detriment to himself. It is, however, a personal obligation. A cannot generally promise C that B will confer a benefit or suffer a detriment in consideration for a promise by C to A, unless, of course, A assumes liability to C for the non-performance of that activity by B. The justification for this is that the consideration has not moved from the promisee.

In *Thomas* v *Thomas* (1842) 11 LJ QB 104, a testator wanted to give a house to his widow. The executors of his will promised the house to the widow 'in consideration of such desire' provided that she promised to keep the house in repair and to pay ground rent of £1 per annum. It was alleged that no binding agreement had been reached because the consideration was expressed to be moving from the testator and not from the widow.

It was held that the promise to repair and to pay £1 per annum ground rent constituted consideration provided by her. She was, therefore, entitled to remain in the house.

There was a similar search for consideration in *Bolton* v *Madden* (1873) LR 9 QB 55. The plaintiff and defendant were both subscribers to a charity and entitled to vote on the distribution of funds at two successive meetings. The plaintiff and defendant agreed that, at the first meeting, the plaintiff would vote for the defendant's chosen candidate, and that the defendant would vote for the plaintiff's chosen candidate. The defendant refused to vote for the plaintiff's candidate.

It was held that the defendant was bound by his promise because the plaintiff had provided consideration in the earlier week by voting for the defendant's preferred candidate.

De La Bere v *Pearson* [1908] 1 KB 280 is similarly an illustration of the need of the court to find consideration moving from the promisee. In this case, the defendants owned a newspaper. They invited readers to apply by letter for financial advice so that the letters could be published. The plaintiff's letter was published. He followed the advice and suffered a loss. He sued. The defendants said that the advice had been given gratuitously and that they were not, therefore, liable.

It was held that the plaintiff had given consideration by writing a letter which could be published, and there was a contract between the plaintiff and the defendants.

Where the only benefit is to the promisee, however, it seems that consideration cannot be found. This is illustrated in *Dickinson* v *Abel* [1969] 1 WLR 295. The occupier and beneficiary under a trust of a farm asked a prospective purchaser of the farm: 'What's in it for me?' The prospective purchaser said that he could have £10,000 if he (the purchaser) bought the farm for £100,000 or less.

It was held that no services were offered by the occupier or expressed by the purchaser. The occupier could not know what was in the mind of the purchaser so that there could not be any contractual consensus as to the consideration to be provided by the occupier. Unlike *The Moorcock* (see section 6.8) no term could be implied which amounted to consideration.

Consideration need not move to the promisor

Where the consideration provided is the suffering of a detriment to the promisee, the consideration cannot move to the promisor.

So in *Carlill* v *Carbolic Smoke Ball Co Ltd* (above), the consideration for the promise by the Carbolic Smoke Ball Co was using the smoke ball which the plaintiff had bought. That conferred no direct benefit on the Carbolic Smoke Ball Co, and so did not move to the promisor. It was, however, a detriment to herself.

In *Tanner* v *Tanner* [1975] 1 WLR 1346, a mistress gave up her rent-controlled flat and moved into a house bought by her lover and brought up the children of their union.

It was held that she had provided consideration by giving up her rent-controlled flat. She had a contractual licence to remain, which was irrevocable until the children were over school age.

The sustaining of the detriment must be part of the bargain struck between man and mistress. In *Horrocks* v *Foray* [1976] 1 WLR 230, the court thought that there would be no consideration in somewhat similar circumstances, because the mistress did not give up anything as part of the bargain.

Megaw LJ said:

'I say ... "(that there was no contractual licence)" ... without going on to consider what I think may well be an extremely difficult barrier in the way of the defendant (the mistress). Suppose that she had established something which otherwise could be regarded as being a contract, where is the consideration for that contract to be found? In *Tanner* v *Tanner*, the consideration was perfectly clear; the lady had given up her rent-controlled flat as part of the bargain that they would move into other accommodation. There is no such consideration here.'

Note also the case of *AEG (UK) Ltd* v *Lewis* (1992) The Times 29 December, in which a cheque was issued, on a voluntary basis, by a daughter to pay for work done by the plaintiffs for her father. No work had been done for her, and when the cheque was stopped, it was because her father was dissatisfied with the work. The question of whether a dishonoured cheque might be deemed consideration was debated, obiter, by the court, but was not in issue here because no right of action lay against the defendant who was a volunteer and not a party to the contract.

Past consideration is not good consideration

The rule is well established. It can be seen in operation in *Roscorla* v *Thomas* (1842) 3 QB 234. The defendant promised the plaintiff that a horse which had been bought by him was sound and free from vice. In fact, it was not.

It was held that the express promise that the horse was sound and free from vice had been made after the sale and, therefore, no consideration for the promise was given.

Similarly, in *Eastwood* v *Kenyon* (1840) 11 Ad & El 438, the guardian of a young girl had raised a loan to pay for her education and maintenance. On her marriage, her husband agreed to repay the amount of the loan. He failed to do so. The guardian sued him.

It was held that there was no liability on the part of the husband because the consideration was past consideration. With reference to the argument that the husband had a moral obligation to repay the loan, the court said that no such argument could exist in English law. It would annihilate any need for consideration at all.

In *Re McArdle* [1951] Ch 669, a promise made 'in consideration of your carrying out certain alterations and improvements to the property' was held by the Court of Appeal to be unenforceable, as all the work had been done before the promise was made.

These cases contrast with that of *Lampleigh* v *Braithwait* (1615) Hob 105. Braithwait had murdered someone (M) and asked Lampleigh to do his best to obtain a pardon for him. Lampleigh journeyed to and from Newmarket for him. Braithwait afterwards promised to pay Lampleigh £100. The court held that the promise to pay £100, coupled with the prior request as part of the same activity, amounted to good consideration.

The principle extrapolated from this case crystallised into its modern form in *Re Casey's Patents* [1892] 1 Ch 104. A and B, who were joint owners of certain patent rights, wrote to C stating: 'In consideration of your services as the practical manager in working our patents we hereby agree to give you one third share of the patents.'

C could rely on this agreement. He was deemed to have given consideration for it. The court made the following observation:

> 'The fact of a past service raises an implication that at the time it was rendered it was to be paid for, and if it was a service which was to be paid for, when you get in the subsequent document a promise to pay, that promise may be treated as an admission which evidences, or as a positive bargain which fixes, the amount of that reasonable remuneration on the faith of which the service was originally rendered. So that here for past services there is ample justification for the promise to give the third share.'

Re Casey's Patents can, therefore, be said to be authority for the view that a subsequent promise to pay for an act done in the past will be good consideration where the plaintiff would be able to recover on a quantum meruit basis. (See Chapter 18). The subsequent agreement fixes the amount of the quantum meruit. Treitel, *The Law of Contract*, suggests that the promise could, alternatively, be regarded as being given in consideration of the promisee's releasing his quantum meruit claim. The decision in *Re Casey's Patents* was approved in 1979 in the case of *Pao On* v *Lau Yiu Long* [1979] 3 All ER 65 PC. The plaintiffs owned issued share capital in a company called 'Shing On'. The defendants were the majority shareholders in a company called 'Fu Chip' in Hong Kong. Two written agreements were entered into.

1. The plaintiffs were to sell shares in 'Shing On' to 'Fu Chip' in exchange for certain shares in 'Fu Chip'.
2. The defendants agreed to buy back just over half of the shares at the same price at a later date.

The purpose of the second agreement was to protect the plaintiffs against a fall in the share prices of 'Fu Chip'. However, as the share prices were expected to rise, the plaintiffs realised that they had contracted a bad bargain. Accordingly, the plaintiffs refused to perform the contracts, unless a different agreement were reached. The defendants chose to avoid litigation by cancelling the second agreement and replacing it by an agreement by the defendants to indemnify the plaintiffs against a drop in the value of the shares. The document of indemnity referred to the first agreement, and incorporated into the guarantee the promise in the first agreement not to sell before a certain date.

In fact, the share prices fell. The defendant failed to idemnify the plaintiff.

The Privy Council held that the promise not to sell before a certain date provided consideration supporting the agreement to indemnify, even though it was made prior to that agreement. The promise had been made in anticipation of some sort of guarantee by the defendant which protected the plaintiff against loss. *Re Casey's Patents* was approved and applied.

The Privy Council, in *Pao On*, laid down the necessary preconditions for an act done before the giving of a promise to constitute consideration for the promise:

1. the act must be done at the promisor's request;
2. the parties must have understood that the act was to be remunerated either by a payment or the conferment of some other benefit; and
3. the payment, or the conferment of a benefit, must have been legally enforceable had it been promised in advance.

Consideration must be sufficient but need not be adequate

The word 'sufficient' in this context is incapable of precise definition. In reality, it is used as little more than shorthand for the body of rules which prevent certain acts or promises from constituting valid consideration even though the rules discussed above may have been satisfied.

Valuation

The court will look to see if the purported consideration contains any value. If it sees that there can be some value, then it will not concern itself with the accuracy of the valuation. That may be so even where the motive for undervaluation is a corrupt one. Equity may intervene but the position at law is unaffected.

In *Chappell* v *Nestlé* [1960] AC 87 the respondents sold gramophone records to consumers of their chocolate products for 1s. 6d. and three wrappers. The question whether the chocolate wrappers formed part of the consideration fell for determination. They were held to be part of the consideration, even though Nestlé only threw them away. It follows that the wrappers would have been good consideration even if no sums had been paid.

Similarly, in *Midland Bank* v *Green* [1981] AC 513, where a husband conveyed an estate to his wife at a very low price to avoid the operation of an option to purchase, the court would not look at the adequacy of the consideration, even though the transaction was in part a gift.

But the act or promise must have some economic value. In *White* v *Bluett* (1853)

23 LJ Ex 36, it was held that a son's promise not to bore his father with complaints (for the father's promise not to sue him on a promissory note) was not good consideration.

Knowledge

It may be the case that a person must know that he is giving value in order to find consideration, though this is still open to debate.

In *Arrale* v *Costain Civil Engineering* [1976] 1 Lloyd's Rep 98, a workman accepted compensation for injury under a Dubai ordinance and in satisfaction of his rights in Dubai and at common law.

It was held that the workman had not lost his right to sue at common law because, at the time he accepted the compensation and entered into the agreement, he did not know he had any rights. He therefore gave no consideration for giving them up.

Compromise of suit

The above case implies that the workman could have provided consideration by giving up rights of which he knew. Similarly, where a person gives up proceedings at law, the mere surrender of the right to continue or start the proceedings is good consideration. Provided that the compromise is reached in good faith, it does not render the consideration invalid if it subsequently transpires that the claim compromised was wholly unfounded.

In *Callisher* v *Bischoffsheim* (1870) LR 5 QB 449, the plaintiff claimed that money was owed to him by the Government of Honduras and others. The defendant offered to pay the plaintiff if he would drop his suit against the Government. The plaintiff did so. The defendant refused to pay. The plaintiff brought an action. The defendant said that the Government of Honduras did not owe any money to the plaintiff, but the court held that was no defence to an action for breach of the agreement of compromise.

Duties owed to third parties

Where a duty is owed to a third party, its performance can also be consideration for a promise by another. The problem was considered in *Scotson* v *Pegg* (1861) 6 H & N 295. A agreed to deliver coal to B's order. B ordered A to deliver the coal to C, who promised A to unload it. A successfully sued to enforce C's promise, it being held that A's delivery of the coal was good consideration for C's promise notwithstanding that A was already bound to so deliver by his contract with B. However, it was also suggested there may have been a separate consideration for C's promise in that A may have had a lien on the coal, which he agreed to release in return for C's promise to unload the coal.

The same question also arose in *Shadwell* v *Shadwell* (1860) 9 CBNS 159, where an uncle promised to pay an annual sum to his nephew on hearing of his intended marriage (at the time a promise to marry was a binding contract that could be sued upon). Although the majority of the Court of Common Pleas held there was consideration for the uncle's promise, the suggested 'consideration' is unconvincing. They suggested that the nephew had made a material change in his position and incurred financial embarrassment, and that there had been a benefit to the uncle in that the welfare of his nephew was an object of interest to a near relative.

The principle that a promise to perform, or the performance of, a pre-existing contractual obligation to a third party can be valid consideration was affirmed by the Privy Council in *New Zealand Shipping* v *Satterthwaite (The Eurymedon)* [1974] 1 All ER 1015, where Lord Wilberforce said:

> 'An agreement to do an act which the promisor is under an existing obligation to a third party to do, may quite well amount to a valid consideration ... the promisee obtains the benefit of a direct obligation ... This proposition is illustrated and supported by *Scotson* v *Pegg* which their Lordships consider to be a good law.'

In *Pao On* v *Lau Yiu* (above), Lord Scarman stated that their Lordships did not doubt the principle.

Duties owed by law

If the duty relied upon to constitute consideration is already owed at law, it may not constitute good consideration. If, however, the promisor agrees to do more than is required at law, the consideration will be sufficient. This contrast can be illustrated by *Collins* v *Godefroy* (1831) 1 B & Ad 950 and *Glasbrook Brothers* v *Glamorgan CC* [1925] AC 270. In *Collins* v *Godefroy,* a plaintiff was subpoenaed to give evidence for the defendant. The plaintiff alleged that the defendant had promised to pay her expenses.

It was held that the defendant was obliged by law to answer to the subpoena, so that giving evidence could not be consideration for the promise to pay the witness's expenses.

The contrasting situation arose in *Glasbrook Bros* v *Glamorgan CC.* The police were under a duty to protect a coal mine during a strike. They were asked by the manager of a coal mine to provide a stronger guard than the police would otherwise have done. A rate was agreed for the provision of this service.

The extra protection was held to be good consideration for the promise by the coal mine manager to pay for it. See also *Harris* v *Sheffield United Football Club* [1987] 2 All ER 838.

A case which is difficult to reconcile with the rationale expressed above is *Ward* v *Byham* [1956] 1 WLR 496. The father of an illegitimate child wrote to its mother from whom he was separated saying that she could have the child and an allowance of £1 per week if she proved that the child was well looked after and happy. The father refused to continue payments after the mother married another man.

The mother was held to be entitled to enforce the father's promise. Denning LJ (as he then was) based his decision on the ground that the mother provided consideration by performing her legal duty to maintain the child. The alternative explanation is that the promise to make the child happy was further consideration. The latter explanation is problematical for two reasons:

1. it may be no more than a provision of natural love and affection; or
2. it may be too uncertain.

This latter view is also difficult to reconcile with *White v Bluett* (above).

Treitel, *The Law of Contract*, prefers the view of Lord Denning MR. He also suggests that, with the exception of the old and somewhat doubtful case of *Collins v Godefroy*, there is no conclusive authority to show that performance of a duty imposed by law cannot be consideration for a promise. In any event, it is hard to see why performance of a duty owed to a third party should be capable of amounting to consideration when performance of a duty owed at law cannot be so capable.

Duties imposed by prior contract with the promisor

The rule is that if A is bound to do something by virtue of a contract with B, performance of the duty or the promise to perform cannot be consideration for a further promise by B.

The same principle is said to be derived also from *Stilk v Myrick* (1809) 2 Camp 317. Some sailors had deserted a ship. The captain of the ship promised to divide their wages among the remaining sailors if they would work the ship home short-handed.

It was held that there was no consideration because the sailors were already bound to work the ship home.

The reliability of this decision is suspect. One of the reports of *Stilk v Myrick* (1809) 6 Esp 129 does not mention consideration at all, but says that the court decided against the sailors on the basis of an earlier decision on the grounds of public policy that sailors might refuse to perform their contracts unless they were granted extra pay. The case is, however, arguably wrong for another reason. The promise to divide the wages of the deserters was made by the ship's master, who was the defendant in the action. The sailors' contracts to work the ship may have been with the ship owners. This question was not raised, at least according to the reports. However, the rule in *Stilk v Myrick* was recognised as still being good law in *North Ocean Shipping v Hyundai Construction (The Atlantic Baron)* [1978] 3 All ER 1170, though being held inapplicable on the facts.

A different conclusion was reached in *Hartley v Ponsonby* (1857) 7 E & B 872. Here the ship became so short-handed as a result of desertion that it was dangerous to sail the ship home with only the remaining crew. The crew were offered increased wages if they sailed the ship home.

The court held that the promise to pay extra money was supported by good consideration. The danger to the sailors discharged them from their original contract. Consequently, they were free to enter into the new contract.

Note that in the case of *Williams v Roffey Bros & Nicholls* [1989] NLJ 1713, it was held (by the Court of Appeal) that when a party to an existing contract later agrees to pay an extra 'bonus' in order to ensure that the other party performs his obligations under the original contract, that the agreement is binding if the party agreeing to pay the bonus has thereby obtained some new practical advantage or avoided a disadvantage.

In the course of his judgment, Glidewell LJ said that following the decision in *Pao On* v *Lau Yiu Long* [1979] AC 614 the state of the law on this subject may be expressed as follows:

1. if A enters into a contract with B to do work for or supply goods or services to B in return for payment from B; and
2. at some time before A has completely performed his obligations under the contract, B has reason to doubt whether A will, or will be able to, complete his side of the bargain; and
3. B therefore promises A an additional payment in return for A's promise to perform his contractual obligations on time; and
4. as a result of giving this promise, B obtains in practice a benefit or obviates a disbenefit; and
5. B's promise is not given as a result of fraud or economic duress on A's part;
6. the benefit to B is capable of being consideration so that B's promise will be legally binding.

This proposition refines and limits the application of the principle in *Stilk* v *Myrick* (1809) 2 Camp 317, but leaves the principle unscathed.

Russell LJ, concurring, noted that in the late twentieth century the rigid approach to *Stilk* v *Myrick* was neither necessary nor desirable. Note, however, that the recent case of *Re Selectmove* [1995] 1 WLR 474 seems to indicate that *despite Williams* v *Roffey Bros & Nicholls* the courts may continue to follow the principal first laid down in *Pinnel's Case* and followed in *Foakes* v *Beer*.

It seems to follow from the proposition that performance of an existing duty cannot be consideration for a new promise that, a fortiori, partial performance of a duty cannot be consideration for a new promise. On the other hand, the introduction of a new element into the existing duty will support a new promise. The cases which are authority for this view are both cases which concern debts. In *Pinnel's Case* (1602) 5 Co Rep 117a, Pinnel sued Cole for £8 10*s.* due on a bond in November 1600. Cole's defence was that at Pinnel's request, he had paid him £5 2*s.* 6*d.* on 1 October, and that Pinnel had accepted this payment in full satisfaction of the original debt.

Though judgment was given for Pinnel on a point of pleading, the court made it clear that, had it not been for a technical flaw, they would have found for Cole on the ground that payment in part had been made on an earlier day than that appointed.

The payment at the request of the plaintiff on an earlier date than is contractually required is a new element, and provides additional consideration to support the discharge of the debt. So payment of a smaller sum accompanied at the creditor's request by the delivery of a chattel is good consideration for a promise to forgo the balance. 'The gift of a horse, hawk or robe, etc in satisfaction is good. For it shall be intended that a horse, hawk or robe, etc might be more beneficial than money.' This observation does not apply to negotiable instruments (such as cheques), even though negotiable instruments are a form of chattel. See *D & C Builders Ltd* v *Rees* [1966] 2 QB 617.

Pinnel's Case is cited as the authority for the proposition that: 'Payment of a lesser sum on the day in satisfaction of a greater sum cannot be any satisfaction for the whole.' The rule was approved by the House of Lords – *Foakes* v *Beer* (1884) 9 App Cas 605 – although Lord Blackburn in the latter case, dissenting in all but name, said the true ratio of the former case was:

> ' … that where a matter paid and accepted in satisfaction of a debt certain might by any possibility be more beneficial to the creditor than his debt, the court will not inquire into the adequacy of the consideration',

and that the further statement that a lesser sum on the day could never be satisfaction was unnecessary and erroneous.

The facts of *Foakes* v *Beer* were that B obtained judgment against F who subsequently asked for time to pay. B agreed to take no proceedings whatever on the judgment in consideration of an immediate payment with the balance paid by instalments. F complied with the terms of the agreement, and paid the whole of the judgment debt, but B thereafter sued for interest on the principal sum and the House of Lords held that she was entitled to succeed on that claim.

Part payment by third parties

Where a third party makes part payment which the creditor accepts as full satisfaction of the debtor's obligation, the creditor cannot then sue the debtor for the balance, for to do so would be a fraud upon the third party. That is not to say, however, that the breach of contract with the third party would be fraud at common law; it would not. For that reason, an alternative explanation for the rule that a third party can discharge a debtor's liability by part payment of the debt has been proffered. The court will not help the creditor to break his contract with the third party by allowing him to recover from the debtor. The third party can intervene so as to obtain a stay of the action. See *Snelling* v *Snelling* [1973] 1 QB 87. It is, of course, necessary that the creditor should have agreed with the third party not to sue the debtor. See *Gore* v *Van Der Lann* [1967] 2 QB 31.

Furthermore, where the part payment is made by a third party against a promissory note, a creditor cannot then sue the debtor on the note. In *Hirachand Punamchand* v *Temple* [1911] 2 KB 330, the court said that the promissory note was extinct as though it had been cancelled. The right of action on a promissory note is, however, distinct from a right of action in contract. The action on the note may be lost even though the contract remedy is not. The reverse is also true.

3.4 Promissory estoppel

Introduction

'Promissory estoppel' is the name that has been given to the equitable doctrine which has as its principal source the obiter dicta of Denning J (as he then was) in *Central London Property Trust Ltd* v *High Trees House Ltd* [1947] 1 KB 130.

Estoppel is a concept known both to law and to equity; estoppel at common law is commonly concerned to prevent a person from denying the existence of facts which he has himself previously asserted; as a rule of evidence, it debars him from leading evidence to rebut his own earlier assertion, where another, in consequence thereof, has acted to his detriment on the faith of the assertion.

Promissory estoppel is a type of equitable estoppel, but the two terms are not interchangeable, because the latter also embraces proprietary estoppel, a more certain and long-established concept. Proprietary estoppel provides that where a person expends money or effort on another's property in the mistaken belief that he has or will thereby acquire an interest in the property and the true owner encourages or acquiesces in the mistake, the latter is estopped, that is, prevented from asserting his full title against the former. Proprietary estoppel is permanent in effect, and may create a positive right of action (compare this with promissory estoppel as elaborated below).

Promissory estoppel is not concerned with facts but with promises and intentions:

> 'Where by his words or conduct one party to a transaction makes to the other an unambiguous promise or assurance which is intended to affect the legal relations between them (whether contractual or otherwise), and the other party acts upon it, altering his position to his detriment, the party making the promise or assurance will not be permitted to act inconsistently with it.' (Snell's *Principles of Equity*.)

The above definition might properly be called the conventional one; it is by no means universally accepted.

Evolution

The modern starting point is *High Trees*, but of necessity reference back must be made to nineteenth-century cases from which the doctrine purports to derive its authority and legitimacy.

The *High Trees* case

In 1937, the defendants leased a block of flats from the plaintiff for 99 years at a rent of £2,500 per annum. By 1940, because of the war, the defendants were unable fully to let the block, and the plaintiffs agreed to reduce the rent to £1,250. In 1945, when conditions had returned to normal and the block was fully let again, the plaintiffs sought to return to the full rent.

Denning J held that the plaintiffs could thereafter recover the full rent because their promise to accept half only was intended to apply during the war whilst the block was not fully let. Such is the ratio decidendi of the case. Promissory estoppel only raises its head in obiter dicta, because his Lordship said that had the plaintiffs sued for the balance in respect of the period 1940 –5, they would not have recovered.

Circumnavigating the authorities

Denning J's obiter dicta caused eyebrows to be raised because of the way he characteristically dealt with apparently immovable obstacles in his path.

The problem his Lordship faced was that, under the lease, the plaintiffs were contractually entitled to £2,500. There was no variation of the contract, no consideration moving from the defendants to support the plaintiffs' bare promise, which according to conventional theory would thus be unenforceable. Up until *High Trees*, it was considered to be an entrenched rule of English law that part payment of a debt did not without more discharge the debtor's liability for the whole amount; *Pinnel's Case* (1602) 5 Co Rep 117a (Court of Common Pleas), affirmed by the House of Lords in *Foakes* v *Beer* (1884) 9 App Cas 605.

Between the contracting parties themselves, the problem was susceptible of a practical solution: if the part payment was made at a time earlier than that stipulated in the contract for payment of the whole sum, the debtor would be discharged – as held in *Pinnel's Case*. The earlier part payment was good consideration for the creditor's promise to accept half, because the debtor was doing something different to that which he was contractually bound to do. Likewise, payments in goods, even if considerably less valuable than the debt in money terms, discharged the debtor. In the immortal words of Jessel MR in *Couldery* v *Bartrum* (1881) 19 Ch D 394:

> 'According to English Common Law a creditor might accept anything in satisfaction of his debt except a less amount of money. He might take a horse, or a canary, or a tomtit if he chose, and that was accord and satisfaction; but by a most extraordinary peculiarity of the English Common Law, he could not take 19*s*. 6*d*. in the pound.'

Thus expressed the rule had little to commend it; it permitted creditors to renege on agreements and, in 1937, the Law Revision Committee recommended its abolition, but although some Commonwealth jurisdictions have adopted this recommendation, no legislative action has yet been taken in England.

How then did Denning J avoid the operation of the rule? He relied on *Hughes* v *Metropolitan Railway Co* (1877) 2 App Cas 439. The appellant landlord served on the respondent tenants a notice to repair within six months; the effect of the respondents' failure to comply being that the appellant could forfeit the lease. Following service of the notice, the parties commenced negotiations for the respondents to buy the lease, which proceeded for almost six months when the appellant terminated them, and sought to forfeit the lease for the respondents' failure to repair. The House of Lords held that, by the negotiations, the appellant impliedly promised that he would not bring proceedings upon the respondents' failure to repair within six months, and that he could not subsequently take advantage of the respondents relying on this.

In *High Trees*, Denning J cited what he regarded as the crucial speech of Lord Cairns in *Hughes*:

> 'It is the first principle upon which all Courts of Equity proceed, that if parties who have entered into definite and distinct terms involving certain legal results – certain penalties or legal forfeiture – afterwards by their own act or with their own consent enter upon a course of negotiations which has the effect of leading one of the parties to suppose that the strict rights arising under the contract will not be enforced, or will be kept in suspense, or held in abeyance, the person who otherwise might have enforced these rights will not be allowed to enforce them where it would be inequitable having regard to the dealings which have thus taken place between the parties.'

For the moment, two short points should be made. First, Lord Cairns cited no authority for his 'first principle' and, secondly, there is no mention anywhere of promissory or, indeed, any other type of estoppel.

It has been said that Denning J revived a moribund case and applied too widely a principle that, on one reading of *Hughes*, concerned only equity's power to mitigate against inequitable forfeiture at common law. This is a little unfair, because *Hughes* had been cited and applied beyond the landlord and tenant context in *Birmingham and District Land Co* v *L & N W Ry* (1888) 40 Ch D 268 where Bowen LJ said:

> 'If persons who have contractual rights against others induce by their conduct those against whom they have such rights to believe that such rights will either not be enforced or will be kept in suspense or abeyance for some particular time, those persons will not be allowed by a court of equity to enforce the rights until such time has elapsed, without at all events placing the parties in the same position as they were before.'

It must, however, be said that certain other authorities relied on by Denning J were somewhat less than convincing. In summary, his Lordship's conclusion was that the effect of *Hughes* was that a promise to accept a smaller sum in discharge of a larger sum, if acted upon, is binding notwithstanding the absence of consideration. This, he said, was a result of the fusion of law and equity; he summarily dealt with *Foakes* v *Beer* by saying that in that case the point had not been considered.

Foakes was not the only authority in Denning J's path. He was also faced with a further decision of the House of Lords in *Jorden* v *Money* (1854) 5 HL Cas 185, where the defendant told the plaintiff on a number of occasions that she did not intend to enforce a debt owed by him to her under a bond and warrant. The plaintiff sought to give effect to these assurances by bringing an action to have the bond released and the debt cancelled. Their Lordships held, insofar as it is possible to extract a ratio decidendi (and the accepted ratio), that only a representation of existing or past fact could give rise to an estoppel, not a mere representation as to intention.

Denning J dealt with this difficulty equally shortly: he said that in *Jorden*, 'the promisor made it clear she did not intend to be legally bound', whereas in *High*

Trees, 'the proper inference was that the promisor did intend to be bound'. Nevertheless, his Lordship paid some respect to the decision by declining to call his equitable principle an estoppel, saying only that it was analogous to estoppel. In subsequent cases, his Lordship has not been so reticent.

Denning J's reasoning analysed

Hughes. Denning J undoubtedly rescued *Hughes* from the obscurity into which it had fallen after the *Birmingham Land* case. Since *High Trees*, it has commonly been cited and relied on (and not just by Lord Denning himself), so it is certainly now accepted as being authority for some principle of equitable relief. It is, however, unlikely that their Lordships appreciated that their speeches would have such profound repercussions, and in all probability considered they were dealing with a straightforward landlord and tenant matter; *Pinnel's Case* and *Jorden* v *Money* were never mentioned.

Foakes v *Beer*. In saying the *Hughes* point was never considered in *Foakes*, Denning J goes halfway to reconciling *High Trees* with *Foakes*. Estoppel was not pleaded in *Foakes* and was, therefore, never discussed (nor of course was it, in terms, in *Hughes*); arguably, if the defendant had taken the point he might have succeeded (and thereby rendered the present discussion superfluous). On the other hand, *Foakes* was only seven years after *Hughes*, and two members of the House of Lords sat in both cases. Perhaps they were in ignorance of the revolution they had initiated?

A possibly crucial factual distinction that is often overlooked is that in *High Trees*, the promise related to future payments (before the rent was due); in *Foakes*, the debt had already accrued. In the former case, the parties' future conduct would thereby be influenced, but can this reasoning apply to a presently outstanding debt? It may be that *High Trees* was correctly decided and that, at the same time, *Pinnel's Case* and *Foakes* remain good law.

Jorden v *Money*. *Jorden* was decided according to equitable principles and cannot be treated as laying down an inconsistent common law rule. Nor is it sufficient for Denning J simply to say that the promisor did not intend to be legally bound. With respect, his Lordship thereby put the cart before the horse. The reason the promisor was not legally bound was *because* the House of Lords held she could not be so bound by a mere representation of intention.

Jorden is a curious case. Lord Cranworth LC said:

> 'I think that the doctrine does not apply to a case where the representation is not a representation of fact but a statement of something which the party intends or does not intend to do. In the former case it is a contract, in the latter it is not'.

In effect his Lordship said that to enforce a representation of intention there must be a contract, and thereby failed properly to draw the distinction between an action upon a representation and an action upon a contract.

Two solutions have been suggested. First, that the criticism levelled at *High Trees* is aimed at the wrong target. *Jorden* may be the case incorrectly decided; the authorities relied on therein do not, it is said, support the limitation on estoppel imposed by that decision. Secondly, less drastically, *Jorden* might be said to lay down the general rule to which *Hughes* and *High Trees* are exceptions; namely, that where there is an existing contractual relationship between the parties, and one makes to the other a promise to vary, suspend or abandon his strict legal rights, he may be prevented from going back on that promise.

Post High Trees

High Trees, it appears, is here to stay, at least for the time being. It has been considered in a considerable number of cases, which are conveniently discussed under a number of headings defining and illustrating its principles and application.

The nature of the promise

The promise must be clear and unequivocal. See *Woodhouse Israel Cocoa Ltd* v *Nigerian Produce Marketing Co Ltd* [1972] AC 741 (HL) and *The Scaptrade* [1983] 2 All ER 763 (CA). Further, as Denning J emphasised in *High Trees*, the promise must be intended to affect legal relations and not be simply a gratuitous indulgence.

See, too, *Baird Textile Holdings Ltd* v *Marks and Spencer plc* [2001] EWCA Civ 274 (alleged obligation on part of defendant to obtain clothing from claimant insufficiently certain to found either contractual obligation or claim based on estoppel).

Contractual relationships and beyond

Can promissory estoppel arise where the parties are not bound by a contractual relationship? In *Hughes* and the *Birmingham Land* case, the parties were contractually bound, as they were in *High Trees*, although Denning J did not specify this as being a necessary precondition. In *Ajayi* v *Briscoe* [1964] 1 WLR 1326, Lord Hodson, giving the opinion of the Privy Council, said that: 'the principle applied when one party to a contract in the absence of fresh consideration agrees not to enforce his right'. In *Hughes,* Lord Cairns expressly referred to his remarks to 'contractual rights'. Further, all the cases relied on by Denning J in *High Trees* were cases of contract. In *Combe* v *Combe* [1951] 2 KB 215, Birkett LJ was prepared to consider that it might apply to a maintenance agreement between a divorced husband and wife, which fell short of being a contract proper but which clearly resembled one. Similarly, in *Durham Fancy Goods Ltd* v *Michael Jackson (Fancy Goods) Ltd* [1968] 2 QB 839, Donaldson J said that an existing contractual relationship was not necessary providing there was 'a pre-existing legal relationship which could, in certain circumstances, give rise to liabilities and penalties'.

Lord Denning endeavoured to go further still in *Evenden* v *Guildford City AFC Ltd* [1975] QB 917, and held that where an employee was promised by his new employer that he would be credited with his years of service for his old employer, which for the purposes of a redundancy payment would greatly increase the lump sum, and on the faith of the promise did not sue his old employer for a redundancy payment, the new employer was estopped from going back on his promise. His Lordship said:

> '[Promissory estoppel] applies whenever a representation is made, whether of fact or law, present or future, which is intended to be binding, intended to induce a person to act on it, and he does act on it.'

and he disclaimed any necessity for a contractual relationship, going considerably further than Birkett LJ and Donaldson J, who thought a legal relationship analogous to contract was required, to say that none at all was necessary.

Evenden was overruled on its facts by the House of Lords in *Secretary of State for Employment* v *Globe Elastic Thread* [1979] 2 All ER 1077 where, on similar facts, their Lordships said promissory estoppel did not apply because, quite simply, there *was* a contract with the employee that he would retain the benefit of his previous years' service. Lord Denning's view was not commented on, but it is submitted that the assertion that there need be no existing legal relationship between the parties for promissory estoppel to apply is not supported by authority, and has serious and unexamined implications for the doctrine of consideration as a whole.

In *Crabb* v *Arun DC* [1976] Ch 179, Lord Denning was prepared to say that promissory estoppel could operate to prevent a person insisting on his strict legal rights 'whether arising under a contract, or on his title deeds, or by statute'. With respect to his Lordship, far from applying the judgment of Lord Cairns in *Hughes*, it extends it far beyond its original context – Lord Cairns was careful to confine his speech to instances where 'parties ... have entered into distinct terms involving certain legal results – certain penalties or legal forfeiture'. In *Brikom Investments Ltd* v *Carr* [1979] 2 All ER 753, Roskill and Cumming-Bruce LJJ expressed their dissent from Lord Denning's view in *Crabb* v *Arun DC*.

A shield not a sword

Here again the question seems to be, if promissory estoppel can create a cause of action on a bare promise, whither the doctrine of consideration? The answer is that the *doctrine operates as 'a shield not a sword'* (*Combe* v *Combe*), that it is defensive in nature, not offensive. As Denning J said in *High Trees*, the doctrine does not create an action for breach of promise, but it will prevent the promissor acting inconsistently with his promise.

In *Combe* v *Combe*, his Lordship expressed concern that the doctrine might be stretched too far and explicitly stated that it did '*not create new causes of action where none existed before*'. (His Lordship's judgment merits close reading in the light of his own remarks in later cases.) Asquith LJ agreed and said that the effect of the doctrine was that 'the promisor cannot bring an action against the promisee which involves the repudiation of his promise or which is inconsistent with it'.

This does not mean that a promisee can never be a plaintiff: if in a contract for the sale of goods a buyer promises not to insist on delivery by the date specified in the contract, and then subsequently refuses to accept the later delivery, it is surmised that the seller could sue for the price and that the buyer would, by his promise, be estopped from asserting that delivery was late.

In *Robertson* v *Minister of Pensions* [1949] 1 KB 227, the defendants refused to pay the plaintiff a disability pension, and the plaintiff sued. Denning J held that by reason of an earlier letter from the defendants to the plaintiff assuring him that his disability had been caused by war service, they were estopped from subsequently asserting the contrary.

As Asquith LJ said in *Combe* v *Combe*, the action was brought not on the promise, but on an independent statutory right which the defendants were estopped from denying.

The orthodox view that promissory estoppel is by definition a defensive doctrine only has been subject to attack. In *Re Wyvern Developments Ltd* [1974] 1 WLR 1097, Templeman J, without much explanation, appeared to think that this was no longer the case and that it could create rights; Lord Denning's judgment in *Evenden* also adopted this approach. The old view was, however, restated by Croom-Johnson J in *Argy Trading Development Co Ltd* v *Lapid Developments Ltd* [1977] 1 WLR 444.

It is true that proprietary estoppel (another form of equitable estoppel) *can* create rights, but this of itself does not seem sufficient to confer a similar quality on promissory estoppel. Its whole history and basis heretofore has been that it deals with promises in a pre-existing contractual framework. To extend it beyond this is to render actionable bare promises unsupported by consideration. What effect will this have on the doctrine of consideration which, according to Denning LJ in *Combe* v *Combe* 'is too firmly fixed to be overthrown by a sidewind'?

An equitable doctrine

Being an equitable doctrine, the promisee can only rely on promissory estoppel if he has himself acted equitably. In the words of the old maxim, 'He who comes to equity must come with clean hands.'

In *D & C Builders Ltd* v *Rees* [1966] 2 QB 617, the defendant owed the plaintiffs £482 for building work done. After failing to pay for several months, the defendant offered £300 or, in effect, nothing. The plaintiffs, as the defendant well knew, were in dire financial straits and were compelled to accept. They subsequently sued for the balance. Lord Denning held that the defendant had held the plaintiffs to ransom by taking advantage of their financial predicament, that there was no true accord between the parties and that accordingly the defendant could not rely on *High Trees* in his defence; it would not be inequitable for the plaintiffs to go back on their promise to accept £300 because it had been extracted by threats.

Acting on the promise

For the promisee to invoke the doctrine of promissory estoppel, he must in some way have acted on the promise, or altered his position in reliance on it. This much emerges with reasonable clarity from *High Trees*, *Ajayi* v *Briscoe* (Privy Council) and *Tool Metal Manufacturing Co Ltd* v *Tungsten Electric Co Ltd* [1955] 1 WLR 761 HL, although in the last two cases the doctrine was only considered en passant. The difficulty lies in the next step in the reasoning. The whole concept of estoppel is based on the principle that it would be inequitable to let the promisor resile on his promise, because the promisee will suffer prejudice or loss as a result, that is, on the faith of the promise he has altered his position to *his detriment*. Is detriment necessary for promissory estoppel?

Prima facie in *High Trees* there was none. Where is the detriment in paying half, when one is liable for the whole? It has been suggested that the defendants did act to their detriment by choosing to remain as tenants of the block on the faith of the plaintiffs' promise.

Whether or not this is so is unclear from the facts as reported and, in any event, appears unlikely in view of the (curious and often unnoticed) fact that the defendant company was a subsidiary of the plaintiffs. Such an exercise is reminiscent of the Court's occasional despairing efforts to find consideration where really none exists (for example, the majority in *Ward* v *Byham* [1956] 1 WLR 496). Lord Denning himself has admitted, extrajudicially, that there was no detriment in *High Trees* and in *W J Alan & Co* v *El Nasr Export and Import Co* [1972] 2 QB 189, has disclaimed detriment as a necessary condition for promissory estoppel.

The point is one of some difficulty. In *Tool Metal* and *Ajayi* v *Briscoe*, the House of Lords and Privy Council respectively simply referred to the promisee 'altering his position' with no mention of the necessity of detriment. It may be that they regarded the point as self-evident and sufficiently embraced within the idea of the promisee 'altering his position'; certainly, it would seem unusual that an equity could be raised by a man who had altered his position to his advantage. The resultant ambiguity of the decisions is that Lord Denning has been able to cite them as supporting his 'no detriment' approach in *Alan* v *El Nasr*.

It is instructive to refer back to the original source of promissory estoppel, *Hughes*. Clearly, the tenants did act to their detriment by failing to repair within the prescribed time, and thereby rendering themselves liable to forfeiture. To this extent, *High Trees* is not on all fours with *Hughes*. The point might be dealt with by saying that the general test is whether, in all the circumstances, it would be inequitable to permit the promisor to go back on his promise. Detriment would clearly be important in determining this, but that it is only a factor (albeit a weighty one) to be considered. To permit the promisor to resile might be, in all the circumstances, inequitable even in the absence of detriment; on the other hand, detriment would not necessarily of itself satisfy the inequitable test.

In *Société Italo-Belge* v *Palm Oils (The Post Chaser)* [1982] 1 All ER 19, Robert Goff J also expressed the view that it is not necessary to show detriment. His Lordship stated, further, that:

'... indeed, the representee may have benefited from the representation, and yet it may be inequitable, at least without reasonable notice, for the representor to enforce his legal rights'.

However, in *Goldsworthy* v *Brickell* [1987] 1 All ER 853, Nourse LJ did regard detriment as a requirement of promissory estoppel. This point was not fully discussed by the Court of Appeal as it was found, on the facts, that a clear and unequivocal representation had not been established. An opportunity to specifically address this issue of detriment as a requirement for an action under promissory estoppel came before the Court of Appeal in *Gillett* v *Holt and Another* (2000) The Times 17 March. The Court stated that when ascertaining whether promises and assurances repeated over a period of many years as to future rights, the entire claim must be examined in the round. Where the assurances given were intended to be relied on, and were infact relied on, it was not then necessary to look for an irrevocable promise since it was the other party's detrimental reliance on the promise which made it irrevocable. The issue is thus settled, ie the innocent party's detrimental reliance will suffice for a proprietory estoppel to operate.

The issue is thus open for decision by the House of Lords should the opportunity arise. With respect to Lord Denning, it requires a deeper analysis than saying (as his Lordship has done extrajudicially) that promises ought to be kept and it is inequitable to permit a man to break a promise. The importance of the doctrine of consideration in the English law of contract means that, in the absence of consideration, as a general rule a man is allowed to do just that.

Suspensive or extinctive?

It has yet to be established beyond argument whether promissory estoppel operates only to suspend rights, that is, that the promisor can reassert his strict legal rights upon giving the promisee reasonable notice that he intends so to do, or whether it may operate totally to extinguish the promisor's rights, that is, is permanent in effect.

It will be remembered that in *High Trees* the defendants were under a continuing liability to pay rent annually under the lease. The doctrine operated suspensively only insofar as the landlords could insist on payment of full rent when wartime conditions had ceased and the block was fully let; at the end of the war, the landlord's rights revived. The contrary hardly seemed arguable because the nature of the landlord's promise was such that it was clear they only agreed to accept half rent during the continuance of the war; when it ceased, the promise no longer applied, nor could it have been understood by either party thereafter to apply. In one sense, however, the promise did extinguish certain of the landlord's rights, namely their rights to the full rent from 1940-5. Denning J held that they were forever estopped from claiming the balance. Suppose the promise, unlike that in *High Trees*, is not limited in nature, but is intended and understood to be permanent in effect? Lord Denning, in *D & C Builders* v *Rees* and *Alan* v *El Nasr*, expressed the view that, in these circumstances, the courts would not permit the promisor to revert to this strict legal right and that the estoppel would be final and permanent. It should be noted that *D & C Builders* did not concern periodical payments, but liability for a single lump sum. If promissory estoppel is to apply to such facts, then it can only be permanent in effect, otherwise *Foakes* v *Beer* will continue in full force and the promisor would be free at a future time to claim the balance; to say that the promisor is temporarily estopped from claiming the balance, but may do so upon giving reasonable notice, renders the estoppel virtually worthless from the promisee's point of view. In *Arrale* v *Costain Civil Engineering Ltd* [1976] 1 Lloyd's Rep 98, Lord Denning said that the rule in *Foakes* v *Beer* was no longer valid and had been replaced by equitable principles. The view preferred here is that *Foakes* remains good in law, but the strictness of the rule is mitigated in equity by promissory estoppel providing the necessary conditions are satisfied.

Other judges have been less certain than Lord Denning about this aspect of promissory estoppel. In *Tool Metal*, the House of Lords permitted the promisors to go back on a promise not to insist upon the payment of compensation for the exploitation of a patented manufacturing process (another case of periodical payments), because the promise was referrable to wartime conditions and could be terminated thereafter by giving reasonable notice.

In *Ajayi* v *Briscoe*, the Privy Council said that the promisor could resile from his promise on giving reasonable notice, which need not be formal notice, giving the promisee reasonable opportunity of resuming his position, but that the promise would become final and irrecovable if the promisee could not resume his former position, thus accepting extinctiveness in principle in certain circumstances.

Promissory estoppel was applied to extinguish all rights by a New Zealand judge in *P* v *P* [1957] NZLR 854. McGregor J held that where the Public Trustee, on behalf of a mentally ill wife, erroneously represented to a husband that the latter's liability to pay maintenance under a deed of separation was discharged by a subsequent divorce, the Public Trustee could not thereafter sue the husband under the deed.

Hughes itself is of little help in this respect. Admittedly, Lord Cairns did not limit his enunciated principle as being suspensive only, but on the facts the promisor's rights were only suspended, and as has already been pointed out, it would be wrong to read too much into the minutiae of his Lordship's speech because he was almost certainly unaware that he was in the act of laying down a principle that would be so closely scrutinised and widely applied.

Again, therefore, it must be said that the matter remains open for argument. The view of Lord Denning does command sympathy and respect. If the promise is such that the promisor unequivocally and permanently abandons his rights, how can a court be said to be preventing the promisor from acting inconsistently with his promise (the very basis of the estoppel) if it subsequently permits him to reassume those rights? It is submitted that the preferred approach is to look at the nature of the promise: if, as in *High Trees* and *Tool Metal*, it is intended to be temporary in application and to reserve to the promisor the right subsequently to reassert his legal rights, the effect will be suspensive only; if, on the other hand, it is intended to be permanent, then there is no reason why in principle or on authority the promise should not be given its full effect so as to extinguish the promisor's rights.

Promissory estoppel – fact or fantasy?

It might be thought to be lamentably late in the day to consider the reality or otherwise of promissory estoppel. The reason why only now the basic premise upon which all the above has been based falls for discussion is that it is only when one has fully understood what promissory estoppel purports to be, that one can stand back and judge the validity or otherwise of the thing itself.

It has been contended that promissory estoppel is not a true estoppel, properly so called. In support of this is cited the judgment of Denning J in *High Trees*, where his Lordship said that the cases from which he derived the *High Trees* principle were 'not really' cases of estoppel. In all probability, his Lordship's guarded language was at least partially motivated by the necessity to give due deference to the decision of the House of Lords in *Jorden* v *Money*, and, further, with all respect to his Lordship, at that stage he had probably not fully thought through the repercussions of his judgment. In later cases, his Lordship has unreservedly adopted the expression 'promissory estoppel'.

Those who argue against the estoppel view have sought to show the close connection between the doctrine and the common law doctrine of waiver or forebearance (see, for example, Treitel). Waiver was developed at common law to mitigate strictness of the rules as to variation, namely, that the terms of an existing contract could only be varied providing both parties furnished consideration and providing any necessary formalities were complied with. Where for the convenience of, and at the request of one party, the other forbears to insist on the precise mode or time of performance specified in the contract, the contract remains unchanged in the sense that there are no variations of its terms, but the party acceding to the request will be said to have waived his right to insist on strict compliance with one or more of them. The promissory estoppel cases, so it is said, are the counterpart in equity, and are better described as being cases of equitable forbearance.

There has so far been no attempt to explain the relationship between waiver and promissory estoppel, there is, indeed, an unfortunate tendency to speak of the two as if there is little or no difference: see *Combe* v *Combe* and, in particular, *Alan* v *El Nasr*. It may be that the answer lies in turning the microscope, not on the promissory estoppel cases, but on the waiver cases. These have always occupied a somewhat anomalous position in the law of contract, and no real attempt to explain them has ever been made (there can be no invocation of equity because the principles were developed by the common law courts before fusion in 1873). In *Charles Rickards Ltd* v *Oppenheim* [1950] 1 KB 616 (a waiver case), Denning LJ described waiver as being 'a kind of estoppel'. This may be the happiest explanation, and if waiver is, at common law, 'a kind of estoppel', then promissory estoppel may legitimately be said to be its specialised counterpart in equity, flowing from *Hughes* v *Metropolitan Rly Co*.

Although the relationship may be close, there are a number of important distinctions.

1. Promissory estoppel may extend beyond mere contractual relationships (see 'Contractual relationships and beyond' above).
2. In the opinion of certain judges, promissory estoppel may create new rights (see 'A shield not a sword' above); waiver can never do this.
3. Promissory estoppel is subject to special equitable principles (see 'An equitable doctrine' above).
4. Promissory estoppel requires the promisee to alter his position (arguably to his detriment) in reliance on the promise (see 'Acting on the promise' above); waiver makes no such demand.
5. Promissory estoppel may be permanent in nature (see 'Suspensive or extinctive?' above); waiver customarily permits the promisor to revert to his strict legal rights upon giving reasonable notice (*Rickards* v *Oppenheim*), though in *Alan* v *El Nasr* Megaw and Stephenson LJJ dealt with the case as being one of 'irrevocable waiver'.

Further complications

The sharp contrast between the views of Lord Denning MR and the more orthodox approach is manifest in the judgments of the Court of Appeal in *Brikom Investments Ltd* v *Carr* [1979] 2 All ER 753. The plaintiff landlords offered 99-year leases to their sitting tenants in four blocks of flats. At that time, the roofs of the blocks were in need of repair. The leases made the tenants liable to pay a contribution towards the repair costs, but the plaintiffs orally represented that they would carry out the repairs at their own expense. After the repairs were completed, the plaintiffs served contribution notices on (1) the first defendant, who was an original lessee and who admitted she would have taken the lease, even if the plaintiffs had not promised to pay for the repairs themselves; (2) the second defendant, who took the assignment of a lease with knowledge of the plaintiffs' representation; and (3) the third defendant, an assignee of an assignee without notice of the representation. The defendants relied in their defence, inter alia, on promissory estoppel.

Lord Denning held the *High Trees* principle in all three cases. As regards the first defendant, his Lordship was not impressed by the fact that she would have taken the lease irrespective of representations, dismissing this as hypothetical and held that she had acted on the promise.

As regards the second and third defendants, he held, simply, that the benefit and the burden ran with the lease to later assignees and assignors, apparently irrespective of whether or not they had notice.

Roskill and Cumming-Bruce LJJ, whilst arriving at the same result as Lord Denning, were careful to distance themselves from his Lordship's reasoning. Roskill LJ said:

> ' ... it would be wrong to extend the doctrine of promissory estoppel, whatever its precise limits at the present day, to the extent of abolishing in this back-handed way the doctrine of consideration'.

His Lordship disagreed with Lord Denning's idea of the estoppel running with the lease, and decided the case partly on the grounds of there being a collateral contract (the benefit of which had been assigned to the second and third defendants). Alternatively, his Lordship said: 'there was a plain waiver by the landlords of their right to claim the cost of these repairs from these tenants' and that this waiver subsisted notwithstanding subsequent assignments and sub-assignments, 'the relevant obligation ... had before the assignment been waived by the landlords'. His Lordship cited *Hughes* v *Metropolitan Rly Co* as supporting the ground of waiver, not promissory estoppel, and said of that case:

> 'For my own part, I would respectfully prefer to regard that as an illustration of contractual variation of strict contractual rights. But it could equally well be put as an illustration of equity relieving from the consequences of strict adherence to the letter of the lease.'

Cumming-Bruce LJ, in a brief judgment, agreed with Roskill LJ.

Regrettably the reasoning in all the judgments is profoundly unsatisfactory.

Lord Denning's judgment may be criticised on three grounds. First, his Lordship held that pre-contractual representations can give rise to an estoppel, whereas existing authority requires a contractual or analogous relationship (see 'Contractual relationships and beyond' above). Secondly, his Lordship appears to dismiss the requirement that the promisee must rely on the promise (see 'Acting on the promise' above), and seems to assert his old view that the unfairness of the promisor going back on his promise is sufficient, irrespective of any prejudice to the promisee. Thirdly, as a matter of property law, his idea of the estoppel running with the lease is unsound. His Lordship regards notice of the estoppel as irrelevant, yet it is a long established rule of property law that a bona fide purchaser for value of a legal estate takes free of equities.

Roskill LJ's judgment too leaves much to be desired. Whilst it is understandable that he refers to promissory estoppel as a 'somewhat uncertain doctrine', and wholly laudable that he is anxious to preserve the doctrine of consideration from underhand attacks, other parts of his judgment commend themselves far less. His Lordship fails to explain why he both rejects promissory estoppel and then applies *Hughes* v *Metropolitan Railway Co*. If, as appears to be the case, his Lordship adheres to the 'equitable waiver' rather than 'promissory estoppel' classification, then he fails to explain what the difference is between the two.

His Lordship regards *Hughes* as being an example of waiver 'as a matter of contract law or equity (call it what you will)', but for the reasons given in (1)–(5) above, it would be wholly wrong to regard the two as being the same; *Hughes* can be authority for one or the other, but not both. Nor can his Lordship be correct in referring to *Hughes* 'as an illustration of contractual variation of strict contractual rights'.

A contractual variation requires consideration and (in appropriate cases) due formality; neither are present in *Hughes,* which cannot, it is submitted, be regarded as a case of 'contractual variation' if his Lordship uses that term in its accepted sense. Unfortunately, therefore, *Brikom* v *Carr* served only to muddy even further already murky waters.

It remains to consider what has been termed 'estoppel by convention'. This may arise where the parties to a transaction act on an assumed state of facts. The effect of estoppel by convention is to preclude the parties from denying those facts. The difference between promissory estoppel and estoppel by convention is that the latter can arise without any representation having been made. If one party makes a mistaken assumption, which is not the result of a representation made by the other party, but is shared by that other party, this may be sufficient for an estoppel by convention to be created.

Thus in *Amalgamated Investment and Property Co* v *Texas Commerce International Bank* [1981] 3 All ER 577, the plaintiff requested the defendant to make advances of money to the plaintiff's subsidiary company, and gave a guarantee to the defendant in respect of those advances. The guarantee was for the repayment of any money advanced *by the defendant.* In order to circumvent the relevant currency restrictions, the defendant advanced money to one of its subsidiaries which, in turn, advanced money to the plaintiff's subsidiary. No money was directly paid by the defendant. On a literal reading, the guarantee did not, therefore, apply to the advances that were made. The plaintiff sought a declaration that it was under no liability to the bank under the guarantee. The Court of Appeal held, however, that the parties had acted on an assumed state of affairs that the guarantee would cover the loans that were actually made. That gave rise to an estoppel by convention, which estopped each party as against the other from questioning the truth of the facts which they assumed to be true.

In a subsequent case, *Keen* v *Holland* [1984] 1 All ER 75, the Court of Appeal was concerned to establish the limitations of estoppel by convention. In the *Amalgamated Investment* case, the parties had established a conventional basis on which they regulated their subsequent dealings. This was not authority for the proposition urged on the court in *Keen* v *Holland* that the mere fact that where the parties had a common view about the legal effect of contract, and that one of them would not to the other's knowledge have entered into it if he had appreciated its true legal effect, they are, without more, estopped from asserting its true legal effect. So broad a proposition could not be deduced from the actual decision in *Amalgamated Investment*, and could not be right.

Concluding thoughts

Promissory estoppel is ripe for examination in the House of Lords. The cases in the Lords in which the doctrine has been discussed have all, ultimately, turned on other issues, and their Lordships' remarks in that House had indicated that their Lordships feel that the time is ready for a pronouncement by the highest court in the land:

'I desire to add that the time may soon come when the whole sequence of cases based on promissory estoppel since the war, beginning with *Central London Property Trust Ltd* v *High Trees Houses Ltd* may need to be reviewed and reduced to a coherent body of doctrine by the courts. I do not mean to say that any are to be regarded with suspicion. But, as is common with an expanding doctrine, they do raise problems of coherent exposition which have never been systematically explored. However, this may be, we are not in a position to carry out this exploration here and in the present proceedings.'

Per Lord Hailsham LC in *Woodhouse* v *Nigerian Produce Marketing*:

'I am unable in any event to agree that any question of estoppel arises. There was a contract with the employee that he would retain the benefit of his previous employment. To convert this into an estoppel is to turn the doctrine of promissory estoppel (the validity or scope of which I do not now examine) upside down.'

Per Lord Wilberforce in *Secretary of State for Employment* v *Globe Elastic Thread Co Ltd*, overruling *Evenden* v *Guildford City AFC Ltd*:

'Pending such consideration, the validity, scope and necessary conditions for the application of promissory estoppel remain uncertain.'

4

Intention to Create Legal Relations

4.1 Aims of the law of contract

4.2 Formation of the contract

4.3 Intention to create legal relations

4.1 Aims of the law of contract

As we have already noted in the Introduction, the common theme underlying all attempts to define the term 'contract' is that there must be agreement. To the extent that, having made such an agreement, the parties must be encouraged to honour their obligations, means that certain rules have been formulated which dictate the degree to which the courts will intervene to enforce an agreement. However, while it may seem to be stating the obvious, it must be remembered that initially (at least in theory) parties voluntarily enter into agreements, free of all pressures or outside forces.

The main aims of contract are usually stated as given below.

1. To realise expectations.
2. To guard against (or allocate) certain commercial risks.
3. To ensure smooth running of the commercial system – *Tsakiroglou and Co Ltd* v *Noblee Thorl GmbH* [1962] AC 93.
4. Not to rescue a party from a bad bargain (see *Tsakiroglou* case, above); however some relief may be afforded to a party in cases of duress or undue influence.
5. To be an instrument of social control (see, for example, employment, sale of goods and consumer credit law).

The remedial goals of a plaintiff in a contract action are traditionally said to be one of three possibilities.

1. Fulfillment of expectation interest. This is often said to be the primary goal: the plaintiff seeks to be put into the position he would have been in had the defendant carried out the contract.
2. Protection of the plaintiff's restitution interest. Here the plaintiff seeks just to be put in the position he was in before he entered into the contract, that is, return of any goods delivered or money paid.

3. Protection of the plaintiff's reliance interest. Here the plaintiff is seeking compensation for work carried out, or expenses incurred in reliance upon the contractual agreement. A good example is the case of *Anglia Television Ltd* v *Reed* [1972] 1 QB 60.

Note: Punishment of the defendant is not a contractual aim (see *Addis* v *Gramophone Co Ltd* [1909] AC 488).

Looking over these aims and goals it becomes clear that, while there must be agreement for a contract to be legally enforceable, enforcement of agreements using the law of contract may achieve certain other underlying purposes as well. (Look, for example, at (3) and (5) of the main aims of contract above.)

4.2 Formation of the contract

General

A plaintiff will not be able to succeed against a defendant, simply because he has suffered loss which has, in some fashion, been induced by the defendant.

He must be able to show that the defendant's conduct has given the plaintiff a course of action in law.

He must be able to show that a contract has been entered into, either with the defendant or his agent or, where a misrepresentation is alleged, with a third party.

If he cannot show that a contract has been entered into, he cannot succeed on an application of the law of contract. He may be able to succeed under the law of torts, or obtain relief in equity, but that does not fall to be discussed in this section.

Elements of contract

Accordingly, it is said that the plaintiff must show four things to exist in order to establish that a contract has been entered into, as listed below.

1. That the parties had an intention to enter into legal relations.
2. That one party made an offer to the other.
3. That the other accepted that offer.
4. That there was an exchange of consideration.

The terms of the agreement must be sufficiently certain, that is, capable of being ascertained, to enable the court to be sure that an agreement has been reached.

Broader questions

It may be argued that the search is less for static ingredients in a 'thing' called a contract than for positive evidence that the plaintiff was justified in relying upon the defendant, and should not, therefore, bear the loss of his disappointed expectation.

The following questions are relevant.

1. Was the plaintiff justified in assuming that there was agreement?
2. Is there any reason to suppose that the parties did not intend their arrangements to have legal results?
3. What is it in the nature of the plaintiff's reliance upon the defendant that would justify the court in interfering on his behalf?
4. If an arrangement was primarily between two or more others, is the plaintiff so closely connected to this arrangement that the court should intervene to give him a remedy?

It is necessary to ask such broad questions because if it is not understood that this seems to be the court's basic approach, the many recent changes that have taken place in this area will be bewildering. These broad issues should be borne in mind when the subject of contractual ingredients is studied through the traditional categories.

Note, in particular, that the courts, in assessing whether or not there has been agreement, apply an objective test. Thus, it is not the function of the courts to ask whether each of the parties believed he had reached agreement; but whether an objective outsider, armed with the same information as the parties possessed at the time of making the contract, would have concluded that they had reached agreement. This objective test is applied in order to achieve the certainty that commercial transactions require. It is a practical approach which has largely displaced the theory prevalent during the nineteenth century that there could be no contract unless there had been a consensus ad idem – a meeting of minds of the contracting parties.

Hence, it is not open to a party to a contract to assert that he did not intend to contract on certain terms, if the evidence shows he accepted an offer containing those terms. Unless, that is, one party can set up one of the four defences of misrepresentation, mistake, duress or undue influence, which may effectively negative apparent agreement.

4.3 Intention to create legal relations

Not every bargain gives rise to a contract. For example, if A says to B, his brother: 'If you drive to the pub, I'll buy the first pint', and B agrees, a reasonable person would not expect that B would be able to sue A when he refuses to buy the first pint. The reason is that the nature of the agreement and the relationship of the parties would lead a reasonable person to believe that there was no contractual intention.

So when will a contractual intention be found? A distinction has to be drawn between agreements which are merely social and/or domestic, and agreements which are commercial in nature.

Social and domestic agreements

The rule where agreements are social or domestic is that there is a *presumption* that the parties do not intend to create legal relations. The leading case is *Balfour* v *Balfour* [1919] 2 KB 571. The defendant, a civil servant based in Sri Lanka, came to England with his wife (the plaintiff) and later returned to Sri Lanka alone, the wife remaining in England for health reasons. The defendant promised to pay the plaintiff £30 per month as maintenance, but failed to keep up the payments. The wife sued.

The court held that the wife could not succeed because:

1. she had provided no consideration for the promise to pay £30; and
2. there was no intention to create legal relations. Where the parties were husband and wife, the onus was on the plaintiff to rebut the presumption that in social and domestic arrangements there was no intention to contract. This she had failed to do.

Note, however, that in *Pettit* v *Pettit* [1970] AC 777, it was observed that though many agreements between husband and wife were not intended to be legally binding, performance of such agreements might well give rise to legal consequences.

Lord Diplock said:

'It would, in my view, be erroneous to extend the presumption accepted in *Balfour* v *Balfour* that mutual promises between man and wife in relation to their domestic arrangements are prima facie not intended by either to be legally enforceable to a presumption that *no* legal consequences should flow from acts done by them in performance of mutual promises with respect to the acquisition, improvement or addition to real or personal property – for this would be to intend what is impossible in law.'

Similarly, in *Jones* v *Padavatton* [1969] 1 WLR 328, Mrs Jones offered a monthly allowance to her daughter if she would go to England and read for the Bar. Her daughter reluctantly gave up her job in America and came to take Bar Finals. She was not very successful. Mrs Jones bought a house in London. She stopped paying the monthly allowance, but she allowed the daughter to live in the house and receive rents from other tenants. Some three years later, Mrs Jones brought an action for possession. The daughter counterclaimed for breach of the agreement to pay the monthly allowance and/or to provide the daughter with accommodation.

It was held that the first agreement may have been made with the intention of creating legal relations, but was only to be deemed to be for a reasonable time; that is sufficient time to enable the daughter to pass her Bar Finals. It had lapsed after five years.

The second agreement was only a family arrangement and there was no intention to create legal relations.

Intention and consideration

In deciding whether there is a contractual intention, it is often difficult to distinguish the intention from the question of whether consideration has been given. Natural love and affection is not consideration recognised at law. That is why no consideration was provided for the wife in *Balfour* v *Balfour*.

Interests in occupation

The presumption against contractual intention is sometimes rebutted where the occupation of real property is concerned. For example, in *Hardwick* v *Johnson* [1978] 1 WLR 683, a mother promised to buy for her son and daughter-in-law a suitable house in which to live. The arrangement was that she would buy it and they would pay her rent at £7 per week. After one year, the marriage broke down. The mother tried to get possession of the house. The daughter-in-law offered £7 per week.

The resulting agreement was held to be a licence for occupation. Lord Denning said that it was equitable and Roskill and Browne JJ said that it was contractual. They were clear that the court has to look at the intention of the parties by forming its own opinion as to what would have been the intention of reasonable men as to the effect of the exchange of promises if it had been present on their minds at the time.

Separation agreements

Furthermore, the presumption may be rebutted where an agreement is reached between spouses who are unhappily married, or about to separate, or separated, but any agreement reached must be expressed in clear, unambiguous terms. In *Meritt* v *Meritt* [1970] 1 WLR 1211, the husband, separated from his wife, agreed in writing to transfer the matrimonial home out of their joint names into her name alone, provided she paid off the remaining mortgage debt.

The husband's promise was held to be legally enforceable after his wife paid off the mortgage. Contrast *Gould* v *Gould* [1970] 1 QB 275.

Intention inferred from 'mutuality'

An illustrative case is *Simpkins* v *Pays* [1955] 1 WLR 975. The defendant, her granddaughter, and the plaintiff, a paying lodger, entered weekly for a newspaper fashion competition in the defendant's name. There was no regular rule concerning the way in which entry fees and postage were shared, but the defendant had told the plaintiff that she would share any winnings. One week a prize of £750 was won; on the defendant's refusal to share the prize, the plaintiff sued for a third and his action was successful.

The arangement was held to be a joint enterprise to which cash was contributed in the expectation of sharing any prize. The court was unable to identify any offer, or acceptance, but said that there was a 'mutuality' about the arrangements.

In *Robertson* v *Anderson* (2003) The Times 2 January, a decision of the Inner House of the Court of Session, it was held that an informal agreement between friends to share a bingo prize was enforceable. Lord Reed said that where a promise or agreement had been made in a purely social context, in most cases it would not be regarded as legally binding. It was, however, essential to look at the particular facts to discover whether they revealed an intention to conclude a contract. Here, the Court of First Instance had been entitled to conclude that it had been an agreement which gave rise to legal consequences. Just as in *Simpkins* v *Pays*, an intention to create legal relations could be inferred. The Court of Session also rejected the contention that the agreement between the parties was a gaming contract and was unenforceable on that ground. As Lord Reed explained, neither party had been making a bet or wager with the other: neither of them could be better or worse off than the other as the result of the game. Their contract had related to gaming, but it was not itself a gaming contract. As to gaming contracts, see particularly s18 of the Gaming Act 1845.

Commercial agreements

Where the agreement is a commercial one, there is a presumption that the parties intended to enter into legal relations. This means that the plaintiff does not have to prove intention in order to succeed; the court will presume its existence. The presumption can, however, be rebutted if a contrary intention is expressed. In *Rose & Frank Co* v *J R Crompton Bros* [1925] AC 445, a commercial agreement stated:

'This agreement is not entered into ... as a formal or legal agreement, and shall not be subject to legal jurisdiction in the law courts.'

The court decided that no legally enforceable contract existed. The appellant company could not recover compensation for the respondent company's refusal to honour its obligation.

Similarly, in *Jones* v *Vernons Pools* [1938] 2 All ER 626, the plaintiff sued on a football coupon which was said to be binding in honour only, but was held not to be entitled to recover.

Again in *Orion Insurance Co* v *Sphere Drake Insurance* [1992] 1 Lloyd's Rep 239 the plaintiffs claimed that the agreement between themselves and the defendants was a goodwill agreement only. The Court of Appeal conceded that from the overall impression (notes, memos, etc) there was no contractually binding agreement.

New England Reinsurance Corporation & First State Insurance Co v *Messoghios Insurance Co SA* [1992] 2 Lloyd's Rep 251, where the sole dealings between the parties consisted of a series of telexes, made it clear that even if the parties refer to a contract between them it may only be an informal agreement binding in honour only. The burden of proof that the agreement relied upon is contractually binding is on the plaintiff seeking to rely on it.

Similarly, the case of *G Percy Trentham Ltd* v *Archital Luxfer Ltd* [1993] 1 Lloyd's Rep 25, referred to the problem. Trentham were the main contractors on a scheme to build an industrial estate. They 'subcontracted' with the defendants to build doors, windows, shutters, etc. The dispute then arose as to defects in the completed work, and the defendants denied that a contract had even been formed.

The Court of Appeal held that even though there were no written documents it was clear from the parties' conduct that contracts existed. The exchanges between them (memos, phone calls, meetings) made it clear that all supported the existence of a binding series of sub-contracts. The defendants could not disprove the contracts' existence.

The parties' intentions may become clear from some collateral contract, that they propose negotiating some other major contract. Whether or not the transactions leading to collateral dealings have the status of a contract may be decided by exactly the same rules (as to parties' intentions) as the main transaction. See, for example *Pitt v PHH Asset Management* (1993) The Independent 6 August, concerning the status of a 'lock-out' agreement.

Rebutting the burden of proof

The question of whether the burden of proof has been rebutted is, however, one of fact. In *Edwards v Skyways Ltd* [1964] 1 WLR 349, an airline pilot was offered a 'golden handshake', that is, a payment expressed to be ex gratia by his employers. They failed to pay. The pilot sued. The employers said that the offer of the ex gratia payment was not intended to be contractually binding.

The burden of proof in a commercial agreement is on the person asserting that no legal effect was intended. The onus was said to be a heavy one and the employers failed to discharge it. In *Manatee Towing Co v Oceanbulk Maritime SA (The Bay Ridge)* [1999] 2 All ER (Comm) 306, the court held that there was no intention to create legal relations in the absence of a conclusive agreement having been reached between the parties. Confirmation of main terms of negotiation on agreement will not do.

A similar conclusion was reached in *Esso Petroleum v Commissioners for Customs and Excise* [1976] 1 WLR 1. Esso supplied garages with 'World Cup' coins. One coin was given away to motorists with every gallon of petrol. The issue, so far as the Customs and Excise were concerned, was whether there had been a contract of sale.

The House of Lords decided by a 4:1 majority that there had been no *sale*. However, three members of the House of Lords thought that there was a contract with regard to the coins – a contract for *supply* – on the basis that Esso had not discharged the burden of proving an absence of contractual intent.

In *Evans v Merzario Ltd* [1976] 1 WLR 1078, a representative of a firm of forwarding agents, with whom the customer had dealt for a long time, said that goods would henceforth be packed into containers and carried below deck. At the time that the statement was made, no specific contract of carriage was designated. It was held that the promise was intended to be legally binding. The Court of Appeal relied on the importance of the place of carriage to the customer, and the fact that the customer would not have agreed to container carriage had that promise not been made.

In *Kleinwort Benson Ltd v Malaysia Mining Corp Bhd* [1989] 1 All ER 785, the plaintiff bank agreed with the defendants to make a loan facility to the defendant's wholly owned subsidiary. As part of the facility arrangement, the defendants furnished to the plaintiffs two 'letters of comfort', each of which stated that 'it is our policy to ensure that the business of (the subsidiary) is at all times in a position to meet its liabilities to you under the (loan facility) arrangements'.

The Court of Appeal held that, on the facts, the letters of comfort were statements of present fact, and not contractual promises as to future conduct. They were not intended to create legal relations, and gave rise to no more than a moral responsibility on the part of the defendants to meet the subsidiary's debt.

Walford v *Miles* [1992] 2 WLR 174, in its progression through the courts, demonstrated that it is perhaps more closely concerned with the question of certainty (see Chapter 5). In this case the plaintiffs entered into negotiations with the defendants over the sale of the defendants' business, and reached the point of the plaintiffs agreeing to obtain a 'comfort letter' from the bank and not to withdraw from the negotiations. The defendants, in return, undertook to break off negotiations with a third party and deal only with the plaintiffs. In fact the defendants not only did not cease negotiations with the rival bidder, they eventually sold the business to that rival. The question arose as to whether this oral agreement was binding.

The House of Lords decided that although the law had, for more than 20 years, directed that an agreement to agree or an agreement to negotiate was not an enforceable contract, there was no reason why in English law, A should not perfectly validly negotiate an enforceable contract with B, that for consideration B would agree not to negotiate with anyone other than A for a fixed period of time. Such agreements, often known as 'lock-out agreements' or some such similar term, have become increasingly common over the last few years.

Unfortunately, however, in *Walford* v *Miles* the agreement was deficient in one respect: it did not specify for how long this arrangement was to continue. This deficiency could not be cured by the court's implying, for example, a requirement that the arrangement should continue for a 'reasonable time' or some similar arrangement. For that reason the arrangement must fail for lack of certainty.

5

Certainty and Form of the Contract

5.1 Certainty

5.2 Form of the contract

5.3 Exceptions to the general rule

5.4 Contracts for the sale of land

5.5 Contracts of guarantee

5.6 Specific contracts required by statute to be in writing

5.1 Certainty

We have examined previously the mechanics of agreement, the process of analysing a transaction or negotiations in order to determine an offer and an acceptance. Even where an offer and acceptance have been established, it may not be clear precisely on what terms the parties have reached agreement. Whilst it is not the function of the courts to make an agreement for the parties, they will not defeat the intention of the parties to contract merely because the agreement has been loosely worded. Gaps in the contract may often be filled by reference to the custom of the trade, or the course of dealings between the parties. If, however, no such reference can be made, or it cannot be objectively determined what the parties intended, then the courts may be forced to conclude that the lack of certainty militates against contractual validity.

Statute

In the absence of express provision in an agreement, statute may be able to provide the missing terms.

Section 8 Sale of Goods Act 1979
(1) The price in a contract of sale may be fixed by the contract, or may be left to be fixed in a manner agreed by the contract, or may be determined by the course of dealing between the parties.

(2) Where the price is not determined as mentioned in subsection (1) above, the buyer must pay a reasonable price.

(3) What is a reasonable price is a question of fact dependent on the circumstances of each particular case.

Section 15(1) Supply of Goods and Services Act 1982

Where, under a contract for the supply of a service, the consideration for the service is not determined by the contract, left to be determined in a manner agreed by the contract, or determined by the course of dealing between the parties, there is an implied term that the party contracting with the supplier will pay a reasonable charge.

Vagueness

If an agreement is too vague to permit a meaning to be given to it, no enforceable contract can be construed. However, courts may be able to find a meaning to an apparently vague term by reference to custom, or to what is reasonable. Further, it may be possible to ignore certain meaningless words and still leave a valid contract. The approach of the courts is indicated by consideration of the following cases.

In *Scammel & Nephew* v *Ouston* [1941] AC 251, the order stated that it was given 'on the understanding that the balance of the purchase price can be had on hire-purchase terms ...' The House of Lords held that the phrase was so vague that it could not be given a definite meaning. There were no usual terms in such a contract to which reference could be made.

In *Hillas & Co* v *Arcos* (1932) 147 LT 503, a seemingly vague phrase was able to be interpreted. The agreement of sale was for timber 'of fair specification'. The parties were persons fully acquainted with the particular trade and, in the light of that, the House of Lords was able to affix a meaning to the phrase.

Nicolene v *Simmonds* [1953] 1 QB 543 illustrates that it may be possible to ignore certain words. A clause of the agreement stated that the sale was subject to 'the usual conditions of acceptance'. There were, in fact, no such usual conditions. The phrase was meaningless and the deletion of the phrase would not impair the validity of the contract.

The Scottish case, *Neilson* v *Stewart* 1991 SLT 523 HL, would, no doubt, be similarly applicable to English cases. In the case, a sale of shares was agreed between seller and purchaser. The agreement included a loan repayment which was to be deferred for one year 'after which time repayment shall be negotiated to our mutual satisfaction'. The purchaser failed to complete the agreement and subsequently argued that the phrase in question rendered the whole agreement unenforceable by reason of uncertainty. The seller's argument was that there were two severable agreements, one for the sale of shares, which was enforceable, and one for the arrangements of the loan, which was not enforceable.

The House of Lords held that in fact both parts of the agreement were enforceable. The parties did not apparently intend the loan to be fixed as to time and manner of payment, all loans were repayable on demand and it was not essential that interest should be payable. Any apparent ambiguities could thus be resolved. The seller's action for damages for breach of contract by the buyer was successful.

The courts are concerned to ascertain whether or not the parties have actually reached agreement. In interpreting the language of the 'agreement', especially where there is a mixture of formal documents, verbal exchanges and later changes made to the basic document (as in the following case), problems may occur as to the construction of language used by the parties. See *Punjab National Bank* v *De Boinville* [1992] 1 WLR 1138 in which the plaintiff bank agreed to finance loans to a company (E Ltd) to purchase oil. One of the terms was that insurance cover be arranged to provide for any loss by the bank. Insurance was placed with various underwriters, most of the work being entrusted to two individual brokers. In all some five different policies were drawn up and assigned by customer to the bank by way of security. Once the first and second policies came into being, the remaining policies were based on simply deleting odd words and phrases and amending them. Thus references to 'assured' became 'a/c E Ltd' and 'net loss' became 'sum assured'. The question arose as to whether, in construing these later policies, regard could be had to the words which had been deleted, to give sense to the words substituted. It was held that since the later policies' construction was dependant on the earliest one, it was permissible to have regard to all aspects of the original policy, including deletions.

It should be noted also that a conditional acceptance is not true acceptance. This should, however, be distinguished from a contract which is conditional, which is quite different. In *Graham* v *Pitkin* (below) the question arose as to whether the condition in question was a condition precedent or not. Conditions of the sort found in this case are common in conveyancing cases, but not in other types of contract. *Graham* v *Pitkin* [1992] 1 WLR 403 concerned a sale of land in which the plaintiff purchasers stipulated a condition that a mortgage be arranged before the contract was considered binding. After considerable difficulty in arranging a mortgage the purchaser decided to pay cash. It was held that the contract was not uncertain or incomplete because of this condition. It was purely for the benefit of the purchaser who might waive the condition if she wished.

Incompleteness

If there is an essential term yet to be agreed, and there is no express or implied provision for its solution, there is no binding contract (*British Bank for Foreign Trade* v *Novinex* [1949] 1 KB 623).

Thus in *May and Butcher* v *R* [1934] 2 KB 17, the agreement provided that the price(s) to be paid and the date(s) of payment should 'be agreed upon from time to time' by the parties. The House of Lords held that there never was a concluded contract between the parties. As Treitel observed, had the agreement been silent on these points, it may have been possible to resolve the matter by reference to the Sale of Goods Act (see above).

There was an arbitration clause in the agreement, but this did not assist in resolution as this clause pre-supposed the existence of a binding contract.

A contrast with the above case is provided by *Foley* v *Classique Coaches* [1934] 2 KB 1, in which there were two related agreements put into separate documents. The one agreement concerned the sale of petrol; the latter agreement stated that the petrol was to be supplied 'at a price to be agreed by the parties in writing and from time to time'. The Court of Appeal was able to distinguish this case from that of *May and Butcher*. Here the agreement for the sale of petrol was acted on for three years; it formed part of a bargain involving the sale of land which had been conveyed; and it contained an arbitration clause, which was construed as applying to any failure to agree as to the price.

It would seem that a distinction must be drawn between an arrangement which is wholly executory on both sides, and one in which one party has performed all the obligations required of him by the agreement. An arrangement providing for 'a price to be agreed' may not constitute a binding contract whilst the matter is still executory, but if one party has completed the obligations required of him, it will be implied from the conduct of the parties that, in the absence of agreement, a reasonable price is to be paid. See *British Bank, etc* v *Novinex* (above).

An agreement will not be void for uncertainty if it provides a means for resolving the matters that are left open. In *Campbell* v *Edwards* [1976] 1 WLR 403 CA, the agreement provided that the price should be fixed by a valuer agreed on by the parties.

Lord Denning MR:

'If two parties agree that the price of property should be fixed by a valuer on whom they agree, and he gives that valuation honestly and in good faith they are bound by it. Even if he has made a mistake they are still bound by it.'

(It would of course, Lord Denning went on to say, be different if there were fraud or collusion.)

In *Sudbrook Trading Estate* v *Eggleton* [1982] 3 All ER 1 HL, the agreement contained the provision for the purchase of the premises by the tenant 'at such price ... as may be agreed upon by two valuers', one to be nominated by each party. The landlord refused to appoint a valuer. The House of Lords interpreted this provision as an agreement to sell at a fair and reasonable price to be assessed by the two valuers. As the landlord had, in breach of his contractual obligation, made the agreed manner of assessment impossible, it was left open to the court to determine on expert evidence what was the fair and reasonable price.

5.2 Form of the contract

General rule

The general rule at common law is that contracts can be made informally. No writing or other document is necessary. A contract made orally is valid and enforceable, unless the contract falls into one of the exceptions set out below.

There may, however, be practical problems of proof when trying to enforce an oral contract in the courts.

The exceptions to the general rule are all imposed by statute. The requirements as to form vary. Some contracts must be made by deed, some in writing, and some must be evidenced in writing.

A *deed* is a document containing all the terms of the agreement, which is signed (by both parties), sealed and delivered. Contracts made by deed are also referred to as specialties. The requirement of a seal dates from times when illiteracy was prevalent. A seal was used in place of a signature. The requirement of a signature to a deed was imposed in 1926 by s72 Law of Property Act 1925.

Alterations

For a deed or other instrument to be rendered invalid by an alteration which was not approved by all parties to it, the party seeking to avoid the contract must show that the alteration was one which was potentially prejudicial to his legal rights or obligations: *Raiffeisen Zentralbank Osterreich AG* v *Crossseas Shipping Ltd* [2000] 3 All ER 274 (space left blank in guarantee subsequently filled in but guarantee enforceable since alteration did not change liabilities under it).

5.3 Exceptions to the general rule

Interests in land

The conveyance of existing legal interests in land, or the creation of new legal interests, must be by deed: s52(1) Law of Property Act 1925.

The grant of a lease for three years or less is excepted from this rule. Such leases may be validly created orally or in writing: s54(2) Law of Property Act 1925.

Contracts within the Statute of Frauds

The Statute, as originally enacted, required that six classes of contract must be supported by written evidence of the existence and terms of the contract before the contract could be enforced by the courts. The object of the Statute was to prevent fraud by witnesses giving false testimony as to the contents of an oral agreement. In practice, it worked badly as it enabled contracting parties to escape from performing their obligations under oral contracts and to avoid liability for breach of contract by relying on the technical defence afforded by the Statute. Hence the Statute was considerably narrowed in its scope by judicial interpretation prior to the repeal of most provisions by the Law Reform (Enforcement of Contracts) Act 1954.

Now only two classes of contract of those originally covered by the Statute of Frauds are required to be evidenced in writing.

1. Contracts of guarantee. The Statute of Frauds still applies to these contracts.
2. Contracts for the sale of land The provisions of the Statute of Frauds were largely reproduced by s40(1) Law of Property Act 1925, so that such contracts were still required to be evidenced in writing. However, s40 has now been abolished and its effect replaced (see below).

Some other contracts are required to be in writing by statute dealing with those specific contracts (see section 5.6).

5.4 Contracts for the sale of land

In 1989, s40 Law of Property Act 1925 was repealed and in effect replaced by the Law of Property (Miscellaneous Provisions) Act 1989.

Section 2 of the 1989 Act provides, inter alia, that:

1. a contract for sale or other disposition of an interest in land can only be made in writing, and only by incorporating all the terms which the parties have expressly agreed in one document, or when documents are exchanged, in each;
2. the terms may be incorporated in a document either by being set out in it, or by reference to some other document;
3. the document incorporating the terms, or when contracts are exchanged, one of the documents incorporating them (but not necessarily the same one) must be signed by or on behalf of each party to the contract.

The effect of this legislation, which became effective on 27 September 1989, is that a contract for sale of land must be in writing, must be signed by each party, and the written document must contain all the terms agreed on. If an agreement does not comply with the statutory requirements, it will not be enforceable as a contract.

However, the statute does *not* apply to contracts made before the Act came into force, and there are also a number of exceptions, the most important of which are: short-term leases of less than three years duration; and contracts made in the course of a public auction. In *Firstpost Homes Ltd* v *Johnson* [1995] 1 WLR 1567, Balcombe LJ stated categorically that he was not prepared to construe s2 by reference to the 'old learning' (ie the wide judicial approach to s40 as manifested in case law prior to 1989: the 1989 Act should be strictly construed.

Note that by virtue of s2(6) 'disposition' has the same meaning as in the old

LPA 1925. 'Interest in land' means any estate, interest or charge in or over land or in or over the proceeds of sale of land.

Note that s1 Law of Property (Miscellaneous Provisions) Act 1989 came into force on 31 July 1990, abolishing previous rules as to the making of deeds. Section 1 abolishes the requirement of sealing for individuals, substituting instead a requirement for signature and attestation by a witness. Section 1 also introduces a new requirement that it should be clear on the face of it that the document is intended to be a deed, and abolishes the old rule that deeds must be made on paper or parchment. For an illustration of the relationship between proprietory estoppel, constructive trusts and s2 LP(MP)A 1989, see the Court of Appeal's decision in *Yaxley* v *Gotts* [1999] 3 WLR 1217: see also *Shah* v *Shah* [2001] 4 All ER 138 (defendants estopped from relying on lack of attestation on deed: they had intended deed to be relied upon and it had been).

'Subject to contract'

The usual rule is that the words 'subject to contract' indicate that no binding contract has been concluded. In the Law Commission's report on which the 1989 Act was based it was said:

'It will still be possible to create contracts by correspondence, so it will still be desirable for the parties to use the formula "subject to contract" on letters which contain, or which refer to documents containing, the terms of the contract, if the letters are signed by a party to the contract. Use of the phrase, however, would not strictly still be necessary in letters written on behalf of the parties.'

Part performance

The doctrine of part performance was developed by equity in response to the Statute of Frauds in accordance with the equitable maxim of not allowing a statute to be used as an instrument of fraud. The doctrine was preserved by s40(2) LPA 1925, which expressly exempted part performance from the effect of s40(1). Section 2 of the 1989 Act does not contain a provision equivalent to s40(2): part performance, it seems, can arise no longer in relation to contracts for the sale of land.

Applications of s2

In *Record* v *Bell* [1991] 1 WLR 853 solicitors for the vendor and purchaser signed a contract for the sale of a house. On the day before exchange of contracts was due, the vendor's solicitor wrote to the purchaser's as to the question of Land Registry records recording the vendor's title. Further communications including another letter and a telephone call followed. The purchaser's solicitor wrote a letter which was to be attached to the contract of sale 'to be a part of the contract'. Later, the queries as to title were resolved.

By the date for completion of the contract, the purchaser had not paid, and so the vendor sought specific performance. The purchaser sought leave to defend on the basis that the contract of sale of the house did not comply with s2 LP(MP)A 1989.

The court held, in granting specific performance of the contract for the sale of the house, that although for that contract to comply with s2 LP(MP)A 1989 (which provides that either the expressly agreed terms for a contract for sale of land should be set out specifically or where the contract referred to some other document in which terms were to be found, that other document should be clearly identified in the contract as signed by the parties) the terms contained in the letters exchanged between the parties' solicitors should be clearly referred to in each of the parts of the contract which were exchanged between the parties. This was clearly not the case.

However, the court found that the vendor's solicitor's letter constituted an offer of a warranty that the vendor would be shown in the Land Registry files as the owner and this offer and its acceptance by the purchaser (as demonstrated by his agreeing to exchange contracts) formed a collateral contract between the parties. This collateral contract was independent of the sale of land and as such outside the provisions of s2 of the Act, and as such could be specifically enforced.

In *Spiro* v *Glencrown Properties* [1991] 2 WLR 931 the question of whether an option to purchase land is within s2 of the LP(MP)A 1989 arose. By a written agreement, the vendor of land granted an option to purchase land. The option could be exercised the same day and take-up of the option was to be signalled by notice in writing given by the purchaser to the vendor or his solicitor. The option agreement was executed in two exchanged parts, each containing the agreed terms and each signed by the party or his solicitor and exchanged. The purchaser took up the option by written notice in the agreed manner, but failed to complete. The question arose as to whether the agreement was within s2 LP(MP)A 1989.

The court held that an option to buy land could be defined as a sale of land within the meaning of the Act. The relevant contract was the agreement creating the option which consisted of two exchanged parts, containing all relevant terms and duly signed by or on behalf of both parties. This duly complied with the requirements of s2 and the contract could not be set aside as unenforceable merely because the taking up of the option required some unilateral action on the part of the purchaser.

Nothing in s2 of the 1989 Act affects the creation or operation of constructive trusts: s2(5) and see *Yaxley* v *Gotts* [2000] 1 All ER 711 (s2(1) did not prevent plaintiff from relying on constructive trust). See, too, Chapter 9, section 9.12, *Braymist Ltd* v *Wise Finance Co Ltd* [2002] 2 All ER 333.

5.5 Contracts of guarantee

Definition

A contract of guarantee is defined in the Statute of Frauds 1677 as 'a special promise to answer for the debt, default or miscarriage of another person'. Such contracts are not enforceable by legal proceedings unless evidenced in writing.

This definition of a contract of guarantee has been further refined by case law. A contract of guarantee now must fall into the form set out below.

1. There must be three parties:

   Creditor: A
   Debtor: B
   Guarantor: C

2. There must be a pre-existing liability between A and B. This liability may arise under a contract, or it may be tortious (*Kirkham* v *Marter* (1819) 2 B & Ald 613).

3. There must be a promise made by C to A that C will discharge B's liability to A if, and only if, B fails to do so himself.

   In *Eastwood* v *Kenyon* (1840) 11 Ad & El 438, it was held that a promise made by C to B did not fall within the statute. The promise must be made by C to A.

Judicial limitations to the statute

The statute has been construed narrowly, in a continuing attempt to limit its application. However, in *Actionstrength Ltd* v *International Glass Engineering IN GL EN SpA* [2002] 4 All ER 468 the Court of Appeal heard that an employer contracted with the main contractor for the building of a factory, and the claimant subcontractor agreed with the main contractor to provide the necessary labour. Because of late payment by the main contractor, the subcontractor threatened to cease work. According to the subcontractor, the employer agreed with the subcontractor that if it remained at work, the employer would ensure that it received any amount due to the subcontractor from the main contractor, if necessary by redirecting moneys due to the main contractor. There was no written note or memorandum of the alleged agreement, so when the subcontractor sued the employer to enforce it the employer relied upon s4 of the Statute of Frauds 1677. Their Lordships said the alleged agreement was unenforceable since, contrary to the subcontractor's contention, s4 of the Statute was not confined to a liability imposed on the promisor's assets generally as distinct from one imposed (as here, according to the subcontractor) on a particular asset or source. It should be noted, though, that the Appeal Committee of the House of Lords gave permission to appeal against this decision.

There are four specific situations which have been held to fall outside the statute's scope.

Substitution of third party for principal debtor

Where the effect of an agreement is to release the principal debtor (B) from his liability to the creditor (A) and put a third party in B's place, then there is no contract of guarantee.

In *Goodman v Chase* (1818) 1 B & Ald 297, a seller of goods was unwilling to fulfil further orders from a buyer unless he was paid, or given security, for goods already supplied. A third party orally promised the seller that he would assume sole responsibility for the payments due for goods already supplied. This was not a contract of guarantee because the third party assumed primary liability for the debt, rather than a liability conditional upon non-payment by the original debtor. The promise was, therefore, not within the statute and hence enforceable without writing.

No principal debtor

There must be a pre-existing liability between the debtor and the creditor. If the agreement is one under which A supplies goods to B in consideration of X's promise to pay for those goods, then B is never liable to pay for the goods. The primary liability is always that of X.

In *Mountstephen v Lakeman* (1871) LR 7 QB 196, the plaintiff was asked to do building works for the Brixham Local Board of Health. On asking how he was to be paid, the chairman of the Board told the plaintiff: 'Go on, Mountstephen, and do the work and I will see you paid.' The Board refused to pay on the grounds that there had never been any contract, express or implied, between it and the plaintiff. He then sued the chairman on his promise to pay. The defendant pleaded that the promise was a guarantee within the statute, and hence unenforceable for lack of writing. It was held that the defendant's promise was not a contract of guarantee as there had never been any liability to the plaintiff on the part of the Board. The primary liability for the payment had been assumed by the defendant from the start. The promise was hence enforceable without writing.

Promises falling within 'Substitution of third party for principal debtor' and 'No principal debtor' above are designated *contracts of indemnity* and are enforceable even though made orally.

Distinction between guarantee and indemnity.

Indemnity: C promises A that he, C, will satisfy an existing or future debt arising out of a benefit conferred on B by A. B is either released from liability to A or is never made liable to pay A.

Guarantee: C promises A that he, C, will satisfy an existing or future liability owed by B to A if B fails to satisfy it himself. B is primarily liable. C is liable only if B defaults.

Guarantee part of larger contract

A guarantee which is merely an incidental part of a larger contract is not within the statute. This covers two types of contract.

Del credere agents is one who, for a commission, introduces buyers to sellers *and* guarantees any liability that may arise under the contract that results from his introduction.

In *Couturier* v *Hastie* (1856) 5 HL Cas 673, the plaintiffs employed the defendants under an oral agreement as del credere agents to sell a shipload of corn. The defendant sold it to X, in ignorance of the fact that at the time of the sale the corn was no longer in a saleable condition. X repudiated the contract when he discovered the condition of the goods, and the plaintiffs sued the defendant on his implied guarantee to pay for the corn if X failed to do so. The defendant pleaded the statute and the lack of writing. The court held that the guarantee was not within the statute, and hence enforceable despite the lack of writing.

The decision must be seen as a matter of public policy rather than one that can be explained by a strict interpretation of the statute.

Guarantees given by the owners of goods to safeguard their possession of those goods. This arises where C has a proprietary interest in goods arising under a contract of sale between himself and B, but there is a lien or charge on the goods in favour of A, arising out of an earlier contract of sale between A and B. In order to obtain undisputed possession of the goods, C guarantees payment to A should B fail to pay.

In *Harburg India Rubber Comb Co* v *Martin* [1902] 1 KB 778, the Court of Appeal held that a guarantee given as merely part of a contract for the sale of goods, or some other agreement, was not within the statute, provided the guarantor was the substantial owner of the goods, and had a proprietary interest in those goods.

Guarantee promise given to protect property

The requirement for contracts in writing does not apply when the guarantee promise is given in order to protect property. See *Fitzgerald* v *Dressler* (1858) 7 CBNS 374.

Summary

Before a contract under which a third party assumes liability for the debt of another falls within the statute, it is necessary to establish the following.

1. That the third party promised a creditor that he would pay the debtor of another.
2. That the agreement on its true construction was intended by the parties to be a guarantee and not an indemnity.
3. That the guarantee does not form part of a larger transaction.

The House of Lords took the opportunity in *Elpis Maritime Co Ltd* v *Marti Chartering Co Inc (The Maria D)* [1991] 3 All ER 785 to discuss in some detail contracts of guarantee. In this case the question of the 'note or memorandum' rule arose. This has already been dealt with in some detail, in the context of sales of land (see section 5.4). In *Elpis* the owners chartered their vessel, The Maria D, to the charterers for a voyage from Izmir, Turkey, to Algeria for the carriage of a cargo of wheat. The contract was negotiated through brokers acting for both sides. Tramp Maritime acted for the owners and Marti Chartering for the charterers. During the course of the negotiations it was insisted that Marti should themselves provide a guarantee, initially only for demurrage, but later extended to include 5 per cent balance of freight. The written charterparty contract as finally drawn up consisted of several sheets. The first page was stamped and signed by Marti 'for and on behalf the charterers as brokers only'; other pages were signed or initialled, but with no indication that Marti were acting as brokers. The final page had stamp and signature for Marti below the heading 'Brokers'. The charterers signed separately.

The charterers failed to pay the $175,533 due for demurrage and freight. Arbitration proceedings awarded the owners this full amount plus interest, but no part of the sum outstanding was paid by the charterers. The owners then brought an action against Marti as guarantors.

The House of Lords found that s4 of the Statute of Frauds 1677 prescribed two separate ways in which a contract of guarantee might be made enforceable: by a written agreement signed by the guarantor; or secondly by a note or memorandum of the agreement. In this case, though the note or memorandum must be in writing and signed by the party to be charged, the basic agreement to guarantee might be verbal.

It was not disputed that there was a verbal undertaking by Marti to guarantee the liabilities of the charterers in respect of freight balance and demurrage. What was in question was whether clause 24 of the main charterparty contract constituted an 'adequate note or memorandum' for the purposes of s4. Clause 24 set out all the terms of the prior oral agreement of guarantee and was signed by Marti on the page containing the clause. The court considered that the question of whether Marti signed the page as brokers or on their own account to be irrelevant.

The charterparty, in whatever capacity Marti signed it, contained a sufficient note or memorandum to make the guarantee enforceable under the Statute of Frauds.

In *Trafalgar House Construction (Regions) Ltd* v *General Surety & Guarantee Co Ltd* [1995] TLR 387 the House of Lords discussed in some detail the meaning of the term 'guarantee'. In this case, the question arose as to whether a bond, provided for in the contract, amounted to a guarantee. Their Lordships held that the courts have always treated a performance bond of this nature as a guarantee. A similar case arose in *Cargill International SA and Another* v *Bangladesh Sugar and Food Industries Corporation* [1996] 4 All ER 563 where Morrison J at the High Court felt that where the nature of the bond was such and, in the absence of clear words to the contrary, if the bond was called at some future stage, parties would have to account with a view to determining their rights and liabilities. Accordingly, he held that the performance bond in this case amounted to a guarantee. An appeal against this decision was dismissed: [1998] 2 All ER 406.

See also Chapter 20, section 20.23 (Consumer guarantees).

5.6 Specific contracts required by statute to be in writing

1. Bills of exchange and promissory notes – ss3(1), 17(2) Bills of Exchange Act 1882.
2. Regulated consumer credit agreements (including hire-purchase agreements) under the Consumer Credit Act 1974.
3. Contracts of marine insurance are void unless made in writing in the form of a policy – Marine Insurance Act 1906.
4. A bill of sale is void unless it is in writing in the statutory form – Bills of Sale Act (1878) Amendment Act 1882.

6

Contents of Contracts

6.1 Introduction

Having established that a contract satisfies the requirements for validity, that is, that there has been an agreement supported by consideration and that it is in the necessary form (where that is required), the next stage is to determine the scope of the obligations incurred by the parties. The first step is to decide whether any statement (whether oral or in writing) forms part of the agreement or precedes the formation of the agreement. We have already seen that some such statements have been construed as invitations to treat, preceding the formation of the contract, and without legal effect.

Where a statement *induces* a contract, it may be construed as a representation, sometimes referred to as a 'mere' representation to distinguish it from terms which form part of the contract. Representations have legal effect, the examination of which we shall undertake later.

The task then is to define the nature and extent of the obligations. This involves determination of the following.

1. The terms of the contract.

2. The relative importance of those terms, that is, whether or not a breach of a term undermines a basic contractual obligation. This is of fundamental importance in determining the remedy available to the innocent party who has suffered a breach of contract.
3. The manner in which the terms formed part of the contract, that is, whether they were expressly provided for, and the rules applicable to, their construction, if not expressly provided for must they be implied by custom, by the courts or by statute.

We shall proceed by firstly examining the distinction between terms and representations and investigating the concept of the collateral contract.

6.2 Terms and representations

Statements made before or at the time of the conclusion of the contract

Problems can arise when statements are made before, or at the time, the contract is concluded. Such statements are usually oral, but may be in writing. The remedies available to a party who has suffered as a result of a false statement will depend on how the law construes the statement. Provided that the statement is not simply a eulogistic commendation of the subject matter of the contract, a common advertising usage, which is regarded as a 'mere puff' without legal significance, it can be one of the following:

1. a promise amounting to a term of the contract which, if unfulfilled, will allow a remedy for breach of contract; or
2. a mere representation, which, if false, will not give rise to an action for breach of contract, but may allow a remedy for misrepresentation; or
3. a collateral contract.

Terms or representations

The task of the court will be to ascertain the intention of the parties. In deciding whether a particular statement was intended to be a term of the contract, or merely amounted to a representation, the court may be guided by a consideration of the following factors.

The importance of the statement
A statement may well be a term of the contract if it is of such importance that if it had not been made the injured party would not have entered into the contract at all.
In *Bannerman* v *White* (1861) 10 CB NS 844, the buyer of hops asked whether sulphur had been used in their cultivation. He added that if it had he would not even bother to ask the price. The seller assured him that it had not. This assurance

was held to be a condition of the contract. It was of such importance that, without it, the buyer would not have contracted.

Similarly, in *Couchman* v *Hill* [1947] KB 54, the buyer asked for the assurance that the heifer he was contemplating purchasing at an auction sale was unserved, as he required it for servicing by his own bull. He also stated that without this assurance, he would not bid. Both the seller and the auctioneer gave him this assurance. The Court of Appeal held that the assurance was a term of the contract, despite the fact that this was in conflict with the printed conditions to which the auction sale was subject, which provided that no warranty was given. In the alternative, the Court of Appeal found that the statement was a collateral contract (collateral contracts are discussed below).

In contrast is the case of *Oscar Chess* v *Williams* [1957] 1 WLR 370. A private seller of a car obtained the sum of £290 in part exchange on the basis that it was a 1948 model. It was, in fact, a 1939 model; the registration book had been fraudulently altered by a previous owner, but the seller was innocent of this. The price of a 1939 model was considerably lower. The plaintiff company, a motor dealer, would still have been prepared to buy the car, but at a 'lower price, had they known the true facts'. The Court of Appeal held, by a majority, that the statement was not a term of the contract. Morris LJ dissented, taking the view that the statement amounted to a condition in the contract; it related, he said, to a vitally important matter.

Did the party making the statement have special knowledge as against the other party?

An important factor may be the relative capability of the parties to know the truth.

Thus in *Harling* v *Eddy* [1951] 2 KB 739, the vendors of a heifer represented that there was nothing wrong with the animal but, in fact, it had tuberculosis from which it died within three months of the sale. A contributory factor in leading the Court of Appeal to decide that the statement was a term of the contract was that the vendors were in a special position to know of the heifer's condition. In his judgment, Lord Evershed MR distinguished the facts before him from what might appear to be similar facts in the earlier case of *Hopkins* v *Tanqueray* (1854) 15 CB 130. In that case, the conversation took place not at the sale, but the day before, and the contract was formed as a result of the sale at the auction and incorporated the conditions set out in the auction particulars.

In *Dick Bentley Productions Ltd* v *Harold Smith (Motors) Ltd* [1965] 1 WLR 623, the statement was made by a motor dealer to a private purchaser that the car had done only 20,000 miles since being fitted with a replacement engine and gearbox. This statement was untrue. A unanimous Court of Appeal held that the statement was a contractual term. Lord Denning MR referred to *Oscar Chess* v *Williams* and said 'in the present case it is very different ... Here we have a dealer, Mr Smith, who was in a position to know, or at least to find out, the history of the car'. See also *Schawel* v *Reade* [1913] 1 Ir Rep 81 and *Birch* v *Paramount Estates* (1956) 167 EG 196 (below).

Was the contract reduced to writing subsequent to the statement?

If the contract is subsequently reduced to writing and the written contract does not incorporate the statement, this would be suggestive of the view that the parties did not intend the statement to be a contractual term.

In *Routledge* v *McKay* [1954] 1 WLR 615, the defendant stated that a motor cycle, the subject matter of the proposed sale, was a 1942 model. In the written contract, signed a week later, no mention was made of the date of the model. It was held, on this point, that what the parties intended to agree on was recorded in the written agreement, and that it would be inconsistent with the written agreement to hold that there was an intention to make the prior statement a contractual term.

However, in *Birch* v *Paramount Estates* (1956) 167 EG 196, the defendants made a statement about the quality of a house. The contract, when reduced to writing, made no reference to the statement. The Court of Appeal regarded the statement as a contractual term. But here the defendants had special knowledge.

The lapse of time between the statement and the conclusion of the contract

This may be a relevant, but by no means a decisive, factor.

In *Bannerman* v *White*, the statement was made virtually at the same time as the conclusion of the contract. In *Routledge* v *McKay*, the lapse of a week between the two events weighed with the court as a factor militating against construing the statement as a contractual term.

On the other hand, in *Schawel* v *Reade* (above), the defendant told the plaintiff, who required a horse for stud purposes, that the animal was 'perfectly sound'. A few days later, the price was agreed and, three weeks later, the plaintiff bought the horse. The statement was held to be a term of the contract, but here again the defendant, who was the owner of the horse, would appear to have had special knowledge.

It must be emphasised that none of the above factors are conclusive. As Lord Moulton makes clear in *Heilbut, Symons & Co* v *Buckleton* [1913] AC 30, they may be criteria of value in deciding whether or not a contractual term is intended, but he said 'they cannot be said to furnish decisive tests ... The intention of the parties can only be deduced from the totality of the evidence ...' (Lord Moulton was commenting on the dicta of A L Smith MR in *De Lassalle* v *Guildford* (see below) in the course of which it was said that 'a decisive test is whether the vendor assumes to assert a fact of which the buyer is ignorant, or merely states an opinion or judgment upon a matter of which the vendor has no special knowledge ...' The use of the phrase 'decisive test' could not, Lord Moulton said, be defended).

A further observation must be made. Prior to the Misrepresentation Act 1967, the distinction between a representation and a contractual term was of more significance than it is today. The primary reason for this is that, before the 1967

Act, the only remedy for an innocent misrepresentation was rescission of the contract. Damages could not be obtained unless the misrepresentation was fraudulent. Moreover, there were (and still are) circumstances in which the right to claim rescission might be lost, leaving the injured party without any remedy.

The Misrepresentation Act introduced the right to obtain damages for certain non-fraudulent misrepresentations, though the measure of damages differs from that of contractual damages. However, damages for a wholly innocent misrepresentation still cannot be obtained while damages for breach of contract can be recovered as of right. The distinction between contractual terms and 'mere' representations remains of importance. This aspect will be dealt with more fully in Chapter 7.

6.3 Collateral contracts

If a promise is not a term of the principal contract, it is possible that it may be enforced as a collateral contract.

This was an important innovation used to circumvent the parol evidence rule, the formerly limited remedies for misrepresentation and privity of contract. The concept of a collateral contract is clearly illustrated by Lord Moulton in *Heilbut, Symons & Co v Buckleton* [1913] AC 30:

> 'It is evident, both on principle and on authority, that there may be a contract the consideration for which is the making of some other contract. "If you will make such and such a contract, I will give you one hundred pounds," is in every sense of the word a complete legal contract. It is collateral to the main contract, but each has an independent existence, and they do not differ in respect of their possessing to the full the character and status of a contract.'

Lord Moulton was also of the view, however, that such collateral contracts should be viewed suspiciously. He said:

> 'Such collateral contracts, the sole effect of which is to vary or add to the terms of the written contract, are therefore viewed with suspicion by the law ... Not only the terms of such contracts but the existence of an animus contrahendi on the part of all parties to them must be strictly shown.'

In an earlier case, the Court of Appeal in *De Lasalle v Guildford* [1901] 2 KB 215 had enforced an oral promise as a collateral contract.

The plaintiff and the defendant negotiated for the lease of a house. The terms of the lease were arranged, but the plaintiff (prospective tenant) refused to hand over the counterpart of the lease which he had signed unless the defendant assured him that the drains were in good order. The defendant gave this assurance, and the counterpart lease was thereafter handed to him. The drains were not in good order, and the plaintiff was held entitled to damages for breach of that undertaking.

This decision appears to be sound despite Lord Moulton's strictures on the dicta of A L Smith MR (see above).

A collateral contract was used for a similar purpose in *City and Westminster Properties* v *Mudd* [1959] Ch 129. The defendant, who had been a tenant of the premises for six years, was accustomed to sleep at the plaintiff's shop. The lease fell for renewal. The plaintiffs inserted a clause for use of the premises to be for 'showrooms, workrooms and offices only'. The defendant asked if he could sleep there. He was told that he could and he signed the lease.

It was held that the promise not to enforce the clause against him was a collateral contract which he could plead in answer to a claim for breach of contract.

The use of a collateral contract to avoid the stringency of written contracts, and where the remedy for misrepresentation is not available or unhelpful, used to be rare. It has, however, become increasingly popular. In *Evans* v *Merzario*, Lord Denning MR thought that the observations of Lord Moulton (above) were largely out of date.

In *Evans* v *Merzario* [1976] 1 WLR 1078, the plaintiffs, who had shipped goods for many years with the defendants who were forwarding agents, agreed to a changeover in the method of shipment to enable goods to be carried in containers. The defendants gave an oral assurance that the goods would be carried below deck on the ship. In fact, goods were carried above deck and the containers were washed overboard in a storm. The printed standard conditions of the forwarding trade enabled the defendants to carry containers above deck if they wished to do so. It was held that the plaintiffs could recover against the defendants. Lord Denning MR said that the promise to carry goods below deck was an enforceable collateral contract. Roskill and Geoffrey Lane LJJ also thought that the oral assurance was an express term of the contract of carriage, which was partly oral, partly in writing and partly by conduct.

Lord Denning explained the use for a collateral contract after the Misrepresentation Act 1967:

> 'We now have the Misrepresentation Act 1967 under which damages can be obtained for innocent misrepresentation of fact. This Act does not apply here because we are concerned with an assurance as to the future. But even in respect of promises as to the future, we have a different approach nowadays to collateral contracts. When a person gives a promise or an assurance to another, intending that he should act on it by entering into a contract, and he does act on it by entering into the contract, we hold that it is binding ...
>
> ... The cases are numerous in which oral promises have been held binding in spite of written exempting conditions.'

Esso Petroleum v *Mardon* [1976] QB 801 was a case which reached a similar conclusion. Esso induced Mardon to enter into a lease for a filling station by negligently misstating to him that the station would have a turnover of 200,000 gallons per year. In fact, it did not. The court decided that Esso, although stating an opinion, also warranted that they had used reasonable care and skill in reaching that opinion. Damages were, therefore, recoverable for breach of that collateral warranty.

Accordingly, it seems that the collateral warranty can be implied as well as express. In *Esso* v *Mardon*, there was no express promise that the opinion had been achieved by the exercise of reasonable care and skill.

In *Eyre* v *Measday* [1986] 1 All ER 488 and *Thake* v *Maurice* [1984] 2 All ER 513, two differently constituted Courts of Appeal declined to find in sterilisation operations collateral warranties that the expected results would be achieved. Although permanent sterility was expected as a result of the operations, the Court of Appeal in both the above cases declined to find that there had been a collateral warranty that the operations would be completely successful.

The collateral contract may also be employed where the main contract is between the plaintiff and a third party. In *Shanklin Pier* v *Detel Products* [1951] 2 KB 854, the plaintiffs, wishing to paint the pier, consulted the defendants, paint manufacturers, who told them that their paint was suitable for the purpose. Acting on the faith of this statement, the plaintiffs caused to be inserted into the agreement with the contractors, who were to paint the pier, a term requiring the use of the defendants' paint. The paint proved unsuitable and the plaintiffs were entitled to damages for breach of the collateral promise. The plaintiffs, entering into the contract with the contractors, furnished consideration for the defendants' promise.

This principle has also been applied in hire-purchase cases where the dealer first sells the article to a finance company and the customer, on the faith of statements made to him by the dealer about the article, then enters into a contract with the finance company. The statements may amount to a collateral promise enforceable against the dealer. See *Andrews* v *Hopkinson* [1957] 1 QB 229. For a further application of the principle, see the Court of Appeal decision in *Wells* v *Buckland Sand & Silica* [1965] 2 QB 170.

6.4 Conditions

The ways in which the obligations under a contract are construed are various. The most important distinction is between those contractual obligations which entitle an innocent party to repudiate a contract in the event of a breach, and those which merely enable a person to claim damages. The classic division is between 'conditions', a breach of which gives the innocent party an option to repudiate, and 'warranties', a breach of which does not. The word 'warranty' is also used to mean a contractual promise, or term, so it is important to have in mind the use to which the word is being put. The word 'condition' also has another meaning. It may mean a stipulation that a contract should be brought to an end, or should not be enforceable, except on the happening of a given event. The condition is then properly called a 'condition subsequent', or a 'condition precedent' respectively.

In addition to the classic division between conditions and warranties, there is a third class of term called an intermediate term or innominate term (the names are interchangeable). This is usually thought to be different from a condition because it is not necessarily certain at the outset whether the term will enable a person to repudiate in the event of its breach. Conditions precedent and conditions subsequent will be examined first.

Condition precedent

Where the operation of an obligation or right is suspended until the happening of a certain event, there is said to be a 'condition precedent'. If the event never happens, the obligation or right never arises.

In *Pym* v *Campbell* (1856) 6 E & B 370, the defendants agreed in writing to buy from the plaintiff a share in an invention. The defendants gave oral evidence that it was not to operate until a third party had approved the invention, and that this had not happened. The court held that there was a condition precedent which had not been satisfied and the plaintiffs could not recover.

Erle J said that the evidence showed that there was never an agreement at all. It does not, however, necessarily follow that there is no agreement. The condition precedent may suspend, rather than negative, the agreement. The performance of the contract was only suspended in *Marten* v *Whale* [1917] 2 KB 480. The plaintiff agreed with X to buy a plot of land subject to the approval by the plaintiff's solicitors of 'title and restrictions'. At the same time, the plaintiff agreed to sell his car to X in consideration of the first agreement and to be simultaneous. He gave possession of the car to X, who sold it to a bona fide purchaser (the defendant) without notice. The plaintiff's solicitor refused to approve the restrictions for the land. The plaintiff sued to recover the car from the defendant.

The solicitor's approval was held to be only a condition precedent to the passing of property in the car, not to the creation of a contract of sale. Once an agreement to sell had been made, X became a buyer in possession and could pass good title under s25 SGA 1893 – now 1979.

It is always a matter of some difficulty to decide whether the failure of a condition precedent prevents the formation of the contract, or merely suspends the obligations created under it. In *Bentworth Finance* v *Lubert* [1968] 1 QB 680, the plaintiff let a car to the defendant who was to pay 24 monthly instalments. The car was delivered without a log book. The defendant did not use the car and refused to pay the instalments. The plaintiff recovered possession of the car and sued for the instalments.

The refusal to supply the log book was held to be the failure of a condition precedent upon which liability for the instalments depended – that is, the contract did not come into existence until the log book was supplied.

Condition subsequent

The obligation of one or both parties may be subject to the condition that it is to be immediately binding, but in the event of a certain occurrence or the ascertaining of certain facts, the obligation will cease to be binding or the party will have the right to avoid the contract.

In *Head* v *Tattersall* (1871) LR 7 Ex 7, A bought a horse from B with a certain description. A was to have the right to return it by a certain day if it did not answer its description. It did not, and A returned the horse before the day. In the meantime, however, the horse had been injured without A's fault. It was held that the contract had been brought to an end by the fulfilment of the condition subsequent. A was entitled to recover the price, and the loss occasioned by the horse's injury fell on B.

When is a term a condition?

Frequently, the terms of a contract are not conveniently labelled by the parties as 'condition' and 'warranty'. Even if the parties do employ such labels, it does not follow that their use may be conclusive as to what may constitute a condition or warranty. For example, if the words 'it is warranted that ...' are used it will not follow that breach of the term will not be a breach of condition. If the parties have not expressed themselves on the issue of what is to be a condition enabling repudiation for breach and what is not, the courts have to decide. This may be a formidable task.

In *Poussard* v *Spiers & Pond* (1876) 1 QBD 410, an actress was employed to play the leading part in a French operetta as from the beginning of its run. She was unable to take up her role until a week after the season had started. The producers, who had had to engage a substitute, refused her services. The court held that her promise to perform as from the first night amounted to a condition and that its breach entitled the producers to treat the contract as discharged.

On the other hand, in *Bettini* v *Gye* (1876) 1 QBD 183, a singer was engaged to sing for the whole of the season in theatres and at concerts. He undertook to appear six days in advance for rehearsals. He only arrived three days in advance. The defendant sought to terminate the contract, but the court held that he could not. The rehearsal clause was subsidiary to the main part of the agreement. Accordingly, it was only a warranty that the singer would arrive six days in advance.

The courts, therefore, seek to distinguish a condition from a warranty by deciding upon the importance of the term to the contract as a whole, and from that decision inferring the intention of the parties.

In *Behn* v *Burness* (1863) 3 B & S 751, the court had to evaluate a statement in a charter party that a ship was now in the port of Amsterdam. The statement was inaccurate, and the question was whether that promise was a condition or a warranty. The term was held to be a condition.

The intention of the parties is to be ascertained at the time of entry into the agreement. In *The Mihalis Angelos* [1971] 1 QB 164, the owners of a vessel let it to charterers for a voyage from Haiphong to Hamburg. The owners said that the vessel was 'expected ready to load about 1st July'. It was found as a fact that there was no reasonable ground for expecting that the vessel would be ready to load on 1 July.

The expected readiness clause was held to be a condition.

6.5 Warranties

It is already suggested that the word 'warranty' is used in a multiplicity of senses. Chitty suggests that:

> '... the emergence of the new category of "intermediate" or "innominate" terms seems likely to have reduced the number of occasions when a term will be classified as a warranty in this sense (the breach of which by one party does not entitle the other to treat his obligations as discharged), almost to vanishing point, save in the very exceptional circumstances where a term has been specifically so classified by statute.'

He is referring principally to the Sale of Goods Act 1979.

6.6 Innominate terms

In *Hongkong Fir Shipping* v *Kawasaki Kisen Kaisha* [1962] 2 QB 26, the defendants chartered the vessel 'Hong Kong Fir' from the plaintiffs for 24 months; the charter party provided 'she being fitted in every way for ordinary cargo service'. It transpired that the engine-room staff were incompetent, and the vessel spent less than nine weeks of the first seven months of the charter at sea because of breakdowns and consequent repairs required to make her seaworthy. The defendants repudiated the charter party and claimed that the term as to seaworthiness was a condition of the contract, any breach of which entitled them to do so. The court decided the term was neither a condition nor a warranty, and in determining whether the defendants could terminate the contract, it was necessary to look at the consequences of the breach to see if they deprived the innocent party of substantially the whole benefit he should have received under the contract. On the facts, this was not the case, because the charter party still had a substantial time to run.

Diplock LJ said:

> 'There are, however, many contractual undertakings of a more complex character which cannot be categorised as being "conditions" or "warranties" ... Of such undertakings all that can be said is that some breaches will and others will not give rise to an event which will deprive the party not in default of substantially the whole benefit which it was intended he should obtain from the contract; and the legal consequences of a breach of such undertaking, unless provided for expressly in the contract, depend upon the nature of the event to which the breach gives rise and do not follow automatically from a prior classification of the undertaking as a condition or warranty.'

Breach of an innominate term will enable the party not in default to treat the contract as repudiated only if the other party has renounced his obligations under the contract; or the other party has rendered his obligations impossible of performance; or the party not in default has been deprived of substantially the whole benefit which it was intended he should obtain from the contract.

A term is most likely to be an innominate term when it is capable of being broken in both a very trivial or a very serious manner, so that a duty to provide a seaworthy ship would fall within this category (*Hongkong Fir* (above)), as could a duty to proceed with 'all convenient speed' to a port of loading (*Freeman* v *Taylor* (1831) 8 Bing 124), and as would an obligation on a shipmaster to obey the charterer's orders (*Federal Commerce & Navigation* v *Molena Alpha* [1979] AC 757). Similarly, a term in a contract for the sale of goods that shipment be in good condition was an innominate term, the breach of which had to be serious as to go to the root of the contract in order for the buyer to reject. This was the case even though the Sale of Goods Act 1979 divides terms only into conditions and warranties: *Cehave* v *Bremer Handelsgesellschaft mbH* [1976] QB 44.

In *Reardon Smith* v *Hansen-Tangen* [1976] 1 WLR 989, two charter parties were in agreement for the charter of a ship to be built at a certain shipyard in Japan. In fact, the ship was built at another shipyard. The charterers sought to reject the vessel on the grounds that the description of the ship was a condition of the contract, any departure from which was a breach of condition of the contract which justified rejection.

The charterers were held not to be entitled to repudiate. In order to reach the decision, the House of Lords looked at the background to the case. Lord Wilberforce expressed the view that 'the court ... must ... place itself in thought in the same factual matrix as that in which the parties were'. In order to place himself in that factual matrix, he asked what was the commercial purpose of the charter parties and what was the factual background against which they were made.

This description has been adopted in subsequent cases by other members of the House of Lords, for example, Lord Scarman in *Bunge* v *Tradax* (below). Notice, however, that he does not regard the expression 'the factual matrix' as describing anything other than the more common 'circumstances of the case'.

The question of whether time was of the essence (a condition) has arisen in a number of cases.

In *United Scientific Holdings* v *Burnley Borough Council* [1978] AC 904, the House of Lords held that the timetable set out in rent review clauses for the taking of pre-defined steps was not of the essence. In contrast, in *Bunge Corporation* v *Tradax Export SA* [1981] 1 WLR 711, the House of Lords thought that in mercantile contracts time would usually be of the essence and not an innominate term.

The distinction between clauses which would be likely to be regarded as innominate terms, and those which would be conditions were illuminated in *Bremer Handelsgesellschaft* v *Vanden Avenne-Izegem PVBA* [1978] 2 Lloyd's Rep 109.

The House of Lords had to consider two clauses.

1. A prohibition of export clause which required the sellers to advise the buyers 'without delay' of impossibility of shipment by reason of a prohibition.
2. A clause setting down a schedule for notifying, and acting upon, the notification of a force majeure occurrence.

The former clause was held to be an innominate term because it would give rise to many varying breaches. The latter was a condition. The stipulation as to time required punctual compliance.

Lord Wilberforce said that the classification of a term as a condition or innominate term is dependent upon: the form of the clause; the relation of the clause to the contract as a whole; and the general considerations of law.

Notably, this categorisation also includes matters of policy, in particular, the question of unfairness to the seller or buyer of restricting the remedy to damages in any given instance. The House of Lords was anxious to convey the impression that they were not constrained to regard any clause as a condition unless there would be demonstrated good reason for doing so.

The last-mentioned case was referred to in *Bunge* v *Tradax* (above) where, similarly, a clause which specified a time was held to be a condition. The buyers in that case had an obligation to give the sellers notice that the vessel nominated for carriage of the goods was ready to load. Notice of readiness was to be given on 13 June. In fact, it was not given until 17 June.

The failure to give notice on time was held to be a breach of condition because the purpose of a clause designating a time for performance was to enable the other party to organise his affairs to meet his own obligations. The need for certainty in commercial contracts was great and to fail to provide certainty would be an unfairness. Time clauses in commercial contracts would generally be conditions, in particular because only one breach is possible; to be late.

Bunge v *Tradax* also disposed of a common fallacy, that is, that whether a clause was a condition or an innominate term was capable of decision only after the breach had occurred. The House of Lords and, in particular, Lord Wilberforce made it plain that the time for determining whether a clause was a condition or an innominate term was at the time of contracting. Lord Wilberforce said:

> 'The test suggested by the appellants was ... (to) ... consider ... the breach actually committed and then decide whether that default would deprive the party not in default of substantially the whole benefit of the contract. They even invoked certain passages in the judgment of Diplock LJ in *Hongkong Fir* to support it. One may observe in the first place that the introduction of a test of this kind would be commercially most undesirable ... I am clear that the submission is unacceptable in law ...'

The judicial approach in determining the intention of the parties as to the classification of a term of the contract is illustrated by the case of *Schuler AG* v *Wickman Machine Tool Sales Ltd* [1974] AC 235 HL. The respondents were the exclusive selling agents in the UK for the appellants' presses. The agency agreement provided:

'It shall be a condition of this agreement that (the respondent) shall send its representative to visit (the six largest UK motor manufacturers) at least once every week.'

The respondents committed some minor breaches of this term, and the appellants terminated the agreement, claiming that by reason of the term being a condition they were entitled so to do.

The House of Lords held that the parties could not have intended that the appellants should have the right to terminate the agreement if the respondents failed to make one of the obliged number of visits, which in total amounted to nearly 1,400. A provision elsewhere in the agreement gave the appellants the right to terminate the agreement if the respondents committed a 'material breach' of the obligations, and failed to remedy it within 60 days of being required to do so in writing. The House of Lords had regard to the fact that the relevant clause was the only one referred to as a 'condition'. Lord Reid felt that it would have been unreasonable for the appellants to be entitled to terminate the agreement for the respondents' failure to make even one visit. But he would have been constrained so to hold were it not for the later provision. The word 'condition' made any breach of the clause a 'material breach', entitling the appellants to give notice requiring the breach to be remedied. But not, as the appellant sought, to terminate the contract forthwith without notice. In a persuasive speech Lord Wilberforce, dissenting, thought that the term was a condition. This view was shared by Stephenson LJ in his dissenting judgment in the Court of Appeal and by Mocatta J at first instance.

In *Lombard North Central plc* v *Butterworth* [1987] 1 All ER 267, the agreement was for the lease of a computer for a period of five years on payment of an initial sum of £584.05, and nineteen subsequent quarterly instalments of the same amount. The agreement provided that the plaintiffs had the right to terminate the agreement if the instalments were not paid punctually. The agreement also contained a clause providing that 'punctual payment of each instalment was of the essence of the agreement'. The Court of Appeal held that though the failure to pay promptly was not repudiatory, this clause had the effect of making failure to pay on time a breach of condition. A failure to pay on time did not normally go to the root of a contract, but the parties were at liberty to make any particular obligation of the essence of their contract and had done so on this occasion.

Finally, to sum up, the attitude of the courts is normally quite straightforward. In *Barber* v *NWS Bank plc* [1996] 1 WLR 641, the Court of Appeal confirmed that if a term was one which admitted only one type of breach, a serious one, then the term *must* be a condition and not an innominate term. In *Re Cosslett (Contractors) Ltd* [1996] 3 WLR 299 the question arose as to whether the contractor's property on site passed to the site owner by virtue of the conditions in the contract. The High Court held that in order to effectively ascertain the parties' obligations under the contract in the event of a breach, conditions must be construed in the context of the contract as a whole and not on it's individual meaning.

6.7 Express terms

All the terms which have been discussed above have been express terms of the contract, that is, the parties have communicated to one another that the form of words is to be a part of the contract between them. It frequently occurs, however, that the parties are at cross-purposes or become at cross-purposes about the meaning of the words used. This difficulty arises particularly in relation to written contracts where rules of law and evidence have been developed to enable one or other party to show what the words in the contract do in fact mean.

These rules can be shortly stated.

1. The aim is to discover the intention of the parties.
2. Their intention must be found in the document itself (although see the observations of Lord Wilberforce in *Reardon Smith* v *Hansen-Tangen* (above)). This is known as 'the parol evidence rule'.
3. The popular meaning of words is to be applied unless the context indicates that some other meaning is intended.
4. Technical words should be given their technical meaning.
5. The contract should be construed so as to avoid absurdity or inconsistency.
6. Mercantile contracts should be construed according to mercantile usage.
7. The courts may look at customs of particular places to interpret the contract.
8. The contract should be read as a whole.
9. Where clauses are inconsistent or repugnant to each other effect should be given to that part which is intended to carry the real intention of the parties on a consideration of the contract as a whole.
10. Where there are printed and written words, greater significance should be placed on the written words as more likely to exhibit a true intention.
11. Where a general word is preceded by several words illustrating a class of behaviour or meaning or intention, the general word shall be limited 'ejusdem generis', that is, it only applies to matters which are in a similar category to the preceding words. For example, the words, 'be destroyed by fire, flood, storm, tempest or other inevitable accident' could not cover losses caused by acts or default of the parties to the contract. See *Saner* v *Bilton* (1878) 7 Ch D 815.

The courts are frequently faced with contracts which present problems of construction. For example, in *G A Estates* v *Caviapen Trustees Ltd* [1993] SLT 1061 the use of the contra proferentem rule was considered by the courts.

In this Scottish case, the plaintiffs, in a sale of land, warranted to the defendants that the land was fit for the purpose of constructing a particular development. The defendants, when they discovered that the land was not suitable for the purpose stated, refused to pay. The plaintiffs sought payment relying on the contra proferentem rule, contending the warranty had been drafted specifically in favour of the defendants and should, if ambiguous, be construed in the manner least favourable to them. The defendants, counterclaiming, argued that the clause was not conceived as a favour to them and was not intended to benefit one party more than another. The contra proferentem rule had no relevance. The court held that, in order for the contra proferentem rule to be justified, the argument that the warranty was a special feature and was never normally included in contracts for sale of land was to be rejected. No special rule of construction (such as contra proferentem) applied here.

In *Richco International* v *Bunge & Co Ltd* [1991] 2 Lloyd's Rep 93, on the other hand, the mercantile expression 'contracts in string' and the repercussions of such 'strings' were considered. Several contracts were negotiated in string. Among the clauses were conditions as to ports of shipment and loading arrangements. The charterers sought to interpret clauses differently in certain aspects of the contract.

Not surprisingly the court decided that, where contracts are in a string, exactly the same meaning must be given to clauses in contracts throughout the chain. The same weighting should also be given to the importance (or lack of it) of similar clauses.

In *West of England Shipowners Mutual Insurance Association (Luxembourg)* v *CRISTAL Ltd, The Glacier Bay* [1996] 1 Lloyd's Rep 370, a case concerning an international agreement, the Court of Appeal was faced with a similar problem of construction regarding a contractual clause. The court had to construe the effect of the words 'sole judge' and whether those words were unchallengeable in English courts. It was held that unless there is clear evidence to the contrary, the courts will seek to give effect to the parties intentions on the terms contracted upon.

The importance of the parties' intention is underlined by the decision of the House of Lords in *Bank of Credit and Commerce International SA* v *Ali* [2001] 1 All ER 961. As part of the bank's extensive reorganisation, a number of its employees, including Mr Naeem, were made redundant. In 1990 Mr Naeem accepted a redundancy package in full and final settlement. When the bank was wound up in 1991 it became clear that part of its business had been carried on in a corrupt and dishonest manner and some employees sought damages for the stigma (and handicap in obtaining other employment) of their association with the bank. The liquidators of the bank rejected these claims, but in *Malik* v *Bank of Credit and Commerce International SA* [1997] 3 All ER 1 the House of Lords ruled that such claims were sustainable in principle. Mr Naeem now wished to pursue such a claim but the liquidators contended that it was barred by his 1990 release. Their Lordships held (Lord Hoffmann dissenting) that, on the proper construction of the release, Mr Naeem's claim was not barred. Lord Bingham of Cornhill explained his approach as follows:

'In construing this [release], as any other contractual provision, the object of the court is to give effect to what the contracting parties intended. To ascertain the intention of the parties the court reads the terms of the contract as a whole, giving the words used their natural and ordinary meaning in the context of the agreement, the parties' relationship and all the relevant facts surrounding the transaction so far as known to the parties. To ascertain the parties' intentions the court does not of course inquire into the parties' subjective states of mind but makes an objective judgment based on the materials already identified. The general principles summarised by Lord Hoffmann in *Investors Compensation Scheme Ltd* v *West Bromwich Building Society* [1998] 1 All ER 98 at 114–115 apply in a case such as this. A party may, at any rate in a compromise agreement supported by valuable consideration, agree to release claims or rights of which he is unaware and of which he could not be aware, even claims which could not on the facts known to the parties have been imagined, if appropriate language is used to make plain that that is his intention. ... But a long and in my view salutary line of authority shows that, in the absence of clear language, the court will be very slow to infer that a party intended to surrender rights and claims of which he was unaware and could not have been aware. ... What, then, of the claim for stigma damages which lies at the heart of this appeal? The bank, through its senior employees, is fixed with knowledge of the bank's insolvency and nefarious practices, although it seems unlikely that those negotiating with the employees were alert to these facts, very carefully concealed from the world. Mr Naeem had no such knowledge. Neither the bank, even when fixed with such knowledge, nor Mr Naeem could realistically have supposed that such a claim lay within the realm of practical possibility. On a fair construction of this document I cannot conclude that the parties intended to provide for the release of rights and the surrender of claims which they could never have had in contemplation at all. If the parties had sought to achieve so extravagant a result they should in my opinion have used language which left no room for doubt and which might at least have alerted Mr Naeem to the true effect of what (on that hypothesis) he was agreeing.'

Rules of evidence

The 'parol evidence rule' is frequently said to derive from the rule in *Goss* v *Lord Nugent* (1833) 5 B & Ad 58:

'... verbal evidence is not allowed to be given ... so as to add to or subtract from, or in any manner to vary or qualify the written contract'.

There are, however, innumerable exceptions to the parol evidence rule.

To show that an implied term is inapplicable
Where the contract is silent on a subject where usually a term would be implied, parol (verbal evidence as to extrinsic matters) evidence is available to show that the usual term should not be implied. So if a person takes out a policy of marine insurance and evidence can show that the ship was unseaworthy, then the implied term of the contract as to seaworthiness can be excluded. See *Burgess* v *Wickham* (1863) 3 B & S 669.

To show when the contract is to commence
In *Pym* v *Campbell* (1856) 6 E & B 370, oral evidence was available to show that a contract for sale of a patent was not to commence until it had been approved by a third party.

To show the capacity of the party acting

In *Wake* v *Harrop* (1861) 6 H & N 768, oral evidence was available to show that an agent was acting as such when signing a charterparty and not as a principal acting on his own behalf – but note that the court indicated that the right to call such evidence existed only in equity where a person was a defendant.

Guidance on the position at law may be given by *Newell* v *Radford* (1867) LR 3 CP 52, where oral evidence could be called to say which party was a buyer and which party a seller in circumstances where that fact was not apparent from the face of the contract.

To defend an action for specific performance

Because an action for specific performance is an action for an equitable remedy, parol evidence may be given by a defendant. In *Martin* v *Pycroft* (1852) 2 De GM & G 785, parol evidence was also given to obtain specific performance of a written lease by giving evidence of an oral promise to pay.

To construe an ambiguous document

But the situation where oral evidence of prior negotiations is given to construe the document by reference to agreed meanings must be distinguished from evidence of prior negotiation alone. See *Robertson* v *Jackson* (1845) 2 CB 412, *Prenn* v *Simmonds* [1971] 1 WLR 1381 and *Arrale* v *Costain* [1976] 1 Lloyd's Rep 98.

Evidence of conduct after the contract is generally inadmissible to show the intention of the parties, unless it relates specifically to the terms of the original agreement. See *James Miller* v *Whitworth St Estates* [1970] AC 583 and *Ferguson* v *Dawson* [1976] 1 WLR 346.

To show a collateral promise

A perhaps classic example of where oral evidence was allowed to reverse the effect of a written agreement was in *City and Westminster Properties* v *Mudd* [1959] Ch 129 (see section 6.3 above).

6.8 Terms implied by the courts

It is a moot point whether the implication of terms into a contract is a question of law, or whether it can, in some circumstances, be a question of fact. Treitel takes the view that the implication may be either of fact or law, whereas Chitty considers that the implication is one of law for the court. There are, in any event, generally said to be two circumstances in which terms are implied at common law.

1. Where the contract does not deal with a matter expressly, but a term is said to be intended by the parties. That intention is discovered by looking at the words of the agreement and their surrounding circumstances.

2. Where the contract does not expressly deal with the matter, but it creates a relationship in which such a term is usually implied.

Treitel treats the first type of implied term as one of fact and the latter as of law.

Intention of the parties

In *The Moorcock* (1889) 14 PD 64, a term was implied that a wharf was safe for the use of ships which contracted to lie at the wharf, so that the plaintiff was able to recover damages against the defendant when his ship was damaged because the water level fell and grounded her.

Bowen LJ gave the classic definition:

'Now, an implied warranty, or as it is called, a covenant in law, as distinguished from an express contract or express warranty, really is in all cases founded upon the presumed intention of the parties and upon reason. The implication which the law draws from what must obviously have been the intention of the parties, the law draws with object of giving efficiency to the transaction and preventing such a failure of consideration as cannot have been within the contemplation of either side; and I believe if one were to take all the cases, and there are many, of implied warranties or covenants in law, it will be found that in all of them the law is raising an implication from the presumed intention of the parties with the object of giving to the transaction such efficiency as both parties must have intended that at all events it shall have.'

Accordingly, the circumstances in which a term will be implied are where its inclusion can be inferred from the agreement. It is sometimes referred to as the 'officious bystander' test for an implied term, because of the test laid down in *Shirlaw* v *Southern Foundries* [1939] 2 KB 206; [1940] AC 701 HL.

'Prima facie that which in any contract is left to be implied and need not be expressed is something so obvious that it goes without saying; so that, if while one of the parties were making their bargain, an officious bystander were to suggest some express provision for it in the agreement, they would testily suppress him with a common, "oh, of course".'

In that case, a company managing director was appointed for ten years. He sought to say (when facing dismissal) that the term implied that the company would not remove him from his directorship in that time and that the Articles of Association would not be altered to enable him to be removed.

The court took the view that the former would be capable of being an implied term, but that the latter would not.

The dividing line between those cases where a term may be implied is narrow and difficult to draw. A few examples illustrate the problem.

In *Luxor* v *Cooper* [1941] AC 108, a term would not be implied that an estate agent was entitled to commission where he introduced a purchaser but no sale followed because the court was not satisfied that both parties, as reasonable men, would have agreed to it if it were suggested to both of them.

In *Reigate* v *Union Manufacturing* [1918] 1 KB 592, no term would be implied that a contract of sole agency was not to be terminated by the principal prematurely ceasing to carry on business. In order for a term to be implied, it must be *necessary* to give business efficacy and not just reasonable.

In *Trollope v NW Metropolitan Hospital Board* [1973] 1 WLR 601, no term as to overrunning on a building contract could be implied because the court could not say which of many types of term was to be implied.

In *Shell v Lostock Garages* [1976] 1 WLR 1187, no term could be implied forbidding abnormal discrimination between competing purchasers of Shell petrol because the parties would not have agreed to such a term. The court indicated that it would always be reluctant to find an implied term where the parties had agreed in the form of a carefully drafted written contract.

In *Courtaulds Northern Spinning v Sibson* [1988] ICR 451 CA, when deciding whether a term should be implied into a contract, the courts should consider what the parties would have agreed if acting reasonably at the time the contract was made.

In *Eyre v Measday* and *Thake v Maurice* (above), the Court of Appeal in both cases refused to imply a term that an undertaking was given that the operations would be successful.

In *Chelsea Football & Athletic Co Ltd v S B Property Co Ltd* [1992] TLR 175 the question of implied terms in a sale of land arose.

In August 1982 a lease for premises, including the Stamford Bridge stadium, was granted by the company to the club, for a period of seven years. At the same time Chelsea Football Club sold the freehold of certain of this land to SB Property. The idea was to give the property company six years to find a developer, the club having an option to purchase the land back if a developer was not found. Exactly three days before the end of the six year period, the company granted a lease of all the land to a company called Crest Homes Ltd for 210 years. Notwithstanding this fact, a week later, the club gave notice that they proposed to exercise their option to purchase the freehold. The property company challenged the validity of this move. By 1991 the property market had collapsed and Crest Homes decided it was expedient to surrender their lease, and SB conceded, contrary to their earlier arguments, that the football club had indeed validly exercised its option.

In late 1991, Chelsea Football Club began a new action, alleging that the property company's delaying tactics amounted to a breach of an implied term and that the club had suffered substantial damages as a result of this delay, because the property market had now collapsed. It was held by the Court of Appeal that there was no indication in the lease that time was to be of the essence, and it could find no justification at all for implying a term into the contract that the parties would do nothing to prevent or delay completion.

It seems the courts will imply a term as to time. In the case of *Zeeland Navigation Co Ltd v Banque Worms (The Foresight Driller II)* [1995] 1 Lloyd's Rep 251, the court held that although as a matter of general principle a business option should be exercised 'within a reasonable time', if no time limit is specified, then the courts will imply such a term in order to give a commercial contract business efficacy. Accordingly, the court held that three months was a reasonable time in this case.

The overriding consideration, however, seems to be that in construing the circumstances in which a term should be implied, the courts will look at the contract itself before going on to look at the parties' intentions as evidenced by the contract and the surrounding circumstances. Only then will it decide as to the reasonableness of implying a term. This was the rationale of the Court of Appeal in *Ali and Others v Christian Salvesen Food Services Ltd* [1997] 1 All ER 721.

This contention was reiterated in *Plant Construction plc v Clive Adams Associates* (2000) The Times 1 March by the Court of Appeal, when it held that a sub contractor carrying out works designed by its employer, to the employer's specific instructions, is contractually obliged by virtue of an implied term (implied by the courts!) to warn the employer when it knows or ought to know that the works are obviously dangerous.

More recently, the Court of Appeal in *Zoan v Rouamba* [2000] 2 All ER 620 reaffirmed the earlier position and stated that the intention of both parties is relevant to the interpretation of a contractual term. The court was in no doubt of the need to find an expressed consensus between the parties to a contract.

The implication of terms was at the heart of the House of Lords' decision in *Equitable Life Assurance Society v Hyman* [2000] 3 All ER 961. The appellant society issued certain policies entitling holders of them to choose annuities at a guaranteed annual rate (GAR). Following a fall in annuity rates, the directors decided to pay policyholders who had chosen GAR a final bonus which was lower than that paid to others. On the face of it, art 65 of the society's articles of association conferred on the directors a discretion wide enough to enable them to adopt this course. However, they asked the court to confirm the validity of their decision.

Their Lordships concluded that such confirmation could not be given. Although art 65 did not contain an express restriction on the directors' powers, such a restriction was to be implied. Lord Steyn explained the position as follows:

> 'If a term is to be implied, it could only be a term implied from the language of art 65 read in its particular commercial setting. Such implied terms operate as ad hoc gap fillers. ... Such a term may be imputed to parties. The process "is one of construction of the agreement as a whole in its commercial setting": *South Australia Asset Management Corp v York Montague Ltd* [1996] 3 All ER 365 at 371, per Lord Hoffmann. This principle is sparingly and cautiously used and may never be employed to imply a term of conflict with the express terms of the text. The legal test for the implication of such a term is a standard of strict necessity. ...
>
> The enquiry is entirely constructional in nature: proceeding from the express terms of art 65, viewed against its objective setting, the question is whether the implication is strictly necessary. ... The supposition of the parties must be presumed to have been that the directors would not exercise their discretion in conflict with contractual rights. These are the circumstances in which the directors of the society resolved upon a differential policy which was designed to deprive the relevant guarantees of any substantial value. In my judgment an implication precluding the use of the directors' discretion in this way is

strictly necessary. The implication is essential to give effect to the reasonable expectations of the parties. The stringent test applicable to the implication of terms is satisfied.'

See also *Clarion Ltd* v *National Provident Institution* [2000] 2 All ER 265 (Securities and Investment Board principles not impliedly incorporated in alleged investment management contract since none of three bases of implication (business efficiency, obvious inference ('officious bystander') and necessity) found to be present). See, too Chapter 11, section 11.5 (*Paragon Finance plc* v *Nash*).

Implied from the relationship between the parties

The classic example of this is *Liverpool City Council* v *Irwin* [1977] AC 236 HL. It was held that it was an implied term of a lease of a maisonette in a council block that the landlord should take reasonable care to keep the common parts of the block in a reasonable state of repair. The House of Lords did not consider *The Moorcock* test to be applicable, but held that the subject matter of the lease and the relationships created by the tenancy demanded, of its nature, the contractual obligation on the landlord.

It seems that courts are reluctant to extend implications from the relationships between the parties beyond the recognised categories of such relationships.

In *Shell* v *Lostock Garages* (above), Lord Denning MR, although tempted to do so, did not find that solus agreements, that is, agreements for the sole distribution of petrol, although increasingly common, yet fell into the category of recognised relationships.

This reluctance by the courts is manifested in *Harvela Investments Ltd* v *Royal Trust Company of Canada* [1984] 3 WLR 1280 CA; [1985] 1 All ER 261 HL.

The vendors of shares put them up for sale to two competing bidders, the plaintiffs and defendants. The notice of sale was made by telex, and expressed itself to be open for a specified period. The vendors bound themselves to sell to the higher of the two bidders, and reserved no right to choose between unequal bids. The defendants sent in an undisclosed bid, to be opened immediately before the period for making a bid expired. When opened, it proved to be made in terms that the defendants' bid fell into two parts: (1) a fixed bid of a specified sum, and (2) a bid to be calculated by reference to the bid made by the plaintiffs and expressed to be 101,000 Canadian dollars in excess of such bid. The defendants elected to make whichever bid should be higher of the two alternatives. Such a method of bidding is termed 'referential'. The plaintiffs, suing to prevent sale to the defendants, argued: (1) the telex was a mere invitation to treat, and (2) a term should be implied into this telex, if it was indeed an offer, to the effect that referential bidding was impermissible. The House of Lords found for the plaintiffs, but the greater consideration of implication of terms appears in the judgment of the Court of Appeal, which seems unaffected on this point.

In his judgment, Waller LJ distinguished the facts before him from those in

Liverpool City Council v *Irwin* (above), which concerned a widespread group, namely landlords and tenants of high-rise flats. Here the case concerned a very small group, namely those vendors who have bound themselves to accept the highest bid and who have not in their offer excluded referential bids. Waller LJ said:

> 'If one considers the position of the reasonable man receiving this offer, would he immediately think that a referential bid would not be allowed? If not are there any other compelling reasons for implying such a term? In my judgment there are not.'

The House of Lords concluded that the parties had by their agreement forbidden referential bidding, thus the 'relationship' basis of implication was unnecessary.

In *Wettern Electric Ltd* v *Welsh Development Agency* [1983] 2 All ER 629, the main issue was whether the licence for the occupation of a factory which had been granted to the plaintiffs included an implied term that the factory was of sound construction and reasonably suitable for the purposes required by the plaintiffs. The court found that although there was no principle that the term was to be implied in licences of land, that is, the legal relationship did not demand it, the term could be implied under *The Moorcock* principle to give business efficacy to the contract.

Thompson v *ASDA-MFI Group plc* [1988] 1 WLR 1093 concerned a share option scheme and the sale of the company. In 1981, the defendants established a savings-related share option scheme for the benefit of employees and their subsidiaries' employees. The plaintiff, employed by a subsidiary, accepted options to subscribe for shares. In 1985, the defendants sold the subsidiary and informed the plaintiff that his options had therefore lapsed. The scheme rules provided, inter alia, that options could only be exercised by employees (para (a)) and that an option would lapse if the holder ceased to be an employee (para (d)). However, the plaintiff contended that the defendants could not rely on their own acts to defeat his rights. The court held that the rules of the scheme took effect and the plaintiff's claim that his opinions had been wrongfully repudiated could not succeed.

Scott J:

> 'Whatever doubt there might previously have been ... the law is now, in my judgement, as stated by Lord Diplock in *Cheall* v *Association of Professional, Executive, Clerical and Computer Staff* [1983] 1 All ER 1130 at 1135. In order to attract the principle that a party is not entitled to rely on his own acts as fulfilling a condition subsequent and bringing a contract to an end, the act must be a breach of duty and (per Lord Diplock):
>
> > "... the duty must be one that is owed to the other party under that contract; breach of a duty whether contractual or non-contractual owed to a stranger to the contract does not suffice."
>
> The principle expressed by Lord Watson in *Mackay* v *Dick* (1881) 6 App Cas 251 at 270 is not, in my view, a principle of English law. The fictional fulfilment of conditions precedent and the fictional non-fulfilment of conditions subsequent may be principles of the civil law; but they are not principles of English law. In this area of the law of contract English law proceeds, in my view, by means of implied terms. If a term can be implied that a party will not do an act that, if done, would prevent the fulfilment of a condition

precedent, then the doing of that act will be a breach of contract; if a term can be implied that a party will not do an act that, if done, would cause a condition subsequent to be fulfilled, then the doing of that act will be a breach of contract. But if a suitable term cannot be implied into the contract then in my judgement, the contract will take effect according to its tenor. The condition precedent will fail and the condition subsequent will be fulfilled.

In the present case, ASDA was entitled to sell its shareholding in [the subsidiary]. The sale did not represent any breach of duty owed to the plaintiff. Nor, for that matter, was the sale wrongful in any other sense. A term to the effect that ASDA would not sell its [subsidiary] shares cannot be implied into the rules. So the rules take effect as they stand.

Paragraphs (a) and (b) ... represent conditions subsequent. The condition in each paragraph was fulfilled as a consequence of the sale of the [subsidiary] shares. Under para (a) the rights under the options ceased to be exercisable. Under para (d) the options lapsed. The conditions were fulfilled by acts of ASDA. That, in my judgement is immaterial because the acts did not represent any breach of the duty owed by ASDA to the plaintiff. In my judgement this action fails and must be dismissed.'

In *Alghussein Establishment* v *Eton College* [1988] 1 WLR 587, it was held that there is an implied term in every contract that neither party is entitled to take advantage of his own breach as against the other party unless there is an express agreement to the contrary.

In employment relationships, the implication of terms is less uncommon. In *Sterling* v *Patchett* [1955] AC 534, it was an implied term in a contract of employment that the employee, who had invented certain processes, was the trustee of his inventions for his employers.

In *Lister* v *Romford Ice and Cold Storage Co* [1957] AC 555, the implied duty of care and skill which an employee owed his employer meant that the employee who had negligently injured a fellow employee, for whom the employer was vicariously liable, was himself liable for the damages which the employer had been obliged to pay to the fellow employee. The employee, in turn, argued that the contract of employment implied a promise to indemnify him from such liability. The House of Lords held by a majority that no such term could be implied.

6.9 Terms implied by custom

Terms may be implied by custom or usage of a particular trade or business, market or locality. The custom must be invariable and certain. A contract may be construed as incorporating a relevant custom unless it is inconsistent with the terms of that contract.

These are examples of terms implied by custom or usage.

Hutton v *Warren* (1836) 1 M & W 466. A tenant established a right to a reasonable allowance for labour expended on the land, even though the lease did not contain a term to this effect.

Lord Eldon v *Hedley Brothers* [1935] 2 KB 1. The usage of a particular trade, the hay trade, was implied into a contract, to vary what would otherwise have been the time property in the goods passed. Section 18 Sale of Goods Act 1979 provides that when goods are subject to being weighed or measured to determine the price, property does not pass until that act is done. The usage in the trade, however, was that when hay was bought in the particular manner relevant in this case, property passed at the time the contract was made, and a term to this effect should be implied into the contract.

British Crane Hire v *Ipswich Plant Hire* [1975] QB 303. The owner of a crane hired it to a contractor who was engaged in the same business. It was held that the owner's terms, which were usual in the business, were binding on the hirer although they had not actually been communicated at the time of hiring. There was, in the view of the Court of Appeal, a 'common understanding' that these terms applied.

Terms of collective agreements between trade unions and employers may be incorporated into individual employees' contracts by implication. The most common basis for such implication will be that the terms of the collective agreement are uniformly observed for the group of workers of which the employee is a member.

Sagar v *Ridehalgh* [1931] 1 Ch 310 and *Donelan* v *Kerby Construction* [1983] IRLR 19. A custom or usage cannot be incorporated into a contract if it is expressly or impliedly excluded by the terms of the contract. Nor can it be incorporated if it is inconsistent with the tenor of the contract as a whole. See also *London Export Corp* v *Jubilee Coffee Roasting* [1958] 1 WLR 661.

6.10 Terms implied by statute

Sale of goods

Certain terms are implied in contracts for the sale of goods. These terms were originally implied by the common law, but they were codified in the Sale of Goods Act 1893, and are now re-enacted (with amendments) in ss12–15 Sale of Goods Act 1979. Note also the amendments introduced by the Sale and Supply of Goods Act 1994 and the Sale and Supply of Goods to Consumers Regulations 2002 to the Sale of Goods Act 1979. The 2002 Regulations implement Directive 1999/44/EC of the European Parliament and of the Council of 25 May 1999 on certain aspects of the sale of consumer goods and associated guarantees. They came into force on 31 March 2003.

Implied terms about title
Section 12 implies a *term* on the part of the seller that he has the right to sell the goods and a warranty of freedom from encumbrance and quiet possession.

Sale by description

Section 13 implies a *term* that, where goods are sold by description, the goods will correspond with the description.

Implied terms about quality

Section 14(2) provides that where the seller sells goods in the course of a business there is an implied *term* that the goods are of satisfactory quality, except where the defects were specifically drawn to the buyer's attention, or, where the buyer examined the goods before the contract was made, regarding defects which that examination ought to have revealed.

Satisfactory quality is defined in s14(2A) and (2B). The general thrust of the definition is that goods should be of a standard that the reasonable person would regard as satisfactory, having regard to all relevant circumstances. For more detail of changes to s14 see Chapter 20.

Implied terms about quality and fitness

Section 14(3) provides that where the seller sells goods in the course of a business and the buyer makes known to the seller (expressly or by implication) any particular purpose for which the goods are being bought, there is an implied *term* that the goods are reasonably fit for that purposes.

Subsections 14(2) and 14(3) overlap to some extent. Both the definition of 'satisfactory quality' and s14(3) refer to 'fitness for purpose'. But if the buyer requires the goods for some particular purpose, he must make this known to the seller.

Sale by sample

Section 15 provides that in the case of a contract for sale by sample, there is an implied *term* that the bulk will correspond with the sample in quality, that the buyer will have a reasonable opportunity of comparing the bulk with the sample, and that the goods will be free from any defect rendering them of unsatisfactory quality, not apparent on reasonable examination of the sample.

Implied terms under the Sale of Goods Act 1979 are considered again, and in more detail, in Chapter 20. They are dealt with here, in outline, as some knowledge of these implied terms is required for an understanding of the Unfair Contract Terms Act 1977 which is dealt with in Chapter 8.

Contracts of hire purchase

Certain terms are implied into all contracts of hire purchase by ss8–11 Supply of Goods (Implied Terms) Act 1973. They relate similarly to title, description, quality, fitness for purpose and sample and correspond very closely to the implied terms in contracts for the sale of goods.

Supply of goods and services

The Supply of Goods and Services Act 1982 implies certain terms into contracts for the supply of goods and services which, prior to this Act, were outside the realm of a statute, but were to some extent governed by the common law. See, for example, the decision of the Privy Council in *Wong Mee Wan* v *Kwan Kin Travel Services Ltd and Others* [1996] 1 WLR 38. See also Chapter 20, section 20.15 et seq where note is made of amendments, implied terms and additional rights contained in the Sale and Supply of Goods to Consumers Regulations 2002.

Part I of the Act deals with contracts for the transfer of property in goods, other than contracts for the sale of goods and hire purchase agreements, and contracts for the hire of goods. There are provisions corresponding to those in the Sale of Goods Act 1979. Thus in the 1982 Act for contracts for the transfer of property in goods, there are implied terms: about title, s2; where transfer is by description, s3; about quality or fitness, s4; where transfer is by sample, s5. And in contracts for the hire of goods, there are, similarly, implied terms: title, s7; description, s8; quality or fitness, s9; sample, s10.

Part II of the Act is concerned with the supply of services and represents an attempt to put into statutory form basic obligations owed by those who provide services. Because of the wide range of services provided to the public, no attempt is made to define a contract for the supply of a service except in the most general terms as 'a contract under which a person ('the supplier') agrees to carry out a service' (s12(1)). Contracts of employment and apprenticeship are specifically excluded.

The basic obligations are those relating to care and skill, time for performance and consideration. In respect of these obligations, certain terms are implied. The Act does not specify whether they are conditions or warranties.

Care and skill

Section 13 provides that in a contract for the supply of a service, where the supplier is acting in the course of a business, there is an implied term that the supplier will carry out the service with reasonable skill and care.

The obligation implied in this section merely restates the law as has been enunciated in many cases. See, for example, *Samuels* v *Davis* [1943] 1 KB 526 (repair of dentures) and *Greaves* v *Baynham Meikle* [1975] 1 WLR 1095 (design of a building).

Time for performance

Section 14 provides, where the supplier is acting in the course of a business, that where the time for the carrying out of the service is not fixed by the contract or by the course of dealing between the parties, there is an implied term that the supplier will carry out the service in a reasonable time. What is a reasonable time is a question of fact.

This section again merely codifies the common law. See *Rickards* v *Oppenheim* [1950] 1 KB 616.

Consideration

Section 15 provides that if the price for the service is not fixed by contract or determined by the course of dealing, the party contracting with the supplier will pay a reasonable charge. What is a reasonable charge is a question of fact.

This section does *not* enable an aggrieved party to re-open the contract if the price, though excessive, is one to which he has agreed.

The Late Payment of Commercial Debts (Interest) Act 1998 which received Royal Assent on 11 June 1998 provides that it is an implied term in a contract to which the Act applies that any qualifying debt created by the contract carries simple interest subject to and in accordance with Part I of the Act. The Act applies to a contract for the supply of goods or services where the purchaser and the supplier are each acting in the course of a business, other than an excepted contract which is defined in s2(1).

By virtue of the Late Payment of Commercial Debts Regulations 2002, s5A is inserted in the Late Payment of Commercial Debts (Interest) Act 1998. This new section, which came into force on 7 August 2002, provides that once statutory interest begins to run in relation to a qualifying debt, the supplier is entitled to a fixed sum (in addition to the statutory interest on the debt). That sum is:

1. for a debt less than £1,000, the sum of £40;
2. for a debt of £1,000 or more, but less than £10,000, the sum of £70;
3. for a debt of £10,000 or more, the sum of £100.

The obligation to pay an additional fixed sum under this new section in respect of a qualifying debt is treated as part of the term implied by s1(1) of the 1998 Act in the contract creating the debt.

7

Misrepresentation

7.1 Introduction

7.2 The misrepresentation must be of fact

7.3 The misrepresentation must have induced the contract

7.4 Fraudulent misrepresentation

7.5 Negligent misstatements at common law

7.6 Representations under the Misrepresentation Act 1967

7.7 Innocent misrepresentation

7.8 Remedies

7.9 Misrepresentation and exclusion clauses

7.1 Introduction

Prior to the enactment of the Misrepresentation Act 1967 (hereinafter MA 1967), the victim of misrepresentation had recourse solely to the courts for rescission of contract or, if fraud could be proven, damages in the tort of deceit. We shall see that the Act of 1967 substantially improved the situation with regard to the remedies available, in addition to widening the context of what constituted a misrepresentation.

We have already seen that contractual terms form the very cornerstone of bargains. Such contractual terms define the rights and obligations of the respective parties to a contract. If a particular term is broken then, dependent on the status of that term, the remedy will lie in breach of contract. The problem which presents itself is: what, if any, remedy lies in respect of incorrect statements inducing a contract, but which are not enshrined in the contract as contractual terms? Inevitably, certain oral statements are made prior to the conclusion of a contract which, although not terms of a contract, have some bearing on whether that contract is or is not concluded. If such a statement turns out to be incorrect, it follows that serious loss could be sustained by the innocent party.

We have already seen from our examination of cases such as *Oscar Chess* v

Williams that the courts have, on occasion, shown a marked reluctance to construe certain undertakings made prior to the contract as terms of that contract.

Development of the concept of the 'mere' representation

The courts developed the concept of the 'mere representation' – being a statement of fact past or present which, though not intended to be a term of the contract, induces the other party to enter into the contract.

At common law, the remedy for misrepresentation was the award of damages for the tort of deceit, where the misrepresentation was fraudulent. Equity developed the remedy of rescission applicable to both fraudulent and innocent misrepresentation. Whilst rescission was a useful remedy, it was subject to the various 'bars' on the right to claim the remedy (see below) and, moreover, an innocent misrepresentation did not allow the award of damages, but only enabled the injured party to recover an indemnity.

However, there have been in recent times two major developments:

1. the decision by the House of Lords in *Hedley Byrne* v *Heller* in 1963 (see below), which provided a remedy in damages for negligent misstatements at common law;
2. the reforms provided by MA 1967.

As a consequence of these developments misrepresentations can now be categorised as given below.

1. Fraudulent misrepresentations.
2. Negligent misstatements at common law.
3. Misrepresentations under s2(1) MA 1967.
4. Innocent misrepresentations.

General requirements

A representation, then, is a statement which is made by one party to the contract to the other, which, although it is not a term of the contract, nevertheless is a reason that induced that other party to enter into the contract. Note that, in certain circumstances, misrepresentation can be by conduct. If the statement is untrue it is a misrepresentation.

For the untrue statement to constitute an actionable misrepresentation it must meet the following requirements:

1. it must be one of fact, not opinion or intention or law;
2. it must have induced the contract.

We shall proceed to examine each of these requirements in turn.

7.2 The misrepresentation must be of fact

Expression of opinion

An expression of opinion, the statement of a belief, incapable of actual proof, will not allow a claim based on misrepresentation.

In *Bisset* v *Wilkinson* [1927] AC 177, the vendor whilst in the process of selling his farm which had not previously been used as a sheep farm, was asked by the plaintiff as to the number of sheep the farm could sustain. An opinion, which turned out to be incorrect, was given.

It was held that this statement was merely the honest expression of an opinion, and not a statement of fact as to the actual capacity of the farm.

However, there can be circumstances in which an opinion is construed as a statement of fact. Where the person giving the opinion was in a position to know the true facts, and it can be proved that the person concerned could not reasonably have held such a view as a result, then in this situation the person's opinion will be treated as a statement of fact.

In *Smith* v *Land and House Property Corporation* (1884) 28 Ch D 7, the plaintiff put up his hotel for sale stating that it was let to a 'most desirable tenant'. The defendants agreed to buy the hotel. The tenant was bankrupt. As a result, the defendants refused to complete the contract and were sued by the plaintiff for specific performance.

The Court of Appeal held that the plaintiff's statement was not mere opinion, but was one of fact.

There is also the view that where a layman relies on an expert's statement and uses such a statement as a positive assertion to back up his own views 'as if they were true facts' liability in misrepresentation will ensue if it turns out to be incorrect. See *Reese River Silver Mining Co Ltd* v *Smith* (1869) LR 4 HL 64.

A more recent case is *Brown* v *Raphael* [1958] Ch 636 CA. The particulars of sale of the reversion on a trust fund stated that estate duty would be payable on the death of the annuitant 'who is believed to have no aggregable estate'. The vendor's solicitors believed this to be true, but had no reasonable grounds for the belief.

It was held that as the vendor was in a stronger position than the purchaser to be able to ascertain the facts, there must be implied a further representation that the vendor had reasonable grounds for his belief. A further example of the manner in which the court may be able to imply a representation appears from the decision in *Laurence* v *Lexcourt Holdings* [1978] 2 All ER 810, in which it was held that the description of premises as offices was a representation not merely as to the physical state of the premises, but contained, by implication, a representation as to the availability of planning permission for the premises to be used as offices.

Some expressions of opinion are mere puffs. The laudatory statements made about a product by sellers or advertisers cannot, for the most part, be regarded as representations. The description of land as 'fertile and improvable' was held not to constitute a representation in *Dimmock* v *Hallett* (1866) 2 Ch App 21.

There may well be liability, however, for more precise claims, ones that purport to be supported by facts and figures. The distinction is between mere laudatory remarks and specific promises or assertions of a factual nature.

Statements or promises as to the future

Representations as to the future will not attract liability in misrepresentation. A statement as to future intention will not be regarded as binding on a person unless the statement is incorporated into a contract. The situation is different if the stated intention is not in fact held. If a person knows that his promise which has induced another to enter into a contract will not, in fact, be carried out, then he will be liable.

In *Edgington* v *Fitzmaurice* (1885) 29 Ch D 459, the directors of a company issued a prospectus inviting subscriptions for debentures stating that the issue was for investment purposes. The plaintiff advanced the money in reliance on that statement and in the erroneous belief that the debenture holders would have a charge upon the property. It transpired that the real object of the loan was to enable the directors to pay off pressing debts.

The Court of Appeal held that the plaintiff was entitled to rescind the contract on the basis of misrepresentation.

Although the statement was a promise of intent, the court held that the defendants had no intention of keeping to such intent at the time they made the statement. The defendants knew that they would not be able to keep their promise.

In recent years, this view has become more prevalent. In *Esso Petroleum* v *Mardon* [1976] QB 801, a petrol company which offered an inaccurate forecast of the probable sales of a filling station was liable in damages to a tenant who contracted with the petrol company on the basis of the forecast.

In *McNally* v *Welltrade International Ltd* [1978] IRLR 497, an employment agency was liable for misrepresentation about a prospective employee's suitability for a job he had applied for.

It seems to follow that the rigidity of the rule that statements of opinion or as to the future are never actionable, is lessening and it may be necessary to analyse anew the traditional formula. One suggestion is that the essence of the rule is not the nature of the statement but the nature of the reliance. If it is reasonable to rely on the statement, then perhaps it should be regarded as actionable.

Misrepresentation cannot be one of law

The rule is simple, the distinction between fact and law is not. If A represents that 'The existing planning permissions cover use of this building as an office', and they do not, is that a misrepresentation of law or fact? It seems that it is a representation of fact: *Laurence* v *Lexcourt Holdings* (above). Where a landlord says that he accepts liability for repairs under a lease that is a representation of fact: *Brikom Investments* v *Seaford* [1981] 1 WLR 863. A statement of foreign law is always regarded as a statement of fact: *Andre et Cie SA* v *Ets Michel Blancs* [1977] 2 Lloyd's Rep 166. In *Cooper* v *Phibbs* (1867) LR 2 HL 149, a distinction was drawn between statements as to private rights and general statements as to the law. By and large, subsequent cases such as those mentioned above have followed that pattern. So if A makes two representations:

1. all contracts which are in writing are enforceable; and
2. this contract of employment between B and C is enforceable because it is in writing.

The former cannot give rise to an action because it is a statement of law (and opinion); the latter may be actionable as it is declaratory of private rights.

Silence

Prima facie silence is not a misrepresentation. Mere non-disclosure is generally not actionable. Remember the maxim is caveat emptor – let the buyer beware. The other party has no duty to disclose problems voluntarily. Thus if one party is labouring under a misapprehension, there is no duty on the other party to correct it. See *Smith* v *Hughes* (1871) LR 6 QB 597.

There are three fundamental exceptions to this rule.

1. The representor must not misleadingly tell only part of the truth. See *Dimmock* v *Hallett* (1866) 2 Ch App 21.
2. Later events falsifying a representation must be disclosed. This includes the situation where an individual makes a false statement believing it to be true. If he subsequently discovers that he was in error, he is under a positive duty to disclose the truth. Similarly, where later events falsify an initially correct assertion, for example, *With* v *O'Flanagan* [1936] Ch 575, where a medical practice became valueless between the time of making the statement and the date of sale. It was held that the vendor should have communicated this.
3. Contracts uberrimae fidei. Certain contracts impose a duty of disclosure. These are known as contracts uberrimae fidei (contracts of the utmost good faith). The main contracts that fall within this category are contracts of insurance, family settlements and contracts where there is a fiduciary relationship. Examples of a fiduciary relationship are: solicitor and client, trustee and beneficiary, bank manager and client, inter-family agreements (though this is not a closed list) but, apparently, not master and servant. See *Bell* v *Lever Bros* [1932] AC 161 and contrast *Sybron Corporation* v *Rochem Ltd* [1983] 2 All ER 707.

Pictorial and other representations

The term 'statement' is not to be interpreted too literally. In *St Marylebone Property Co Ltd* v *Payne* (1994) 45 EG 156, the use of a photograph taken from the air, printed with the addition of arrows (misleadingly) indicating the extent of the boundaries, was held to convey a statement of fact. As to inducement see section 7.3 (following). The plaintiffs relied on the photographs and never actually saw the land until the auction sale was completed. This was held to amount to actionable misrepresentation.

The Chancery Division recently held that where a representation by conduct induced a contract, it may be tantamount to an actionable misrepresentation. This was stated in *Spice Girls Ltd* v *Aprilla World Service BV* [2000] EMLR 478 where the participation of a pop group in making a film advertising certain goods constituted a representation by conduct of an intention of the group that it would not break up during the term of the advertising contract. The court held that it was a continuing representation which the group had a duty to correct when it was/or became untrue.

7.3 The misrepresentation must have induced the contract

Reliance

There can be no liability in respect of a falsehood which does not induce the party to enter into the contract. The best illustration of this in operation is where A makes a false statement as an inducement for B to contract, but B contracts regardless, either knowing the statement to be false, or not even being aware of the statement in the sense that it did not influence his mind.

There will be no reliance, and hence no inducement, in the following circumstances.

1. The misrepresentation did not come to the plaintiff's notice. Thus where false reports of a company's financial affairs had been published but the plaintiff had not read them. See *ex parte Biggs* (1850) 28 LJ Ch 50.
2. The plaintiff relied not on the misrepresentation but on his own judgment. In *Attwood* v *Small* (1838) 6 Cl & F 232, the plaintiffs negotiated with the defendant for the sale of certain mines. The plaintiffs asked questions as to the capabilities of the property. The defendant's answer was verified by persons appointed by the plaintiffs. Six months after the sale was complete, the plaintiffs found that the defendant's statement had been inaccurate, and they sought to rescind on the ground of misrepresentation.

   The court held that the plaintiffs could not rescind the contract since they had not been induced to contract by the defendant's statement, but rather by their own engineer's report.

   It must be stressed that this rule applies in cases of innocent (and probably negligent) misrepresentation, but not where the misrepresentation was fraudulent. See *S Pearson & Son* v *Dublin Corporation* [1907] AC 351.

   If, however, a plaintiff has been induced to enter into a contract by a misrepresentation, it is no answer to say that he had been afforded the means of verifying it. Thus in *Redgrave* v *Hurd* (1881) 20 Ch D 1, a party was induced to purchase a solicitor's house and practice by innocent misrepresentations as to the value of the practice. He was allowed rescission even though the books and papers which he had been invited to examine, and did not, would have revealed the falsity of the representations.

In *Central Railway Co of Venezuela* v *Kirsch* (1867) LR 2 HL 99, the defendants issued a prospectus which contained representations which were untrue and deceptive. The plaintiffs were given the opportunity of inspecting certain reports and plans which supplied the correct data. It was held that it is not sufficient to mitigate a falsehood by giving the victim a chance to verify the statement from plans and documents. What would be the position if the plaintiffs checked the plans and documents (which contained the true position), and concluded that such inspection verified the statement made initially? Presumably the result would have been different.

It is not necessary for the plaintiff to show that the misrepresentation was the only inducement for him to enter into the contract. In *Edgington* v *Fitzmaurice* (above), there were two inducing factors. One was the statement of intent, where no such intention was held, the other was the plaintiff's own erroneous belief as to the security afforded by the debentures. The fact that the plaintiff could not rely on the latter did not disentitle him to relief.

The question of reliance was considered by the Court of Appeal in the context of a claim in tort based on negligence in *JEB Fasteners* v *Marks, Bloom & Co* [1983] 1 All ER 583. The plaintiffs wished to take over a company with the principal object of acquiring the services of the two directors. During the period of negotiations, the defendants produced some audited accounts. The figures in the accounts were inaccurate. The plaintiffs were aware that there was inaccuracy, but were not aware of the extent of the inaccuracy. The take-over was unsuccessful, and the plaintiffs sustained considerable loss as a result. The trial judge found that the plaintiffs did 'rely on' the accounts in the sense that they had studied the accounts before the take-over, and the picture presented by the accounts encouraged them to continue with the take-over. However, the judge found that because the motive for the take-over was to obtain the services of the company's two directors and the plaintiffs had formed their own view of the value of the company's stock, the plaintiffs would have proceeded in any event. There was an appeal on the ground that this approach was illogical.

The Court of Appeal upheld the judgment on the grounds that there was sufficient evidence to support the finding that there had been no 'true reliance'.

Stephenson LJ said that in the context of negligent misrepresentation, the false representation had to play a real and substantial, although not necessarily decisive, part in inducing the plaintiff to act.

In the case of fraudulent misrepresentation, there is a rebuttable presumption that, if a false statement is of such a nature that it would be likely to play a part in the decision of a reasonable person, it is presumed to have done so unless the representor satisfies the court to the contrary: see *County NatWest Ltd* v *Barton* [2002] 4 All ER 494. In that case the Court of Appeal approved the approach of Hutley JA in *Australian Steel and Mining Corp Pty Ltd* v *Corben* [1974] 2 NSWLR 202. In the course of his judgment Hutley JA said:

'A person who knows that an erroneous belief is entertained does not, unless a fiduciary relationship exists, have any obligation to dissipate such a belief or to correct a position reached upon such a belief, but when asked after the decision has been reached a question which touches the belief upon which it has been reached and he answers falsely he ... has induced all those acts which flow from the continuing belief.'

Materiality

Treitel argues that a misrepresentation has no effect unless it is material. He says (the *Law of Contract*):

'That is, it must be one that would affect the judgment of a reasonable man in deciding whether, or on what terms, to enter into the contract; or one that would induce him to enter into the contract without making such enquiries as he otherwise would make.'

Chitty states that there is no clear authority denying relief to a representee who has, in fact, been influenced by a representation which would not have influenced a reasonable man, and submits that where the representor knows or ought to know that the statement will be acted upon, the representee ought not to be denied relief. See also *Museprime Properties Ltd* v *Adhill Properties Ltd* [1990] 36 EG 114 (below).

7.4 Fraudulent misrepresentation

Once misrepresentation has been established, it is necessary to direct the enquiry into the nature of the misrepresentation. A misrepresentation is fraudulent in the three instances set out by Lord Herschell in *Derry* v *Peek* (1889) 14 App Cas 337, where it is made with knowledge of its falsity, or without belief in its truth, or recklessly not caring whether it is true or false.

The victim of a fraudulent misrepresentation has the following courses of action open to him as listed below.

1. He may affirm the contract and claim damages for the tort of deceit.
2. He may rescind the contract and claim damages as aforesaid.
3. He may plead fraud as a defence to an action against him for breach of contract.

The remedies of rescission and for damages will be discussed further below.

Certain points should be noted in connection with fraudulent misrepresentation. The onus probandi is on the plaintiff – he who asserts fraud must prove it: see, however, *County NatWest Ltd* v *Barton*, above.

7.5 Negligent misstatements at common law

An important development in the common law was initiated by the decision of the House of Lords in *Hedley Byrne* v *Heller* [1964] AC 465. The plaintiffs in this action had suffered loss by extending credit to a certain firm. They had been induced to do so by a reference, carelessly given by that firm's bank, which, in effect, vouched for the firm's creditworthiness. The bank escaped liability because of a disclaimer clause – the reference was stated to have been given 'without responsibility'. But the House of Lords made it clear that, without this clause, the bank would have owed a duty to the plaintiffs.

The importance of this case lies in its recognition that the duty arises not only in situations of fiduciary and contractual relationships, but also in situations where there is a 'special relationship' between the parties. This special relationship will arise where the representor has (or purports to have) some special skill or knowledge, and knows (or should know) that the representee will rely on the representation.

The main impact of the case for the law of contract was the clear emergence of the category of negligent misrepresentation for which a remedy lay in damages. But this has been somewhat overtaken by the enactment of MA 1967.

7.6 Representations under the Misrepresentation Act 1967

Section 2(1) of the Act provides:

> 'Where a person has entered into a contract after a misrepresentation has been made to him by another party thereto and as a result thereof he has suffered loss, then, if the person making the misrepresentation would be liable to damages in respect thereof had the misrepresentation been made fraudulently, that person shall be so liable notwithstanding that the misrepresentation was not made fraudulently unless he proves that he had reasonable ground to believe and did believe up to the time the contract was made that the facts represented were true.'

This section requires analysis.

It is clear that where the representation had induced the contract, there is no need to prove a 'special relationship'. See *Howard Marine* v *Ogden* [1978] QB 574.

It reverses the burden of proof. Once the representee has proved that there has been a misrepresentation which induced him to enter into the contract, the onus is on the representor to prove both his belief in the truth of the representation and reasonable ground for his belief.

Section 2(1) also applies where the representation is made by an agent on behalf of the contracting party (see *Gosling* v *Anderson* (1972) 223 EG 1743), but the agent is not personally liable (see *The Skopas* [1983] 2 All ER 1).

The effect of s2(1) was considered by the Court of Appeal in *Howard Marine* v

Ogden (above). The defendants wished to hire two barges from the plaintiffs. The plaintiffs quoted a price for the hire in a letter which made no mention of the carrying capacity in weight of the barges. During subsequent negotiations, in response to a query, the plaintiffs' representative gave a figure for the carrying capacity, which though an honest answer was incorrect. The figure was given on the basis of the representative's recollection of the figure given in Lloyd's Register. The correct figure appeared in shipping documents which the representative had seen, but had forgotten. Because of their limited carrying capacity, the defendant's work was held up. They refused to pay the hire charges. The plaintiffs sued for the hire charges and the defendants counter-claimed damages. By a majority, the Court of Appeal found the plaintiffs liable under s2(1).

Lord Denning MR (dissenting) held that:

1. there was no collateral warranty;
2. there was nothing giving rise to a duty of care which would make the plaintiffs liable for negligent misstatement at common law;
3. the plaintiffs had discharged the burden of proof imposed by s2(1).

Bridge and Shaw LJJ held that there was no collateral warranty, but held the plaintiffs liable under s2(1) as the evidence adduced by the plaintiffs was not sufficient to show that their representative had an objectively reasonable ground for disregarding the carrying capacity figure given in the shipping document and preferring the figure in Lloyd's Register. Shaw LJ also held that the plaintiffs were liable for breach of their common law duty of care in making the representation. Bridge LJ expressed doubts on this point.

The recent case of *Gran Gelato Ltd* v *Richcliff Group Ltd* [1992] 1 All ER 865 makes it clear that as a general principle the defence of contributory negligence may be available in cases of negligent misrepresentation.

Section 2(2) of the Act provides that where the representee is entitled to rescission the court may, if it considers it equitable to do so, award damages in lieu of rescission. The court will consider the nature of the representation, the loss that would be caused if the contract were upheld, and the loss that would be caused to the representor if rescission were granted. Damages may be awarded under s2(2) whether or not the representor is liable under s2(1), but any award under s2(2) shall be taken into account in assessing the representor's liability under s2(1). This principle was upheld by the Queen's Bench Divisional court in the case of *Zanzibar* v *British Aerospace (Lancaster House) Ltd* (2000) The Times 28 March, where the court awarded damages in lieu of rescission, as established by s2(2) Misrepresentation Act 1967.

7.7 Innocent misrepresentation

The Act has only to a limited extent altered the position with regard to innocent misrepresentation, that is, where the representor has discharged the burden of proof imposed by s2(1).

Prior to the Act, the only remedy available for innocent misrepresentation was rescission, which as we shall see may be a doubtful remedy. Damages were not obtainable, but Equity devised a measure of compensation, known as indemnity compensation, for loss directly attributable to innocent misrepresentation. The difference between indemnities and damages is illustrated by the case of *Whittington v Seale-Hayne* (1900) 82 LT 49. The plaintiffs, poultry breeders, were induced to enter into a lease of property belonging to the defendants by an oral representation that the premises were in a sanitary condition. The lease that was later executed did not contain this representation, which was not, therefore, a term of the contract. The premises were, in fact, insanitary. The terms of the lease required the plaintiffs to pay rent to the defendants and rates to the local authority, and they were also obliged to effect certain repairs to the premises. The plaintiffs could recover these expenses as they were bound under the lease to make these payments. They could not recover removal expenses and consequential loss as these did not arise from obligations imposed by the lease.

MA 1967 allows by s2(2) damages in lieu of rescission, but this modification of the law is subject to certain limitations:

1. it is within the discretion of the court;
2. the award of damages is in lieu of rescission; a plaintiff cannot rescind and be awarded damages for innocent misrepresentation, whereas he can be entitled to both remedies for fraudulent or negligent misrepresentation;
3. it is not yet clear what the measure of damages is under s2(2).

7.8 Remedies

Damages

For fraudulent misrepresentation, the measure of damages is tortious; in tort the purpose of an award of damages is to put the injured party in the position he would have been in if the wrong had not been committed. The contractual measure is designed to put such party in the position he would have been in if the contract had been performed, that is, if the promise were true. The House of Lords recently affirmed this in *Smith New Court Securities Ltd* v *Citibank NA* [1997] AC 554.

On 21 July 1989, the plaintiff purchased a parcel of shares in Company F at a price of 82.25p per share in a deal totalling over £23 million. It was subsequently discovered that this transaction had been induced by a fraudulent misrepresentation. In September 1989, the shares in Company F fell dramatically in value because of a (totally unconnected) fraud. The plaintiff eventually sold the shares in Company F at a great loss, and brought an action against the defendants claiming that they had been induced to enter into the contract by fraudulent misrepresentation. The main issue was the value of the shares and assessment of damages.

The Court of Appeal accepted that there had been fraudulent misrepresentation and assessed damages on the basis of the difference in price between what was actually paid and what the shares would have fetched on the open market. The House of Lords reaffirmed the decision of the Court of Appeal with regard to the finding of fraudulent misrepresentation, but reversed the decision of the Court of Appeal in relation to the measure of damages. Their Lordships felt that the amount recoverable by the plaintiffs was the difference between the contract price and the amount actually realised by the plaintiffs on the resale of the shares.

Their Lordships felt that, but for the causative influence of the fraudulent misrepresentation, the plaintiffs would not have suffered a loss and as such, damages must be assessed on the basis of losses accruing or flowing naturally out of the fraud.

Normally, in tort actions, an award of damages is limited by the test of remoteness, that is, the defendant will be liable only for damages that were reasonably foreseeable.

In *Doyle* v *Olby (Ironmongers) Ltd* [1969] 2 QB 158, however, Lord Denning MR said that:

'The defendant is bound to make reparation for all the actual damage directly flowing from the fraudulent inducement ... It does not lie in the mouth of the fraudulent person to say that they could not have been reasonably foreseen.'

In the recent case of *East* v *Maurer* [1991] 2 All ER 733 the Court of Appeal stated that the 'reparation for all actual damage' as indicated by Denning in *Doyle* v *Olby* would include loss of profits. The assessment of loss of profits was, however, to be made on a tortious basis, that is, placing the plaintiff in the same position he would have been in, had the wrong not been committed. The result is that damages for loss of profits caused by a fraudulent misrepresentation must be based on the level of profits that might have been expected, had the false misrepresentation not been made, rather than on the basis of a contractual warranty that a particular state of affairs should continue. The overall effect of such an approach may well result in the amount of damages to be awarded for loss of profits being reduced. This case should also be considered in the light of *Royscott* v *Rogerson* (see below).

There is a conflict of views as to whether or not exemplary damages can be awarded for the tort of deceit. This question was raised, but not decided, in *Archer* v *Brown* [1984] 2 All ER 267 where the court held, however, that the plaintiff was entitled to aggravated damages for the distress he had suffered.

For negligent misrepresentation at common law the measure of damages is in tort, the normal rule applies that the loss must be reasonably foreseeable. See *Esso Petroleum* v *Mardon* [1976] QB 801.

The measure of damages under s2(1) MA 1967 is not made entirely clear by the wording of the subsection. The language employed suggests that a tortious measure was envisaged. However, in *Watts* v *Spence* [1976] Ch 165, the court gave damages for loss of bargain under s2(1), that is, the contractual measure. That decision was not followed in *Sharneyford Supplies* v *Edge* [1985] 1 All ER 976, where the matter was fully considered by Mervyn Davies J, who decided that the tortious measure was the correct one to apply. (The actual decision of Mervyn Davies J was reversed by the Court of Appeal – [1987] 1 All ER 588 – but not on this point.)

In *Royscott Trust Ltd* v *Rogerson* [1991] 3 WLR 57 it was held that the tortious measure of damages was the true one. In that case a car dealer agreed to sell a car on HP to a customer for a cash price of £7,600, of which the customer was to pay a deposit of £1,200. These amounts were mistakenly stated as £8,000 and £1,600 respectively to the finance company and all future transactions were based on these figures.

The customer paid part of the sum due to the finance company, but in 1987 he dishonestly sold the car; and later ceased to make any payments. The amount unpaid by that time was, the finance company claimed, £3,625. They based this figure on the difference between the amount repaid to them by the customer and the amount £6,400 which they had advanced to the car dealer. The figures supplied to the finance company, however, had been mistakenly set too high, and the finance company sued the car dealer for innocent misrepresentation and claimed damages under s2(1) Misrepresentation Act 1967.

The Court of Appeal held that the measure of damages recoverable under s2(1) MA 1967 was a tortious rather than contractual one. The finance company was entitled to recover damages in respect of all losses occurring as a natural consequence, including unforeseeable losses, subject to the normal rules on remoteness. It was in any event a foreseeable event that a customer buying a car on HP might dishonestly sell the car. The act by the customer was not a novus actus, the chain of causation was unbroken. The car dealers were liable for innocent misrepresentation and the finance company could claim the £3,625 plus interest. Recently, the Court of Appeal in *Downs and Another* v *Chappell and Another* [1996] 3 All ER 344, a case concerning fraudulent misrepresentation, held that the plaintiffs' damages have to be assessed by reference to what they have lost as a result of entering into the transaction. The measure of damages must, therefore, reflect the true or actual loss sustained by the plaintiffs. In an article by Jeremy Stuart-Smith QC and Anna de Chassirow recently (NLJ Practitioner 9 June 2000), the issue of recovery of damages after misrepresentation was raised. In *Avon Insurance plc* v *Swine Fraser Ltd* (2000) The Times 20 January, Rix J of the Commercial Court held that various causes of action may be asserted when misrepresentation is alleged. In considering the availability of s2(1) Misrepresentation Act 1967, he stated that s2(1) is potentially the smart missile in a claimant's legal armoury, but as with many exocet, it needs to be handled with care. It cannot be assumed that the slightest inaccuracy in a statement or document will bring the section into play. The decision therefore raises doubt about the correctness of *Royscott*. It further suggests that *Royscott* is ripe for revision.

There is considerable uncertainty as to the measure to be applied when damages are awarded in lieu of rescission under s2(2) MA 1967. Both Treitel and Chitty are of the view that damages under s2(2) may be lower than the damages awarded under s2(1). Chitty suggests the possibility of a special measure to compensate the representee for the loss of his right to rescind. In Cheshire and Fifoot (11th edn pp286–7), the view is expressed that compensation should be limited to an indemnity.

This issue was considered by the High Court in *Thomas Witter Ltd* v *TBP Industries Ltd* [1996] 2 All ER 573, where the court held that the measure of damages for breach of contract and/or for misrepresentation is the same.

When the damages involve assessment of open market values, the House of Lords case of *Smith New Court Securities Ltd* v *Scrimgeour Vickers (Asset Management) Ltd* [1996] 4 All ER 769 is of particular relevance.

On 21 July 1989, the plaintiff purchased a parcel of shares in company F at a price of 82.25p per share – a deal totalling over £23 million. It subsequently was found that this transaction had been induced by a fraudulent misrepresentation. In September 1989, the shares in company F fell dramatically in value, because of a (totally unconnected) fraud. The plaintiff eventually sold the shares in company F at a great loss, and pursued an action against Scrimgeour Vickers and other defendants claiming that they had been induced to enter the contract by fraudulent misrepresentation. The main problem arose as to the value of the shares and assessment of damages.

The Court of Appeal accepted that there had been fraudulent misrepresentation and would assess damages as being the difference in price between what was actually paid and what the shares would have fetched on the open market. On appeal, the House of Lords reaffirmed the decision of the Court of Appeal with regards to the finding of fraudulent misrepresentation, but reversed the decision of the Court in relation to the measures of damages. Their Lordships felt that the amount of damages recoverable by the plaintiffs was the difference between the contract price and the amount actually realised by the Plaintiffs on the resale of the shares.

The Court of Appeal's decision in *Clef Aquitaine SARL* v *Laporte Materials (Barrow) Ltd* [2000] 3 All ER 493 is significant in so far as, in consequence of the defendant's deceit, the claimant made less profit as opposed to an initial loss. Relying on *East* v *Maurer* [1991] 2 All ER 733 which was approved by Lord Steyn in *Smith New Court Securities Ltd* v *Scrimgeour Vickers (Asset Management) Ltd* [1996] 4 All ER 769, by way of damages the trial judge awarded the claimant the difference between the prices paid and the prices which would have been paid but for the deceit.

Their Lordships concluded that this decision (including the exercise of the judge's assumed discretion to award simple interest only) should not be disturbed. Simon Brown LJ said:

'I have ... reached the conclusion that there is no absolute rule requiring the person deceived to prove that the actual transaction into which he was induced to enter was itself loss-making. … It will sometimes be possible, as it was here, to prove instead that a different and more favourable transaction (either with the defendant or with some third party) would have been entered into but for the fraud, and to measure and recover the claimants' loss on that basis.'

Rescission

Rescission is available for any of the categories of misrepresentation. A contract can be rescinded by giving notice to the representor, but this is not always necessary. In *Car and Universal Finance* v *Caldwell* [1965] 1 QB 525, the owner of a car was induced by fraud to sell his car to a rogue, who disappeared and could not be traced. On discovering the fraud, the owner notified the police and the Automobile Association. These actions were held sufficient to rescind the contract, so that an innocent third party who had bought the car from the rogue acquired no title to it.

It has recently been established that it is not necessary to prove conclusively that reliance was placed on a misrepresentation, if it is conceded by all parties that misrepresentation has in fact taken place.

In *Museprime Properties Ltd* v *Adhill Properties Ltd* [1990] 36 EG 114, a sale by auction of three properties, the particulars wrongly represented the rents from the properties as being open to negotiation. The statements in the auction particulars and made later by the auctioneer himself misrepresented the position with regard to rent reviews. In fact, on two of the three properties, rent reviews had been triggered and new rents agreed.

The plaintiff company successfully bid for the three properties – commercial and residential premises in Finchley – and discovered the true situation. They commenced an action for rescission. The defendant company countered with the defence that the misrepresentations were not such as to induce any reasonable person to enter into a contract. It was held that the plaintiffs had established and, indeed, the defendants conceded, that misrepresentation had occurred. Any material misrepresentation is a ground for rescission.

The judge referred, with approval, to the view of Goff and Jones: *Law of Restitution*, that the question whether representations would have induced a reasonable person to enter into a contract was relevant only to the onus of proof. Here the plaintiffs had established their claim to rescission of the contract on the ground of material misrepresentation. Reliance was, therefore, of no further relevance. The plaintiffs were awarded return of their deposit and damages in respect of lost conveyancing expenses.

Limits to rescission

There are several bars, or limits, to the right to rescind for misrepresentation.

If the representee has affirmed the contract

See *Long* v *Lloyd* [1958] 1 WLR 753.

In *Peyman* v *Lanjani* [1985] Ch 457, the Court of Appeal held that the plaintiff had not lost his right to rescind because, knowing of the facts which afforded this right, he proceeded with the contract, unless he also knew of the right to rescind. The plaintiff here did not know he had such right. As he did not know he had such right, he could not be said to have elected to affirm the contract.

See also *Production Technology Consultants* v *Bartlett* [1988] 25 EG 121, in which the plaintiff bought a freehold house which had been divided into four flats from the defendant at an auction. The particulars supplied at the auction innocently failed to say that one of the flats was let on a 99-year lease. Before completion, the lease was sent to the plaintiff's solicitors, but without waiting, the plaintiff completed the transaction, then sued for damages under s2(1) of the MA 1967.

While, at first instance, the court held that by completing he had exhausted his remedies, on appeal the CA held that the plaintiff, while having lost his right to rescind, still retained the right to sue for damages.

Note that the point at which the existence of the 99-year lease became known to the solicitors became the point at which constructively knowledge was imputed to the plaintiff; his decision to complete was assumed to be affirmation and his right to rescind lost.

This case demonstrates, however, the courts' right to award damages in lieu, even when the right to rescind is lost for some reason.

If the representee has not acted within a reasonable time

See *Leaf* v *International Galleries* [1950] 2 KB 86. However, this may not be a bar in the case of fraudulent misrepresentation. See *Armstrong* v *Jackson* [1917] 2 KB 822.

If restitution is impossible

See *Clarke* v *Dickson* (1858) EB & B 148 and *Erlanger* v *New Sombrero Phosphate Co* (1878) 3 App Cas 1218. See also the Australian case of *Vadasz* v *Pioneer Concrete (SA) Pty Ltd* (1995) 130 ALR 570, where the court held that even if rescission could not be granted ab initio, equity might operate to set aside the contract entirely.

If third parties have acquired rights in the subject matter of the contract

Phillips v *Brooks* [1919] 2 KB 243.

Two previous bars to rescission have been removed by MA 1967. Prior to the Act, it was doubtful whether the right to rescind for innocent misrepresentation survived if the misrepresentation had become a term of the contract. Section 1(a) now provides that a person shall be entitled to rescind notwithstanding that the misrepresentation has become a term of the contract if he would otherwise have been so entitled without alleging fraud.

Before the Act, there were decisions to the effect that certain contracts could not be rescinded for innocent misrepresentation after they had been 'executed', for example, contracts for the disposition of an interest in land and the sale of shares. This has now been reversed by s1(b).

7.9 Misrepresentation and exclusion clauses

Section 3 MA 1967 as substituted by s8 Unfair Contract Terms Act 1977 provides that:

> 'If a contract contains a term which would exclude or restrict:
> (a) any liability to which a party to a contract may be subject by reason of any misrepresentation made by him before the contract was made; or
> (b) any remedy available to another party to the contract by reason of such a misrepresentation,
> that term shall be of no effect except insofar as it satisfies the requirement of reasonableness as stated in s11(1) of the Unfair Contract Terms Act 1977; and it is for those claiming that the term satisfies that requirement to show that it does.'

The requirement of reasonableness will be considered in the ensuing chapter on exclusion clauses.

There is one point to observe at this juncture. It may be difficult to draw a distinction between a clause excluding liability and one defining the authority of, for example, an agent. See *Overbrooke Estates* v *Glencombe Properties* [1974] 1 WLR 1335, in which it was held that a provision in the particulars of sale did not constitute an exclusion clause but a limitation on the apparent authority of the auctioneers.

8

Exclusion Clauses

8.1 Introduction

An exclusion or exemption clause is one which purports to exclude wholly, or in part, liability for certain breaches of contract or for the happening of certain events. If the exclusion is only partial, then the clause may be called a 'limitation of liability clause'. The courts have always been wary of such clauses and this is reflected in common law on the topic. More recently, the Unfair Contract Terms Act 1977 (UCTA) marks the beginning of the present statutory controls.

The importance of UCTA is not only that it covers a wide range of potential clauses in different types of contract, but that it also has a real effect on the older common law rules. The provisions of common law and UCTA co-exist in many contracts. In some contracts, only parts of the Act will apply; to some contracts, UCTA does not apply at all, the contract being governed entirely by common law. Note also that EC Directives, increasingly of importance in English domestic law, now affect exclusion clauses. The EC Directive 93/13 gave rise to the Unfair Terms in Consumer Contracts Regulations 1994 which came into effect on 1 July 1995. These Regulations were subsequently repealed and replaced with the Unfair Terms in Consumer Contracts Regulations 1999 which came into force on 1 October 1999. These Regulations are dealt with towards the end of this chapter (section 8.9).

The main thrust of the Regulations is that any term which has not been individually negotiated is to be regarded as unfair, if it creates substantial inequality between the parties to the detriment of the consumer. A term is to be regarded as not being individually negotiated if it has been drafted in advance and the consumer has had no say in its wording or effect. (This is particularly likely in standard-form contracts.) The Annex to the Directive contains an illustrative (but not exhaustive) list of such terms, including:

1. those with the object or effect of excluding or limiting liability of the seller or supplier;
2. those terms automatically extending a contract of fixed duration if the consumer does not indicate otherwise;
3. terms allowing the seller/supplier to alter the contract unilaterally;
4. terms which seek to limit consumers' rights to take legal action, eg by requiring disputes to go to arbitration rather than to court.

It is, therefore, necessary to be familiar with the common law as well as the statutory rules governing exclusion clauses.

At common law, in order for an exclusion clause to be binding, it must have been incorporated as a term of the contract. The courts have evolved stringent tests to check whether the relevant clause is incorporated. There are two main ways in which an exclusion clause may be incorporated: by advance notice to the other party that the exclusion is to be a term of the contract, and by the signature of the party agreeing to be bound by the exclusion clause.

When the incorporation is by virtue of notifying the other party, in advance, of its inclusion, then three situations should be noted: notice by display; notice in a document; and notice by a course of dealing.

8.2 Notice by display

Notices exhibited in premises which purport to exempt liability for loss or damage are common. For example: 'Car parked at owner's risk' in a car park, or 'The Management undertake no liability for loss or damage occasioned to customer's apparel' in a cloakroom, are instances of notices which are intended to have contractual force. Whether such clauses do have contractual force is dependent upon whether the notice is in a position where it can be seen before or at the time of entry into the contract. A leading case is *Olley* v *Marlborough Court* [1949] 1 KB 532. A husband and wife arrived at a hotel. They paid for their board and residence in advance. They went to the hotel room. A notice was displayed in the room exempting the hotel from liability for loss or damage to items left in the room. During their stay, the wife's fur coat was stolen.

The contract was held to have been made before the notice was seen, so that the contractual liability could not unilaterally be transferred back to the hotel guests. See also *Thornton* v *Shoe Lane Parking* [1971] 2 QB 163.

8.3 Notice in a document

There are five questions which should be asked.

1. Is the document contractual?
2. Has reasonably sufficient notice been given?
3. Is the clause unusual?
4. Could acceptance have been avoided?
5. When is the contractual dealing concluded?

A case heard in the Australian Court of Appeal provides a useful illustration of items (1)–(5) above. In *Dillon* v *Baltic Shipping Co* (*The Mikhail Lermontov*) [1991] 2 Lloyd's Rep 155 the plaintiff and her daughter booked a cruise on the 'Mikhail Lermontov' by paying a deposit. One week later they received a document headed 'Booking Form CTC Cruises'. This form contained, inter alia, the clause:

'Contract of Carriage for travel as set out ... will be made only at the time of issuing the tickets and will be subject to conditions and regulations printed on the tickets ...'

Having paid the balance, the plaintiff received tickets containing terms and conditions, limiting the shipping line's liability for personal injury and death. Just over a week into the cruise, the liner struck a rock and sank. The plaintiff suffered personal injury and nervous shock.

The plaintiff claimed damages for personal injuries, loss of property and loss of the enjoyment of the holiday. The defendants argued that limitation clauses, referred to on the ticket, formed part of the conditions of the contract and that they were entitled to rely on them. The court held that the statement in the initial brochure (supplied on receipt of the deposit) was insufficient to draw the attention of the customer to the fact that limitation clauses were contained in the ticket terms and conditions. The issue of a ticket with terms and conditions printed in full occurred after payment of the balance and a firm contract of carriage was already in existence. At the time the contract of carriage came into force, the plaintiff had not had a reasonable opportunity to see and agree to the conditions and terms referred to, and which the defendants sought to impose on all the passengers when tickets were delivered, which was about a month or more later.

Exclusion or limitation clauses thus referred to, on the ticket, could not be said to be incorporated into the contract and could not be relied upon.

Is the document contractual?

Where the clause is contained in a document, it is still essential that the clause is incorporated into the contract. A document proffered after the contract has been made cannot contain any terms of the contract, and so cannot be binding upon the recipient. For example, A makes an offer to B. B accepts. After he has done so, he gives A a sheet of 'Terms and conditions'. These are not part of the contract between A and B.

Even where the document which contains terms and conditions is proffered before the contract is concluded, the document must be one on which a person could reasonably expect to find 'terms and conditions'. The test is that of the expectation of 'the reasonable man'. The narrowness of the distinction between documents upon which the reasonable man would, and would not, expect to find contractual terms, can be illustrated by a comparison of the following four cases.

In *Parker* v *South Eastern Railway* (1877) 2 CPD 416, the plaintiff was given a ticket which read 'see back' in exchange for luggage left at a railway cloakroom. The reverse of the ticket contained exclusion clauses for loss or damage to the luggage.

The plaintiff was held to be bound by the exclusion clause because notice of the clauses had been given, and the notice was sufficient 'in all the circumstances of the case'.

In *Chapelton* v *Barry UDC* [1940] 1 KB 532, deck chairs were stacked by a notice asking the public who wished to use the deck chairs to get tickets and retain them for inspection. The plaintiff paid for two tickets for chairs, but did not read them. The reverse of the ticket contained exclusion clauses from liability for personal injury. The plaintiff was injured when a deck chair collapsed. It was held that the defendant could not rely on the exclusion clause because it was not contained in a contractual document. No one would have assumed that the ticket was anything but a receipt. Even if the ticket had been a contractual document, it was given to the plaintiff after he had accepted the offer to hire the chair.

In *McCutcheon* v *David MacBrayne* [1964] 1 WLR 125, exclusion clauses were contained in 27 paragraphs of small print contained inside and outside a ferry booking office and in a 'risk note' which passengers sometimes signed.

The exclusions clauses were held not to be incorporated.

A different type of case is *Burnett* v *Westminster Bank* [1966] 1 QB 742. The plaintiff had accounts at branches A and B of the defendant bank. A new cheque book for branch A contained a notice that the cheques in the book would be applied to the account for which they had been prepared. No notice of contractual terms had been contained in previous cheque books. The plaintiff attempted to debit account B by writing on the cheque. The bank's computer failed to read the handwritten instruction, and the wrong account was debited. The court decided that the words in the cheque book were not contained in a contractual document and were therefore ineffective.

Has reasonably sufficient notice been given?

In *Parker*, the House of Lords held that the notice must be reasonably sufficient in all the circumstances of the case. This is a question of fact. The court must look at all the circumstances and the situation of the parties. See also *Vine* v *Waltham Forest London Borough Council* [2000] 4 All ER 169 (claim of motorist parking on private land not defeated by notice warning of clamping she had not seen).

It has become almost axiomatic that where a document contains terms and conditions on its reverse, it must refer to them on the face of that document.

In *Sugar* v *London, Midland and Scottish Railway* [1941] 1 All ER 172, the words 'for conditions see back', which appeared on the face of the document, was obliterated by the date stamp.

It was held that reasonably sufficient notice had not been given.

In *Richardson Spence & Co* v *Rowntree* [1894] AC 217, the plaintiff contracted with the defendant to be taken as a passenger on a steamer from Philadelphia to Liverpool. The fare was paid and the plaintiff received the ticket, which was folded up and in part obliterated by red ink. She knew that the ticket contained writing, but not that it contained terms.

The court held that no reasonably sufficient notice had been given.

The requirement is only that *reasonably* sufficient notice be given. It is an objective and not a subjective test. If the plaintiff has a peculiarity not common to the rest of the population, such that he does not know of the terms, he will not be protected by his ignorance if a reasonable man would have known of them.

In *Thompson* v *LMS Railway* [1930] 1 KB 41, the plaintiff was injured when she stepped off a train which had stopped before reaching the platform. Her ticket contained terms which referred to timetables which limited liability. She could not read the words on the ticket because she was illiterate.

She was held to be bound by the clauses limiting liability. A reasonable man would have been able to read the ticket and to know that exclusion clauses in the railway timetable could be referred to and were incorporated in the contract.

If the defendant knows of the peculiarity, the same result does not follow. In *Geier* v *Kujawa* [1970] 1 Lloyd's Rep 364, a notice in English was displayed in a car to the effect that passengers travelled at their own risk. A German passenger who was known to speak no English travelled in the car. The passenger was not bound by the term.

An interesting case which illustrates the application of the objective test occurred in *Smith* v *South Wales Switchgear* [1978] 1 All ER 18. A contractual document provided that the contract incorporated general conditions of business which were available on request. There were three editions of the general conditions, the last of which was March 1970. No copy had been requested, although the 1969 conditions had been supplied by mistake.

The 1970 version of the conditions was held by the court to be incorporated into the contract. It was common experience that trading conditions were revised from time to time. The meaning which could be reasonably attributed to the reference was that the conditions referred to were the current conditions.

Does it make any difference that the clause is unusual?

It seems that the more unusual or unreasonable the clause, the more difficult it may be to incorporate it into the contract at common law. This is principally an argument promoted by Lord Denning MR. He first made this observation in *Spurling* v *Bradshaw* [1956] 2 All ER 121, where he suggested that 'the more unreasonable the clause is the greater the notice which must be given of it'. He expressed like views in *Thornton* v *Shoe Lane Parking* [1971] 2 QB 163. In that case, a ticket was issued from an automatic machine in a car park. The car park premises contained a notice which was visible on approach that all cars were parked at owner's risk. The ticket, which was issued as the driver approached, emerged from the machine. He would take the ticket and drive on. The ticket contained printed wording that it was issued subject to conditions displayed inside the premises. The conditions inside the premises were in small print and very wide, and excluded liability for damage to cars and customers. The plaintiff was not held to be bound by the notice displayed inside the premises.

Lord Denning said that the clause was so wide and destructive of rights that, in order to be effective, it would have to have a red hand pointing to it and be printed in red ink.

Megaw LJ said that when a restriction was not usual, the defendant must show that he had fairly brought to the notice of the other party his intention to attach an unusual condition.

In *Interfoto Picture Library Ltd* v *Stiletto Visual Programmes Ltd* [1988] 1 All ER 348, the Court of Appeal re-affirmed the principle that where a condition in a contract was particularly onerous or unusual, and would not generally be known to the other party, the party seeking to enforce that condition had to show it had been fairly and reasonably brought to the other party's attention. Their Lordships stressed that this was a general principle of law and was not confined to exclusion clauses.

This approach was adopted by the Court of Appeal in *O'Brien* v *MGN Ltd* (2001) The Times 8 August. The *Daily Mirror* launched a scratchcard game on 29 April 1995. On 25 June the claimant bought a newspaper that came with a game card. On the card was printed 'Full rules and how to claim see *Daily Mirror*'. Rule 5 provided: 'Should more prizes be claimed than are available in any prize category for any reason, a simple draw will take place for the prize.' The claimant's copy of the *Daily Mirror* 3 July contained a card indicating two sums of £50,000. As was required, he telephoned the mystery hotline and a message indicated that he had won that amount. As it turned out, no fewer than 1,472 people made the same claim. The newspaper announced a special draw for one £50,000 prize and for a further £50,000 to be shared by other cardholders. The claimant received £34 as a share of that sum. The game was designed and the cards printed to produce only one or two £50,000 prizes each week. Someone responsible for determining winning combinations had made a mistake. In the claimant's action to recover the full prize, the issue was whether the contract between the parties incorporated the newspaper's instant scratch card rules. Their Lordships were satisfied that this question had properly been answered in the affirmative by the trial judge. Applying the judgments of Bingham and Dillon LJJ in *Interfoto Picture Library Ltd* v *Stiletto Visual Programmes Ltd*, Hale LJ said the test was whether the newspaper could be said fairly and reasonably to have brought the rules to the notice of the claimant and whether those rules were particularly onerous or unusual. Rule 5, although it turned an apparent winner into a loser, was neither onerous or outlandish. It merely deprived the claimant of a windfall for which he had done very little in return. In the particular context of the game, her Ladyship was satisfied that the newspaper had done just enough to bring the rules to the claimant's attention. There was a clear reference to the rules on the face of his card and they could be discovered from the newspaper office or from back issues of the paper.

Could acceptance have been avoided?

The observances of the Court of Appeal in the *Shoe Lane* case support the proposition that if the plaintiff cannot resile from his prior intention to conclude the contract at the time when notice is given, the exclusion clause will not have been incorporated into the contract.

Have the contractual negotiations been concluded?

This is, of course, always a question of fact rather than law, but an interesting illustration of the difficulties which present themselves arose in *Levison* v *Patent Steam Carpet Cleaning Co* [1977] 3 All ER 498. The owner of a carpet requested that it be picked up and taken away for cleaning. When the cleaning company called for it, the owner was presented with a document containing exclusion clauses. He signed it. The cleaning company took away the carpet and a further rug.

The exclusion clauses were held to be incorporated into the contract, although they did not cover a fundamental breach. The reasoning is difficult to ascertain, although the Court of Appeal were unanimous. Lord Denning MR thought that the exclusion clauses were incorporated by a course of dealing and, in any event, the contract was not concluded until the signature of the form. Sir David Cairns and Orr LJ thought that the document would have been part of the contract even in the absence of a course of dealing. The most promising suggestion was on the basis of a novation (see below). During the telephone conversation, only a carpet had been mentioned, whereas the contract subsequently was for a rug plus a carpet. The alternative way of looking at this suggestion is to say that the telephone conversation was only an invitation to treat, but this seems artificial in the light of the detail of agreement which had been achieved. (Lord Denning's judgment on the fundamental breach question must be read in the light of *Photo Production* v *Securicor Transport Ltd* – see below.)

8.4 Notice by a course of dealing

If notice has not been given by display as in a contractual document, it may have been given by 'a course of dealing'. This situation will arise where the parties have dealt together in the past on a number of occasions such that one party can be presumed to know the terms and conditions upon which the other operates. It does not seem to matter that the party against whom the clause is used does not know in fact what those terms are, provided that he has had every opportunity to find out what they are.

In *Henry Kendall* v *William Lillico* [1968] 2 All ER 444, the parties had contracted on more than 100 occasions in the years preceding the contract which was broken. On each occasion, there was a verbal contract which was followed by a 'sold note'. The 'sold note' contained conditions. They would not have been incorporated into the first few contracts. On the other hand, the recipients knew that the notes contained conditions, but they had not read them. Their conduct in continuing to trade evinced an intention to be bound by the conditions.

In contrast with the above is *McCutcheon* v *David MacBrayne Ltd* (above). The plaintiffs' agent had dealt with the defendants on many occasions. Sometimes he had signed a 'risk note', and sometimes he had not. The risk note contained conditions. On this occasion no risk note was signed.

The plaintiffs were not bound by the conditions, according to the court. There was no course of conduct because there was no consistency of dealing.

In *Hollier* v *Rambler Motors* [1972] 2 QB 71, Salmon LJ held that three or four transactions over a period of five years could not be described as 'a course of dealing'.

In *British Crane Hire* v *Ipswich Plant Hire* [1975] QB 303, the facts were that both parties were companies engaged in hiring out earth-moving equipment. The defendants needed a dragline crane urgently, and they contacted the plaintiffs by telephone. Subsequently, a printed form containing conditions arrived. In the previous year, there had been two occasions when the plaintiff contracted on those terms, with the defendant, although that was not known to the defendant's manager at the time of contracting. The court held that the terms would be incorporated into the contract, not by a course of dealing, but because there was a common understanding between the parties, who were in the same line of business, that any contract would be on these standard terms.

If there had been some bizarre element in the terms and conditions relied upon by the plaintiff, the same result may not follow, because there could not then be a 'common understanding'. That observation would seem to follow from Sir Eric Sachs' judgment. It may not follow from that of Lord Denning MR. He thought that the mere fact that one party knew that the other would contract on conditions was sufficient regardless of what those conditions might be. He said that he:

> ' ... would not put it so much on the course of dealing but rather on the common understanding which is to be derived from the conduct of the parties, namely, that the

hiring was to be on the terms of the plaintiff's usual conditions ... it is just as if the plaintiffs had said "We will supply it on our usual conditions" and the defendants had said "of course, this is quite understood".'

Sir Eric Sachs emphasised the distinction between the position then before him, and the position where the parties are in wholly different walks of life, as in *Hollier*'s case (above) – where one, for instance, is an expert in a line of business and the other is not.

8.5 Signature

The effect of signing a written document was distinguished from the mere receipt of a notice in *Parker* v *South Eastern Railway* (above).

Mellish LJ said:

'Where an action is brought on a written agreement which is signed by the defendant the agreement is proved by proving his signature, and, in the absence of fraud it is wholly immaterial that he has not read the agreement and does not know its contents.'

This dictum was conclusively adopted in *L'Estrange* v *Graucob* [1934] 2 KB 394. The plaintiff was a café owner. She agreed to buy an automatic slot machine from the defendants. The agreement was to pay by instalments and it contained an exemption clause which the plaintiff signed. The machine was faulty and the plaintiff purported to terminate the agreement. The court held that she could not do so because she was bound by the exclusion clause which she had signed.

Scrutton LJ observed:

'In cases in which the contract is contained in a railway ticket or other unsigned document, it is necessary to prove that an alleged party was aware, or ought to have been aware, of its terms and conditions. These cases have no application when the document has been signed. When a document containing contractual terms is signed, then, in the absence of fraud, or I will add, misrepresentation, the party signing it is bound, and it is wholly immaterial if he has read the document or not.'

8.6 Avoiding or qualifying the clause

The severity of the rule that signature will incorporate the clause can be mitigated in a number of ways.

If there has been a misrepresentation

In *Curtis* v *Chemical Cleaning and Dyeing Co* [1951] 1 KB 805, the plaintiff took a white satin wedding dress to the defendant's shop for cleaning. She was asked to sign a receipt containing an exemption clause. She asked for an explanation. She was told that it exempted liability from certain risks and, in the present instance, from the risk of damage to the beads and sequins in the dress. In fact, the clause purported to exempt liability for damage howsoever caused. The dress was stained.

Because of the misrepresentation, the exemption clause could not be relied on. This has been subsequently endorsed in a number of cases, for example, *Jacques* v *Lloyd D George & Partners* [1968] 2 All ER 187.

If there is an independent oral undertaking

In *Couchman* v *Hill* [1947] KB 54 (see Chapter 6), a promise was given that a heifer was 'unserved'. This was untrue and an exemption clause excluded liability for warranties. The Court of Appeal found that the promise was nonetheless a term of the contract and, *alternatively*, that it was a collateral contract. (See Chapter 6, section 6.3.)

If the plea of 'Non est Factum' can be upheld

(This plea 'it is not my deed' is dealt with in Chapter 10.)

If there has been fraud

Although see *Tullis* v *Jacson* [1892] 3 Ch 441. The parties to a building contract agreed that an arbitrator's decision was to be final, and was not to be set aside for any pretence, suggestion, charge or insinuation of fraud. The court stated that the award would be upheld and would not be set aside even if it had not been made in good faith.

Notably, this case dealt in terms with the question of fraud, so that the parties had clearly addressed their minds to the question of fraud. The fraud to which they had so addressed their minds was not their own fraud. This case, therefore, has no relevance to the proposition that the party cannot exclude liability for his *own* fraud. Furthermore, it is a case which has attracted some criticism, for example, that of Scrutton LJ in *Czarnikow* v *Roth, Schmidt & Co* [1922] 2 KB 478 at 488.

In *S Pearson & Son* v *Dublin Corporation* [1907] AC 351, the plaintiffs agreed to do work for the defendants. The plaintiffs had a duty to satisfy themselves that the plans were accurate. This clause would not avail the defendants if the plans were fraudulent.

On the question of whether the parties could specifically exclude liability for their own fraud, the House of Lords made the following observations:

Lord Loreburn:

'No one can escape liability for his own fraudulent statements by inserting a clause in a contract that the other party shall not rely on them.' (He thought that a person could exclude liability for his agent's fraud, however.)

Lord Halsbury:

'No craft or machinery in the form of contract can estop a person who claims that he has been defrauded from having that question of fact submitted to a jury.'

Lord James:

'When the fraud succeeds, surely those who designed the fraudulent protection cannot take advantage of it ... As a general principle I incline to the view that an express term that fraud shall not vitiate a contract could be bad in law.'

8.7 Interpreting the clause

Where there has been a fundamental breach or a breach of a fundamental term

The first issue is the meaning of the expressions 'fundamental breach' and 'term'. A fundamental breach may be the breach of a fundamental term, but it could also be any other breach of contract which defeats the main purpose of the contract. A fundamental term (a phrase which has attracted great and, no doubt, well-deserved criticism as indistinguishable in principle from the description 'condition'), is one which is at the root of the contract so that it governs its main purpose.

Where there has been a breach of a fundamental term or a fundamental breach, it is a question of construction whether the exclusion clause is drafted sufficiently widely to apply to the breach. In *Suisse Atlantique Société d'Armament Maritime* v *Rotterdamsche Kolen Centrale* [1967] 1 AC 361, a charterparty contained a clause limiting damages to $1,000 per day for each lay-day beyond the permitted number (that is, days spent waiting in port). The number of excess days was 150. The owners claimed a greater loss. It was held that, in fact, the clause was an agreed damages clause and not an exclusion clause so that the question of fundamental breach did not arise and, even if it had, the clause would have been effective.

However, the House of Lords went on to say that as a rule of *construction* (not of law), an exemption clause should not, in the absence of clear words, be applied to breaches which tended to defeat the main purpose of the contract.

This was re-affirmed in *Photo Production* v *Securicor Transport Ltd* [1980] AC 827. The defendants agreed to provide a visiting patrol service to the plaintiffs' factory at £8 15*s*. per week. The contract contained an exemption clause to the effect that the defendants 'should not be responsible for any injurious act or default by any employee of the company unless such act or default could have been foreseen and avoided by the exercise of due diligence on the part of the company as his employer'. In fact, a patrolman deliberately lit a fire and the factory was substantially burnt down.

The defendants were held to be protected by the exemption clause. The view expressed in *Harbutt's Plasticene Ltd* v *Wayne Tank and Pumps Co Ltd* [1970] 1 QB

447 that a breach of contract by one party, accepted by the other as discharging him from his further obligations under the contract, brought the contract to an end and, together with it, any exemption clause, was disapproved. The proper question was whether, as a matter of construction, the exemption clause relieved the defendants from liability. Here, there was an apportionment of the risk as between plaintiff and defendant, and the risk of arson was not accepted by the defendant.

The distinction between an exclusion clause and limitation of liability and agreed damages arose again for discussion in *Ailsa Craig Fishing* v *Malvern Fishing* [1983] 1 All ER 101. The appellants owned a boat which sank in Aberdeen Harbour. The vessel was a complete loss. The respondents were required by contract with inter alia the appellants to provide continuous security cover for the boat. The contract contained two contentious clauses and the issues were:

1. whether they were available to the respondents even though the respondents had completely failed to comply with the contract; and
2. how the clause was to be interpreted.

The court said that the clause was one which limited liability, and that the contract had to be construed as a whole to see whether the limitation of liability clause should apply to a fundamental breach. Although a limitation of liability clause had to be clearly and unambiguously expressed and construed contra proferentem, it should be given its ordinary and natural meaning. This should be construed less rigidly than an exemption clause because it would be more likely to accord with the true intention of the parties.

Note that the *Ailsa Craig Fishing* case was of particular importance with regard to limitation clauses.

While it is difficult to see just *why* limitation clauses should be construed less rigidly than an exclusion clause, the distinction has nevertheless been approved in *George Mitchell* v *Finney Lock Seeds* (1983) (see below).

The contra proferentem rule

It has already been indicated that the clause should be construed contra proferentem, that is, against the interests of the person seeking to rely on it. Accordingly, where a clause fails to deal with a specific matter, it will not be deemed to cover that matter. A few examples will illustrate the point.

In *Lee & Son (Grantham) Ltd* v *Railway Executive* [1949] 2 All ER 581, the plaintiffs leased a warehouse from the defendants. In the lease was a clause which purported to exempt liability for loss and damage which would not have arisen but for the tenancy. The goods were damaged by a spark which gave rise to a fire. It was held, on a construction contra proferentem, that the loss did not arise from the relationship of landlord and tenant, and so the clause was not applicable to exempt liability for the loss.

In *Webster* v *Higgins* [1948] 2 All ER 127, a term in a hire-purchase contract said that no warranty, condition or description is given. It was held that the clause did not exempt liability for an undertaking which had already been given.

In *Wallis, Son & Wells* v *Pratt & Haynes* [1911] AC 394, a provision that a seller gave no 'warranty, express or implied' did not exclude him from liability for breach of a condition

In *Houghton* v *Trafalgar Insurance* [1954] 1 QB 247, the insurance policy excluded the insurer from liability 'whilst the car was carrying any *load* in excess of that for which it is construed'. It was held that the clause did not exclude liability where the car was carrying an excess number of passengers.

Similarly, in *Computer and Systems Engineering plc* v *John Lelliott Ltd* (1991) The Times 21 February, a standard form contract excluded liability for 'flooding or burst pipes'. Damage was caused to the plaintiff's property by a fractured sprinkler pipe. The court interpreted the clause literally and strictly and held that the damage caused was not within the meaning of the exclusion clause. The plaintiff could claim compensation.

The continuity of this trend is illustrated by the recent New Zealand case of *Kelly* v *National Insurance Company of New Zealand* (1995) 1 NZLR 641 where the court held that the phrase 'in transit' must be given its ordinary meaning. Similarly in *Middleton* v *Wiggins* (1995) The Independent 31 August, the Court of Appeal approached the question of construction in a strict and literal sense.

Exclusion clauses: enforcement by the party in breach

The case of *Micklefield* v *SAC Technology Ltd* [1990] IRLR 218 concerned an employment contract and was, as such, excluded from the operation of the Unfair Contract Terms Act 1977 by Schedule 1 paragraph 1 of that Act.

A company director was employed under a service agreement which, inter alia, allowed him to apply for share issues. An exclusion clause in the agreement provided that this privilege would lapse if, for any reason, he ceased to be employed by the company. He was dismissed without notice, wrongfully and in breach of contract. His employers held that since the exclusion clause said ceased to be employed 'for whatever reason', they could legitimately refuse to issue the shares applied for by the plaintiff some two weeks before he was wrongfully dismissed. The plaintiff argued that he should be permitted to recover damages for loss of the option to take up shares.

The court declared that the principle that a party could not be permitted to take advantage of his own wrong was not a strict rule of law and could, in fact, be excluded. Provided the clause in question was decisive and explicit, it would be within either party's right to incorporate such a clause. The clause in question was sufficiently clear and specific, and would apply. The plaintiff was refused damages.

Negligence

The Unfair Contract Terms Act now renders clauses purporting to exclude liability for negligence largely ineffective (see below), but even where the statute does not apply, the courts have required clear words to satisfy the exclusion of liability for negligence.

Where a party can be made liable on some ground other than negligence, the clause will be construed as applying to that other ground, and not to negligence. The principle was stated by Lord Greene MR in *Alderslade* v *Hendon Laundry* [1945] KB 189 as follows:

> '... where the head of damage in respect of which limitation of liability is sought to be imposed by such a clause is one which rests on negligence and nothing else, the clause must. be construed as extending to that head of damage, because if it were not so construed it would lack subject-matter. Where, on the other hand, the head of damage may be based on some ground other than that of negligence, the general principle is that the clause must be confined to loss occurring through that other cause to the exclusion of loss arising through negligence. The reason for that is that if a contracting party wishes in such a case to limit his liability in respect of negligence, he must do so in clear terms, and in the absence of such clear terms the clause is to be construed as relating to a different kind of liability and not to liability based on negligence.'

The reasoning behind this approach was made clear in *Gillespie Brothers* v *Roy Bowles Transport* [1973] QB 400, where Buckley LJ said:

> '... it is inherently improbable that one party to the contract should intend to absolve the other party from the consequences of the latter's own negligence. The intention to do so must therefore be made perfectly clear for otherwise the court will conclude that the exempted party was only to be free from liability in respect of damage occasioned by causes other than negligence for which he is answerable.'

In *Smith* v *South Wales Switchgear* [1978] 1 All ER 18, the House of Lord held that a clause did not contain an express provision excluding liability for negligence unless it contained the word 'negligence', or some synonym for 'negligence'.

The courts have distinguished between cases where the defendant could be held liable only if he were negligent, and cases where liability could arise from some other cause. Thus in *Hollier* v *Rambler Motors* (above), the clause purported to exclude liability 'for damage caused by fire to customers' cars on the premises'. The Court of Appeal held that the clause did not apply to negligence. Fire could occur from a large variety of causes, only one of which is negligence on the part of the occupier of the premises.

This case should be compared with that of *Rutter* v *Palmer* [1922] 2 KB 87, where the clause provided that 'customers' cars are driven by our staff at customers' sole risk'. It was held that the clause excluded liability for negligence, as the garage was *only* liable where such loss was due to negligence.

8.8 The Unfair Contract Terms Act 1977

Ambit of the Act

The Act applies to contract terms and to notices which are non-contractual, and which purport to exclude or restrict liability in tort. It seeks to limit the circumstances in which terms and notices restricting or limiting liability may apply, but it does not affect the basis of liability, nor does it apply to any other 'unfair' terms. The Act, furthermore, does not affect the issues of incorporation and interpretation which must be left to the common law.

Generally, the Act can be said to cover three areas.

1. The exclusion or restriction of liability for negligence (defined in s1(1)) to apply to a contractual duty of care, a tortious duty of care and a common duty of care under the Occupiers Liability Act 1984.
2. The exclusion or restriction of liability for certain terms implied by statute into sale of goods contracts, hire purchase agreements and some other supply contracts.
3. Some contract terms which exclude or limit liability for breaches of contract, or which purport to entitle the other party to render a contractual performance substantially different from that which was reasonably expected of him.

The general effect of the Act

Where the act or omission complained of is covered by an exemption clause or limitation of liability clause, the Act may:

1. render it wholly ineffective;
2. render it effective only in so far as it may satisfy the requirement of reasonableness.

Although the Act only applies to clauses which 'exclude or restrict' liability, those words have an extended meaning. Section 13 provides:

'(1) To the extent that this Part of this Act prevents the exclusion or restriction of any liability it also prevents –
(a) making the liability or its enforcement subject to restrictive or onerous conditions;
(b) excluding or restricting any right or remedy in respect of the liability, or subjecting a person to any prejudice in consequence of his pursuing any such right or remedy;
(c) excluding or restricting rules of evidence or procedure;
and (to that extent) ss2 and 5 to 7 also prevent excluding or restricting liability by reference to terms and notices which exclude or restrict the relevant obligation or duty.
(2) But an agreement in writing to submit present or future differences to arbitration is not to be treated under this Part of this Act as excluding or restricting any liability.'

Thus the Act will apply to terms: imposing a time limit for making claims, s13(1)(a);

limiting a buyer's right to reject defective goods, s13(1)(b); stating that acceptance of goods shall be regarded as proof of their conformity with the contract, s13(1)(c).

Business liability and dealing as a consumer

Apart from s6 (implied terms in sales of goods and hire purchase agreements), the Act is concerned with terms which purport to exclude business liability. The person intended principally to benefit from the Act is the person who is dealing as a consumer. A distinction is drawn between a person who is dealing as a consumer, and a person who is not. Section 12, as amended by the Sale and Supply of Goods to Consumers Regulations 2002, provides:

> '(1) A party to a contract "deals as consumer" in relation to another party if –
> (a) he neither makes the contract in the course of a business nor holds himself out as doing so; and
> (b) the other party does make the contract in the course of a business; and
> (c) in the case of a contract governed by the law of sale of goods or hire purchase, or by s7 of this Act, the goods passing under or in pursuance of the contract are of a type ordinarily supplied for private use or consumption.
> (1A) But if the first party mentioned in subsection (1) is an individual paragraph (c) of that subsection must be ignored.
> (2) But the buyer is not in any circumstances to be regarded as dealing as consumer –
> (a) if he is an individual and the goods are second hand goods sold at public auction at which individuals have the opportunity of attending the sale in person;
> (b) if he is not an individual and the goods are sold by auction or by competitive tender.
> (3) Subject to this, it is for those claiming that a party does not deal as consumer to show that he does not.'

('Business' includes a profession and government, local government, local authority or public authority activities, s14.)

The Court of Appeal gave consideration to the question of 'dealing as a consumer' in *R & B Customs Brokers Co Ltd* v *United Dominions Trust Ltd* [1988] 1 All ER 847. The plaintiff company had purchased a car from the defendant company for the use of one of its directors. It was held that where a transaction was only incidental to a business activity, a degree of regularity was required before a transaction could be said to be an integral part of the business carried on and so entered into in the course of that business. Since here the car was only the second or third vehicle acquired by the plaintiffs, there was not a sufficient degree of regularity capable of establishing that the contract was anything more than part of a consumer transaction.

Negligence liability

This is set out in s2 of the Act:

> '(1) A person cannot by reference to any contract term or to a notice given to persons

generally or to particular persons exclude or restrict his liability for death or personal injury resulting from negligence.

(2) In the case of other loss or damage, a person cannot so exclude or restrict his liability for negligence except in so far as the term or notice satisfies the requirement of reasonableness.

(3) Where a contract term or notice purports to exclude or restrict liability for negligence a person's agreement to or awareness of it is not of itself to be taken as indicating his voluntary acceptance of any risk.'

This is a section which only applies to business liability which, so far as death or personal injury resulting from negligence is concerned, can no longer be excluded or restricted. Liability for other types of negligence can be excluded or restricted, but only in so far as the contract term or notice satisfies the requirement of reasonableness within s11(1) (below).

Subsection (3) seems to be an attempt to distinguish between the exclusion or restriction of liability and the defence of volenti non fit injuria.

Note that s2(1) does not preclude the wrongdoer from making arrangements with a third party as to sharing or bearing the burden of compensating the victim. See *Thompson* v *T Lohan (Plant Hire) Ltd* [1987] 2 All ER 631.

If, however, a clause purports merely to transfer liability to a third party, but has the effect of excluding all liability on the part of the wrongdoer, such clause *will* fall within the Act. See *Phillips Products* v *Hyland* [1987] 2 All ER 620.

Liability arising in contract

Section 3 provides:

'(1) This section applies as between contracting parties where one of them deals as consumer or on the other's written standard terms of business.

(2) As against that party, the other cannot by reference to any contract term –

(a) when himself in breach of contract, exclude or restrict any liability of his in respect of the breach; or

(b) claim to be entitled –

(i) to render a contractual performance substantially different from that which was reasonably expected of him, or

(ii) in respect of the whole or any part of his contractual obligation, to render no performance at all,

except in so far as (in any of the cases mentioned above in this subsection) the contract term satisfies the requirement of reasonableness.'

It would seem that the expression 'deals on the other's written standard terms of business' applies even where these standard terms are the terms of a third party – so that the National Conditions of Sale drawn up by the Law Society for the benefit of vendors and purchasers of land would be within the scope of s3 of the Act.

Section 3(2)(b)(i) would appear to apply to contracts with tour operators, which contain provisions entitling the tour operators to arrange accommodation or transport other than that specified. A contract for concert tickets providing that the management reserves the right to cancel the concert at any time might be subject to s3(2)(b)(ii).

See, too Chapter 11, section 11.5 (*Paragon Finance plc* v *Nash*).

Unreasonable indemnity clauses

An indemnity clause is one where a party agrees to reimburse losses sustained by another whether on the happening of a specified event or not. Section 4 of the Act applies to such a clause. The liability against which an indemnity is sought must be a business liability, and the person who is benefited by the clause is the consumer. He is not bound by the clause unless it satisfies the requirement of reasonableness. An example of the situation in which such a clause may be used is to indemnify a car hire company against third party claims arising out of the hirer's use of the car.

Section 4 provides:

'(1) A person dealing as consumer cannot by reference to any contract term be made to indemnify another person (whether a party to the contract or not) in respect of liability that may be incurred by the other for negligence or breach of contract, except in so far as the contract term satisfies the requirement of reasonableness.
(2) This section applies whether the liability in question –
(a) is directly that of the person to be indemnified or is incurred by him vicariously;
(b) is to the person dealing as consumer or to someone else.'

Guarantee of consumer goods

Section 5 prevents the implementation of terms or notices in manufacturer's guarantees which exclude or restrict liability for the negligence of the manufacturer or distributor for loss or damage from defects in the goods:

'(1) In the case of goods of a type ordinarily supplied for private use or consumption, where loss or damage
(a) arises from the goods proving defective while in consumer use; and
(b) results from the negligence of a person concerned in the manufacture or distribution of the goods,
liability for the loss or damage cannot be excluded or restricted by reference to any contract term or notice contained in or operating by reference to a guarantee of the goods.
(2) For these purposes –
(a) goods are to be regarded as "in consumer use" when a person is using them, or has them in his possession for use, otherwise than exclusively for the purposes of a business; and
(b) anything in writing is a guarantee if it contains or purports to contain some promise or assurance (however worded or presented) that defects will be made good by complete or partial replacement, or by repair, monetary compensation or otherwise.
(3) This section does not apply as between the parties to a contract under or in pursuance of which possession or ownership of the goods passed.'

Sales and hire-purchase

Section 6 deals with both business and non-business liability, and makes some clauses totally ineffective and others subject to the test of reasonableness. It provides:

'(1) Liability for breach of the obligations arising from –
(a) s12 of the Sale of Goods Act 1979 (seller's implied undertakings as to title, etc);
(b) s8 of the Supply of Goods (Implied Terms) Act 1973 (the corresponding thing in relation to hire-purchase);
cannot be excluded or restricted by reference to any contract term.
(2) As against a person dealing as consumer, liability for breach of the obligations arising from –
(a) ss13, 14 or 15 of the 1979 Act (seller's implied undertakings as to conformity of goods with description or sample, or as to their quality or fitness for a particular purpose);
(b) ss9, 10 or 11 of the 1973 Act (the corresponding things in relation to hire-purchase),
cannot be excluded or restricted by reference to any contract term.
(3) As against a person dealing otherwise than as consumer, the liability specified in subsection (2) above can be excluded or restricted by reference to a contract term, but only in so far as the term satisfies the requirement of reasonableness.
(4) The liabilities referred to in this section are not only the business liabilities defined by s1(3), but include those arising under any contract of sale of goods or hire-purchase agreement.'

Notice that the requirement of reasonableness referred to is that under s11(2) of the Act, which refers the reader to the guidelines set out in Schedule 2. See below.

Miscellaneous contracts under which goods pass

Section 7 applies to contracts (other than sale or hire-purchase) for the supply of goods now governed by the Supply of Goods and Services Act 1982:

'(1) Where the possession or ownership of goods passes under or in pursuance of a contract not governed by the law of sale of goods or hire-purchase, subsections (2) to (4) below apply as regards the effect (if any) to be given to contract terms excluding or restricting liability for breach of obligation arising by implication of law from the nature of the contract.
(2) As against a person dealing as consumer, liability in respect of the goods' correspondence with description or sample, or their quality or fitness for any particular purpose, cannot be excluded or restricted by reference to any such term.
(3) As against a person dealing otherwise than as consumer, that liability can be excluded or restricted by reference to such a term, but only in so far as the term satisfied the requirement of reasonableness.
(3A) Liability for breach of the obligations arising under s2 of the Supply of Goods and Services Act 1982 (implied terms about title etc in certain contracts for the transfer of the property in goods) cannot be excluded or restricted by reference to any such term.
(4) Liability in respect of –
(a) the right to transfer ownership of the goods, or give possession; or
(b) the assurance of quiet possession to a person taking goods in pursuance of the contract,

cannot (in a case to which subsection (3A) above does not apply) be excluded or restricted by reference to any such term except in so far as the term satisfies the requirement of reasonableness.

(5) This section does not apply in the case of goods passing on a redemption of trading stamps within the Trading Stamps Act 1964 or the Trading Stamps Act (Northern Ireland) 1965.'

The requirement of reasonableness

Section 11 has already been referred to. It provides:

'(1) In relation to a contract term, the requirement of reasonableness for the purposes of this Part of this Act, s3 of the Misrepresentation Act 1967 and s3 of the Misrepresentation Act (Northern Ireland) 1967 is that the term shall have been a fair and reasonable one to be included having regard to the circumstances which were, or ought reasonably to have been, known to or in the contemplation of the parties when the contract was made.

(2) In determining for the purposes of ss6 or 7 above whether a contract term satisfies the requirement of reasonableness, regard shall be had in particular to the matters specified in Schedule 2 to this Act; but this subsection does not prevent the court or arbitrator from holding, in accordance with any rule of law, that a term which purports to exclude or restrict any relevant liability is not a term of the contract.

(3) In relation to a notice (not being a notice having contractual effect), the requirement of reasonableness under this Act is that it should be fair and reasonable to allow reliance on it, having regard to all the circumstances obtaining when the liability arose or (but for the notice) would have arisen.

(4) Where by reference to a contract term or notice a person seeks to restrict liability to a specified sum of money, and the question arises (under this or any other Act) whether the term or notice satisfies the requirement of reasonableness, regard shall be had in particular (but without prejudice to subsection (2) above in the case of contract terms) to:

(a) the resources which he could expect to be available to him for the purpose of meeting the liability should it arise; and

(b) how far it was open to him to cover himself by insurance.

(5) It is for those claiming that a contract term or notice satisfies the requirement of reasonableness to show that it does.'

These guidelines specified in s11(2) appear in Schedule 2:

' "Guidelines" for application of reasonableness test

The matters to which regard is to be had in particular for the purposes of ss6(3), 7(3) and (4), 20 and 21 are any of the following which appear to be relevant –

(a) the strength of the bargaining positions of the parties relative to each other, taking into account (among other things) alternative means by which the customer's requirements could have been met;

(b) whether the customer received an inducement to agree to the term, or in accepting it had an opportunity of entering into a similar contract with other persons, but without having to accept a similar term;

(c) whether the customer knew or ought reasonably to have known of the existence and extent of the term (having regard, among other things, to any custom of the trade and any previous course of dealing between the parties);

(d) where the term excludes or restricts any relevant liability if some condition is not complied with, whether it was reasonable at the time of the contract to expect that compliance with that condition would be practicable;

(e) whether the goods were manufactured, processed or adapted to the special order of the customer.'

The requirement of reasonableness was considered by the House of Lords in *George Mitchell* v *Finney Lock Seeds* [1983] 2 All ER 737. The purchasers of cabbage seeds were supplied with commercially useless seed of the wrong description so that their crops were lost. The contract contained an exclusion clause which purported to limit the liability of the seller to the cost of the seeds, some £200. The purchasers' claim was for damages of £61,513 for breach of contract.

The House of Lords held: although a limitation clause was to be construed contra proferentem, it was not subject to the very strict principles of construction applicable to clauses of complete exclusion of liability; the limitations clause was enforceable at common law. Lord Bridge observed that the *Photo Production* case (above) 'gave the final quietus to the doctrine that a "fundamental breach" of contract deprived the party in breach of the benefit of clauses in the contract excluding or limiting his liability'. However, the test of reasonableness (imposed by an enactment now superseded by s6(3) UCTA) was not satisfied. The reasons for this were: that it appeared that the normal practice of the seller was not to rely on the limitation clause, but to negotiate settlements of reasonable claims; the breach was due to the seller's negligence; and the seller could have insured against the loss without materially raising his charges.

A contrasting case is *R W Green* v *Cade Bros Farm* [1978] 1 Lloyd's Rep 602. Here the contract was for the sale of seed potatoes by potato merchants. The contract limited the liability of the sellers to returning the price. The potatoes proved to be infected with a virus. As the potatoes were uncertified, and hence cheaper, Griffiths J upheld the limitation clause as reasonable. However, he struck down as unreasonable a clause requiring the buyers to give notice of a claim within three days of delivery.

In *Stag Line Ltd* v *Tyne Shiprepair Group Ltd* [1984] 2 Lloyd's Rep 211, it was held, in respect of a shiprepairing contract, that a term excluding liability for economic loss was reasonable, but a term that the shipowner should have no remedy unless he returned the vessel to the shiprepairer's yard for repair, was unreasonable.

The House of Lords considered the question of the exclusion of liability for negligence and whether such exclusion meets the requirement of reasonableness in hearing appeals in the two cases of *Smith* v *Eric S Bush* and *Harris* v *Wyre Forest District Council* [1989] 2 All ER 514. (The appeals were heard together.)

In the first case, the plaintiff applied to a building society for a mortgage and signed an application form which stated that a copy of the survey report and valuation would be given to the plaintiff. The form contained a disclaimer to the effect that neither the society nor its surveyor warranted that the report and valuation would be accurate, and that the report and valuation would be supplied without any acceptance of responsibility. The plaintiff subsequently received a copy of the report which contained a disclaimer in terms similar to those on the application form. The report stated that no essential repairs were required. On the strength of that report, and without obtaining an independent survey, the plaintiff purchased the house. In their inspection of the house, the surveyor had observed that certain chimney breasts had been removed, but had not checked to see whether the chimneys above were adequately supported. Eighteen months after the plaintiff purchased the house, bricks from the chimney collapsed and fell through the roof, causing considerable damage.

In the second case, the plaintiffs applied to a local authority for a mortgage to enable them to purchase a house. The local authority instructed their valuation surveyor to carry out a valuation. The plaintiffs signed an application form which stated that the valuation was confidential and was intended solely for the information of the local authority, and that no responsibility was accepted for the value or condition of the property by reason of the inspection and report. The surveyor valued the house at the asking price of £9,450, and the local authority offered to advance the plaintiffs 90% of that sum subject to certain minor repairs being done to the house. The plaintiffs, assuming that the house was worth at least the amount of the valuation and that the surveyor had found no serious defects, purchased the property for £9,000 without obtaining an independent survey. Three years later, they discovered that the house was subject to settlement, was virtually unsaleable and could only be repaired, if at all, at a cost of more than the purchase price.

In affirming the decision of the Court of Appeal in *Smith,* and reversing the Court of Appeal's decision in *Harris,* the House of Lords held that a valuer who valued a house for a building society or a local authority owed a duty of care to the purchaser of the house. However, the valuer could disclaim liability to exercise reasonable skill and care by an express exclusion clause, but such a disclaimer had to satisfy the requirement of reasonableness in s2(2) of the Act. In both these cases, it would not be fair and reasonable to impose on the purchasers the risk of loss arising from the incompetence or carelessness on the part of the valuers. The disclaimers were, therefore, not effective to exclude liability for the negligence of the valuers.

In his speech, Lord Griffiths said that it was impossible to draw up an exhaustive list of factors to be taken into account in deciding whether an exclusion clause met the requirement of reasonableness, but these certain matters should always be considered.

1. Were the parties of equal bargaining power?
2. In the case of advice, would it have been reasonably practicable to obtain the advice from an alternative source, taking into account considerations of costs and time?
3. How difficult is the task of being undertaken for which liability is being excluded?
4. What are the practical consequences of the decision on the question of

reasonableness? This involves the sums of money at stake and the ability of the parties to bear the loss, which raises the question of insurance.

The 'practical consequences' referred to in point 4 (above) were among a number of factors taken into account in considering *St Albans City and District Council* v *International Computers Ltd* [1996] 4 All ER 481 CA.

A computer firm was sued by the local authority that had hired them to assess population figures on which to base community charges. The standard contract used by the computer firm contained an exclusion/limitation clause restricting liability to £100,000. The database supplied to the plaintiffs was seriously inaccurate and resulted ultimately in the local authority sustaining a loss of £1.3m. As well as considering the orthodox criteria in assessing reasonableness as defined in s11(4) (eg, insurance, equality of bargaining power), the court also took into account practical considerations, particularly that if the loss was not paid for by the defendants or their insurers, the loss would be ultimately fall on the ordinary people of St Albans.

The case of *Davies* v *Parry* [1988] BTLC 236 concerned the question of whether a disclaimer, seeking to absolve a surveyor from liability for negligence in the preparation of a valuation report, was reasonable. It was held that whether or not such a clause was reasonable depended on the facts of each case and, in particular, whether it was reasonable to assume that such a report would be relied on by non-experts, that is, potential buyers.

The test of reasonableness and the ambit of s11(1) was further considered in *Flamar Interocean Ltd* v *Denmac Ltd (The Flamar Pride and Flamar Progress)* [1990] 1 Lloyd's Rep 434.

The owners of the two vessels claimed damages for breach of contract against the defendants, the technical managers of the vessels. The contract(s) in question was a ship's management contract for each vessel, pertaining to pre-delivery inspection of the vessels, maintenance inspections, insurance and so on. The question arose as to whether the technical managers (the defendants) could rely on an exclusion clause in the contract.

It was held that, under s2(2) UCTA 1977, a person could not exclude or restrict his liability for negligence, save insofar as the clause might satisfy the test of reasonableness. It was incontestable that there had been negligence, in (inter alia): (1) failure to require adequate and thorough pre-delivery tests to be carried out; (2) failure to engage someone with experience of refrigerated vessels; and (3) failure to provide liability insurance cover.

Potter J remarked:

> 'The clauses in question did not satisfy the test of reasonableness as laid out in s11(1) of the UCTA, providing that the term shall be fair and reasonable having regard to the circumstances "which were, or ought to have been, known to, or in the contemplation of the parties, at the time when the contract was made". The exclusion clause could not be relied on by the defendants.'

The Act prevents evasion of its provisions by means of a secondary contract

Section 10 provides:

> 'A person is not bound by any contract term prejudicing or taking away rights of his which arise under or in connection with, the performance of another contract, so far as those rights extend to the enforcement of another's liability which this part of the Act prevents that other from excluding or restricting.'

A possible application of this section is to an attempt to exclude liability under an agreement for the sale of an article by means of a secondary maintenance agreement.

The case of *Tudor Grange Holdings Ltd* v *Citibank NA and Another* [1991] 4 All ER 1 helps to cast further light on s10 of the UCTA 1977. The section was aimed at controlling future exemptions and exclusions rather than retrospectively limiting or adjusting liability.

At a hearing in chambers the defendant bank and others applied to have an action by the plaintiff company struck out. Judgment was given in open court. By a deed of release, dated March 1989, the plaintiffs purported to release Citibank and its associates from 'all claims, demands and causes of action prior to the date hereof'. The question arose as to whether this release was, under s10 UCTA 1977, reasonable. The argument lay that it was not, and since it failed to satisfy the test of reasonableness it could not be binding.

The court repudiated this argument and held that s10 was held not to be intended to cover the present situation; it did not cover settlements and compromises on events that had already occurred. In the view of the court the Act was aimed soley at exemption clauses, clauses modifying future liability – it was not concerned with retrospective claims or settlements. Since s10 did not apply to the deed of release which bound the plaintiffs, it (the deed) formed a complete defence to the claims against the banks.

Exceptions

The Act does not apply to the following.

1. The liability of people not acting within the course of business (except s6).
2. Insurance contracts.
3. Certain parts of contracts relating to land.
4. Apart from s2(1), which does apply, contracts of marine salvage, such as towage, charterparties of ships or hovercraft, contracts for the carriage of goods by ship or hovercraft.
5. The s2(1) and (2) do not apply to contracts of employment except in favour of the employee.
6. Contracts for the international supply of goods.

Save as set out above, a contract properly governed by English law may not include provisions excluding the Act. A person cannot exclude liability by choosing a foreign law wholly or mainly to avoid the Act.

Note that despite the exceptions listed above, a contract may be deemed not to come into any of the given categories because, despite appearances, the court looks at the ultimate purpose of the contract. See, for example, the Scottish case of *Melrose* v *Davidson* 1993 SLT 611, where the court decided that the exclusion clause was not part of a contract concerning land (one of the excepted categories) but was concerned with the provision of a loan to buy land. The exclusion clause was therefore ineffective under the Unfair Contract Terms Act 1977.

8.9 The Unfair Terms in Consumer Contracts Regulations 1994 and 1999

The 1994 Regulations introduced a new concept of unfairness, over and above the provisions of the Unfair Contract Terms Act 1977. The 1994 Regulations were repealed and replaced by the Unfair Terms in Consumer Contracts Regulations 1999 which came into force on 1 October 1999.

No fundamental changes were made by the 1999 Regulations. In most respects, it mirrors the 1994 provisions. The test as to 'unfairness' remains the same, namely:

'A contractual term which has not been individually negotiated shall be regarded as unfair, if, contrary to the requirement of good faith, it causes a significant imbalance in the parties' rights and obligations under the contract, to the detriment of the consumer.'

An indicative and non-exhaustive list of the terms which may be regarded as unfair is to be found in Schedule 2 to the 1999 Regulations.

Briefly the following observations may be made of the 1999 Regulations.

1. All the factors and circumstances surrounding the contract will be taken into consideration in deciding the issue of unfairness.
2. The scope of the Regulations has been extended to cover contracts relating to employment, succession rights, rights under family law and company law (incorporation and organisation).
3. A revised definition of 'consumer' and 'seller or supplier' is given by the Regulations. 'Consumer' means a natural person acting for purposes outside his trade, business or profession. 'Seller or supplier' means someone acting for the purposes of his trade, business or profession, whether publicly or privately owned.
4. The powers possessed by the Director-General of Fair Trading have now been extended. The following regulatory bodies may now exercise these powers: the Information Commissioner; the Director-General of Water, Gas and Electricity; and the Consumers Association (a non-governmental organisation) has also been given a similar power in respect of seeking injunctions.

Director General of Fair Trading v *First National Bank plc* [2002] 1 All ER 97 was the first case to reach the House of Lords on the 1994 Regulations. The Director General sought an injunction, alleging that a contractual term included in the bank's standard conditions of business on which it provided credit to consumers was unfair. The effect of an agreement incorporating the relevant term was that where the bank obtained judgment against a borrower, interest was payable by the borrower at the contractual rate on the outstanding principal plus accrued interest unpaid at the date of judgment until the judgment was discharged by payment. Had this term not been included, the obligation to pay interest would have merged in the judgment. The agreement did not specifically draw this term to the borrower's attention. Evans-Lombe J ([2000] 1 All ER 240) refused the injunction, but the Director General's appeal ([2000] 2 All ER 759) was allowed since, in their Lordships' view, the term did not satisfy the Regulations' requirements as to fairness.

The House of Lords allowed the bank's appeal. As Lord Bingham explained, reg 4(1) of the 1994 Regulations provided the test of an unfair term as any term which, contrary to the requirement of good faith, caused a significant imbalance in the parties' rights and obligations under the contract to the detriment of the consumer. On balance the term in question could not properly be said to cause a significant imbalance in the parties' rights and obligations under the contract to the detriment of the consumer in a manner or to an extent which was contrary to the requirement of good faith.

9

Capacity

9.1 Introduction

Prima facie the law presumes that everyone has capacity to contract. A few classes of person are in a special position and each of these is here considered.

9.2 Minors

General

Who is a minor?

Anybody who is under 18 years is a minor: s1 Family Law Reform Act 1969. A person becomes legally 18 years at the commencement of the day which is his birthday: s9 Family Law Reform Act 1969.

The issues involved

These are that the minor must have some contractual capacity so that he can survive; and unfairness to the other party to a transaction with him ought to be avoided, where possible; but, exploitation of a person who may lack insight into the nature of legal transactions by reason of his age, ought to be avoided. The parents of a minor are not liable for his contracts unless they acted as his agent in law.

There are two kinds of contract

1. Contracts for necessaries (which are valid).
2. Voidable contracts.
   At common law these are of two types:

   a) those binding on the minor, unless he repudiated them during minority or within a reasonable time thereafter; and
   b) those which were not binding upon him, unless and until he ratified them after attaining his majority.

9.3 Necessaries

Necessary goods

What are necessary goods?

There are goods 'suitable to the condition of life of the ... (minor) and to his actual requirements at the time of the sale and delivery': s3(3) Sale of Goods Act 1979. It must be shown, first, that the class into which the goods fall is capable of being described as necessary, and, secondly, that the goods supplied, even if within such a class, were actually necessary at the time of the contract. See *Chapple* v *Cooper* (1844) 13 M & W 252.

Thus, given the style of dressing at the time, a waistcoat would fall into a class of objects capable of being called 'necessary', but the eleven fancy waistcoats supplied to an undergraduate in *Nash* v *Inman* [1908] 2 KB 1 were not deemed to be necessary to him. Clothes, food, drink, medicine, etc will fall within the definition of necessaries. The onus of showing that the goods are necessaries lies on the supplier. See *Nash* v *Inman* (above).

Executory contracts for necessary goods

It is not entirely certain whether a minor is bound by an executory contract for necessary goods. Section 3(2) Sale of Goods Act provides that a minor must pay a reasonable price for 'necessaries sold and delivered' and, as we have seen, 'necessaries' are defined in s3(3) in relation to 'the time of the sale and delivery'. What if the goods are sold but not yet delivered? Can the minor repudiate the contract before delivery?

The answer depends on whether the minor is liable in re: that is, because he has received the item in question, or by virtue of of consensus: that is, because he made the contract in the first place. The wording of s3 suggests that the goods must be 'necessary' both when the infant buys them and when they are delivered (if these two happenings are at different times). This implies that the basis of the minor's liability is that he has been supplied with the goods. Moreover, the requirement of s3 is for the minor to pay 'a reasonable price' which may not be the contract price. This does not support a contractual liability. In *Nash* v *Inman*, Fletcher Moulton LJ said that the minor was liable because he had been supplied, and not because he had contracted. Buckley LJ, however, said that the minor had a limited capacity to contract, and a contract for necessaries was one that the minor could make.

The position remains in doubt, but in *Roberts* v *Gray* [1913] 1 KB 520, it was held that an infant is bound by an executory contract for necessary services and education. Treitel (6th edn p413) considers that no distinction should be drawn between goods and services on this point.

Necessary services

These would include contracts by an infant for legal and medical assistance. In *Chapple* v *Cooper* (above), a contract by a widow for her husband's funeral was a contract for a necessary. A trading contract, is not, however, a necessary.

Contracts for necessaries must be for the benefit of the minor taken as a whole

If it contains terms which are harsh and onerous, the contract will not be enforceable against the infant. See *Fawcett* v *Smethurst* (1914) 84 LJ KB 473. Similarly, in *Flower* v *London and North Western Railway* [1894] 2 QB 65, a contract of carriage, which contained a clause exempting the defendants from liability for injury to the minor even if caused by negligence. It was void as against the minor.

Loans for necessaries

At common law it has been held that a minor cannot be made liable on a loan to him to purchase necessaries. See *Darby* v *Boucher* (1694) 1 Salk 279. But the common law position is not beyond doubt. See Treitel (1957) 73 LQR 194. By statute the former position was that contracts of loan were declared to be 'absolutely void'. This provision was contained in the Infants Relief Act 1874, but this Act has now been repealed by the Minors' Contracts Act 1987.

If the loan is actually spent on necessaries, it can be recovered (or such part of it as may have been so spent) in equity. See *Marlow* v *Pitfield* (1719) 1 P Wms 558.

A person who purchases necessaries at the request of a minor may be able to recover against the minor under an agency.

Contracts for service, apprenticeship and education

Contracts of service are valid if the service is, taken as a whole, beneficial to the minor, for example, an apprenticeship, or articles of clerkship, which may on occasions appear exploitive, but which have beneficial consequences long term. See *Clements* v *L & NW Railway* [1894] 2 QB 482. However, an apprenticeship was said to be oppressive, and not beneficial, in *De Francesco* v *Barnum* (1890) 45 Ch D 430, where the dancing master stipulated in the contract that his pupil should not accept remunerative engagements without his consent during the apprenticeship, nor marry until it was over.

On the other hand, there was an interesting clash of values in *Chaplin* v *Leslie Frewin (Publishers) Ltd* [1966] Ch 71. A minor made a contract to sell the story of his disreputable life; Lord Denning MR concluded that:

'... it is not for his good that he should exploit his discreditable conduct for money, no matter how much he is paid',

but Dankwerts and Winn LJJ considered the contract beneficial in so far as Chaplin was well paid at a time when he would otherwise have had to rely on National Assistance. The scandal, the majority felt, would not be harmful, for there was 'clear proof that he had no taste nor decency' and 'no right to claim to any reputation'.

If he is grossly underpaid for his services, the contract would, unless there were off-setting, long-term benefits, be held invalid.

Other beneficial contracts

Some other beneficial contracts, but not all contracts, for example, trading contracts (see *Cowern* v *Nield* [1912] 2 KB 419), will be binding on a minor. In *Doyle* v *White City Stadium* [1935] 1 KB 110, a minor who was a professional boxer contracted with the British Boxing Board of Control and agreed to adhere to the rules of the Board.

The contract was held to be binding on him because he could not have earned his living otherwise.

See also *Denmark Productions* v *Boscobel Productions* [1969] 1 QB 699.

9.4 Voidable contracts

Valid until repudiated

Voidable contracts generally are contracts which subsist unless and until avoided as contrasted with void contracts, which are a complete nullity ab initio. In the case of minors' voidable contracts, only one party, the minor, may avoid them. The rules as to liability are that once the minor has avoided the contract, he avoids liabilities which accrue after that date, but remains bound to meet obligations which have already arisen. See *Blake* v *Concannon* (1870) Ir R 4 CL 323. He cannot receive back money that was paid prior to the date of his avoiding the contract. See *Steinberg* v *Scala (Leeds) Ltd* [1923] 2 Ch 452. A minor applied for and was allotted shares in a company. She paid the amounts due on allotment and on the first call. She then attempted to repudiate the whole contract.

It was held that, although she could repudiate while under age, she could not recover moneys paid. She had received the very consideration she bargained for even though she had not been paid any dividend.

What kinds of contract are voidable?

1. Real property contracts.
2. Contracts involving shares.
3. Partnership agreements.
4. Marriage settlements.

Why?

In none of the above categories could the contracts be considered as for 'necessaries', except a contract for a lease of tenancy which would, in that event, be valid. Thus, if they were not voidable, they would have to be void. If so, the minor would have no obligation to make any payments, and could retain the benefit he had obtained. This may prove unjust to the other party in any transaction, but particularly so in these types of contract for they envisage reciprocal liability extending over a period of time.

There are, of course, other types of contract which involve such long-term reciprocal liability, notably contracts of hire-purchase, and these are void, except in so far as they are for necessaries. The reason is that the categories of voidable contracts became frozen in the late nineteenth century, and have not been added to. Perhaps they should be – this whole area of law is ripe for reform by legislation.

How are minors' voidable contracts avoided?

This is usually accomplished by notice, which the minor may revoke before he attains his majority. Notice that he wishes to avoid a voidable contract must be given before the minor becomes 18 years old, or within a reasonable time thereafter. What is reasonable time varies with the circumstances, but in a marriage settlement case Lord Watson said that a 'period of four years and eight months ... cannot possibly be regarded as a reasonable time'. See *Edwards* v *Carter* [1893] AC 360.

Contracts valid when ratified

At common law, all contracts which are not enforceable against the minor during his minority may be ratified by him when he attains his majority. Upon ratification, they become enforceable. The common law position has been restored by s1(a) Minors' Contracts Act 1987, which repeals the former provisions of the 1874 Act prohibiting ratification.

9.5 The Minors' Contracts Act 1987

As previously noted, the Infants Relief Act 1874 (which invalidated certain contracts and prohibited actions to enforce contracts ratified after majority) no longer applies – s1(a) of the 1987 Act. The new Act provides protection to creditors of minors in respect of guarantees. Section 2 provides that:

'Where –
(a) a guarantee is given in respect of an obligation of a party to a contract made after the commencement of this Act, and
(b) the obligation is unenforceable against him (or he repudiates the contract) because he was a minor when the contract was made,
the guarantee shall not for that reason alone be unenforceable against the guarantor.'

9.6 Liability of a party contracting with a minor

So far in this discussion it is the minor's liability which has been considered. Generally, the rule is that lack of capacity is a personal advantage, so that the person contracting with the minor cannot rely upon it to invalidate the contract. To permit that to happen would transform the advantage to the minor into a disadvantage. Accordingly, a minor can recover damages from a person who refuses to peform his part of the contract. He would not, however, be able to obtain an order for specific performance: not, at least, unless he had himself performed the contract, because there would not be mutuality. See *Flight* v *Bolland* (1824) 4 Russ 298.

9.7 Liability of a minor in tort

A minor cannot be sued for an act which was within the contemplation of a void contract. In *Fawcett* v *Smethurst* (1914) 84 LJ KB 473, a minor hired a car to fetch a bag from the station. On the way he met a friend. He drove on further than the station. During the extra journey, the car accidently caught fire and was damaged.

He was not held to be liable in tort as the extra journey did not take his actions out of the scope of the contract.

A similar finding was made in *Jennings* v *Rundall* (1799) 8 Term R 335, where a minor hired a horse and injured it by riding it too hard. On the other hand, in *Burnard* v *Haggis* (1863) 14 CB (NS) 45, a minor who hired a mare 'merely for a ride' and was warned that she was unfit for jumping was held liable for her death when jumped by his friend.

In *Ballett* v *Mingay* [1943] KB 281, a minor was liable when he improperly parted with a microphone that he had hired.

The rule that a minor is not liable in tort applies, not only where he commits a tort in breaking the invalid contract, but also where he commits a tort in procuring it.

In *R Leslie Ltd* v *Sheill* [1914] 3 KB 607, it was held that a minor could not be sued in deceit for inducing an adult to lend him money by fraudulently misrepresenting his age.

9.8 Restitution

Equity had the power to order the restoration of gains obtained by a minor under a contract unenforceable against him. This equitable power is now enshrined in statute. Section 3 Minors' Contracts Act 1987 provides that:

'(1) Where –
(a) a person ("the plaintiff") has after the commencement of this Act entered into a contract with another ("the defendant"), and
(b) the contract is unenforceable against the defendant (or he repudiates it) because he was a minor when the contract was made,
the court may, if it is just and equitable to do so, require the defendant to transfer to the plaintiff any property acquired by the defendant under the contract, or any property representing it.
(2) Nothing in this section shall be taken to prejudice any other remedy available to the plaintiff.'

9.9 Mentally disordered persons

There are two categories.

1. If a person is certified by two medical practitioners as being incapable of dealing with his property, then the court will have control over his property, and will delegate the day-to-day management of it, often to a relative, who will then be accountable to the court: Part VII Mental Health Act 1983. The person certified cannot then dispose of any of his property.
2. If there has been no certification, the contract may be set aside:

   a) if the other party knew of the disorder;
   b) if the disordered person did not understand the transaction by reason of his disorder.

The contract may be ratified by the disordered person once the disorder has ceased temporarily or permanently.

A person who supplies necessaries (see section 9.2) may recover a reasonable price, therefore, even if he knew of the disorder: s3 Sale of Goods Act 1979.

9.10 Persons who are drunk

The contract may be set aside if: one party was very drunk and this prevented his understanding the transaction, and the other party knew of this.

Note *Gore* v *Gibson* (1843) 13 M & W 623. The drunken person is liable to pay a reasonable price for necessaries, and may in any event ratify the contract when he is sober.

9.11 Partnerships

Section 1 of the Partnership Act 1890 stipulates that partnership is the relation which subsists between persons (which may include a body corporate) carrying on a business in common with a view of profit. However, the relation between members of any company or association which is registered as a company under the Companies Acts or formed or incorporated by any other Act of Parliament or letters patent or Royal Charter is not a partnership within the meaning of that Act. All property and rights and interests in property originally brought into the partnership or acquired, whether by purchase or otherwise, on account of the firm (the collective description of those who have entered into partnership with one another), or for the purposes and in the course of the partnership business, must be held and applied by the partners exclusively for the purposes of the partnership and in accordance with the partnership agreement: s20(1) of the 1890 Act.

Every partner is an agent of the firm and his other partners for the purpose of the business of the partnership; and the acts of every partner who does any act for carrying on in the usual way business of the kind carried on by the firm of which he is a member bind the firm and his partners, unless the partner so acting has in fact no authority to act for the firm in the particular matter, and the person with whom he is dealing either knows that he has no authority, or does not know or believe him to be a partner: s5 of the 1890 Act. Subject to any general rule of law relating to the execution of deeds or negotiable instruments, an act or instrument relating to the business of the firm done or executed in the firm-name, or in any other manner showing an intention to bind the firm, by any person thereto authorised, whether a partner or not, is binding on the firm and all the partners: s6. Every partner in a firm is liable jointly with the other partners for all debts and obligations of the firm incurred while he is a partner: s9.

Limited partnerships

Although there are exceptions (eg, in the case of solicitors and accountants), a limited partnership must not consist of more than twenty persons. There must be one or more persons called general partners, who are liable for all debts and obligations of the firm, and one or more persons called limited partners, who at the time of entering into the partnership have contributed a sum or sums as capital or property valued at a stated amount, and who are not liable for the debts or obligations of the firm beyond the amount so contributed. A limited partner must not during the continuance of the partnership, either directly or indirectly, draw out or receive back any part of his contribution, but if he does so he is liable for the debts and obligations of the firm up to the amount so drawn out or received back. A body corporate may be a limited partner: s4 of the Limited Partnerships Act 1907.

A limited partner must not take part in the management of the partnership business, and has no power to bind the firm. However, if he does take part in the management of the partnership business he is liable for all debts and obligations of the firm incurred while he does so as though he were a general partner: s6(1) of the 1907 Act. Subject to the provisions of the 1907 Act, the Partnership Act 1890 and the rules of equity and of common law applicable to partnerships, except so far as they are inconsistent with the express provisions of the 1890 Act, apply to limited partnerships: s7 of the 1907 Act.

Limited liability partnerships

A new form of legal entity introduced by the Limited Liability Partnerships Act 2000, a limited liability partnership is a body corporate with legal personality separate from that of its members. It has unlimited capacity and, except in so far as the 2000 Act otherwise provides, the law relating to partnerships does not apply to it: s1 of the 2000 Act. The first essential for a limited liability partnership to be incorporated is two or more persons associated for carrying on a lawful business with a view to profit who must have subscribed their names to an incorporation document: s2(1)(a).

Except as far as otherwise provided by the 2000 Act or any other enactment, the mutual rights and duties of the members of a limited liability partnership and the mutual rights and duties of a limited liability partnership and its members, are governed by agreement between the members, or between the limited liability partnership and its members, or, in the absence of agreement as to any matter, by any provision made in relation to that matter by regulations under s15(c) of the 2000 Act. An agreement made before the incorporation of a limited liability partnership between the persons who subscribe their names to the incorporation document may impose obligations on the limited liability partnership (to take effect at any time after its incorporation): s5.

Every member of a limited liability partnership is the agent of the limited liability partnership. However, a limited liability partnership is not bound by anything done by a member in dealing with a person if the member in fact has no authority to act for the limited liability partnership by doing that thing, and the person knows that he has no authority or does not know or believe him to be a member of the limited liability partnership. Where a member of a limited liability partnership is liable to any person (other than another member of the limited liability partnership) as a result of a wrongful act or omission of his in the course of the business of the limited liability partnership or with its authority, the limited liability partnership is liable to the same extent as the member: s6(1), (2), (4).

9.12 Corporations

Chartered corporations

A chartered corporation is created by Royal Charter. It has full contractual capacity so far as the other contracting party is concerned, but if it exceeds what it is authorised to do by its charter, the Attorney-General may bring proceedings to revoke the charter, or a member may seek a declaration that the contract is invalid. See *Pharmaceutical Society* v *Dickson* [1968] 2 All ER 686.

Statutory corporations

A statutory corporation is one which has been set up in the manner prescribed by statute. For example, after the Local Government Act 1972, virtually all local authorities in England and Wales are statutory corporations. Probably the most common type is the incorporated company, which can be created by individuals following the procedure laid down in the Companies Act 1985.

Incorporated companies

Any two or more persons associated for a lawful purpose may, by subscribing their names to a memorandum of association and otherwise complying with the requirements of the Companies Act 1985 in respect of registration, form an incorporated company, with or without limited liability. A company so formed may be either:

1. a company having the liability of its members limited by the memorandum to the amount, if any, unpaid on the shares respectively held by them ('a company limited by shares');
2. a company having the liability of its members limited by the memorandum to such amount as the members may respectively thereby undertake to contribute to the assets of the company in the event of its being wound up ('a company limited by guarantee'); or
3. a company not having any limit on the liability of its members ('an unlimited company'): s1(1), (2) of the Companies Act 1985.

A company's memorandum must include a statement as to its objects and, in principle, any contract entered into outside the scope of the stated objects is ultra vires and therefore void: see, eg, *Ashbury Railway Carriage and Iron Co* v *Riche*

(1875) LR 7 HL 653 (agreement to purchase railway concession beyond company's objects and could not be ratified even by whole body of shareholders). However, this position has been much modified.

Section 3A of the 1985 Act provides that where the company's memorandum states that the object of the company is to carry on business as a general commercial company, the object of the company is to carry on any trade or business whatsoever, and the company has power to do all such things as are incidental or conducive to the carrying on of any trade or business by it. Again, s35(1) provides that the validity of an act done by a company shall not be called into question on the ground of lack of capacity by reason of anything in the company's memorandum. However, it remains the duty of the directors to observe any limitations on their powers flowing from the company's memorandum; and action by the directors which, but for subsection (1), would be beyond the company's capacity may only be ratified by the company by special resolution: s35(3). In favour of a person dealing with a company in good faith, the power of the board of directors to bind the company, or authorise others to do so, is deemed to be free of any limitation under the company's constitution: s35A(1). A party to a transaction with a company is not bound to enquire as to whether it is permitted by the company's memorandum or as to any limitation on the powers of the board of directors to bind the company or authorise others to do so: s35B.

As to company contracts, a contract may be made:

1. by a company, by writing under its common seal, or
2. on behalf of a company, by any person acting under its authority, express or implied;

and any formalities required by law in the case of a contract made by an individual also apply, unless a contrary intention appears, to a contract made by or on behalf of a company: s36.

A contract which purports to be made by or on behalf of a company at a time when the company has not been formed has effect, subject to any agreement to the contrary, as one made with the person purporting to act for the company or as agent for it, and he is personally liable on the contract accordingly: s36C(1).

In *Braymist Ltd* v *Wise Finance Co Ltd* [2002] 2 All ER 333 Braymist Ltd contracted to sell Wise Finance Co Ltd a parcel of land. At the time, Braymist was in the process of incorporation: its solicitors (Sturges) signed the agreement as agents and solicitors for it. Wise did not know that Braymist had yet to be incorporated. Sturges sought to enforce the contract against Wise by virtue of s36C(1) Companies Act 1985 and the judge found in their favour. He also concluded that the signing of the agreement by Sturges as agents satisfied the requirements of s2 Law of Property (Miscellaneous Provisions) Act 1989. The Court of Appeal decided that the judge's decision on both points had been correct: Wise's appeal was dismissed. Judge LJ said:

'The critical question for decision is whether s36C(1) of the Companies Act 1985 not only provides a remedy for a person (A) who has purported to enter into a contract with a company when it was unformed (the narrow view) but also imposes obligations enforceable against A's wishes by the person purporting to act for or as agent of the unformed company (B). ... The insurmountable difficulty with the narrow view is that it requires s36C(1) to be read as if it created a complete option for someone in A's position, but never for someone in B's position, either to adopt or reject the contract, a choice to be made unilaterally by him, for good, bad, or no reason. The statutory language could, of course, have been drafted so to provide. Instead s36C(1) specifies that contract has "effect", language remote from the concept of an "option" or, as here, the wish of the party in A's position to be protected from the consequences of the deemed contract simply because the bargain is no longer as commercially attractive as it once was. Accordingly, dealing with the issue as a matter of construction, I prefer the broad rather than the narrow view of the meaning and effect of s36C(1).'

Arden LJ added:

'Section 2 of the 1989 Act refers to signature "by or on behalf" of a party. In my judgment, having concluded that Sturges is a party to the agreement by virtue of s36C and that there is no common law bar to enforcement of the contract by Sturges, in my judgment Sturges is properly to be treated as having signed the agreement on its own behalf for the purposes of s2. I reach this construction in order to make both sections work properly together. Otherwise, Sturges having shown that it is entitled to enforce the contract under s36C would be unable to do so because of over-literal construction of s2 of the 1989 Act. I agree with the judge that this cannot be the policy of s2. My interpretation does no violence to the language: Sturges did sign the contract. Because it renders ss36C and 2 more efficacious, in my view the judge's consideration is to be preferred.'

Section 36A of the 1985 Act makes provision with respect to the execution of documents by a company. A document is executed by a company by the affixing of its common seal, but a company need not have a common seal and, whether or not it has one, eg, a document signed by a director and the secretary of a company, or by two directors of a company, and expressed (in whatever form of words) to be executed by the company has the same effect as if executed under the common seal of the company. In *OTV Birwelco Ltd* v *Technical and General Guarantee Co Ltd* [2002] 4 All ER 668, following a management buy-out, the new company usually traded under the original company's name. The new company entered into a performance bond with the defendant surety, in respect of a contract with the claimant. The bond was made by deed in which, and on its seal on which, the new company used the original company's name. The new company ceased trading: could the claimant enforce the bond? Judge Thornton QC held that it could, since (1) s36A Companies Act 1985 did not require a company to use its registered name rather than its trading name in the body of a deed, and (2) non-compliance by the new company with s350 of the 1985 Act did not render the bond a nullity nor make the claimant's third party rights created by the bond unenforceable by the claimant against the defendant. Section 350 provides that a company which has a common seal shall have its name engraved in legible characters on the seal; and if its fails to comply with this subsection it is liable to a fine.

Other corporate bodies

A body corporate, other than a company incorporated under the Companies Act 1985 or a limited liability partnership, may make a contract under seal or, provided the person making it has been duly authorised, in writing or by word of mouth: Corporate Bodies' Contracts Act 1960, as amended.

10

Mistake

10.1 Introduction

It has been said that there is no single coherent doctrine of mistake in English law. Certainly, the single word 'mistake' can have so many different meanings it really indicates little more than a distant connection between assorted instances in which for various reasons the parties may, in everyday language, be said to have been 'mistaken'. The rules relating to mistake, when more closely examined, may be found to have more to do with other areas of contractual law, such as offer and acceptance and the formation of contracts generally.

The effect of a mistake at common law is that when the mistake is operative, it usually operates to make the contract void ab initio. No property will pass under it and no obligations can arise under it. The effect is literally that the law assumes there never has been a contract. Because of the fundamental importance of this doctrine insofar as sale of goods is concerned (no title may pass under a void contract), the courts have always been reluctant to extend the doctrine of operative mistake.

As often happens, equity has stepped into the breach (see section 10.6). In equity, the contract may be voidable. Property will pass and obligations will arise unless or until the contract is avoided. However, the right to rescission may be lost in a number of cases and avoidance of the contract will be impossible.

10.2 Types of mistake

This is an area which abounds with confusing terminology. No two authorities seem agreed as to the forms mistake may take and, often, the same terminology is used to cover different forms of mistake.

Cheshire and Fifoot adopt the threefold classification of unilateral, common and mutal mistake. Unilateral is where A makes a mistake and B knows that A is mistaken. In mutual mistake, each party mistakenly makes a wrong assumption as in *Raffles* v *Wichelhaus* (see below). In common mistake, both parties make exactly the same mistake as in *Solle* v *Butcher* (see below). Other authorities (such as Anson) combine all forms of mistake into either unilateral or mutual.

There are also other, really unrelated, doctrines concerned with documents. In the first type of case, there may be a simple transcription error in drawing up the contract, so that in its written form it does not accurately reflect what the parties agreed earlier. Secondly, a party may assert that the document containing his signature is not the document he thought he was signing. These will be dealt with below (see section 10.5).

For the purposes of this book, the terms 'mutual' and 'unilateral' mistake only will be used. Thus a *mutual mistake* is one when the parties have arrived at a genuine agreement in the erroneous belief that some fact lying at the heart of the contract is true, when it is not.

A *unilateral mistake* is one where though superficially the parties appear to be in agreement, in fact, there is no genuine agreement and no binding contract has been concluded.

In the first case, mutual mistake, if both parties, on becoming aware of the true state of affairs, regret making the agreement, they may usually extricate themselves from the contract without recourse to the courts. Problems arise where one party, though originally mistaken, is unwilling to surrender an advantage gained under the contract that has resulted.

In the second case, unilateral mistake, here again if the parties themselves recognise that despite appearances they have not truly come to any agreement, there is no great problem, and they can usually extricate themselves without resorting to the courts. However, where one party continues to assert that an agreement exists, on terms he mistakenly understood to form the basis of the contract, then litigation may become necessary.

10.3 Mutual mistake

Bell v Lever Brothers Ltd

The concept of mutual mistake was extensively examined by the House of Lords in the leading case of *Bell* v *Lever Bros* [1932] AC 161.

The appellants were employed by a subsidiary company of the respondents and, during their term of office as chairman and vice-chairman respectively, they committed breaches of duty by certain speculative dealings. This conduct would have entitled the respondents to terminate their contracts without notice.

The appellants became redundant after company reorganisation, and large payments were made to them by the respondents, at that time unaware of their misconduct. When the appellants' misconduct came to light, the respondents sought rescission of the redundancy agreements and return of the sums paid.

At first instance, it was found that the appellants had never sought to actively conceal their past misconduct, and they simply did not appreciate its likely effect. In other words, the agreements were entered into under a mutual mistake.

By a 3-2 majority, the Lords held the agreements to be valid and binding.

It is generally agreed that the effect of *Bell* v *Lever Bros* is to confine the doctrine very narrowly. Specific types of mistake will be considered shortly, but it is convenient first to consider what their Lordships said concerning the general nature of common law mistake. Both Lords Atkin and Thankerton agreed that the mistake must be a false and fundamental assumption going to the root of the contract, and which both parties must be taken to have had in their minds at the time the contract was made as being the basis of their agreement. What is required is more than simply one party being able to demonstrate that had he known the true facts, he would never have made the contract. Lord Thankerton said:

'The phrase "underlying assumption by the parties", as applied to the subject matter of a contract, may be too widely interpreted so as to include something which one of the parties had not necessarily in his mind at the time of the contract; in my opinion it can only properly relate to something which both must have necessarily accepted in their minds as an essential and integral element of the subject matter.'

Applying this test to *Bell* v *Lever Bros*, it clearly was not satisfied. As Lord Atkin said, the respondents got exactly what they bargained for, release of the contracts, and it was immaterial that the same objective would have been achieved by other means, or that had they known the true facts, they would not have made the bargain. The discovered facts could not be said to destroy the identity of the contract.

In *Sheikh Brothers Ltd* v *Ochsner* [1957] AC 136, the appellants, who were lessees of an estate in Kenya, granted the respondent a licence to cut and manufacture sisal on the estate. The terms of the licence provided that the respondents should deliver to the appellants 50 tons of manufactured sisal fibre per month. It transpired that the net yield of the estate was insufficient to comply with this condition. *Bell* v *Lever Bros* was cited to the Judicial Committee, and the contract was held to be void.

Examples of contracts void under English law because of a sufficiently false and fundamental assumption, all preceding *Bell* v *Lever Bros* and which must, therefore, be read subject to it, are as follows.

Scott v *Coulson* [1903] 2 Ch 249. The parties entered into a contract for the assignment of a life insurance policy wrongly believing that the object of the policy was still alive. The contract was held to be void and the vendor recovered the policy and the moneys payable under it on the assured's death.

Galloway v *Galloway* (1914) 30 TLR 531. The parties entered into a separation deed, believing themselves to be husband and wife. In fact, they had not contracted a valid marriage, the deed was held to be void and the man not liable to make the payments promised under it.

Griffiths v *Brymer* (1903) 19 TLR 434. The plaintiff contracted to hire a room from the defendant to watch the King's coronation procession. Shortly before the contract was made, the procession was cancelled. The plaintiff recovered moneys paid to the defendant on the grounds that the agreement was made on a missupposition of facts which went to the whole root of the contract.

An example of a case subsequent to *Bell* v *Lever Bros* is *Norwich Union Fire Insurance Society* v *Price* [1934] AC 455. The respondents shipped a cargo of lemons, insured under a policy of marine insurance, with the appellants. In the belief that the lemons had been damaged by an insured–against peril, and sold in consequence, the appellants paid over the insurance moneys. In fact, the lemons had not been damaged and had been sold because they were ripening. The Judicial Committee of Privy Council held that the appellants could recover the moneys as having been paid under a mistake of fact. The mistake was 'vital' and the contract was therefore void. The Judicial Committee said there was nothing in *Bell* v *Lever Bros* to suggest otherwise.

See also *Rover International* v *Cannon Film Sales* [1989] 1 WLR 912. Here a mutual mistake as to an essential question of fact meant that the contract was held to be void ab initio. Both parties were under the mistaken impression that a contract entered into earlier was valid. In fact, it was not. All their subsequent dealings were grounded on this mistaken belief. On appeal it was held since all agreements between the parties, and monies paid pursuant to such agreements, were based on a mutual mistake of fact, then any such agreements must be void ab initio and any monies paid be returned.

Having considered the general approach of the law to the problem of mutual mistake, three specific areas of contract, which have generated much case law, will now be considered. They are mistake as to quality; mistake as to the existence of the subject matter; and mistake as to title. In *Bell* v *Lever Bros*, Lord Atkin gave examples of all three.

Mistake as to quality

In the ordinary course of events, a mistake as to quality will not avail a party seeking to avoid a contract. He will usually be taken to have received the article or goods that constituted the subject matter of the contract and which the vendor contracted to supply. The buyer's only remedy may be to sue for breach of condition or warranty, providing there is some term in the contract relating to quality. The situations in which the contract may be void for mistake as to quality were said by Lord Atkin to be where:

> '... it is the mistake of both parties, and is as to the existence of some quality which makes the thing without the quality essentially different from the thing as it was believed to be.'

He came to this conclusion on consideration of *Kennedy* v *Panama Royal Mail Co* and *Smith* v *Hughes.*

In *Kennedy* v *Panama Royal Mail Co* (1867) LR 2 QB 580, the plaintiff applied for shares in the defendant company in reliance on a prospectus which stated wrongly, but in good faith, that the company had concluded a contract with the Government of New Zealand to carry mails.

The shares were allotted to him and subsequently fell in value. On discovering the true facts, the plaintiff brought an action to recover the money he had paid for the shares. Dismissing the action, the Court of Queen's Bench held that the plaintiff had received that which he had contracted for, namely shares in the defendant company, and that the invalidity of the contract with the New Zealand Government did not make them different in substance. Blackburn J said that the difference must be:

> '... such as to show that there is a complete difference in substance between what was supposed to be and what was taken, so as to constitute a failure of consideration.'

Smith v *Hughes* (1871) LR 6 QB 597 involved a contract for the sale of oats by sample. The defendant wished to purchase old oats, but the oats sold to him by the plaintiff were new oats and useless for the defendant's purpose. The Court of Queen's Bench held that even if both parties believed the oats to be old oats, there would nevertheless be a binding contract.

In the light of these cases, the problem seems to be exactly when a mistake as to quality will avoid a contract. As has been said with some justification, if a mistake as to £50,000 (the sum at issue in *Bell* v *Lever Bros*) is not fundamental, then what is? The speeches in the House of Lords offer some assistance. Lord Atkin gave the following examples of contracts that would not be avoided.

1. Where a buyer purchases a horse believing it to be sound, pays accordingly, and would not have bought the horse had he known that it was, in fact, unsound. In the *absence of any contractual term as to soundness,* the buyer is bound.
2. Both buyer and seller believe a painting to be an old master; in reality it is a copy. If there is no representation or warranty the buyer has no remedy (contrast *Peco Arts* v *Hazlitt Gallery* [1983] 3 All ER 193, where the decision was, however, on the question of limitation of action).
3. A buyer purchases a house which, unbeknown to him, is uninhabitable, the contract is valid.
4. In the sale of a roadside garage, the buyer is unaware that shortly a by-pass route

will be constructed to divert a substantial amount of traffic and thus business elsewhere; he has no remedy.

As with much of the law of mistake, mistake as to quality is defined by exclusion, and examples of where the plea might have or has succeeded are rare. In the Court of Appeal in *Bell* v *Lever Bros*, Greer LJ said that the contract would be void where the intention was to buy and sell a racehorse whereas, in fact, the animal was a carthorse. This example may be usefully contrasted with Lord Atkin's unsound horse. Three more cases in which the plea failed should also be mentioned.

In *Harrison & Jones Ltd* v *Bunten and Lancaster Ltd* [1953] 1 QB 646, the buyers agreed in writing to purchase from the sellers '100 bales of Calcutta kapok, sree brand', equal to an exhibited sample. Both parties believed it to be pure kapok consisting of sree cotton, but the commodity turned out to be a mixture containing bush cotton and commercially inferior. Pilcher J said that although the mistake may be fundamental from the point of view of the purchaser, the fact that the parties were unaware that the goods commercially thus described lacked a particular quality did not affect the validity of the contract.

In *Leaf* v *International Galleries* [1950] 2 KB 86, the plaintiff purchased from the defendants a painting which both mistakenly believed to be by Constable. The plaintiff sought rescission for misrepresentation, but the Court of Appeal said, obiter, that although the mistake may have been in one sense essential or fundamental, it did not avoid the contract.

The facts in *Peco Arts* (above) were substantially similar, but there was no decision on this point. It is clear, therefore, that although a particular quality may be of great importance to the contracting parties themselves, the courts look at the matter in a slightly different way by considering the essential nature of the subject matter, and not necessarily giving any weight at all to the hopes, desires and disappointments of the parties.

In *Solle* v *Butcher* [1950] 1 KB 671, the defendant let a flat to the plaintiff at a rent of £250 pa. Both parties assumed that in view of the considerable alterations that had been carried out on the property, it was in law a 'new' flat and no longer subject to rent control. The assumption was incorrect, and the maximum permitted rent was £140, and the plaintiff sought the return of the rent overpaid. The defendant in his counterclaim alleged that the lease was void for mistake. The Court of Appeal held that although there was a mutual mistake as to fact, the contract was not void. Denning LJ took a robustly critical view of the doctrine of mistake at common law (to be dealt with later), but the case is important because Bucknill LJ agreed that the mistake was not sufficient to avoid the contract. It has been argued that if ever a mistake as to quality were to operate, then it should be here, because the difference between a rent-controlled and a de-controlled flat is such as to make the one essentially different from the other. The opposite view is that the difference is simply as to commercial value, which will rarely, if ever, afford grounds for avoiding a contract. If the latter view is correct, and on balance it may be preferred, the case still illustrates the extent to which the mistake must be 'an essential and integral element' of the subject matter of the contract. It is suggested that the case does not hold that a mistake as to substance, as opposed to quality, can never operate.

There is a comparative dearth of authority in which contracts have been held to be void for mistake as to quality/substance – the following cases may be considered:

Gompertz v *Bartlett* (1853) 2 E & B 849. In a contract for the sale of a bill of exchange, the parties assumed it to be a valid unstamped foreign bill; in fact, it was an inland bill and therefore invalid. The purchaser was able to recover the purchase price on the grounds that the contract was void.

In *Nicholson and Venn* v *Smith-Marriott* (1947) 177 LT 189, table linen was advertised at a sale by auction as being 'with the crest of Charles I and the authentic property of that monarch'. The linen was Georgian and, in consequence, the buyer recovered damages though the judge was of the opinion that the buyer could have treated the contract as void. In *Solle* v *Butcher*, Denning LJ disagreed with this conclusion.

In attempting to produce a coherent exposition of the above law, it has been suggested that the test to apply in a given situation is whether the parties can be said to use the quality in question to identify the thing that is the subject matter of the contract, such that if it lacks this quality, the contract is void, per *Bell* v *Lever Bros.* Thus in *Bell*, the parties, if asked, would have replied that they were contracting for a service agreement, not an 'unbroken' service agreement; in *Nicholson and Venn*, the parties would have said that the contract was for the sale of Carolean table linen, and in Lord Atkin's examples of an unsound horse and an uninhabitable house, the answer would be that the contracts concerned a horse and a house respectively. His example of an old master would not necessarily fit into this text, and presumably the parties' answer in *Leaf* v *International Galleries* would have been that they were dealing with a Constable painting, which, in fact, it was not.

Apart from its obvious uncertainties, the principal weakness of this test is that it is really only a useful rule of thumb and no more. It fails to answer the essential point of why certain articles may be identified by their quality, and why others may not be. The significance of a fundamental mistake as to quality, for the mistake to operate, lies in the importance that the Court attach to the quality taking into account the pre-contractual negotiations of the parties (if any), and the express and implied terms of their final agreement. Such an approach has led to a further attempt to restate the law relating to mistake as to quality, by rejecting the quality/substance distinction as being both arbitrary and imprecise.

Glanville Williams (1945) 23 Can Bar Rev has argued that there is no 'metaphysical' substance independent of qualities, and that qualities considered compositely produce the essence of the substance of an article. Arguably preferable, instead, is to look at the matter from the point of view of exactly what the parties intended and undertook when entering into the contract. Ignoring the possibility of any term implied by statute (for example, Sale of Goods Act 1979), a mistake as to quality would normally have one of two possible results – applying the rule caveat emptor, the risk, that the goods were not of the quality that the parties believed them to be, will fall on the buyer, and he will have no remedy; or the seller may be held to have expressly or impliedly warranted that the goods were of the assumed quality and the buyer will have an action for damages.

Generally, it is argued, a mutual mistake as to quality will fall into either category, but there may be special circumstances in which, on the true construction of the contract, neither party could be held to have accepted the risk that the subject matter of the contract might be what in fact it proves to be, and to enforce the contract would cause either or both to have imposed upon them contractual obligations that the parties never intended to create. In such a situation, the contract would be void. This solution accords with the general object of the doctrine of common law mistake, that in exceptional cases contractual liabilities should be discharged because of matters unknown to the parties that render the contract utterly different to the contract that they intended to make.

In *Associated Japanese Bank International Ltd* v *Credit du Nord SA* [1988] 3 All ER 902, the effect of mistake as to quality was subject to detailed examination by Steyn J. His Lordship observed that the decision in *Bell* v *Lever Brothers* had been interpreted as virtually excluding mistake as to quality being operative at common law. He referred, in particular, to the judgments of Lord Denning in *Solle* v *Butcher* and *Magee* v *Pennine Insurance Co*, and the arguments advanced in Cheshire, Fifoot and Furmston's *Law of Contract* (11th edn pp225–6). In his view, this interpretation did not do justice to the speeches of the majority in that case. Lord Atkin had recognised that mistake as to quality might well operate to nullify consent, although in limited circumstances, when he held that:

> '... a mistake will not affect assent unless it is the mistake of both parties, and is as to the existence of some quality which makes the thing without the quality essentially different from the thing as it was believed to be'.

Lord Thankerton had enunciated almost precisely the same test. Steyn J adopted the test formulated by Lord Atkin and held further that a party who seeks to rely on such a mistake to avoid the contract must have had reasonable grounds for the belief which gave rise to the mistake.

After a careful examination of the speeches in *Bell*, he concluded that the majority view was that there did exist a narrow, but perceptible, doctrine of common mistake where the mistake renders the subject matter of the contract essentially and radically different from the subject matter the parties believed to exist.

Mistake as to the existence of the subject matter

In *Bell* v *Lever Bros*, Lord Atkin clearly contemplated that where there was an agreement to purchase a specific article, and the article had perished prior to the making of the contract, then the contract was void and the parties' consent was nullified, with the qualification that the seller would be liable in damages if he knew this when the contract was concluded.

In addition, s6 Sale of Goods Act 1979 provides that:

> 'Where there is a contract for the sale of specific goods, and the goods without the knowledge of the seller have perished at the time when the contract was made, the contract is void.'

However, the cases suggest that the matter is not as plain as it might appear. Section 6 was widely believed to embody in statute form the principle of law to be found in *Couturier* v *Hastie* (1856) 5 HL Cas 673. The plaintiffs agreed to sell and the defendant to buy a cargo of Indian corn, which, unknown to both of them, had deteriorated to such an extent in transit that it had been sold en route to England in order to minimise losses, as it would not have survived the remainder of the voyage. The contract included a policy of insurance, and the plaintiffs alleged that the defendant had bought a chance, that is, he had taken a commercial risk as to whether or not the corn existed and, in any event, he had the insurance policy, and was therefore liable to pay the agreed price. The defendant argued that the contract was for the sale of specific goods, and that as the plaintiffs were unable to sell them, he was not bound to pay. It should firstly be noted that the case was not decided on the grounds of mistake, nor was the contract held to be void, though the inference to be drawn from the judgments is that it was. The Court of Exchequer Chamber and the House of Lords decided that it was a contract for specific goods, and that because the plaintiffs could not deliver them, they were unable to sustain an action for the price. This is equally well a finding that there has been a total failure of consideration.

If the case is correctly cited as dealing with non-existent subject matter, then it follows a number of earlier decisions in the nineteenth century to the same effect.

In *Strickland* v *Turner* (1852) 7 Exch 208, the plaintiff purchased an annuity and, unknown to the parties, the annuitant was already dead. He was able to recover the price paid, the consideration having totally failed.

In *Hitchcock* v *Giddings* (1817) 4 Price 135, the plaintiff bought a remainder in fee expectant upon an estate tail which had in fact been barred. The plaintiff recovered his purchase money.

It can be seen from these two cases, and also from *Couturier* v *Hastie*, that a buyer is not liable for the price where the seller has completely failed to deliver that which he promised, and as such they merely illustrate a total failure of consideration. If a contract is void for mistake, it is void ab initio and the buyer need not pay the price, and if he has done so then he may recover it. The two concepts thus have this much in common, and because they may often have the same effect, some confusion has arisen in distinguishing between them.

In *Barrow, Lane and Ballard Ltd* v *Phillips & Co* [1929] 1 KB 574, the plaintiffs contracted to sell the defendants 700 bags of nuts, believed by both parties to be lying in a warehouse. In fact, at the time the contract was made, 109 had disappeared, apparently stolen, and before the defendants tried to take delivery of them, a further 450 went missing. The contract was held to be void under s6.

Wright J said that where a contract relates to specific goods which do not exist, the case is not to be treated as one in which the seller warrants the existence of those specific goods, but one in which there has been a failure of consideration and mistake. As a matter of law, a failure of consideration is a breach of contract for which the injured party may recover damages, to be assessed in accordance with the principles of *Hadley* v *Baxendale* (1854) 9 Exch 341. He may content himself with merely recovering the price paid; this is, however, his only remedy in a case of mistake, and may be substantially less than the sum he would recover as damages. In this respect, therefore, the statement of Wright J is misleading, and the problems that may be caused by treating the matter in this way arose in a particularly acute form in *McRae* v *Commonwealth Disposals Commission* (1950) 84 CLR 377.

The defendants accepted the plaintiff's tender of £285 for the purchase of a wrecked oil tanker, described as laying on Jourmaund Reef, off Papua New Guinea. There was no such reef, nor any wrecked tanker in the indicated area, and in consequence of this, and of having incurred considerable expense in preparing the salvage operation, the plaintiff sued for damages for breach of contract. At first instance, the judge held himself bound by *Couturier* v *Hastie* to hold that the contract was void, but on appeal in the High Court of Australia, it was held that the defendants had warranted that the tanker existed and were liable accordingly. *Couturier* had been concerned with the construction of the terms of the contract, and was not to be regarded as an authority on mutual mistake; it was decided on the grounds of a failure of consideration and not with reference to the validity or otherwise of the contract. Had this been at issue, it would have been necessary to decide whether there was an implied condition precedent that the corn existed at the time the contract was made, and that if it did not, the parties were to be excused. The court held in the present case that no such term could be implied; the buyer relied on and acted on the assertion of the seller that the tanker existed, and there was no common assumption of fact to lead to the conclusion that the creation of contractual obligations depended on the correctness of the assumption.

As an Australian case, *McRae* is of only persuasive authority in the English courts. The decision has, in fact, led to a wide reappraisal of the law relating to non-existing goods (res extincta).

Slade, at (1954) 70 LQR 385, argues that, since *McRae*, the doctrine of mutal mistake had become redundant and that there will in every case be a binding contract unless the implied term precedent referred to in the judgment is present in the contract.

Atiyah, at (1957) 73 LQR 340, adopts a similar approach to *Couturier* v *Hastie*. He says that the case is open to four possible interpretations.

1. The contract was void for mistake. Such an explanation is dismissed as being discredited because the case had nothing to do with mistake. Strictly this is true;

the case was not decided in mistake, nevertheless, their Lordships probably did have the concept of mistake in their minds when they formed their judgments. Atiyah is therefore correct in as much as the case is not a binding authority on mistake, as the court held in *McRae*.

2. The contract was void for attempting the impossible; that there can never be a contract for the sale of a res extincta because a contract must have subject matter. Atiyah replies that whether or not this is so depends on the intention of the parties. The seller may contract that the goods exist, and although he may in reality have nothing to sell, that does not mean that the contract also does not exist. The obligation on the seller may be an absolute one, just as it may be to prevent the doctrine of frustration operating.

3. The contract is void on the grounds of a condition precedent; and

4. that it illustrates that a party cannot enforce a contract where there is a failure of consideration. He considers these possibilities together, and says that there are three alternatives: (1) that if there are no goods there is no binding contract, or (2) the buyer is not absolutely bound to pay, or (3) the seller is liable for non-delivery. *Couturier* only decided (2), and it is sufficient for the buyer to establish either (1) or (3) as in neither case is he liable to pay the price.

Couturier, *Hitchcock* and *Strickland* are, therefore, distinguished leaving *McRae* as good law concerning the validity of a contract for non-existent goods.

In a previous edition, Cheshire and Fifoot had suggested that *McRae* would not be followed, for a number of reasons, which in the light of modern developments now seem incorrect.

In fact, as has been noted, though only of persuasive authority, *McRae* has led to considerable rethinking of the law on res extincta. Certainly, *McRae* suggests that the operation of this area of mistake is extremely limited and subject to stringent restrictions.

Mistake as to title

In *Bell* v *Lever Bros*, Lord Atkin said that where unknown to both parties the buyer already possesses legal title to that which the seller purports to transfer to him, then the transaction is inoperative in law because the transfer is impossible. He cited *Cooper* v *Phibbs* (1867) LR 2 HL 149. A agreed to take the lease of a fishery from B, though contrary to the belief of the parties at the time, A was tenant for life of the fishery and B had no title. The House of Lords granted rescission in equity, though Lord Atkin was of the opinion that the contract was void at common law and regarded the case as analogous to a situation where a contract is void for mistake owing to non-existent subject matter (above).

The principle is a restricted one, however, and it must not be thought that when a seller 'sells' to the buyer what is already the buyer's in law, the contract is thereby avoided. Although the seller may have no title, as a rule this will not mean there is no contract; the effect will be that the seller is in breach of contract as being unable to perform his obligations and correspondingly unable to enforce the contract himself. It will still be open to the buyer to sue. Thus in the case of the sale of goods, s12(1) of the 1979 Act provides that there is:

> '... an implied term on the part of the seller that in the case of a sale he has a right to sell the goods, and in the case of an agreement to sell he will have such a right at the time when the property is to pass'.

Generally, the contract will only be avoided when there is no implied term or warranty as to title, where it would be correct to say that the parties have regarded ownership of the subject matter as being, in the words of Lord Thankerton, 'an essential and integral element' of it.

Negligence

There is no English authority as to the position where the mutual mistake entertained by the parties is caused by the failure of one party to take reasonable care. Section 6 only precludes from its scope a case where the seller knew the goods had perished, that is, effectively fraud, and the normal rule would apparently apply to cases of negligence.

The suggestion to the contrary is to be found in *McRae*, where the defendants were held to be guilty of the 'grossest negligence' in that they knew that the buyer would rely on their assertion that the tanker existed, and they took no steps to verify what they were asserting. In such circumstances, the guilty party cannot rely on mutual mistake:

> 'In these circumstances it seems out of the question that they should be able to assert that no contract was concluded. It is not unfair or inaccurate to say that the only "mistake" the plaintiffs made was that they believed what the Commission told them.'

The common sense of this view appears unimpeachable, subject only to the caveat that normally in contract questions of fault are not relevant because liability in contract is strict. *McRae* is noted in (1952) 68 LQR 30, where it is suggested that the law would be in an extraordinary state if a defendant, however unequivocally he has represented a state of affairs as existing, is entitled to plead mistake and avoid liability to a plaintiff who has relied on his representation of fact. The law relating to mutual mistake is, therefore, to be qualified by a rule that in such a case, an estoppel will arise against the representor. Having regard to the present trend of decisions against holding contracts void for mistake, it is safe to say that a court would regard negligence as important where a defendant sought to escape liability, as in *McRae*. Note also that new cases are coming before the courts in which fault is for the first time becoming relevant in contract cases. (See Chapter 16.)

Mutual mistake and frustration

The distinguishing feature between a contract which is void for mistake and a contract which is frustrated, is the time of the occurrence of the event. If the vitiating factor occurs *before* the contract is made and the parties are in ignorance of it, the contract may be void for mutual mistake. If, on the other hand, the event occurs after the contract is made, the contract will be frustrated. It may not always be easy to ascertain the time of the relevant event.

In *Amalgamated Investment and Property Co* v *John Walker & Sons* [1976] 3 All ER 509, the plaintiffs contracted to buy a valuable property from the defendants. Shortly afterwards, the local authority 'listed' the building so that it could not be pulled down or altered. The value of the property was greatly reduced. The plaintiffs argued that the contract was void for mistake. They said that the relevant event was not the listing of the building, but the administrative decision to list the building. This occurred before the contract was made. The court decided that the relevant act was the official act of listing the building which occurred only after the contract was made. Mistake did not apply since the building was not listed when the contract was signed. Nor was the contract frustrated. The parties were aware of the risk that the building might be listed, and it was a risk the plaintiffs had to bear.

10.4 Unilateral mistake

In the cases discussed above, the parties have been under a mutual misapprehension, that is, they have both made the same mistake. In this section, the matters to be considered concern instances where the mistake is made by one party only or, more exceptionally, though both are mistaken each is as it were differently mistaken. The difference between mutual and unilateral mistake may be illustrated by contrast; in the former the parties are agreed on the terms of the contract and have apparently concluded a binding agreement, it is the existence or non-existence of facts unknown to the parties that operates to negative or nullify their agreement. In unilateral mistake, the mistake occurs at the time the 'contract' is concluded (a void contract is, of course, no contract at all), and the effect of the unilateral mistake is such that these parties are, unknowingly, not, in fact, in agreement at all. In this respect, the cases concern as much offer and acceptance as mistake, and turn on the principle that no contract can be formed if there is no correspondence between the offer and the acceptance. In considering whether there is a concluded agreement, the intention of the parties is usually to be construed objectively, and whatever one party's real intention is, if the language used may be reasonably construed to mean what the other party reasonably believed it to mean, then a contract will exist.

It will be necessary for the party seeking to avoid the agreement to show either that there is such ambiguity that it is impossible reasonably to impute any agreement to the parties' dealings; or that the other party has knowingly accepted an offer in terms different to those in which it was intended to be by the offeror.

These matters will be considered under the following headings.

1. Where the parties are at cross purposes.
2. Where there is a mistake as to the terms of the contract.
3. Where there is a mistake as to identity: parties not inter praesentes.

Where the parties are at cross purposes

In order to succeed under this heading the party seeking to avoid the contract must show that it would be impossible, by applying the objective test, to decide that the parties intended the contract to take one form rather than another. If the 'reasonable man' test leads to the conclusion that, in the objective approach, the contract could be understood in one sense only, both parties will be bound by the contract in this sense. The following cases illustrate the circumstances under which the court will hold that there is no concluded contract.

Raffles v *Wichelhaus* (1864) H & C 906. In a contract for the sale of cotton, the goods were specified as being those 'to arrive ex Peerless from Bombay'. Two ships called the Peerless had recently sailed from Bombay, the one to which vendors believed the contract referred had left in December, whereas the buyers believed the cotton to be on board a ship that had sailed in October. There was no evidence to ascertain to which of the two ships the contract related, and the ambiguity was held to prevent a binding contract coming into existence.

In *Falck* v *Williams* [1900] AC 176, the parties used a code for business purposes, and the plaintiff sent to the defendant an offer in code by telegraph. The message was unpunctuated and could be understood in one of two senses, the plaintiff intending it in one sense and the defendant accepting it in the other. The Privy Council held that in the absence of any evidence to resolve in which sense the offer might reasonably be said to have been intended, no contract had been concluded.

In *Scriven Bros & Co* v *Hindley & Co* [1913] 3 KB 564 the defendants wished to purchase a quantity of hemp being offered for sale by the plaintiffs by auction. Prior to the sale, the defendants inspected a sample of the hemp, but unknown to them there was also some tow for sale, in similar bales and bearing identical markings. Tow is a commercially inferior commodity; but there was nothing in the auction catalogue to distinguish between the different goods, and the defendants bid for and had knocked down to them a quantity of tow at a price extravagant for the defendants' purposes. The plaintiffs sued for the price. Lawrence J held that the defendants' conduct did not suggest, according to the objective test, that they intended to buy tow; the offer and acceptance did not coincide, the parties were never ad idem as to the subject matter of the sale, and no contract existed.

The effect of the objective test is that negligence or blameworthiness is relevant in deciding whether, despite a party's private intentions, he may objectively be held to have entered into a contract. The concept, therefore, has something in common with the approach of the High Court of Australia in *McRae* (above). In each case, carelessness will prevent a party from asserting that the contract is void. In *McRae,* he is estopped, here he is bound by the impression he induced the other party reasonably to hold.

Where there is a mistake as to the terms of the contract

Here the objective test gives way to a subjective one, because the law is concerned not with reasonable inferences, but with circumstances in which one party is actually aware of the other party's mistake.

The grounds on which one party may avoid a contract because the other knew of his mistake are, at common law, narrowly and finely drawn. Generally, in English law, parties are assumed to possess equal bargaining power, and are treated accordingly. The rule is caveat emptor, let the buyer beware, and it is upon the contracting parties to ensure, in concluding an agreement, that it properly represents their intentions and desires. Certain contracts, for example, contracts of insurance, do impose duties on the parties to make a full and frank disclosure regarding contractual matters, but at common law in the absence of, for example, a misrepresentation, there is no such duty. Of course, this position has been eroded by statute which now affords much consumer protection. The position being considered here is one of classic common law contract, and the rule is this: that it is only where one party is mistaken as to the nature of the promise made by the other party, and the other is aware of the mistake, that the contract is void.

Thus, for example, in a contract for the sale of a painting, it is insufficient that the buyer thinks he is purchasing a Rembrandt, even if the buyer is aware of this delusion. It must be the case that the seller knows that the buyer thinks that he, the seller, is contracting to sell the painting as being by Rembrandt, but, in fact, the seller is simply selling it as a painting with no undertaking as to its origin. The mistake must be more than merely being in relation to the subject matter, it must be as to the nature of the offer the seller is making regarding the subject matter.

This can be illustrated by *Smith* v *Hughes* (1871) LR 6 QB 597. In a contract for the sale of oats by sample, the defendant buyer wished to purchase, and alleged the plaintiff had described the goods as being, 'old oats'. The plaintiff denied he had thus described them; the oats were new oats and of no use to the defendant. The trial judge left the following questions to the jury.

1. If the plaintiff had described the oats as 'old oats', then should the defendant succeed?
2. If the word 'old' was not used, did the plaintiff believe the defendant believed or was under the impression that he was agreeing to buy 'old oats' and, if so, should the defendant succeed?

The Court of Queen's Bench held that the second question had not been phrased with sufficient clarity to draw the jury's attention to the difference between the plaintiff knowing or believing that the defendant thought the oats were 'old', and his knowing or believing that the defendant thought that he was contracting to sell him oats as 'old oats'. Only in the latter case is there any operative mistake as to the nature of the offer which renders the contract void.

Thus, in *Hartog v Colin and Shields* [1939] 3 All ER 566, the plaintiff accepted the defendants' offer to sell 30,000 hare skins at a given price per pound. The previous negotiations had been conducted on the basis of a price per piece, as was the custom of the trade, and the evidence showed that at the rate per pound, the overall price would be absurdly low. The plaintiff sought to enforce these terms. Singleton J held the plaintiff could not reasonably have supposed that the offer contained the defendants' true intention; he must have known that the defendants were mistaken as to the offer made by them regarding the price, and the contract was void as a result.

Where there is a mistake as to identity: parties not inter praesentes

The most difficult area in unilateral mistake is where a contract is void because one contracting party was unaware of the true identity of the other party. Normally, it is said, the identity of the person with whom one contracts is immaterial; this will be particularly so in, for example, a shop sale or a public auction, for example, *Dennant v Skinner & Colborn* [1948] 2 KB 164.

At a car auction sale, several cars were knocked down to a bidder who, for the purposes of the memorandum of sale, gave his name as King of King's of Oxford, which was false. On the strength of this, he was allowed to take the cars away in return for a worthless cheque. It was held the property passed to him when the hammer fell; being an auction, his identity was immaterial. To avoid the contract for mistake as to identity, the matter must be material to the contract. It should firstly be borne in mind that a person may not accept an offer which he knows, or ought to know, is addressed to a third person.

In *Boulton v Jones* (1857) 2 H & N 564, the defendant had, over a period of time, established a course of dealing with one Brocklehurst. The two had a running account against which the defendant set-off sums owed to him by Brocklehurst. Unknown to the defendant, the plaintiff took over Brocklehurst's business, and when the defendant ordered goods from Brocklehurst, the plaintiff executed the order without informing him of the changed circumstances. The defendant refused to pay for the goods, and the plaintiff sued for the price. The Court held that the defendant was not liable, and Pollock CB said:

'Now the rule of law is clear, that if you propose to make a contract with A, then B cannot substitute himself for A without your consent, and to your disadvantage, securing to himself all the benefit of the contract.'

It may be that the crucial factor in this case was the existence of the defendant's right to set-off Brocklehurst's debts against his account, and conceivably had this not been the case, then he might never have sent the order in the first place. As a statement of law, the ratio decidendi is undoubtedly correct, but it may be that the rule only applied to small businesses or to contracts involving some personal element, and that in the present day when large, impersonal commercial concerns predominate, it will be less readily applied. Further, it may be that what is important is the company's standing, and (in law) its independent legal personality, and not the persons who either manage or own it.

A further qualification is that a party may not avoid a contract by merely asserting that the offer was, in fact, addressed to some third person. As is the case where the parties are at cross purposes as to offer and acceptance, the test is objective; one must ask how the reasonable man in the offeree's position would have interpreted the offer. If the irresistible conclusion is that he would have reasonably believed that the offer was addressed to him, then his acceptance will be effective.

Upton-on-Severn RDC v *Powell* [1942] 1 All ER 220. In consequence of a fire on his property, the defendant telephoned the Upton police and asked them to send for the fire brigade. The police called the Upton fire brigade, who duly put out the fire. It subsequently transpired that although the defendant was in the Upton police area, his property fell within the province of the neighbouring Pershore fire brigade, and the plaintiff sought to recover payment for the services of the Upton fire brigade. It was held that the Upton fire brigade had acted reasonably in effect, in accepting the defendant's offer, and could recover reasonable remuneration for their services.

The converse of this situation is the proposition that no valid contract is concluded when a person accepts an offer reasonably believing that the offer is from someone other than the actual offeror, and the offeror is aware of this. This is a logical corollary, because just as a party cannot accept an offer not made to him, there is no intention to contract with the person with whom the agreement is apparently concluded.

In *Cundy* v *Lindsay* (1878) 3 App Cas 459, one Blenkarn, a rogue, ordered a quantity of handkerchiefs from the respondents giving his address as 37 Wood Street, Cheapside, and signing the signature to make it appear as if the order came from Blenkiron & Co, a reputable firm of 123 Wood Street, and already known to the respondents. The respondents wrote to and sent goods to Benkiron & Co of 37 Wood Street, and the rogue sold the goods to the appellants who purchased them bona fide. In the Queen's Bench Division, Blackburn J held that although the rogue had obtained the goods by false pretences, the respondent had intended to contract with the addressee of 37 Wood Street, and that the contract, though voidable for fraud, was at first valid, and the appellants therefore acquired good title. The Court of Appeal and the House of Lords thought differently. Lord Cairns said:

> 'I ask the question, how is it possible to imagine that in that state of things any contract could have arisen between the respondents and Blenkarn, the dishonest man? Of him they knew nothing and of him they never thought. With him, they never intended to deal. Their minds never even for an instant of time rested upon him, and as between him and them there was no consensus of mind which could lead to any agreement or any contract

whatever. As between him and them there was merely the one side to a contract where, in order to produce a contract, two sides would be required.'

Had Blenkarn been an honest man, and if nothing had put him on inquiry that the respondents did not intend to deal with him, then a valid contract would have been concluded, following *Upton* v *Powell.*

The crucial fact in *Cundy* was the question of identity. Lindsay's never intended to contract with Blenkarn, but with Blenkiron & Co. Suppose, however, that they intended so to do, having being induced by Blenkarn to believe that he was a reputable firm not a rogue?

This problem arose in *King's Norton Metal Co Ltd* v *Edridge Merrett & Co Ltd* (1897) 14 TLR 98. The plaintiffs were metal manufacturers, and received a letter requesting a quotation for a quantity of rivet wire purporting to come from 'Hallam & Co' on headed notepaper containing a drawing of a large factory and details of its overseas depots and agencies. The plaintiffs delivered the quotation and, in reply to orders, despatched the wire to Hallam & Co. The scheme was a fraud by a rogue, one Wallis, who never paid for the wire and resold it to the defendants. The plaintiffs claimed its return on the grounds that the contract was void. The Court of Appeal held that it was voidable only, because the plaintiffs had always intended to deal with the person who wrote the letter, and as there was no such entity as Hallam & Co, this clearly was Wallis. The property had, therefore, passed to him, and he could in turn pass good title to the defendants. The distinction drawn from *Cundy* v *Lindsay* was that here there was no mistake as to the identity of the offeror, but simply to his attributes. They thought he was a solvent international company; in reality he was a rogue.

Two conclusions are commonly drawn from these two cases: (1) that to succeed in the case of a mistake as to identity, there must be an indentifiable third party with whom one intended to contract (considered shortly); (2) the mistake must be as to identity and not attributes. This approach has been the subject of much academic and judicial criticism, and as a practical test has been compared in its value (or lack of it) with the quality/substance distinction enunciated in *Bell* v *Lever Bros*, that has proved so difficult to apply (above).

In *Lewis* v *Averay* (below), Lord Denning MR said:

' ... this is a distinction without a difference. A man's very name is one of his attributes. It is also a key to his identity. If then he gives a false name, is it a mistake as to his identity or a mistake as to his attributes? These fine distinctions do not make good law'.

It should also be noted that his Lordship, current to his reformulation of the law of mistake, is of the opinion that the contract in *Cundy* v *Lindsay* was voidable only.

Glanville Williams, at (1945) 23 Can Bar Rev 278, has argued that the distinction between identity and attributes is based on a fundamental misconception, namely, that they are treated as being two inherently different things which is, in reality, not the case. What the courts have chosen to call a mistake as to identity is, in fact, a mistake as to attributes. Despite this compelling reasoning, the distinction persists, and was relied on by Megaw LJ, sitting alongside Lord Denning in *Lewis* v *Averay*.

Treitel suggests a compromise, that where the attribute is used to identify a person, either as an individual or as being a member of a particular class of persons, then a mistake in this respect nullifies the contract. He adds two qualifications; first that an attribute as to credit-worthiness can never render a contract void, this is something which the parties must risk in the course of their dealings. Secondly, that the law makes certain presumptions as to identity, for example, that in a contract concluded by letter, the presumption is that it is the intention to contract with the writer of the letter. A further such presumption is considered under the next heading.

Mistake inter praesentes

Mistake as to identity is further complicated by the difficulty of fitting into the analysis a sukare face to face). Prima facie the offeror will be presumed to have intended to contract with the person in front of him. Thus, in *Phillips* v *Brooks* [1919] 2 KB 243, a man called North entered the plaintiff's shop and asked to see some jewellery, and selected some pearls and a ring, of total value £3,000. He wrote a cheque, saying as he did so, 'You see who I am. I am Sir George Bullough', a person known by reputation to the plaintiff, and gave an address which the plaintiff checked in a directory. The plaintiff allowed North to take the ring away, valued £450, and North pledged it with the defendants for £350, who took it bona fide and without notice of the fraud. When North's cheque was dishonoured, the plaintiff sought the return of the ring, claiming the contract was void. The issue was whether the plaintiff intended to sell the ring to the person present in the shop, or whether the offer was directed at Sir George Bullough only. It was held that the plaintiff's intention was the former; he may have thought his customer was Bullough, but the evidence did not bear out the argument that the offer was made to him alone.

The inference that the judge drew was that the parties intended to thus contract. Two cases have gone the other way.

In *Hardman* v *Booth* (1863) 1 H & C 803, the plaintiff went to the office of Thomas Gandell & Co, where a clerk by the name of Edward Gandell was employed, though Thomas Gandell was the sole owner of the firm. The clerk dishonestly persuaded the plaintiff that he was, in fact, a partner in the firm, and induced the plaintiff to send goods to Gandell & Co, being addressed to 'Edward Gandell & Co'. The clerk pledged the goods with the defendant as security for advances, and the plaintiff sued for their return. It was held that the plaintiff's offer related to the firm 'Thomas Gandell & Co' only, and the clerk, knowing this, could not purport to accept the offer for himself, and the contract was void.

In *Lake* v *Simmonds* [1927] AC 487, the appellant was a jeweller, and he had in the past made a number of small sales to a woman, Esme Ellison, who described herself as the wife of a wealthy customer, Van der Borgh. He permitted her to take away two extremely valuable necklaces 'on approval' to show to her 'husband'. She was, in fact, Van der Borgh's mistress, and she absconded with the jewelry. The appellant sought to claim for the loss on his insurance policy which excluded liability for jewelry 'entrusted to a customer', but covered theft. The question turned on whether there was a contract between the jeweller and Ellison, and the House of Lords held there was no contract; the jeweller intended to deal with the wife of Van der Borgh, and that was the reason he parted with the goods. This was held to be a mistake as to identity and not merely attributes. *Phillips* v *Brooks Ltd* was distinguished on the ground that the sale had been concluded before North made his claim to be Bullough, the effect of which had been to affect the mode of payment the jeweller was prepared to accept and to induce him to let North take the ring away. It should be stated that although this is an arguable interpretation of the facts, it was in no way at the heart of the decision of the case, and Horridge J did not rely on it. Further, in *Lake* v *Simmonds,* this line of reasoning was adopted by Viscount Haldane alone, and is not supported by the other speeches. The logical conclusion of the chain of thought is that if North had at the outset announced himself as Sir George Bullough, the contract would have been void because the jeweller intended to contract with Bullough only, as the jeweller in *Lake* was held to have intended to contract with the wife of Van der Borgh only.

Another case in which the apparent intention to contract with the person immediately present was rebutted is *Ingram* v *Little* [1961] 1 QB 31. The plaintiffs were three elderly ladies who advertised their car for sale. A rogue calling himself Hutchinson visited their home and agreed to purchase the car for £717. When he tried to make payment by cheque, they refused to accept it, and to persuade them otherwise he told them what he claimed to be his full name and address and of his local business interests. One of the plaintiffs checked his details in a telephone directory at the local post office, and found them apparently correct. As a result he was permitted to take the car away in return for his cheque, which was dishonoured. The defendant bought the car from him in a good faith. The majority of the Court of Appeal held the contract was void. Pearce LJ said that after the initial refusal to take a cheque, the parties became involved in a credit sale in which the identity of the purchaser was of the utmost importance, and that the plaintiffs were only prepared to sell after checking his name and address; they were said to attach importance to the individuality of Hutchinson of the given address, and his Lordship would not disagree with the trial judge's finding that the plaintiff's offer was capable of acceptance only by the true Hutchinson.

Devlin LJ dissenting said that the evidence merely showed that if the plaintiffs had known the truth about the rogue, they would not have contracted with him, something that is at the bottom of every contract voidable for fraud. Their mistake as to his identity did not matter; even if he had been Hutchinson, this was no guarantee that his cheque would have been met. It was as to his creditworthiness that they were mistaken, and this was not a fact at the basis of the contract, but only a belief that each contracting party has that the other will honour his promise.

Lewis v *Averay* [1972] 1 QB 198 is at odds with the decision in *Ingram* v *Little*. The plaintiff advertised his car for sale and a rogue called round to see it and offered to buy it, claiming to be the actor 'Richard Greene'. He signed a cheque for £450 'R A Green' and asked to take the car away with him. The plaintiff asked for proof of his identity, and the rogue showed him an admission pass to Pinewood Studios in the name of 'Richard A Green'. The plaintiff, in consequence, allowed him to take the car. The cheque was dishonoured and the defendant purchased it bona fide for £200. The Court of Appeal held that the contract with the rogue was voidable only, that the plaintiff had failed to show that he did not intend to contract with the person actually present.

Lord Denning MR endorsed the judgments in *King's Norton Metal* and *Phillips* v *Brooks* and said:

> 'When two parties have come to a contract – or rather what appears, on the face of it, to be a contract – the fact that one party is mistaken as to the identity of the other does not mean that there is no contract, or that the contract is a nullity and void from the beginning. It only means that the contract is voidable, that is, liable to be set aside at the instance of the mistaken person, so long as he does so before third parties have in good faith acquired rights under it.'

The other two members of the court were less sweeping in their judgments, though nonetheless critical of the decision in *Ingram* v *Little*. Phillimore LJ thought it turned on its 'very special and unusual facts', and Megaw LJ held that, in both cases, the mistake was simply as to attributes, namely the rogue's creditworthiness, and that identity was not a matter of vital importance.

In the light of this decision, it is probably correct to say the presumption against holding a contract void where it is concluded inter praesentes, is very strong indeed, and the facts would have to be very special (more so than in *Ingram* v *Little*) to rebut it. A possible formulation is suggested in a note in (1972) 88 LQR 161; that the test ought to depend on an analysis of the terms of the agreement between the parties, and that where they meet face to face it is not usual to regard their identity as a vital term of the contract, but that a different conclusion will be reached if the seller has made it clear that the purchaser's identity is an essential point. It is suggested that this is a fair resolution of the authorities as they stand at present.

Lord Denning's view in *Lewis* v *Averay* found support in the Twelfth Report of the Law Reform Committee (1966) Cmnd 2958, which recommended that where goods are sold under a mistake as to the buyer's identity, the contract should, so far as third parties are concerned, be voidable not void. This also suggests that the members of the Committee thought that this can only be established by legislative enactment and is not as yet, despite his Lordships' judgment, part of the English law of contract.

The Committee also considered the suggestion of Devlin LJ in *Ingram* v *Little* that the courts should be given a power to apportion in such cases. The importance of such a concept will be readily appreciated. The authorities concern, almost universally, the problem as to who should suffer the loss caused by a rogue's fraudulent activities, the original vendor seeking to re-establish title to the goods by proving the contract was void, or the third party who has acquired the goods from the rogue, bona fide for value without notice of the fraud? Devlin LJ suggests that the:

> '... loss should be divided between them in such proportion as is just in all the circumstances. If it be pure misfortune, the loss should be borne equally; if the fault or imprudence of either party has caused or contributed to the loss, it should be borne by that party in the whole or in the greater part.'

The Committee considered that such a power would be undesirable, because it would create uncertainty in an area of the law where certainty and clarity are particularly important, that it would be likely to increase litigation; and it would make it difficult for businessmen to obtain reliable legal advice or assess the likely financial outcome of their dealings and insure against the risks involved. In particular, the Committee highlighted the practical and procedural difficulties where there were more than two persons involved, that is, where there was a string of innocent purchasers.

An innocent third party might face the gravest problems in showing that the vendor was negligent; after all, that was a transaction to which he was not a party and about which he knows nothing. Also, the Committee disagreed with Devlin LJ regarding the position when the original vendor is not at fault, and was unable to see why, if he has a right in law to retain title to his chattel, he should be penalised, although his behaviour has fallen below the required standard.

It is not clear if the Committee was correct in fearing an increase in litigation and complications in apportionment. It may be that in the majority of cases it would simply be a matter of apportioning between seller and third party, and that usually there is no entangling chain of purchasers. Additionally, the view that it would make life difficult for businessmen is also arguable; Devlin LJ was probably contemplating private sales, which are where real injustices do arise. It seems unlikely that the power of apportionment would be an intolerable extra burden on businessmen. It might finally be said that although such a discretionary power would create a degree of uncertainty, it cannot be stated with confidence that the law is as clear and as certain as the Committee seems to think it is.

In the cases considered above, in all but *King's Norton Metal Co*, the offeror has contemplated making a contract with a clearly identifiable third party, be he Brocklehurst, Sir George Bullough, or Richard Greene. It is suggested that it need not be the case that the third person need be alive, or even have ever existed. This was impliedly the view of Lord Haldane in *Lake* v *Simmonds* and, whatever the correctness of the decision, it seems that in principle providing A can show that he made an offer to B in the erroneous belief that he was making an offer to C (whether or not C existed), then if B knew or reasonably ought to have known this, the contract would be void. *King's Norton* would be distinguished on the grounds that the contract was made with the author of the letter and as such was not an identifiable third party; it was the party with whom the seller had been corresponding, albeit fraudulently masquerading under another name.

It must be conceded, however, that the judge was of the opinion that an independent third party, that is, Hallam & Co would have had to exist in order to avoid the contract, and it would follow that a belief in a non-existent third party would not avail the seller. Bearing in mind the Court's increasing reluctance to permit the plea of mistake at common law, although the proposition that the third party need not, in fact, exist may be based on sound legal reasoning, it might not meet with approval when argued.

A further refinement to this hypothesis is where A makes an offer to B in the belief that B is not B (but otherwise does not entertain any belief as to his identity). Goodhart (1941) 57 LQR 228 has illustrated that such a case is fundamentally different to the one where A believes that B is C. Generally in the postulated case, the offer has been made to B, and whether or not he is aware that A would not have made the offer had he known B's identity, he may accept it, although it may be voidable at the suit of A. The contract will only be void ab initio if A proves an express or implied term in the contract, either that B is not B, or else that the offer is not one capable of acceptance by B. In such a case, there would be a mistake as to the terms of the contract known to B which would avoid the contract. See *Smith* v *Hughes*, *Hartog* v *Colin & Shields* (above). Thus in *Said* v *Butt* [1920] 3 KB 497, the plaintiff, a theatre critic knowing that the manager of a theatre would refuse to sell a ticket to him, employed a third party to buy on his behalf. The court held that, because he knew the theatre would not contract with him, he could not, by using an agent, cause the theatre to so contract against their knowledge and contrary to their express refusal. It is rare that such a term is ever expressly incorporated into a contract, and the job of the courts is, therefore, to consider where such a term may properly be implied into the contract.

In *Sowler* v *Potter* [1940] 1 KB 271, in May 1938, the defendant was convicted under the name of Ann Robinson of permitting disorderly conduct in a café. In July she began calling herself Ann Potter, and obtained from the plaintiff the lease of certain property in that name. The agent who conducted the negotiations over the lease with the defendant for the plaintiff said in evidence that he knew of the record of Ann Robinson, and had he known that the two were one and the same, he would not have completed the contract. Accordingly, the plaintiff alleged that the lease was void. The judge concluded that the agent thought he was entering into a contract with someone other than Ann Robinson, and said that in the grant of a lease, as between landlord and tenant, the consideration of identity was a vital element in the contract, and that the plaintiff's mistake rendered it void ab initio.

This case has been criticised – Goodhart (1941) 57 LQR 228 and judicially by Lord Denning MR in *Solle* v *Butcher* and *Lewis* v *Averay* – and is probably no longer to be regarded as good law. *King's Norton Metal Co* was apparently not cited to Tucker J in *Sowler* v *Potter*, and that case is authority that it is not enough that had the seller known the true facts about the buyer, he would not have entered into the contract, his motive for contracting is in this respect not relevant. It cannot be reasonably argued that at the time the lease was granted, it was uppermost in the agent's mind that the lessee should not be Ann Robinson and, therefore, no term could be implied into the offer that Ann Robinson was excluded from it and the contract would be voidable only. The case is really on all fours with *King's Norton Metal Co*, which has subsequently been affirmed, and must be the preferred authority.

The rule that a contract will only be void where A contracts with B thinking B is some identifiable third party, C, was criticised by Wilson in (1954) 17 MLR 515, who argues that the third party approach is only a useful guide for proving mistake, and that in any given situation what is important is that A should show an absence of an intention to contract with B. The example is given that if A refuses to deal with B, and B therefore disguises himself as C, the contract is void because A will be held to have intended to deal with C, whereas if B merely conceals his own identity, the contract is not void, there being no identifiable third party. This is said to be artificial, and is a conclusion only reached because of self-imposed limitations on the doctrine of mistake. Wilson suggests the question to be posed is: Did A intend to contract with B, with whom he has apparently entered into legal relations? and not 'With whom did A intend to contract?' Thus the case where A intends to contract with C is merely illustrative of an intention not to contract with B, and ought not to be the central point around which the law revolves. He relies on the writings of the French jurist Pothier, who said that where the consideration of the person with whom a party is willing to contract enters as an element into the contract, an error in this respect destroys consent and annuls the contract.

The contrary view, first cogently set out by Goodhart at (1941) 57 LQR 228 (above), is put in reply by Unger in (1955) 18 MLR 259. He argues, first, that Wilson's approach would have the effect of extending the doctrine of mistake at common law, and that it should be the policy of the law to uphold contracts rather than destroy them. Secondly, he says that Wilson's thesis, laying emphasis as it does on the alleged logical inconsistency of the third party approach, completely ignores the fact that even where there is no third party, the contract is still voidable and the full range of equitable remedies is available, at the court's discretion, to do justice between the parties, and that any inconsistency there may be is of little consequence. Thirdly, and perhaps least convincingly, he says that the third party approach goes hand in hand with the identity/attributes distinction considered above. In view of the criticism this distinction has attracted, this point must be taken with care.

The importance of third party purchasers for value in the mistake cases previously discussed has already been considered. The final point for inquiry in this section is whether it is possible for a third party to intervene and allege that a contract is void for mistake where the contracting parties themselves choose not to do so. The issue has not yet been considered by the English courts, but was raised in the New Zealand case: *Fawcett* v *Saint Merat* [1959] NZLR 952.

The plaintiff advertised her car for sale and the defendant, accompanied by a

Mrs D, made an offer to purchase it, which was accepted. The plaintiff gave the defendant possession of the car and of the certificate of registration in return for a post-dated cheque, which was subsequently dishonoured. Judgment in default was obtained against the defendant but never satisfied. In the meantime, Mrs D, representing that she was the plaintiff, sold the car to the claimant company, and the plaintiff sought to satisfy the judgment by issuing a writ of sale under which the car was seized from the company by the sheriff. As the plaintiff had obtained judgment, it was not open to her to argue that the original contract between her and the defendant was voidable, because by suing on it she had affirmed it. To succeed she therefore had to show that the sale between Mrs D and the claimant company was void and that no title passed. Hardie Boys J held, following *Phillips* v *Brooks* and distinguishing *Hardman* v *Booth*, that the company had intended to contract with the person present, identified by sound and hearing, that is, Mrs D; the offer was not made to the plaintiff only. Secondly, he held that the plaintiff was not allowed to raise 'in the name of one of the contracting parties' the question of mistake as to identity so as to have the contract avoided, relying on an absence of any authority that such an action 'would lie'. Guest (1960) 76 LQR 207 argues that where a contract is void at common law, it is void ab initio, and that therefore the plaintiff is not raising the invalidity 'in the name of one of the contracting parties', but is asserting it on his own behalf. Further, *Lake* v *Simmonds* allowed an insurer to argue that the appellant jeweller had made a valid contract with a third party. His conclusion is that a third party has locus standi to intervene, but that here the plaintiff should be estopped from so doing because by her conduct in parting with the car registration certificate and accepting a post-dated cheque in return, she had armed the defendant with the appearance of being the owner of the car.

Some such restriction would be necessary, or the doctrine would appear to have some very odd results, for example, if the defendant in *Boulton* v *Jones* had accepted the goods from the plaintiff, would it be open to a third party to allege that the contract was void and that the property never passed? It may be that the courts would look to see if the third party had some legitimate interest for intervening, and only permit it in such circumstances.

Some cases concerning mistaken identity are more complex. Because the fraud involved in the case below took some considerable ingenuity to set up, the parties might be said to be inter praesentes, or not, depending on the exact stage at which one considers the mistake as to identity to have occurred.

In *Citibank NA* v *Brown Shipley & Co Ltd*; *Midland Bank* v *Brown Shipley & Co Ltd* [1991] 2 All ER 690, in several separate transactions involving different banks a person claiming to be a signatory of a company's account at one bank (the issuing bank) telephoned another bank (the receiving bank) with a request to buy substantial amounts of foreign currency, payment to be made by a bankers' draft issued by the issuing bank. The caller then telephoned the issuing bank, instructing them to prepare this bankers' draft to be drawn on the company's account. This the issuing company did: they handed the draft over to a messenger who purported to be from the company, in exchange for a letter that purported to confirm the telephone instructions, with forged signatures. The draft was then paid to the receiving bank, who after checking that the draft was genuinely issued by the issuing bank and had been issued in the ordinary course of business, paid the cash to the fraudster. In due course the receiving bank presented the draft to, and were paid by, the issuing bank. When the fraud was finally discovered the issuing bank brought an action against the receiving bank to recover the value of the draft on the basis that title in the draft had never passed to the receiving bank, as it could not derive good title from the fraudster, and the banks did not have a contract between them. The court decided that it was irrelevant that the delivery of the bankers' draft from the issuing bank to the receiving bank with the authority of the issuing bank established a voidable contract between the two banks.

The fact that the issuing bank had mistakenly dealt with a fraudster instead of the company with whom they thought they were dealing did not affect the formation of the contract between the two banks; admittedly the fraudster, because of mistaken identity had no title, but he was merely a 'conduit'. Title did not have to pass from the fraudster to the receiving bank. Of the two innocent parties, the issuing bank must bear the loss.

Mistake at common law – an appraisal of the different views

It will be appreciated from what has already gone before that explaining mistake at common law poses many problems. Some writers have concluded that these problems are not simply concerned with the interpretation of cases, but with the more fundamental point that, in fact, on consideration it is the case that authorities treated as being concerned with mistake are, in fact, not authority for this at all, and as Slade says at (1954) 70 LQR 405 the whole thing is a 'myth'. Some of these arguments will now be considered.

Cheshire and Fifoot (1944) 60 LQR 175, and *Law of Contract*, argue that, since *Bell* v *Lever Bros*, mutual mistake will now only operate where the mistaken assumption is that the very subject matter of the contract is in existence, and that the wide language of the speeches suggesting that any false and fundamental assumption will suffice is not borne out by the decision in the case. The argument is that if, in Lord Atkin's words, 'the new state of facts makes the contract something different in kind from the contract in the original state of facts' renders the contract void, then if this test was not satisfied in *Bell* v *Lever Bros*, it will hardly ever be. The conclusion is that if the subject matter has ceased to exist, then there is nothing on which a binding contract can operate, and the parties have thus attempted the impossible. The reply is that, first, their Lordships in their speeches explained why the contract in *Bell* was not different in kind under the newly discovered facts, namely, that it was still possible of performance entirely in the way the parties had envisaged it at the outset. Regarding non-existent subject matter, it is suggested that the learned editors fail to appreciate both the correctness and the importance of the decision in *McRae*.

A forceful attack on the traditional doctrine of mistake at common law is to be found in the judgments of Lord Denning, and in the writings of Atiyah and Slade. Thus in *Solle* v *Butcher*, Denning LJ (as he then was) said:

> 'All previous decisions on this subject must now be read in the light of *Bell* v *Lever Bros*. The correct interpretation of that case, to my mind, is that once a contract has been made, that is to say, once the parties, whatever their inmost states of mind, have to all outward appearances agreed with sufficient certainty in the same terms on the same subject matter, then the contract is good unless and until it is set aside for failure of some condition on which the existence of the contract depends, or for fraud, or on some equitable ground. Neither party can rely on his own mistake to say it was a nullity from the beginning, no matter that it was a mistake which to his mind was fundamental, and no matter that the other party knew that he was under a mistake. A fortiori if the other party did not know of the mistake, but shared it.'

And he reiterated this view in *Magee* v *Pennine Insurance Co Ltd* [1969] 2 QB 507.

Atiyah (1975) 73 LQR 340, and Atiyah and Bennion (1961) 24 MLR 421, argue for the implied term theory considered under 'Mistake as to the existence of the subject matter' above, that is that the risk of the facts on the basis of which the buyer and seller concluded their agreement not being correct will normally lie on either one or the other, and that only if there is an implied condition precedent that the contract will be inoperative if the facts are not as they are believed to be, are the parties discharged from their obligations.

Slade (1954) 70 LQR 405 adopts a similar stance, and starts from the proposition that a mistake as such may be a ground for affording a party some relief in equity, but in itself is irrelevant at law. A contract is void at law only if there is an implied term as referred to above, or if offer and acceptance are found on a true interpretation to be divergent. He divides the cases into three categories.

1. Where one party is unaware of the other's true intention.
2. Where one party is aware of the other's true intention.
3. Where the parties contract under the same mistaken assumption.

Where one party is unaware of the other's true intention

This is simply a question of whether one party has accepted the other's offer on the terms in which one party could enforce in court; if so, there is a contract. Because of the objective approach to offer and acceptance, a party is, in effect, estopped from denying the existence of a contract where his mistake is self-induced. The corollary of this is that the parties are not bound where the offer and acceptance are ambiguous. The general rule, therefore, is that if offer and acceptance are in identical terms, judging objectively, there is a contract.

Where one party is aware of the other's true intention

Here the approach is subjective; the promisor is not bound to fulfil a promise in a sense in which the promisee knew at the time of the promise he did not intend it. Thus in *Hartog* v *Colin & Shields*, there was no consensus as to terms.

Where the parties contract under the same mistaken assumption

Under this heading, Slade argues the implied term theory, and cites *Pope & Pearson* v *Buenos Aires New Gas Co* (1892) 8 TLR 758 per Lindley LJ: 'the defendants might have succeeded if they could have proved that it was an implied condition of the contract that it was not to be binding unless the information ... was correct', and Lord Atkin in *Bell* v *Lever Bros*: 'the proposition does not amount to more than this, that if the contract expressly or impliedly contains a term that a particular assumption is a condition of the contract, the contract is avoided if the assumption is not true.'

He further argues that because it must be the presumed intention of both the parties, it is almost impossible to imply such a term regarding the quality of the subject matter, and that is why the contract in *Leaf* v *International Galleries* was not void. The conclusion is, therefore, that it is the Court's task to discover what are the terms, express or implied, of the offer and acceptance.

As statements of the law, (1) and (2) are almost unarguable, and it is really a matter of classification whether such matters should be treated as ones of 'mistake' or of offer and acceptance. It is sufficient for present purposes that examiners treat them as separate topics falling within mistake.

The real difficulty arises under (3). There is a danger of relying too much on extracts from *Bell*, the judgments of which are not obviously clear as is desirable. The proposition Lord Atkin refers to is immediately qualified by the statement that it does not take the Court very far in its inquiry in ascertaining whether a contract contains such a term, and his Lordship warns against constructing for the parties contracts which they have not in terms made, by importing implications which would appear to make the contract more businesslike and more fast. It is suggested that the general approach of the majority in *Bell* is that there is scope for an independent doctrine of mistake. Grunfield (1952) 15 MLR 297 argues that in the judgments of neither Lord Atkin nor Lord Thankerton is there to be found the severe curtailment of the function of the common law of contractual mistake, which is the primary feature of Lord Denning's restatement of the law in *Solle* v *Butcher* and subsequent cases. This, it is submitted, is correct; what the court was trying to do in *Bell* was to define the circumstances in which the doctrine operated, not to deny its very existence, and the judgments proceeded on the basis that certain types of mistake will avoid a contract. The conclusion that may tentatively be drawn is that the doctrine operates, where on the true construction of the contract, it is apparent that it was never the intention of the parties that the contract should apply to the newly discovered situation. Some support may be derived from an article by Wade 7 CLJ 341, one of the few writers to support the decision in *Bell* v *Lever*

Bros. He argues that the correct approach following that case is as follows: that the subject matter of the contract consists of all the points that are contained within the contract as agreed by the parties, and those points which are outside it go at most to motive and are irrelevant in mistake. If the parties intend their agreement to depend for its validity on any one fact, they must state this in the contract, that is, the distinction is between what they ask for and the test, which is, did each party get what he bargained for? If either did not, as the result of a common error between the parties, then there must have been a mistake within the terms of the contract. This was not the case in *Bell*, where respondents did get what they bargained for; it was simply a bad bargain. Therefore, if it is possible for the agreement to be executed exactly according to its terms, there is a valid contract and no mistake. This is, in a sense the reverse of the implied term theory, in which the parties must have made provision for the contract to be inoperative for mistake, whereas in the suggested approach, the contract does not operate because the parties have not made provision for these unexpected facts. The jurisprudential difference is fundamental; the end result may be much the same, because in either case the court is considering the application of the terms of the contract. Depending on which view is adopted, the matter is initially considered from opposite ends but, by a course of construction, the two may well strike common ground in the middle.

In this context the decision of the Court of Appeal in *Great Peace Shipping Ltd* v *Tsavliris Salvage (International) Ltd, The Great Peace* [2002] 4 All ER 689 is highly significant. While taking a cargo of iron ore from Brazil to China, the Cape Providence suffered serious structural damage in the South Indian Ocean. The appellants offered and had accepted their salvage services on standard terms. On finding that it would take five or six days for a tug to reach the Cape Providence, and since there was serious concern for the safety of the crew, through brokers the appellants sought a merchant vessel in the vicinity of the Cape Providence. The brokers were told, by a respected source, that the respondents' vessel, the Great Peace, was about 12 hours (35 miles) away and they agreed with the respondents that it would go to the rescue, again on standard terms. In fact, the Great Peace was 39 hours (410 miles) away from the Cape Providence and, by chance, another vessel, the Nordfarer, passed by and provided the necessary assistance. The appellants contracted directly with the Nordfarer's owners for these services and instructed the brokers to cancel the contract with the respondents. The respondents claimed damages for breach of contract, a claim which the appellants resisted on the ground of common mistake or, alternatively, that the facts had given rise to a right to rescind the contract in equity. Their Lordships concluded that the respondents would succeed since the mistake as to the distance between the two vessels had not rendered the services that the respondents' vessel was in a position to provide something essentially different from those which the parties had agreed. Lord Phillips MR said:

'... what we are here concerned with is an allegation of a common mistaken assumption of fact which renders the service that will be provided if the contract is performed in accordance with its terms something different from the performance that the parties contemplated. This is the type of mistake which fell to be considered in *Bell* v *Lever Bros Ltd* [1932] AC 161. We shall describe it as "common mistake", although it is often alternatively described as "mutual mistake". ... We agree ... that, on the facts of the present case, the issue in relation to common mistake turns on the question of whether the mistake as to the distance apart of the two vessels had the effect that the services that the Great Peace was in a position to provide were something essentially different from that to which the parties had agreed. ... The appellants would have wished the contract to be performed but for the adventitious arrival on the scene of a vessel prepared to perform the same services. The fact that the vessels were further apart than both parties had appreciated did not mean that it was impossible to perform the contractual adventure. The parties entered into a binding contract for the hire of the Great Peace. That contract gave the appellants an express right to cancel the contract subject to the obligation to pay the "cancellation fee" of five days hire. When they engaged the Nordfarer they cancelled the Great Peace. They became liable in consequence to pay the cancellation fee. There is no injustice in this result.'

At first instance Toulson J held that equity neither gave a party a right to rescind a contract on grounds of common mistake nor conferred on the court a discretion to set aside a contract on such grounds: *Solle* v *Butcher* [1950] 1 KB 671 had been wrongly decided. The Court of Appeal shared this view. The Master of the Rolls said:

'In this case we have heard full argument, which has provided what we believe has been the first opportunity in this Court for a full and mature consideration of the relation between *Bell* v *Lever Bros Ltd* and *Solle* v *Butcher*. In the light of that consideration we can see no way that *Solle* v *Butcher* can stand with *Bell* v *Lever Bross Ltd*.'

10.5 Non est factum

Where a person, by signing a document, enters into contractual relations with another party, it may be possible for him to avoid liability under the contract if he signed the document under a mistaken belief as to the essential nature of the document, by raising the plea 'non est factum', namely, that 'it is not my deed'. This is an exception to the general rule that a person who signs a document is bound by it, whether or not he reads it or understands it, and was originally applicable where the mistaken party was unable to read the document owing to illiteracy or blindness; further, it could also only be pleaded where the document was, in fact, a deed. The plea has evolved through judicial decision such that now it applies to any written contract, and though some special circumstance must now attach to the mistaken party, it no longer needs to be inability to read.

The nature of the mistake

To define and delineate the nature of the mistake to which the plea may successfully be raised has proved difficult. The former approach was that the mistake must be as to the character of the document as opposed to its contents, and this was exemplified in *Howatson* v *Webb* [1907] 1 Ch 537 affirmed; [1908] 1 Ch 1.

The defendant was the trustee and nominee of land held for a solicitor, who induced the defendant to sign deeds which he believed were deeds of transfer. In fact, one of them was a mortgage to a third party as security for a loan, and the third party subsequently transferred the mortgage to the plaintiff. Warrington J held that the plea of non est factum failed because the defendant had been told that the documents were deeds relating to the property, and they did so relate, and his mind was therefore applied to dealing with the property, he was simply mistaken as to contents.

As a workable distinction, to differentiate between character and contents left much to be desired. It attracted criticism similar to that levelled against the substance/quality distinction in *Bell* v *Lever Bros*, and against the contrast between attributes and identity, *King's Norton Metal Co* v *Edridge Merrett & Co* and *Cundy* v *Lindsay* (above). In the case of non est factum, the unworkable rule was eventually rejected in the leading case in the House of Lords *Gallie* v *Lee* [1971] AC 1004 (*sub nom Saunders* v *Anglia Building Society*).

The plaintiff gave the deeds of her leasehold interest in the house in which she resided to her nephew, P, for him to raise money on its security providing that she could continue to reside there rent free until her death. She knew that a friend of P's, L, was helping him to arrange the loan, and L requested her to sign a document to this end. She had broken her spectacles and signed the document unread, though in reply to her inquiry she was told that it related to the gift by deed to her nephew. The document thus signed conveyed the house by sale to L, who did not pay the price, and subsequently mortgaged the house to a building society. The House of Lords, affirming the Court of Appeal, held that the object of the exercise was to raise money for the nephew, and that this would have been equally achieved by the alternative means envisaged by P and L, and would have been so achieved had L been honest, as by the plaintiff's original plan. Their Lordships rejected the test used in *Howatson* v *Webb*, and preferred to say, in the words of Lord Pearson, that it must be the case that the document was 'fundamentally different' or 'radically different' or 'totally different' to what the mistaken party believed it to be. Other terms employed by their Lordships were that the difference must be 'serious', 'essential' or 'very substantial'.

Undoubtedly, the new test is considerably more satisfactory than the character/contents approach. It now means, for example, that a mistake as to the size of a financial transaction – where an undertaking or guarantee is, in fact, for £10,000 rather than the £1,000 it is believed to be – could give rise to the plea. Formerly, it would have been excluded as being a mistake relating to contents only.

Equally, if the difference between £10,000 and £1,000 is fundamental, the borderline case of £1,000 to £5,000 or £2,000 cannot be answered with confidence. Nor is it clear whether the nature of the mistake should be considered in an objective or subjective sense – the difference between £10,000 and £1,000 might be fundamental to an improverished law lecturer, but not necessarily to a multi-millionaire. In the test's flexibility, is also its uncertainty, and it may be that the end result is not very different – where a mistake is fundamental or radical, it would not strain judicial reasoning too much to classify the difference as being one of character as opposed to contents. Nevertheless, *Gallie* v *Lee* is probably logically and academically a happier solution to the difficulty, so long as the degree of discretion that lies in the Court's hands is appreciated.

As examples of cases in which the plea succeeded, reference may be made to two cases which, although decided before *Gallie* v *Lee*, are correct on their facts, even if the reasoning thereto could not stand with the new propositions formulated by their Lordships.

In *Foster* v *Mackinnon* (1869) LR 4 CP 704, the defendant, an elderly gentleman, was induced to indorse a bill of exchange, having been told that it was merely a guarantee and not having seen the face of the bill. The bill was later indorsed to the plaintiff who sued on it. Byles J held it invalid:

'... not merely on the ground of fraud ... but on the ground that the mind of the signer did not accompany the signature; in other words, that he never intended to sign and therefore in contemplation of law never did sign the contract to which his name is appended'.

Likewise, in *Lewis* v *Clay* (1898) 67 LJQB 224, at the request of a third party, one N, the defendant signed in a number of cut-open spaces on otherwise concealed documents, believing he was witnessing N's signature. In reality, he had signed promissory notes in favour of the plaintiff worth approximately £11,000. The plea succeeded on the grounds that promissory notes were altogether different to merely attesting a formal signature. See *Lloyds Bank* v *Waterhouse* (1991) 10 Tr LR 161.

Who may plead non est factum?

From originating as a plea to protect the illiterate, it appeared at one time as if the doctrine had been sufficiently extended such as to make it available to all persons. In *Gallie* v *Lee*, the House of Lords sought to disabuse lawyers of this idea. Lord Pearson said that the plea was open to persons who, for some permanent or temporary reason (not limited to blindness or illiteracy), are incapable of both reading and sufficiently understanding the deed or other document to be signed, that is, that such persons must be unable to understand to the extent that they are unable to detect a fundamental difference between the actual document, and the document as the signer had believed it to be. Lord Reid spoke of persons unable to understand the purport of a particular document, whether due to defective education, illness, or innate incapacity, and Lord Wilberforce included senile persons. It is apparent that normally a literate person of full understanding and capacity will be unable to plead non est factum.

Note that non est factum may not be used by a party who, having granted a power of attorney to another, finds that the power of attorney has been abused; or, the power having not been properly allocated, is used by a person who is incompetent. In *Norwich & Peterborough Building Society* v *Steed* [1992] 3 WLR 669, a power of attorney was granted to his mother by the defendant. She never properly understood the concept of power of attorney and was tricked into signing the necessary documents for the sale of the defendant's house at a very low price. The plea of non est factum could not be used by the defendant.

Negligence

Surprisingly, the effect of the signer's negligence was in considerable doubt until *Gallie* v *Lee*. One might have presumed that in view of the special nature of the plea, it was essential for the signer to show that he had not contributed to his mistake by failing to take reasonable care. However, prior to *Gallie* v *Lee*, the authoritative decision was that of the Court of Appeal in *Carlisle & Cumberland Banking Co* v *Bragg* [1911] 1 KB 489, in which it was held that negligence did not prevent a party from raising the plea, except in the special case of negotiable instruments where an indorser or an acceptor owes a duty to every subsequent bona fide holder for value. The Court clearly had tortious principles in mind in coming to the decision, and held that the plaintiff's loss was not caused by the signer's negligence, but by the fraud of a third party who had induced the defendant to sign a document without reading it. In *Gallie* v *Lee*, the House of Lords said that the tortious concept of a duty of care to one's neighbour had no relevance here, and it was simply a question of whether the signer had acted reasonably or carelessly in signing the document. Lord Wilberforce said that the signer has the responsibility of the normal man of prudence, and that the onus of proof lies on him to prove that he acted carefully. In considering this, the Court may pay particular attention to the nature of document signed and, in general, will consider all the circumstances of the case.

Mistake as to identity

The plea is not applicable where A signs a document believing it to be in favour of B whereas, in fact, it is in favour of C, thus it was that the plea failed in *Howatson* v *Webb* and *Gallie* v *Lee*. The rationale has been suggested as being that even if a party cannot understand a document, normally by reading it he would be able to discern to whom it is made out.

Ignorance

The essence of the plea is that there must be a mistake as to the essential nature of the document, thus to sign in complete ignorance of what is contained within does not permit the plea.

In *Gillman* v *Gillman* (1946) 174 LT 272, a wife signed a document in ignorance of its contents. In fact, it was a separation deed, and shortly afterwards her husband left her.

The court held that she was bound by the deed.

Nor is the plea applicable to documents signed in blank; it pertains only to documents that as and when signed impose some liability on the signer.

For a detailed analysis of *Gallie* v *Lee* see Stone (1972) 88 LQR 190.

Non est factum and undue influence

It may be useful to remember that although non est factum may not lie as a defence – at least against a third party – other defences may be available, for example, duress or undue influence (although the extent to which the latter can be of assistance may be limited). Undue influence was a defence, nevertheless, in *Avon Finance Co Ltd* v *Bridger* [1985] 2 All ER 281 CA: a son induced his elderly parents to sign a mortgage in favour of a moneylender as security for a loan to him. The parents were in the course, as they believed, of selling their house and not executing a mortgage.

The parents were held to be negligent in executing the mortgage deed and, therefore, could not rely upon non est factum as against the plaintiff. They could, however, rely on a defence of undue influence. The plaintiffs had sufficient notice of the circumstances to be bound by the equity.

10.6 Mistake in equity

In view of the uncertainties discussed above concerning the operation of mistake at common law, the courts are making increasing use of the special remedies available in equity that enable the court to do justice between the parties, whilst refraining from making the all or nothing decision on the validity of the contract which it must do at common law. In equity, the contract is not void ab initio, and the old rule was that equity will follow the law such that if the contract is valid at law, in general, the Court will not intervene. The scope of the new equitable jurisdiction that the courts have been claiming for themselves will be considered in the light of the three equitable remedies available, which are: specific performance; rectification of a written agreement; and rescission.

Specific performance

Where one party to a contract refuses to perform his part of the bargain, the other party may request the court to make an order for specific performance, which directs the party in breach to carry out the contract in accordance with its terms. The remedy is discretionary and the court will usually not order specific performance where damages would adequately compensate the injured party. In mistake in contract, although damages might fail to do this, the remedy will be refused, at the Court's discretion, where it would be inequitable to permit the plaintiff to enforce the contract on the terms in which it stands. Thus in *Webster* v *Cecil* (1861) 30 Beav 62, the defendant, having previously refused the plaintiff's offer of £2,000 for certain land which he had put up for sale, wrote to the plaintiff offering to sell the land for £1,250, which the plaintiff accepted. The defendant had intended to offer the land for £2,250 and, in the light of the previous dealings, the plaintiff must have known that the defendant had made a mistake. The contract was probably void at law, *Hartog* v *Colin and Shields* (above), but the plaintiff brought an action for specific performance. This was refused, and the plaintiff was left 'to bring such action at law as he might be advised'.

Specific performance may also be refused in the case of mutual mistake: *Grist* v *Bailey* [1967] Ch 532. The plaintiff agreed to buy a house, freehold, from the defendant, 'subject to the existing tenancy thereof'. Although the market value of the house with vacant possession was £2,250, the contract price was only £850 because both parties believed that the sitting tenant was protected by the Rent Acts. This was wrong and the tenant left the house shortly afterwards. Goff J, following *Solle* v *Butcher*, held the mistake did not make the contract a nullity at law, but that it was a mutual fundamental misapprehension which enabled the defendant to resist the action for specific performance. In addition, the defendant was granted rescission of the contract.

In the case of unilateral mistake, specific performance will be refused if the plaintiff had contributed, albeit innocently and unintentionally, to the defendant's mistake.

In *Denny* v *Hancock* (1870) LR 6 Ch App 1, intending to bid for a property being sold by auction, the defendant inspected a plan which showed the western side bounded by shrubs or trees. He located what he thought were the marked trees, bounded by an iron fence. In fact, these were not marked on the plan, and the real boundary was denoted by stumps, which were so covered by shrubs that they could not easily be seen. The Court of Appeal held that he had been misled by both the plan and the actual state of the grounds, and that his mistake was 'occasioned by at least crassa negligentia on the part of the vendor' and specific performance was refused.

The position is more difficult where the defendant's mistake is in no way attributable to the plaintiff's conduct, but is, nevertheless, a reasonable mistake to make in the circumstances. The following cases may be contrasted.

In *Malins* v *Freeman* (1837) 2 Keen 25, at a sale of land by auction, the defendant mistakenly thought that because lot 2, the property of the plaintiff, had been sold, lot 3 was the lot he wished to buy, that is, the land to be offered for sale after the plaintiff's land. In fact, lots 1–5 belonged to the plaintiff, and lot 3 was knocked down to the defendant. It was held that although the defendant was 'hurried and inconsiderate', he had never intended to enter into this contract, and it would be inequitable to compel him to perform it.

In *Tamplin* v *James* (1880) 15 Ch D 215, an inn and adjoining premises were being offered for sale by auction, and exhibited plans clearly showed that two plots of land at the rear were not included in the sale. The defendant purchased this property in the belief that the lot did include the additional two plots, and sought to resist an action for specific performance. Baggallay LJ said:

'But where there has been no misrepresentation and where there is no ambiguity in the terms of the contract, the defendant cannot be allowed to evade the performance of it by the simple statement that he has made a mistake'.

The cases are not easily reconciled because, in each, unlike *Denny* v *Hancock*, the fault lay with the purchaser, and it would be a futile exercise to attempt to define the degree of fault in each case, except that the standard of care must be that approved in *Tamplin* v *James* that if there was no reasonable ground for the defendant's mistake, specific performance should be ordered. One explanation of the cases is that even if the mistake is unreasonable, then the contract should not be enforced where it would cause hardship to the defendant, and that in *Malins* v *Freeman* the defendant would have been forced to complete the purchase of an entirely different piece of land to the one he intended to buy, whereas in *Tamplin* v *James* the difference was arguably peripheral. The solution is a neat one, though it leaves a degree of uncertainty in predicting which way a court will decide. As the relief sought is discretionary, this is to a certain extent inevitable, and one must confine oneself to saying that particular cases will turn on their particular facts. This conclusion is reinforced by the judgment at first instance in *Van Praagh* v *Everidge* [1903] 1 Ch 434.

At a sale of land by auction, the order of sale was clearly displayed on a notice affixed to the auctioneer's rostrum and was also given on a number of distributed handbills. The defendant bid for and had knocked down to him a property other than the one he wished to purchase. It was held that the mistake was entirely due to his own fault, and the plaintiff could succeed in an action for specific performance.

Rectification

The remedy of rectification is available where by a mistake a written document does not accord with the true agreement between the parties. In these circumstances, the court has the equitable power to rectify the agreement so as to bring it into line with the true agreement. The mistake is not in the agreement, but in the way it has been written down: *Mackenzie* v *Coulson* (1869) LR 8 Eq 368 'Courts of Equity do not rectify contracts; they may and do rectify instruments purporting to have been made in pursuance of the terms of the contracts' per James VC.

As with specific performance, the remedy is discretionary, and to obtain rectification, three conditions must be satisfied.

1. There must be no other suitable alternative remedy. That which is omitted from the instrument may be enforceable as a collateral contract; a voluntary rectification will suffice, although unlike a decree it is not retrospective and may be less advantageous; or the matter may be solved by construction of the agreement, and in reported cases omitted words have been read into an agreement; words incorrectly included have been ignored; and '£1,000' has been read as '£100', *Elliott* v *Freeman* (1863) 7 LT 715. In these instances, rectification is unnecessary.

2. There must be very weighty evidence to establish the mistake. The burden of proof is on the party seeking rectification, though the standard is not that of the criminal trial (beyond reasonable doubt), *Joscelyne* v *Nissen* [1970] 2 QB 86 (see below). It must, therefore, be possible to adduce evidence of what the parties intended prior to the execution of the document; if their dealings were on an uncertain basis, the document will be treated as the best evidence of their intentions, and an action for rectification will be unlikely to succeed.

3. There must be a mistake common to all parties. This is the most important condition and may be sub-divided into three categories.

   First, the parties must have come to an agreement, though this need not be in itself an enforceable contract; it is sufficient that the parties have agreed certain common terms that will be included in their agreement, and to this end the court will usually look for some outward expression of accord.

   Secondly, it must be shown that it was the parties' continuing and unchanged intention that the common term be included in the written agreement up to the time of its execution.

   In *Joscelyne* v *Nissen* [1970] 2 QB 86, the plaintiff shared a house with the defendant, his daughter, and it was orally agreed that she should take over his car-hire business and, in return, he would continue to reside in the house, but she would pay all the household expenses, including the cost of gas, coal and electricity. The subsequent written agreement failed to incorporate this term, and after paying these bills for some time, she then refused to do so on the grounds that she was not bound so to do under the written contract. The father sought to have the contract rectified. The court held that the agreement that she should make such payments had continued up until the time of the execution of the document, and it should be rectified accordingly.

   Thirdly, the written document must clearly fail to represent the agreement.

   In *Frederick Rose (London) Ltd* v *William Pim & Co Ltd* [1953] 2 QB 450, the plaintiff company received from their Egyptian house an order for 'Moroccan horsebeans described here as feveroles'. Not being familiar with 'feveroles', they consulted the defendants who explained that it was merely another term for horsebeans. The parties concluded an oral contract for the sale of horsebeans in Egypt. It was discovered that horsebeans were not 'feveroles' as the Egyptian house had requested, and the plaintiffs sought to rectify the contract to include the word feveroles in order that they could then claim for damages for breach of contract. The Court of Appeal refused the application because there was no disparity between the oral and the written agreements. Both had referred to horsebeans which had duly been delivered. The mistake of the parties lay in failing to apprehend that horsebeans and feveroles were different commodities.

In *Craddock Brothers Ltd* v *Hunt* [1923] 2 Ch 136, the plaintiffs orally agreed to sell to the defendants a house, excluding an adjacent yard. In the subsequent written agreement, the yard was included, and in the deed of conveyance the whole of the property was transferred to the defendants. The plaintiff was held entitled to rectification of both the written agreement and the conveyance.

An interesting example of the court's exercise of its discretion to permit rectification was in *Re Slocock's Will Trusts* [1979] 1 All ER 358. The plaintiffs were beneficiaries under a will, and in order to administer the proceeds of sale of land held on trust for them, a management company was formed and nominal shareholdings taken out. The first plaintiff wished to surrender her share of the money to the second and third plaintiffs in order to reduce or avoid tax. By a solicitor's mistake, the executed deed transferred only her shares in the management company and not her beneficial interest in the proceeds of sale. The plaintiff sought rectification to give effect to their common intention. Graham J granted the application and held that the parties were entitled to legitimately arrange their affairs in order to avoid paying tax, and it was not a ground to refuse to exercise the discretion to rectify because the Crown would be deprived of revenue.

Rectification is granted in only exceptional cases where the mistake is unilateral, because such a mistake normally fails to reflect the intentions of only one of the parties to the agreement, and the issue is likely to be whether or not the parties ever agreed that the alleged term should be incorporated in the contract. Rectification may be granted in cases involving fraud and misrepresentation, and estopped where one party knows of the mistake in the document, but fails to correct it. He will be estopped from resisting rectification on the grounds that the mistake is unilateral.

In *Agip SpA* v *Navigazione Alta Italia SpA* [1984] 1 Lloyd's Rep 353, the Court of Appeal insisted that rectification can only be ordered in a case of unilateral mistake where the other party has actual knowledge of the mistake.

The Court of Appeal in *Commission for the New Towns* v *Cooper (Great Britain) Ltd* [1995] 2 WLR 677, recently reaffirmed the rule that rectification may be awarded in cases of unilateral mistake if the other party has deliberately induced that mistake by fraudulent misrepresentation or some other form of deliberate deception. Quite clearly in such cases the need to achieve justice between the parties overrides the condition that there must be a mistake common to all parties.

Rescission

Of the three equitable remedies, rescission is the most controversial in operation for two reasons. First, it is said that the Courts are rescinding contracts which are valid at common law, and that in the absence of, for example, misrepresentation or fraud, the parties should be bound by their bargains and left to pursue their remedies at common law, if any. Secondly, rescission is often granted on certain terms, and this is said to be exercise of a power not justified by authority. To consider these views, rescission as it has evolved through the cases must be considered. It should also be borne in mind that rescission operates to set a transaction aside, and to put the parties in the position they were in prior to the contract.

Unilateral mistake

Similar considerations apply here to those discussed above concerning the refusal of specific performance for unilateral mistake, that there must be some vitiating element in the transaction that would make it inequitable to refuse to permit a party to rescind, because the other is in some way guilty of misrepresentation, negligence or unfair dealing.

In *Torrance* v *Bolton* (1872) LR 8 Ch App 118, property was being offered for sale by auction, and in the advertisement for the sale was described as an 'absolute freehold reversion'. It was only revealed by the auctioneer at the time of sale that it was, in fact, subject to three mortgages. The plaintiff was deaf and did not hear the announcement, and he bid for the property on the faith of the advertisement and it was sold to him. The sale was rescinded because the buyer was clearly under a misapprehension induced by the seller, and Lord Denning has said that the court held that it 'had power to set aside the contract whenever it was of opinion that it was unconscionable for the other party to avail himself of the legal advantage which he had obtained'.

The case could, perhaps, have been decided in misrepresentation, but the wide language of the judgments indicated that this 'advantage' need not affect the validity of the contract.

As a general rule, equity will not allow a person who has simply entered into a bad bargain to escape from it on the ground of mistake: *Clarion Ltd* v *National Provident Institution* [2000] 2 All ER 265.

Mutual mistake

Cooper v *Phibbs* (above). It will be recalled that the appellant agreed to take the lease of a fishery from the respondents to which, in fact, he was already entitled. The contract was set aside in equity. In *Bell*, Lord Atkin thought it was void at law, but in *Solle* v *Butcher* Denning LJ agreed with the decision and said the mistake as to title did not render the lease a nullity, it was liable to be set aside on such terms as the Court thought just. The terms were that the respondents should have a lien on the fishery to the amount which they had spent in improving it. The equitable doctrine was expressed as follows: 'If the parties contract under a mutual mistake and misapprehension as to their relative and respective rights, the result is, that the agreement is liable to be set aside as having proceeded upon a common mistake.'

The case is regarded as the starting point of two related ideas: first, that where a contract is not void for mistake at common law, it may be set aside in equity if the mistake is, nevertheless, fundamental; secondly, that in thus setting aside, the Court may impose such terms as seem to it to be just.

The first principle was adopted in *Huddersfield Banking Co Ltd* v *Henry Lister & Son Ltd* [1895] 2 Ch 273. The defendant company went into liquidation and the plaintiffs, as mortgagees of the company's mills and fixtures therein, claimed to be entitled to the looms in the mills. If the looms were not fixtures, they would have had no claim on them, and the looms would pass to the liquidator. Upon inspection of the premises by both parties, it was agreed that the looms were not attached to the mills and were, therefore, not fixtures, and the plaintiffs agreed to a consent order for their sale. It later became known that the looms had been attached to the mills when the mortgage was executed, and they had been wrongfully loosened by a third party. The bank sought to have the consent order set aside for common and mutual mistake, and the court held, following *Cooper* v *Phibbs*, that the agreement was concluded on the basis of a common mistake as to a material fact, and it had the jurisdiction to set the order aside.

The importance of the court's power of rescission, if these two cases are correct, is considerable: it allows valid contracts to be set aside in equity. How would this apply to the facts of *Bell* v *Lever Bros*? The matter was raised in a case turning on remarkably similar facts: *Magee* v *Pennine Insurance Co Ltd* [1969] 2 QB 507.

The plaintiff purchased a motor car for his son to drive, and on his insurance proposal form, mistakenly, but innocently, stated that he, the plaintiff, held a licence. The defendants accepted the proposal and later the car was seriously damaged in an accident. The two sides came to an agreed settlement regarding the damage, but the defendants subsequently discovered the plaintiff's incorrect statement on the proposal form, which would enable them to repudiate liability. On the authority of *Bell* v *Lever Bros* and *Solle* v *Butcher*, the majority of the Court of Appeal held the contract was not void at law, but that there was a common mistake which was fundamental to the whole agreement. Lord Denning side-stepped the factual similarities, simply saying that *Bell* had given 'enough trouble ... already'. Winn LJ, dissenting, said that although there was a misapprehension as to rights there was no misapprehension as to the subject matter of the contract, and the case fell within the ratio decidendi of *Bell* v *Lever Bros*.

In a note at (1969) 85 LQR 454, it is argued that *Magee* on its facts cannot be properly distinguished from *Bell* – in both there was an assumption that the contract comprised was valid and enforceable. The appropriate test advocated in such cases is: is there an express or implied term in the compromise that the contract is valid and enforceable and, if there is not, the agreement will be effective whatever the mistake as in *Bell*. What is important is to concentrate on the interpretation of the terms of the promisor's promise.

This argument is similar to the implied term theory regarding non-existent goods, that is, that it approaches the problem from the point of view of the allocation of risk; which of the parties undertook to bear the possibility that the common assumption was false?

The difficulty is that frequently they have not addressed their minds to the issue at all, and an order to find such an implied term would usually involve a degree of judicial creativity normally eschewed in the field of contract.

It may also be noted that an important factual distinction is that in *Bell*, the money had actually been paid over, in *Magee*, the plaintiff was suing the insurance company for the agreed sum. No reference is made to this in *Magee*, but it may be common sense to treat payment over of the money in such cases as discharging all obligations and liabilities once and for all.

Putting the defendant to his election

This has been described as equitable election, and has arisen where a plaintiff has been seeking rectification on the ground of unilateral mistake. As was noted above, rectification is usually only avalable in a case of mutual mistake; there is, however, a line of cases holding that in certain circumstances where a plaintiff seeks rectification and the mistake is not mutual, the defendant is given the choice to either submit or to have the contract rescinded.

In *Garrard* v *Frankel* (1862) 30 Beav 445, the parties were negotiating over the lease of some property, based on a rent of about £230 pa. When the lease was executed, the figure was incorrectly written in by the plaintiff as £130. It was held that the defendant must have been aware of the mistake, and should not be permitted to take advantage of it, and he was put to his election of rectification or rescission.

In *Paget* v *Marshall* (1884) 28 Ch D 255, the plaintiff offered to let a block of houses to the defendant, and mistakenly failed to exclude from his offer the first floor of one of the houses, which he had intended to keep for his own use. On the plaintiff's action for rectification 'the defendant was put to his election'. The court made no finding of fraud on the part of the defendant, but was of the opinion that he was aware of the mistake.

The problem with these decisions is that they appear to offer two illogical and irreconcilable alternatives: on the one hand if the parties were never ad idem, the contract ought to be rescinded, and might even be void at law; and if they did agree, then either the document records that agreement or it must be rectified. The cases were approved in *Solle* v *Butcher* by Denning LJ, and have been said to exemplify the flexible use of equitable remedies to achieve justice between the parties, and the effect is to put the parties back in their original position prior to the conclusion of the contract.

Their standing is now in grave doubt following *Riverlate Properties Ltd* v *Paul* [1975] Ch 133. The defendant leased a maisonette from the plaintiff, who intended that the former should be liable for half of the cost of exterior and structural repairs. In the lease liability rested entirely on the plaintiff, who, as a result, sued for rectification or, alternatively, rescission. The action was dismissed by the Court of Appeal, which held that there was no power to grant such relief in the case of unilateral mistake where it has neither been caused by the other party, nor was the other party aware of it.

Russell LJ said that to do so would be to venture into the field of moral philosophy, if it considered setting aside a good bargain because one party had made a miscalculation or other mistake, or because one party had obtained the goods at a bargain price. *Garrard* and *Paget* were said to turn on the fact that in both the defendant was aware of the plaintiff's mistake and was trying to take advantage of it. As such, the court still has the power to intervene, though apparently now only with a view to rectification, and it has no jurisdiction to offer rescission as an alternative. To this extent, *Garrard* and *Paget* must be taken to be disapproved and overruled. The decision in *Riverlate Properties* has effectively stopped optimistic plaintiffs from trying to withdraw from unfavourable transactions in the absence of any other mitigating factors. (For a note on this case see (1974) 90 LQR 439.)

Whether *Riverlate* represents the start of a reversal or at least a halting of the line of authority conferring on the courts a wide power to intervene in equity on the ground of mistake remains to be seen. Before this case, it could be stated with confidence that the courts were developing new equitable tools. The first recent authority was *Solle* v *Butcher* (above).

It will be recalled that the parties erroneously believed a house was no longer rent controlled, and let it at a higher than permitted rent, and when the plaintiff sought to recover the rent overpaid, the defendant counterclaimed that the lease was void and should be rescinded. The court held that the parties were under a common mistake of fact in believing that the flat was no longer rent controlled, and that the plaintiff should, on rescission of the lease, be permitted either to accept it or to take a new lease at the rent originally agreed which it was not permissible for the landlord to recover.

Denning LJ relied heavily on *Cooper* v *Phibbs* and *Huddersfield Banking Co Ltd*, and said those cases were in no way impaired by *Bell* v *Lever Bros* which, if it had been considered on equitable grounds, might have been decided differently. His Lordship was clearly thinking of rescission for mutual mistake as to a fundamental fact. The judgment depends on accepting that *Bell* either as a matter of law, or anyway in reality, has laid down that a contract will not be void at law for mistake (see discussion of this above), and that mistake is now only relevant in equity. Mistakes said to make a contract voidable were described as follows:

1. unilateral mistake: where there has been a material misrepresentation, whether or not it is fraudulent or fundamental; or where one party knowing the other is

mistaken about the terms of an offer or the identity of the person by whom it is made, lets him remain under his delusion and concludes the contract on that basis;

2. mutual mistake: where the parties are under a common misapprehension, either as to facts or as to their relative and respective rights, provided that the misapprehension was fundamental and that the party seeking to set it aside was not himself at fault.

One might also add a caveat that it should be inequitable to allow the party contending there is a valid contract to insist on his strict contractual rights.

Regarding the question of fault under (2), Goff J in *Grist* v *Bailey* said that the point was not entirely clear, and that it must denote some degree of blameworthiness beyond the mere fault of having made a mistake: 'question is, how much, or in what way?'. The matter was considered in *Laurence* v *Lexcourt Holdings Ltd* [1978] 2 All ER 810.

In 1971, the plaintiff obtained permission to use the ground and part of the first floors of a property it owned for offices. In 1974, they offered to let the first and second floors of the property as offices to the defendants for 15 years, completely forgetting that the planning permission did not cover the whole building. The defendants assumed permission did exist, accepted the offer and took possession immediately without making any of the usual searches or enquiries. When the defendants learned of the true facts, they immediately vacated the building. The plaintiffs sued for specific performance, and the defendants counterclaimed for rescission on the grounds of, inter alia, common mistake. Deputy Judge Dillon QC held, following *Solle* v *Butcher* and *Grist* v *Bailey*, the mistake was fundamental, and that although the defendants were imprudent in proceeding without checking on the planning permission, they did not owe a duty of care to the plaintiff's forgetfulness or mistake, they were therefore not disentitled from relying on the mistake.

This new doctrine of equity thus appears well established, and it seems that in practice where there is an element of fundamental mistake in a contract, that a party is now more likely to obtain a remedy in equity than at common law. The criticisms that have been levelled against the doctrine have been principally that it has developed on the basis of tenuous authority, and that as a matter of strict law (or rather equity) it is unsupportable. Slade, at (1954) 70 LQR 385, has argued that equity may intervene in the following circumstances only.

1. If one party is unaware of the other's true intention, for example, on the seller's version of the events in *Smith* v *Hughes*, then rescission may only be granted if there is misrepresentation or fraud, though it may at its discretion refuse to order specific performance.

2. If one party is aware of the other's true intentions, then if the contract is not void and there is not misrepresentation, the court grants rescission. Denning LJ in *Solle* v *Butcher* thought that where one party knew the other was mistaken as to the terms of the offer, an action for rescission would lie but, as Slade points

out, such a contract is void at law, *Smith* v *Hughes*, and although Denning LJ considered nowadays that the contract would be set aside in equity, the line of authority is too firmly established to regard it without more as overruled. Slade also argues in the case of error in persona, that where the other party knows of the mistake, the contract would be voidable for misrepresentation, but if there was no representation, for exampe, the rogue never claimed to be anyone in particular, there would be no jurisdiction to grant rescission.

3. His strongest criticism is of Denning LJ's views on the position where the parties are under a common misapprehension. He argues that in *Cooper* v *Phibbs*, there was an active, albeit innocent misrepresentation that the would–be lessor had good title to the fishery, and that the rest of the judgment was therefore obiter dicta and, on a true reading of the case, Lord Westbury could not be said to have intended to lay down the wide rule that he is commonly held to have done. He also makes the point, considered in a note at (1950) 66 LQR 169, that the power the court exercised in relation to the parties' relative and respective rights was derived from the fact that the vendor had a valid lien for the amount he had spent on improving the fishery prior to the 'contract', and the court was, therefore, able to place terms on which it permitted the appellant to rescind. The conclusion is that *Cooper* can hardly be said to support the view that the court has the equitable power to set aside a valid lease because it considers that it would be unconscionable for the lessee to enforce it, or that it may impose terms on the parties when doing so. *Solle* v *Butcher*, Slade suggests, is wrongly decided on four counts.

a) There is no suggestion in *Cooper* that contracts not void at law may be set aside in equity.

b) That case is authority for setting aside void contracts.

c) The terms imposed in *Cooper* related to existing rights which would have been enforced independently.

d) *Bell* v *Lever Bros* was concerned with equity as well as the common law.

This last point is interesting in view of Denning LJ's suggestion in *Solle* that *Bell* might have been decided differently in equity. The action in Bell was, in fact, for the equitable remedy of rescission, and it is argued that the correct interpretation of the case is that as the contract was valid at common law, their lordships considered that no equitable relief could be sought in the absence of fraud, misrepresentation or the like.

Supporters of *Solle* v *Butcher* – and academically these are few and far between – argue that as the doctrine of mistake at common law is so narrow in operation (witness the almost total lack of recent authority), it is important that the courts should have a residuary discretion in order to impose a just solution where the exceptional case warrants it. It is conceded that this represents a radical extension of present (or in the light of recent cases) past principles, but this is justified principally on grounds of policy rather than authority. Bearing in mind *Riverlate Properties,* it may be that no precise limits can be drawn with respect to this new doctrine pending a possible pronouncement on it by the House of Lords.

Loss of the right to rescission
A party may lose the right to rescind in one of three ways.

By acquiescence. When a person has full knowledge of the facts giving him the right to rescind, and he elects to waive his right and affirm the contract, the right is lost forever. Mere possession of the knowledge is not itself acquiescence, but failure to act after acquiring it may be treated as evidence of an intention to waive the right.

Impossibility of restitutio in integrum. The contract is valid until set aside, and may be incapable of rescission where the parties cannot be restored to their original position. However, the rule is not strictly applied, and it is not necessary to restore the parties to their previous state in every detail.

When considering the 'right' to rescission it should be borne in mind that this is an equitable remedy and one which the courts may refuse to grant; not only should restitution be impossible to achieve, but also even if possible it would be inequitable to restore the parties to their original position. See *William Sindall plc* v *Cambridgeshire County Council* [1994] 1 WLR 1016. Here, land was purchased in early 1989 for development. Preliminary enquiries failed to discover a private foul sewer running just under the surface of the land in question. The main problem was that the land was steadily declining in value because of the recession. While accepting that there had been mistake (but not misrepresentation) the courts refused to grant rescission on the grounds that to do so would be inequitable. The land was now worth only half its value when purchased, and to order the defendants to return the purchase price and interest would be unfair in the circumstances.

Intervention of third parties. When the third party is a bona fide purchaser for value, the right is lost; it is not lost when he is a volunteer.

10.7 Common law and equity considered

Given that there is still such a thing as operative mistake at common law, one of the hardest things to define is precisely how this, and the doctrine of mistake in equity, operate side by side. Historically, common law and equity developed as separate jurisdictions, each having its own particular remedies, and neither relying on the other in coming to a decision. The two systems were fused by the Supreme Court of Judicature Act 1873, and with the remedies of both systems now available in one court, the decision in any given case has depended upon the nature of the action brought by the plaintiff. Thus in *Cundy* v *Lindsay*, *King's Norton Metal* and *Phillips* v *Brooks* the plaintiffs alleged the contract was void at common law, and the cases decided accordingly. The trend is now to plead mistake in equity; in *Laurence* v *Lexcourt Holdings* the common law was not mentioned and *Bell* v *Lever Bros* never cited. (It should be remembered that a party may not raise at trial matters that have not been pleaded.)

The present difficulty has arisen in the light of the robust view asserted by Denning LJ in *Solle* v *Butcher* and repeated in *Magee* v *Pennine Insurance* that contracts are no longer void for mistake at common law, except where the mistake has prevented the formation of any contract at all, and that mistake cases now fall to be decided in equity. However desirable such a solution may be, Grunfeld, at (1952) 15 MLR 297, had shown that Lord Denning's reasoning is based on an incorrect interpretation of the systems of law and equity before the 1873 Act. On the one hand, Lord Denning suggests that the Courts of Equity would take it for granted that a contract was valid at law, that there was a presupposition that this was the case. Grunfeld says there is virtually not a scintilla of authority to support this view; they approached the matter straightforwardly in equity, indifferent to the common law. Alternatively, his lordship suggests that the courts would first look to see if the contract was valid at law before applying equity, which Grunfeld says is based on a misreading of *Cooper* v *Phibbs*, and Grunfeld then argues for a complete substitution of equity for the common law. Subsequent cases have shown that this is what Lord Denning is doing in practice, even if his judgment in *Solle* allows some scope for common law mistake.

The contrary argument is that although since the Act of Fusion, where equity and common law conflict, the former prevails; mistake in contract is not an example of conflict, but of the complementary operation of law and equity, and that equitable remedies only become relevant once it is known the contract is valid at law. Thus in *Grist* v *Bailey*, where a house was sold at undervalue because the parties believed the sitting tenant was protected by statute, Goff J said:

'... the first question which arises is one of law, namely, what is the effect of common mistake? The leading case on this subject is *Bell* v *Lever Bros*. This is, of course, binding upon me and if exhaustive is really fatal to the defendant since it lays down very narrow limits within which mistake operates to avoid a contract.'

His Lordship held the contract valid at common law, and then applied the rules of equity derived from *Solle* v *Butcher*:

'Then I have to decide first, was there a common mistake in this case? Secondly, was it fundamental? And perhaps thirdly was the defendant at fault?'

The learned judge granted rescission in equity as a result of a fundamental common mistake.

It should be borne in mind, as Goff J said, that operative mistake at common law is now very restricted, and a mistaken party's best chance of success will be in equity. Common law will still be important in cases involving third party bona fide purchasers; the vendor's only hope of keeping title to his goods after being cheated out of them by a rogue, will be to show the contract was void at law, and that title never passed.

11

Duress and Undue Influence

11.1 Introduction

11.2 The common law doctrine of duress

11.3 The equitable rules of undue influence

11.4 The limited, and now suspect, principle of inequality of bargaining power

11.5 The protection afforded by certain statutory provisions

11.1 Introduction

We have examined, in earlier chapters, the situations in which a party may be afforded relief where he has been induced to enter into a contract by a misrepresentation, and the circumstances in which a contract may be void or voidable because a party has contracted on the basis of mistake.

We now turn to examine the situations in which the law gives relief to a person where the contract into which he has entered has been obtained by some form of improper pressure. It is important to emphasise at the outset that, for the law to intervene, the pressure must be 'improper'. People may be compelled to enter into unfavourable transactions by a number of factors: the demands of their own personal circumstances; the lack of an alternative source for the benefit they seek; or, more generally, the bargaining strength of the other party to the transaction. It would be contrary to all legal principle to permit a party to escape from the consequences of a transaction into which he has freely and voluntarily entered merely because of the restraints imposed upon him in the exercise of his freedom. However, there are situations in which the pressure is such that the victim of such pressure cannot be said to have acted freely and voluntarily. For certain forms of improper pressure, the law does afford the victim relief. The kinds of improper pressure that are recognised fall within the following categories.

1. The common law doctrine of duress.
2. The equitable rules of undue influence.
3. The limited, and now suspect, principle of inequality of bargaining power.
4. The protection afforded by certain statutory provisions.

We shall proceed to a consideration of each of these in turn.

11.2 The common law doctrine of duress

The origin of duress

The original common law of duress confined the doctrine within very narrow limits. Only duress to the person was recognised during the nineteenth century, and this required actual or threatened violence to the victim. Instances of duress to the person, in these terms, are rare in the present day. A modern example of such duress is *Barton* v *Armstrong* [1976] AC 104. A decision of the Privy Council, in which A threatened B with death if B's company did not pay a substantial sum of money to A. This is an important decision on the question of whether or not the victim would have entered into the contract but for the threat. This question provoked a difference of opinion both in the Court of Appeal of New South Wales and in the Privy Council. It will be considered further, below.

The nineteenth century limitation on duress meant that it could not be applied to 'duress of goods'. If a person, unlawfully detained, or threatened to detain, another's goods, this was not considered to be sufficient duress to enable a contract to be avoided. Note *Skeate* v *Beale* (1840) 11 Ad & El 983. There is a line of decisions to this effect in the nineteenth century.

However, while *Skeate* v *Beale* lays down the rule that a contract entered into in pursuance of a threat to retain goods cannot be thereby set aside, there is a wider restitutionary rule to the effect that money paid to obtain the release of goods wrongfully retained, or to avoid their seizure, may be recovered in an action for money had and received.

In *Maskell* v *Horner* [1915] 3 KB 106, tolls were levied on the plaintiff under a threat to seize goods and close down his business in a market. These tolls were, in fact, demanded with no right in law, and the Court of Appeal held the plaintiff entitled to recover the tolls paid, even though the payments had been made over a considerable period of time. Lord Reading CJ said:

> 'If a person pays money, which he is not bound to pay, under the compulsion of urgent and pressing necessity or of seizure ... he can recover it as money had and received.'

The distinction between the *Skeate* v *Beale* line of cases and the decision in *Maskell* v *Horner* is hard to follow, and it has been pointed out that the peculiar result would follow that although an agreement to pay money under duress of goods is enforceable, sums paid in pursuance of such an agreement by the coerced can be recovered in an action for money had and received.

A line of decisions prior to *Maskell* v *Horner* had upheld this wider restitutionary rule. It was said by Lord Denman CJ in *Skeate* v *Beale* that the distinction between that case, and the ones involving the application of the restitutionary rule, was that in the former the agreement had been entered into not compulsorily, but voluntarily. This was strongly criticised (though obiter) by Kerr J in *Occidental Worldwide Investment Corp* v *Skibs A/S Avanti (The Siboen and The Sibotre)* [1976] 1 Lloyd's Rep 293.

Kerr J said that *Skeate* v *Beale* would not justify a decision that:

'If I should be compelled to sign a lease or some other contract for a nominal but legally sufficient consideration under an imminent threat of having my house burnt down or a valuable picture slashed through without any threat of physical violence to anyone, I do not think that the law would uphold the agreement.'

This view was endorsed by Mocatta J in *North Ocean Shipping* v *Hyundai Construction (The Atlantic Baron)* [1979] QB 705. In the light of the modern developments of duress, it would seem that *Skeate* v *Beale* is no longer good law.

The effect of duress

Before discussion of the modern developments, it is necessary to examine the effect of duress. It is clear that if duress is established, it makes the contract voidable at the instance of the victim, not void.

This is emphasised because in some of the cases we shall be considering language is used in the judgments which might give the contrary impression. The use of the term 'to vitiate consent' (employed in *Pao On* – see below – and *The Siboen and The Sibotre*) suggests that duress destroys or negatives consent. If there were no consent, the contract would be void. However, it is clear from the tenor of the judgments being considered and, as Lord Scarman made explicit in *Universe Tankships* v *ITF* (below), the effect of operative duress is to make the contract voidable.

Duress in the modern law

A forerunner to the modern developments in contract was the decision in the law of torts by the House of Lords in *Rookes* v *Barnard* [1964] AC 1129, where the hitherto neglected tort of intimidation was revived and expanded in its application to trade union activities. Prior to this decision, it had been thought that the 'unlawful means', which is an essential ingredient of the tort, involved some form of physical violence. The concept of unlawful means was extended to include a threat of a breach of contract.

In *Morgan* v *Fry* [1968] 2 QB 710, Lord Denning MR defined the tort of intimidation as follows:

'The essential ingredients are these: there must be a threat by one person to use unlawful means (such as violence or a tort or a breach of contract) so as to compel another to obey his wishes and the person so threatened must comply with the demand rather than risk the threat being carried into execution. In such circumstances the person damnified by the compliance can sue for intimidation.'

In *D & C Builders* v *Rees* [1966] 2 QB 617 (which has been previously considered in connection with promissory estoppel), Lord Denning equated the undue pressure brought to bear on the plaintiffs with the tort of intimidation.

The relationship between duress and the tort of intimidation finds expression in the words of Lord Scarman in *Universe Tankships* v *ITF* [1982] 2 All ER 67, where his Lordship said that: 'duress, if proved, not only renders voidable a transaction into which a person has entered under its compulsion but is actionable as a tort, if it causes damage or loss'.

In recent times, the courts have extended the concept of duress from its earlier confines so as to recognise that certain forms of commercial pressure could amount to economic duress. The first modern case to make this clear was *The Siboen and The Sibotre*. At a time of recession in the shipping trade and a sharp fall in the market rates of hire of vessels, the charterers of two ships renegotiated the rates of hire, after a threat by them that they would go bankrupt and cease to trade if instalments under contracts of hire were not lowered. Since they also represented that they had no substantial assets, this would have left the owners with no effective legal remedy. It was especially coercive for the owners, who would have had to lay up the vessels and would then have been unable to meet mortgages and charges – a fact known by the charterers. The threats themselves were false in that there was no question of the charterers being bankrupted by high rates of hire.

Kerr J rejected the earlier confines of duress. But, he said, commercial pressure was not, in itself, enough to constitute duress. 'The court must', he said, 'be satisfied that the consent of the other party was overborne by compulsion so as to deprive him of any animus contrahendi.'

This would depend on the facts in each case. Kerr J considered that the owners would have been entitled to set aside the renegotiated rates on the ground of economic duress, but that on the present facts their will and consent had not been 'overborne' by what was ordinary commercial pressures.

In the subsequent case of *The Atlantic Baron* (above), Mocatta J confirmed that duress could take the form of economic duress. The facts were: under a ship construction contract, the building company demanded a 10 per cent increase in instalments from the owners largely because of a devaluation of the US dollar. The owners did pay the increased rate demanded from them, although they protested that there was no legal basis on which the demand could be made. The owners were commercially compelled to pay since, at the time of the threat, they were negotiating a very lucrative contract for the charter of the ship to be built. Mocatta J decided that this constituted economic duress. The illegitimate pressure exerted by the building company was their threat to break the construction contract. Where, accordingly, a threat to break a contract had led to a further contract, that contract, even though it was made for good consideration, was voidable by reason of economic duress. However, the right to have the contract set aside could be lost by affirmation. By their delay in taking any action, once they were free of the duress, the owners had affirmed the contract. Furthermore, the judge held the fact that it was not the owner's intention to affirm did not entitle them to avoid the contract if that intention had not been indicated to the building company.

The Privy Council had occasion to consider economic duress in *Pao On* v *Lau Yiu* [1980] AC 614, Lord Scarman read the judgment of the board. Their Lordships agreed with the observations of Kerr J in *The Siboen and The Sibotre* that in a contractual situation, commercial pressure is not enough. There must be present some factor 'which could be regarded as a coercion of his will so as to vitiate his consent'. The material factors to consider were, Lord Scarman said:

1. whether the person alleged to have been coerced did or did not protest;
2. whether at the time of the alleged coercion he did or did not have an adequate legal remedy;
3. whether he was independently legally advised; and
4. whether after entering into the contract he took steps to avoid it.

His Lordship drew attention to the decisions of American judges which stressed the *effectiveness* of the alternative legal remedy. Thus, it would appear, it is no answer to an allegation of duress that the victim had a legal remedy which, in due course, he could have pursued.

A further important development was in *Universe Tankships* v *ITF* (above). In this case, the ITF, a trade union, had 'blacked' one of the plaintiffs' (a Liberian company's) ships, The Universe Sentinel, in port for sailing under a flag of convenience, only releasing the ship on payment of a large sum of money, part paid to the union welfare fund. The shipowners succumbed, made the payment and then sought to recover it as having been made under economic duress. Most of the judgments of the House of Lords were concerned with the union's statutory defence under the Trade Union and Labour Relations Act 1974, but they did find that the payments could be recovered – the House of Lords not challenging the Court of Appeal's finding of economic duress.

Lord Diplock stated that the rationale of economic duress is:

'... that his apparent consent was induced by pressure exercised on him by that other party which the law does not regard as legitimate, with the consequence that the consent is treated in law as revocable unless approbated either expressly or by implication after the illegitimate pressure has ceased to operate on his mind'.

Lord Scarman dealt with the two elements in the wrong of duress: that is, pressure amounting to compulsion of the will of the victim; and the illegitimacy of the pressure exerted.

In his discussion of 'compulsion', Lord Scarman modified the approach previously adopted by Kerr J in *The Siboen* and by the Privy Council in *Pao On*. His Lordship said:

'Compulsion is variously described in the authorities as coercion or the vitiation of consent. The classic case of duress is, however, not the lack of will to submit but the victim's intentional submission arising from the realisation that there is no other practical choice open to him ... The absence of choice can be proved in various ways, eg by protest, by the absence of independent advice, or by a declaration of intention to go to law to recover the money paid or the property transferred ... But none of these evidential matters goes to the essence of duress. The victim's silence will not assist the bully, if the lack of any practicable choice but to submit is proved.'

In the present case, Lord Scarman observed:

> 'There was no protest at the time, but only a determination to do whatever was needed as rapidly as possible to release the ship.'

A significant feature of this judgment is its departure from the previously stringent requirement of *The Siboen* and *Pao On* that the victim's will and consent should have been 'overborne' by the pressure. This approach of Lord Scarman was cited and approved by the Court of Appeal in *B & S Contractors v Green* [1984] ICR 419

The decision in *Universe Tankships* also involves the clear rejection by the House of Lords of the contention on behalf of the defendants that a plea of duress requires the party guilty of the duress to realise that his victim is acting under it.

The concept of economic duress received further recognition in the recent case of *Atlas Express Ltd v Kafco (Importers and Distributors) Ltd* [1989] 1 All ER 641. Also, see *Vantage Navigation Corp v Suhail* [1989] 1 Lloyd's Rep 138.

While it adds little that is new to the doctrine of economic duress, the recent decision in *Dimskal Shipping Co SA v International Transport Workers' Federation (The Evia Luck)* [1991] 4 All ER 871 is a useful reminder of the fact that the pressure applied must be improper in the legal sense.

The Evia Luck was a ship owned by the plaintiffs, a Panamanian registered company whose vessels sailed under the Panamanian flag of convenience. The International Transport Workers Federation (ITF) had been conducting a long campaign against flags of convenience. While the ship was in harbour in Sweden, it was boarded by agents of ITF, who informed the master, and the owners, that the ship would be blacked and loading would not be continued until the company entered into certain agreements with ITF. These included payment of back pay to the Greek and Filipino crew, new contracts of employment at higher wages and guarantees for future payments. At first the owners would not agree and the ship was in fact blacked. Yielding to pressure, the company agreed to sign the various agreements, which were expressly declared to be governed by English law. The company incurred loses of some £100,000 or more, due to delays in loading and sailing, and having to pay backpay to the crew.

They sought a declaration that the agreements were void on the grounds of duress and claimed restitution of all sums paid under such void agreements.

The House of Lords in discussing what constituted economic duress, said the fact that ITF's conduct was quite legal in Sweden was irrelevant. In stipulating that the agreements were to be governed by English law, the defendants had to accept English law as the proper law of conduct. Under English law a contract obtained by duress was voidable, and improper economic pressure (blacking the ship) constituted one form of duress. The owners were thus entitled to avoid the agreements they entered into because of pressure from ITF.

Note that in this country it is the actual pressure in making the contract which must be improper. Unlike, for example, the USA, the courts make no distinction between substantive and procedural unfairness. Substantive unfairness (when the actual terms of the contract are heavily and unfairly balanced in favour of one party) is as much a ground in the USA for declaring a contract void for unfairness (economic duress) as procedural unfairness would be. However several authorities, notably Trietel, have pointed out that the concept may be acquiring some support in this country (see *Hart* v *O'Connor* [1985] 2 WLR 214).

Pressure

The initial point to be observed is that it is not necessary to show that the duress was the sole cause of the victim's entry into the transaction.

In *Barton* v *Armstrong* (above) a case, it will be recalled, concerning duress to the person, the Privy Council held that if A's threats were a contributory reason for B entering into the transaction, B was entitled to relief. Once the duress had been established, the onus was on A to show that it had no bearing on the making of the contract. The Court of Appeal of New South Wales, by a majority, had taken the contrary view, holding that the onus was on B to show that, but for the duress, he would not have entered into the contract. The Privy Council allowed the appeal against that decision.

The presence or absence of duress is illustrated by consideration of the facts in *Atlantic Baron*, *The Siboen* and *Pao On*. Duress having been established in the former case, but not in the latter two. In *Pao On*, there had been unanimity amongst the judges in the courts below that the party alleging duress had not been subject to coercion. They had formed the opinion that he had considered the matter, chosen to avoid litigation, and formed the opinion that the risk in entering into the transaction was more apparent than real. There was, in short, no coercion. The Privy Council was not disposed to take a different view, but even if it had been it would not have substituted its opinion for that of the judges below on a question of fact.

The illegitimacy of the pressure

Threats to commit unlawful acts

Prima facie the threat to commit an unlawful act would constitute illegitimate pressure. It is not certain, however, that all threats to commit a breach of contract would, of necessity, be so regarded. Changes in circumstances, short of frustration of the contract, may make it commercially impossible for a party to continue the performance of a contract on the terms originally concluded. Pressure brought to bear on the other party to renegotiate the terms might not be regarded as illegitimate. There is a US authority to this effect: *Goebel* v *Linn* (1882) 47 Mich 489. In *Pao On*, the pressure for a variation might be regarded as legitimate as it was necessary to remedy the inadequacy of the original transaction. Recently, in *Alf Vaughen & Co Ltd (In Receivership)* v *Royscot Trust plc* [1999] 1 All ER (Comm) 856, the Chancery Division stated that to amount to economic duress, there must be a threat to commit an unlawful act and only then will there be illegitimate pressure

– mere exercise of a bargaining right under a contract will not amount to duress or undue commercial pressure. Hence, the court in the instant case was convinced that the defendants were only exercising their contractual rights as owners.

Threats to commit a lawful act

For such threats to constitute duress can only be rare. It cannot, as a rule, be illegitimate for a person to threaten to do what he is lawfully entitled to do. If, however, it is coupled with a demand which is itself illegitimate, the pressure will assume the nature of the illegitimacy. Lord Scarman in *Universe Tankships* cites blackmail as an example.

In *Scolio Property* v *Cote* (1992) Supreme Court of Western Australia (unreported), after the auditors had been in, it was apparent that the defendant, an employee of the plaintiff company, had misappropriated large sums of money. Allegedly both parties signed a deed, in which the defendant promised to pay back the money missing. He defaulted and the plaintiff brought proceedings for that sum. Although the threat was undoubtedly made, it was quite legitimate to threaten to call the police in such cases and so it did not amount to duress.

Threats not to contract

As in 'Threats to commit a lawful act', a threat not to contract is usually no more than the exercise of a lawful right. There are, however, salvage cases where contracts for extortionate payments have been refused enforcement or set aside. See *The Rialto* [1891] P 175 and *The Crusader* [1907] P 196.

Note that the courts have recently, in *CTN Cash and Carry Ltd* v *Gallaher Ltd* [1994] 4 All ER 714, refused to extend duress to include the concept of 'lawful act' duress. In this case, under pressure, the plaintiffs paid a disputed invoice presented by the defendants. The pressure took the form of a threat to withdraw credit facilities – a right the defendants had, quite legitimately, reserved to themselves in the original agreement between them. The Court of Appeal, while recognising that the defendants' method of obtaining payment was 'unattractive', declared itself unwilling for policy reasons to extend the concept of duress. They refused to declare that the defendants had obtained payment of the disputed invoice by duress. See above, the relevance of *Alf Vaughen & Co Ltd (In Receivership)* v *Royscot Trust plc* [1999] 1 All ER (Comm) 856.

Threats to institute civil proceedings

Such threats can, again, rarely amount to illegitimate pressure. Apart from certain limited categories, there is no general tort of maliciously instituting civil proceedings. See *Metall und Rohstoff AG* v *Donaldson Lutkin & Jenrette Inc* [1989] 3 All ER 14 at p51.

Warnings

At common law it was once thought necessary to distinguish a threat from a warning. See *Biffin* v *Bignall* (1862) 7 H & N 877 and *Cumming* v *Ince* (1847) 11 QB 112. Chitty (25th edn para 495) suggests that this distinction is untenable in modern law.

Remedies for duress

As has been previously submitted, it is now clear that the effect of duress is to make the contract voidable, not void. The injured party will, therefore, be entitled to have the contract set aside for operative duress, unless he has expressly or impliedly affirmed it (see above).

As duress has been equated with the tort of intimidation (see the judgments of Lord Denning MR in *D & C Builders* and Lord Scarman in *Universe Tankships*), it would follow that a remedy for damages would lie in tort. (For the measure of damages for the tort of intimidation, see *Rookes* v *Barnard*, above.) There is, as yet, no authority on the question of whether or not an injured party who has affirmed the contract may nevertheless recover damages in tort. Chitty (para 501) has the view that damages should be recoverable, since otherwise a party who has lost the right to avoid the contract is left without a remedy for a clearly unlawful act.

11.3 The equitable rules of undue influence

Undue influence is an equitable doctrine. It must be kept distinct from the common law concept of duress. The equitable rules developed in consequence of the originally narrow confines of the common law.

The basis of the equitable doctrine was explained in *Allcard* v *Skinner* (1887) 36 Ch D 145 where Cotton LJ said:

'First, where the Court has been satisfied that the gift was the result of influence expressly used by the donee for the purpose; second, where the relations between the donor and donee have at or shortly before the execution of the gift been such as to raise a presumption that the donee had influence over the donor. In such a case the Court sets aside the voluntary gift, unless it is proved that in fact the gift was a spontaneous act of the donor acting under circumstances which enabled him to exercise an independent will and which justified the Court in holding that the gift was the result of a free exercise of the donor's will. The first class of cases may be considered as depending on the principle that no one shall be allowed to retain any benefit arising from his own fraud or wrongful act. In the second class of cases the Court interferes, not on the ground that any wrongful act has in fact been committed by the donee, but on the ground of public policy, and to prevent the relations which existed between the parties and the influence arising therefrom being abused.'

This passage requires elucidation in the light of Lord Scarman's speech in *National Westminster Bank* v *Morgan* (below). First, although the transactions in question were gifts in *Allcard* v *Skinner*, Cotton LJ did not exclude the applicability of his observations to other transactions. Secondly, the presumption of undue influence only arises where the transaction is one of manifest disadvantage to the party conferring the benefit. Thirdly, the principle involved is not one of vague public policy, but the prevention of victimisation of one party by another.

It is necessary to examine, therefore, (1) express influence; and (2) influence presumed from the special relationship between the parties.

Express influence

In this category, the onus of proving that the gift or contract was the result of improper pressure is on the party seeking to avoid the transaction. An example is *Williams* v *Bayley* (1866) LR 1 HL 200, where a promise to pay money was set aside because it was obtained by a threat to prosecute the promisor's son.

Influence presumed from a special relationship

A transaction can be set aside in equity where undue influence is presumed from the relationship between the parties. The presumption can be rebutted (see below), the onus is on the party receiving the benefit to show that it was not obtained by undue influence. See *Powell* v *Powell* [1900] 1 Ch 243.

These are relationships where undue influence is presumed.

1. Parent and child – *Wright* v *Vanderplank* (1855) 2 K & J 1.
2. Solicitor and client – *Wright* v *Carter* [1903] 1 Ch 27.
3. Doctor and patient – *Mitchell* v *Homfray* (1881) 8 QBD 587.
4. Trustee and beneficiary – *Ellis* v *Barker* (1871) LR 7 Ch App 104.
5. Religious adviser and disciple – *Roche* v *Sherrington* [1982] 1 WLR 599.

The presumption does not apply between husband and wife. See *Bank of Montreal* v *Stuart* [1911] AC 120, *Kings North Trust* v *Bell* [1986] 1 WLR 119 CA and *Midland Bank* v *Shephard* [1988] 3 All ER 17.

A presumption of undue influence might arise, even though the parties were husband and wife, in particular circumstances of dependency coupled with mutual trust. See *Simpson* v *Simpson* (1988) The Times 11 June.

In the case of master and servant, a recent decision, *Mathew* v *Bobbins* (1980) 256 EG 603, has held that servants are not today dominated by their masters, and as a result of modern employment legislation, there is no longer any presumption of undue influence.

There have been a number of reported cases in this area of the law since the mid 1970s. We shall consider, first, the decisions of the Court of Appeal and the House of Lords respectively in *Lloyds Bank* v *Bundy* [1975] QB 326 CA and *National Westminster Bank* v *Morgan* [1985] 1 All ER 821 HL.

What is critical in the application of the equitable doctrine is the nature of the transaction. This principle is not a new one, but has been re-emphasised by Lord

Scarman in *Morgan*. His Lordship referred to the judgment of Lindley LJ in *Allcard* v *Skinner*, where Lindley LJ had said:

'Where a gift is made to a person standing in a confidential relation to the donor the Court will not set aside the gift of a small amount simply on the ground that the donor has no independent advice. In such a case, some proof of the exercise of the influence of the donee must be given. The mere existence of such influence is not enough in such a case; ... But if the gift is so large as not to be reasonably accounted for on the ground of friendship, relationship, charity or other ordinary motives on which ordinary men act, the burden is upon the donee to support the gift.'

Lord Scarman also referred to a passage in the judgment of Lord Shaw in *Poosathurai* v *Kannappa Chettiar* (1919) 47 Ind App 1, which is apparently not elsewhere reported and which he (Lord Scarman) regarded as of critical importance:

'It must be established that the person in a position of domination has used that position to obtain unfair advantage for himself, and so as to cause injury to the person relying upon his authority or aid. Where the relation of influence, as above set forth, has been established, and the second thing is also made clear, namely that the bargain is with the "influencer" and in itself unconscionable, then the person in a position to use his dominating power has the burden thrown upon him, and it is a heavy burden, of establishing affirmatively that no domination was practised so as to bring about the transaction, but that the grantor of the deed was scrupulously kept separately advised in the independence of a free agent.'

As Lord Scarman observes, the doctrine applies not only to transactions of gift. A commercial relationship can become one in which one party assumes a role of dominating influence over the other.

Sir Eric Sachs in *Bundy* held that there were no finite categories of the special relationship. Such relationship, he said, tended to arise where someone relied on the guidance or advice of another, where the other was aware of that reliance and where the person on whom reliance is placed obtains a benefit from the transaction. This must be read subject to the requirement that the transaction was wrongful in itself as set out in the quotations given above.

It is necessary at this juncture to examine the facts in the two cases under discussion. In *Lloyds Bank* v *Bundy*, a guarantee was given to the bank by an elderly farmer, a customer of the bank, for his son's indebtedness. The guarantee was secured by a mortgage of Bundy's house in favour of the bank. It was held that as Bundy was liable to be influenced by the bank, which was obtaining a benefit, there was a duty on the bank to ensure that Bundy formed an independent judgment on the transaction. This duty the bank had failed to discharge. The obligation undertaken by Bundy was an onerous one; he had mortgaged his house to the hilt and it did not appear that his son's financial circumstances were likely to improve.

Sir Eric Sachs made it clear that, in ordinary circumstances, a bank does not incur the duty consequent upon a special relationship where it obtains a guarantee from a customer. But he said that:

'... once ... it is possible for a bank to be under that duty, it is, as in the present case, simply a question for "meticulous examination" of the particular facts to see whether that duty has arisen. On the special facts here it did arise and it has been broken.'

In *National Westminster Bank* v *Morgan,* the husband and wife owned a home jointly. The husband was unable to meet his mortgage commitments and made refinancing arrangements with the bank secured by a mortgage in favour of the bank over the matrimonial home. The bank manager called at the home to get the wife to execute the charge. She did not wish the charge to cover her husband's business liabilities. The bank manager assured her, in good faith but incorrectly, that it did not. It was, in fact, unlimited in extent and could, therefore, extend to all the husband's liabilities to the bank, though it was the bank's intention to confine it to the amount needed to refinance the mortgage. The wife had not received independent legal advice before executing the mortgage. The husband and wife fell into arrears with their payments, and the bank obtained an order for possession of the home. Shortly afterwards, the husband died without owing the bank any indebtedness for business advances. The wife contended that she had executed the mortgage because of undue influence and that it should be set aside. Lord Scarman made the only speech and his findings may be summarised as follows.

1. A transaction would not be set aside on the grounds of undue influence unless it could be shown that it was manifestly disadvantageous to the party alleged to be influenced.
2. The basic principle was not a vague public policy, but the prevention of victimisation of one party by another. On this point, Lord Scarman, with whose speech all their Lordships concurred, referred to the 'public policy' principle formulated by Cotton LJ in *Allcard* v *Skinner* (above). He stressed that it would be an error in applying the principle to ignore the requirement that the transaction was itself wrongful.
3. The transaction in the instant case was not unfair to the wife.
4. Although the doctrine of undue influence could extend to commercial transactions, including those between banker and customer, it could not be maintained on the present facts that the relationship was one in which the banker had a dominating influence.
5. The bank, therefore, was not under a duty to ensure that the wife had independent advice.

Note that in *Bank of Credit and Commerce International SA* v *Aboody and Another* [1989] 2 WLR 759, the Court of Appeal in disallowing an appeal by a wife alleging undue influence, held that there was no manifest disadvantage to the wife; and there was a strong probability the wife would have entered the transaction anyway.

The issue of whether a wife could set aside a bank's charge on the grounds of undue influence was again considered by the court in *Dunbar Bank plc* v *Nadeem and Another* [1998] 3 All ER 876. It was held that so long as the wife is able to prove that that the bank held constructive notice of the undue influence of the husband, she would be entitled to set aside the charge against the bank.

The court emphasised that, for the presumption of undue influence to arise, the parties relationship must be one based on trust, so as to be described as one of fiduciary. Furthermore, in *Mahoney* v *Purnell and Others (Baldwin and Another, Third Parties)* [1996] 3 All ER 61, the court held that where such a relationship was abused, the courts may use its inherent powers to award fair compensation in equity to the plaintiff.

Lord Scarman's use of the expression 'dominating influence' was the subject of much scrutiny by the Court of Appeal in the recent case of *Goldsworthy* v *Brickell* [1987] 1 All ER 853.

The Court held that in order for the presumption to arise that a transaction had been procured by the undue influence of one person over another, there had to be a relationship wherein the latter had ceded such a degree of trust or confidence to the former that the former was in a position to influence the latter into effecting the transaction. But it was not necessary to show that the person in whom the trust and confidence had been placed had assumed a dominating influence over the other. The Court thought that the decision of the Privy Council in *Poosathurai* v *Kannappa Chettiar* (above), which was much relied on by Lord Scarman, was not an accurate statement of English law on undue influence.

Nourse LJ referred to a number of leading cases, in particular, *Tufton* v *Sperni* [1952] 2 TLR 516, from which it clearly appeared that the presumption arose from a relation of trust and confidence, well short of domination. Nourse LJ doubted that the House of Lords in *Morgan* intended to the contrary, but if they did his Lordship respectfully disagreed with them, and observed that such holding was not necessary to the decision in that case. His Lordship added that it was to his mind inconceivable that the House of Lords intended, sub silentio, to overrule *Tufton* v *Sperni* and many other leading cases.

Parker LJ held the view that Lord Scarman had used the expression 'dominating influence' merely as a convenient means of describing a relationship in which one party was in a position to exercise influence over the other.

For Sir John Megaw it was beyond belief that the House of Lords could have intended to change the law by defining undue influence by reference to the words 'domination' or 'dominating'.

The Court of Appeal reiterated that the presumption of undue influence did not arise unless the transaction in question was manifestly and unfairly disadvantageous to the person alleged to be influenced. See also *Cornish* v *Midland Bank* [1985] 3 All ER 513 and *Woodstead Finance* v *Petrou* (1986) 136 NLJ 188.

Where a creditor entrusts the task of obtaining the signature of a debtor to an agreement to a person whom the creditor knows is in a position to influence the debtor, the transaction is liable to be set aside. See *Avon Finance* v *Bridger* [1985] 2 All ER 281 and *Kings North Trust* v *Bell* (above). In the absence of such knowledge, the creditor will not be tainted by the undue influence. See *Coldunell* v *Gallon*

[1986] QB 1184, *Midland Bank* v *Perry* [1988] 1 FLR 161 and *Bank of Baroda* v *Shah* [1988] 3 All ER 24.

As to knowledge, including constructive knowledge, of undue influence on the debtor, see the recent cases of *Barclays Bank* v *O'Brien* [1993] 3 WLR 786 and *CIBC Mortgages plc* v *Pitt* [1993] 3 WLR 802. Both these cases concerned constructive knowledge (or what might be deemed to be so) on the part of creditors. In relation to the equitable rules of undue influence, the Court of Appeal recently, in the cases of *Banco Exterior Internacional SA* v *Thomas and Another* [1997] 1 All ER 46 and *Barclays Bank plc* v *Thomson* [1997] 4 All ER 816, held that where the bank had discharged its primary duty in advising the spouse of a borrower to seek independent legal advice, then any undue influence exercised upon that spouse cannot be imputed to the bank by way of constructive notice. In both these cases the wives were claiming that there was constructive notice of the undue influence on the bank's part. The Court of Appeal in both cases rejected this argument.

Conversely, in *Barclays Bank plc* v *Boulter and Another* [1997] 2 All ER 1002, the Court of Appeal held that the burden of proof was on the bank to plead and prove that it did not have constructive notice of the misrepresentation. If the bank is unable to discharge this burden, then liability follows. In this case the wife successfully argued that the bank had constructive notice of the undue influence and misrepresentation exercised on her by the husband.

Rebutting the presumption

As has been indicated, where the presumption of undue influence arises it can be rebutted. The usual way of doing this is by showing that the other party had independent advice before entering into the transaction.

In *Inche Noriah* v *Shaik Allie bin Omar* [1929] AC 127, the Privy Council was also of the view that independent advice might be effective even though it was not taken. It must be given, however, in that case 'with a knowledge of all the relevant circumstances and must be such as a competent and honest adviser would give if acting solely in the interests of the donor.'

Where the influence is particularly strong, it may be necessary to show that the adviser approved the transactions and that his advice was followed: see *Powell* v *Powell* [1900] 1 Ch 243.

The matter was considered and explained by Blackburne J in *Naidoo* v *Naidu* (2000) The Times 1 November. His Lordship said that, once the presumption of undue influence arose, the wrongdoer, or anyone else concerned to uphold the transaction, had to prove, if the presumption was to be rebutted, that the complainant entered into the transaction as the result of the free exercise of an independent will. That requirement would not be satisfied merely by showing that the complainant understood what he or she was doing and intended to do it: it had to be shown that the complainant was either free from the influence of the alleged wrongdoer or had been placed by receipt of independent legal advice in an equivalent position. One way of proving that the transaction was entered into as a result of the free exercise of the complainant's independent will was by showing that the complainant entered into it only after its nature and effect were explained by some independent and qualified person fully informed of the material facts. However, where the complainant was subject to continuing undue influence this was not enough: in such circumstances the adviser's duty was to satisfy himself that his client was free from improper influence, ie, that he or she was able to reach an independent decision on his or her own.

Again, in *Dunbar Bank plc* v *Nadeem and Another* [1998] 3 All ER 876 the Court of Appeal found that a transaction had not been manifestly disadvantageous to the wife. However, their Lordships stressed that where a transaction is set aside for presumed undue influence, the wife or husband (as the case may be) would have to make restitution in respect of all that she had obtained from the transaction.

The extent of a lender bank's duty to a surety wife was established by the House of Lords in *Royal Bank of Scotland plc* v *Etridge (No 2) and Other Appeals* [2001] 4 All ER 449. These were appeals in eight cases, each of which arose out of a transaction in which a wife charged her interest in her home in favour of a bank as security for her husband's indebtedness, or the indebtedness of a company through which he carried on business, and the wife later asserted she signed the charge under the undue influence of her husband. In seven of the appeals the bank sought to enforce the charge signed by the wife and claimed an order for possession of the matrimonial home, but the wife raised a defence that the bank was on notice that her concurrence in the transaction had been procured by her husband's undue influence. The eighth appeal concerned a claim by a wife for damages for negligence from a solicitor who advised her before she entered into a guarantee obligation of this character. In the event, five of the appeals (including that in relation to the negligence claim) were allowed and the other three were dismissed. Lord Scott of Foscote observed that in each of the wife v bank appeals, the transactions pre-dated *Barclays Bank plc* v *O'Brien* [1993] 4 All ER 417 and, therefore, the bank did not have the advantage of the guidance provided by Lord Browne-Wilkinson. The question to be asked in each of these cases was whether, at the time the security was granted to the bank, the bank's perception of the risk that the grant might have been procured by the husband's impropriety was such as to have required the bank to take some additional steps to satisfy itself that she understood the nature and effect of the transaction. His Lordship helpfully summarised as follows his views about the principles that apply and the practice that should be followed in surety wife cases:

'(1) The issue as between the surety wife and the lender bank is whether the bank may rely on the apparent consent of the wife to the suretyship transaction. (2) If the bank knows that the surety wife's consent to the transaction has been procured by undue influence or misrepresentation, or if it has shut its eyes to the likelihood that that was so, it may not rely on her apparent consent. (3) If the wife's consent has in fact been procured by undue influence or misrepresentation, the bank may no rely on her apparent consent unless it has good reason to believe that she understands the nature and effect of the transaction. (4) Unless the case has some special feature, the bank's knowledge that a solicitor is acting for the wife and has advised her about the nature and effect of the transaction will provide a good reason for the purposes of (3) above. That will also be so if the bank has a reasonable belief that a solicitor is acting for her and has so advised her. Written confirmation by a solicitor acting for the wife that he has so advised her will entitle the bank to hold that reasonable belief. (5) So, too, a sufficient explanation of the nature and effect of the transaction given by a senior bank official would constitute good reason for the purposes of (3) above. (6) If there are any facts known to the bank which increase the inherent risk that the wife's consent to the transaction may have been procured by the husband's undue influence or misrepresentation, it may be necessary for the bank to be satisfied that the wife has received advice about the transaction from a solicitor independent of the husband before the bank can reasonably rely on the wife's apparent consent. (7) If the bank has not taken reasonable steps to satisfy itself that the wife understands the nature and effect of the transaction, the wife will, subject to such matters as delay, acquiescence, change of position etc, be able to set aside the transaction if her consent was in fact procured by undue influence or misrepresentation. (8) Subject to special instructions or special circumstances, the duty of a solicitor instructed to act for a wife proposing to stand as surety, or to give security, for her husband's debts is to try and make sure that she understands the nature and effect of the transaction. (9) In all surety wife cases the bank should disclose to the surety wife, or to the solicitor acting for her, the amount of the existing indebtedness of the principal debtor to the bank and the amount of the proposed new loan or drawing facility. (10) Subject to (9) above, a creditor has no greater duty of disclosure to a surety wife than to any other intending surety.'

As to the solicitor negligence claim, his Lordship said that what he (the solicitor) needed to do, and, on the judge's findings, did do, was to try and make sure that the wife understood the nature and effect of the document she was being asked to sign. On the facts, Lord Scott was satisfied that the solicitor had discharged that duty. The facts of the eight cases, and the reasons for their Lordships' decisions in each of them, are to be found in the speeches of Lord Nicholls of Birkenhead, Lord Hobhouse of Woodborough and Lord Scott of Foscote.

It is interesting to compare this decision with *Longstaff* v *Birtles* [2002] 1 WLR 470 where the Court of Appeal held that a solicitor proposing to buy property from, or to sell property to, a client (or, possibly, a former client) is under a duty to cause him to obtain independent advice.

Loss of the right

The right to have the contract set aside for undue influence is barred by affirmation after the influence has ceased; delay; and third party rights.

Unconscionable bargains

Equity may also give relief where advantage is taken of a 'poor and ignorant man'. See *Fry* v *Lane* (1880) 40 Ch D 312. There are three more recent decisions: *Cresswell* v *Potter* [1978] 1 WLR 255n (decided in 1968) and *Backhouse* v *Backhouse*

[1978] 1 WLR 243. In *Barclays Bank plc* v *Schwartz* [1995] TLR 452 the Court of Appeal reaffirmed the court's discretion in equity to set aside contracts where one of the parties is so vulnerable, and in such a weak bargaining position, that any purported 'agreement' would be harsh and unconscionable. However, the court doubted whether in this case the so-called vulnerable party could claim illiteracy and unfamiliarity with the English language as evidence that the bank had taken advantage of a 'poor and ignorant man'. The court discovered that he had, despite his so-called 'disability', carried on a lucrative business career in the United Kingdom for some years. While the court recognised the concept of a harsh and unconscionable bargain, they believed that their power to set aside such a bargain should be used in only the most limited circumstances.

11.4 The limited, and now suspect, principle of inequality of bargaining power

In *Lloyds Bank* v *Bundy*, Lord Denning MR, after examining duress, the various forms of improper pressure and unconscionable bargains, sought to derive a general principle from these categories. They all rested on inequality of bargaining power. He said:

> 'By virtue of it, English law gives relief to one, who, without independent advice, enters into a contract on terms which are very unfair or transfers property for a consideration which is grossly inadequate, when his bargaining power is grievously impaired by reason of his own needs or desires, or by his own ignorance or infirmity, coupled with undue influences or pressures brought to bear on him by or for the benefit of the other.'

The principle did not, Lord Denning said, depend on proof of any wrongdoing. This principle was an alternative ground for his decision in *Bundy*. The other members of the Court of Appeal based their decision on undue influence, and did not find it necessary to express an opinion on Lord Denning's principle.

In subsequent cases, Lord Denning reiterated his view that English Law recognises this principle: *Clifford Davis* v *WEA Records* [1975] 1 WLR 61 and *Levison* v *Patent Steam Carpet Cleaning Co* [1978] QB 69. Some support for the principle is derived from the speech of Lord Diplock in *Schroeder Music Publishing* v *Macaulay* [1974] 1 WLR 1308, but Lord Diplock was dealing with the particular problem of standard form contracts in the context of restraint of trade. There has been little other judicial support for inequality of bargaining power as a general principle.

In *Pao On* v *Lau Yiu* (above), Lord Scarman stated that, where duress was not established, to treat the unfair use of a dominant bargaining position as a ground for invalidating a contract was unnecessary for the achievement of justice and unhelpful in the development of the law. In *Burmah Oil* v *Bank of England* (1981) The Times 4 July, the court rejected the argument that inequality of bargaining power is of itself a ground of invalidity. In *Alec Lobb (Garages)* v *Total Oil* [1985] 1 All ER 303, the plaintiff sought to have the transaction set aside on the grounds, inter alia, that the bargain was harsh and unconscionable. It was argued that because of Total's superior economic position and the financial pressures faced by the plaintiff, the parties were in a position of unequal bargaining power, and that, in this situation, the test should be whether the terms of the contract were fair and reasonable.

The Court of Appeal rejected this as a proposition of law. Dillon LJ observed that it was seldom in any negotiation that the bargaining position of the parties was absolutely equal. 'The Courts', said Dillon LJ, 'would only interfere in exceptional cases where as a matter of common fairness it was not right that the strong should be allowed to push the weak to the wall.' Concepts of unconscionable conduct and the exercise by the dominant party of coercive power would then be brought in.

The plaintiffs' shortage of money, the fact that they were already tied to Total by mortgages and had no alternative sources of finance, all of which was known to Total, did not render the transaction unconscionable. It was also clear, in the present case, that no pressure had been placed on the plaintiffs, who had taken independent advice from their accountants and solicitors. Total had been reluctant to enter into the transaction.

Most recently in *National Westminster Bank* v *Morgan* (above), Lord Scarman said:

> 'I question whether there is any need in the modern law to erect a general principle of relief against inequality of bargaining power. Parliament has undertaken the task – and it is essentially a legislative task – of enacting such restrictions upon freedom of contract as are in its judgment necessary to relieve against the mischief: for example, the hire-purchase and consumer protection legislation, of which the Supply of Goods (Implied Terms) Act 1973, Consumer Credit Act 1974, Consumer Safety Act 1978, Supply of Goods and Services Act 1982 and Insurance Companies Act 1982 are examples. I doubt whether the courts should assume the burden of formulating further restrictions.'

The most recent cases tend to confirm Treitel's view that it is unlikely that the principle will find literal acceptance in English law. The recent widening of the scope of duress has, Treitel observes, greatly reduced the need for such a principle.

11.5 The protection afforded by certain statutory provisions

Brief mention must be made of the Consumer Credit Act 1974, which empowers the court to 'reopen' any 'extortionate credit bargain', and the Fair Trading Act 1973, which controls practices which 'subject customers to undue pressure' and which cause the terms of certain transactions to be so adverse to consumers as to be inequitable. Many of the provisions of the 1973 Act will be revised and updated when the Enterprise Act 2002 is brought into force.

The extent of the protection provided by s138 of the 1974 Act was considered by the Court of Appeal in *Paragon Finance plc* v *Nash* (2001) The Times 25 October.

The claimant lender sought possession of the defendants' property on the ground that they were in arrears with their mortgage interest payments. The mortgage contained a variable interest clause. The defendants contended that there was an implied term that the lender would act reasonably in relation to interest rates and that the lender was in breach of it, that the mortgage was an extortionate credit bargain within s138 of the Consumer Credit Act 1974 and that there had been a breach of s3 of the Unfair Contract Terms Act 1977. These contentions were rejected: the claimant's action was successful. While their Lordships agreed that there was an implied term that the rate of interest would not be set dishonestly, for an improper purpose, capriciously or arbitrarily, in all the circumstances it was impossible to say that the lender's discretion was being exercised in any of these ways. The total charge for credit was central to a consideration of whether a credit bargain was extortionate, as the language of s138 of the 1974 Act made clear. The allegation that the rate of interest was grossly exorbitant within s138(1)(a) had no real prospect of success. As to the alleged breach of s3 of the 1977 Act, their Lordships rejected the defendants' submission that they were reasonably entitled to expect that, in performing its side of the bargain, the lender would not apply rates substantially out of line with those applied by comparable lenders to borrowers in comparable situations, and found no breach of s3(2)(b). Dyson LJ concluded that the Consumer Credit Act 1974 provided borrowers with only limited protection from the working of the free market. The court could intervene only where a bargain was grossly unfair to the borrower, either because the payments required to be made were grossly exorbitant or grossly contravened ordinary principles of fair dealing. Nothing less would do.

12

Privity of Contract

12.1 Introduction

The traditional approach to the rights and liabilities which are subject to a contract is to assert that they can vest only in a party to the contract. This is because the law only seeks to enforce bargains supported by consideration. Such a bald assertion does, however, in some cases, cause hardship and, in recent years, a departure may be witnessed from the strict application of that rule. See, for example, *Jackson* v *Horizon Holidays* (below). Where the rule has not been departed from it has been distinguished, and complex analyses of factual situations have resulted in the discovery of consideration where, at first glance, there was none to be found. See, for example, *New Zealand Shipping* v *Satterthwaite (The Eurymedon)*.

236

12.2 Privity and consideration

A party can either be privy to the agreement or to the consideration. It is disputed whether the rule that consideration must move from the promisee is the same as, or different from, the rule that only a party to the agreement can sue. See Furmston (1960) 23 MLR at pp383–4. English judges have acted ambivalently and referred to both rules interchangeably. The two rules are capable, however, of being distinguished. Chitty on contracts furnishes an example:

> 'A man might ... promise his daughter to pay £1,000 to any man who married her. A person who married the daughter with knowledge of and in reliance on such a promise might provide consideration for it, but could not sue on it as it was not addressed to him.'

That is to say, he was not party to the agreement. A person can be party to an agreement, but not provide consideration. If, at the request of A, B promises C that he (B) will pay A £50 pa if C will dig his garden, A can be said in one sense to be 'party' to the agreement, but he does not provide consideration. A will not be able to enforce the contract.

Kepong Prospecting v *Schmidt* [1968] AC 810 is a decision of the Privy Council which supports the view that the doctrine of privity is distinct from the rule that consideration must move from the promisee.

12.3 Circumstances falling outside the rule

There are some circumstances in which the rule that only a party to the contract can enforce it, does not apply. These situations are not properly regarded as 'exceptions' to the rule because the question of privity is not in issue if the situation exists.

Collateral contracts

In *Shanklin Pier* v *Detel Products* [1951] 2 KB 854, the plaintiffs had employed contractors to paint a pier. They told them to buy paint made by the defendants. The defendants had told them that the paint would last for seven years. It only lasted for three months.

The court decided that the plaintiffs could sue the defendants on a collateral contract. They had provided consideration for the defendants' promise by entering into an agreement with the contractors, which entailed the purchase of the defendants' paint. See also *Andrews* v *Hopkinson* [1957] 1 QB 229 and *Wells* v *Buckland* [1965] 2 QB 170 referred to in Chapter 6.

The court was able to find consideration moving from the plaintiffs – *Shanklin Pier* – without substantial difficulty. The case of *Charnock* v *Liverpool Corporation* [1968] 1 WLR 1498 gives rise to some doubts about the presence of consideration. The plaintiff's car was damaged. A contract existed between his insurance company and a garage (the defendant) for repairing the plaintiff's car. It was held that there was also a collateral contract between the plaintiff and the defendant to do the repairs within a reasonable time. The court found that the consideration was the leaving of the car at the garage. This was not, of course, a detriment to the plaintiff, but it was a benefit to the garage.

There must, however, be an intention to create a collateral contract before that contract can be formed. In *Alicia Hosiery Ltd* v *Brown Shipley Ltd* [1970] 1 QB 195, the owner of goods in a warehouse pledged them to a bank. The owner then sold to a buyer. The bank gave the buyer a delivery order addressed to the warehouseman (to instruct the warehouseman to give delivery of the goods). The warehouseman refused. The buyer sued the bank on a collateral contract. It was held that there was none.

A well-established example of a collateral contract is that which arises between the seller of goods and a bank when a buyer opens an irrevocable letter of credit in favour of the seller. When the buyer 'opens' the letter of credit, it means that a contract has been formed between the buyer of goods and the bank wherein the bank undertakes to pay the seller. Once the bank informs the seller, it seems that there is a collateral contract. But where is the consideration? There are two possible solutions: first, that the bank was making a unilateral offer to the seller which was accepted by performance of the contract between the buyer and seller; and, secondly, that the seller provided consideration by forbearing to sue the buyer for the price.

Under the Consumer Credit Act 1974, a dealer who conducts preceding negotiations for a 'regulated agreement' is, in certain circumstances, deemed to do so as agent of the creditor as well as in his actual capacity. The representation can, therefore, make the company liable under the main contract, while the dealer may still be liable on the representation as a collateral contract.

In *Sandeman Coprimar SA* v *Transitos y Transportes Integrales SL* (2003) The Times 13 February it appeared that the parties had entered into a contract for the carriage of goods from Spain to Scotland. One of the sub-contractors lost the goods. The trial judge held that the claimants had implicitly authorised the conclusion of a chain of contracts on terms to be found in the Convention for the International Carriage of Goods by Road and that, in those circumstances, the sub-bailment of each party was on the terms of all the Convention conditions, whether by application of the doctrine of bailment on terms or under principles of the law of contract. The Court of Appeal upheld this decision. As Lord Phillips MR explained, where a bailor consented to and thereby authorised a sub-bailment on terms, all the terms agreed between the bailee and the sub-bailee, in so far as they were applicable to the relationship of the bailor and the sub-bailee, applied as between the bailor and the sub-bailee. That result also followed from the application of the principles of the law of contract. Where a bailee had the consent, and thus the authority of the bailor to enter into a sub-bailment on particular terms and did so, and where those terms purported to govern the relationship between the sub-bailee and the bailor as well as between the sub-bailee and the bailee, all the elements of a collateral contract binding on the sub-bailee and the bailor would be present. There would be privity, via the agency of the bailee, and no difficulty in identifying consideration, at least if the terms were capable of resulting in benefit to each of the parties.

Multi-partite agreements

Clubs or unincorporated associations

Where a person joins a club or other unincorporated association, he may contract with all the other members, even though he may not know any of them. For example, in *Clarke* v *Dunraven* [1897] AC 59 HL, the owners of two yachts entered them in a regatta. Each owner undertook in a letter to the secretary to obey all the rules of the club. These included a rule that members were to pay 'all damages' caused by fouling. 'The Satanita' fouled 'The Valkyrie'. The owner sued the owner of 'The Satanita'. The owner of 'The Satanita' relied on a statutory limitation of liability to £8 per ton on the registered tonnage of the ship. The owner of 'The Valkyrie' said that the promise to pay 'all damages' excluded the statutory provision.

The owner of 'The Valkyrie' could rely on the promise to pay 'all damages' because a contract between them on the terms specified with the club was formed, either when they entered the race, or at the latest at the time of sailing.

In contrast, in *Ellesmere* v *Wallace* [1929] 2 Ch 1, people entering horses for races were held to be contracting with the Jockey Club and not among themselves.

Companies

The position is not dissimilar where a person becomes a member of an incorporated body. The Companies Act 1985 provides that the Memorandum and Articles of a company (which contain its rules) bind the company and its members as though signed and sealed by each member, and amount to a covenant between each member and every other member.

Agency

A person may contract as agent for a third party (his principal). The principal is then bound and the agent is not privy to the contract and cannot (generally) sue or be sued upon it. Sometimes problems arise regarding sub-agencies. An agent can create privity of contract between himself and a sub-agent. See Chapter 19.

12.4 Attempts to impose liabilities on third parties (prior to the Contracts (Rights of Third Parties) Act 1999)

The general rule is that a contract only binds the parties to it. The reason that this is so, is that C is a stranger to the contract effected between A and B. In *Taddy* v *Sterious* [1904] 1 Ch 354, the plaintiffs were manufacturers of tobacco and they stipulated that this tobacco should not be sold under a fixed minimum price. Some tobacco was sold by the plaintiffs to a wholesaler, and a term of this contract was 'that acceptance of the goods will be deemed a contract between the purchaser and Taddy & Co, that he will observe these stipulations'. The contract also provided that:

> 'In the case of purchase by a retailer through a wholesaler the latter shall be deemed to be an agent for Taddy & Co.'

The wholesalers resold the tobacco to the defendants who had notice of this condition but, nevertheless, sold the tobacco at below the prescribed price. Taddy & Co brought an action against the defendants on three grounds.

1. The printed notice amounted to a contract between themselves and the defendants – the court held that this was not so, there was no contract between the plaintiff and the defendant.
2. The wholesaler was only an agent of the plaintiff – the court rejected this view as their 'agent' did not agree to any of the terms of agency.
3. The doctrine of restrictive covenants should be extended to manufactured goods – the court rejected this argument as it went against common sense.

There are various ways in which the strict harshness of this rule may be circumvented.

1. The creation of a lien (where goods are entrusted to a person who has a right to retain them pending payment. So, if A contracts with B – a common carrier – that goods belonging to C should be carried from London to Newcastle to be paid for by C, C is not bound by the obligation under the contract between A and B, but he may not be able to get his goods from B because B has a right to retain them pending payment. This right is called a lien).
2. The creation of an equitable interest or irrevocable lience. In *Binions* v *Evans* [1972] Ch 359, a purchaser of land was bound by a promise made by the vendor of the land to an occupant of a cottage that the occupant could remain in the cottage for the rest of her life. The purchaser took with notice of this promise. He would not have been bound by the promise if he had no notice.
3. The law of tort. In *Lumley* v *Gye* (1853) 2 E & B 216, the plaintiff had employed Johanna Wagner as an opera singer. The defendant induced her to refuse to perform because he wanted her to sing in his opera house. He was liable for his wrongful interference with contractual rights. The same rule may apply where a stranger to a contract uses a chattel in a manner which is inconsistent with a party's contractual rights. He may be liable in conversion as in the tort of wrongful interference. See *British Motor Trade Association* v *Salvadori* [1949] Ch 556, where A bought a car, convenanting with B that he would not resell it for one year without offering it to B. C bought the car with notice of the covenant within one year of the contract. He was held to be liable in tort for wrongful interference with the contractual rights of B.

Equity may impose liability although the common law does not

The principal application of the imposition of liability in equity is in relation to negative covenants which may, if certain conditions are satisfied, run with the land and bind purchasers of it to observe the covenants for the benefit of adjoining owners. The leading case is *Tulk v Moxhay* (1848) 2 Ph 774. The plaintiff who owned several houses in Leicester Square sold the garden in the centre of the Square to one Elms, who covenanted that he would keep the gardens and railings around them in their present condition and continue to allow individuals the use and enjoyment of the gardens.

The land in question was sold to the defendant although the conveyance to him did not contain the convenant in similar terms. The defendant did know of the restriction contained in the contract between the plaintiff and Elms. The defendant announced that he was going to build on the land, and the plaintiff, who was still owner of several adjacent houses, sought an injunction to restrain him from doing so.

It was held that the covenant would be enforced in equity against all subsequent purchasers with notice. The reason for this decision was partly due to the defendant acting as he did whilst knowing of the plaintiff/Elms covenant and the plaintiff, it was said, must also have some interest in the land in question. The injunction was granted.

Attempts have been made to extend the operation of a restrictive covenant to cover contracts for the hire of ships as well as contracts restraining certain uses of land. The leading case is *Lord Strathcona Steamship Co v Dominion Coal Co* [1926] AC 108. The plaintiffs, Dominion Coal Co, had a charter right of the Lord Strathcona, and during the period of the charter, the ship was sold to the defendants who refused to let the plaintiffs use the ship in accordance with the terms of the charter. The plaintiffs sought an injunction to stop the defendants retaking the ship, but the defendants argued that as they were not privy to the contract (original charter contract) they could not be bound. Strictly speaking, the plaintiffs would have lost if they had sued in contract but, instead, they asked the court to extend the doctrine of *Tulk v Moxhay* from land to sea. The Judicial Committee of the Privy Council agreed to this and so the plaintiffs succeeded. *Strathcona* has been heavily criticised mainly because, under the doctrine of *Tulk v Moxhay*, an essential condition was that the plaintiff kept an interest in the *land*. There cannot be an analogy with ships in which case. The judgment was couched in such wide terms that it could have been applied to all chattels.

There is some doubt today as to whether the decision has much legal status due to Diplock J's judgment in *Port Line Ltd v Ben Line Steamers Ltd* [1958] 2 QB 146. A ship chartered to the plaintiffs by its owners for 30 months was sold to the defendant within this period. The defendant agreed to honour the charter. However, the ship was soon requisitioned by the government and compensation was paid to the defendant. The plaintiffs sued the defendant for compensation. Diplock J (as he then was) held that even if the *Strathcona* case was rightly decided it could not be applied to this case as (1) the defendant was not in breach of any duty by his act – it was the government who had acted, and (2) the plaintiff had not sought an injunction but *financial compensation*, which was thus outside the ambit of *Tulk* v *Moxhay* – also the defendants did not know of the plaintiff's actual charter rights.

The point about *Tulk* v *Moxhay* is that it opened a possible line of argument extending the ambit of the exception to the doctrine of privity. The argument raised in *Tulk* v *Moxhay* was naturally attractive to the lawyers of the time in that it presented a way round the doctrine. Thus, it came as no surprise to see the *Tulk* v *Moxhay* argument being raised in subsequent cases. You will recollect that the courts rejected the view that an agreement between A and B with regard to goods could run with the goods so as to bind C (*Taddy* v *Sterious*). In the *Strathcona* case (above), it was held by the Privy Council that a third party could effectively be bound by an agreement made between two parties and to which he was thus not a party.

Diplock J (as he then was) said in *Port Line*:

'The *Strathcona* case, although decided over thirty years ago, has never been followed in the English courts and has never come up for direct consideration.'

In *Bendall* v *McWhirter* [1952] 2 QB 466, Denning LJ said:

'It seems, therefore, that in this case for the first time after more than 30 years that an English court has to grapple with the problem of what principle was really laid down in the *Strathcona case*, and whether that case was rightly decided. The difficulty I have found in ascertaining its ratio decidendi, the impossibility which I find of reconciling the actual decision with well-established principles of law, the unsolved and, to me, insoluble problems which that decision raises combine to satisfy me that it was wrongly decided. I do not propose to follow it. I naturally express this opinion with great diffidence, but having reached a clear conclusion it is my duty to express it.

If I am wrong in my view that the case was wrongly decided, I am certainly averse from extending it one iota beyond that which, as I understand it, it purported to decide. In particular, I do not think that it purported to decide (1) that anything short of actual knowledge by the subsequent purchaser at the time of the purchase of the charterer's rights, the violation of which it is sought to restrain, is sufficient to give rise to the equity; (2) that the charterer has any remedy against the subsequent purchaser with notice except a right to restrain the use of the vessel by such purchaser in a manner inconsistent with the terms of the charter; (3) that the charterer has any positive right against the subsequent purchaser to have the vessel used in accordance with the terms of his charter.'

12.5 Attempts to impose benefits on third parties (prior to the Contracts (Rights of Third Parties) Act 1999)

If A and B cannot impose liabilities on C, the corollary of this rule would logically seem to be that neither can they confer benefits on him or, more importantly, C cannot enforce such benefit by contractual action in the courts. The reason is simple: C is not a party to the bargain between A and B. The leading case on this aspect is *Tweddle* v *Atkinson* (1861) 1 B & S 393. The plaintiff married Mr Guy's daughter. The plaintiff's father and Mr Guy effected an agreement whereby each would pay a sum of money to the plaintiff. Both the fathers reneged on this agreement and subsequently died. The executor faced a problem due to the fact that the plaintiff sued the executor of Mr Guy for the sum promised. Crompton J:

> 'It is admitted that the plaintiff cannot succeed unless this case is an exception to the modern and well-established doctrine of the action of assumpsit. At the time when the cases which have been cited were decided the action of assumpsit was treated as an action of trespass upon the case, and therefore in the nature of a tort; and the law was not settled, as it now is, that natural love and affection is not a sufficient consideration for a promise upon which an action may be maintained; nor was it settled that the promisee cannot bring an action unless the consideration for the promise moved from him. The modern cases have, in effect, overruled the old decisions; they shew that the consideration must move from the party entitled to sue upon the contract. It would be a monstrous proposition to say that a person was a party to the contract for the purpose of suing upon it for his own advantage and not a party to it for the purpose of being sued. It is said that the father in the present case was agent for the son in making the contract but the argument ought also to make the son liable upon it. I am prepared to overrule the old decisions, and to hold that, by reason of the principles which now govern the action of assumpsit, the present action is not maintainable.'

Wrightman J:

> 'Some of the old decisions appear to support the proposition that a stranger to the consideration of a contract may maintain an action upon it, if he stand in such a near relationship to the party from whom the consideration proceeds, that he may be considered a party to the consideration. But there is no modern case in which the proposition has been supported. On the contrary, it is now established that no stranger to the consideration can take advantage of a contract, although made for his benefit.'

The rule in effect laid down by *Tweddle* v *Atkinson* has become accepted as one of the tenets of the common law.

Lord Haldane LC remarked in *Dunlop* v *Selfridge* [1915] AC 847:

> 'My Lords, in the law of England certain principles are fundamental. One is that only a person who is a party to a contract can sue upon it. Our law knows nothing of a jus quaesitum tertio arising by way of contract.'

The facts in this case were that Dunlop sold tyres to a wholesaler who sold them to Selfridges. Part of the contract of sale between the wholesaler and Selfridges was that Selfridges should pay compensation to Dunlop if they sold the tyres at below the fixed minimum price. Selfridges later sold below the minimum price and refused to pay compensation. They were sued by Dunlop for breach of contract.

The House of Lords held that Dunlop were not entitled to succeed. They were seeking to enforce a right in a contract to which they were not a party. The argument that the wholesalers were the agents of Dunlop was also rejected.

In *Scruttons* v *Midland Silicones Ltd* [1962] AC 446, a contract was made between a shipping company and a chemical manufacturer concerning the transportation of drums of chemicals. It was agreed that in case of damage by the shipping company, their liability would not exceed £500. A stevedore company damaged the drums and damage was above the £500 limit. They pleaded that they could rely on the provisions of the contract and only pay £500.

As they were strangers to the contract it was held that they could not rely on its rights – and so they were liable to pay compensation by way of damages.

Scruttons v *Midland Silicones* (above) should be read in the light of *New Zealand Shipping* v *Satterthwaite (The Eurymedon)* [1975] AC 154, in which, on similar facts, the stevedore was able to rely on the provisions of the contract between the cargo owner and carrier. It was said that the bill of lading (which evidences the contract between the cargo owner and the carrier) brought into existence a bargain, initially unilateral, but capable of becoming mutual, between the shipper and the stevedore, made through the carrier as agent, which became a full contract when the stevedore performed services by unloading the goods. The performance of the services was for the benefit of the shipper, and the consideration was that the stevedore should have the benefit of the exemptions in the bill of lading.

This has been affirmed in *Port Jackson Stevedoring* v *Salmond and Spraggon (The New York Star)* [1981] 1 WLR 138. However, in the more recent case of *Southern Water Authority* v *Carey* [1985] 2 All ER 1077, subcontractors sought to rely on a limitation of liability clause in a main contract. They were held not to be entitled to the benefit of the clause in the absence of evidence that the main contractor had authority from the subcontractors at the time of making the contract. See *Darlington Borough Council* v *Wiltshier Northern Ltd and Another* [1995] 1 WLR 68.

12.6 Creation of a benefit by equity

Trusts

Although contractual rights cannot be established for a stranger, a trust can occur, conferring benefits on such a person, giving rights that can be legally enforced. Any form of property can form a trust. If A and B contract, B promising to pay C £100, then C cannot sue for the £100, because he is a stranger to the contract. But, if it can be proved that A and B had not created a contract but a *trust*, then A, the trustee, or C, the beneficiary, under the trust can sue for the £100 – in equity.

In *Re Flavell* (1883) 25 Ch D 89 a contract between two parties provided that in the event of one of the parties' death, the widow would be entitled to certain payments. The action was brought by one such widow. Her claim in contract failed, but she succeeded in equity as she managed to show to the court that she was the beneficiary under a trust made by the above parties in her favour.

Compare this decision, however, with *Re Schebsman* [1944] Ch 83. Schebsman was employed by a Swiss company, who agreed that his appointment should be ended by means of a golden handshake to the value of £5,500 to be paid in instalments and in the event of death to his widow. The widow sued for the failed payment, but it was held that she would fail as she could show no evidence of a trust. (In contract she failed because she was not privy to the contract.)

It appears from these two cases that two conditions must be fulfilled in order for the court to be convinced of the existence of a trust.

1. There must be a clear intention to create a trust; the words 'trust' and 'beneficiary' need not be used, although it would clarify matters if they were.
2. It must be clear that the parties did not intend to *alter* in any way whatever, the rights they had created, for example, if A and B make a contract to pay C £100, they have created a non-enforceable benefit to C (non enforceable by C) and C cannot sue. But if A and B create a trust, their freedom to modify the trust is curtailed.

That is, a £100 trust cannot be altered/reduced. In *Re Schebsman,* the court thought that this condition was lacking because it appeared that the employee and the employer still had the freedom to negotiate the golden handshake.

Commentary

One can derive an analysis of the discussion above on the equitable concept of trust in the following terms:

If A and B make an agreement for the benefit of C, C cannot enforce that contract since he is not a party to it. However, if they make a trust – or a trust is implied – then one of two analyses is relevant.

1. In the first instance of A and B making a trust for the benefit of C, C is a beneficiary of the trust created between A and B. The Law of Trusts indicates that provided all the parameters of trusts are satisfied then, C, as a beneficiary, can enforce the trust in his own right.
2. But in the instance of a trust being implied from a contractual situation, the analysis seems to be different.

For example, A agrees with B that B will do something for C. If a trust can be implied per *Flavell* above, then, it seems that A is the trustee for B of his own contractual rights. Thus A is, in effect, holding his own contractual rights for the benefit of C in trust. If that is the case, then C as a beneficiary of A's contractual rights can enforce the trust by virtue of those 'trust rights'.

The possibility stated in (2) above has been accepted by the courts. In *Les Affreteurs Reunis Société Anonyme* v *Leopold Walford* [1919] AC 801, it is suggested that although it is theoretically possible for a trust still to be found in these situations, it must be clear beyond a peradventure that a trust was intended. In

Knight v *Knight* (1840) 3 Beav 148 at 173, Lord Langdale referred to the required three certainties:

1. certainty of words,
2. certainty of subject matter; and
3. certainty of objects.

Vandepitte v *Preferred Accident Insurance Corporation of New York* [1933] AC 70 held that:

> 'It is not legitimate to import into the contract the idea of a trust when the parties have given no indication that such was their intention. To interpret this contract as creating a trust would, in my judgment, be to disregard the dividing line between the case of a trust and the simple use of a contract made between two parties for the benefit of a third.'

Since the Privy Council decision in the above case, there has been very little mention of the trust concept in English courts in the context of privity.

Restrictive covenants

The benefit of a restrictive covenant can also run with land from vendor to purchaser. See *Tulk* v *Moxhay* (above).

12.7 Section 56 Law of Property Act 1925

Lord Denning MR believed that privity of contract never really existed as true law, and that the only reason it was recognised was due to constant erroneous interpretations over the years. He claims that the LPA 1925 puts this belief into statute form.

Section 56 LPA 1925:

> 'A person may take an interest in land or other property or the benefits concerning land or other property although he may not be named a party to the conveyance or other instrument.'

In both *Smith and Snipes Hall Farm Ltd* v *River Douglas Catchment Board* [1949] 2 KB 500 and *Drive Yourself Hire Co Ltd* v *Strutt* [1954] 1 QB 250, Lord Denning launched his campaign against privity — he argued that s56 LPA 1925 was intended to destroy the whole doctrine altogether. Certainly, the words are wide enough to support Denning's view. But it was questionable whether it was wise to take one section out of the context of an entire Act and use it to displace an established doctrine. Lord Denning's view was rejected by other judges in succeeding cases, but it was not until *Beswick* v *Beswick* [1968] AC 58 that the matter came before the House of Lords.

By a written agreement, PB assigned his business as a coal merchant to his nephew JB; in consideration, JB agreed to employ PB as a consultant at £6.50 pw for the rest of his life and, further, to pay PB's wife an annuity of £5 pw for her life after PB's death. PB's wife was not privy to the contract. After PB's death, JB only paid one sum of £5 to the widow and then refused to pay any more. The widow sought an order for specific performance of the agreement in her capacity as *executrix/administratrix* of the estate of her husband and in her *personal capacity*..

At first instance, the judge decided against the widow because he saw no evidence of a trust, and he rejected Lord Denning's interpretation of s56 LPA 1925 (above).

The Court of Appeal, with Lord Denning sitting, decided in favour of the widow however, basing their judgment on s56 LPA 1925 and on the fact that she was the administratrix of her husband's estate.

The House of Lords decided in favour of the widow on the *sole* ground that she was the administratrix of her husband's estate.

Lord Denning's view was rejected outright, the House of Lords holding that s56 should not be taken outside its context despite the wideness of the wording.

12.8 Remedies of the contracting party

Consideration must be given of (1) specific performance, and (2) damages.

Specific performance

This remedy was allowed in *Beswick*. It is, however, a discretionary remedy which will be examined in more detail in Chapter 15.

Damages

The majority view in *Beswick* v *Beswick* was that the widow qua administratrix would have been able to recover only nominal damages. This is presumably based on the general principle that, in an action for damages, the plaintiff cannot recover more than he has lost as a result of the breach. The estate would not have suffered any direct loss. Lord Upjohn was of the view that the basis for the conclusion that only nominal damages would be available is that the promisee had no other assets. Presumably he meant that had the promisee had other assets, they would have had to be diverted from the estate to keep the widow, and the estate would have sustained damage.

The question of the extent to which a contracting party may recover for loss sustained by a stranger who is intended to benefit from the contract was raised in *Jackson* v *Horizon Holidays* [1975] 1 WLR 1468. The plaintiff entered into a contract for himself and his family. The holiday provided failed to comply with the description given by the defendants in a number of important respects.

At first instance, the plaintiff recovered damages including a sum for mental distress. The defendants appealed against the amount of the damages.

In the Court of Appeal, James LJ, in dismissing the appeal, regarded the damages as compensation for the plaintiff's own distress. The plaintiff had, however, brought the action on behalf of himself and his family. Lord Denning MR thought the amount awarded was excessive compensation for the plaintiff himself, but he upheld the award on the ground that the plaintiff had made a contract for the benefit of himself and his family, and that he could recover for their loss as well as for his own. Lord Denning accepted as an established rule of law that if A makes a contract for the benefit of B, A can sue on the contract for the loss sustained by B as a result of the breach.

In *Woodar Investment Development* v *Wimpey Construction* [1980] 1 WLR 277, the House of Lords rejected the basis on which Lord Denning had arrived at his decision, and reaffirmed the view that a contracting party cannot recover damages for the loss sustained by the third party.

Their Lordships did not dissent from the actual decision in *Jackson*, which they felt could be supported either because the damages were awarded for the plaintiff's own loss; or because booking family holidays or ordering meals in restaurants calls for special treatment.

The facts of the *Woodar* case were: a contract for the sale of land provided that on completion the purchaser should pay £850,000 to the vendor and also £150,000 to a third party. The vendor claimed damages for wrongful repudiation. In fact, there was found to be no wrongful repudiation, but the House of Lords expressed the above views. At the same time, they suggested that the position at law might be unsatisfactory.

In *Forster* v *Silvermere Golf and Equestrian Centre* (1981) 125 Sol Jo 397, Dillon J refered to the results produced by the application of the rule that parties to the contract can only recover their personal loss as 'a blot on our law and most unjust'. The plaintiff had transferred land to the defendant who undertook to build a house on it and to allow the plaintiff and her children to live in it rent free for life.

It was held that she could recover damages for her own loss, but not for the loss of the rights of occupation which her children might have enjoyed after her death.

Promises not to sue

If A promises B for consideration not to sue C, can B prevent this?

In *Gore* v *Van Der Lann* [1967] 2 QB 31, the Court of Appeal held that B could only obtain a stay of proceedings if there was a definite promise by A not to sue C; and B must have a sufficient interest in the enforcement of a promise, for example, where B would be exposed to a legal liability to C if A sues.

It is not clear that a 'sufficient interest' was required in *Snelling* v *Snelling Ltd* [1973] 1 QB 87. Three brothers lent money to a family company of which they were directors. They agreed that if one of them resigned he should forfeit any money due to him by the company. One resigned and sued the company. The company relied on the agreement. Because a company has an independent legal personality, it was not a party to the agreement. The brothers applied to be joined as defendants, adopted the defence and counter-claimed for a declaration that the loan was forfeit.

Ormrod J held that they were entitled to the declaration and that it was a proper case for the stay of proceedings.

12.9 Statutory exceptions

Certain exceptions to the doctrine of privity have been created by statute, including price maintenance agreements; and certain contracts of insurance enforceable in favour of third parties.

For example, under s148(4) Road Traffic Act 1972, an injured party may recover compensation from an insurance company once he has obtained judgment against the insured person. However, the most notable and significant exception is the Contracts (Rights of Third Parties) Act 1999 which came into force in May 2000.

12.10 The Contracts (Rights of Third Parties) Act 1999

In 1937, the Law Revision Committee recommended in its 6th Interim Report that:

> 'Where a contract by its express terms purports to confer a benefit on a third party it shall be enforceable by the third party in his own name subject to any defences that would have been valid between the contracting parties.'

The subsequent failure of the legislature to act on this recommendation prompted the remark by the House of Lords in *Woodar* v *Wimpey* (above) that if Parliament did not soon act, the courts would be forced to.

Consequently, in 1996, the Law Commission published a report (No 242) and a draft Bill which sought to introduce statutory reforms in this area. The Bill, now an Act, namely the Contracts (Rights of Third Parties) Act 1999, received the Royal Assent on 11 November 1999. It came into force in May 2000 and has the effect of allowing strangers to enforce contracts made for their benefit. It also gives them the use of all the standard contractual remedies to do with the contract, and emphasises for good measure that they can now be validly exempted from liability pursuant to a contract as well as being given rights to sue for breach of it.

Whilst the Act focuses on the benefit issue, it remains silent on the issue of imposing a burden on third parties.

The Act is short and only has ten sections, out of which the first eight are relevant.

Section 1:   Outlines the ways in which a third party may have a right to enforce contractual terms, particularly s1(1)(a), (b) and 1(2).

Section 2:   Outlines the utility of exclusion clauses and matters relating to variation and rescission of contract.

Section 3:   Provides the defences available to a promisor where a third is seeking to enforce a contract.

Section 4:   Outlines the rights of the promisee to enforce any term of the contract. Note that s1 does not affect any right of the promisee in terms of enforcement.

Section 5:   Provides protection to the promisor from incurring double liability as against the promisee and a third party.

Section 6:   States the contracts which are specifically excluded from the application of this Act.

Section 7:   Deals with supplementary provisions relating to third parties – eg the Unfair Contracts Terms Act 1977 and the Limitation Act 1980.

Section 8:   Provides for arbitration provisions.

Whilst this Act has the potential of making significant changes in the way in which contracts can be enforced by third parties, it must nonetheless be remembered that the main contracting parties are still in control and thus may agree to exclude the application of the provisions of the new Act.

13

Illegality

13.1 Introduction

Different methods of classification of illegal contracts have been adopted by writers, some of whom prefer to classify illegal contracts according to the effects of the illegality. The effects, however, vary, depending on the nature of the contract and the behaviour of the parties. For example, one or both parties may be prevented from suing on the contract at all, or one or both parties may be prevented from suing on a particular undertaking, or, if the doctrine of severance applies (see below), one or both parties may be prevented from suing on part of a particular undertaking. The classification that is adopted here is into: contracts contrary to some principle of law; and contracts contrary to public policy.

Contracts in restraint of trade fall into the second category but are dealt with separately because of their importance. We shall examine, first, the types of illegal contracts and then the effect of the illegality.

13.2 Contracts which break the law

It is traditional to distinguish the situation where the object of a contract is the deliberate infringement of the provisions of a statute or a statutory instrument or the

251

common law, then the court will not enforce that contract regardless of whether the infringement is a civil or a criminal one; or where the law has been broken through carrying into effect the terms of a contract, then that contract may be upheld as valid at the instance of a party who was ignorant of such breach of the law or who innocently caused the breach.

Contracts which break the criminal law

Contracts to commit a crime

If a contract has as its object the deliberate commission of a crime, then it is illegal and the courts will not enforce it.

In *Bigos* v *Bousted* [1951] 1 All ER 92, the defendant wished to send his daughter to Italy for health reasons, but because of Exchange Control Regulations could not get sufficient funds out of the country to make her an adequate allowance while abroad. He contracted with the plaintiff that if she made £150 of Italian money available to his daughter in Italy, he would give her £150 in England and gave the plaintiff some share certificates as security. The whole transaction failed and the defendant sought recovery of his share certificates.

The court would not aid the defendant to recover his share certificates as the whole transaction was illegal.

Property under the contract to be used for unlawful purposes

The contract itself may be legal, but the purpose to which its subject matter is to be put may not. If the plaintiff enters into a contract with the defendant knowing that the defendant is going to use the subject matter for an illegal purpose, then it will not be enforceable.

In *Langton* v *Hughes* (1813) 1 M & S 593, the plaintiff sold the defendant Spanish juice, isinglass and ginger. The plaintiff knew the defendant was a brewer and that he intended to use these ingredients in flavouring his beer. In fact, the use of anything other than hops or malt in flavouring beer was illegal. The plaintiff sued the defendant for the price of the goods.

The plaintiff was held not to be entitled to recover anything, he knew the defendant was going to use them for a purpose contrary to statute.

The contract performed in an unlawful manner

The manner in which the contract is performed may be sufficient to turn it into a contract which is prohibited by statute.

In *Anderson* v *Daniel* [1924] 1 KB 138, the plaintiff sold the defendant some agricultural fertilizer, but failed to give him an invoice showing the composition of it as statute required.

It was held that he could not recover the price since he had not performed the contract in the only manner which was permitted by statute.

The question may arise whether the purpose of the statute is merely to penalise conduct or, in addition, to prohibit performance of the contract.

In *St John's Shipping* v *Joseph Rank Ltd* [1957] 1 QB 267, the defendant's defence to a claim by the plaintiff for freight was that the plaintiff had so overloaded his ship with the cargo in respect of which the freight was claimed, that the ship had been submerged below the load line, which was a statutory offence.

It was held that although the plaintiff's conduct was an offence, it did not affect the contract between the plaintiff and the defendant.

'A court should not hold that any contract or class of contract is prohibited by statute unless there is a clear implication, or "necessary inference" as Parke B put it that the statute so intended. If a contract has as its whole object the doing of the very act which the statute prohibits it can be argued that you can hardly make sense of a statute which forbids an act and yet permits to be made a contract to do it; that is a clear implication' per Devlin J.

The problem of illegality is expressly dealt with in some statutes, for example, the Trades Description Act 1968 states that a contract for the supply of goods is not void merely because it contravenes that Act. This raises the question whether, if the plaintiff sells the defendant a television set, can he recover the price if he fails to give notice of the transaction to the Post Office as required by statute?

Contracts to idemnify against criminal liability
A contract to idemnify a person against liability resulting from the deliberate commission of a crime cannot be enforced at law.

In *Askey* v *Golden Wine Co* [1948] 2 All ER 35, the plaintiff, a wholesaler, was fined as a result of breaches of the Food and Drugs Act and had to refund money to retailers. The breaches were due to his own gross negligence and failure to prevent them when he could have done so. He sought to recover the loss from the suppliers of the goods.

The court held that it would be against public policy to allow him to recover this loss, which was incurred through his own fault.

It is clearly established that a contract to indemnify a person against a crime which requires mens rea is illegal. See *Colburn* v *Patmore* (1834) 1 C M & R 73. However, where the offence is one of strict liability, it appears that a person can recover an indemnity for the innocent commission of such an offence.

In *Gregory* v *Ford* [1951] 1 All ER 121, X was employed to drive the defendant's lorry which had third party insurance as required under s35 Road Traffic Act 1930. However, there were conditions attached to the insurance. X had an accident while on an errand for the defendant and it transpired that the insurance policy was inoperative. The plaintiff sued the defendant for damages and the defendant in turn claimed to be indemnified by X. X argued the defendant had a duty to insure him against third party risks. The court held that there was no duty on the defendant to insure X against third party risks merely because he was their servant. However, X was entitled to assume that it was an implied term of his contract of employment that he should not be asked to do anything unlawful. He was entitled to assume the lorry was lawfully insured and was, therefore, not liable to indemnify the defendant.

Contracts which break the civil law

Contract to commit a civil wrong
If the contract is to deliberately commit a civil wrong, such as to assault a third party (*Allen* v *Rescous* (1677) 2 Lev 174), or give fraudulent preference to a creditor (*Cockshott* v *Bennet* (1788) 2 TR 763), it is illegal and unenforceable.

If the parties are ignorant of the fact that by the contract they are committing a civil wrong, then it is not illegal. Therefore, if X agrees to sell Y goods which, in fact, belong to a third party, both are liable in conversion. However, no case seems to have held such contracts illegal and s12 Sale of Goods Act 1979 would appear to lend support to the theory that they are not.

If one of the parties to the contract knows that the contract is illegal, for example, where the seller of goods knows they belong to a third party, then it appears that only the innocent party is entitled to rely on the contract.

In *Clay* v *Yates* (1856) 1 H & N 73, the plaintiff agreed to print a book for the defendant which had a libellous dedication. The plaintiff discovered afterwards that the dedication was libellous and printed the book without it. He then claimed the cost of printing the book. The defendant argued it was an entire contract and that the plaintiff could not recover anything as he had only given part performance.

It was held that there was an implied undertaking to pay for so much of the book as was lawful, on a quantum meruit basis.

Whether a contract to break a contract is illegal is not, as yet, clearly decided. In some instances it is clear that the courts will declare such contracts bad on grounds of public policy. Lauterpacht in his article in 52 LQR 494 (1936) suggests that the proper approach is to accept that a contract to break a contract is illegal and unenforceable, and then to inquire what exceptions are engrafted onto that rule.

In *Edwin Hill* v *First National Finance Corporation plc* [1989] 1 WLR 225, the defendant bankers held a charge on land scheduled for redevelopment. The defendants agreed to pay the developer the necessary funds, provided the plaintiffs were replaced by other architects. The plaintiffs sued claiming damages against the defendants for procuring breach of the contract that they had with the developer. The Court of Appeal held that the defendants' interference with the plaintiffs' contract was justified as being in defence and protection of an equal and superior right of the defendants to be repaid under the legal charge.

This suggests that certain types of contract while prima facie illegal may be defensible on the grounds of public policy.

Contract to indemnify against civil liability
If the civil wrong is deliberately committed, then it appears that the general rule is

that any contract of indemnity in respect of that wrong is illegal, for example, if X publishes a libel at the instigation of Y he cannot recover an indemnity from Y. See *W H Smith* v *Clinton* (1909) 99 LT 840. Where, however, the tendency of such a contract would be to restrict the circulation of the libel as published in a communication which the parties have agreed is to remain confidential, it would appear that an indemnity is recoverable if any liability is incurred through its disclosure. See *Weld-Blundell* v *Stephens* [1920] AC 956.

Where a civil wrong is innocently committed, then the general rule is that the plaintiff can sue on a contract of indemnity. Therefore, an employer can insure himself against civil liability for the tort of his employee, whether or not it is a crime, and he can obtain an indemnity for torts committed by one employee on another from the wrongdoer under the contract of employment. See *Lister* v *Romford Ice and Cold Storage Co* [1957] AC 555.

Where a civil liability arises out of the commission of a crime, the rule is that any contracts to indemnify are not effective.

In *Gray* v *Barr* [1971] 2 QB 554, the plaintiff shot and killed his wife's lover. He had an insurance policy which indemnified him against liability through causing death, and consequently sought to be indemnified under it for damages he had paid to the lover's estate.

The court decided the plaintiff's actions in shooting the defendant amounted to manslaughter and, as a matter of policy, he should not recover as armed violence should be deterred.

For further application of this principle, see *Re K (deceased)* [1985] 1 All ER 403.

In two exceptional cases, the plaintiff may recover where he is liable in civil law for a crime, where the crime is one of strict liability (see *Gregory* v *Ford* (above)); and under a motor insurance policy where the crime is committed negligently, but not if it is committed deliberately.

In *Tinline* v *White Cross Insurance* [1921] 3 KB 327, the plaintiff, a motorist, insured against 'accidental personal injury' to third parties, killed a third party through negligent driving. He was convicted of manslaughter and later was successfully sued by the estate of the third party. The plaintiff sought to recover from the insurers the damages he paid. It was held that he could recover from the insurers.

Contracts to waive rights conferred by statute

Whether a statutory right can be waived depends upon its overall purpose, and upon whether the intention of the statute would be frustrated by 'contracting out'. This is, therefore, the application of the provisions of public policy to the decision, because the courts will not allow the intentions of Parliament to be frustrated.

In *Johnson* v *Moreton* [1980] AC 37, the House of Lords held that a tenant could not contract out of the protection provided by s24 Agricultural Holdings Act 1948, because to do so would undermine the purpose of the Act.

Contract is illegal per se

The making of the contract itself may amount to an illegality and, in such circumstances, it may not only remain unenforced by the court but, in addition, it may be punishable with a fine or imprisonment. This is true, for example, of a conspiracy to defraud.

Therefore, if the purpose of a contract is to perpetrate a fraud on the prospective shareholders of a company (see *Begbie* v *Phosphate Sewage Co Ltd* (1875) LR 10 QB 491), the contract is illegal and criminal.

Contracts declared illegal by statute

Although the statute itself may not be repealed, the impact of certain sections of it may be diminished by subsequent legislation. Consider *City Index* v *Leslie* [1991] 3 All ER 180.

The plaintiff company carried on a business which included wagers on the stock market index movements. The defendant opened a credit account with the plaintiff company, and after a number of unsuccessful bets owed the company nearly £35,000. He stated he was unable to pay. The plaintiff company sued for the amount outstanding on the basis that, although betting and wagering contracts had for many years been unenforceable under the Gaming Act 1845, the Financial Services Act 1986 meant that such wagers were now exempt from the effect of the 1845 Act.

Section 63 Financial Services Act 1986 was held to cover wagers entered into by way of business with a party entitled to trade under the Act. (The plaintiff company was a member of the Association of Futures, Brokers and Dealers and recognised by the Secretary of State.) Such wagers on differences in the market are 'investments' for the purposes of the Act, and the buying and selling of such forecasts are excluded from the unenforceability provisions of the Gaming Act 1845. The full sum owed was, therefore, not considered to be an 'illegal' contract and, as such, was recoverable.

The exemption from gaming legislation of many City 'deals' is now to be found in s412 of the Financial Services and Markets Act 2000 and the Financial Services and Markets Act 2000 (Gaming Contracts) Order 2001.

13.3 Contracts contrary to public policy

Contracts to pervert the course of justice

Concealing and compounding crimes

Any agreement to conceal a crime is illegal and against public policy. See *Gardside* v *Outram* (1857) 26 LJ Ch 113.

Though the question as to whether if, in order to obtain information relating to crimes a promise to proceed no further by, say, the police, would be contractually binding, has never been tested in the courts.

The compounding of an offence other than treason is not an offence, except where it falls within s5 Criminal Law Act 1967, which provides that anyone:

> '... who knows or believes that an arrestable offence has been committed and that he has information which might be of material assistance in securing the prosecution or conviction of any offender for it is guilty of an indictable offence if he accepts, for not disclosing that information, any consideration other than (a) the making good of loss or injury occasioned by the offence or (b) the making of reasonable compensation for that loss or injury'.

Where an agreement is an offence under s5 it is not enforceable in law.

If the agreement is not to initiate a prosecution or report an offence to the police, then it may be considered as stifling a prosecution and contrary to public policy.

Again, the question as to whether it would be contrary to public policy if the plaintiff has a civil claim arising out of an offence and he compromises this with the defendant has not been tested in a court of law, nor whether it would make any difference if he offered not to report the matter to the police.

But note *Fulham Football Club Ltd* v *Cabra Estates plc* [1994] 1 BCLC 363 in which a development company and a local authority applied separately for planning consent to redevelop land. The plaintiffs covenanted with the development company that, for a substantial fee, they would not in any way support the council's application, including the provision of witnesses or evidence at any resultant public inquiry. Later, however, despite the covenant, the plaintiffs refused to support the development company, arguing that any agreement was void by reason of illegality. At first instance they were successful. The development company appealed. The Court of Appeal held that no agreement which required the giving of false evidence, or purported to prevent a witness responding to subpoena could be legal; it would always be contrary to public policy. But in commercial transactions such as this, involving disposition of land, an agreement to refrain from objecting, or to support, such a scheme would be considered valid. The plaintiffs could not rely on the rule concerning public policy to ignore the covenant they had agreed to as illegal. It would be an enforceable agreement and the defendants' appeal succeeded.

Interfering with proceedings

It is illegal to conduct criminal proceedings so that a person's name shall not be mentioned, or shall only be mentioned in a manner that does not damage or implicate him. An agreement not to appear and give evidence is illegal. A contract with a person who has 'stood bail' as a surety to indemnify the amount that the surety has stood is illegal and unenforceable. It is also an indictable offence.

Fraudulent preferences

Agreements to prefer creditors (who are unsecured) in winding up and bankruptcy proceedings are illegal and unenforceable. They may be set aside by statute, which declares them void rather than unenforceable.

Contracts with police informers

In *Carnduff* v *Rock* [2001] 1 WLR 1786 the claimant alleged that he had orally agreed with officers of the West Midlands force that he would provide information and assistance to enable the investigation of suspected criminals and that in return he would be paid reasonable remuneration. He sought to recover payment for information allegedly provided. The Court of Appeal held (Waller LJ dissenting) that here, at least, the claim was against the public interest and it would be struck out. As Laws LJ explained, the very business of trying the claim would transfer the difficult and delicate business of tracking and catching serious professional criminals from the confidential context of police operations to the glare of a court of justice.

Contracts which oust the jurisdiction of the courts

Such contracts are contrary to public policy as they would have the effect of evading many peremptory rules of law.

In *Anctil* v *Manufacturers Life Insurance* [1899] AC 604, a clause in an insurance policy provided that it should be 'incontestable' in certain events. The plaintiff attempted to sue on it and it was held that this clause did not stop the court from deciding if he had an insurable interest.

Maintenance agreements

The House of Lords decided in *Hyman* v *Hyman* [1929] AC 601 that a wife could not validly contract with her husband not to apply for maintenance on a divorce, and that a contract of that kind did not prevent her from applying. For a recent application of this, see *Sutton* v *Sutton* [1984] 1 All ER 168.

Arbitration

It is perfectly legal to have a clause in an agreement to refer a matter to a private tribunal for a decision before going to court. But, if such a clause deprives the parties of their right to go to court, it is contrary to public policy and void.

In *Czarnikow* v *Roth, Schmidt & Co* [1922] 2 KB 478, a contract for the sale of sugar contained a clause that all disputes should be referred to arbitration, but that the arbitrator should not be required by any party to state a special case for the court to decide a point of law.

The clause was held to be an attempt to deprive the court of its jurisdiction to decide points of law and was, therefore, contrary to public policy.

The parties to a contract are, however, at liberty to make it a condition precedent of going to court that arbitration should have taken place.

In *Scott* v *Avery* (1856) 5 HLC 811, an insurance policy contained a clause providing that the assured should not be 'entitled to maintain any action on his policy until the matters in dispute shall have been referred to and decided by arbitrators ... and the obtaining of the decision of such arbitrators is hereby declared to be condition precedent to the right of (the assured) to maintain any action'.

The clause was declared valid – it did not oust the jurisdiction of the court, but only laid a timetable for when that jurisdiction arose.

Maintenance and champerty

Maintenance is the unjustified meddling in, support of, or instigation of litigation by a person who has no concern or interest in it. A contract, for example, in which X agrees to help Y finance litigation to have Z's will set aside when X has no interest in the will may be within this category.

Champerty is where a person who is maintaining another extracts an agreement for a share in the winnings of the action. For example, X, a solicitor, agrees to help Y who is poor, to bring an action in defamation against Z, provided Y gives X 50 per cent of the damages recovered.

Both maintenance and champerty were formerly a crime and a tort, but by ss13 and 14 Criminal Law Act 1967 both were abolished as such. However, the Act went on to provide that such abolition would 'not affect any rule of law as to the cases in which a contract is to be treated as contrary to public policy or otherwise illegal'. Therefore, a contract concerning maintenance or champerty is still illegal.

The leading case is *Martell* v *Consett Iron Co Ltd* [1955] Ch 363. An association for the protection of rivers from pollution supported an action by one of its members in connection with a river that ran through his land. The defendant said that the action was unlawfully maintained.

Danckwerts J, whose decision was upheld by the Court of Appeal, held that 'support of legal proceedings based on a bona fide community of pecuniary interest or religion or principle or problems', did not constitute maintenance.

The area of maintenance and champerty was re-examined by the Court of Appeal and House of Lords in *Trendtex Trading Corporation* v *Credit Suisse* [1982] AC 679. The issue arose out of a purported assignment of the right to litigate. The plaintiff sold cement. Payment was to be by confirmed letter of credit. The bank failed to honour the letter of credit. The plaintiff sued. After the Court of Appeal hearing, the plaintiff assigned the right to sue to Credit Suisse to whom the plaintiff was very substantially indebted. Credit Suisse then assigned the right to a third party. Subsequently, the plaintiff thought that the transfer of the right to sue was undervalued. As part of the indebtedness to Credit Suisse arose out of the cement contract and the financing of litigation, the plaintiff then claimed that the agreement was champertous. The House of Lords held that the assignment was void.

The Court of Appeal had held it valid and Oliver LJ said that as the defendants had a close commercial relationship with the plaintiff, which would have justified them maintaining the action and participating in the profits, he could see no reason why they should not have the right to litigate as well.

Lord Denning MR saw no reason why the benefit of the right to sue should not be assignable, given that the benefit of the contract before breach is assignable. But note: that this would not extend to purely personal actions, nor where the assignment was to a solicitor. Such assignments would be champertous.

The House of Lords held that it was void here because the assignment was the first step in a transaction which involved further assignment to the third party. Lord Roskill thought that Oliver LJ should have distinguished between the interest necessary to support an assignment of a cause of action, and an interest necessary to justify maintaining the cause of action. It does not follow that the interest is the same. It was necessary to show that there was a commercial interest in the enforcement of the claim before the assignment would be valid. The burden of proof is on the assignee.

In *Picton Jones & Co* v *Arcadia Developments* [1989] 3 EG 85, the plaintiffs, who were a firm of surveyors, agreed to act for the defendants in relation to the aquisition of some amusement arcades. Their fees were only to be payable 'in the event of ultimate success'.

Though the plaintiffs were successful in carrying out their assignments, the defendants refused to pay, stating that the contract was one of champerty and, as such, illegal and unenforceable. Further, they alleged that entering such contracts was contrary to rules established by the plaintiffs' professional institute and, as such, contrary to public policy and illegal.

Judgment was given to the plaintiffs since, first, the doctrine of champerty was confined to agreements regarding the outcome of litigation. Also, secondly, the fact that a professional institution forbids a particular type of contract does not necessarily mean that it is contrary to public policy and thus illegal.

It was worth considering, in view of the Code of Practice issued by the Bar Council in which 'contingency fees' were introduced for the first time, whether maintenance and champerty, in particular, were obsolete. In *Bevan Ashford (A Firm)* v *Geoff Yeandle (Contractors) Ltd (In Liquidation)* [1998] 3 All ER 238 Sir Richard Scott V-C decided that a conditional fee agreement sanctioned for proceedings by s58 of the Courts and Legal Services Act 1990 and by the Conditional Fee Agreements Order 1995 made thereunder was free from any public policy objection in relation to arbitration proceedings in pursuance of that particular cause of action. However, in *Hughes* v *Kingston upon Hull City Council* [1999] 2 WLR 1229 the Queen's Bench Divisional Court held that a contingency fee arrangement in criminal proceedings was unenforcable.

Interestingly, the Court of Appeal in *Thai Trading Co (A Firm)* v *Taylor and Another* [1998] 3 All ER 65, held that the position now is that the courts will not find anything unlawful in a solicitor acting for a party to litigation to agree to forego all or part of his fee if he loses, provided he does not seek to recover more than his ordinary profit costs and disbursements if he wins. This reasoning was in fact applied in the *Bevan Ashford* case (above), but it was rejected by the Court of Appeal in *Awwad* v *Geraghty & Co* [2000] 1 All ER 608: see section 13.5.

The Court of Appeal had another opportunity to consider the position in *Factortame Ltd* v *Secretary of State for the Environment, Transport and the Regions (No 2)* [2002] 4 All ER 97. It having been decided that the claimant fishing companies were entitled to compensatory damages in respect of the United Kingdom Government's breach of Community law, the claimants agreed to pay a firm of accountants 8 per cent of the final settlement received as their fees for preparing and submitting the claimants' claims for damages. The claimants sought to recover these fees as costs, but the Secretary of State resisted this claim, contending – unsuccessfully – that the agreement as to fees was champertous. Lord Phillips of Worth Matravers MR said:

> 'The costs judge concluded that the ... agreements [with the accountants] lacked the characteristics that might have rendered them contrary to public policy under the vestigial remnants of the law of champerty. As we considered the evidence and heard the argument unfold we became increasingly convinced that he was correct. Reflection after reserving our judgment has not shaken that conclusion. The claimants had been brought low by the initial wrong done to them and by the costs and stress of prolonged litigation in which no quarter was given. They were faced with an extraordinarily complicated task in proving the damage that they had suffered and there was a real risk that lack of funds might result in their losing the fruits of their litigation. The ... agreements ensured that they continued to enjoy access to justice. They did this without putting justice in jeopardy. The ... agreements were not champertous.'

His Lordship affirmed that s58 Courts and Legal Services Act 1990 does not apply to expert witnesses and the court considered that it would be in a very rare case indeed that the court would be prepared to consent to an expert being instructed under a contingency fee agreement. Here, the accountants were not expert witnesses: they had engaged others to perform that role.

Contracts promoting sexual immorality

Contracts which fall within this category are those which promote extramarital sexual intercourse. Pictures, books and films which are illegal by virtue of the Obscene Publications Act 1959 fall within the category of contracts which break the law.

A promise by a man to pay a woman money, either to become his mistress or to secure the continuance of cohabitation, used to be thought illegal. See *Franco* v *Bolton* (1797) 3 Ves 368. Any bond given after cohabitation to secure payment on such promises was, likewise, illegal. It does not follow that the same remains true. Values change and stable domestic relations between unmarried couples are no longer regarded as a departure from the norm. In recent cases, the illegality of these domestic relations has not been raised and, probably, would not be welcomed. An example of a case where a contract (a contractual licence) was found is *Tanner* v

Tanner [1975] 1 WLR 1346. A married man who had twins by his mistress, provided her with a house. When the man subsequently attempted to evict her, it was held that there was an implied contract that she could remain there. The consideration provided by her was the relinquishment of a rent-controlled flat.

If the payment does not promote immorality by promoting cohabitation, then it is not illegal. Thus, a promise to pay money to a woman with whom a man has in the past cohabited is not illegal, it is a contract which lacks consideration in any case. See *Beaumont* v *Reeve* (1846) 8 QB 483. A gift by a man to a woman either during or after cohabitation is also, without more, valid. See *Ayerst* v *Jenkins* (1873) LR 16 Eq 275.

Contracts which have the effect of promoting prostitution are illegal. Thus, a contract to hire out a brougham to a prostitute for her profession is illegal. See *Pearce* v *Brooks* (1866) LR 1 Ex 213. But, apparently, it is not illegal to contract to wash a prostitute's linen which included a quantity of gentlemen's nightcaps. See *Lloyd* v *Johnson* (1798) 1 B & P 340.

Contracts to lease premises to prostitutes for their profession are illegal, but a contract to let a room to a prostitute who practises her profession at another place is valid 'because persons of that description must have a place to lay their heads'. See *Appleton* v *Campbell* (1826) 2 C & P 347.

Contracts concerning family matters

Contracts relating to divorce or separation
A contract by the parties to divorce proceedings is invalid if made with a corrupt intention, for example, where one party bribes the other to institute the proceedings or to deceive the court on certain matters relevant in the proceedings like family finances. But, bona fide attempts to come to arrangements which overcome the difficulties resulting from a broken marriage are valid.

In *Brodie* v *Brodie* [1917] P 271, an agreement was made between a man and a woman, who felt obliged to marry after the woman gave birth to a child, that they would not live together after the marriage. This was held to be invalid.

Spouses who are already married may agree to separate and, if they are already separated, they may make further agreements concerning their position. Where spouses attempt reconciliation, then any agreements relating to future separation are valid as it may aid the reconciliation. See *Harrison* v *Harrison* [1910] 1 KB 35.

Contracts to marry
By s1 Law Reform (Miscellaneous Provisions) Act 1970, actions for breach of promise to marry were abolished. Prior to this, only a promise by a married man to marry was unenforceable as against public policy on the ground that it tended to promote sexual immorality. However, a promise of marriage between the decree nisi and decree absolute was, then, permissible.

Marriage brokerage contracts

An undertaking for reward to procure a marriage between two parties is against public policy and void. The same rule applies if the contract is merely to find a marriage partner for a client. See *Hermann* v *Charlesworth* [1905] 2 KB 123. This rule, if still applicable nowadays, raises an interesting question as to the status of contracts between marriage bureaux and their clients.

Contracts in restraint of marriage

A contract which attempts to restrain or prevent a party from marrying is void and against public policy. See *Lowe* v *Peers* (1768) 4 Burr 2225. But a contract which deters a person from marrying by providing some inducement which will end when he or she marries is not void, for example, a promise to let a house to a person until marriage is valid. See *Gibson* v *Dickie* (1815) 3 M & S 463.

Contracts to assign parental rights

A contract to transfer parental rights and liabilities is against public policy and void. Therefore, if X agrees to sell his child to Y, it is illegal. But a separation agreement between husband and wife for one or the other to relinquish such rights is valid – s1(1) Guardianship Act 1973.

Contracts interfering with government or foreign relations

Procurement of public offices and honours

Contracts for the sale of public appointments, such as a directorship in a public company, are contrary to public policy and void. Likewise, any agreement to pay money to procure an honour for the payer is also contrary to public policy, as it may result in improper methods being employed. It is also an offence under the Honours (Prevention of Abuses) Act 1925. See *Parkinson* v *Royal College of Ambulance* [1925] 2 KB 1.

Contracts by employees and members of public authorities

By s117 Local Government Act 1972, any officer with a direct or indirect pecuniary interest in a contract entered into by a local authority must declare his interest and can take no fees or rewards beyond his ordinary remuneration. Formerly, at common law, it was an offence for a public officer to accept a bribe or show favour. See *Re Wallace* [1920] 2 Ch 274.

Contracts to deceive public authorities

If a contract is made either to conceal or misrepresent facts to a public authority or body, for example, tax returns to the Inland Revenue, then it is illegal and void.

In *Alexander* v *Rayson* [1936] 1 KB 169, the plaintiff let a service flat to the defendant for £1,200 by a contract which was drawn up in two separate documents. In the first document, the defendant agreed to pay £450 for the flat and services and, in the second, the defendant agreed to pay £750 for the flat and services and the use of a refrigerator. The purpose was to deceive the local authority in respect of rates. The contract was declared illegal and unenforceable.

If a contract is an attempt to evade the provisions of a statute, the purpose of which is to protect one of the contracting parties, then it is illegal.

In *Farrell* v *Alexander* [1976] 2 All ER 721 the defendant wished to assign the unexpired term of four years of her tenancy to the plaintiff. The assignment was to be done by means of a surrender by the defendant to her landlord, who would grant the plaintiff a new lease and, as a term of the agreement, the plaintiff was to pay the defendant £4,000 for fixtures and fittings, although they were worth much less. The plaintiff claimed that the balance of the £4,000 was an illegal premium under the Rent Acts. It was declared that the plaintiff was entitled to recover so much as exceeded the value of the fixtures and fittings. This was because the Rent Act only made the excess recoverable and not the whole sum.

Contracts which interfere with foreign relations

Where a contract has as its object the doing of an act illegal by the law of a friendly foreign country, it is illegal and void.

In *Regazzoni* v *KC Sethia* [1958] AC 301, a contract was made to export Indian jute to Italy with the ultimate purpose of re-exporting it from Italy to South Africa. Indian law prohibited the export of goods to South Africa and the contract could only be performed by making false declarations as to the destination of the jute.

The court would not help the plaintiff to enforce the contract as it was an attempt to contravene Indian law.

If a contract has as its purpose the breach of the customs regulations of a foreign country or aiding terrorists to attack that country, it is illegal. See *De Wutz* v *Hendricks* (1824) 2 Bing 314.

The public policy of a friendly foreign state could not of itself prevent the enforcement of a contract in England. But if the contract was contrary to English public policy, and the same public policy applied in the friendly foreign country, the combination of the two factors would prevent enforcement. See *Lemenda Trading Co Ltd* v *African Middle East Petroleum Co Ltd* [1988] 1 All ER 513.

See also *Howard* v *Shirlstar Container Transport Ltd* [1990] 1 WLR 1292, where the defendant company agreed to pay the plaintiff £25,000 to 'remove' from Nigeria an aircraft belonging to them. He flew the aircraft out of Lagos without obtaining the necessary clearance and in breach of air traffic controls. After pursuit by a Nigerian Air Force plane, he made a forced landing in the Ivory Coast; the plane was impounded and later returned to Nigeria.

The defendant company said that because the contract required the plaintiff to 'successfully' remove the aircraft from Nigerian airspace, he had not performed the contract as agreed and they were, therefore, justified in withholding the agreed fee.

On a strictly technical interpretation the aircraft had (for a short time) left Nigeria and, therefore, the full sum was payable. A court would not allow a person to benefit from an illegal act, whether or not arising under foreign law, if to do so would be an affront to public conscience. Whether an illegal act might be considered against public policy was a question of fact in each case. In this case, the plaintiff's illegal act had been to save his own and his crew's lives and, on hearing that this would have been an acceptable defence under Nigerian law, the court permitted the plaintiff to recover the full amount.

Contracts to trade with the enemy
Under the Trading with the Enemy Act 1939, it is an offence to trade or attempt to trade with the enemy. Contracts to trade with the enemy are therefore illegal.

An enemy is anyone voluntarily resident or carrying on business in an enemy territory (*Porter* v *Freudenberg* [1915] 1 KB 857), and if the contract tends to aid the economy of the enemy that is sufficient.

Contracts interfering with personal liberty

If a contract imposes conditions on an individual which restrict his liberty unduly without cause it is illegal.

In *Horwood* v *Millar's Timber and Trading Co* [1917] 1 KB 305, the plaintiff borrowed money from the defendant on terms that the plaintiff would not, without the defendant's written consent, leave his job, dispose of his house, borrow more money or move home. The contract imposed unreasonable restrictions on the plaintiff's liberty and was, therefore, held to be void.

Restrictions imposed by a father on his son would not appear to fall within this category provided there are reasons for them.

In *Denny* v *Denny* [1919] 1 KB 583, a son who associated with gamblers, swindlers and other disreputable characters went bankrupt. His father promised to pay his debts and an allowance provided he did not become bankrupt again and reformed his character, gave up these friends, did not go within 80 miles of Piccadilly Circus without his father's consent, and did not have any contract with moneylenders, bookmakers or their servants. The contract was held to be valid; it was an attempt by a father to act for his son's moral benefit and not intended to restrict his liberty merely for commercial reasons.

13.4 Covenants in restraint of trade

Where a contract contains a covenant in restraint of trade, it will generally only be the covenant which is unenforceable (or part of it) and not the whole contract. The whole contract will be unenforceable, of course, if the promise to restrict trading activities is the only consideration moving from the promisee, for example, if the contract is: 'I will give you £100 if you will agree not to sell fish in the United

Kingdom.' If the promise not to sell in the UK is unenforceable, the whole contract may fail.

All covenants in restraint of trade are prima facie unenforceable at common law. They become enforceable only if they are reasonable.

Definition of restraint of trade

The leading case is *Esso Petroleum Co* v *Harper's Garage (Stourport) Ltd* [1968] AC 269 (see below). Various definitions were attempted, or not, as the case may be.

Lord Reid would not attempt to define the dividing line between contracts which are, and contracts which are not, in restraint of trade.

Lord Wilberforce: 'no exhaustive test can be stated – probably no non-exhaustive test'. The common law has often (if sometimes unconsciously) thrived on ambiguity and it would be mistaken, even if it were possible, to try to crystallise the rules of this, or any aspect of public policy, into neat propositions. The doctrine of restraint of trade is one to be applied to factual situations with a broad and flexible rule of reason.

Lord Hodson adopted a test attempted by Diplock LJ in *Petrofina (Great Britain) Ltd* v *Martin* [1966] Ch 146:

'A contract in restraint of trade is one in which a party (the covenantor) agrees with any other party (the covenantee) to restrict his liberty in the future to carry on trade with other persons not parties to the contract in such manner as he chooses.'

Lord Morris thought that the above was a helpful exposition, but not to be taken too literally. He also referred to dicta of Lord Denning MR in the *Petrofina case*:

'Every member of the community is entitled to carry on any trade or business he chooses and in such manner as he thinks most desirable in his own interests, so long as he does nothing unlawful; with the consequence that any contract which interferes with the free exercise of his trade or business, by restricting him in the work he may do for others, is a contract in restraint of trade. It is invalid unless it is reasonable as between the parties.'

Lord Pearce:

'Somewhere there must be a line between those contracts which are in restraint of trade ... and those contracts which merely regulate the normal commercial relations between the parties.'

Note, for example, the case of *Watson* v *Prager* [1991] 1 WLR 726 in which the relationship between a professional boxer and his manager was held to come within the ambit of restraint of trade. The court held that the contract was not a normal commercial contract freely entered into by both parties, but was, by virtue of the British Boxing Board of Control's monopoly, to be subject to more stringent than usual judicial supervision. The contract would only be enforced if it was reasonable. Reasonableness would be tested by the nature of the terms, not how fairly or otherwise the defendant had adhered to conditions laid down by the BBBC. The fact that the manager had negotiated higher than average 'purses' did not alter the fact he was unilaterally able to agree the 'purse' for fights; the plaintiff was unable to negotiate on his own behalf. This was unreasonable, even if the actual sums negotiated were good.

The court decided that the contract contained restrictions on the plaintiff which were restrictive and unreasonable and was therefore unreasonable as a whole.

The origin of modern law is in the speech of Lord Macnaghten in *Nordenfelt* v *Maxim Nordenfelt Guns & Ammunition Co* [1894] AC 535 from which the proposition emerged that: although a covenant in restraint of trade is prima facie unenforceable, it will become enforceable if it is reasonable. Note that the recent case of *Allied Dunbar* v *Frank Weisinger* [1987] IRLR 60 has confirmed that the proper test is to consider whether the restraint is reasonably necessary for the protection of the interests of the covenantor. The concept of 'proportionality' in testing a covenant in restraint of trade is *not* a valid test. The matters which are pertinent in assessing reasonableness are the legitimate interests of the parties; and the public interest.

The criteria for determining reasonableness will depend on the nature of the transaction in which the restraint is imposed.

Although the categories of covenants in restraint of trade are not closed, the bulk of case law falls into the following categories: sale of a business and employment; restrictive trading; solus agreements; and others.

Sale of a business and employment

Covenants which restrain an employee's activities after the termination of the employment have always been construed more zealously than covenants which restrict the trading activities of the vendor of a business. The reason is that there is a greater parity of bargaining power between the vendor and purchaser of a business than between an employee and employer. That does not mean, however, that the court will go to extravagant lengths to find a covenant restricting the employee's activities void. In *Home Counties Dairies* v *Skilton* [1970] 1 WLR 526, the defendant (a milkman) covenanted that he would not serve or sell 'milk or dairy produce' to any customer or former customer of his employer for a period of one year. It was argued that this was too wide, because it would prevent him from working in a grocer's shop.

From the obvious intentions of the parties, the court held that the clause was intended to apply only to occupation as a roundsman, which was a business similar to that of his employer. The clause was reasonable.

The legitimate interests which can be protected by an employer are less than those which can be protected by the purchaser of a business. Whereas the purchaser of a business can be deemed to be entitled to the goodwill of the business free of competition, the same is not true of an employer. He cannot protect himself against competition, but only against the use of something in which he has a proprietary interest, such as a list of customers. See *Fitch* v *Dewes* [1921] 2 AC 158.

Although an employer's principal concern is likely to be about soliciting customers, it does not follow that this is the only interest which he can protect. In *Eastham* v *Newcastle United Football Club* [1964] Ch 413, Wilberforce J thought that other covenants in restraint might protect legitimate interests and be enforceable. In that case, he was considering the 'retain and transfer' system (where an employee could not transfer sides without the consent of both the sides from which, and to which, he wished to change). In fact, he did not find that this was an interest to be protected.

Reasonableness

Nature of the relationship with the covenantee's customers

The nature of the relationship which the vendor or employee would have had with customers of a business is relevant. For instance, a covenant imposed on the bookkeeper of a small business not to deal with customers or former customers of the business is unlikely to be reasonable because the employee would not have come into contact with the customers and would not be in a position to solicit them.

Area of restraint

The area to which an employee or vendor can be limited in plying his trade is a matter which goes to the reasonableness of the clause. Again, it may follow that a purchaser of a business has a greater interest to protect than an employer and can impose wider restraints.

In *Nordenfelt* v *Maxim Nordenfelt Guns and Ammunition* [1894] AC 535, a worldwide restraint was held valid. N entered into a contract for the the sale of his worldwide business. He undertook not to compete with it (inter alia) in the trade or business of guns, gun making, explosives, etc, for 25 years or anywhere in the world. The clause was held valid in so far as set out above. Certain words were deleted.

On the other hand, in *Mason* v *Provident Clothing* [1913] AC 724, a covenant by a canvasser, employed to sell clothes in Islington, not to enter into a similar business within 25 miles of London was held void. The area was too large.

In *Spencer* v *Marchington* [1988] IRLR 392, a restrictive covenant to prevent a former employee being engaged in a similar business within a radius of 25 miles of the ex-employer's business was too wide and contrary to public policy.

The case of *Briggs* v *Oates* [1991] 1 All ER 407 concerned a restraint of trade clause as agreed between solicitors. The solicitor's contract of employment with the firm contained a restriction that he would not set up in practice on his own, nor go to any rival firm, within a five mile radius of his present employers. The restriction was to last for five years. The court found that the restrictions were reasonable and binding.

Scope of restraint

Only those activities which pose a threat to an employer's legitimate interests may be covered. So in *Attwood* v *Lamont* [1920] 3 KB 571, the plaintiff carried on business as a draper, tailor and outfitter in Kidderminster. The defendant, who was head cutter and manager of the tailoring department, agreed that he would not at any time carry on the trades of tailor, dressmaker, general draper, milliner, hatter, haberdasher, or outfitter within 10 miles of Kidderminster. It was decided that only the restraint of him as a tailor was reasonable. Note that the Court of Appeal refused to apply the 'blue pencil test' below.

In *Clarke* v *Newland* [1991] 1 All ER 397, a restraint of trade clause covering members of a medical partnership contained a clause agreeing 'not to practise in the area of the practice'. The Court of Appeal had to consider not only what the exact 'practice area' was, but also whether the phrase meant that the defendant could not practise as a medical practitioner of any sort, or whether the bar was simply applicable to general medicine.

Duration of the restraint

In *Fitch* v *Dewes* (above), a life-long restraint was upheld. The circumstances in which this may be upheld, however, were said in *Fellowes* v *Fisher* [1976] QB 122 to be rare.

Public interest

It is frequently said that a covenant will be void if it is contrary to the public interest. There is little direct authority. In *Wyatt* v *Kreglinger & Fernau* [1933] 1 KB 793, the employers of a wool broker promised him a pension on his retirement provided that he did not re-enter the wool trade and did nothing to their detriment. He claimed for arrears of his pension, but the court declared that he could not recover. One of the reasons given in the judgments was that the stipulation against competition was contrary to the public interest.

In *Deacons* v *Bridge* [1984] 2 All ER 19, the Privy Council upheld a restraint on a former partner in a firm of solicitors the effect of which was that he would not act as a solicitor in Hong Kong for a period of five years for any client of the firm or any person who had been a client during the three years preceding his departure from the firm. Their Lordships did not consider that a five-year restriction was unreasonable, and also thought that such a restriction was reasonable in the public interest.

In *Kerr* v *Morris* [1986] 3 All ER 217, the Court of Appeal held that a restraint on a doctor, a member of a partnership practising within the National Health Service, which precluded him from practising within a certain area, or treating patients of the partnership, was not contrary to the public interest.

Restrictive trading

Where suppliers and acquirers contract not with each other but suppliers contract inter se, and acquirers contract inter se, the rules about restraint of trade do not cease to apply. It is, however, more difficult to discover the interest that deserves to be protected.

In *English Hop Growers* v *Dering* [1928] 2 KB 174, hop growers undertook to deliver their crops to a central selling agency to avoid 'cut-throat' competition during a period of surplus. The agreement was held to be valid.

Compare *McEllstrim* v *Ballymacelligot Cooperative Society* [1919] AC 548. An association of farmers in Ireland promised to buy all the milk produced by its members in the area. The members promised not to sell milk to anyone except the association. The agreement was declared invalid, because no farmer could withdraw from the association without the consent of the association, and that consent could be unreasonably withheld.

An agreement was held invalid in a more recent case because it would be prejudicial to a group of people, even though it would not prejudice the general public.

In *Kores Manufacturing* v *Kolok Manufacturing* [1959] Ch 108, both organisations produced carbon paper and typewriter ribbons. They agreed not to employ each other's former employees for five years after leaving that employment. The area of restraint was declared to be too wide. It covered all employees no matter what they knew, and was of excessive duration.

Solus agreements

Many of these agreements have arisen between oil companies and garage proprietors, and some in respect of tied public houses. The leading case is *Esso Petroleum* v *Harper's Garage* [1968] AC 269. The defendants had undertaken to purchase from the plaintiffs petrol for two filling stations operated by them. In one case, the promise was of four years and five months duration. In respect of the other filling station, the agreement was for 21 years. It was held that the agreement for four years and five months was valid; that the agreement for 21 years was not valid. Further, as the purchase of the filling station was secured by a mortgage in favour of the plaintiffs containing the covenant, the covenant would be regarded as a clog on the equity of redemption of the mortgage.

In *Alec Lobb (Garages)* v *Total Oil* [1985] 1 All ER 303 CA, in 1969 the plaintiffs' garage business was in financial straits. In return for financial support from the defendants, they granted to the defendants a 51-year lease of their premises at a full market rent, then took for themselves an underlease (a 'leaseback') at a low rent for 21 years, which contained a tie to buy all their petrol from the defendants for a period of at least seven, and possibly as much as 21 years. In 1979, the plaintiffs sued to have the lease set aside and the exclusive purchase agreement declared void as being in unreasonable restraint of trade. The Court of Appeal held the exclusive sale agreement valid, and refused to set aside the lease.

The court had regard to the overall transaction, in particular (1) it was a rescue operation, benefiting the plaintiffs; (2) there was ample consideration for the grant of the lease to the defendants; (3) there were break clauses in the underlease; and (4) there was a public interest in encouraging a transaction which enabled a plaintiff to continue trading. See also *Amoco* v *Rocca Bros* [1975] AC 561 and *Cleveland Petroleum* v *Dartstone* [1969] 1 WLR 116.

Other agreements

The categories of restraint of trade are not closed, although the approach of the courts is that it is a rule which should be extended only cautiously.

In *Pharmaceutical Society of Great Britain* v *Dickson* [1970] AC 403, a rule of the Society which restricted the trading of chemists was invalid. A majority view was that this was because it was in restraint of trade.

Also, in *Greig* v *Insole* [1978] 1 WLR 302, a restriction on cricketers was held to be in restraint of trade.

13.5 Enforcement of illegal contracts

Where the contract itself is prohibited

If the contract itself is prohibited by law, then it is unenforceable and neither party to it can plead ignorance or innocence as an excuse.

The party which instigated the illegality will not be able to enforce the contract itself in any circumstances; thus, in *Pearce* v *Brooks* (above), the owner of a brougham who let it to a prostitute, knowing it was for the purposes of her profession, could not sue for the hire fee.

Any attempts by either party to enforce a contract prohibited by law by indirect means will be nullified by the court. Therefore, if the contract provides for arbitration, the court will set aside any awards made by the arbitrator, *David Taylor* v *Barnett Trading Co* [1953] 1 WLR 562. The Court of Appeal recently, in *Birkett* v *Acorn Business Machines Ltd* (1999) The Times 24 August, held that the courts have an overriding duty in the public interest not to order enforcement of a contract that is tainted by illegality, even where the illegality is not pleaded, provided the court can eliminate any other possible defences with confidence. Hence, contracts which aim to defy the law and public interest would be declared as unenforcable by the courts.

If either party to an illegal contract commits wrongs which are independent of the contract, then the court will recognise and enforce remedies for such wrongs.

In *Edler* v *Auerbach* [1950] 1 KB 359, the plaintiff let premises to the defendant under an illegal lease which was unenforceable by either party. The defendant removed a bath from the premises and promised the plaintiff he would replace it at the end of the tenancy. He failed to do so and the plaintiff sued for damages. It was held that the defendant's promise was independent of the illegal lease and, therefore, the plaintiff could recover damages for the failure to replace the bath. This principle was recently illustrated by the Court of Appeal in the case of *Mohamed* v *Alaga & Co (A Firm)* [1999] 3 All ER 699. The plaintiff (M) (a Somalian), a professional translator of the Somali language, brought an action against the defendant (a firm of solicitors) based on an alleged oral contract. M contended that he would introduce Somali asylum seekers to the defendant in return for one-half of any fees received from the Legal Aid Board by the defendant. M would also assist in the translation and 'getting-up' of the case. M claimed that the solicitors had breached the agreement by failing to make the agreed payments. M therefore sued for breach of contract and claimed in the alternative a reasonable price for work carried out at the solicitors' expense. Lightman J, in the first instance, struck out the plaintiff's action on the grounds that the contract was illegal and hence unenforceable and that the alternative claim in restitution was therefore not maintainable. M appealed.

The Court of Appeal allowed the appeal in part. Whilst holding that the agreement itself was an illegal contract and as such would not be enforced by the court, the alternative claim for reasonable remuneration for services rendered would be allowed.

It would have defeated public policy to allow a non solicitor to enlist the court's aid to enforce an agreement which the solicitor was prohibited from making in the light of r7a of the Solicitors' Practice Rules 1990 made by the Law Society. This did not, in the Court's view, taint the plaintiff's alternative claim for restitution, which the Court viewed as a quantum merit claim as opposed to one for the recovery of consideration under the unlawful contract.

The question received further consideration by the Court of Appeal in *Awwad* v *Geraghty & Co* [2000] 1 All ER 608. Before the making of orders authorising conditional fee agreements in proceedings for libel, Awad Awwad brought such proceedings and Geraghty & Co, solicitors, acted for him. They agreed that the solicitors would be paid at their full rate if Awwad won and at a lower rate if he lost. Awwad accepted a payment into court but, when the solicitors sent him a bill at the lower rate, he refused to make any payment. Their Lordships concluded that, since the agreement had been unlawful when it was made, it would not be enforced and, in these circumstances, the solicitors were not entitled to payment on a quantum meruit or any other basis. May LJ explained the position as follows:

> 'Although no doubt not every trifling breach of the Solicitors' Practice Rules would render a transaction with which it was concerned unenforceable, in my view an arrangement to receive a contingency fee contrary to r8(1) would make the fee agreement which it comprised unenforceable. That was the conclusion of this court where there was a breach of r7 of the Solicitors' Practice Rules, which forbids fee sharing, in *Mohamed* v *Alaga & Co* [1999] 3 All ER 699. In the context of enforceability, I can see no distinction

of substance or quality between an unlawful contingency fee agreement and an unlawful agreement to share professional fees. The facts of the present case are stronger against enforceability than were those in *Mohamed*'s case. Geraghty & Co are solicitors seeking to enforce an arrangement which, as the judge found, Miss Geraghty knew to be contrary to the rules of her profession. In *Mohamed*'s case, the plaintiff was not a solicitor and it was assumed that he was unaware of any prohibition on fee sharing agreements.'

Contrary to views expressed by the Court of Appeal in *Thai Trading Co* v *Taylor* [1998] 3 All ER 65 (see section 13.3), in *Awwad* their Lordships were not persuaded that there was any difference in substance between an agreement to charge a fee or an enhanced fee if the client wins and an agreement to forgo some or all of the fee if he loses.

In *Callery* v *Gray (Nos 1 and 2)* [2002] 3 All ER 417 the House of Lords heard that, following a motoring accident in which he had suffered minor injuries, the claimant entered into a conditional fee agreement with his solicitors providing for a success fee of 60 per cent. A few days later he took out an after-the-event insurance policy (premium £350) to protect himself against the possibility of liability for the defendant's costs. On the same day, his solicitors sent the defendant a letter before action. The claim was settled before proceedings were issued and the defendant agreed to pay the claimant's reasonable costs and disbursements. Since the parties were unable to agree the amount of costs and disbursements, the claimant commenced costs-only proceedings. The district judge reduced the success fee to 40 per cent but allowed the premium; on appeal, the judge upheld the district judge's decision; on a further appeal the Court of Appeal upheld the judge as to the premium but reduced the success fee to 20 per cent. The appeal against the Court of Appeal's decision was dismissed, although Lord Scott of Foscote would not have allowed recovery of the insurance premium. Lord Bingham of Cornhill said:

'There are none the less two reasons which lead me to the conclusion that the House should not intervene. The first is that the responsibility for monitoring and controlling the developing practice in a field such as this lies with the Court of Appeal and not the House, which should ordinarily be slow to intervene. The House cannot respond to changes in practice with the speed and sensitivity of the Court of Appeal, before which a number of cases are likely over time to come ... I would [also] decline to intervene because, as the Court of Appeal repeatedly stressed, the present issues arise at a very early stage in the practical development of the new funding regime, when reliable factual material is sparse, market experience is meagre and trends are hard to discern ... I feel sure that district and costs judges, circuit judges and in the last resort the Court of Appeal can be relied on to maintain a fair and publicly beneficial balance between competing interests.'

Indeed, a refinement in the approach to these matters may be seen in the decision of the Court of Appeal in *Halloran* v *Delaney* [2003] 1 All ER 775. Their Lordships concluded that judges concerned with questions relating to the recoverability of a success fee in simple claims which are settled without the need to commence proceedings should now ordinarily decide to allow an uplift of 5 per cent on the claimant's lawyers' costs (including the costs of any costs-only proceedings which are awarded to them) unless persuaded that a higher uplift is appropriate in the particular circumstances of the case.

For the present position as to which conditional fee agreements may be enforced, see ss58 and 58A of the Courts and Legal Services Act 1990, as substituted by s27(1) of the Access to Justice Act 1999. When in force, s58B of the 1990 Act, as inserted by s28 of the 1999 Act, will make provision as to the enforceability of litigation funding agreements.

Where the contract is lawful but performance is not

If the contract is lawful but the method of performance is one which *both parties knew is illegal*, then both parties are without remedies in enforcing it.

In *Ashmore, Benson & Pease* v *A V Dawson Ltd* [1973] 1 WLR 828, the plaintiff contracted with the defendant that the defendant should carry two 25 ton loads of goods for him by using lorries which could not lawfully carry more than 20 tons apiece. Both the plaintiff and the defendant knew this and, in consequence, the goods were damaged. It was held that the plaintiff's claim for damages for the goods must be rejected as he not only knew of the illegality, but also permitted the defendant to perform in such illegal manner in the hope of saving the expense of having the goods carried on three vehicles or two 25 ton vehicles.

As already mentioned above, Lord Devlin, in the *St John Shipping case*, drew a distinction between cases where the law penalises conduct and cases where the law penalises conduct and, in addition, makes that conduct an illegal mode of performing a contract.

A contract may be lawful in its formation, but one party intends to use it for illegal purposes while the other party is innocent of these purposes. The general rule is that the innocent party will not be affected by the illegal intentions of the guilty party.

If the innocent party, or indeed both parties, make a *mistake of law*, either in making the contract or concerning the consequences, then the general rule does not apply and the contract is unenforceable.

In *J M Allan* v *Cloke* [1963] 2 QB 340, a roulette wheel was let for the purpose of playing roulette royale at a country club. The parties honestly believed that this game was lawful when, in fact, it was not. The hirer sued for his hiring fee.

The court decided that the parties had a 'common design to use the subject matter for an unlawful purpose' and, therefore, the contract was illegal and neither party could enforce it.

Where the innocent party makes a *mistake of fact* as to the circumstances which will give rise to illegality, then he may be able to enforce the contract. The test for deciding whether he can enforce the contract is unclear, and the best solution to the problem seems to be that proposed by Devlin LJ in *Archbolds* v *S Spanglett Ltd* [1961] 1 QB 374 that one should consider whether declaring the contract illegal and denying a remedy to an innocent party will further the principles on which the contract has been declared illegal. In particular, he referred to contracts which are illegal by statute:

> 'I think that the purpose of this statute is sufficiently served by the penalties prescribed for the offender; the avoidance of the contract would cause grave inconvenience and injury to innocent members of the public without furthering the object of the statute.'

In *Archbolds* v *S Spanglett Ltd*, the defendant contracted to carry the plaintiff's whisky in a van which was not licensed to carry goods belonging to a third party. The plaintiff did not know that the van was not so licensed to carry his whisky and that the defendant was committing an offence thereby.

Since the plaintiff did not know that as a fact the van was improperly licensed, it was held he could recover damages for the defendant's breach of the contract.

In *Re Mahmoud and Ispahani* [1921] 2 KB 716, the plaintiff was licensed to sell linseed oil to licensed dealers. The defendant fraudulently misrepresented to the plaintiff that he was a licensed dealer, and was thereby able to purchase some linseed oil from the plaintiff. It was an offence to buy or sell linseed oil without a licence. The plaintiff sued to enforce the contract.

The court held that even if the plaintiff lacked the mens rea of the offence, he still could not enforce the contract because both parties were prohibited from entering into the contract. It was illegal from its inception and, even though the plaintiff was an innocent party, he was without remedy.

It is possible to conclude that *Re Mahmoud* could be distinguished from the *Archbolds* case on the basis that the former contract was illegal as formed, while the latter was illegal as performed. However, this is not a suitable test to distinguish between cases where the innocent party can enforce his rights, and where he cannot because, in several cases, the contract has been enforced where its formation was illegal, for example, *Bloxsome* v *Williams* (1824) 3 B & C 232.

The plaintiff bought a horse from the defendant on Sunday. The defendant was a licensed horsedealer and, under the Sunday Observance Act 1677, he was prohibited from selling horses on Sunday and committed an offence if he did so. The plaintiff did not know the defendant was a dealer. The defendant breached the contract and the plaintiff sued for damages. It was held that the plaintiff could recover damages for breach of contract.

In *Phoenix Insurance* v *Adas* [1987] 2 All ER 155, Kerr LJ summarised the position with regard to the statutory prohibition on contracts as follows:

> '(i) Where a statute prohibits both parties from concluding or performing a contract when both or either of them have no authority to do so, the contract is impliedly prohibited: see *Mahmoud and Ispahani*'s case [1921] 2 KB 716, [1921] All ER Rep 217 and its analysis by Pearce LJ in the *Archbolds* case [1961] 1 All ER 417, [1961] 1 QB 374 with which Devlin LJ agreed.
> (ii) But where a statute merely prohibits one party from entering into a contract without authority and/or imposes a penalty on him if he does so (ie a unilateral prohibition) it does not follow that the contract itself is impliedly prohibited so as to render it illegal and

void. Whether or not the statute has this effect depends on considerations of public policy in the light of the mischief which the statute is designed to prevent, its language, scope and purpose, the consequences for the innocent party, and any other relevant considerations.'

The Court of Appeal was considering the effect of the carrying on of insurance business without proper authorisation in breach of statute, where the statute only provided for criminal sanctions. It was held that the statute prohibited the business of effecting and performing contracts of insurance in the absence of proper authorisation and, therefore, such contracts were unenforceable and void. The Court of Appeal applied the decision of Parker J in *Bedford Insurance* v *Instituto de Reseguros de Brasil* [1985] QB 966. The contrary decision of Leggat J in *Stewart* v *Oriental Fire and Marine Insurance* [1985] QB 988 was overruled.

If the innocent party is unable to enforce the contract he may have alternative remedies

1. Where such contract has been induced by misrepresentation. See *Shelley* v *Paddock* [1980] QB 348.
2. Where it is possible to rely on a collateral contract.

In *Strongman* v *Sincock* [1955] 3 All ER 90, the plaintiff, a firm of builders, agreed to modernise houses belonging to the defendant, an architect. It was illegal to do this work without licences, and the defendant promised to get these. The plaintiff did the work and the defendant only got some licences, and refused to pay for the work for which he did not get licences on the ground that the contract was illegal.

The building contract was held to be illegal and the plaintiff could not sue on it. The plaintiff could, however, support an action for damages based on the defendant's breach of his collateral promise to obtain the licences.

13.6 Severance

If the contract is only partly illegal, then it may not be totally unenforceable. In *Wallis* v *Day* (1837) 2 M & W 273, Lord Abinger said:

> 'The defendant demurred on the ground that the covenant being in restraint of trade was illegal, and that therefore the whole contract was void. I cannot, however, accede to that conclusion. If a party enters into several covenants, one of which cannot be enforced against him, he is not therefore released from performing the others.'

There can be no severance if one of the promises is to do an act which is itself a criminal offence or contra bonos mores; in such cases, the whole transaction is regarded as void.

In the majority of cases where severance is allowed, the contracts have been concerned with restraint of trade. It has been used in the cases in two ways, either to cut out the offending promise altogether, or to nullify so much of it as is repugnant.

Excluding consideration

If the whole of the consideration for a promise is illegal, then the promise is unenforceable and void.

In *Lound* v *Grimwade* (1888) 39 Ch D 605, the plaintiff was promised £3,000 by the defendant in return for an undertaking not to take legal proceedings in respect of a fraud which the defendant had committed. The court held that the plaintiff could not enforce payment of the £3,000 as the main consideration was to do an illegal act, that is, stifle a prosecution, and was as such inseverable.

If the main consideration for a promise is lawful, then the court will enforce the contract, even if the contract is supported by subsidiary illegal consideration.

In *Goodinson* v *Goodinson* [1954] 2 QB 118, a contract was made between a husband and wife who were separated to the effect that the husband would pay the wife a weekly sum of maintenance and, in consideration, the wife would indemnify him against all debts incurred by her, would not pledge his credit and would not take any proceedings for maintenance.

The promise by the wife not to sue for maintenance was held to be void as it ousted the jurisdiction of the courts, but it was not the main consideration provided by the wife. Therefore, her promise on maintenance would be excluded and the contract upheld.

In *Alec Lobb* v *Total Oil* (above), the question of severance did not arise for decision in the Court of Appeal as the court had held that the restraint of trade clause was reasonable. Dunn LJ, in an exhaustive review of the authorities, nevertheless conducted an investigation into the law on this point. He formulated the principle of law on severance as follows:

> '... if the valid promises are supported by sufficient consideration, then the invalid promise can be severed from the valid even though the consideration also supports the valid promise. On the other hand if the invalid promise is substantially the whole or main consideration for the agreement then there will be no severance.'

On the present facts, Dunn LJ had the view that the main consideration was that given for the lease, and the transaction was not dependent on the tie clause (the restraint of trade) in the underlease. Waller LJ agreed.

In *Carney* v *Herbert* [1985] 1 All ER 438 Privy Council, the respondents owned shares in a company. They entered into contracts to sell their shareholding to a company controlled by the appellant. The proceeds of sale were to be cash, payment secured by certain guarantees from the purchaser and (the term which rendered the sale potentially illegal) secured also by mortgages on land owned by the very company which issued the shares subject matter of the sale. Without doubt, the purported mortgages were illegal, but the question arose whether such illegality was so much a part of the sale agreement and guarantees as to render them also illegal and unenforceable. The privy Council severed the mortgages from the sale agreement, and enforced the latter. In the words of the judgment of the entire Board:

> 'Subject to a caveat that it is undesirable, their Lordships venture to suggest that, as a general rule, where parties enter into a lawful contract of, for example, sale and purchase, and there is an ancillary provision which is illegal but exists for the exclusive benefit of the plaintiff, the court may and probably will ... permit the plaintiff, if he so wishes, to enforce the contract without the illegal provision.'

Excluding promises

This is concerned with reducing the scope of a promise so as to exclude a part which is illegal and, thereby, making the contract enforceable. In order that this can be done, three conditions must be satisfied.

The promise itself must be capable of severance

Promises which are illegal in themselves are incapable of severance, for example, a criminal or immoral promise. There may, however, be some grounds for believing that a promise made without mens rea, as required by the relevant crime, may be severable.

The 'blue pencil' test must be applied

The illegal promise must be amenable to severance by merely drawing a blue pencil through the offending words. The court will not redraft the covenant so that it makes sense, or add or substitute words for the same purpose.

In *Mason* v *Provident Clothing & Supply Co Ltd* [1913] AC 724, a contract in restraint of trade provided that a canvasser should not enter into a similar business, (that is, selling clothes), 'within 25 miles of London'. An application was made to substitute 'in Islington'. This amounted to redrafting the covenant and not severance and could not be done by the court.

Mason's case would appear to imply that severance is only possible under the blue pencil test with regard to the actual words of the contract. It is not possible to sever the covenant by limiting definitions in the covenant itself.

The nature of the contract must remain unaltered by severance

If the result of severance is that the contract becomes entirely different to that as envisaged by the parties, then the court will not order severance. In *Marshall* v *NM Financial Management Ltd* [1995] 1 WLR 1461, for example, when the restrictive clause was severed from the contract, it continued to be a standard principal/agent agreement unaltered in its general effects. The contract as a whole still reflected the intentions of the parties.

At one time, a distinction existed between contracts between employer and employee, and contracts between purchaser and vendor. In the former, severance would only be permitted where the restraint or restriction on an employee was trivial. However, it is now clear that this view is no longer held by the courts and, if it is possible, as a matter of construction, to interpret the contract as containing two separate covenants, one of which can be deleted without altering the nature of the contract, then the court will do this.

In *Attwood* v *Lamont* [1920] 3 KB 571, the plaintiff owned a general outfitters business in Kidderminster which had several departments, each with a supervisor who signed a contract that he would not after leaving the plaintiff's service: 'be concerned in any of the following trades ... a tailor, dressmaker, general draper, milliner, hatter, haberdasher, gentlemen's, ladies' or children's outfitter within 10 miles of Kidderminster'. The defendant, the supervisor in the tailoring department, started up a tailor's shop and the plaintiff, attempting to enforce the covenant, admitted that it was too wide and should be limited to tailoring only. The court decided that severance as proposed by the plaintiff would alter the nature of the covenant, which was intended to protect the whole business and not merely part of it and, therefore, could not be effected. Further, the clause could not be regarded as a series of covenants for the protection of each department.

A contrasting case is *Goldsoll* v *Goldman* [1915] 1 Ch 292. The seller of imitation jewellery undertook that he would not deal in real or imitation jewellery in the United Kingdom, or certain named places abroad, for two years. The covenant was too wide in area as the seller had not traded abroad, and in the subject matter as he had scarcely dealt in real jewellery. It was held, however, that the reference to the places abroad and to real jewellery could be severed.

If the 'blue pencil' test is satisfied, the court still will not order severance if the result is to change the nature of the contract.

In *British Reinforced Concrete Engineering* v *Schelff* [1921] 2 Ch 563, the plaintiff, who made and sold road reinforcement in the UK, bought the defendant's business, which was solely concerned in selling road reinforcements. The defendant covenanted not to 'directly or indirectly carry on or be concerned or interested in or act as a servant of any person concerned or interested in the business of the manufacture or sale of road reinforcements in any part of the United Kingdom'.

The covenant was held to be too wide, and it could not be severed as it was one entire covenant. Further, the blue pencil test could not be applied to it in any case as it made the covenant worse instead of better, particularly in relation to the wide and offending phrase: 'in any part of the United Kingdom'.

13.7 Recovery of money or property paid or transferred under an illegal contract

The courts will not help the parties to enforce an illegal contract, and the general rule is that the court will not assist either party to an illegal contract to recover money paid or property transferred under the contract. Since the parties have embarked on an illegal transaction, they can expect no assistance from the court in respect of it and if money is paid or property passes, this will not be interfered with even if it appears unjust.

The courts' attitude may be summed up in the phrase, 'the loss lies where it falls'. Several exceptions exist where the court will aid a party to recover property or money.

Recovery authorised by statute

A statute may provide for the protection of a class of persons by making payments of money or property transferred to them under the illegal contract recoverable.

Under s125 Rent Act 1977, the payment of a premium in consideration of being granted a tenancy is illegal and an offence, and is expressly stated to be recoverable by the paying party, that is, the tenant. However, the Act also allows for the fact that payments may be made for fittings and fixtures in a lease, and provides that any excess payment for these is also a premium and recoverable. See *Farrell* v *Alexander* (above) as an example.

In some older statutes, certain conduct is made an offence, but nothing is said as to the recovery of property where such conduct is the basis of a contract. In such cases, it appears one must look to see for what purpose the statute was passed before allowing recovery of money or property.

In *Green* v *Portsmouth Stadium* [1973] 2 QB 190, the plaintiff, a bookmaker, was charged an entrance fee in excess of that permitted by statute at a racecourse. It was held that he could not recover it as the relevant Act only made such conduct an offence, and was silent as to whether the excess was recoverable and, in any case, it was passed to regulate racecourses and not to protect bookmakers.

Repudiation of illegal purpose

If a party who has entered an illegal contract repudiates that contract or the illegal purpose in the contract in time, then the law will assist him to recover money or property under the contract. Some authorities refer to this as repentance, but this does not always reflect the repudiating party's state of mind!

Two conditions must be satisfied.

The repudiation must be in time

There can be no recovery of money or property if the party who is attempting to recover has already begun to perform the illegal purpose or has accepted illegal performance.

In *Kearley* v *Thomson* (1890) 24 QBD 742, the plaintiff paid the defendant £40 not to appear at his friend's public examination in bankruptcy. The defendant stayed away from the examination, but before the friend was discharged from bankruptcy, the plaintiff claimed the £40 back.

The court held that there had been a partial carrying into effect of the illegal purpose in a substantial manner since the plaintiff had intended to interfere with the course of justice and achieved his object to some extent.

In *Taylor* v *Bowers* (1876) 1 QBD 291, the plaintiff, who was being pressed by his creditors, fraudulently assigned some machinery to X to prevent it falling into their hands. He then called several creditors' meetings, but failed to reach a settlement with the creditors. The plaintiff then claimed the machinery from the defendant who had obtained it from X knowing of the fraudulent scheme. The illegal purpose of defrauding the creditors had not been carried out, and the plaintiff could, therefore, recover the machinery.

Repudiation must be voluntary

If the party is forced to repudiate by either a third party or a repudiation of the illegal contract by the other party, he cannot recover his property. Further, if the illegal transaction proves abortive, but only after a party has participated in it, then there can be no voluntary repudiation.

Oppression

Where a party is forced to enter into an illegal contract, then he can recover his money or property back at any stage, either before or after performance. Oppression is, for these purposes, given a wide meaning, and may include the circumstances in which the contract was made. The use of the word 'forced' in the first sentence of this paragraph may sometimes give a misleading impression. Certainly, if the parties are not 'in pari delicto', that is, not on an equal footing, with one party at a marked disadvantage, oppression is more likely to apply.

In *Kiriri Cotton Co* v *Dewani* [1960] AC 192, the plaintiff paid his landlord, who was committing an offence by accepting it, a premium for a flat. However, the relevant statute, then the Rent Restriction Ordinance, did not expressly provide that such premiums were recoverable.

The plaintiff was not to blame for attempting to evade the Ordinance, but his landlord was. He was using his property rights to exploit those in need of a roof over their head. The plaintiff therefore had but little choice if he wanted a home, and would qualify as 'oppressed'.

Fraud

Where a party enters into the contract in reliance on a fraudulent misrepresentation, then he can recover his money or property given under the contract even if it was illegal. For these purposes, an innocent misrepresentation is insufficient.

In *Hughes* v *Liverpool Victoria Legal Friendly Society* [1916] 2 KB 482, the plaintiff took out a life insurance policy on the advice of the defendant's agent on the life of a person in which he had no insurable interest. The contract was therefore illegal.

The plaintiff could recover the money he had paid as he had entered into the contract as a result of a fraudulent representation.

Mistake

Where there has been a mistake of fact, then it may be possible to recover money or property under the illegal contract. In *Oom* v *Bruce* (1810) 12 East 225, the parties to an insurance policy, one of whom was a Russian, were unaware of the fact that war had broken out between Britain and Russia at the time they effected the policy, and it was held that the premium was recoverable.

Where there has been a mistake of law, then there can be no recovery of money or property. See *Harse* v *Pearl Assurance Co* [1904] 1 KB 558.

Recovery other than under illegal contract

In several cases, a party may recover money paid or property given under the contract by means which do not require reliance on the contract.

Goods transferred under illegal contract

It is settled law that property in goods can pass under an illegal contract. See *Singh* v *Ali* [1960] AC 167. Therefore, if the property has passed from the seller to the buyer and the goods have been delivered either to the buyer or his agent, the seller will not be able to get them back.

Where goods are pledged, hired or lent under an illegal contract, then a right to possession passes when the goods are transferred. This right to possession will endure until it is brought to an end either by effluxion of time, or the occurrence of certain events, and until then the transferor cannot recover the goods. However, if the hirer, for example, commits a fundamental breach of contract, then his right to possession may come to an end otherwise than under the illegal contract, and the transferor can recover the goods.

In *Bowmakers* v *Barnet Instruments* [1945] KB 65, the defendant possessed machine tools under several illegal hire-purchase agreements. They failed to pay the instalments due, and sold some of the goods, but kept the rest. The plaintiffs claimed damages for conversion of all the goods.

The plaintiffs did not have to found their claim on the illegal contract or plead illegality to support their claim, they could rely on their title. The hirer's right to possession had come to an end by fundamental breach of contract by selling the thing hired to him, and the plaintiffs could, therefore, recover their property.

Note: it is unclear in the *Bowmaker* case whether the contract provided for the hirer's right of possession to determine on any breach. But it is assumed that this must have been the case as the plaintiffs recovered the whole goods back, including those the defendant had not sold and with respect to these, it is established law that failure to pay instalments is not a fundamental breach of contract.

Goods obtained under an illegal contract

Since property can pass in goods from the seller to the buyer under an illegal contract, the buyer has all the usual remedies to protect his property even if he pays nothing for them in return. Thus, if the seller attempts to recover them, the buyer can sue for them or their value. See *Singh* v *Ali* (above).

This rule operates irrespective of whether the goods have actually been delivered to the buyer.

In *Belvoir Finance Co* v *Stapleton* [1971] 1 QB 210, the plaintiff agreed to finance the purchase of cars by one Belgravia from one Francis. Each purchase was effected by two contracts: the sale of the car by Francis to the plaintiff, and the letting on hire-purchase by the plaintiff to Belgravia. In fact, these contracts were illegal. Although the plaintiff had never acquired possession of the cars, as Francis delivered them directly to Belgravia, it was held that the plaintiff could recover the cars from Belgravia in an action for conversion.

Money paid under an illegal contract

Where money is paid under an illegal contract, the general rule is that it is irrecoverable.

Where money is paid as a deposit to a stakeholder under an illegal contract, it can be recovered so long as the stakeholder has not paid it over as instructed. See *O'Sullivan* v *Thomas* [1895] 1 QB 698.

13.8 Collateral agreements

Any agreement which is made to help with the performance of an illegal contract is itself illegal and unenforceable. Thus, an insurance policy on an illegal agreement is illegal (see *Toulmin* v *Anderson* (1808) 1 Taunt 227) and any loans or payments of money to aid the performance of an illegal contract are also illegal (see *M'Kinnell* v *Robinson* (1838) 3 M & W 434).

If an agreement is in itself legal, it will not, however, be rendered illegal merely because a collateral transaction to aid or further its performance happens to be illegal. Therefore, if a charterparty is itself legal, it will not be invalidated merely because a policy of insurance relating to it is illegally drawn up. See *South Western Mineral Co* v *Ashmore* [1967] 1 WLR 1110.

14

Frustration

14.1 Introduction

14.2 Initial development of the doctrine

14.3 Tests for frustration

14.4 Examples of frustration

14.5 Scope of the doctrine

14.6 Effects of frustration

14.1 Introduction

The doctrine of frustration operates in situations where it is established that due to subsequent change in circumstances, the contract is rendered impossible to perform, or it has become deprived of its commercial purpose by an event not due to the act or default of either party.

This is not to be confused with initial impossibility, which may render the contract void ab initio. See Chapter 10 and s6 Sale of Goods Act 1979, *Couturier* v *Hastie* (1856) 5 HL Cas 673 and *Barrow Lane & Ballard* v *Phillips* [1929] 1 KB 574.

Originally, the law declared that if a man bound himself by contract, then that man was absolutely bound notwithstanding anything which may subsequently have transpired making it difficult or impossible to perform the contract.

> 'It amounts to this: when the law casts a duty upon a man which, through no fault of his, he is unable to perform he is excused from non-performance; but if he binds himself by contract to do a thing, he cannot escape liability for damage by proof that as events turned out performance is futile or even impossible.'

In *Paradine* v *Jane* (1647) Aleyn 26, the classic statement of the concept appears in the above, a Civil War case involving dispossession of tenants by one Prince Rupert of the Rhine. The tenant pleaded that he should be relieved under the contract with the landlord for he had been evicted and thus had obtained no material benefit from the lease.

He was held liable under the lease – broadly, for the reasons given in the extract above.

The 'absolute' approach to the determination of a legal problem is harsh without doubt, and the subsequent evolution of the doctrine of frustration bears witness to this.

14.2 Initial development of the doctrine

The turning point away from absolutist construction of contractual obligation came with the decision in *Taylor* v *Caldwell* (1863) 3 B & S 826.

Caldwell agreed to let a music hall to Taylor so that four concerts could be held there. Before the date of the first concert, the hall was destroyed by fire. Taylor claimed damages for Caldwell's failure to make the premises available. The court held that the claim for breach of contract must fail since it had become impossible to fulfil. The contractual obligation was dependent upon the continued existence of a particular object.

The interesting point to note was that until this time, the law refused to acknowledge that a party could be relieved from a contract unless there was some express condition entitling him to be so relieved in the event of subsequent impossibility.

Blackburn J gave the judgment of the Court of Queen's Bench, holding that the defendants were not liable under the contract.

The rationale of this decision was (broadly) as follows.

1. The doctrine of 'sanctity of contracts' does not apply where the contract is subject to conditions express or *implied*.
2. The doctrine of 'sanctity' only applies, therefore, to contracts based on positive or absolute promises.

Blackburn J stated the principle in the following terms:

'The principle seems to us to be that, in contracts in which the performance depends on the continued existence of a given person or thing, a condition is implied that the impossibility of performance arising from the perishing of the person or thing shall excuse the performance.

In none of the cases is the promise other than positive, nor is there any express stipulation that the destruction of the person or thing shall excuse the performance; but that excuse is by law implied, because from the nature of the contract it is apparent that the parties contracted on the basis of the continued existence of the particular person or chattel.'

From this he was able to derive in the particular case that the contract was subject to the implied condition that the music hall would continue to exist and that, if it did not, the parties were to be relieved of their obligations.

14.3 Tests for frustration

There are principally two tests which compete for recognition as the test for frustration:

1. The 'radical change in the obligation' test. This was adopted by the majority of the House of Lords in *Davis Contractors Ltd* v *Fareham UDC* [1956] AC 696. It is also sometimes referred to as 'the construction test'.
2. The implied term theory, as in *Taylor* v *Caldwell* (above). Contrast *Blackburn Bobbin & Co* v *Allen* [1918] 2 KB 467.

Notably, in *National Carriers* v *Panalpina (Northern) Ltd* [1981] AC 675, Lord Wilberforce was reluctant to choose between the theories. He took the view that they merged one into the other and that the choice depends upon 'what is most appropriate to the particular contract under consideration'.

This observation is criticised by Chitty. He gives four reasons why it does matter which test is chosen. (He favours the 'radical change in the obligation' test.)

1. Although it is possible that the two tests arrive at the same conclusion in the majority of cases, there may be borderline cases which could produce a different result if one test rather than the other were applied. It is reasonable that parties should be able to know in advance the view that a court may take and avoid litigation rather than seeking the intervention of the court to see which one the court may think 'most appropriate'.
2. The application of the implied term test (which Chitty denigrates as artificial) may prevent a proper understanding of the court's function.
3. The implied term test might be treated as a matter of fact, whereas the question of whether a contract has been frustrated is really one of law.
4. Lord Reid suggested in the *Davis* case that if the 'radical change' test were applied, the ordinary rules about the admissibility of extrinsic evidence could apply. (Note, however, that the ordinary rules of evidence could also apply to the implied term test.)

Atiyah (*An Introduction to the Law of Contract*) suggests that these two theories are not mutually inconsistent, but signify attempts to answer different questions. One can find support for all the various theories in decided cases and, ultimately, most attempts to define the 'basis' of the doctrine of frustration are unsatisfactory.

The 'radical change in the obligation' test

This has been upheld in two recent cases: in *Pioneer Shipping Ltd* v *BTP Tioxide Ltd* [1982] AC 724 and *National Carriers* v *Panalpina* (above).

Lord Simon restated the test in the latter case at p63:

'Frustration of a contract takes place when there supervenes an event (without default of either party and for which the contract makes no provision) which so significantly changes the nature (not merely the expense or onerousness) of the outstanding contractual rights and/or obligations from what the parties could reasonably have contemplated at the time of its execution that it would be unjust to hold them to the literal sense of its stipulations in the new circumstances; in such case the law declares both parties to be discharged from further performance.'

Lords Reid and Radcliffe in the *Davis* case found that the application of this test was a three-tiered process. It necessitated the following.

1. To construe the contractual terms in the light of the contract and surrounding circumstances at the time of its creation.
2. To examine the new circumstances and decide what would happen if the existing terms are applied to it.
3. To compare the two contractual obligations and see if there is a radical or fundamental change.

Accordingly, it is the nature of the *obligation* that must have changed, and not just the circumstances.

The implied term theory

Following the *Pioneer* and *Panalpina* cases, this test can be regarded as abandoned, although it is significant in the development of the doctrine of frustration. The traditional exposition is found in the speech of Lord Loreburn in *FA Tamplin SS Company Ltd* v *Anglo–Mexican Petroleum Products Company Ltd* [1916] 2 AC 397:

'A court can and ought to examine the contract and the circumstances in which it was made, not of course to vary but only to explain it, in order to see whether or not from the nature of it the parties must have made their bargain on the footing that a particular thing or state of things would continue to exist.

And if they must have done so, then a term to that effect will be implied, though it be not expressed in the contract ... In most of the cases it is said that there was an implied condition in the contract which operated to release the parties from performing it, and in all of them I think that was at bottom the principle upon which the Court proceeded.

It is, in my opinion, the true principle, for no court has an absolving power, but it can infer from the nature of the contract and the surrounding circumstances that a condition which was not expressed was a foundation on which the parties contracted ... Were the altered conditions such that, had they thought of them, the parties would have taken their chance of them, or such that as sensible men they would have said "if that happens, of course, it is all over between us".'

The traditional criticism of this test directed itself at the artificial implication of a term to deal with a situation which the parties would not have contemplated.

14.4 Examples of frustration

Destruction of the specific object essential for performance of the contract

See *Taylor* v *Caldwell* (above). Note s7 Sale of Goods Act 1979.

Personal incapacity where the personality of one of the parties is significant

In *Condor* v *The Barron Knights* [1966] 1 WLR 87, a drummer engaged to play in a pop group was contractually bound to work on seven nights a week when work was available. After an illness, Condor's doctor advised that it was only safe to employ him on four nights a week, although Condor himself was willing to work every night. It was necessary to engage another drummer who could safely work on seven nights each week.

The court held that Condor's contract of employment had been frustrated in a commercial sense. It was impracticable to engage a stand-in for the three nights a week when Condor could not work, since this involved double rehearsals of the group's music and comedy routines.

Compare this with *Phillips* v *Alhambra Palace Co* [1901] 1 QB 59. One partner in a firm of music hall proprietors died after a troupe of performers had been engaged.

The contract with the performers was held not to be frustrated because the contract was not of a personal nature, and could be enforced against the surviving partners.

In *Graves* v *Cohen* (1929) 46 TLR 121, the court held that the death of a racehorse owner frustrated the contract with his employee, a jockey, because the contract created a relationship of mutual confidence.

In *FC Shepherd & Co* v *Jerrom* [1986] 3 All ER 589 CA, it was held that a sentence of imprisonment imposed on an employee was capable of frustrating the employee's contract of employment if the sentence was such that it rendered the performance of the contract radically different from that which the parties contemplated when they entered into the contract.

The non-occurrence of a specified event

See *Krell* v *Henry* [1903] 2 KB 740. Henry hired a room from Krell for two days, to be used as a position from which to view the coronation procession of Edward VII, but the contract itself made no reference to that intended use. The King's illness caused a postponement of the procession. It was held that Henry was excused from paying the rent for the room. Holding of the procession on the dates planned was regarded by both parties as basic to enforcement of the contract.

Compare this with *Herne Bay Steamboat Company* v *Hutton* [1903] 2 KB 683. Herne Bay Steam Boat Company agreed to hire a steamboat to Hutton for a fee of £250 for a period of two days for the purpose of taking passengers to Spithead to cruise round the fleet and see the naval review on the occasion of Edward VII's coronation. The review was cancelled, but the boat could have been used to cruise round the assembled fleet. It was held that the contract was not frustrated. The holding of the naval review was not the only event upon which the intended use of the boat was dependent. The other object of the contract was to cruise round the fleet, and this remained capable of fulfilment.

Also see *Amalgamated Investment and Property Co* v *John Walker* [1977] 1 WLR 164.

Interference by the government

In *Metropolitan Water Board* v *Dick Kerr & Co* [1918] AC 119, Kerr & Co agreed to build a reservoir for the Water Board within six years. After two years, Kerr & Co were required by a wartime statute to cease work on the contract and to sell their plant. The contract was held to be frustrated because the interruption was of such a nature as to make the contract, if resumed, a different contract.

Supervening illegality

In *Denny, Mott & Dickson* v *James Fraser* [1944] AC 265, a contract for the sale and purchase of timber contained an option to purchase a timber yard. By a wartime control order, trading under the agreement became illegal. The appellants wanted to exercise the option. The order had frustrated the contract so the option could not be exercised.

In a similar case, *Re Shipton Anderson and Harrison Brothers* [1915] 3 KB 676, a contract was concluded for the sale of a quantity of wheat lying in a warehouse. The Government requisitioned the wheat, in pursuance of wartime emergency regulations, for the control of food supplies, before it had been delivered, and also before ownership in the goods had passed to the buyer under the terms of contract of sale.

It was held that the seller was excused from further performance of the contract as it was now impossible to deliver the goods due to the Government's lawful requisition.

Notice that where there is a supervening illegality, the parties cannot rely on the contractual terms to prevent the contract being frustrated. See *Ertel Bieber* v *Rio Tinto* [1918] AC 260. Apart from this exception, the parties can contract with the frustrating event in mind. This will prevent frustration.

Delay

Inordinate and unexpected delay may frustrate a contract. The problem is to know how long a party must wait before the delay can be said to be frustrating. In *Pioneer Shipping Ltd* v *BTP Tioxide Ltd* [1982] AC 724, Lord Roskill said:

'... it is often necessary to wait upon events in order to see whether the delay already suffered and the prospects of further delay from that cause, will make any ultimate performance of the relevant contractual obligations "radically different" from that which was undertaken by the contract. But, as has often been said, businessmen must not be required to await events too long. They are entitled to know where they stand. Whether or not the delay is such as to bring about frustration must be a question to be determined by an informed judgment based on all the evidence of what has occurred and what is likely thereafter to occur. Often it will be a question of degree whether the effect of delay suffered and likely to be suffered, will be such as to bring about frustration of the particular event in question.'

Also see *Jackson* v *Union Marine Insurance* (1873) LR 10 CP 125. A ship was chartered in November 1871 to proceed with all possible despatch, danger and accidents of navigation excepted, from Liverpool to Newport where it was to load a cargo of iron rails for carriage to San Francisco. She sailed on 2 January, but the next day ran aground in Caernarvon Bay. She was refloated by 18 February and taken to Liverpool, where she underwent extensive repairs, which lasted till August. On 15 February, the charterers repudiated the contract.

Such time was so long as to put an end in a commercial sense to the commercial speculation entered upon by the shipowner and the charterers. The express exceptions were not intended to cover an accident causing such extensive damage. The contract was to be considered frustrated.

Leases

In *Cricklewood Property and Investment Trust* v *Leightons Investment Trust* [1945] AC 221, the House of Lords held unanimously that there was no frustration of a long-term building lease by the imposition of building restrictions following the outbreak of war. On the question of whether a lease could ever be frustrated, Lords Russell and Goddard thought that it could not because it created an estate in land which could not be defeated, even though some purpose for which the parties wished to use the land might become prohibited. Viscount Simon and Lord Wright, on the other hand, thought that a lease could be frustrated in rare circumstances, such as an earthquake or flood.

The question arose again in the *Panalpina* case. This concerned a ten-year lease of a warehouse. By a temporary order, the street, which gave the only access to the warehouse, was closed. On the question of whether the lease was frustrated, it was held that, since the closure was expected to last only a year or more, which would leave three or more years of the lease left to run, the lease was not frustrated. The House of Lords were anxious to say that, in principle, a lease could be frustrated. They cited with approval a passage from Corbin '*Contracts*':

'If there was one principal use contemplated by the lessee, known to the lessor, and one that played a large part in fixing rental value, a government prohibition or prevention of that use has been held to discharge the lessee from his duty to pay the rent. It is otherwise if other substantial uses permitted by the lease and in the contemplation of the parties, remain possible to the lessee.'

Frustration of contract by constant revision

McAlpine, Humberoak Ltd v *McDermott International Inc* (1992) 58 Build LR 1 raised the question of whether continual alteration of the contractual terms could be said to give rise to frustration.

Both parties signed a contract for construction of an oil rig: the defendants were one among a large number of sub-contracting firms. Delays occurred in the plaintiffs' work, largely caused, the plaintiffs argued, by the late submission of large numbers of revised drawings which hindered production. The defendants' counterclaim suggested among other arguments, that the contract was in fact frustrated by the constant revision of plans.

The Court of Appeal stated that the numerous revisions of plan did not transform the contract so as to frustrate it. Indeed, the contract provided for changes of instruction in the form of new construction drawings. Also, since the contract was signed retrospectively, some months after work had begun, the parties were both fully aware of changes necessary at the time of signing the contract.

14.5 Scope of the doctrine

'The doctrine of frustration must be applied within very narrow limits', per Viscount Simonds in *Tsakiroglou and Company* v *Noblee Thorl GmbH* [1961] 2 All ER 179.

More recently, Lord Roskill said that the doctrine of frustration was 'not lightly to be invoked to relieve contracting parties of the normal consequences of imprudent commercial bargains'. See *Pioneer Shipping* v *BTP Tioxide* [1982] AC 724.

The doctrine is subject to the following limitations.

The doctrine cannot override express contractual provision for the frustrating event

However, this does not apply if the supervening event is illegality. See *Ertel Bieber* v *Rio Tinto* (above).

The mere increase in expense or loss of profit is not a ground for frustration

See *Davis Contractors* v *Fareham UDC* [1956] AC 696. The plaintiff agreed to build 78 houses in eight months at a fixed price. Due to bad weather, and labour shortages, the work took 22 months and cost £17,000 more than anticipated. The builders said that the weather and labour shortages, which were unforeseen, had frustrated the contract, and that they were entitled to recover £17,000 by way of quantum meruit. The court stated that the fact that unforeseen events made a contract more onerous than was anticipated did not frustrate it.

Also see *Tsakiroglou* v *Noblee Thorl* (above). Tsakiroglou agreed to sell Sudanese groundnuts to Noblee, the nuts to be shipped from Port Sudan to Hamburg, November/December 1956. As a result of the 'Suez crisis', the Suez Canal was closed from 2 November 1956 until April 1957. Tsakiroglou failed to deliver, arguing that shipment round the Cape was commercially and fundamentally different.

The contract was held not to be frustrated. Tsakiroglou were, therefore, liable for breach – the change in circumstances was not fundamental. (Note that there was no implied term that the shipment should be via Suez; also, the nuts would not have deteriorated on the longer journey.)

Frustration must not be self-induced

In *Maritime National Fish* v *Ocean Trawlers* [1935] AC 524, Maritime chartered from Ocean a vessel which could only operate with an otter trawl. Both parties realised that it was an offence to use such a trawl without a government licence. Maritime was granted three such licences, but chose to use them in respect of three other vessels, with the result that Ocean's vessel could not be used. It was held that the charterparty had not been frustrated, consequently Maritime was liable to pay the charter fee. Maritime freely elected not to license Ocean's vessel, consequently their inability to use it was a direct result of their own deliberate act.

The burden of proving events which prima facie frustrate the contract lies on the party relying on frustration. If there is an allegation that the frustration is self-induced, the burden then shifts to the person alleging self-inducement. See also *Joseph Constantine* v *Imperial Smelting* [1942] AC 154.

The question of self-induced frustration arose before the House of Lords in *Paal Wilson* v *Blumenthal* [1983] AC 854. Where there had been a delay in proceeding with an arbitration which had been caused by breaches by both parties of their mutual obligations to one another to avoid delay, the House of Lords held that the fact that the parties were under a mutual obligation to keep the arbitration moving meant that neither party could claim that delay by the other party had frustrated the agreement to arbitrate.

Dealing with the requirements for frustration Lord Brandon said:

> 'There are two essential factors which must be present in order to frustrate a contract. The first essential factor is that there must be some outside event or extraneous change of situation, not foreseen or provided for by the parties at the time of contracting, which either makes it impossible for the contract to be performed at all, or at least renders its performance something radically different from what the parties contemplated when they entered into it. The second essential factor is that the outside event or extraneous change of situation concerned, and the consequences of either in relation to the performance of

the contract, must have occurred without either the fault or the default of either party to the contract.'

Neither requirement had been met in the present case. The contract had not been subject to an extraneous event, but simply to the delay of the parties, and that delay was a breach by each party of its obligation.

In *FC Shepherd & Co* v *Jerrom* (above), although the employee was to blame for the offence for which he was sentenced, this was not a case of self-induced frustration. The employee could not plead his own default in order to establish a claim for unfair dismissal. Lawton LJ also held that the frustrating event was not the offence, but the outside event of the sentence imposed by the court.

In *Lauritzen AS* v *Wijsmuller BV* [1990] 1 Lloyd's Rep 1, the defendant agreed to transport the plaintiff's drilling rig by one of two transportation units. One unit was sunk and the defendant refused to use the other transportation unit. Two questions arose.

1. Did the extra time and cost involved entitled the plaintiff to treat the contract as frustrated?
2. If it was frustrated, could the contract be considered as terminated by self-induced frustration?

14.6 Effects of frustration

Frustration discharges the contract automatically: no question of election of one of the parties (compare with breach). However, this discharge does not relate back to the making of the contract, therefore, on principle, rights and liabilities already acquired up to the termination of the contract remain intact; only subsequent obligations are discharged. Accordingly, in the case of *Chandler* v *Webster* [1904] 1 KB 493, the Court of Appeal held that the loss would lie where it fell. However, this case was subsequently considered unjust and was overruled in *Fibrosa* v *Fairbairn* [1943] AC 32, where the House of Lords held that money paid over on a total failure of consideration was recoverable. This case, however, was equally inflexible: recovery was dependent upon a total failure of consideration, and there was no provision for restitution of prefrustration expenditure by one of the parties. As a result, Parliament intervened with the Law Reform (Frustrated Contracts) Act 1943.

The Law Reform (Frustrated Contracts) Act 1943

This statute remedies the defects of the common law. The main provisions of the Act are outlined in s1 as follows:

'(2) All sums paid or payable to any party in pursuance of the contract before the time when the parties were so discharged (in this Act referred to as "the time of discharge") shall, in the case of sums so paid, be recoverable from him as money received by him for the use of the party by whom the sums were paid, and, in the case of sums so payable, cease to be payable:

Provided that, if the party to whom the sums were so paid or payable incurred expenses before the time of discharge in, or for the purpose of, the performance of the contract, the court may, if it considers it just to do so having regard to all the circumstances of the case, allow him to retain or, as the case may be, recover the whole or any part of the sums so paid or payable, not being an amount in excess of the expenses so incurred.

(3) Where any party to the contract has, by reason of anything done by any other party thereto in, or for the purpose of, the performance of the contract, obtained a valuable benefit (other than a payment of money to which the last foregoing section applies) before the time of discharge, there shall be recoverable from him by the said other party such sum (if any) not exceeding the value of the said benefit to the party obtaining it, as the court considers just, having regard to all the circumstances of the case ...'

Section 1(6) allows an action given by subs1(3) to be brought against one party even though the benefit was bestowed on a third party.

Section 2(3) permits contracting out.

Section 2(4) enables severance of a part of a contract which has been performed from a part which has been frustrated, but only where a part of a contract 'can properly be severed from the remainder of the contract'.

The effect of s1(2)

Section 1(2) provides three rules.

1. All sums actually paid at the time of discharge are recoverable.
2. All sums payable at the time of discharge cease to be payable.
3. The party to whom the sums were paid or payable at the time of the discharge may be allowed, if the court considers it just and equitable, to retain or recover the whole or part of the sums paid or payable if he has incurred expenses in, or for the purposes of, performing the contract. Recovery will not be allowed of any amount in excess of the expenses incurred.

Recovery for expenses is only allowed from sums 'paid or payable' at the time of discharge. If, therefore, the party incurring the expenses had not stipulated for prepayment, he will not be able to obtain recovery. In *Gamerco SA* v *ICM/Fair Warning (Agency) Ltd* [1995] 1 WLR 1226 the court held that if expenses are incurred by the defendants, they have the right to have these losses offset against any advance payments made before the frustrating event which must (by virtue of s1 of the 1943 Act) be returned once the contract has been frustrated. But, Garland J made it clear that the defendants must offer proof of expenses incurred before the court will exercise its discretionary right to offset such a sum against any money paid at the time of discharge.

The effect of s1(3)

There is academic controversy over the meaning of 'valuable benefit': one school of thought holds the view that it should be construed widely, for example, if a painter begins work on X's house, and the house is burnt down before completion of the job, X is nevertheless deemed to have received a benefit. A Canadian case on this problem, *Parsons Brothers v Shea* (1965) 53 DLR (2d) 86, favours this view.

A case has occurred which has discussed, inter alia, the meaning of the words 'valuable benefit'. In *BP Exploration v Hunt* [1982] 1 All ER 925, the defendant had a licence to explore the Libyan desert for oil. The defendant agreed to assign to the plaintiff a half share in the oil concession, and the plaintiff undertook to explore from its own resources and make payments to the defendants. There was a revolution in Libya. The plaintiff's half share was expropriated in 1971. In 1973, the defendants' share was expropriated. The plaintiffs said that the contract was frustrated in 1971, and that payments to the defendant could be recovered under s1(3) of the Act.

Held: (at first instance and in the Court of Appeal) that the plaintiff could recover those sums under the Act that had been paid to the defendant together with interest. In the House of Lords, the only points taken by the defendant were whether the agreement was entered into with a view to the events that occurred and whether interest was payable.

Robert Goff J examined the relationship between the subsections at length. The following principles can be extracted from his judgment.

1. The Act was designed to prevent unjust enrichment.
2. Under subs1(3), the court is not concerned with restitution of value for net benefits, but with achieving justice between the parties. Subsection 1(2) may be concerned with the net benefit being the benefit to one party less an appropriate deduction for expenses incurred by him.
3. The court should, however, try to achieve consistency between these two sections, because they flow from the same principle (preventing unjust enrichment).
4. The Act was *not* designed to do certain things: for example, to apportion the loss between plaintiff and defendant; or to put the parties in the position they would have been in if the contract had been performed; or to restore the parties to the position they were in before the contract was made.
5. The valuable benefit should be the end product of services rendered and not just the service itself. He takes the example set out above:

> 'Suppose that a contract for work on a building is frustrated by a fire which destroys the building and which, therefore, also destroys a substantial amount of work already done by the plaintiff. Although it might be thought just to award the plaintiff a sum assessed on a quantum meruit basis, probably a rateable part of the contract price, in respect of the work he has done, the effect of s1(3)(b) will be to reduce the award to

nil, because of the effect, in relation to the defendant's benefit, of the circumstances giving rise to the frustration of the contract.

... This will not be so in every case, since in some cases the services will have no end product; for example, where the services consist of doing such work as surveying, or transporting goods.

In each case it is necessary to ask the question: what benefit has the defendant obtained by reason of the plaintiff's contractual performance?'

6. The date of valuing the benefit is the date of frustration.
7. A just sum is restitutionary. If money has been paid, then it is recoverable. If the benefit does not consist of money, it is the reasonable value of the plaintiff's performance. In the case of services, it is reasonable remuneration. In the case of goods, it is a reasonable price.

The Court of Appeal, although suggesting that unjust enrichment was an inappropriate expression to use in connection with frustrated contracts, did not overturn this approach. It was not a live issue in the House of Lords.

Exclusion from the Act

Four types of contract are excluded.

1. Certain charterparties (voyage charterparties).
2. Contracts for carriage of goods by sea.
3. Insurance contracts.
4. Contracts for the sale of specific goods which perish.

15

Discharge of the Contract – Performance, Agreement and Breach

15.1 Introduction

15.2 Performance: the general rule

15.3 Modification of the general rule

15.4 Stipulations as to time of performance

15.5 Agreements

15.6 Bilateral discharge

15.7 Unilateral discharge

15.8 Breach

15.1 Introduction

In the previous chapter, we examined the circumstances in which the parties to a contract could be discharged of their obligations by the frustration of the contract. We turn now to an examination of discharge of contractual obligations by performance, by agreement and by breach.

The performance of his obligations by a contracting party discharges that party from his obligations under the contract. It should be noted that unless a term of the contract is expressly stated to have effect after the existence of the contract has ceased, all restrictions, liabilities and duties end with the discharge or breach of the contract. This principle was reiterated by the Court of Appeal recently in *Raiffeisen Zentralbank Osterreich AG* v *Crossseas Shipping Ltd and Others* [2000] 3 All ER 274 where it was held that an alteration to a deed or instrument, made after signature by one of the parties without the other's knowledge, nullified the agreement only when the charge altered the parties' rights and obligations. Discharge materialises where the would-be avoider is able to demonstrate that the alteration was potentially prejudicial to his legal rights or obligations under the instrument.

In *Harrods Ltd* v *Schwartz-Sackin & Co Ltd* [1991] FSR 209 the plaintiffs terminated their contract with the defendants, who had operated the fine arts department at Harrods. One of the clauses in the contract was a no-advertising clause – that the defendants would not indicate their connection with Harrods, or use Harrods' name in any way. Once the contract had been ended, the defendants began to advertise their previous association with Harrods, who sought an interlocutory injunction to stop this.

The Court of Appeal held that unless a clause is specifically and expressly worded so as to make it clear that its effect is to continue beyond the existence of the contract, no such effect will be implied. All restrictive clauses terminate along with the contract.

What constitutes performance is the subject matter of our initial discussion. The parties may elect to discharge their obligations under the original contract by a subsequent agreement so to do.

A party who fails to perform his obligations under the contract is in breach of contract. It is perhaps unnecessary to state that what constitutes a breach depends on the terms of the contract. We have seen in Chapter 6 that certain breaches entitle the injured party to treat the contract as repudiated. If he elects to do so, he is himself discharged of his obligations under the contract, and is able to seek a remedy against the party in breach.

15.2 Performance: the general rule

Generally, parties must perform *precisely* all the terms of the contract in order to discharge their obligations.

Note that the question of whether a contract must be *personally* performed came before the courts in *Southway Group Ltd* v *Wolff* (1991) 57 Build LR 33. The question as to whether a contract must be performed in person arose in this contract for services. Before the sale of a warehouse and adjoining land was completed with the plaintiffs, B agreed to carry out certain improvements in accordance with outline specifications. The question asked was whether B could then subcontract the work to an independent contractor. B had entered into a resale agreement with the defendants and then on purchase of the land had delegated all obligations.

The Court of Appeal decided that where, as in this case the essence of the contract lay in the provision of a special skill or expertise, the party who had agreed to provide the skill or expertise did not have the right to unilaterally delegate the responsibility to another person.

In contracts for the sale of goods, the Sale of Goods Act 1979 contains strict rules. Section 30 affords the buyer the right to reject goods if the seller delivers less or even more goods than he contracted to sell. Section 13 imposes the condition that the goods must correspond with the description. An illustration of the precise requirement of this section appears from *Re Moore and Landauer & Co* [1921] 2 KB

519. Tins of fruit delivered in cases of 24 and not the stipulated cases of 30 constituted a breach of s13.

The decision in this case is now, perhaps, doubtful. It was criticised as being excessively technical by Lord Wilberforce in *Reardon Smith Line* v *Hansen-Tangen* [1976] 3 All ER 570 at p576.

A classic example of hardship caused by this rule is *Cutter* v *Powell* (1795) 6 Term Rep 320. A seaman who was to be paid his wages after the end of a voyage died just a few days away from port. His widow was able to recover none of his wages because he had not completed performance of his contractual obligation.

The strict rule as to performance is mitigated in a number of instances.

15.3 Modification of the general rule

Divisible contracts

It is a question of construction whether a contract is entire or divisible. An *entire* contract is one where the agreement provides that complete performance by one party is a condition precedent to contractual liability on the part of the other party. With a *divisible* contract, part of the consideration of one party is set off against part of the performance of the other. Divisible contracts are frequently to be found in the building trade, for example, where a builder agrees to build a house for £2,500, with £1,000 to be paid on completion of the foundations, £1,000 on erection of the superstructure, and £500 six months after completion of the house in accordance with the specifications. Then, if after the foundations are laid the builder fails to do any further work, he can, nevertheless, recover £1,000.

However, in *Sumpter* v *Hedges* [1898] 1 QB 673, the plaintiff had agreed to erect upon the defendant's land two houses and stables for £565. He did part of the work to the value of about £333 and then abandoned the contract. The defendant completed the buildings.

The plaintiff could not recover the value of the work done, as he had abandoned the contract; and see below, as to acceptance of partial performance.

Acceptance of partial performance

Where the plaintiff to whom the promise of performance was made receives the benefit of partial performance of the promise under such circumstances that he is able to accept or reject the work and he accepts the work, then the promisee is obliged to pay a reasonable price for the benefit received. But it must be possible to infer from the circumstances a fresh agreement by the parties that payment shall be made for the goods or services in fact supplied.

In *Christy* v *Row* (1808) 1 Taunt 300, a ship freighted to Hamburg was prevented 'by restraint of princes' from arriving. Consignees accepted the cargo at another port *to which they had directed it to be delivered.*

The consignees were held liable upon an implied contract to pay freight pro rata itineris (contract implied from their directions re alternative port of delivery).

In *Sumpter* v *Hedges* (above), Collins LJ said:

'Where, as in the case of work done on land, the circumstances are such as to give the defendant no option whether he will take the benefit of the work or not, then one must look to other facts than the mere taking of the benefit in order to ground the inference of a new contract. In this case I see no other facts on which such an inference can be founded. The mere fact that a defendant is in possession of what he cannot help keeping, or even has done work upon it, affords no ground for such an inference. He is not bound to keep unfinished a building which in an incomplete state would be a nuisance on his land.'

Completion of performance prevented by the promisee

Where a party to an entire contract *is prevented by the promisee* from performing all his obligations, then he can recover a reasonable price for what he has in fact done on a quantum meruit basis in an action in quasi-contract.

In *Planché* v *Colburn* (1831) 8 Bing 14, the plaintiff was to write a book on 'Costume and Ancient Armour' for a series, and was to receive £100 on completion of the book. After he had done the necessary research but before the book had been written, the publishers abandoned the series. He claimed alternatively on the original contract and on a quantum meruit. The claim on the original contract seems to have disappeared in the course of the argument but, on the alternative submission, it was held that:

1. the original contract had been discharged by the defendants' breach (or, more properly, that the plaintiff had accepted the defendants' breach as discharging the contract);
2. no new contract had been substituted;
3. the plaintiff could obtain 50 guineas as reasonable remuneration on a quantum meruit. This claim was independent of the original contract and was based on quasi-contract.

Substantial performance

When a man fully performs his contract in the hope that he has done all that he agreed to do, or has supplied all he agreed to supply, but subject to defects of so minor a character that he can be said to have *substantially* performed his promise, it is regarded as far more just to allow him to recover the contract price diminished by the extent to which his breach of contract lessened the value of what was done, than to leave him with no right of recovery at all.

The doctrine of substantial performance dates back to the judgment of Lord Mansfield in *Boone* v *Eyre* (1779) 1 Hy Bl 273n. In *Dakin & Co* v *Lee* [1916] 1 KB 566, builders promised to build a house according to specification and failed to carry out exactly all the specifications, for example, concrete not 4 feet deep as specified, wrong joining of certain rolled steel joists and concrete not properly mixed.

The Court of Appeal held that the builders were entitled to recover the contract price, less so much as ought to be allowed in respect of the items found to be defective.

Note that in requiring a standard of substantial performance, the court must not apply an excessively strict standard. In *Ateni Maritime Corporation* v *Great Marine* (1991) Financial Times 13 February the buyers agreed to buy a ship under a contract based on a Norwegian Standard Sale form. The contract provided, inter alia, that if on arrival the ship was in any way so defective as to affect its certification, the defects would be made good at the seller's expense. The work should be to the satisfaction of a named third party, the classification society. The propeller was found to be severely damaged. A damages award against the sellers was appealed by them, on the grounds that in assessing damages the judge had applied too high a standard.

The Court of Appeal held that the buyers could not complain if the sellers did no more than was necessary to obtain a clean certificate. They were not able to demand the sellers did work that would restore it to its pre-contractual condition. The buyers were only entitled to such damages as would cover the cost of reasonable repair work.

Tender of performance

Tender of performance is equivalent to performance in the situation where one party cannot complete performance without the assistance of the other and the one party makes an offer to perform which the other refuses.

In *Startup* v *M'Donald* (1843) 6 M & G 593, the plaintiffs agreed to sell 10 tons of oil to the defendant and to deliver it to him 'within the last 14 days of March', payment to be in cash at the end of that period. Delivery was tendered at 8.30 pm on 31 March. The defendant refused to accept or pay for the goods because of the late hour.

The tender was held to be equivalent to performance and the plaintiffs were entitled to recover damages for non-acceptance.

Rolfe B said:

'In every contract by which a party binds himself to deliver goods or pay money to another, he in fact engages to do an act which he cannot completely perform without the concurrence of the party to whom the delivery or the payment is to be made. Without acceptance on the part of him who is to receive, the act of him who is to deliver or to pay can amount only to a tender. But the law considers (the latter) as having substantially performed it if he has tendered the goods or the money ... provided only that the tender has been made under such circumstances that the party to whom it has been made has had a reasonable opportunity of examining the goods or the money tendered, in order to ascertain that the thing tendered really was what it purported to be. Indeed, without such an opportunity an offer to deliver or pay does not amount to a tender.'

Where goods are tendered they must be correct in quantity and quality.

Where *money* is tendered as payment, it must be in the form of 'legal tender' or such other form as is agreed, for example, a cheque.

To amount to a valid tender of money, the party seeking to perform must produce the correct sum of money (change cannot be required) in the form of 'legal tender', that is, Bank of England notes for any amount; gold coins for any amount; coins of cupro-nickel or silver exceeding 10p in value for any amount up to £10; coins of cupro-nickel or silver of not more than 10p in value up to £5; coins of bronze for any amount up to 20p. See s2 Coinage Act 1971.

If the party making the tender of payment is sued for breach of contract, he must make payment of the sum tendered into court, whereupon the costs of the action will be borne by the plaintiff. See *Griffith* v *School Board of Ystradyfodwg* (1890) 24 QBD 307.

It is the duty of the party obliged to pay to seek out his creditor and, if he sends the money in any way and it is lost in the course of transit, the risk is on the debtor, and he will have to pay again, unless the creditor requests a particular manner of delivery, for example, by post, in which case the debtor will be discharged as long *as he exercises reasonable care* even where the money is lost in transit, viz the risk is on the creditor.

Where there is a valid tender of *goods,* the party tendering is discharged, but where there is a tender of *money,* although the debtor is absolved from further obligation to tender, the obligation to pay the debt, when called upon, remains.

15.4 Stipulations as to time of performance

At common law

The principle used to be that, in the absence of evidence of a contrary intention, time was essential, even though it has not been expressly made so by the parties. Thus, at common law, a party who did not perform on time could not perform his part of the contract late and enforce the contract against the other party. This rule was modified in part by s41 Law of Property Act 1925 which provides:

> 'Stipulations in a contract, as to time or otherwise, which according to the rules of equity are not deemed to be or to have become of the essence of the contract, are also construed and have effect at law in accordance with the same rules.'

The effect of this section in that, if time is not of the essence, late performance does not give rise to a right to terminate, but does give rise to a right to damages. See *Raineri* v *Miles* [1981] AC 1050.

In equity

Equity does not regard time as of the essence of a contract as long as the stipulations as to time can be disregarded without injustice to the parties, and, generally, in contracts for the sale of land, they can be disregarded because the delay of one party does not usually deprive the other of the substance of his bargain. However, even in equity time may, in certain circumstances, be regarded as of the essence of a contract.

1. Where the contract expressly provides that time 'is of the essence', or uses other clear words to the same effect. Then equity will give effect to the manifest intention of the parties. This view was shared by the Privy Council recently in the case of *Union Eagle Ltd* v *Golden Achievement Ltd* [1997] 2 All ER 215 (Privy Council) where their Lordships agreed that the established principles of equity dictate that only where the contract expressly provides that time is of the essence will equity award the appropriate equitable remedy. In this case, the action for specific performance failed.

2. Time can be made of the essence by the giving of notice (during the currency of the contract) to perform within a reasonable time. What amounts to a reasonable time is a question of fact depending on the circumstances of each case.

   In *Rickards (Charles)* v *Oppenheim* [1950] 1 KB 616, the defendant ordered a Rolls Royce chassis early in 1947, and in July the plaintiffs agreed that a body should be built for it within six or seven months. The body was not completed seven months later, but the defendant agreed to wait another three months. At the end of this period, the body was still not built. The defendant gave a final notice that if the work was not finished within a further four weeks, he would cancel the order. The body was not finished. The defendant cancelled the order.

   Held: by giving the final indulgence and indicating that time was of the essence, and giving reasonable notice of that condition, he was not to be regarded in breach of the agreement. It was the plaintiff who was in breach.

   In *British & Commonwealth Holdings plc* v *Quadrex Holdings Inc* [1989] 3 WLR 723, the two companies entered into a written agreement to divide between them different divisions of a third company in which they were both interested. Initially, no time limit was set, but following delays, the plaintiffs served on the defendant company a notice making time 'of the essence' and setting a date for completion.

   The Court of Appeal held that while normally the plaintiffs would undoubtedly be within their rights to issue such a notice, their own conduct was not blameless. Because the plaintiffs' status was not that of an innocent party, their ability to issue a notice, making time 'of the essence', was in doubt.

3. Where from the nature of the surrounding circumstances or from the subject matter of the contract it is clearly essential that the stipulation as to time should be observed, for example, where ripe bananas or a short lease are the subject matter of the contract.

Stipulations as to time in conditional contracts

Note that contractual stipulations as to time may occur, not only as to the time by which performance must be completed but also, in certain types of conditional contracts, the dates by which certain contingent events must take place.

In *Millers Wharf Partnership Ltd* v *Corinthian Column Ltd* (1990) 61 P & CR 461 the plaintiffs agreed to grant the lease of a flat to the defendants, on condition that the plaintiffs should obtain planning permission for redevelopment by a certain date. Either party should have a right of rescission if planning permission was not obtained by the relevant time. The plaintiffs obtained planning consent, some months after the due date. The defendants eventually exercised their power of rescission. The plaintiffs argued that since the due date had passed and the condition had not been fulfilled yet the defendants had not rescinded, then they had lost the right to rescind. The obtaining of planning consent, the condition on which the contract depended, had been fulfilled by a later date; the defendants had waived their right to rescind by not acting immediately once it became apparent planning permission would not be obtained in the time specified.

The court held, however, that the right to rescind still existed. Planning permission had not been obtained by the due date and the plaintiffs' delay in seeking rescission was not to be taken as evidence of waiver.

See *Thornton* v *Abbey National plc* (1993) The Times 4 March for further guidance as to construction of contracts where stipulations are made as to timing of the performance of the contract.

15.5 Agreements

Eodem modo quo oritur, eodem modo dissoluitur – what has been created by agreement may be extinguished by agreement.

An agreement by the parties to an existing contract to extinguish the rights and obligations that have been created is itself a binding contract, provided that it is either made under seal or supported by consideration. Accordingly, a distinction needs to be drawn between agreements which are executed on one side, where the party seeking to be released must show that he has been giving consideration for the release, or that the release is under seal, and agreements which are wholly executory, where consideration may be found in the mutual release by each party of his rights under the contract.

Discharge by deed is equally effective as regards unilateral or bilateral discharge but where the agreement for discharge is not under seal, the legal position varies according to whether the discharge is bilateral or unilateral.

15.6 Bilateral discharge

This occurs whenever *both* parties to the contract have some right to surrender, as where the contract is in no way performed by either party, or is partly performed by one or both sides to the contract. Where neither party has performed his obligations, the contract is said to be executory.

The agreement by the parties to discharge their contract may be designed to have one of several effects:

1. the parties may intend to rescind their present agreement and nothing more, for example, R has agreed to make weekly deliveries of new materials to J as from 1 July. In June, both parties agree to the termination of the contract (*accord and satisfaction*); or
2. the parties may intend rescission plus agreement on the terms of a new contract as where A has agreed to supply B with a Ford Escort and, by agreement, his contract is rescinded and A agrees to supply B with a Renault 5; or
3. the parties may agree on the variation of an existing contract, for example, where delivery dates are changed for the convenience of both parties. Here, the parties intend to deal on the varied terms of basically the same contract.

The main area of discussion as regards the above surrounds the situation where the original contract is one for which the law requires either that it be in writing, or that there be written evidence of it.

Accord and satisfaction

'Accord and satisfaction is the purchase of a release from an obligation whether arising under a contract or tort by means of any valuable consideration, not being the actual performance of the obligation itself. The accord is the agreement by which the obligation is discharged. The satisfaction is the consideration which makes the agreement operative.' *British Russian Gazette* v *Associated Newspapers* [1933] 2 KB 616.

Thus, where there is an agreement mutually to release the other from the obligations under the first agreement, there is an accord and satisfaction.

See, on the question of agreement, the case of *Stour Valley Builders* v *Stuart* (1993) The Times 9 February, in which the Court of Appeal stressed the importance of the fact that there must be agreement between the parties for accord and satisfaction to apply.

Rescission

Although the law requires writing or written evidence for the formation or forceability of certain types of contract, *no* writing is required for their discharge. Thus, where an oral agreement seeks to provide for the rescission of such a contract and the creation of another in its place, the oral words will effectively discharge the existing contract, but if the new contract is of a type required to be evidenced in writing, then it will fail, for lack of writing, to be legally effective.

For example, where A enters into a written contract for the sale of Blackacre to B and later the parties orally agree that instead of selling Blackacre to B, A shall sell Whiteacre, the effect of the oral agreement is to discharge A from his obligation to convey Blackacre to B, but the agreement fails to give B any enforceable rights in respect of Whiteacre.

A rescission and substitution of a new contract is different from a variation, which merely changes or qualifies one or more of the existing contractual provisions. An example of rescission and substitution arose in *Morris* v *Baron* [1918] AC 1. Because there was a substituted agreement, the court drew the necessary inference that the original contract was discharged by rescission. A written contract was entered into for the sale and purchase of dates. A dispute arose and legal proceedings commenced. The parties agreed that the action and counter-claim should be withdrawn, and that an extension should be given to the buyer for payment of a sum owed by him under the contract, and that he should have an option to purchase the goods remaining due, instead of being bound to take delivery.

The House of Lords held that the original contract of sale was discharged by the executory agreement.

A contract under seal has always been capable of oral dissolution in equity. Since the Judicature Act 1873, the equitable rule has prevailed. This formula is now embodied in s49 Supreme Court Act 1981.

Novation

This is the name given to a particular type of discharge by agreement. It occurs where there are two contracts each with a creditor and debtor, and the same person is the debtor under the second contract and the creditor under the first. The creditor under the second contract agrees for the release of his own debtor and to accept the debtor under the first contract, and the debtor under the first contract agrees to pay the creditor under the second contract in return for his creditor's promise to release him.

For example, A owes B £100. C owes A £100. C agrees to pay £100 to B in return for A's promise to release him. B agrees to release A in return for C's promise of £100. A agrees to release C in return for C's promise to pay off A's debt to B.

Old contracts: C – £100 – A   A – £100 – B

New contract: C – £100 – B

All are parties to the agreement and all three give consideration. The first contracts are discharged and a new one is created.

Variation

The parties may effect a variation by modifying or altering the terms of the original agreement. In *Berry* v *Berry* [1929] 2 KB 316, husband and wife entered into a separation deed whereby the husband promised to pay to the wife a certain sum each year for her support. Subsequently, they agreed in writing to vary the agreement.

The variation was held valid and enforceable, and could be set up as a defence to an action on the deed.

So it seems that an oral or written agreement may be sufficient to vary a deed (compare the situation under the parol evidence rule, which relates to the *formation* of the contract and not the variation of it). An oral or written agreement may not be sufficient, however, to vary a contract which is required by law to be in writing or evidence in writing. See *Gross* v *Nugent* (1833) 5 B & Ald 58.

The vendor of certain land contracted to make a good title, and this he was unable to do. The purchaser by oral agreement agreed to accept the defective title, but later failed to complete. The vendor brought an action to enforce the contract, that is, the written contract as orally varied.

The court held against the vendor on the ground that there was no written evidence of the contract he wished to enforce.

Note: probably the purchaser could have enforced the original contract (subject to the possible effect of waiver – see later) because the variation of the original contract was ineffective. But if the oral agreement were construed as a rescission of the original contract and its replacement by a new contract, then there would be nothing for the purchaser to enforce.

So the distinction whether the oral agreement was intended by the parties to extinguish the original contract altogether and create a new one, or merely vary the original contract, can be crucial. It is a question of fact to be determined in the light of all the circumstances of each particular case.

See *British and Benington Ltd* v *NW Cachar Tea Co* [1923] AC 48, *Morris* v *Baron* (above) and *United Dominions Corporation (Jamaica) Ltd* v *Shoucair* [1969] 1 AC 340.

A variation should also be distinguished from:

1. a collateral agreement. This is concluded before the contract is entered into or under which one party agrees not to enforce a term of the main agreement. See *City & Westminster Properties* v *Mudd* [1959] Ch 129;
2. the mere elucidation of the contract by correcting mistakes or filling in details.

Waiver

Where one party voluntarily accedes to a request by another party to forbear his right to strict performance of the contract, or where he represents to another that he will not insist upon his right to strict performance of the contract, the court may hold that he has *waived* his right to performance as initially contemplated by the parties. Under the ordinary pressures of commerce and industry, such as postal delays and labour troubles, it frequently arises that it is not possible for one of the parties to keep strictly to the terms of his contract.

For example, the seller of goods may ask the buyer to let him deliver less than the agreed number of items one month, and make up the number on later monthly deliveries. If the buyer agrees, he is said to *waive* his strict rights under the contracts.

The waiver may be oral, written or inferred from conduct, even where the contract itself is one which is required by law to be in, or evidenced in, writing. In *Besseler Waechter Glover & Co v Derwent Coal* [1938] 1 KB 408, Goddard J said at p416:

> 'If the parties agree to rescind their original contract and to substitute it for a new one, the latter must be evidenced in writing; so, too, if as a matter of contract the parties agree that the terms of the original agreement shall be varied, the variation must be in writing. But if what happens is a mere voluntary forbearance to insist on delivery or acceptance according to the strict terms of the written contract, the original contract remains unaffected and the obligation to deliver and accept the full contract quantity still continues ... It does not appear to me to matter whether the request comes from one side or the other, or whether it is a matter which is convenient to one party or to both. What is of importance is whether it is a mere forbearance or a matter of contract.'

The effect of the waiver is that, in the absence of reasonable notice requiring contractual performance (if that is possible – it would not be possible where compliance with a time period has been waived), the party extending the forbearance will not be permitted to sue, and the party in whose favour the waiver has been granted will not be able to rely on the contractual obligations of the parties to allege that the other is in breach. For example, in *Levy v Goldberg* [1922] 1 KB 688, the defendants agreed in writing to buy cloth from the plaintiffs during a specified period. The defendants asked the plaintiffs not to deliver within that period. When the plaintiffs effected delivery subsequently, the defendants refused to accept delivery. The plaintiffs sued. The defendants said that the plaintiffs were in breach as the oral terms were insufficient to vary the contract (which was then required by the Statute of Frauds to be evidenced in writing). It was held that the plaintiffs had waived their contractual rights to insist on delivery during the contractual period, and so they were entitled to maintain their action against the defendants.

In *Hartley v Hymans* [1920] 3 KB 475, a buyer of cotton agreed to allow the seller to make late delivery. It was held that he was liable in damages for refusing to take delivery after the contract period had expired.

In *Leather Cloth Co v Hieronimus* (1875) LR 10 QB 140, a buyer of goods to be shipped via Ostend agreed that they could be shipped via Rotterdam. The goods were lost. The buyer was still held liable for the price because he had assented to the altered mode of performance.

Proctor & Gamble Philippine Manufacturing Corpn v *Peter Cremer GmbH* [1988] 3 All ER 843 is an interesting recent case on waiver. In two contracts for copra cake being shipped from the Philippines, the buyers sought to repudiate on the grounds that the bills of lading were incorrectly dated. In fact, the cargo had not in any event been completely loaded on time, but was 11 days late. The court decided that if a party has a right to reject, which he is not aware of, he cannot be held to have waived his rights of rejection, since he is ignorant that such rights exist.

An example of the revocable nature of waiver is provided in *Rickards* v *Oppenheim*, the facts of which are set out above. The defendant (the buyer) had waived his original rights as to time of delivery, but could give reasonable notice that a new final date was to be complied with and treat the contract as at an end if that date was not complied with.

Of course, there must be circumstances in which the waiver cannot be revoked, for example, where the goods have been lost in the *Hieronimus* case and, possibly, where transportation via Rotterdam had already occurred.

The position relating to waiver at common law is also open to objection on the ground that, in effect, it often makes enforceable a promise which is unsupported by consideration, being given for the benefit of one party only.

The cases on waiver have much in common with the doctrine of promissory estoppel, which has been discussed in Chapter 3. See obiter dicta of Denning LJ in *Rickards* v *Oppenheim*:

> 'If the defendant, as he did, led the plaintiffs to believe that he would not insist on the stipulation as to time, and that, if they carried out the work, he would accept it, and they did, he could not afterwards set up the stipulation to regard to time against them. Whether it be called waiver or forbearance on his part, or an agreed variation or substituted performance, does not matter. It is kind of estoppel. By his conduct he evinced an intention to affect their legal relations. He made, in effect, a promise not to insist on his strict legal rights. That promise was to be acted on, and was in fact, acted on. He cannot afterwards go back on it.'

Although in many instances waiver and promissory estoppel produce the same results, there is authority for the view that the doctrines must be kept distinct. See *Brikom Investments* v *Carr* [1979] QB 467.

Provision for discharge in the contract itself

The contract can provide for discharge in its terms, for example, upon certain breaches of contract, or upon the occurrence of certain events, such as the bankruptcy of a party or conviction of a criminal offence, or on an event unconnected with the parties, or upon the giving of notice by one party. A common illustration of these provisions is found in partnership agreements. See also *Head* v *Tattersall* (above, 6.4).

15.7 Unilateral discharge

This takes place where only one party has rights to surrender. Where one party has entirely performed his part of the agreement, he is no longer under obligations but has rights to compel the performance of the agreement by the other party.

For example, A agrees to sell 1 cwt of coal to B for £X and A delivers the coal only to find out that B has suddenly incurred a tremendous expense. A, out of sympathy, agrees that B shall not pay for the coal. But where is the consideration moving from B in support of A's promise to forgo his right to the £X? There is none. There is merely a bare promise from A.

For unilateral discharge, unless the agreement is under seal, consideration must be furnished in order to make the agreement enforceable.

In this context, the agreement is termed the *accord,* and the consideration which makes it binding is known as the *satisfaction.* See above under 'Bilateral discharge'.

The Bills of Exchange Act 1882 provides an exception to the general rule that a unilateral discharge requires consideration: where the holder of a bill of exchange or promissory note unconditionally renounces his rights against the acceptor, the bill is discharged. The renunciation must be in writing, or the bill must be delivered up to the acceptor.

15.8 Breach

The nature of a breach

A failure to perform the terms of a contract constitutes a breach. As we have seen in Chapter 6, not all breaches entitle the innocent party to treat the contract as repudiated. In some cases tortious liability (as well as contractual) may arise from breach of contract; for example, in the case of *Holt and Another* v *Payne, Skillington and Another* (1996) 77 BLR 51, the plaintiff alleged negligence in the conduct of the defendant's duties under the contract. The court held that where a duty of care arose between the parties to a contract, wider obligations could be imposed by the duty of care in tort than that arising under a contract. In *Modahl* v *British Athletic Federation Ltd* (1999) The Times 23 July the House of Lords stated that only failure to perform the terms of a contract constitutes a breach. Anything else, for example, ignorance of a third party's (potential) breach which may affect the contract as between the plaintiff and defendant will not necessarily be tantamount to a failure to discharge contractual obligations between the parties to the contract itself.

A breach does not automatically discharge a contract. Indeed, note the case of *Thornton* v *Abbey National plc* (1993) The Times 4 March, in which the Court of Appeal ruled that where a breach of contract occurs which in no way disadvantages the plaintiff, the defendants may, effectively, take advantage of their own breach of contract. It is simply that a sufficiently serious breach (breach of a condition or a breach with serious consequences) will give the innocent party the option of treating the contract as repudiated (viz treating the contract as 'at an end'). It is not rescinded ab initio, and the word rescission is, accordingly, a misleading term to use. The word 'repudiation' is more satisfactory. When a contract is said to be 'at an end', it means that the innocent party or, in some cases, both parties are discharged from further performance of their primary obligations under the contract, but in place of the primary obligation a secondary obligation may arise. This secondary obligation is (usually) to pay a monetary compensation for the non-performance. See also, *Photo Production Ltd* v *Securicor Transport Ltd* [1980] AC 827.

Note: the innocent party may choose to continue with the contract and simply sue for damages.

The doctrine of repudiatory breach does not apply to partnership agreements. Accordingly, a partner's conduct amounting to a repudiatory breach of the partnership agreement, accepted by the innocent partner, does not bring about the automatic dissolution of the partnership: *Mullins* v *Laughton* (2002) The Times 27 December.

Anticipatory breach

Where the breach occurs before the time fixed for performance, this is known as anticipatory breach. One preliminary question is to ascertain whether, once repudiation has been communicated to the innocent party, that party accepts the repudiation or not. In *Vitol SA* v *Norelf Ltd* [1996] 3 WLR 107, the repudiating party notified the other that they considered the contract at an end. However, no action was taken by the innocent party, either to act on the repudiation or to affirm the contract, on receipt of this information. The Court of Appeal stated that inactivity did not show the party's intentions one way or another and did not amount to acceptance of repudiation or serve as affirmation either. On appeal, the House of Lords reversed the Court of Appeal's decision stating that on repudiation of a contract, the aggrieved party could elect whether to accept the repudiation or affirm the contract, and that an acceptance required no particular form provided the aggrieved party clearly and unequivocally demonstrated to the repudiating party that he was treating the contract as terminated.

The innocent party is not under any obligation to wait until the date fixed for performance before commencing his action, but may immediately treat the contract as at an end and sue for damages. Alternatively, he may affirm the contract by treating it as still in force. The innocent party has this right of election, and is bound by his choice. If within a reasonable time he does not indicate that he accepts the other party's repudiation so that the contract is discharged, then the contract remains open for the benefit of, and the risk of, both parties.

The breach was accepted in *Hochster* v *De La Tour* (1853) 2 E & B 678. An employer told his employee (a travelling courier) before the time for performance arrived that he would not require his services. The courier sued for damages at once. He was held entitled to do so. See also *Frost* v *Knight* (1872) LR 7 Ex 111.

The breach was not accepted in *Avery* v *Bowden* (1855) 5 E & B 714. A charterparty provided that a ship should proceed to Odessa and there take a cargo from the charter's agent. The ship arrived at Odessa and the master demanded a cargo, but the agent could not provide one. The ship's master continued to ask for one. A war broke out. The charterer sued. The court held (inter alia) that if the agent's conduct amounted to an anticipatory repudiation of the contract, the master had elected to keep the contract alive until it was discharged by frustration on the outbreak of war.

It appears that the right to keep the contract alive subsists even where the innocent party is increasing the amount, and not mitigating, the damages which he may receive from the party in breach. In *White & Carter* v *McGregor* [1962] AC 413, the appellants (advertising contractors) agreed with the respondent (a garage proprietor) to display advertisements for his garage for three years. The respondent repudiated the agreement and cancelled on the same day. The appellants refused to cancel and performed their obligations. They sued for the contract price. The court held (by a majority of 3:2) that they were entitled to the full contract price.

Where a party elects to treat the contract as continuing, that is, he 'affirms' the contract, the affirmation can be regarded as a species of waiver. The innocent party waives his right to treat the contract as repudiated (see, for example, s11 Sale of Goods Act 1979) and may be 'estopped' from changing his election.

In *Panchaud Freres SA* v *Etablissements General Grain Co* [1970] 1 Lloyd's Rep 53, buyers of maize rejected it on a ground which was subsequently found to be inadequate. Three years later, they discovered that the grain had not been shipped within the period stipulated for in the contract. They, therefore, sought to justify their rejection on this ground.

They were held to be not entitled to do so. Lord Denning MR stated that the buyers were estopped by their conduct from setting up late delivery as a ground for rejection because they had led the sellers to believe they would not do so.

If a party elects to affirm a contract after an anticipatory breach by the other party, he is not absolved from tendering further performance of his own obligations under the contract. Accordingly, if a repudiation by anticipatory breach was followed by affirmation of the contract, the repudiating party could escape liability if the affirming party was subsequently in breach of the contract. See *Fercometal Sarl* v *Mediterranean Shipping Co SA* [1988] 2 All ER 742.

Whether the anticipatory breach amounts to a repudiation depends on the actual circumstances of the case:

> '… you must examine what (the) conduct is to see whether it amounts to a renunciation, to an absolute refusal to perform the contract … and whether the other party may accept it as a reason for not performing his part.'

per Lord Selborne in *Mersey Steel and Iron Co* v *Naylor Benzon & Co* (1884) 9 App Cas 434 at 438–9.

The difficulty that can arise in determining whether the conduct amounts to a repudiation is illustrated by a comparison of two decisions in the House of Lords.

In *Federal Commerce and Navigation* v *Molena Alpha* [1979] AC 757, the owners of the ship gave instructions not to issue bills of lading without which the charterers would not be able to operate the ship. The owners believed that they were entitled to take these measures. This belief did not weigh with the House of Lords, their Lordships holding that their conduct constituted a wrongful repudiation of the contract.

In *Woodar Investment* v *Wimpey Construction* [1980] 1 WLR 277, in a contract for the sale of land, the purchasers sought a right to rescind the contract. The right to rescind was afforded by the contract, but was only exercisable on grounds which did not, in fact, exist. The purchasers' motive was to escape from an unprofitable transaction, but they honestly believed that they were entitled to the right they brought.

The House of Lords held, by a majority, that the purchasers' conduct did not amount to a repudiatory breach. Lord Wilberforce distinguished this case from *Molena Alpha* by drawing a distinction between the erroneous assertion of a view, as here, and threatening a breach with serious consequences, as in *Molena Alpha*.

Lords Salmon and Russell, dissenting, held the view that the two cases were identical.

Cheshire and Fifoot suggests three possible grounds of distinction between these two cases.

1. In *Woodar*, there was no call for the sellers to take immediate action, they could have tested their rights by legal process.
2. In *Woodar*, the time for completion was some way off, if the purchasers had actually refused to complete this would then have amounted to a repudiation.
3. In *Molena Alpha*, the gap between repudiation and performance was fairly short, and the pressure on the charterers accordingly greater.

Recently, the Privy Council also considered the topic of repudiatory breach in *Vaswani* v *Italian Motors (Sales & Services) Ltd* [1996] 1 WLR 270. The issue before the Judicial Committee in this instance was one of proper construction of the contract and the court looked at the performance, intention and state of mind of the parties.

Questions of whether or not repudiation can be established often arise in contracts for the sale of goods where delivery or payment is to be made by instalments.

In *Mersey Steel and Iron* (above), the buyers were acting under the genuine, but mistaken, belief that they could not continue making payments without leave of the court, because of the initiation of insolvency proceedings. It was held that this conduct could not be construed as a repudiation.

Some guidance is given by the Court of Appeal in *Maple Flock Co Ltd* v *Universal Furniture Products (Wembley) Ltd* [1934] 1 KB 148 where it was stated that whether, in an instalment contract, a certain breach could be treated as repudiation is to be determined by considering, first, the ratio quantatively which the breach bears to the contract as a whole and, secondly, the degree of probability or improbability that the breach will be repeated.

In *Decro-Wall International* v *Practitioners in Marketing* [1971] 1 WLR 361, a company was persistently – though only slightly – late in making payments under the contract. This was not held to constitute a repudiation because the other party had not been prejudiced by the late payments, except in having to pay a small amount of interest on the outstanding sums, which could have been recovered from the party in default; moreover, there was no reason to doubt that payment would be made as soon as the goods in question had been disposed of. See also *Afovos Shipping* v *Pagnan* [1983] 1 All ER 449 where the House of Lords affirmed the principle that the doctrine of anticipatory breach related only to repudiation arising out of fundamental breach. The delay, in this instance in paying one instalment of hire, did not amount to a fundamental breach. The cases of *Alfred C Toepfer International GmbH* v *ITEX Itagrani Export SA* [1993] 1 Lloyd's Rep 360 and *Vitol SA* v *Norelf Ltd* [1996] 3 WLR 107 have considered further the question of what amounts to a repudiatory breach.

16

Remedies for Breach of Contract – Damages

16.1 Introduction

As we have seen from the discussion in earlier chapters, a breach of contract may be of such a nature that the injured party is justified in treating the contract as discharged. In such a case, the normal remedy of the injured party is to obtain damages for the breach to compensate him for the promise to him not being fulfilled, as well as to repudiate the contract. Alternatively, he may limit his remedy to damages. Not every breach of contract will entitle a person to treat himself as discharged, of course. Where a breach has only been a breach of warranty, the only remedy at common law is damages. The right to repudiate does not arise.

Equity may assist

By declaration
Damages for breach of contract may not always be satisfactory as a remedy. If the

injured party feels that he made a bad bargain in the first place in entering into the contract, he may choose to obtain a declaration that the contract is terminated.

Specific performance

It may be the case that damages are an inadequate remedy to the injured party, for example, there may be no satisfactory substitute for that which the injured party had bargained for, as in a contract for the sale of a specific piece of land. In such cases, the appropriate remedy will be specific performance of the contract itself.

Injunction

Damages may be a useless remedy to the injured party who may seek specific performance of the contract in such cases. However, the breach may take the form of doing something contrary to the terms of the contract, for example, where an employee agrees not to go into competition against his employer or to work for his employer's competitors. The appropriate remedy there will be an injunction to restrain the defaulting party from acting in breach of contract.

Account of profits

Where other remedies fail to provide an adequate response to a breach of contract, exceptionally the remedy of account of profits may be available. *Attorney-General* v *Blake, Jonathan Cape Ltd third party* [2000] 4 All ER 385 was such an exceptional case. For part of the time that the defendant Blake was a member of the Secret Intelligence Service (SIS) he was an agent of the Soviet Union. He was convicted of spying offences, but he escaped from prison and fled to Moscow. The third party published his autobiography and this constituted a breach of the contractual undertaking which the defendant had given when first he was employed by the SIS. The Attorney-General contended that the Crown was entitled to recover from the third party publisher the defendant's profits arising from this breach of contract. The House of Lords accepted this contention and concluded that the Attorney-General was entitled to an account of profits and a declaration that he was entitled to be paid a sum equal to that owing to the defendant from his publisher.

In so far as there is a conflict, in this regard, between the decision of Brightman J in *Wrotham Park Estate Co Ltd* v *Parkside Homes Ltd* [1974] 2 All ER 321 and the decision of the Court of Appeal in *Surrey County Council* v *Bredero Homes Ltd* [1993] 3 All ER 705, their Lordships preferred the former.

Quasi-contractual remedies

Restitution for total failure of consideration

If the injured party had performed his side of the contract but has not received counter-performance in full, then the appropriate remedy may be restitution in respect of his own performance, for example, where the injured party has paid the price for the goods which he has not received.

Quantum meruit

In cases where the injured party has performed, under the contract, work the value of which exceeds what would have been due to him if the contract had been fully performed, then he may claim on a quantum meruit the value of that work already done. Such a claim will be quasi-contractual in nature.

16.2 Damages

General

Damages are meant to compensate the injured party for any consequences of the breach of contract which the law recognises. The underlying principle is to put the injured party financially as near as possible, into the position he would have been in had the promise been fulfilled.

Damages are assessed on the actual loss to the plaintiff, and not on the gain to the defendant. They are compensation, not punishment.

In *Teacher* v *Calder* [1889] 1 F (HL) 39, a financier broke a contract by which he agreed to invest £15,000 in the business of a timber merchant; instead, he invested the same sum in a distillery. The court held that the timber merchant's damages were to be based on the loss to his business – not on the much larger profits the financier had derived from investing in the brewery.

An exception exists to this rule in cases concerning a contract for the sale of land; here, the defendant must hand over the profits. In *Lake* v *Bayliss* [1974] 1 WLR 1073, the position was explained: the vendor is considered to be a trustee of the land for the purchaser after the contract is made. Therefore, if the vendor wrongfully resells the land to a third party, the purchaser is entitled to the proceeds of sale, even though they may exceed his loss.

If there has been no actual loss inflicted on the plaintiff as a result of the breach, he may still, in rare circumstances, recover damages. There is no rule of law that liability without payment does not constitute a recoverable loss: *Total Liban SA* v *Vitol Energy SA* [2000] 1 All ER 267.

In *Penarth Dock Engineering* v *Pound* [1963] 1 Lloyd's Rep 359, the defendant bought a floating dock from the plaintiff but failed to remove it from its berth within the stipulated time. The plaintiff claimed damages on the basis that he was deprived of the use of the berth during the time it was there in breach of the agreement. The defendant argued that the plaintiff should get only nominal damages, as he would not have made any use of the berth anyway. It was held that the defendant should pay a fair rental value for the berth.

The general principle to be observed is that: *there must be a loss to the plaintiff (claimant) in consequence of the breach*. Loss is widely defined and includes any harm to a person or his property and any other injury to his economic position. The plaintiff will be awarded *substantial damages* for such losses, and they will be based on the compensatory principle. If no such loss has been sustained, he will only be able to recover *nominal damages*.

See, for example, *Surrey County Council* v *Bredero Homes Ltd* [1992] 3 All ER 302 in which nominal damages only were awarded to a local authority who had waited so long to make a claim that they had lost any rights to enforce the covenant they had claimed was breached. The loss of the value of the right to enforce the covenant (for instance by injunction) meant that the plaintiffs' failure to act no longer had any contractual rights to enforce.

Substantial damages are only recoverable if the plaintiff's position has been adversely affected. In *Staniforth* v *Lyall* (1830) 7 Bing 169, a shipowner who claimed damages for a charterer's breach to load his ship could not recover as he had found an alternative and more profitable means of employing the ship in the meantime.

Exceptionally, damages may be recovered where it is found that it was within the contemplation of the parties to a contract that any breach of it would cause loss to an identifiable stranger to it, but this does not apply where it was intended that the stranger should have a direct claim in respect of such a breach: *Panatown Ltd* v *Alfred McAlpine Construction Ltd* [2000] 4 All ER 97.

Exemplary damages are not normally awarded in breach of contract. Such damages are awards of sums far greater than the pecuniary loss suffered by the plaintiff (see below).

C & P Haulage v *Middleton* [1983] 1 WLR 1461 illustrates the general proposition that the victim of a breach should not make a profit out of it, and that to recover substantial damages, the plaintiff must show actual loss suffered.

See also Chapter 19, section 19.3 (damages for breach of warranty of authority).

Compensation for the plaintiff's loss

There are several ways in which the plaintiff can be compensated for his loss; the plaintiff is entitled to choose whichever form of compensation he feels is most appropriate to his case.

Loss of bargain
Damages for loss of bargain are assessable to put the plaintiff 'so far as money can do it … in the same situation as if the contract had been performed'.

In a contract for the sale of goods which are defective, the plaintiff will, under this heading, be entitled to damages reflecting the differences between the price paid under the contract and the actual value of the defective goods.

Reliance loss
Damages to put the plaintiff in the position he would have been, if the contract had never been made, by compensating him for expenses he has incurred in his abortive performance. Under this heading, expenses which the plaintiff was never obliged to incur may be recovered.

In *McRae* v *Commonwealth Disposals* (1950) 84 CLR 377, the plaintiff recovered £3,000 spent on sending out a salvage expedition to salvage a wrecked tanker, in a specified position, which they had purchased from the defendant. The tanker had never, in fact, existed. Reliance loss incurred before the contract was entered into may be recovered in certain instances.

In *Anglia Television* v *Reed* [1972] 1 QB 60, the plaintiffs incurred expenses in preparation for filming a television play. They subsequently entered into a contract with the defendant to play the leading role. The defendant repudiated the contract. The plaintiffs tried hard to find a substitute but failed, and had to abandon the play. The plaintiffs sued the defendant for expenses of production amounting to £2,750 incurred by the plaintiffs on production before the contract.

They were held to be entitled to recover the whole of the wasted expenditure:

'Mr Reed must have known perfectly well that much expenditure had already been incurred on director's fees and the like. He must have contemplated – or at any rate, it is reasonably to be imputed to him – that if he broke his contract, all the expenditure would be wasted, whether or not it was incurred before or after the contract.' (per Lord Denning MR.)

Compare *C & P Haulage* v *Middleton* (above) where the expenditure was wasted, not because of the defendant's breach, but because the contract was unwise.

Restitution

Where a bargain is made, and the price paid, but the defendant fails to deliver the goods, then the plaintiff is entitled to recover the price paid plus interest thereon.

Choosing the claim

The plaintiff's choice in the above claims is limited to an extent. In loss of bargain, he must give some evidence of the value of his expectations and, if he is unable to do so, or his expectations are so speculative that no value can be put on them, then he is limited to claims in reliance loss and restitution. Further, if he wishes to pursue his remedy on a claim for restitution, then he must show a total failure of consideration.

The plaintiff's choice of claim may be aided by the fact that more than one of the claims is available to him; for example, both loss of bargain and reliance loss may be available. In such cases, the plaintiff can combine the claims.

In *Millar's Machinery Co* v *David Way* (1935) 40 Com Cas 240, the plaintiff bought some machinery which was installed in his factory and paid for. However, the machinery was not in accordance with the specifications laid down by the contract and the plaintiff rejected it. It was held that the plaintiff could recover the price (restitution), installation expenses (reliance loss) and the net loss resulting from the breach (loss of bargain).

The plaintiff is limited in combining his claims to the extent that he cannot recover the same loss more than once.

In *Cullinane* v *British 'Rema' Manufacturing Co* [1954] 1 QB 292, the plaintiff contracted to buy a clay pulverising plant from the defendant which should have pulverised clay at 6 tons per hour.

The plant never, in fact, pulverised clay at more than 2 tons per hour, and the plaintiff claimed damages under five headings.

1. Cost of buildings to house plant, less break up value.
2. Cost of plant less residual value.
3. Cost of ancillary plant less its residual value.
4. Interest on capital sums under the three headings above.
5. Loss of profit which would have been made on 6 tons per hour from date of installation of plant to date of trial.

The court held that the first three headings could not be awarded as damages as the plaintiff was attempting to recover both the whole of his original capital loss, and the whole of the profit he could have made. It was really a self-evident proposition as a claim for loss of profits could only be founded on the footing of capital expenditure.

For example, if a buyer pays for goods in advance which are not delivered, he cannot have both his payment (restitution) and the full value of the goods at the time of delivery (loss of bargain).

In *CCC Films* v *Impact Quadrant Films* [1984] 3 WLR 245, this case illustrates the choice of claim available – wasted expenditure or loss of profits. It makes the logical point that if the victim of the breach is claiming wasted expenditure because he cannot begin to estimate the expectation loss, then it would be impossible to make him have to prove at least sufficient expectation loss to cover the wasted expenditure. The onus falls on the defendant to prove that the expenditure would not have been recovered had the contract been performed.

The *CCC Films* decision will operate happily when the object of the contract is to make a profit. It produces difficulties for cases similar to *Anglia TV* v *Reed*, where the object of the contract is not to make a profit. The TV company expected to make their profits from increased advertising revenue if the programme was a success. Hutchinson J fails to deal with those problems.

Students will only understand all the cases in this area if they keep in the back of their minds the distinction the Court of Appeal failed to make clear in *Cullinane* v *British 'Rema'*. 'Loss of profits' is used in two senses – loss of *gross* profit and loss of *net* profit, that is, after deduction of the necessary spending to earn that pure profit.

Claims can be made combining reliance loss + restitution + net profit, but *not* combining reliance loss + restitution + gross profit.

For example, A contracts to buy a washing machine from B to install in his laundry to increase the capacity of his business. A spends £10 altering his premises in preparation and £100 in consideration for the new machine. The machine is installed but, in breach of contract, breaks down the next day losing A the chance of doing C's washing. A would have charged C £8 for this comprising £5 for electricity, soap powder, wear and tear on the machine and £3 pure profit.

A can sue B for   £10   +   £100   +   £3
                          (Reliance)   (Restitution)   (Expectation
                                                           net profit)

Incidental and consequential losses

Incidental losses are those which the plaintiff incurs after the breach has come to his notice. They include the administrative costs of buying a substitute, or sending back defective goods, or hiring a replacement in the meantime.

Consequential losses may be loss of profits, for example, reliance loss, or further harm such as personal injury or damage to property. Thus, if the defendant sells the plaintiff a cow which is diseased and infects the plaintiff's other cows, then the plaintiff can claim for not only damages in selling a defective cow, but the losses caused to the other cows. The High Court in *British Sugar plc* v *NEI Power Projects and Another* (1997) The Times 21 February held that consequential loss meant such loss as the plaintiffs could prove over and above that which arose as a direct result of such breaches as the plaintiff could prove in accordance with *Hadley* v *Baxendale*.

Contributory negligence

Until comparatively recently, contributory negligence was not considered relevant in assessing damages for breach of contract.

There have, however, been a number of interesting cases, mainly at first instance, concerning this issue. See *AB Marintrans* v *Comet Shipping Co Ltd* [1985] 3 All ER 442 and *Basildon DC* v *J E Lesser (Properties)* [1985] 1 All ER 20.

The Court of Appeal decision in *Forsikringsaktieselskapet Vesta* v *Butcher* [1988] 2 All ER 43 looked carefully at these earlier cases. In *Forsikringsaktieselskapet*, the plaintiffs, a Norwegian insurance firm, insured a Norwegian fish farm and re-insured 90 per cent of the risk with London underwriters. It was a condition of the insurance that a 24-hour watch be kept on the farm; the owners said this could not be arranged. The plaintiffs telephoned the brokers and awaited confirmation that a non-continuous security arrangement was acceptable. Because of a breakdown in communications, the brokers never followed this up, and the reinsurers were never aware that a 24-hour watch was not being kept.

A severe storm resulted in heavy losses of fish. Although even if there had been a 24 hour-watch, losses would have been the same, the reinsurers repudiated liability on the ground inter alia of the breach of the 24-hour watch condition. The main issue was whether, on the facts of the case, the court had power to apportion under the Law Reform (Contributory Negligence) Act 1945, and thus reduce the damages recoverable by the plaintiffs.

The Court of Appeal held that the 1945 Act might apply in a number of categories of case:

'Three categories in particular can be conveniently identified:

1. Where the defendant's liability arises from some contractual provision which does not depend on negligence on the part of the defendant.
2. When the defendant's liability arises from a contractual obligation which is expressed in terms of taking care (or something similar) but does not correspond to a common law duty of care which would exist in the given case independently of contract.
3. Where the defendant's liability in contract is the same as his liability in the tort of negligence independently of the existence of any contract ...'

The Court of Appeal agreed that the present case was an example of category (3), and that in category (3) the defendant must be allowed to raise the defence of contributory negligence, so that the result of the case would be much the same whether the plaintiff chose to sue in contract or in tort. Though, ultimately, the Court of Appeal decided contributory negligence did not apply in the instant case, in *Barclays Bank plc* v *Fairclough Building Ltd* [1994] 3 WLR 1057 it was made quite clear that contributory negligence might be taken into consideration in assessing damages. The court said that in appropriate circumstances, a defendant could offer a defence based on apportionment of liability under the 1945 Law Reform (Contributory Negligence) Act even when the claim was based on strict contractual duty.

16.3 Remoteness of damage

Hadley *v* Baxendale

Not every type of damage caused to the plaintiff as a result of the breach of contract will be recoverable. If the loss flowing from the breach of contract is too remote then it cannot be recovered. Losses, to be recoverable, must have been within the reasonable contemplation of the parties.

In *Hadley* v *Baxendale* (1854) 9 Exch 341, a shaft in the plaintiff's mill broke and had to be sent to the makers at Greenwich to serve as a pattern for the production of a new one. The defendant agreed to carry the shaft to the makers but, in breach of contract, delayed it so that a stoppage of several days occurred at the plaintiff's mill. The plaintiff claimed damages for £300 for loss of profits during this period, and was awarded £50. The defendant appealed. It was held that there were two principles upon which the jury should have been directed:

'Where the parties have made a contract which one of them has broken, the damages which the other party ought to receive in respect of such breach of contract should be such as may fairly and reasonably be considered as either arising naturally, ie according to the usual course of things, from such breach of contract itself, or such as may be reasonably supposed to have been in the contemplation of both parties at the time they made the contract as the probable result of the breach' (per Alderson B).

Damages are recoverable under two limbs under *Hadley* v *Baxendale*.

1. Damages which may fairly and reasonably be considered as arising naturally.
2. Damages which may reasonably be supposed to have been in the contemplation of the parties at the time of the contract.

If the loss resulting from the damage falls within either category under *Hadley* v *Baxendale*, then it is recoverable. Therefore, in *Hadley* v *Baxendale*, as the stoppage was not the natural consequence of the delay, the defendant was not liable under the first limb. He was not liable under the second limb either, as this required that the damage, that is, the stoppage would be contemplated by both parties at the time of the contract, as a probable result of the breach. The plaintiff had only told the defendant that the shaft was the broken shaft from a mill; if he had told the defendant that the mill would be idle if there was any delay, then the defendant might have tried to limit his liability as he would then, in the circumstances, have been clearly in breach.

The first limb covers loss which would usually be expected to result from the breach. The second limb will only operate where special circumstances under which the contract was actually made are communicated to the defendant by the plaintiff.

Developments after Hadley *v* Baxendale

Both rules can be put together to say what ought the reasonable man in the defendant's position to know and expect.

In *Victoria Laundry* v *Newman Industries* [1949] 2 KB 528, Victoria Laundry wished to expand business and needed a new boiler. Newman Industries wished to supply one, but delivered six months late after a road accident. During this time, Victoria Laundry were losing profits the new boiler would have earned, and this included certain lucrative contracts for the Ministry of Supply. Victoria Laundry claimed these profits as damages.

Newman Industries knew nothing of these orders and could not be held responsible for this loss. But Newman Industries, as an experienced firm, must have known that the new boiler was needed to cut losses or increase profits, thus they were liable for a reasonable sum representing some loss along those lines.

The Court of Appeal took the opportunity to review and restate the principles governing the measure of damages in the *Victoria Laundry* case, and Asquith LJ found six propositions which emerged from the authorities:

'(i) It is well settled that the governing purpose of damages is to put the party whose rights have been violated in the same position, so far as money can do so, as if his rights have been observed. This purpose, if relentlessly pursued, would provide him with a complete indemnity for all loss de facto resulting from a particular breach however improbable, however unpredictable. This in contract at least is recognised as too harsh a rule. Hence:

(ii) In cases of breach of contract the aggrieved party is only entitled to recover such part of the loss actually resulting as was, at the time of the contract, reasonably foreseeable as liable to result from the breach.

(iii) What was at the time reasonably foreseeable, depends on the knowledge then possessed by the parties or, at all events, by the party who later commits the breach.

(iv) For this purpose knowledge "possessed" is of two kinds – one imputed, the other actual. Everyone, as a reasonable person, is taken to know "the ordinary course of things" and consequently what loss is liable to result from a breach of that ordinary course. This is the subject matter of the "first rule" in *Hadley* v *Baxendale*, but to this knowledge, which the contract-breaker is assumed to possess, whether he actually possesses it or not, there may have to be added in a particular case knowledge which he actually possesses of special circumstances outside the "ordinary course of things", of such a kind that a breach in those special circumstances would be liable to cause more loss. Such a case attracts the operation of the "second rule" so to make the additional loss also recoverable.

(v) In order to make the contract-breaker liable under either rule it is not necessary that he should actually have asked himself, "What loss is liable to result from a breach?" As has often been pointed out, parties at the time of contracting contemplate, not the breach of the contract, but its performance. It suffices that, if he had considered the question, he would as a reasonable man, have concluded that the loss in question was liable to result.

(vi) Nor, finally, to make a particular loss recoverable, need it be proved that on a given state of knowledge the defendant could, as a reasonable man, forsee that a breach must necessarily result in that loss. It is enough if he could foresee it was likely to so result.'

The principles relating to remoteness of damage were further considered in the House of Lords in 1967 and given greater refinement.

In *The Heron II* [1969] 1 AC 350, the owner of 'Heron II' agreed to carry a cargo of sugar from Constanza (Rumania) to Basrah (Iraq). The voyage normally took 20 days but, in breach of contract, this voyage took 29 days. In those nine days, the Basrah sugar market fell and the plaintiff suffered loss of profit.

The plaintiff was held to be entitled to damages for loss of profit since the defendant knew there was a sugar market in Basrah. The whole matter was a question of the likelihood of what the defendant knew; it was quite likely that the plaintiff was intending to sell on the sugar market:

'The present case is one in which no special information was given to the carrier as to what the charterers intended to do with the goods after they arrived at Basrah. In those circumstances in deciding what damages would fairly and reasonably be regarded as arising, if the delivery of the goods was delayed, I think that such a shipowner must reasonably have contemplated that, if he delivered the sugar at Basrah some nine or ten days later than he could and should have delivered it, then a loss by reason of a fall in the market price for sugar at Basrah was one that was liable to result or at least was not unlikely to result' (per Lord Morris).

In *The Heron II*, the House of Lords did not agree upon a general formulation. Lords Morris, Hodson and Pearce generally approved these propositions. Lords Reid and Upjohn modified the propositions in part.

Neither was happy with the words 'foreseeable' or 'reasonably foreseeable' in the *Victoria Laundry* formation. Lord Upjohn said:

'It is clear that on the one hand the test of foreseeability as laid down in the case of tort is not the test for breach of contract; nor on the other hand must the loser establish that the loss was a near certainty or odds-on probability. I am content to adopt as the test a "real danger" or a "serious possibility". There may be a shade of difference between these two phrases, but the assessment of damages is not an exact science and what to one judge or jury will appear a real danger may appear to another judge or jury as a serious possibility.'

All the members of the House of Lords used phrases to denote the degree of probability of loss resulting from the breach which would be recoverable.

Lord Reid: 'not unlikely', which meant, he thought, a degree of probability considerably less than an even chance but, nevertheless, not very unusual and easily foreseeable.

Lord Morris: 'not unlikely to occur', or 'liable to result'.

Lord Hodson: 'liable to result'.

Lords Pearce and Upjohn: 'a real danger', or 'a serious possibility'.

Four of them thought that the colloquialism 'on the cards' should not be used – the phrase employed by Asquith LJ in *Victoria Laundry*.

Effects of 'the two limbs'

Losses which occur 'in the ordinary course of things' only are recoverable under the first limb

In *Pilkington v Wood* [1953] Ch 770, the plaintiff bought a house in Hampshire and his solicitor, in breach of contract, negligently failed to notice that the house had a defective title, and was held liable for the amount by which the house's value had been lessened by the title not being good. The plaintiff shortly afterwards took up work in Lancashire and suffered added loss as the house was hard to resell.

The solicitor was held not liable for the latter loss as he could not anticipate that the plaintiff would shortly move.

If the parties are not ad idem in their contemplation of the use for which the subject matter of the contract is needed, then no loss is recoverable beyond that which would have resulted if the intended use had been that reasonably within the contemplation of the defendant.

In *Cory v Thames Ironworks Co* (1868) LR 3 QB 181, the defendant agreed to supply the plaintiff with the hull of a floating boom derrick, but delivered it six months late. The defendant reasonably believed the plaintiff intended to use the hull as a coal store. If this belief was well founded, then the plaintiff's loss would have been £420. But, unknown to the defendant, the plaintiff intended to use the hull for a new method of transferring coal from colliers to barges, and lost profits of £4,000. The plaintiff claimed £420 damages. The defendant argued that this represented a loss not actually suffered. The court held that there would be 'no hardship or injustice' in awarding the plaintiff £420 when he had lost a larger amount.

However, it is doubtful if damages could be recovered for a loss suffered which is quite different in kind from that which would have occurred in the ordinary course of things. For example, if A sells B poisonous dog food and B eats the dog food himself and dies, could B's executor sue A for the loss of a dog? See, for example, the recent case of *Seven Seas Properties* v *Al Essa* [1993] 3 All ER 577 in which the plaintiffs, having kept secret their intention to resell property quickly from the defendants, were held unable to claim from the defendants additional damages caused by delay in completion. The defendants were not to know that the plaintiffs had in fact made an agreement to sell on the property, at a considerable profit, before that property had even been acquired by them.

Knowledge of special circumstances

The defendant's knowledge of special circumstances under the second limb is not in itself sufficient to make him liable. There must be knowledge and acceptance by the defendant of the purpose and intention of the plaintiff.

In *Horne* v *Midland Railway* (1873) LR 8 CP 131, the defendant contracted to carry a consignment of shoes to London by 3 February, but delivered a day late. As a result of the delay, the plaintiff lost an opportunity of selling the shoes at an exceptionally high price. It was held that the defendant was not liable for this loss, although he knew the plaintiff would have to take the shoes back if they were not delivered by 3 February, he did not know the plaintiff would lose an exceptionally high profit.

In *Simpson* v *L & N Railway* (1876) 1 QBD 274, the defendant contracted to carry the plaintiff's samples of cattle food from an agricultural show at Bedford to another at Newcastle. He delivered certain goods to an agent of the defendant at Bedford showground. The goods were marked 'must be at Newcastle by Monday certain'. No express reference was made in the contract of carriage to the Newcastle show. The samples arrived at Newcastle after the show was over.

The defendant was held to be liable for loss of profits which the plaintiff would have made had the samples reached Newcastle on time. The plaintiff's purpose and intention could readily be inferred from the circumstances, which clearly indicated that the contract was one to carry samples to the Newcastle show and not simply to Newcastle.

Therefore, if the defendant could anticipate circumstances leading to an extra loss to the plaintiff on the facts known to him if the contract was breached, he will be liable. For example, a seller will be liable to a buyer for loss of profit on a sub-sale of which he knew.

Type or kind of loss

The test of remoteness determines whether the plaintiff is entitled to damages, and not the quantum.

In *Wroth* v *Tyler* [1974] Ch 30, the defendant contracted to sell his house to the plaintiff, but later refused to complete the transaction in breach of contract. In the meantime, house prices rose sharply and the plaintiff claimed the difference between the contract price and the market value at the date of the trial. The defendant argued that he should not be liable for the full difference between the contract price and the market price, because he could not have contemplated the exceptionally large rise in house prices between 1971 and 1973. However, he admitted he could have contemplated some rise in house prices. The court stated that the defendant might escape liability for a type or kind of loss which he could not have contemplated, but there was no authority to show that the quantum should be contemplated.

However, the test does not mean that the defendant is liable for all losses once liability has been founded. In the *Victoria Laundry* case, the defendant was only held liable for a reasonable amount of the profits, not for the actual amount of profits the plaintiff lost on not having the contracts for the Ministry of Supply.

Accordingly, whether or not a plaintiff may recover damages depends substantially upon the type of loss that the court is prepared to identify. So, in *Parsons* v *Uttley Ingham* [1978] QB 791, the court thought that it was within the contemplation of the parties that a hopper which was unfit for its purpose of storing food in a suitable condition for feeding pigs might lead to 'illness' of, or 'physical injury' to, the pigs, even though the pigs had died of a rare intestinal disease, which could not have been foreseen. See the judgment of Scarman LJ, in particular, on remoteness of damage in contract and in tort.

16.4 Causation

Where remoteness of damage is in issue between the parties, there will be no dispute about whether the breach caused the state of affairs leading to the damage. The issue will be whether that state of affairs was one which the law should recognise as permitting the plaintiff to recover damages for the breach.

Where causation is in issue between the parties, the dispute between the plaintiff and the defendant will be whether the state of affairs which the plaintiff alleges caused him damage, was one which resulted from a breach at all.

One event in the sequence of events leading to a loss might not be held to be the cause of the loss, for example, a shipowner is not liable to a charterer if, as a result of delay, the ship ran into a typhoon, as such a catastrophe may occur anywhere. See *The Monarch SS Co Case* [1949] AC 196.

If there are two causes of the state of affairs resulting in damage, and both causes co-operate and have equal efficacy, one will be sufficient to carry a judgment for damages.

In *Smith, Hogg & Co* v *Black Sea Insurance* [1940] AC 997, a shipowner was held liable to a charterer in damages for loss of a cargo which had been caused by a combination of perils of the sea and the unseaworthiness of the ship. The latter was sufficient to carry a claim for damages.

An intervening act of a third party which itself causes the loss, or aggravates the loss, caused by the defendant's breach, will not absolve the defendant from liability if the intervening act was reasonably foreseeable – *Victoria Laundry* and *The Heron II* principles.

In *Weld–Blundell* v *Stephens* [1920] AC 956, the plaintiff employed an accountant, the defendant, to investigate the affairs of a company he had invested in. The defendant's partner negligently dropped a letter from the plaintiff in the office of the company's manager, which the manager picked up and showed to his directors, who sued the plaintiff in libel and won. The plaintiff sued the defendant for breach of contract to recover the damages he paid out in the libel action. The court declared that the claim must be dismissed since (1) the plaintiff's liability for libel existed apart from contract, and (2) the loss was not caused by breach of contract, but by the act of the company's manager showing the letter to the directors. This was an act the defendant could not have foreseen.

In *De La Bere* v *Pearson* [1908] 1 KB 280, the defendant was held liable for loss where he recommended a dishonest stockbroker to the plaintiff who wished to make investments, even though it was the dishonest stockbroker who caused the losses.

In *Stansbie* v *Troman* [1948] 2 KB 48, a painter in breach of contract after he had completed decorations, left unlocked a house, which was later burgled by thieves.

The defendant was held liable for the value of goods taken as this was exactly the sort of loss he should have guarded against and foreseen.

Where loss is suffered on two or more separate occasions, the question will arise as to causation, limitation of actions and, possibly, the Latent Damage Act 1986 (see below). In *Iron Trade Mutual Insurance Co* v *Buckenham* [1989] 2 Lloyd's Rep 85, the plaintiffs were underwriters and brokers agents. The defendant firm were insurance and re-insurance brokers. From 1981, the defendants began refusing to pay out on certain contracts and, in 1984, they repudiated the contracts altogether, alleging that the contracts were voidable for non–disclosure of material facts. The plaintiffs sued the brokers for losses occasioned by this, framing their action in contract and tort. The defendants' main defence was limitation – the contracts were mainly from 1976 to 1981.

Three questions arose.

1. When did the plaintiffs' cause of action accrue?
2. Could the plaintiffs rely on the Latent Damage Act as a means of delaying the limitation period?
3. If the LDA, applied, what was the relevant starting date for the purposes of the Act?

The decision of the court, based as it was on the three questions listed above, found that the Act had no application to claims founded on contract, even when the duty concerned is simply a contractual duty to take reasonable care. Therefore, the questions as listed need not be considered further.

The issue of causation was once again examined by the Court of Appeal in the case of *County Ltd and Another* v *Girozentrale Securities* [1996] 3 All ER 834 and the court, in keeping with the doctrine of precedent, held that where causation is in issue between parties, the paintiff will be successful so long as he proves that the loss or damage sustained is attributable to the breach caused by the defendants in performing the contract.

16.5 Measure of damages

Damages will be quantified on one of three bases as stated above.

1. Reliance loss, that is, cost to the plaintiff of reliance on the contract.
2. Restitution, that is, benefits obtained by the defendant under the contract.
3. Loss of bargain, that is, the plaintiff claims to be put in the same position as if the contract had been performed.

The last named requires further investigation.

Loss of bargain

Where the plaintiff claims for loss of bargain and that he be put in the position as if the contract had been performed, two bases of assessment are available: cost of cure; and difference in value.

In *Peevyhouse* v *Garland Coal Co* (1962) 382 P 2d 109, a coal company took a mining lease of farmland, covenanting to restore the land to its original state at the end of the lease. The work at the end of the lease would have cost $29,000, while the result of not doing it would reduce the value of the land by only $300. It was held that damages for the company's failure to do the work should be assessed at the latter sum.

In the majority of cases where there is a discretion, the court will exercise this to use the most appropriate basis of assessment in the case. Certain prima facie rules exist for working out the appropriate mode of assessment.

1. In sale of goods contracts if a defect can be cured at a reasonable cost, the cost of cure will be awarded, otherwise the difference in value is awarded.
2. In building contracts, cost of cure basis is usual, and the builder must put the defects right. However, if the cost of cure is greater than the whole value of the building, then only the difference in value will be awarded. See *Morris* v *Redland Bricks* [1970] AC 652. This issue was recently considered by the House of Lords in *Ruxley Electronics and Construction Ltd* v *Forsyth* [1995] 3 WLR 118, though the impact of this decision does, in fact, go far beyond rectification of faulty building work and affects measure of damages generally. In the context of building contracts (in *Ruxley* the construction of a swimming pool) if the building work is defective then normally the measure of damages would be the cost of whatever it takes to rectify the work. But if, as in *Ruxley*, the work is such that, despite the fault, the structure is perfectly serviceable, and the cost of

ordering rectification and possibly total reconstruction is out of all proportion to the advantages such rectification might have, then the court will not award such a sum. In *Ruxley*, for example, the swimming pool was not as deep as specified, yet it was perfectly safe to dive into. To award the cost of digging it out and rebuilding it, simply to add an extra three or four inches of depth, would be unfair and unjust. Instead the court ordered the payment of a much smaller sum by way of compensation for loss of amenity.

3. Certain statutes prescribe which method of assessment is to be used, for example, s18 Landlord and Tenant Act 1927, the difference in value is to be used.

Actual and market values

Where damages are based on the difference in value principle, then market values may be taken into account to assess the plaintiff's loss.

If there is a market value against which the plaintiff's loss can be assessed, then the loss will be, prima facie, quantified by reference to it, but other factors may be taken into account.

Where the defendants fail to deliver goods or render services, then the plaintiff can go into the market and obtain these goods or services at the prevailing price. Therefore, the plaintiff's damages will be the difference between the market price and the price of the goods or services in the contract. See *Watts, Watt & Co v Mitsui* [1917] AC 227. It was held that if a carrier completely fails to deliver goods which he has contracted to carry, then the owner of the goods is entitled to their market value at the place and time fixed for delivery.

Under s51 Sale of Goods Act 1979, where a seller wrongfully neglects or refuses to deliver the goods to the buyer, the buyer may maintain an action against the seller for damages for non-delivery. But such an action will not allow the seller to recover for anything more than the difference between the market value and the actual value: see, eg, *Barry v Heathcote Ball & Co (Commercial Auctions) Ltd* [2001] 1 All ER 944 which is noted in Chapter 2, section 2.2 (*Auction sales*). Therefore, the plaintiff will not be able to recover any losses incurred by reason of not being able to make sub-sales.

In *Williams v Agius* [1914] AC 510, coal was sold at 16*s*. 3*d*. per ton. The buyer resold an equivalent amount at 19*s*. per ton. When the seller failed to deliver, the market price was 23*s*. 6*d*. The buyer went into the market to buy coal at 23*s*. 6*d*. and claimed damages.

The buyer was held to be able to recover the difference between 16*s*. 3*d*. and 23*s*. 6*d*. The fact he had made a sub-sale at 19s was irrelevant, and the seller could not take advantage of this.

The sub-sale is irrelevant in assessing damages whether it was above or below the market price.

In *Williams v Reynolds* (1865) 6 B & S 495, cotton was sold to the plaintiff at 16*s*. 3/4*d*., and the plaintiff resold it at 19s. 3/4*d*. The defendant failed to deliver when the market price was 18*s*. 1/4*d*. The plaintiff failed to go into the market at that time to purchase to satisfy his sub-sale and market prices subsequently rose.

The plaintiff could only recover 1*s*. 1/2*d*. per ton damages as he should have gone into the market and mitigated. He was not entitled to the difference between the purchase price (16*s*. 3/4*d*.) and the sub-sale price (19*s*. 3/4*d*.).

Therefore, the defendant may not be allowed to take advantage of a sub-sale, as *Williams* v *Agius* illustrates. However, the plaintiff is at the same time permitted to have any mitigation which he undertakes taken into account, and the fact he goes into the market to do so is considered. If he fails to mitigate, then this is held against him.

Sub-sales are taken into consideration on one exceptional occasion, where the contract is one for specific or particular goods.

In *Re Hall and Pim's Arbitration* (1928) 139 LT 50, a cargo of wheat was sold for 51*s*. 9*d*. per quarter and resold by the buyer for 56*s*. 9*d*. per quarter. The seller refused delivery when the market price was 53*s*. 9*d*. It was held that the seller was liable for the difference between 51*s*. 9*d*. and 56*s*. 9*d*. The market price was to be disregarded because the buyers could not buy this particular cargo, which they had resold, on the market.

Late delivery as opposed to non-delivery has entitled the court to take into account a sub-sale.

In *Wertheim* v *Chicoutimi Pulp* [1911] AC 301, the defendant sold the plaintiff 3,000 tons of wood pulp for delivery in November at 25*s*. a ton. The pulp was not delivered until the following June. In November, the market value was 70*s*. per ton but in June it was only 42*s*. per ton. The plaintiff had in fact resold at 65*s*. per ton.

The plaintiff was held to be entitled to damages of 5*s*. per ton, that is, the difference between the actual price and the market price at the agreed date of delivery, 65*s*. and 70*s*. He was not entitled to the difference between 42*s*. 6*d*., the market price in June, and 70*s*., the market price at the agreed date for delivery.

The latter, that is, damages of 27*s*. 6*d*. would allow the plaintiff to make a profit out of the breach.

It is submitted that the above is incorrect since the plaintiff would not have been making a profit out of the breach but, instead, his sub-sale would appear to have given the defendant the advantage of the plaintiff's business acumen.

Where there has been a delivery of goods which are defective, then the loss will, prima facie, be the difference between the market value and the value of the goods actually delivered. The sub-sale above or below the market price is ignored unless the sub-sale concerns some sort of unique goods. If the buyer chooses, he may reject the defective goods and then demand restitution of the price paid.

If the buyer refuses to accept and pay for goods, then the seller can go into the market and sell the goods at the prevailing price. The seller is not entitled to any damages if he sells in the market above the contract price, but he can claim for loss of bargain if he sells below the contract price.

The House of Lords recently in *Banque Bruxelles SA* v *Eagle Star Insurance Co*

Ltd [1996] 3 WLR 87 held that the actual amount of loss recoverable should reflect the difference between the valuation and the correct market value.

On the issue of whether the plaintiff is entitled to recover damages for total loss, the Court of Appeal in *St Albans City and District Council* v *International Computers Ltd* [1996] 4 All ER 481 held that the award of damages must be proportionate to the amount of loss actually sustained. The Court of Appeal in *Bence Graphics International Ltd* v *Fasson UK Ltd* [1997] 1 All ER 979, held that the correct measure of damages should be the actual loss suffered by the plaintiff under or arising from a breach of contract for onward sales and not the difference between the value of goods at the time of delivery to the buyer and the value they would have had if they had fulfilled the warranty.

Where there is no market

In the case of non-delivery of such goods, the court will assess the loss as best it can on the evidence before it. Relevant facts may include loss of the goods, their carriage and a reasonable profit.

In *The Arpad* [1934] P 189, sale of a cargo of wheat which was not marketable. The plaintiff made a sub-sale at 36*s.* per quarter, but the wheat was never delivered. The court did not assess the plaintiff's damages at the difference between the purchase price and, in this case, the sub-sale price since the court decided the price of other wheat in the market ought to be considered in any case.

Failure to accept and pay for goods which do not have a market will result in damages being quantified by reference to the actual proceeds of a sub-sale, so long as such sub-sales are reasonable.

Loss of profit

If the plaintiff has lost profit on the resale of the subject matter of the contract because of the defendant's breach, then the defendant will only be liable for this, subject to the rules above, if he should have reasonably seen or contemplated that the plaintiff was going to make a resale.

If the defendant wrongfully refuses to accept and pay for the goods, then the plaintiff can sue for the loss of profit on that transaction in certain circumstances.

In *Thompson* v *Robinson (Gunmakers) Ltd* [1955] Ch 177, the defendant bought a Vanguard car from the plaintiff, and later refused to accept and pay for it. The plaintiff's profit would have been £61. It was held that where, as here, the supply of Vanguard cars exceeded the demand, had the plaintiff found another customer and sold to him as well as the defendant, then there would have been two sales and two profits. Therefore the defendant was liable for £61.

If there is a limited number of sales which the plaintiff could make because of, for example, shortages of the goods or services he is supplying, then there will be no damage for loss of profits if the defendant defaults.

In *Charter* v *Sullivan* [1957] 2 QB 117, the defendant bought a Hillman Minx car from the plaintiff but refused to accept it. The plaintiff's profit would have been £97, but he failed to recover this from the defendant as he could only sell as many cars as he could get from the makers. Note that assessment of damages in loss of profit cases is based on tortious principles (*Beoco Ltd* v *Alfa Laval Co Ltd* (1994) The Times 12 January).

Two cases, *Western Web Offset Printers Ltd* v *Independent Media Ltd* [1995] TLR 510 and *White Arrow Express Ltd* v *Lamey's Distribution Ltd* [1995] TLR 430 illustrate the problems of quantifying (*Western Web*) and proving loss of profits (*White Arrow*). In the first case the plaintiffs claimed, successfully, that the effects of the recession should be taken into account when assessing loss of profits. In the second case, the problems of establishing loss, where no proof can be offered one way or another were highlighted. In *White Arrow* the plaintiffs, who ran a mail order business, had negotiated with the defendants special rates for an 'enhanced' delivery service, which they never apparently received. However, in the light of the fact that they could put no monetary value on the loss of this service, nor offer any suggestion as to how such loss of profits might be calculated, the Court of Appeal declined to offer anything other than purely nominal damages.

A clearer guidance was given by the Court of Appeal in *ELO Entertainment Ltd* v *Grand Metropolitan Retailing Ltd; Lyons* v *Grand Metropolitan Retailing Ltd* [1999] 1 All ER (Comm) 473, where it stated that valuation on the basis of negotiations between buyer and seller was a better and more reliable way of assessing quantum, in so far as loss of profits are concerned.

Damages for distress and inconvenience (see below)

These are always assessed fairly stringently. The case of *Watts* v *Morrow* [1991] 1 WLR 1421 concerned inter alia the measure of damages for 'distress and inconvenience' caused by a negligent surveyor's report. The Court of Appeal felt that subject to certain restricted categories of exceptions damages for distress and inconvenience had little part to play in contractual compensation and an award of £4,000 was drastically reduced to £1,500.

16.6 Type of damage recoverable

In *Addis* v *Gramophone Co Ltd* [1909] AC 488, Lord Atkinson said:

> 'I have always understood that damages for breach of contract were in the nature of compensation, not punishment.'

The general rule of law applicable to such cases was in effect stated by Cockburn CJ, in *Engell* v *Fitch* (1868) LR 3 QB 314, at 330:

'By the law of England as a general rule, a vendor, who from whatever cause fails to perform his contract, is bound, as was said by Lord Wensleydale in the case referred to, to place the purchaser, so far as money will do it, in the position he would have been had the contract been performed.'

To the above principle there are exceptions. In some cases, as a matter of policy, or because of inherent difficulties in assessing whether any actual damage has occurred, damages are irrecoverable. In other cases, exemplary damages are recoverable because the type of breach is looked upon by law as socially reprehensible and, therefore, is discouraged in this way. Finally, damages are recoverable in circumstances which do not readily fall within the compensatory principle.

Damages which are irrecoverable

Injury to reputation

If the plaintiff's reputation in injured as a result of a breach of contract, then he cannot recover damages for this in addition to damages for the breach itself. The plaintiff's remedy in these circumstances is in tort, for example, defamation, and he should pursue the appropriate remedy in tort.

In *Hurst* v *Picture Theatres Ltd* [1915] 1 KB 1, the plaintiff was forcibly ejected from a cinema seat for which he had paid 6*d*. He brought an action in tort for assault and false imprisonment and not in contract, and recovered £150 damages. Much of this £150 was compensation for the injury the plaintiff had suffered to his reputation; such damage would clearly have been irrecoverable in contract. Indeed, the damages recoverable in contract would appear to have been minimal – probably only the 6*d*. price of the seat.

However, in *Malik* v *Bank of Credit and Commerce International SA* [1997] 3 All ER 1 the House of Lords held that, in appropriate cases, damages could in principle be awarded for loss of reputation caused by breach of contract. Furthermore, provided a relevant breach of contract was established and the requirements of causation, remoteness and mitigation were satisfied, financial loss in respect of damage to reputation caused by breach of contract could be recovered for breach of a contract of employment.

In that case their Lordships concluded that since the defendant bank had promised, in an implied term of the contracts of employment, not to conduct a dishonest or corrupt business, the promised benefit being employment by an honest employer which benefit did not materialise, the appellants were entitled to damages if they proved that they were handicapped in the labour market in consequence of the bank's corruption. When some former employees claimed such damages the Court of Appeal (*Bank of Credit and Commerce International SA* v *Ali (No 2)* [2002] 3 All ER 750) accepted that, in these particular circumstances, the handicap had to be proved in every particular case. Jonathan Parker LJ explained the position as follows:

'I accept ... that had the [former employees] succeeded in establishing a general prejudice in the employment market against former employees of BCCI as a result of stigma, it would have been open to them to invite the Court to infer that but for that general prejudice a claimant would have succeeded in obtaining – albeit not a particular job – a job of a particular type or at a particular level of salary. In the event, however, the judge found as a fact (as in my judgment he was entitled to do) that no such general prejudice existed. Absent general prejudice, it was necessary for the [former employees] to prove that stigma was an effective cause of the failure of their job applications on what the judge described as a "job-specific" basis. In other words, it was necessary for them to show that stigma was an effective cause of the failure of a particular job application. That too they failed to do on the findings of the judge (findings which, once again, he was in my judgment entitled to make).'

Injury to feelings

The plaintiff may be able to recover damages for such injuries in tort, but in contract such damages are irrecoverable.

In *Addis* v *Gramophone Co Ltd* [1909] AC 488, the plaintiff could be dismissed by his employers on six months' notice, which he was given but, at the same time, a new manager was appointed to take his place and the plaintiff was prevented from acting as manager. The plaintiff claimed damages for the harsh and humiliating manner in which he was dismissed, as well as for loss of salary and commission after his dismissal. The plaintiff was held only to be entitled to the commission and salary he had lost, and not to damages because his dismissal was harsh and humiliating:

'I can conceive nothing more objectionable and embarrassing in litigation than trying in effect an action of libel or slander as a matter of aggravation in an action for illegal dismissal' (per Lord Atkinson).

The principle established in *Addis* was reaffirmed by the Court of Appeal in *Bliss* v *South East Thames Regional Health Authority* [1985] IRLR 308.

The question arose again in *Johnson* v *Gore Wood & Co* [2001] 1 All ER 481. In the context of an alleged breach of contract, the House of Lords was required to consider, inter alia, the appellant's claims for general damages for mental distress, and for aggravated damages based on the fact that the manner of commission of the respondent firm's wrong was 'such as to injure his pride and dignity'. Their Lordships concluded (with one dissentient) that these claims could not succeed. Lord Goff of Chieveley said:

'I agree ... that, as a matter of principle, damages on these grounds are not generally recoverable: see *Addis*; *Watts* v *Morrow* [1991] 4 All ER 937 ... It is true that there has in recent years been a softening of this principle in certain respects see ... *Malik* v *Bank of Credit and Commerce International SA* [1997] 3 All ER 1, but none of these developments has, so far as I can see, gone so far as to allow recovery on the broad grounds here pleaded.'

See also *Johnson* v *Unisys Ltd* [2001] 2 All ER 801 where the House of Lords held that an employee has no right of action at common law to recover financial losses arising from the unfair manner of his dismissal which allegedly caused him a nervous breakdown, making it impossible for him to find other employment.

Failure to make title to land

No damages are recoverable in this situation in the absence of fraud because of 'the peculiar difficulty in making a title to land in England'.

Elliott v *Pierson* [1948] 1 All ER 939 per Harman J applying the rule laid down by the House of Lords in *Bain* v *Fothergill* (1874) LR 7 HL 158.

In *Sharneyford Supplies Ltd* v *Edge* [1987] 1 All ER 588, the Court of Appeal expressed the view that now that registered title to land is general the rationale for the rule in *Bain* v *Fothergill* is no longer valid and the rule should be abolished.

Note that s3 Law of Property (Miscellaneous Provisions) Act 1989 did, finally, abolish the rule in *Bain* v *Fothergill* as from September 1989.

Now that the rule of *Bain* v *Fothergill* has been formally abolished, the following case is of interest.

In *Grangeville Marketing Inc* v *Seven Seas Properties Ltd* [1990] EGCS 23, in a contract for the sale of land there occurred, because of delay, a breach of contract; the vendor's delay was due to an inability to show good title. The plaintiff claimed damages for loss of profit on a prompt resale of the property in question, and loss of profit from renovating the property and selling individual flats. The defendant conceded that the delay amounted to breach of contract, but argued that the delay was caused by defect in title, and the plaintiff was precluded by the rule in *Bain* v *Fothergill* from recovering for loss or profit of the failure of the bargain.

A certificate was granted for leave to appeal direct to the House of Lords. It was for the Appellate Committee of the House of Lords to consider whether the rule in *Bain* v *Fothergill* (which had been criticised and subsequently abolished by s3 Law of Property (Miscellaneous Provisions) Act 1989, as from September 1989) should be applied in the present case.

On the face of it, it seems unlikely that the rule will, after so much criticism, be resurrected in any form whatsoever.

Exemplary damages

Dishonoured cheque

Where a cheque is wrongfully dishonoured, a trader on whose account it is drawn is entitled to substantial damages without pleading and proving actual damages.

In *Gibbons* v *Westminster Bank Ltd* [1939] 2 KB 882, this exception would appear from the cases to apply to traders only, and seems to be based on the principle that commercial reputation must be protected. If this is so, then not only is there an exception to the rule that damages are irrecoverable for injury to reputation, but that the exception operates merely on the proof of the cheque being dishonoured.

A non-trader would appear to be capable of recovering damages for dishonour of his cheque only if he pleads and proves them and then only as compensation.

In *Kpohraror* v *Woolwich Building Society* [1996] 4 All ER 119, the Court of Appeal stated that a person who is not a trader could recover substantial rather than nominal damages in contract for loss of credit or business reputation resulting from a cheque being wrongly dishonoured by the bank.

Wrongful eviction

Under the Rent Act 1977 and Protection from Eviction Act 1977, a landlord who fails to give the appropriate notice to quit to his tenant will be liable for exemplary damages if he then attempts to wrongfully evict him. See *Drane* v *Evangelou* [1978] 1 WLR 455 as an example.

Other types of damage

Damage to commercial reputation

If the plaintiff's cheques are dishonoured and he is a trader, then he will have alternative remedies. But, if a plaintiff's commercial reputation is damaged in other ways, then he may recover.

In *Anglo-Continental Holidays* v *Typaldos Lines* [1967] 2 Lloyd's Rep 61, a travel agent recovered damages for loss of 'goodwill' from a shipowner who broke a contract to supply passengers with accommodation on a pleasure cruise.

The plaintiff may even be able to recover damages for loss of an opportunity to enhance his commercial reputation.

In *Herbert Clayton* v *Oliver* [1930] AC 209, an actor or author it was held, could recover damages for 'loss of publicity', but not for injury to existing reputation.

If the plaintiff's commercial reputation is damaged because he has been supplied with defective goods by a manufacturer or wholesaler, then he may recover damages. See *Cointat* v *Myham* [1913] 2 KB 220.

Discomfort, vexation and disappointment

In *Jarvis* v *Swan Tours* [1973] 2 QB 233, the plaintiff, a solicitor, went on a Swan Tour and, as a result, he sued for damages because the hotels fell short of the standards promised, and the buses were not of the standard promised. It was held that the plaintiff could recover damages for the disappointment and discomfort he had been caused as a result.

And see again *Jackson* v *Horizon Holidays* – discussed in Chapter 12 – where the plaintiff was allowed damages for distress and disappointment when his holiday fell far short of the defendant's promises.

There is, however, a limit to damages for distress for breach of contract. In *Bliss* v *South East Thames Regional Health Authority* [1987] ICR 700, Dillon LJ stated that such damages should be confined to cases 'where the contract which has been broken was itself a contract to provide peace of mind or freedom from distress'. In *Hayes* v *James and Charles Dodd* [1990] 2 All ER 815, Staughton LJ said that:

'... it might be that the class was somewhat wider than that. But it should not include any case where the object of the contract was not comfort or pleasure or the relief of discomfort, but simply carrying on a commercial activity with a view to profit.'

Subsequently, the Court of Appeal made it clear, in *Alexander* v *Rolls Royce Motor Cars Ltd* [1995] TLR 254, that they were not prepared to extend the circumstances in which damages for distress or disappointment might be granted. In this case the plaintiff had argued that the purchase of a Rolls Royce had been the culmination of a lifelong ambition, and that when the garage concerned had not repaired it properly or quickly enough he had suffered distress and inconvenience. The Court of Appeal, while accepting that there was breach of the contract to repair, were not prepared to award damages for the plaintiff's 'emotional anguish' while his Rolls Royce was being repaired.

In *Farley* v *Skinner* [2001] 4 All ER 801 the claimant had been interested in buying a property some 15 miles from Gatwick International Airport. He had engaged the defendant surveyor and specifically asked him to investigate whether the property would be affected by aircraft noise and told him that he did not want to buy a property on a flight path. In his report, the defendant said that he thought 'it unlikely that the property will suffer greatly from such noise, although some planes will inevitably cross the area'. The plaintiff bought the property and had it modernised but, after he had moved in, he discovered that the property was markedly affected by aircraft noise: indeed, it was not far from a navigation beacon around which aircraft circled awaiting a landing slot. Nevertheless, he decided not to sell the property, but he claimed damages against the surveyor. The House of Lords concluded that his claim would be successful and, although it was at the very top end of possible awards in cases of this kind, the trial judge's award of £10,000 for non-pecuniary damage would be restored. The claim had not been defeated by the claimant's reasonable decision not to move out of the property.

Lord Clyde:

'The object of the request to consider the risk of aircraft noise was very plainly to enable the plaintiff to determine the extent of the peace and quiet which he could enjoy at the property. It would be within the contemplation of the defendant that if the noise was such as to interfere with the occupier's peaceful enjoyment of the property the plaintiff would either not buy it at all or live there deprived of his expectation of peace and quiet. Each of these consequences seems to me to flow directly from the breach of contract so as to enable an award of damages to be made on one or other basis. The present case can in my view qualify as one of the exceptional cases where a contract for peace or pleasure has been made and breached, thereby entitling the injured party to claim damages for the disappointment occasioned by the breach.'

As Bingham LJ observed in *Watts* v *Morrow* [1991] 4 All ER 937, 'a contract-breaker is not *in general* liable for any distress, frustration, anxiety, displeasure, vexation, tension or aggravation which his breach of contract may cause to the innocent party', but there are exceptions to this rule and this claim was within one of those exceptions.

In passing, it is interesting to note that *Hatton* v *United Kingdom* (36022/97) [2002] 1 FCR 732 the European Court of Human Rights said that the increase in the level of noise caused by aircraft using Heathrow airport at night since 1993 was a breach of the applicants' right to respect for their private and family lives and their homes as guaranteed by art 8 of the European Convention for the Protection of Human Rights and Fundamental Freedoms. The applicants were each awarded £4,000 for non-pecuniary damages.

Currency of damages

In the normal way of things, the currency in which damages are actually estimated and awarded has little significance. The amount will be the same, whatever foreign currency is nominated. In a very few cases, however, the choice of currency may make a considerable difference to the fairness, or otherwise, of the award.

In *The Texaco Melbourne* [1992] 2 Lloyd's Rep 303 following a breach of contract, it fell to be decided whether damages should be paid in US dollars or Ghanaian cedis.

The court held that in deciding such a matter regard should be had to the currency in which the loss was felt, but also to what was fair and equitable. Although the ship owners had felt the loss in cedis, because the value of the cedi had fallen drastically since the time of the contract, and because of stringent Ghanaian currency controls, it would be more reasonable to quantify the award in dollars.

The issue of currency arose once again in the case of *OT Africa Line Ltd* v *Vickers plc* [1996] 1 Lloyd's Rep 700. Here the court placed importance on the defendant's final offer of settlement which was made in pound sterling as opposed to the previous negotiations of settlement which were made in terms of dollars. The court stated that the defendant's offer to settle was conclusive on any objective approach and no surrounding circumstance for which the defendants might refer could undermine this conclusion.

Inconvenience

In *Bailey* v *Bullock* [1950] 2 All ER 1167, a solicitor failed to take proceedings to recover his client's house for him and was held liable in damages for the inconvenience caused by reason of the client having to live with his wife's parents for two years.

In *Cook* v *Spanish Holidays* (1960) The Times 6 February, a honeymoon couple recovered damages for the disappointment and inconvenience caused to them by a travel agent who failed to provide them with holiday accommodation.

Diminution of future prospects

In *Dunk* v *George Waller* [1970] 2 QB 163, an apprentice was wrongfully dismissed, but had he been allowed to complete his apprenticeship he would have got a certificate entitling him to certain jobs at certain wages. Without this certificate, his chances were lessened and he claimed damages for diminution of future prospects. He was held to be entitled to damages on this basis as the object of his apprenticeship was to enable him to get better employment.

In *Edwards* v *SOGAT* [1971] Ch 354, the plaintiff was wrongfully expelled from a trade union which resulted in his loss of employment. It was held that he could recover damages for the loss of employment opportunities which would follow from this.

Speculative damages

If the plaintiff's loss is the chance of doing something or benefiting from doing something, and this contingency is outside the control of the parties, then he is entitled to damages if the defendant's breach of contract denies him this chance.

In *Chaplin* v *Hicks* [1911] 2 KB 786, the plaintiff recovered damages for loss of the chance to take part in a beauty contest.

Speculative damages are usually a last resort since if the plaintiff could prove the value of his loss, then he could claim for loss of bargain. In *Simpson* v *L & N Railway* and *Victoria Laundry* v *Newman Industries*, the loss of profits on contracts which might have been made were speculative in character.

There can be no damages for the loss of a chance which depends entirely on the discretion of the defendant and he exercises this discretion against the plaintiff.

In *Lavarack* v *Woods of Colchester Ltd* [1967] 1 QB 278, the defendant contracted to employ the plaintiff at £4,000 pa plus such bonus, if any, as the defendant should from time to time determine. The defendant wrongfully dismissed the plaintiff and, afterwards, discontinued their bonus scheme, but increased salaries in lieu of the bonus.

The question arose as to whether the plaintiff's damages be increased to include increase in salary in lieu of bonus.

The plaintiff was not held to be entitled to the increase in salary in lieu of bonus. His contract provided only for £4,000 pa plus bonus. The defendant was under no contractual obligation to the plaintiff to continue the bonus, and the fact that it was discontinued meant the plaintiff was only entitled to £4,000.

Quantification of speculative damages requires a valuation of the expected benefit and an assessment of the plaintiff's chances of getting it. Therefore, if the lost chance was that of entering a beauty contest, the plaintiff can only recover for this lost chance and not the full prize which she might have won.

16.7 Mitigation of damages

It is the duty of every plaintiff to mitigate his loss, that is, to do his best not to increase the amount of damage done.

There are three rules.

1. The plaintiff cannot recover for loss which is consequent upon the defendant's breach of contract where the plaintiff could have avoided the loss by taking reasonable steps.
2. The plaintiff cannot recover for any loss he has actually avoided, even though he took more steps than were necessary in compliance with the rule above.
3. The plaintiff may recover loss incurred in taking reasonable steps to mitigate his loss, even though he did not succeed.

Avoidable loss

The plaintiff must minimise the loss resulting from the breach by taking all reasonable steps available to him. If he fails to do so, then he cannot recover anything in respect of that extra loss.

In *Payzu v Saunders* [1919] 2 KB 581, the plaintiff agreed to buy certain goods from the defendant over a period of nine months with payment within one month of delivery, and deliveries monthly. The plaintiff failed to make prompt payment for the first instalment, and the defendant, in breach of contract, refused to deliver any more instalments under the contract, but offered to deliver the goods at the contract price if the plaintiff paid cash on delivery of the order. The plaintiff refused this and claimed damages, these being the difference between the contract price and the market price. It was held that the plaintiff had permitted himself to sustain a large measure of the loss which, as prudent and reasonable people, they ought to have avoided. He had the cash available to meet the defendant's demands and could have mitigated by purchasing off the defendant at the contract price as the defendant offered, instead, of going into the market to purchase at a higher price. He was, therefore, not entitled to damages.

However, not every new offer by the defendant will be regarded as one which the plaintiff must accept in order to mitigate the effects of the breach. In a contract of employment situation, if the plaintiff is wrongfully dismissed for alleged dishonesty made before others, he need not return if his employer offers to take him back. Similarly, if the plaintiff is wrongfully dismissed, he need not take a labouring job where he previously had a professional job. If, however, the plaintiff is offered alternative employment by an employer who has wrongfully dismissed him without cause, then the plaintiff must accept this in mitigation if it is a reasonable alternative.

In *Brace v Calder* [1895] 2 QB 253, the common law in the area of dismissals from employment has now been largely superseded by the statutory provisions of the Employment Protection (Consolidation) Act 1978.

The plaintiff is not expected to take risks in order to mitigate losses caused by the defendant's breach.

In *Pilkington v Wood* [1953] Ch 770, a solicitor in breach of contract obtained for the plaintiff a house which had a defective title. The plaintiff tried to sue the solicitor, who argued that the plaintiff should have mitigated by suing the vendor under the covenants for title under s76 LPA 1925. As the court remarked:

> 'The so-called duty to mitigate does not go so far as to oblige the injured party, even under an indemnity, to embark on a complicated and difficult piece of litigation against a third party ... it is no part of the plaintiff's duty to embark on the proposed litigation in order to protect his solicitor from the consequences of his own carelessness' (per Harman J).

The plaintiff must not take unreasonable steps which would actually increase the loss; if he does, he will not recover such losses. Therefore, if the plaintiff is aware of the defendant's breach, he must not continue to incur expense in order to prepare for performance when it is clear the defendant will not accept it.

In *Gebruder Metalmann* v *NBR* [1984] 1 Lloyd's Rep 614, Gebruder Metalmann sold goods to NBR, both being dealers in sugar. NBR repudiated the contract before the date for delivery of the goods, and Gebruder Metalmann accepted the repudiation. On the question whether the proper date for assessment of damages was the date the repudiation was accepted, or the date performance should have been made by delivery, the Court of Appeal held that the correct date was the date for delivery, subject to the seller doing everything reasonable, between the date of repudiation and the date for delivery, to sell the goods or otherwise mitigate its loss.

This case illustrates the need for the mitigating step taken to be *reasonable*, and where there are two reasonable courses of action open to the plaintiff, either will be sufficient to mitigate the damage. See also, *Kaines UK Ltd* v *Osterreichische Warrenhandelgesellschaft Austrawaren Gesellschaft mbH* [1993] 2 Lloyd's Rep 1, as to dates of assessing compensation in anticipatory breach.

No recovery for avoided loss

If the plaintiff obtains any benefits as a result of his mitigation, these must be brought into account; for example, if the plaintiff is wrongfully dismissed and then finds a comparable job elsewhere, the earnings of this job will be taken into account in assessing damages for wrongful dismissal. Other benefits which accrue to the plaintiff, but which he was not bound to do in mitigation, may be taken into account.

A benefit in order to be considered as received in mitigation, must be a direct benefit resulting from the breach and not a collateral benefit.

In *British Westinghouse* v *Underground Electric Rly of London* [1912] AC 673, A agreed to supply B with turbines of stated efficiency, but supplied less efficient ones, which used more coal. B accepted them and used them for some years before replacing them with turbines which were even more efficient than those specified in the contract with A. After replacement B, claimed damages from A.

B was held to be under no duty to mitigate by buying new turbines, but since he had done so, the financial advantages he had gained from new turbines had to be taken into account. Thus, as B's saving in coal exceeded the cost of the new turbines, he was not entitled to damages. If B had claimed damages before buying the new turbines, A would have had no defence.

If P insures against a loss which may occur in the event of a breach, then this cannot be relied on by the defendant as mitigation, since it is a collateral benefit.

Note *Bradburn* v *GW Rly* (1874) LR 10 Ex 1. The defendant cannot rely on a profitable sub-sale by the plaintiff as mitigation either. See also *Williams* v *Agius* (above).

Mitigation and anticipatory breach

The duty to mitigate does not apply to compel an innocent party to accept an anticipatory breach of contract, even though by failing to do so the plaintiff can increase the defendant's liability. See *White & Carter* v *MacGregor*.

Compare with *Clea* v *Bulk Oil* [1984] 1 All ER 129. C chartered a ship to B. After a year (the charter was for two years), the ship broke down and was put in for repairs. B informed C that it no longer wanted the ship, but C carried out the repairs and, on their completion, offered the ship as ready once again; again B said it was not wanted. C took no steps to find an alternative charterer, and kept the ship fully crewed. On the question whether C was entitled to continue performance of the contract, or should have repudiated it and sued for damages, Lloyd J refused to interfere with the arbitrator's finding that C should have accepted the repudiation made on completion of the repairs, and could not recover the cost of hire under the charterparty; instead C had to sue for breach of contract.

In this case, Lloyd J confirmed the general principle that the victim of a repudiation of contract has a right to choose whether to accept the repudiation and bring the contract to an end, or to waive the repudiation and contined his performance of it. Where the contract is a continuing one, and the parties have future obligations under it, this right must be subject to the court finding that a victim has no 'substantial interest' in continuing to perform, and must repudiate: in *White & Carter* there was such an interest.

16.8 Liquidated damages clauses

General

The parties to the contract may make a genuine assessment of the losses which are likely to result in the event of a breach, and stipulate that such sum shall be payable in the event of a breach of contract.

Such clauses enable a party to know his liability in advance. If, however, the clause is not an assessment of losses, but intended as punishment on the contract-breaker, then the clause is a penalty clause and is void.

Note in this context the recent Privy Council case of *Golden Bay Realty Ltd* v

Orchard Twelve Investments Ltd [1991] 1 WLR 981 in which it is made clear that contracts drawn up in statutory form cannot be said to incorporate penalty clauses.

A contract made in Singapore for the sale of commercial property was made in accordance with the relevant statutes as applicable locally. This included the Sale of Commercial Properties Act 1979, which provided inter alia that if the vendor failed to complete by the prescribed date he should pay liquidated damages, calculated as according to the SCP Act. The vendors failed to complete on the appointed day and were thus liable to pay the purchaser liquidated damages until he did finally complete, some two years later. The vendor appealed against this payment on the basis that it amounted to a penalty clause.

The Privy Council, supporting the Singapore Court of Appeal, refused relief from the provisions of the Act; holding that where the terms and conditions of a contract are prescribed by legislation, the usual rules as to penalty clauses do not apply. The vendor was not entitled to question the validity of the provision relating to liquidated damages by claiming it was penal in nature. Regardless of the purpose of the Act, damages were entitled to be recovered, calculated in accordance with the statutory formula.

A liquidated damages clause will be effective in the event of a breach, and the plaintiff will not recover more than that sum. No action for unliquidated damages will be allowed. Where the clause is a penalty clause, then in an action for breach of contract it is disregarded.

The Privy Council has recently made it clear that the desirability of achieving certainty in commercial contracts dictates that wherever possible liquidated damages clauses should be incorporated (see *Philips Hong Kong Ltd* v *Attorney-General of Hong Kong* (1993) 61 Build LR 41).

Penalty or liquidated damages?

The parties may often be in dispute over whether the clause was a penalty or a liquidated damages clause. Various rules have been formulated to deal with such contingencies.

The mere fact that a payment is described in a contract as a 'penalty' is not, of itself, decisive. The court will look at the construction of the clause itself and the surrounding circumstances and may, on these, conclude that what is described as a penalty clause is, in fact, a liquidated damages clause. See *Kemble* v *Farren* (1829) 6 Bing 141.

In *Dunlop Pneumatic Tyre Co* v *New Garage* [1915] AC 79, Lord Dunedin laid down three rules concerning penalty clauses.

1. The use of the words 'penalty' or 'liquidated damages' may prima facie be supposed to mean what they say, yet the expression used is not conclusive.
2. The essence of a penalty is a payment of money as in terrorem of the offending party; the essence of liquidated damages is a genuine convenanted pre-estimate of damage. See *Clydebank Engineering* v *Don Jose Ramos* [1905] AC 6.

3. Whether a sum stipulated is penalty or liquidated damages is a question of construction to be decided upon the terms and inherent circumstances of each particular contract, judged as of the time of making the contract, not as at the time of breach.

In *Public Works Commissioners v Hills* [1906] AC 368, Lord Dunedin then mentioned four tests which would prove helpful, or even conclusive, in deciding if the clause was a 'penalty' or 'liquidated damages'.

First, it will be held to be a penalty if the sum stipulated for is extravagant and unconscionable in amount in comparison to the greatest loss that could conceivably be proved to have followed from the breach. For example, if a builder contracts to do work worth £50 with a clause stipulating that he pay £1m if he fails to do the work, it is clearly a penalty.

Secondly, it will be held to be a penalty if the breach consists only in not paying a sum of money, and the sum stipulated is a sum greater than the sum which ought to have been paid. For example, a clause to make a debtor pay £1,000 if he failed to pay £50 on the due day.

In cases under this category, the rule will apply even if the contract is in every respect a fair one. Thus, in *Betts v Birch* (1859) 4 H & N 506, a contract for the sale of the furniture and stock in trade of a public house which contained a clause for the payment of £50 if either party should default, was held to be a contract with a penalty clause even though the bargain was fair.

In subsequent cases, the courts have attempted to overcome the effects of this rule by narrow construction. The cases on this point were decided before the *Dunlop* case and whether they are still good law is undecided. If they are, equity would, in many cases, be able to strike down the bargains as unconscionable.

In *Proctor Loan Co v Grice* (1880) 5 QBD 592, a debtor owing a debt payable in instalments, promised that on default on any instalment he would pay the whole balance.

This clause was held not to be penal as it only accelerated, rather than increased, the liability of the debtor.

In *Wallis v Smith* (1892) 21 Ch D 243, a contract to develop a building estate stipulated that the defendant was to pay £500 on signing and £5,000 on the occurrence of 'any substantial breach'. The defendant failed to pay the £500 on signing and repudiated the whole contract.

The failure to pay the £500 was held not to be a substantial breach, but the plaintiff could recover the £5,000 from the defendant in any case because the defendant had repudiated the whole contract.

Thirdly, there is a presumption (but no more) that it is a penalty when:

' ... a single lump sum is made payable by way of compensation on the occurrence of one or more or all of several events, some of which may occasion serious and others but trifling damage' (Lord Watson in *Lord Elphinstone v Monkland* (1886) 11 App Cas 332).

Finally, it is no obstacle to the sum stipulated being a genuine pre-estimate of damage, that the consequences of the breach are such as to make precise pre-estimation almost an impossibility.

In *Dunlop Pneumatic Tyre Co* v *New Garage* [1915] AC 79, the defendant bought tyres from the plaintiff and agreed not to: tamper with manufacturer's marks; sell below the list price; sell to any person blacklisted by the plaintiff; exhibit or export tyres without the plaintiff's consent. The defendant agreed to pay £5 for every tyre he sold or offered in breach of the agreement. In breach, the defendant sold to the public below the list price.

The provision for payment of £5 was held not to be penal. Looking at the language of the contract itself, the character of the transaction and the circumstances, it was clear that the provision was to prevent a price war and so protect the plaintiff's sales. The clause was, therefore, an attempt to estimate damage at a certain figure and as the figure was not extravagant, it could only be concluded that it was a bargain to truly assess damages and not a penalty clause.

In *Jobson* v *Johnson* [1989] 1 WLR 1026, in a transaction for the transfer of shares in a football club, provision was made for default. The Court of Appeal held that whether a particular clause was penal or not was entirely a question of construction, to be decided in the light of circumstances at the time of making the contract.

Careful drafting of a contract may, however, enable a party to circumvent the rules relating to penalty clauses as appears from the case of *Lombard North Central plc* v *Butterworth* [1987] 1 All ER 267. A contract of hire provided that should the defendant default in the payment of any one instalment, he would be required to pay all past arrears of the hire charges, plus all future charges for the entire remaining period of hire. The Court of Appeal held that the term was a penalty. The plaintiffs, however, recovered the same sum as damages, as under the agreement punctual payment was a condition, the breach of which entitled the plaintiffs to repudiate the contract and recover damages for the loss of the whole transaction.

It is no surprise that the courts take each case on its own facts and merits. In *Lordsvale Finance plc* v *Bank of Zambia* [1996] 3 WLR 688, the High Court examined whether an agreement providing for an increased rate of interest in the event of a default (an indemnity clause), amounted to a penalty clause, and held that where such a default clause contained nothing in the nature of a penalty, then it was fully enforceable.

Clauses which underestimate damages

Where the contract has underestimated damages in the event of a breach, either because of inflation, or through bad bargaining, then damages will be limited to the amount stipulated by the contract.

A distinction may be drawn in such cases between a pure limitation clause, which specifies that damages shall be limited to a maximum figure of, for example, £10,000, and that the plaintiff can have such loss as he can prove up to this limit, and liquidated damages clauses. In the former, the plaintiff, as stated, can only receive what he proves. Thus, if he can only prove £100 damages, he will receive only £100. In the latter, the plaintiff will, on proving the breach, receive the stipulated sum regardless of whether these damages were above or below that amount, subject to the rule about penalty clauses.

In *Cellulose Acetate* v *Widnes Foundries* [1933] AC 20, the defendant agreed to build a chemical plant for the plaintiff in 18 weeks. If it took longer than this, they agreed to pay 'by way of penalty £20 per working week'. The defendant completed 30 weeks late, and the plaintiff lost £5,850 as a result of the delay. The defendant argued they were only liable for £600 damages.

The plaintiff was held only to be able to recover £600. The clause was not a penalty clause although it was described as such, because its object was not to act in terrorem. The parties must have known that the actual loss would be more than £20 per week, and the clause would, therefore, appear to have been an attempt to limit liability. However, the clause was not a pure limitation clause, because it also fixed the minimum payable for delay. The defendant would, therefore, still have had to pay £20 per week had the plaintiff lost less.

If the clause is, in fact, a penalty clause, then as it is void, the plaintiff can ignore it and sue for his actual loss.

In *Wall* v *Rederiaktiebolaget Luggude* [1915] 3 KB 66, it was held that a shipowner could disregard a penalty clause and sue for the actual loss he suffered where it exceeded the amount of the penalty. If the clause provides for a payment in excess of the loss and is a penalty clause, it is unclear whether the plaintiff can rely on it. However, it would appear wrong to allow the plaintiff to take the benefit of such clauses when he can ignore them when they are to his detriment.

If the clause has been affected by inflation, then it would appear that the only remedy for the parties is to revise it themselves. However, it may be possible as a matter of construction to have it revised by the court, if it is clear that the clause is no longer effective for the purposes envisaged by the parties. See *Staffs Area Health Authority* v *Staffs Waterworks* [1978] 3 All ER 769 at p777 per Lord Denning MR.

Payments which are not liquidated damages

Some contracts stipulate for payment of a particular sum on the happening of certain events other than breach of the contract itself. These payments are not liquidated damages, and the distinction between liquidated damages and penalties is inapplicable.

In *Alder* v *Moore* [1961] 2 QB 57, the defendant, a professional footballer, received £500 from an insurance company for an injury which was supposed to have disabled him. He signed a declaration that he would not play professional football again and that 'in the event of infringement of this condition, he will be subject to a penalty of the amount paid him in settlement of his claim'. The defendant began playing football four months after signing the declaration and the plaintiff sought recovery of the £500. The defendant argued the clause was a penalty and that the underwriters had suffered no loss by his playing football again. It was held that this was a contract for the payment of a certain sum in a certain event which was not a breach of contract, and that the event having happened, the sum was payable. See also *Exports Credit* v *Universal Oil Products* [1983] 2 All ER 205.

Problems arise where a clause contains provision for payments on the occurrence of several different events and some of these are penal and some are not. The problem is usually associated with hire purchase agreements. The rules are as follows.

1. If the clause stipulates for payment on the hirer's breach, then the clause is penal and void. See *Cooden Engineering* v *Stanford* [1953] 1 QB 86.
2. If the agreement is determined on some ground other than the hirer's breach, then the law as to penalties does not apply. For example, where the hirer exercises his right to return the goods. See *Associated Distributors* v *Hall* [1938] 2 KB 83.
3. Where the agreement contains a minimum payment clause, then it will be regarded as penal unless the minimum payment is very small. See *Lamdon Trust* v *Murrell* [1955] 1 WLR 391. A minimum payment clause which provided for the payment of three-quarters of the hire-purchase price on determination, was held to be penal, because it was payable regardless of whether the hirer defaulted on the first or last instalment.

   Any attempts to apportion the minimum payment clause according to the seriousness of the breach is disapproved of. In *Bridge* v *Campbell Discount* [1962] AC 600, the plaintiff bought a car on hire-purchase and paid a deposit plus one monthly instalment. He could not keep up the payments and returned the car to the finance company. Clause 9 of the agreement required the plaintiff to pay, by way of depreciation, such sum as would make his total payments up to two-thirds of the purchase price (£206 in this case). Although this clause was to compensate for depreciation, it in fact decreased the amount payable, the longer the plaintiff kept the goods and continued the payments.

   The clause was held to be penal because if the plaintiff was liable to pay the:

   '... penal sum of £206 without relief of any kind ... It means that equity has committed itself to this absurd paradox: it will grant relief to a man who breaks his contract but will penalize the man who keeps it' (per Lord Denning).

Withholding payments

This can often be a penalty unless the contract stipulates that there will be no payment until performance is completed.

In *Gilbert-Ash* v *Modern Engineering* [1974] AC 689, a subcontractor was entitled to payments on the issue of architects' certificates, but the main contractor had, in the same contract, the right to withhold or suspend payments if the subcontractor 'failed to comply with any provisions' of the contract. This provision was held to be invalid as a penalty clause.

16.9 Deposit and part payment

Where a contract provides that the purchaser makes a part payment in advance, then this is recoverable by the plaintiff unless the contract provides to the contrary.

A deposit is a guarantee that the contract will be performed, and it is normally irrecoverable unless the contract specifies to the contrary. In most cases, the deposit, will also be regarded as part satisfaction of payment, for example, in contracts for the purchase of land, a deposit of 10 per cent is normal by the purchaser. This will be retained by the vendor if the purchaser fails to complete the contract but, in any event, if the purchaser completes it is regarded as part of the purchase price unless the contract provides to the contrary.

A deposit differs from a penalty in that it is payable before, not after, the breach. However, there is in substance no real difference between a deposit and a penalty.

In *Pye* v *British Automobile Commercial Syndicate* [1906] 1 KB 425, a car dealer agreed to buy ten cars, and paid a 'deposit' of £300 to be forfeited if he refused to accept any of the cars. He broke the contract and claimed back the £300. The forfeiture clause was held not to be penal because a breach was likely to have serious consequences for the seller's whole selling organisation and, therefore, their precise loss could not be assessed accurately in advance. Whether or not the dealer could have got his 'deposit' back if the clause had been a penalty clause seems open to doubt.

Where a deposit is made on the purchase of land, then under s49(2) of the Law of Property Act 1925 the court can order repayment of the deposit even though it was not penal. However, in *Omar* v *El-Wakil* (2001) The Times 2 November the parties contracted for the sale and purchase of land and the claimant paid a deposit of £110,000. Neither party was able to complete. The claimant sought the return of his deposit: the Court of Appeal concluded that his claim could not succeed. As Arden LJ explained, since neither party was able to complete, under the contract the purchaser was not entitled to the return of his deposit as of right. Although s49(2) of the Law of Property Act 1925 provided for the return of deposits paid under contracts for the sale of land at the court's discretion, on the facts such discretion was not to be exercised in favour of the claimant. Where a purchaser could not himself perform, the circumstances which made it appropriate for the court to exercise its discretion under s49(2) in his favour were exceptional. Inability to complete was exactly the risk the deposit was intended to guard against.

Where payment is to be by instalments and there is a forfeiture clause for default, the purchaser may obtain relief in two situations.

1. If the purchaser was willing and able to perform, then equity may extend the time for payment and/or order repayment of the forfeited payments. See *Starside Properties* v *Mustafa* [1974] 1 WLR 816.
2. If the purchaser was not willing and able to perform, he will not get his instalments back unless it is unconscionable for the vendor to keep them.

Mussen v *Van Diemen's Land Co* [1938] Ch 253 concerns sale of land for £321,000 with the price payable in instalments. The defendant could rescind if the plaintiff defaulted in payment. The plaintiff, in fact, defaulted after payment of £42,000 and claimed the return of this. The court held that the plaintiff's claim must be rejected as he had freely entered the contract on agreed terms, which included terms that instalments paid were forfeited on default. If, however, the plaintiff had paid 90 per cent of the price, then it may well be regarded as unconscionable to allow the defendant to keep this.

16.10 Action for an agreed sum

General

This is an action for an agreed sum and neither more nor less. For example, the price of goods delivered or agreed remuneration for work done. Such actions differ from damages in that there are no questions of remoteness or quantification. The question is whether the plaintiff is entitled to the agreed sum, and the defendant will usually raise defences that either the goods were defective, or the work done unsatisfactorily.

Requirements for the action

The duty to pay the price must have arisen. Whether this has actually occurred will depend on the terms of the contract itself.

In *Mount* v *Oldham Corporation* [1973] 1 QB 309, a private school taking state scholars had an agreement with the Corporation for payment of fees which stipulated that fees were payable in advance. On the introduction of the comprehensive system, the Corporation withdrew pupils from the school without giving the customary one term's notice. It was held that the headmaster could sue for fees payable in advance.

Section 49(2) Sale of Goods Act 1979 provides that if payment is to be made on a certain day irrespective of delivery, then the seller can sue for the price any time after that day.

In *Workman* v *Lloyds Brasileno* [1908] 1 KB 968, the plaintiff was constructing a ship for the defendant which was to be paid for by instalments. The seller was held to be entitled to sue for instalments as they became due.

The conduct of the injured party

The plaintiff can elect to terminate the contract and sue for damages which will take account of any sums payable under the contract but, in such cases, sums due after the contract terminated, under the terms of the contract, cannot be claimed.

The plaintiff can elect to treat the contract as still subsisting, and claim for what is due to him under it. In such cases, the plaintiff has done all that is required of him. For example, a seller who has delivered goods can sue for the price. But if the plaintiff has not done all that is required of him under the contract, he cannot bring an action for an agreed sum.

In *Denmark Productions* v *Boscobel Productions* [1969] 1 QB 699, a singer wrongfully repudiated a contract with his agent and the latter could not continue performance without the co-operation of the singer.

Despite the fact that the agent could not perform without the co-operation of the guilty party, he could not be permitted to bring an action for an agreed sum, and could only claim for damages.

If the plaintiff continues performance after repudiation of the contract by the other party, he may be regarded as having an option which he, the plaintiff, has exercised to continue the contract and he can claim for agreed sums under the contract.

In *White and Carter Councils* v *MacGregor* [1962] AC 413 (and see above), the plaintiffs agreed to advertise the defendant's garage business on their litterbins for three years. The payment was to be 2*s.* per week for plates on litterbins and 5*s.* per annum towards the cost of a plate. The defendant repudiated on the day the contract was made, but the plaintiff nevertheless made the plates and displayed them. Then he sued for the full amount due on the contract.

The defendant's repudiation did not bring the contract to an end, but only gave the injured party an option as to whether to go on with the contract, but since the plaintiff had affirmed the contract it remained in full effect:

'It is settled as a fundamental rule of the law of contract that repudiation by one of the parties to a contract does not itself discharge it ... It follows that, if, as here, there was no acceptance (of the breach), the contract remains alive for the benefit of both parties and the party who has repudiated can change his mind, but it does not follow that the party at the receiving end of the proffered repudiation is bound to accept it before the time for performance and is left to his remedy in damages for breach' (per Lord Hodson).

If the plaintiff cannot perform without the co-operation of the defendant, then the contract will be at an end, and the plaintiff can only get damages. If the plaintiff could only have carried on with the defendant's co-operation, in the *MacGregor* case he would have only got damages in the circumstances. In *Sanders* v *Neale* [1974] 3 All ER 327, the plaintiff was wrongfully dismissed from his employment, and it was held he could only obtain damages and not an agreed sum.

In the *MacGregor* case, much depends on commercial considerations. If there is a small demand for the plaintiff's goods, then it may be reasonable for him to carry on with the contract. However, if demand is strong, the plaintiff would be acting unreasonably in not accepting repudiation, and may be penalised for not mitigating his loss. However, it is arguable that mitigation only applies to damages and not to an action for an agreed sum. Similarly, the plaintiff is entitled to continue performance where he would injure his repudiation if he discontinued, or when he has already entered contracts with third parties, to honour his contract with the defendant. In short, the rule in the *MacGregor* case will not be applied if the injured party has no 'substantial or legitimate interest' in completing performance. See *Clea* v *Bulk Oil* (above).

17

Remedies for Breach of Contract – Equitable Remedies

17.1 Specific performance: introduction

There are cases where damages, although obtainable for the breach, are an inadequate remedy because they will not give the plaintiff adequate compensation for his loss. For example, the plaintiff may have contracted to purchase a particular plot of land from the defendant for which compensation can provide no satisfactory equivalent in the event of the defendant's breach.

Specific performance is an equitable remedy for breach of contract. The court has a discretion to order specific performance where it is just and equitable to do so. The plaintiff is not entitled to it as of right.

Note, however, that while specific performance (and other equitable remedies) may not be available as of right, any attempt in a contract to exclude such remedies will be void. In *Quadrant Visual Communications Ltd* v *Hutchinson Telephone (UK) Ltd* [1993] BCLC 442 in a contract made between the two parties one particular clause apparently purported to exclude equitable remedies. The Court of Appeal held that once there was a request for an equitable remedy (in this case specific performance) its discretion could not be fettered. Whatever the construction of the clause it was the decision of the court alone as to whether to grant or refuse any equitable remedy.

17.2 When damages are an inadequate remedy

If the plaintiff can show that damages are inadequate, then the court may entertain his claim for specific performance. Damages will be inadequate in the following cases.

Where the plaintiff cannot get a satisfactory substitute

Where land or other premises are involved, their specific performance is readily granted as the law takes the view that a buyer is not readily compensated by damages.

Antiques, valuable paintings and other irreplaceable items may be the subject of an action for specific performance. See *Nutbrown* v *Thornton* (1804) 10 Ves 159. Specific performance was ordered of a contract to supply machinery or plant which could not be readily obtained elsewhere. For instance, in *Co-operative Insurance Society Ltd* v *Argyll Stores (Holdings) Ltd* [1996] 3 WLR 27, the Court of Appeal addressed the question of whether a covenant could be specifically enforced. The Court in this case allowed the appeal and granted an order for specific performance on the basis that (apart from the fact that damages were an inadequate remedy), the defendants had deliberately breached the terms of the contract.

In cases where the plaintiff has contracted to obtain services of a personal quality from the defendant, for example, to sing or take part in a film, then he will *not* get specific performance, but may obtain an injunction.

Where damages are difficult to assess

For example, specific performance will be ordered of a contract to sell or pay annuities.

Where the amount allowable as damages is not a secure financial equivalent

In *Beswick* v *Beswick* [1968] AC 58, A promised B to pay an annuity to C in consideration of B's transferring the goodwill of the business to A. It was held that, although the promise did not give C any right of action, because she was not a party to the contract (see Chapter 12), it could be specifically enforced by B's personal representative against A. This was because damages would have been purely nominal as the promisee or his estate had suffered no loss. A would have been unjustly enriched by being allowed to retain the entire benefit of the other contracting party's performance without performing his own promise.

Section 52 Sale of Goods Act 1979. The court has a discretion to order specific performance in the case of 'specific or ascertained goods'. This discretion is heavily influenced by pre-1893 equity cases and is used very sparingly.

Note *Behnke* v *Bede Shipping* [1927] 1 KB 649, a decree of specific performance was granted in the case of a ship.

However, in *Cohen* v *Roche* [1927] 1 KB 169, the court refused specific performance to a buyer of a set of Hepplewhite chairs saying that they were 'ordinary articles of commerce and of no special value or interest'. It was crucial in this case that the buyer was contracting with a view to resale and not to use. If the latter had been the case the result, it is submitted, would have been different.

In *Re Wait* [1927] 1 Ch 606, a case which failed under s52 because the goods were not 'specific or ascertained', Atkin LJ said the 'only remedy by way of specific performance was a statutory one'. This dictum appears to have been departed from in one recent case.

In *Sky Petroleum* v *VIP Petroleum* [1974] 1 All ER 954, the plaintiff agreed to buy all its petrol from the defendant for ten years, that is, unascertained goods. In November 1973, the defendant purported to terminate the contract for alleged breach of contract by the plaintiff. The plaintiff sought an interlocutory injunction in the circumstances, restraining the defendant from withholding petrol supplies because petrol shortages meant the plaintiff had either to get petrol from the defendant or close down since no alternative sources were available. It was held that the plaintiff could get an injunction to restrain the defendant.

It would appear that the court grants specific performance according to the appropriateness of that remedy in the circumstances of each case. In this case, an injunction was granted for unascertained goods despite s52 and *Re Wait*. Damages would not have been an adequate remedy since the plaintiff could not have gone to the market to buy petrol.

17.3 Factors considered in awarding specific performance

Mutuality

There must be mutuality before specific performance is available. Therefore, the plaintiff can only have this remedy if the contract can also be enforced by the defendant.

There will be no mutuality if there exist some unperformed obligations of the plaintiff which cannot by their nature be enforced, for example, personal service contracts or contracts requiring constant supervision.

'The court does not grant specific performance unless it can give full relief to both parties' per Lord Cranworth LC in *Blackett* v *Bates* (1865) LR 1 Ch App 117 at 124.

The date of the hearing and not the date of the contract is the relevant time for dealing with mutuality. See *Price* v *Strange* [1977] 3 All ER 371:

'The time at which the mutual availability of specific performance and its importance must be considered is, in my opinion, the time of judgment, and the principle to be applied can, I think, be stated simply as follows: the court will not compel a defendant to perform his obligations specifically if it cannot at the same time ensure that any unperformed obligations of the plaintiff will be specifically performed' (per Buckley LJ).

In *Sutton* v *Sutton* [1984] 1 All ER 168, the court held that lack of mutuality might have been a good argument while the contract was executory but, by the time the case came before the court, the plaintiff had performed her side of the agreement, and it was too late for the defendant to rely on that defence.

Hardship

This is a ground for not ordering specific performance where it would cause the defendant hardship. In *Denne* v *Light* (1857) 8 De GM & G 774, the court refused to order specific performance against the buyer of farmland, which was wholly surrounded by land belonging to others, and over which there was no right of way.

A rare modern case where specific performance was refused on this ground is *Patel* v *Ali* [1984] 1 All ER 978. Specific performance may be refused against the defendant on grounds of hardship where the cost to the defendant is wholly out of proportion to the benefit which performance will confer on the plaintiff.

Unfairness

The court will refuse the remedy to the plaintiff if he has acted unfairly or dishonestly. The equitable principle is that the plaintiff must come to equity with clean hands. See *Coatsworth* v *Johnson* (1886) 54 LT 520 and *Walters* v *Morgan* (1861) 3 De GF & J 718, where the defendant agreed to grant the plaintiff a mining lease over land he had just bought. Specific performance was refused as the plaintiff had produced a draft lease and induced the defendant to sign the agreement in ignorance of the value of the property. The plaintiff had hurried the defendant into signing the lease before he knew the value of the property.

Mere inadequacy of consideration is not a ground for refusing specific performance, *Collier* v *Brown* (1788) 1 Cox CC 428, unless it is coupled with factors such as mistake or fraud.

Conduct of the plaintiff

Specific performance will be refused if the plaintiff fails to perform a promise which induced the defendant to contract.

In *Lamare* v *Dixon* (1873) LR 6 HL 414, the plaintiff induced the defendant to agree to take a lease of cellars by orally promising they would be made dry. The promise had no effect as a misrepresentation as it related to the future. The court refused the plaintiff specific performance since he had made no attempt to perform his promise. See also *Shell* v *Lostock Garages* [1976] 1 WLR 1187.

Impossibility

Equity will do nothing in vain, thus specific performance will not be ordered, for example, against the defendant who has contracted to sell land which he either does not own, or has already conveyed elsewhere. See *Castle* v *Wilkinson* (1870) LR 5 Ch App 534.

Supervision

The court is reluctant to grant specific performance where this would require constant supervision.

In *Ryan* v *Mutual Tontine Assoc* [1893] 1 Ch 116, a lease of a service flat provided that the lessors should provide a porter who was to be 'constantly in attendance'. It was held that this undertaking could not be specifically enforced. It would require 'that constant superintendence by the court which the court has always in such cases declined to give'.

In *Posner* v *Scott-Lewis* [1987] Ch 25, however, the court granted an application for specific performance of a lessor's covenant to employ a resident porter for certain duties. Mervyn Davies J distinguished the facts before him from those in *Ryan*, where supervision of the execution of the undertaking had been required. Here neither personal services, nor a continuous series of acts, were required, but merely the execution of an agreement containing provision for such services.

Contracts to cultivate a farm in a particular manner, keep an airfield in operation, deliver goods in instalments, etc, have not been enforced for this reason.

It has been argued that supervision is only a factor to be taken into account and is not a bar to specific performance.

In *Luganda* v *Service Hotels* [1969] 2 Ch 206, a mandatory injunction ordering the defendant to allow the plaintiff, who had been wrongfully locked out of a room in a hotel, to resume his residence was granted. This shows that the court attaches more importance to the plaintiff's interest than the difficulty of supervision.

Uncertainty

The agreement must be definite enough to be enforced both legally and specifically, that is, the court must be able to formulate its decree.

In *Joseph* v *National Magazine Co* [1959] Ch 14, the defendant undertook to publish an article to be written by the plaintiff, but could not agree with him as to the precise wording. It was held that specific performance must be refused as there was no definite manuscript, publication of which could be ordered.

Delay

There is no limitation period for obtaining specific performance, however, the plaintiff should pursue his remedy within a reasonable time, otherwise the equitable doctrine of laches may operate to bar his claim, that is, 'equity assists the vigilant, not the indolent'.

If both sides regard the contract as a leisurely transaction, then the plaintiff may obtain specific performance after two years. See *Lazard Bros* v *Fairfield Properties* (1977) 121 SJ 793.

If the plaintiff takes possession of land relying on his equitable title, then he may obtain a decree for specific performance of the contract regardless of the delay. See *Williams* v *Greatrex* [1957] 1 WLR 31.

17.4 Particular contracts

Contracts involving personal service

The court will not order specific performance of these contracts. Section 16 Trade Union and Labour Relations Act 1974 states that no court shall compel an employee to do any work by ordering specific performance of a contract of employment, or by restraining the breach of such contract by injunction.

An employer cannot be forced to employ somebody against his wishes, and the general rule is that the court will not order re-engagement of an employee, but will, instead, award compensation. In one case, however, an employer was forced to retain an employee he dismissed.

In *Hill* v *CA Parsons Ltd* [1972] Ch 305, the plaintiff was employed by the defendant for 35 years. Within two years of retirement, which would mean certain pensions etc, the defendant ordered the plaintiff to join a certain trade union, which he refused to do and got a month's notice.

The notice was held to be wholly inadequate and a breach of contract which required six if not 12 months' notice. An interim injunction was granted so that the plaintiff's employment continued.

In all contracts involving personal service, the equitable principle applies. Thus in *Chinnock* v *Sainsbury* (1861) 30 LJ Ch 409, an agreement to allow an auctioneer to sell certain works of art could not be specifically enforced, and in *England* v *Curling* (1844) 8 Beav 129, an agreement to enter into a partnership could not be specifically enforced.

An industrial tribunal can order reinstatement or re-engagement under the provisions of the Employment Protection (Consolidation) Act 1978.

Building contracts

The general rule is that a contract to erect a building cannot be specifically enforced. Several reasons exist for this, such as the following.

1. Damages may be an adequate remedy as the owner can engage another builder.
2. The contract may be too vague and not describe the building with sufficient certainty.
3. Specific performance may cause difficulties relating to supervision.

Where the first two reasons are not applicable, the court will in effect ignore the third and order specific performance.

In *Wolverhampton Corp* v *Emmons* [1901] 1 KB 515, the plaintiff acquired land for an improvement scheme and sold part of it to the defendant, who covenanted to demolish houses on it and build new ones. The demolition was carried out and plans for new houses approved.

Specific performance would be ordered since the defendant's obligations were precisely defined by the plans, and damages would be inadequate because the defendant had possession of the site, and the plaintiff could not get the work done by employing another contractor.

Entire and severable contracts

Where the court cannot grant specific performance of a contract as a whole, it will not interfere to compel specific performance of part of that contract. Where parts of a contract are severable, specific performance of each part can be separately granted. See *Odessa Tramway* v *Mendel* (1878) 8 Ch D 235.

17.5 Specific performance and third parties

In *Beswick* v *Beswick* (above), the House of Lords granted specific performance of a contract for the benefit of a third party. Three points were stressed in that case as forming the basis of the decision.

1. The promisee's remedy at law was inadequate. The damages he could recover would only be nominal.
2. The promisor had received the entire consideration for his promise.
3. The contract could have been specifically enforced by the promisor if the promisee had failed to perform his part of transferring the business.

Specific performance could be ordered of a promise to pay a single lump sum to a third party. See *Gurtner* v *Circuit* [1968] 2 QB 587. The equitable remedy need not have been available in a similar two-party case. It is sufficient if there was a common law remedy available in such a two-party case.

17.6 Injunction: introduction

A court may be able to restrain a party from committing a breach of contract by injunction. The remedy is most appropriate where the contract contains a negative stipulation, by which the defendant precludes himself from acting in a manner inconsistent with his positive contractual obligations.

17.7 Types of injunction

There are three types of injunction commonly available.

1. *Interlocutory injunction* – this is designed to regulate the position of the parties pending a hearing.
2. *Prohibitory injunction* – this orders the defendant not to do something, for example, X contracts with Y to obtain all the beer for his pub from Y. A prohibitory injunction could be issued to prevent him buying from Z.
3. *Mandatory injunction* – this orders the defendant to undo something he has agreed not to do.

Unlike specific performance, the defendant cannot resist a prohibitory injunction on the ground that it is burdensome to him.

Interlocutory injunctions

These could possibly be used to prevent a breach of contract by the defendant before it actually occurs. The circumstances in which this is likely to occur are hard to envisage, but the rules governing the grant of such an injunction were laid down by the House of Lords in *American Cyanamid* v *Ethicon* [1975] 1 All ER 504. The basis of this case is that the plaintiff must show there is a serious issue to be tried at the trial, and that the balance of convenience is in his favour in granting the injunction. See also *Fellowes* v *Fisher* [1976] QB 122, where the subject matter of a contract is in danger of being moved out of the jurisdiction in a case where a claim for damages or for an agreed sum is being heard and the sale of that subject matter is likely to be used to pay the damages, then it would appear that the plaintiff can apply for an interlocutory injunction to restrain the defendant from removing the subject matter from the jurisdiction. Such injunctions are known as 'Mareva' injunctions. See also *Mareva Compania Naviera* v *International Bulk Carriers* [1980] 1 All ER 213.

Prohibitory and mandatory injunctions

These will not be granted if the effect is to directly or indirectly compel the defendant to do acts for which the plaintiff could not have specific performance. Thus an employee cannot be restrained from committing a breach of his positive obligation to work (s16 TULRA 1974, above).

A service contract may, however, contain certain express negative obligations, which can be enforced by injunction without compelling the defendant to work or infringing the rule that the plaintiff could not have obtained specific performance.

In *Lumley* v *Wagner* (1852) 1 De GM & G 604, the defendant contracted to sing for the plaintiff in his theatre for three months and, at the same time, not to sing elsewhere during this time without the plaintiff's consent. A third party, one Gye, offered the defendant a larger sum to sing for him.

The court stated that they had no power to make the defendant sing or encourage her to sing at plaintiff's theatre. However, the court could persuade her to do so by preventing her singing elsewhere by imposing an injunction to the effect.

Lumley v *Wagner* has been criticised, particularly as regard the perilous position in which it puts those who have agreed, and later refuse to perform, personal contracts. In *Giles* v *Morris* [1972] 1 WLR 307, Megarry J pointed out that if an artist was ordered to sing and did it badly or wilfully, he would be in contempt of court. If it was not wilful, then there would be no contempt of court. As it is exceedingly difficult to define wilful and unwilful, the defendant is thus given the benefit of the doubt. An injunction may well put so much economic pressure on the defendant that he decides to perform and to perform badly as above.

Since an injunction can put so much economic pressure on the defendant in certain cases, it is tantamount to making him perform the positive part of the contract.

In *Warner Bros* v *Nelson* [1937] 1 KB 209, the defendant, an actress, agreed to act for the plaintiff and, at the same time, not to act or sing for anybody else for two years without the plaintiff's written consent, and no other employment could be taken up during this period without the plaintiff's consent.

The defendant could be restrained by injunction from breaking this undertaking. She would not be forced to act for the plaintiff because she could earn a living by doing other work.

The law seems to be moving away from this rule in the *Warner Bros* case and it appears that an injunction will not now be granted unless it leaves the defendant with some reasonable alternative means of earning a living.

In *Page One Records* v *Britton* [1968] 1 WLR 157, The Troggs, a pop group, contracted to appoint the plaintiff their sole agent and manager for five years, and agreed not to act themselves in such capacity and not to appoint any other person for that time. They fell out with the manager and wanted to replace him. The plaintiff sought an injunction. It was held that an injunction must be refused because to grant it would, in effect, compel The Troggs to continue to employ the plaintiff, and thus would amount to enforcing the performance by the plaintiff of a contract for personal services.

The above principles have been applied in cases where contracts of employment have included clauses requiring the employee not to work for competitors or set up in competition for a certain period after he has left the employment. In these cases, an added complication exists, for the court will not grant an injunction if the clause in the contract is too wide.

In *The Littlewoods Organisation* v *Harris* [1978] 1 All ER 1026, the plaintiff, was a large mail order firm who employed the defendant as a divisional director to plan their catalogues in advance. The defendant's contract of service included a clause which provided 'in the event of the determination of this Agreement ... the (defendant) shall not at any time within 12 months after such determination enter into a contract of service with Great Universal Stores'. Great Universal Stores was the plaintiff's only rival in the mail order business, but they also had, like the plaintiff, a chain of shops. The defendant resigned from the plaintiff on the offer of a job by Great Universal Stores. The plaintiff sought an injunction. The defendant argued it should not be granted as it was wider than necessary to protect the plaintiff's business.

Such a covenant, although drafted in general terms, could be construed in a sense that was not unreasonably wide, and the court should construe it in that sense to render it valid and enforceable. In the circumstances, it was clear the clause was intended to protect confidential information and trade secrets and it would be limited as such.

In *Evening Standard* v *Henderson* [1987] ICR 588, the defendant had undertaken not to work for his employer's competitors during the duration of his employment. In breach of contract, he gave his employer two months' notice of termination, instead of the required twelve months. The plaintiffs offered to pay him his wages for the remaining ten months and successively claimed an injunction to prevent him from working for a rival newspaper for that period.

A sole distributorship agreement may also be enforced by injunction. In *Decro-Wall International* v *Practitioners in Marketing* [1971] 1 WLR 361, a manufacturer was restrained from breaching a 'sole distributorship' agreement in that he was prevented from disposing of the goods in any other way. However, the court would not order him to keep up the positive part of the convenant to keep up the distributor's supplies.

Lastly, it seems that the court will not grant an injunction, if the negative stipulation is not expressed. See *Mortimer* v *Beckett* [1920] 1 Ch 571. An apparent exception is *Hivac* v *Park Royal Scientific Instruments* [1946] Ch 169, but that can also be explained on the basis that the court was seeking to prevent breach of an employee's duty of confidentiality which is implied by law.

17.8 Damages in lieu of specific performance or injunction

Damages were originally only available at common law. However, s2 Chancery Amendment Act 1858 gave the Court of Chancery the power to award damages in lieu of specific performance (now s50 Supreme Court Act 1981) commonly referred to as Lord Cairns' Act.

See s50 Supreme Court Act 1981, where the Court of Appeal or High Court has jurisdiction to entertain an application for an injunction or specific performance, it may award damages in addition to, or in substitution for, an injunction or specific performance.

In contractual cases, other than those concerning land, there is little point invoking s50 SCA 1981 where there is a valid contract and a breach of this is proved. However, the plaintiff may invoke the Act on two occasions.

1. Damages may be awarded under the Act even though there is no completed cause of action. See *Leeds Industrial Co-operative Society* v *Slack* [1924] AC 851. In such cases, it would not be possible to get damages at common law, for example, damages in lieu of a quia timet injunction and damages for breach of a restrictive covenant to which the defendant was not a party.
2. Damages awarded to the plaintiff may be greater under the Act than at common law. Damages under the Act are assessed in the same manner as at common law. But, where damages are awarded at common law, the principle is that such damages are normally assessed as at the date of the breach, a principle which is recognised and embodied in s51 Sale of Goods Act 1979.

This is not an absolute rule and if 'it would give rise to injustice, the court has power to fix such other date as may be appropriate in the circumstances' (per Lord Wilberforce in *Johnson* v *Agnew* [1980] AC 367). The plaintiff obtained a decree of specific performance on a contract for the sale of a house to the defendant. The plaintiff had bought a new house in the meantime and he could not keep up the mortgage instalments on the house he had sold to the defendant. The mortgagee took possession and sold the house making specific performance impossible. The plaintiff then claimed to have the specific performance decree cancelled and damages in lieu of specific performance requested. The date of breach of the contract was about 21 January 1974, the decree of specific performance was drawn up and entered on 26 November 1974, and specific performance became impossible on 3 April 1975, when the mortgagee took possession and sold. The Court of Appeal fixed the date of assessment of damages at 26 November 1974, but in the House of Lords it was held that damages should be assessed as at 3 April 1975:

> 'As the vendors acted reasonably in pursuing the remedy of specific performance the date on which that remedy became aborted (not being the vendor's fault) should logically be fixed as the date on which damages should be assessed' (per Lord Wilberforce).

Damages may often be awarded in addition to specific performance but, again, the only clear examples of use of this are in contracts for the sale of land.

In *Grant* v *Dawkins* [1973] 1 WLR 1406, the vendor's title to land was subject to an encumbrance which amounted to a breach of contract. The plaintiff, it was held, could get specific performance of what title the defendant had, plus damages based on the cost of discharging the encumbrance.

18

Quasi-contract

18.1 Introduction

18.2 Action for money had and received

18.3 Action for money paid

18.4 Liability to account

18.5 Quantum meruit

18.1 Introduction

Quasi-contract is also called restitution. It has been described by Lord Wright in *Fibrosa Spolka Akcynja* v *Fairbairn Lawson Combe Barbour Ltd* [1943] AC 32 in the following terms:

> 'It is clear that any civilised system of law is bound to provide remedies for what has been called unjust enrichment or unjust benefit, that is, to prevent a man from retaining the money of, or some benefit derived from, another which it is against his conscience he should keep. Such remedies in English law are generically different from remedies in contract or in tort, and are now recognised to fall within a third category of the common law which has been called quasi-contract or restitution.'

As to what constitutes 'unjust enrichment', see the case of *Barclays Bank* v *Hammersmith and Fulham LBC* (1991) The Times 27 November in which the Court of Appeal decided that it was proper to look at the state of mind of both payer and payee at the time the payments were made. See also *Halifax Building Society* v *Thomas* [1995] TLR 385, in which the Court of Appeal examined, in some detail, the meaning of the term 'unjust enrichment'. Further opportunities arose for the Court of Appeal to scrutinise 'unjust enrichment' in the following cases: *Kleinwort Benson Ltd* v *Birmingham City Council* [1997] QB 380 and *Portman Building Society* v *Hamlyn Taylor Neck (A Firm)* [1998] 4 All ER 202. In both cases the actions failed as the plaintiffs could not establish that the defendants had been unjustly enriched at the plaintiffs' expense. This was also the view of the House of Lords in *Kleinwort Benson Ltd* v *Glasgow City Council (No 2)* [1997] 4 All ER 641 where the principle that a claim in restitution is based on the establishing of unjust enrichment was once against re-affirmed.

In a leading text, *The Law of Restitution* by Goff and Jones J, it is argued that these exceptional decisions should be classified under a category separate from contract or tort, namely restitution. The approach would bring the English law of obligations more in line with the Roman classification, the latter having a well-defined law of restitution. Goff and Jones's book has been cited with approval by the courts.

However, as quasi-contract has traditionally been viewed as part of the law of contract (see Theories, below) – and is often associated with the subject in practice – it is necessary to examine the topic in outline.

There are three main quasi-contractual actions: the action for money had and received; the action for money paid; and a quantum meruit claim.

Cases concerning quasi-contract do not come before the courts very often. The New Zealand case, *Meates v Westpac Banking Corporation* (1990) The Times 5 July, is therefore interesting, though of persuasive authority only.

The government of New Zealand had issued a number of formal documents as part of a project to establish new industries. The project never came into effect, but the appellants claimed that as a result of conversations, press statements and so on, they had understood that the government was prepared to indemnify them. They had incurred considerable expenses.

It was held that as a general rule, governments and large corporations intend ultimately to be bound only by formal written documents. Any *implied* undertaking made verbally, therefore, in the face of the written documents' express terms, could not be enforced. No quasi-contractual obligation existed.

Meates v Westpac, being a New Zealand case, was of persuasive authority only, but a remarkably similar case – *Regalian Properties plc v London Docklands Development Corporation* [1995] 1 WLR 212 – has recently appeared before the Chancery Division of the High Court. It, too, made it clear that expenses incurred preparatory to a contract may not be recovered by way of an action in quasi-contract should the contract prove, for whatever reason, abortive.

18.2 Action for money had and received

This is an old common law action that, in many ways, resembled the equitable trust remedy. It was gradually extended to cover situations where money was paid by mistake or under a consideration that had totally failed. The action is usually available in the situations below.

Money paid under a mistake of fact

The classic test was formulated by Bramwell B in *Aiken v Short* (1856) 1 H & N 210:

'In order to entitle a person to recover back money paid under a mistake of fact, the mistake must be as to a fact which, if true, would make the person paying liable to pay the money; not where, if true, it would merely make it desirable that he should pay the money.'

This test may, however, be too narrow. In *Kerrison* v *Glyn, Mills, Currie & Co* (1912) 81 LJKB 465, the House of Lords permitted recovery of money mistakenly paid in anticipation of a future liability.

In *Morgan* v *Ashcroft* [1938] 1 KB 49, Greene MR sought to confine the law to 'cases where the only mistake is as to the nature of the transaction', although the test of Bramwell B was criticised as being too narrow.

In *Larner* v *LCC* [1949] 2 KB 683, payments made by a local authority in the mistaken belief that it was under a moral obligation to pay were recovered. The authority had voluntarily promised 'until further order' to pay all their employees on war service the difference between their service pay and their civilian pay. Larner was overpaid because he did not tell the authority that he had had increases in his service pay. He defended the action on the basis that the payments were voluntary.

The payments were held not to be voluntary, even though there was no legal obligation to pay. The local authority had 'for good reasons of national policy, made a promise to the men which they were in honour bound to fulfil. The payments were not mere gratuities. They were made as a matter of duty.'

In *Friend's Provident* v *Hillier Parker May & Rowden* [1996] 2 WLR 123, the Court of Appeal was faced with the question of whether an action could be struck out on the grounds of mistake of fact. Here, the Court of Appeal held that where the plaintiffs were labouring under a mistake of fact, then they were also entitled to any notional interest paid out by them in respect of the contract.

The nature of the mistake

The general view seems to be that a person can recover for a mistake which is less grave than the mistake required before a contract may be rescinded, so that mistakes as to creditworthiness and arithmetic have not prevented recovery. See *Kerrison* v *Glyn, Mills, Currie* (above) and *Weld-Blundell* v *Synott* [1940] 2 KB 107.

In *National Westminster Bank plc* v *Somer International (UK) Ltd* [2002] 1 All ER 198 the Court of Appeal heard that the defendant company sometimes received payments from its customers in dollars directly into its dollar account with the claimant bank. Knowing that the defendants were expecting to receive from their customer Mentor a payment of between $US70,000 and $US80,000, having received a payment of $US76,708 from Moffett intended for another of the claimants' customers, the claimants notified the defendants that the moneys they were expecting had been received into their account. On hearing this, the defendants released to Mentor further goods to the value of £13,180. Some nine months later, having discovered their mistake, the claimants notified the defendants that the payment received had been credited to their account in error and requested repayment. By this time, Mentor had ceased to trade and had effectively disappeared. The claimants now sued to recover the payment of $US76,708 and it was held that they were entitled to recover the amount mistakenly credited to the defendants' account less the value of the goods subsequently sent by the defendants to Mentor. As Peter Gibson LJ explained:

> 'The test is whether it would be unconscionable and inequitable for the recipient of the moneys mistakenly paid to retain the moneys having regard to what the recipient did in reliance on the representation made to him. I fully accept that the Court, when assessing detriment, should not apply too demanding a standard of proof because of the practical difficulties faced by a defendant conducting a business who has been led to believe that the moneys paid by mistake are his ... But in view of the clear findings of fact made by the judge as to the extent of the detriment suffered by [the defendants] and in particular his outright rejection of the argument that [they were] induced to forgo the opportunity to pursue Mentor for payment, I am not able to accede to [counsel for the defendants'] submission that this is a case where it would be unjust not to give full effect to the estoppel. On the contrary, the circumstances here, as found by the judge, are such that the disparity between the $US76,708 mistakenly credited to [the defendants] and £13,180, being the value of the goods despatched by [the defendants] in reliance on the bank's representation, makes it unconscionable and inequitable for [the defendants] to retain the balance.'

In reaching this conclusion, their Lordships followed the decision of the Court of Appeal in *Scottish Equitable plc* v *Derby* [2001] 3 All ER 818 (defence of change of position requires some causal link between mistaken receipt of overpayment and defendant's change of position which makes it inequitable for recipient to be required to make restitution). See also Chapter 3, section 3.4.

Mistake as the cause of payment

Notably in *Barclays Bank* v *Simms & Cooke* [1980] QB 677, Goff J preferred the test of whether the mistake *caused* the payment to any test relating to the nature of the mistake made. He went on to say that there were, however, three circumstances in which no recovery would be possible.

1. Where the payer intends that the payee shall have the money in any event, and is deemed in law so to intend.
2. Where the payment is made for good consideration – especially the discharge of a debt from payer to payee.
3. Where the payee has, or is deemed in law to have, changed his position in good faith as a result of the payment.

Other limitations on the power to recover

1. In submission to a claim or under a compromise of a claim.
2. Where recovery would be contrary to public policy. In *Morgan* v *Ashcroft*

(above), the plaintiff, a bookmaker, overpaid the defendant on a betting account. He sued to recover the amount of the over-payment. It was held that the court would not recognise wagering contracts as giving rise to legal and enforceable obligations.

3. Where the plaintiff has not asked for repayment before commencing proceedings. This may, alternatively, only go to the issue of costs, but see *Kelly* v *Solari* (1841) 9 M & W 54 at p58, which has now been effectively overruled. See below.

4. Where there is only a mistake of law and not a mistake as to private rights. See *Cooper* v *Phibbs* (1867) LR 2 HL 149, *Solle* v *Butcher* [1950] 1 KB 671 and *Kiriri Cotton* v *Dewani* [1960] AC 192.

   In the latter case, Lord Denning MR may have thrown some doubt on the general proposition by saying that:

   > 'The true proposition is that money paid under a mistake of law, by itself and without more, cannot be recovered back ... If there is something more in addition to a mistake of law – if there is something in the defendant's conduct which shows that of the two of them, he is the one primarily responsible for the mistake – then it may be recovered back.'

   In overruling *Kelly* v *Solari* (1841), the House of Lords in *Kleinwort Benson Ltd* v *Lincoln City Council and Other Appeals* [1998] 4 All ER 513 stated that English law should now recognise that there is a general right to recover money paid under a mistake, whether of fact or law, subject to the defences available in the law of restitution.

   The plaintiff in *Nurdin & Peacock plc* v *D B Ramsden & Co Ltd* [1999] 1 All ER 941 was allowed to recover all the overpayments made under a mistake of law and/or fact. The Chancery Court stated that all that needs to be proven by the claimant is that, but for the mistaken belief, it would not have made the payments and that the mistake was directly relevant to the payments.

   There is some indication that this may be true where money has been paid under compulsion, but the broadest sense of this dictum has not been followed.

5. Where the payee can show that the payer is estopped he has to show three things:

   a) that the payer was either under a duty to give accurate information, which he failed to do or gave inaccurate information, or that the payer made a clear misrepresentation;

   b) that the inaccurate information led him to believe that the money could be treated as his own;

   c) that he has, as a result, changed his position, so that it would be inequitable for the payer to be able to recover the money.

Failure of consideration

Most of the cases are concerned with contracts where consideration is provided on one side, but not furnished on the other. For example, where a party 'sells' a car to which the seller has no title, to a purchaser, no title can pass. There is, accordingly, a total failure of consideration for the price of the car. This will still be a total failure of consideration even though the 'purchaser' has had the use of the car.

In *Butterworth* v *Kingsway Motors* [1954] 1 WLR 1286, a 'purchaser' had a car for nearly a year, during which time it had depreciated in value nearly £500.

He was, nevertheless, entitled to recover the full purchase price on a total failure of consideration. See also *Rowland* v *Divall* [1923] 2 KB 500 (below) and *Karflex* v *Poole* [1933] 2 KB 251.

There must, however, be a total failure of consideration. A partial failure is not sufficient. So, where goods are merely defective or an insufficient quantity is supplied, there will only be a partial failure of consideration and the action for money had and received will fail.

In line with this reasoning, the Privy Council in *Murray Stanley Goss* v *Laurence George Chilcott* [1996] 3 WLR 180 held that where the plaintiff can successfully establish failure of consideration, then he would be entitled to restitution.

Returnable and non-returnable benefits

1. If the plaintiff has received only a partial or a defective performance, then he may be entitled to rescind the contract. If, in these circumstances, he is able to return to the defendant what he has received under the contract, then this will work a total failure of consideration and allow the plaintiff to recover any money he has paid. See *Baldry* v *Marshall* [1925] 1 KB 260.
2. The requirement that the plaintiff must restore what he has received in this case is inapplicable where the defect in the goods is an inability to restore them, for example, where the defendant had not title to them, and the true owner took them off the plaintiff.
3. If the plaintiff has used the subject matter of the contract so as to derive a benefit from it, then there is no failure of consideration and he cannot use this method. In *Hunt* v *Silk* (1804) 5 East 449, an agreement for a lease provided that the plaintiff was to get immediate possession. The defendant, the landlord, was to do certain repairs, and the lease was to be executed in 10 days with £10 payable by the plaintiff on execution. The plaintiff took possession and paid the £10 in advance, but the defendant failed to repair. The plaintiff as a result, vacated the premises.

    The plaintiff could not claim his £10 on total failure of consideration. He had received benefits under the contract already.

Benefits different in kind

1. If the plaintiff receives a benefit different in kind to that he bargained for, then he will not be held to have received consideration, but rather a total failure of consideration is presumed and he is entitled to have his money back.

   In *Rowland* v *Divall* [1923] 2 KB 500, the plaintiff, a car dealer, bought a car from the defendant for £334, repainted it and resold it for £400. The car was, in fact, stolen, which was unknown to any of the parties and the police seized it. The plaintiff repaid his customer £400 and sued the defendant for £334. The insurance company which took the car sold it to the plaintiff for £260, and the defendant, relying on this, paid £260 into court on the basis this was the limit of his liability.

   The plaintiff could recover the £334 as there had been a total failure of consideration. He did not get what he paid for, viz a car with good title, and as the plaintiff was a dealer, he bought with a view to resale and title was essential to him.

2. The principle in *Rowland* v *Divall* has, however, also been applied in cases where the car was bought for private use.

   In *Butterworth* v *Kingsway Motors* (above), the plaintiff bought a car off the defendant for £1,275 and used it for almost a year. It, in fact, belonged to a finance company under a hire-purchase agreement, and they claimed its return. The plaintiff immediately claimed his £1,275, but 10 days after this the hire-purchase instalments were paid up, so that a good title could have been fed to the plaintiff.

   The question whether there was a total failure of consideration was determined at the time the plaintiff asked for his money back, and not later when the writ was issued. Thus the plaintiff was entitled to succeed, even though he had a year's use of the car for nothing.

3. Unlike *Rowland* v *Divall*, the purchaser in *Butterworth*'s case was purchasing a car for his own use; this he bargained for and obtained. It is hard to conclude that title was of paramount importance to him. The decision has been heavily criticised.

4. In both of the above cases, the unfairness of restitution is evident. The defendant had to return the purchase price in full and no set-off was allowed in respect of the plaintiff's use. In damages, the plaintiff would have brought such benefits into account, but it appears restitution is often a bounty for the plaintiff.

Restitution and damages

Because it is often difficult to quantify the plaintiff's precise loss, it has become common in contracts for the sale of goods to use the price paid as the figure at which damages are assessed for the sake of convenience.

In *Harling* v *Eddy* [1951] 2 KB 739, the defendant sold a cow which was warranted healthy but was, in fact, diseased, and later died. The plaintiff recovered the price paid as one of the items of damages for breach of warranty.

Void contracts

If the plaintiff pays money under a void contract, then this can be recovered by him, but not if it is merely illegal. A series of cases concerning interest rate swap agreements have appeared before the courts over the past few years since late 1989.

In *Kleinwort Benson Ltd v Birmingham City Council* [1996] 4 All ER 733 the Court of Appeal affirmed the fact that a claim in restitution rests upon the plaintiff proving that the defendant had been unjustly enriched at the plaintiffs expense.

In another case concerning the same plaintiffs, *Kleinwort Benson Ltd v Glasgow City Council* [1996] 2 All ER 257, the Court of Appeal addressed the issue of jurisdiction stating that so long as the matter fell within the convention of the Civil Jurisdiction and Judgments Act 1982, the English courts would have jurisdiction. The House of Lords in *Westdeutsche Landesbank Girozentrale v Islington London Borough Council* [1996] 2 All ER 961 (also a case involving interest swap agreements) held that the court had no power to award compound interest in such cases in the absence of an express or implied agreement or custom. At best, simple interest under s35A Supreme Court Act 1981 could be awarded.

Other cases which essentially share common features with the cases mentioned above are; *Barclays Bank plc v Glasgow City Council* [1994] 4 All ER 865, *Kleinwort Benson plc v Sandwell Borough Council* [1994] 4 All ER 890, *Kleinwort Benson Ltd v South Tyneside Metropolitan Borough Council* [1994] 4 All ER 972 and *Morgan Grenfell and Co Ltd v Welwyn Hatfield District Council (Islington London Borough Council, Third Party)* [1995] 1 All ER 1.

They establish that interest rate swap agreements are ultra vires the powers of a local authority to contract and are consequently void ab initio. They are *not* betting or wagering contracts. Where money has been paid by a bank or finance house to a local authority the mere fact that the contract is null and void will not preclude the courts granting restitution in quasi-contract.

Money paid under compulsion

The categories under which restitution may be ordered are broader than those for which rescission of contract is available, and cover, for example, money paid as a result of wrongful demands which are not accompanied by threats of violence.

18.3 Action for money paid

This action lies for money paid by the plaintiff to a third party for the defendant's benefit. Originally, the payment had to be at the defendant's request, but the law was later prepared to imply such a request in certain circumstances. The action is usually available in the following situations.

Compulsory discharge of another's liability

> 'Where the plaintiff has been compelled by the law to pay, or being compellable by law, has paid, money which the defendant was ultimately liable to pay, so that the latter obtains the benefit of the payment by the discharge of his liability; under such circumstances the defendant is held indebted to the plaintiff in the amount' (per Cockburn CJ in *Moule* v *Garrett* (1872) LR 7 Ex 101).

Recovery is subject to three main conditions.

1. The plaintiff's payment must have been compulsory in the sense that he must be under an immediate or ultimate obligation to make the payment. See *Exall* v *Partridge* (1799) 8 TR 308 and *Brook's Wharf & Bull Wharf* v *Goodman Bros* [1937] 1 KB 534.
2. The plaintiff must not have officiously exposed himself to the liability in making the payment. See *England* v *Marsden* (1886) LR 1 CP 529 and *Owen* v *Tate* [1975] 2 All ER 129.
3. The plaintiff's payment must have discharged a liability of the defendant. See *Receiver for Metropolitan Police District* v *Croydon Corporation* [1957] 2 QB 154.

Necessitous intervention

Roman law allowed a quasi-contractual action to a person who intervened to protect another's property in an emergency: English law, however, has traditionally refused such an action. See *Falcke* v *Scottish Imperial Insurance Co* (1886) 34 Ch D 234. Certain exceptions can be found, for example, agency of necessity, and a general principle may be emerging: *Sims* v *Midland Ry* [1913] 1 KB 103, *Poland* v *John Parr* [1917] 1 KB 236 per Scrutton LJ, *Re Rhodes* (1890) 44 Ch D 94 and *Owen* v *Tate* (above) per Scarman LJ.

18.4 Liability to account

A liability to account may arise:

1. where the defendant is under an obligation to pay money or property to the plaintiff which has been received from a third party; or
2. where the plaintiff is entitled to be subrogated to (placed in the shoes of) another against a third party.

Defendant acknowledging that he will pay the plaintiff at the request of the third party whose funds he holds

The nature of the legal obligation is explained in *Griffin* v *Weatherby* (1868) LR 3 QB 753 by Blackburn LJ:

> 'Even since the case of *Walker* v *Rostron* it has been considered as settled law that where a person transfers to a creditor on account of a debt, whether due or not, a fund actually existing or accruing in the hands of a third person, and notifies the transfer to the holder of the fund, although there is no legal obligation on the holder to pay the amount of the debt to the transferee, yet the holder of the fund may, and if he does promise to pay to the transferee, then that which was merely an equitable right becomes a legal right where indicated in the transferee, founded on the promise; and the money becomes a fund received or to be received for and payable to the transferee, and when it has been received an action for money had and received to the use of the transferee lies at his suit against the holder.'

This principle was applied and extended in *Shamia* v *Joory* [1958] 1 QB 448. The defendant owed more than £1,300 to Y. Y requested the defendant to pay £500 to Y's brother. The plaintiff later received a cheque for £500. The cheque was not met. The defendant failed to write another, although he promised to do so. It was held that the plaintiff could recover under the principle in *Griffin* v *Weatherby*; the defendant had in his hands 'a fund' from which the money could be paid, because he had a monetary liability to another.

Stakeholders

A stakeholder is an agent who holds money on instructions to make payment of the money lodged when instructed to do so. If he makes payment before he is instructed to do so, he will be liable to his principal.

Agent or employee receiving a secret bribe or profit

The principal or employer is entitled to claim any secret bribe or commission which is received by his agent or employee. Evidence of a corrupt motive on the part of the agent or employee is not necessary. Also, where a person wrongfully usurps an office belonging to the plaintiff, the plaintiff is entitled to all the fees and profits obtained by the usurper.

Constructive trusts

The law on constructive trusts is sometimes said to be an equitable restitutionary remedy.

Subrogation

Subrogation is the stepping 'into the shoes of' another, that is, assuming the legal rights and liabilities by displacement of that other. It is a restitutionary remedy which arises principally in contracts of insurance so as to allow an insurer who pays a claim under a policy of indemnity to enforce the rights of the insured person arising out of that loss against any third party. The right to be subrogated may also lie under contracts of guarantee; in an indorser of a Bill of Exchange; under a loan to an infant for necessaries in respect of sums so spent; or under an irrecoverable loan (see, eg, *Crantrave Ltd* v *Lloyds Bank plc* [2000] 4 All ER 473 (bank not entitled to debit customer's account amount mistakenly paid on its behalf)).

18.5 Quantum meruit

Where a contract is terminated by breach

In *Planché* v *Colburn* (1831) 8 Bing 14, the plaintiff contracted with the defendants to write a volume for publication in 'The Juvenile Library'. After he had started, the defendants withdrew the series.

The plaintiff was held to be able to recover reasonable remuneration for work already done.

When a contract is void

In *Craven-Ellis* v *Canons Ltd* [1936] 2 KB 403, the plaintiff was entitled to recover quantum meruit even though he had been appointed managing director under a void contract. Greer LJ said that the obligation to pay was imposed by a rule of law and not by contract. It is, therefore, restitutionary in nature.

Quantum meruit to fix a price or remuneration

It has already been seen that quantum meruit is implied where the parties fail to fix a contract price or remuneration. See *Foley* v *Classique Coaches* [1934] 2 KB 1.

19

Agency

19.1 Introduction

An agent is a person appointed by a principal to bring the principal into a contractual relationship with third parties. The agent is merely the instrument used in forming the contract; he is not a party to it and need not have contractual capacity. The principal becomes a party to the contract and must have contractual capacity.

The agent may be one of the following.

1. A universal agent: appointed to act for the principal with no limitation on powers.
2. A general agent: appointed to act in transactions of a class – a banker, a solicitor
3. A special agent: appointed for one particular purpose.

Note that the agency relationship may bear some resemblance to other types of relationship. In *Comet Group plc* v *British Sky Broadcasting* [1991] TLR 211 it was held that a promotion contract was not the same as the agency relationship. A contract between British Satellite Broadcasting and Comet, whereby Comet would promote BSB's equipment, operated until BSB's merger with Sky Television in 1990. At that point BSB instructed Comet to suspend all further sales of BSB equipment. The contract made provision expressly for the period until February 1991. The action taken by BSB in November 1990 represented a considerable

375

financial loss to Comet. BSB attempted to argue that the promotion contract was a form of agency and cited cases such as *Rhodes* v *Forwood* (1876) 1 App Cas 256 and *Hamlyn* v *Wood* [1891] 2 QB 488, all of which had in common that the court had declined to imply into the contract a term that the principal would continue in business until the expiry of the term agreed. Comet argued that the contract was not one of agency and that BSB's conduct amounted to a repudiation of the contract giving rise to an action for damages.

The court agreed with the latter argument, holding that the contract differed from agency in a number of respects, most notably in that Comet were required to purchase at the outset £13m of equipment.

It should be noted that the Commercial Agents (Council Directive) Regulations 1993 (SI 93/3053) and Commercial Agents (Council Directive) (Amendment) Regulations 1993 (SI 93/3173) came into operation as of January 1994. These Regulations are now in force.

The Regulations represent considerable changes in English agency law. They cover only 'commercial agency' agreements and are part of an attempt by the EU to coordinate the laws of all Member States, prior to the inception of the Single Market.

Prior to these Regulations, there was little statutory law in England governing agency contracts; by and large the parties themselves negotiated terms, and if for any reason the agency contract failed to cover the situation, then common law rules would be used to imply additional terms.

The new Regulations cover all new agreements, and those subsisting as of January 1994. They cover most contingencies from appointment to duties of principal and agent, remuneration and termination. Many Regulations are mandatory and cannot be avoided or excluded. Certain new rights are introduced (for example, under regs 16 and 17, an agent may have a right to compensation on termination of agency). Often Regulations merely give statutory form to long-established common law rules.

The term 'commercial agent' is exhaustively defined, both specifically (a 'self-employed intermediary, who has continuing authority to negotiate the sale and/or purchase of goods on behalf of another person ... or to negotiate and conclude the sale and/or purchase of goods on behalf of and in the name of the principal') and by means of negative provisions excluding certain categories of person from the definition. Nonetheless, there is a certain degree of ambiguity in the definition and it is thought that attempts may be made to circumvent the rules (by, for example, appointing an agent for a series of one-off transactions to defeat the 'continuing authority' requirement in the definition). Certainly the rules as a whole are not clearly drafted and it seems likely that as cases begin to arrive on the doorsteps of the courts for interpretation, further amending regulations will prove necessary.

19.2 Appointment of an agent

The agent is usually appointed by a contract between himself and his principal; here the agent must have contractual capacity if this contract is to be enforceable between principal and agent. The appointment may be made in the following ways.

Express

Generally, this may be in any form, but if the agent is to be authorised to contract under seal, his appointment must be by a deed which is called a 'power of attorney'.

Implied

This form of authority usually arises out of an express appointment and covers: acts necessary for the performance of the express agency; and acts in the ordinary course of the agent's business. See *Ryan v Pilkington* [1959] 1 WLR 403. The owners of a hotel instructed an estate agent to find a purchaser for a private hotel. He accepted a deposit from a prospective purchaser 'as agent' of the owners. It was held that the estate agent acted within the ostensible scope of his authority, although he was not expressly authorised to accept deposits.

Note the special example of the wife who, during cohabitation, is presumed to have her husband's authority to pledge his credit for necessaries suitable to their system of living, unless the husband instructed the trader not to supply goods on credit to his wife; or the husband forbade his wife to pledge his credit; or the wife had an adequate allowance to cover the purchase of necessaries. See *Miss Gray Ltd v Cathcart* (1922) 38 TLR 562. A trader sued a husband for £215 being the price of clothing supplied to his wife.

The husband was held not liable since he gave his wife an allowance of £960 a year. The household was sufficiently supplied with the goods in question.

In *W A Ellis Services Ltd v Wood* (1993) 31 EG 78 it was made clear that in the absence of strong evidence as to the existence of a trade custom or usage no term will be implied by the courts. Thus, in this case, the agents' contention that right to payment out of the proceeds of the sale of property was a 'customary term' was dismissed; the courts would not imply it.

Ratification

A form of retrospective appointment by way of adoption or confirmation; if at the time of the transaction the agent has no authority, either because he is not an agent or is an agent but is exceeding his authority, the principal may subsequently adopt the contract, and the agent is then treated as having been authorised to enter into it from the very beginning, for example, *Bolton Partners v Lambert* (1889) 41 Ch D 295.

Ratification is only possible in these situations.

1. The agent is contracted as an agent for a named principal. See *Keighley, Maxsted & Co v Durant* [1901] AC 240. R was authorised by K & Co to buy wheat at an agreed price from D. R exceeded his authority and purchased at a higher price in his own name, but intending to buy for K & Co. Later, K & Co agreed to buy the wheat at the higher price, but then refused to take delivery.

   K & Co were held not liable to D since R's contract had not been ratified by K & Co. Where a person contracts on his own behalf, with an undisclosed intention to benefit another, that other person cannot ratify the contract so as to make himself liable on it.

2. The principal had contractual capacity when the contract was made and also at the time of ratification. See *Kelner v Baxter* (1866) LR 2 CP 174. A company was in the process of being formed to buy a hotel. A contract was made 'on behalf' of the company, by three promoters of the scheme, to buy wine for £900 from K. The company was eventually formed, the wine was consumed, but the company went into liquidation before payment for the wine.

   The promoters were held personally liable on the contract, not the company. A principal did not exist at the time of contracting, consequently, the contract was inoperative unless binding on the promoters who signed it.

3. Ratification is of the whole contract.
4. Ratification takes place within a reasonable time.
5. The principal has full knowledge of all material terms or intends to ratify whatever those terms may be.

By operation of law ('agency of necessity')

This arises without any agreement where the agent is compelled by some emergency to act on behalf of the principal. It usually arises when the agent is in possession of property of the principal, and has to act to preserve that property, for example, *GNR v Swaffield* (1874) LR 9 Exch 132. S sent a horse by train. It arrived at its destination without anyone meeting it. The station master put the horse in a livery stable and claimed reimbursement of charges from S.

S was held liable to pay. Being unaware of S's identity or his address, the station master was obliged to make suitable arrangements for the horse.

The agent can only act when it is impossible to obtain instructions from the principal; compare *Springer v Great Western Rail Co* [1921] 1 KB 257. The railway company agreed to carry tomatoes from Jersey to London for S. The ship arrived late in Weymouth and the railway employees were on strike. The tomatoes were sold since the railway company feared that they would not be in saleable condition on eventual arrival in London.

There must be an actual and definite commercial necessity for the creation of the contract. See *Prager v Blatspiel, Stamp & Heacock Ltd* [1924] 1 KB 566. P, a fur dealer in Bucharest, asked B Ltd, London dealers, to buy and deliver skins worth £19,000. P paid the purchase price, but delivery was prevented by the First World War. B Ltd sold the skins.

B Ltd were held to be liable for conversion. The skins were not likely to deteriorate if properly stored, consequently, there was no necessity for the sale.

Note that, because of improved communications, agency of necessity is rare nowadays. The whole question of agency of necessity needs review as a matter of some urgency, in the light of modern conditions.

The case of *The Choko Star* [1990] 1 Lloyd's Rep 516 raised the question as to whether the master of a ship had authority to sign a Lloyd's Open Form for cargo (as opposed to salvage of the ship itself). In the initial hearing, the court held that there was implied (and hence apparent) authority to do so stemming from the authority vested in the mastership from the owners and/or shippers.

On appeal, the Court of Appeal held that there was no such implied authority and only the ancient rules as to agency of necessity might apply. The doctrine of agency of necessity confers, usually on shipmasters, certain authority by operation of law given certain conditions relating to emergency. Of those conditions, the requirement that consultation between ship's master and owners/shippers should not be possible gives most difficulty in these days of virtually instantaneous communications.

The Court of Appeal reached the decision that the doctrine of agency of necessity would apply here, given certain circumstances.

By estoppel ('holding out')

This is not really an appointment at all; it involves a representation made by the principal to a third party by which the third party is led to believe that the principal has appointed 'A' as his agent; if the third party acts on that belief, the principal is estopped from denying the fact of agency.

In *Spiro v Lintern* [1973] 1 WLR 1002, L's wife arranged for estate agents to sell his house. She entered into a written contract with S to sell it to him. The wife lacked authority to make such a contract. L led S to believe that he was to be the purchaser by allowing S to buy L's furniture and instruct an architect to carry out repairs. The wife eventually sold the house for a higher price by exercising L's power of attorney recently executed by him in her favour. It was stated that S was entitled to specific performance of the contract of sale and possession from the present occupier. L had represented by his conduct that his wife had proper authority to act as she did towards S. The representations were so precise and unequivocal as to amount to an estoppel.

19.3 Authority of an agent

Actual authority

The principal is bound by any act which he has expressly or impliedly authorised the agent to do on his behalf. Although the normal measure of damages for breach of a warranty of authority is the difference between the contract price and the market price, that measure is not appropriate where the claimant's failure to recoup his loss in the market is a consequence of the defendant's breach of warranty: *Habton Farms* v *Nimmo* (2003) The Times 7 February. In that case the Court of Appeal held that the seller of a racehorse, which had died in the seller's hands after the conclusion of a contract of sale containing a warranty that the buyer was acting for a principal, was entitled to the full contract price.

Ostensible (or apparent) authority

This includes the implied powers of a general agent to bind the principal by any act in the ordinary course of the agent's business (even though this has been expressly prohibited by the principal – unless the third party knows this – see *Watteau* v *Fenwick*) and authority conferred by the principal holding out 'A' as his agent to the third party, although the agent has not been appointed as such. The third party usually has to rely on the agent's ostensible authority, as he is not normally in a position to know the actual terms of the appointment.

In *Watteau* v *Fenwick* [1893] 1 QB 346, H was the owner of an hotel and later the manager for its new owner. H was forbidden to buy cigars on credit. W supplied cigars on credit at H's request believing him still to be owner of the hotel.

H was held to be acting within the scope of his usual authority as manager. F was liable to pay W for the cigars. F could not, as against W, set up any secret limitation of H's usual authority.

19.4 Relationship of principal and agent

Duties of agent to principal

These are to carry out the terms of the agency, including the following.

1. The exercise of reasonable care and skill; probably a higher standard of care is imposed upon a paid agent that upon a gratuitous agent.
2. Disclosure of any relevant information to the principal. In *Keppell* v *Wheeler* [1927] 1 KB 577, K employed W to sell a house. W failed to inform K of a higher offer that was made after K had provisionally agreed to sell to another 'subject to contract'. W was liable to pay K the difference between the sale price and the higher price not communicated. *PCW Syndicates* v *PCW Reinsurers*

[1996] 1 WLR 1136 makes it clear, however, that it would be unrealistic to expect an agent to disclose his fraud to his principal.

Unlike ordinary agency, estate agents, who by their very nature act for numerous principals, several of whom might be competing and whose interests would conflict, do not have such an extensive fiduciary duty. Failure to inform the plaintiff of what might seem important material information was not a breach of the estate agent's fiduciary duty.

In *Kelly v Cooper* [1992] 3 WLR 936, the plaintiff instructed the defendant, an estate agent, to sell his house and the terms were a percentage of the selling price as commission. The estate agent had also been approached by the owner of an adjoining property to sell his house for him. The agent showed both properties to a prospective purchaser who purchased the adjoining house immediately. The agent did not inform the plaintiff of this and when approached sold at the first asking price. Had he been alerted by the agent to the fact that the purchaser had already bought the property next door and wanted to link the two properties he could probably have got far more. He refused to pay the agent's commission. The Privy Council held that the agent had acted properly in the circumstances and his commission could not be withheld.

See also the case of *McCullagh v Lane, Fox & Partners Ltd* [1996] 1 EGLR 35, in which the Court of Appeal held that an estate agent owed no duty of care toward a purchaser in respect of negligent misstatement. Moreover, under the provisions of the Unfair Contract Terms Act 1977, estate agents can rely on disclaimers.

3. Disclosure of any personal interest in the contract to the principal. In *Armstrong v Jackson* [1917] 2 KB 822, A employed J, a stockbroker, to buy some shares for him. J sold some of his own shares to A and sent A a false contract note suggesting a purchase on the open market from a third party.

   The court declared that J had failed to carry out his proper duties as agent, consequently, A could rescind the contract of sale.

4. Not to disclose confidential information to third parties.

5. Not to delegate his authority unless this is authorised, customary or necessary. Note that if a valid delegation is effected, the agent still remains personally liable to the principal for proper performance of the contract.

6. To account for all money and other property received for the principal, and to keep proper accounts of all transactions.

7. Not to make any secret profit out of the agency, not to take a bribe from the third party; if he does, the principal may:

   a) recover the profit from the agent;
   b) refuse to pay commission or other remuneration;
   c) dismiss the agent without notice;
   d repudiate the contract out of which the profit arose. In *Shipway v Broadwood* [1899] 1 QB 369, B agreed to buy a pair of horses from S provided X, a

veterinary surgeon, examined them and found no faults. X was bribed by S to give a certificate of soundness. After purchase, B discovered that the horses were not sound. He returned them and stopped payment of a cheque given to S.

B was not liable on the cheque. He could rescind the contract because of S's bribery. It was unnecessary to determine whether X had been biased as a result of receiving the bribe;

e) sue the agent or the third party for damages for any loss suffered; the damages are awarded without deduction of the amount of the secret payment recovered by the principal. In *Salford Corporation* v *Lever* [1891] 1 QB 168, L, a coal merchant who supplied coal to the S Corporation from time to time, was induced by H, the corporation's gas manager, to charge 1s. a ton extra and hand over the money secured to H personally, otherwise supplies would be taken from elsewhere. The corporation recovered this bribe, which amounted to £2,329, from H, and now sued to recover the same amount from L as the excess over and above the proper price that should have been charged.

L was found guilty of fraud which was separate and distinct from H's fraud. Both L and H were separately liable to pay the corporation money secured by their individual frauds;

f) prosecute the agent or the third party or both under Prevention of Corruption Act 1906.

See, for example, *AMF* v *Hashim* [1993] 1 Lloyd's Rep 543 on the rights of a principal in cases of bribery.

Rights of agent against principal

1. To be remunerated for his services, if expressly or impliedly agreed by the principal.
2. To be indemnified by the principal for any expenses properly incurred. In *Christophorides* v *Terry* [1924] AC 566, C employed T to buy cotton. C failed to settle his account, so T sold the cotton at a loss of over £6,000. T had to pay the sellers of the cotton out of his own pocket.

   It was held that C must indemnify T for losses suffered by acting on C's behalf lawfully and in execution of his authority.

   In *Davison* v *Fernandes* (1889) 6 TLR 73, F told his stockbroker D to sell some shares believing the price quoted to him by D to be Ex Div, that is, F could keep dividend recently paid by the company. In fact, the price quoted was Cum Div, that is, D had to hand over a sum equal to the dividend to the purchaser.
3. To a lien on any goods of the principal in his possession for the amount due to him from the principal.
4. To stop goods in transit to the principal if he is personally liable for the price.

19.5 Principal and agent and third parties

Contracts for disclosed principal

If an agent indicates to a third party that he is contracting only as the agent, whether he names his principal or not, the contract is between the principal and the third party, and the agent will not normally be liable on it.

The agent may be liable, however:

1. if he expressly or impliedly assumes personal liability;
2. if he signs a written contract in his own name;
3. by trade usage or custom;
4. on a bill of exchange, under s26 Bills of Exchange Act 1882 or s108 Cheques Act 1948;
5. if he is actually contracting on his own behalf;
6. if he executes a deed in his own name, unless he is acting under a power of attorney for a named principal;
7. if acting as a receiver for debenture holders, s369 Cheques Act 1948;
8. if, acting for an unnamed principal, he refuses to identify the principal.

For example, see *Foalquest Ltd* v *Roberts* [1990] 21 EG 156. A financial consultant claimed various items of remuneration for services rendered. Whether he was so entitled depended on the true liability of the agent acting for the company with which he had dealt. The agent claimed to have acted throughout as agent for a disclosed principal and never to have assumed or accepted personal liability.

The court had looked to the objective intention of both parties, examining the form and terms of the contract and the surrounding circumstances. The Court of Appeal felt that in this case there was no reason to overturn the initial assessment of the position. There was no evidence to indicate that the agent purported to bind himself personally.

To a large extent the agent's personal liability (or lack) of it is a matter of determining the parties' intentions. In *Badgerhill Properties* v *Cottrell* [1991] BCLC 805, in making contracts for work with the defendant, X, the director of the plaintiff company, drew up contracts on headed notepaper bearing the company name. Against his own name on this paper X had written 'director' in brackets. The company sued the defendant for non-payment for work done, while the defendants counter-claimed that the work was defective. The question arose as to whether X was personally liable, whether he had been acting on his own behalf or that of the principal company.

The Court of Appeal held that whether X was acting on his own behalf depended to some degree on the intention of the parties. The language of the contract, the fact that the company name appeared on the headed paper, the fact that the company's trading name appeared in the contract all seemed to indicate that the defendant was trading with whoever called themselves by the trade name of the company. The fact that the word agent did not appear was not enough to prevent the contract's being construed as a contract of agency.

Contracts for undisclosed principal

Here the fact of agency is concealed altogether. The third party has an option: he can sue the agent on the contract or he can sue the principal when he discovers his existence; but he must make an election and is bound by it: he cannot sue one and then, having obtained judgment, sue the other, for example, *Clarkson, Booker Ltd* v *Andjel* [1964] 2 QB 775. Andjel booked airline tickets through C Ltd, a firm of travel agents. Later, P & M Ltd claimed that the booking was made on their behalf, so C Ltd asked them for payment. Further correspondence indicated that C Ltd regarded both Andjel and P & M Ltd as being liable. After issuing a writ against P & M Ltd, the company became insolvent. Proceedings were then commenced against Andjel. It was held that C Ltd had not unequivocally elected to sue only P & M Ltd with full knowledge of all the relevant facts. They had not lost their right to sue Andjel as agent. In *Boyter* v *Thomson* [1995] 3 WLR 36 it was held by the House of Lords that in a case where the fact of agency is not disclosed, the third party may, when he discovers the existence of the principal, sue that principal for breaches of s14 Sale of Goods Act 1979 (as amended).

The principal can enforce the contract against the third party unless:

1. the agent had no authority at the time of contracting;
2. the agent's identity was material to the contract;
3. the principal allowed the agent to contract on terms incompatible with agency, for example, as 'owner'. The third party can set up against the principal any defences he had against the agent before he discovered the existence of the principal.

Unauthorised acts of agent

Two situations may arise.

1. If the agent, although not in fact authorised, acts within his ostensible authority, the principal is liable on the contract. The agent is not (but he may be liable to the principal for breach of duty).
2. If the act is outside the agent's actual and ostensible authority, the principal is not liable, but the agent is liable to the third party for breach of warranty of authority, even though the agent acted in good faith, believing he had authority, for example, *Yonge* v *Toynbee* [1910] 1 KB 215. T instructed the solicitors (W) to defend an action for libel against him brought by Y. T went insane before commencement of the action, thereby revoking the solicitors' authority to act. W being unaware of this event delivered a defence to the action. Y asked for the claim to be struck out and costs against W because W acted without authority.

Since W had impliedly warranted that they had authority to act when this was not so, thus they were personally liable for Y's costs.

Note: insanity of a principal revokes the agent's authority, but that principal is liable on a contract made with a third party who had no notice of the insanity. See *Drew* v *Nunn* (1879) 4 QBD 661.

19.6 Termination of agency

By act of parties

The termination of agency by act of parties may arise where:

1. the transaction is completed;
2. there is mutual agreement between the agent and the principal;
3. the agent renounces his appointment;
4. the principal revokes the appointment, except in those cases where the agent's authority is irrevocable, as where the agent's authority is 'coupled with an interest', such as a debt due from the principal to the agent, the authority being given as security, or where a power of attorney is expressed to be irrevocable and is given to secure a proprietary interest of the agent or the performance of an obligation owed to the agent; the power cannot be revoked without the agent's consent so long as the agent has that interest or is owed that obligation. Section 4 Powers of Attorney Act 1971.

By operation of law

The termination of agency by operation of law may arise in these cases.

1. The principal dies, or becomes bankrupt or insane (in case of insanity, notice of termination must be given to the third party).

   In *Drew* v *Nunn* (above), N permitted his wife to buy boots and shoes from D over a period of time. N went insane in 1873 but recovered by 1877. During this period, D supplied goods to N's wife on credit, unaware of D's condition.

   N's insanity had not revoked his wife's authority to purchase from D, thus N was liable to pay for them.
2. Supervening illegality or frustration, for example, by destruction of subject matter; death or insanity of the agent.

   In *Stevenson & Sons* v *Cartonnagen Industrie* [1918] AC 239, an English company, contracted with a Germany company, C, to be their sole agents in Britain and their partners here for the manufacture of certain goods.

   The contract of agency had been terminated by the outbreak of war between the two countries in 1914. The partnership between the two companies was dissolved.
3. By lapse of time without agency being performed.

Effects of termination

Yasuda Fire & Marine Insurance Co of Europe Ltd v *Orion Marine Insurance Underwriting Agency Ltd and Another* [1995] 2 WLR 49 makes it clear that even where an agency contract has been terminated, for whatever reason, the rights and duties of the parties may extend beyond the termination of the relationship. Regardless of whether the agency relationship is set up by contract, provided any contract does not expressly exclude such consequences, there may be circumstances which necessitate principal and agent continuing to deal together. In *Yasuda*, for example, even though the agency contract had ended, it was a matter of practical necessity that the principal retained the means of consulting files and records held on computerised databases by the agent underwriters. Although the agent retained property of the databases, the principal must be allowed to consult them, in order to ascertain what risks had been underwritten by the agent, otherwise the principals could not continue to function in business.

It is noteworthy that where the termination results in one party suffering a loss, then the courts will not hesitate to compensate that party for the loss, provided that the loss accrues as a direct result of the termination of the contract. This was illustrated in *Page* v *Combined Shipping and Trading Co Ltd* [1997] 3 All ER 656.

19.7 Factors

A factor is defined as a mercantile agent having in the customary course of his business as such agent, authority either to sell goods, or to consign goods for the purpose of sale, or to buy goods or to raise money on the security of goods (s1 Factors Act 1889). This definition should be known and also the circumstances in which, under s2 of that Act, a factor can pass a good title in goods although not authorised to do so by the owner.

Definition of factor

Lord Denning said in *Rolls Razor Ltd* v *Cox* [1967] 1 QB 552, that a factor is:

> 'an agent:
> (i) entrusted with the *possession* of goods of several principals, or sometimes only one principal,
> (ii) for the purpose of sale *in his own name* without disclosing the name of his principal, and
> (iii) he is remunerated by a commission.'

It is the first two of these characteristics that distinguish factors from *brokers*. Moreover, since a factor has possession of his principal's goods, he has a lien on them for the balance of his account with the principal; the broker has no such lien.

Transfer of title by factor

A person claiming a title to goods under s2 must show:

1. that the owner of the goods consented to the factor having possession as such;
2. that the factor was acting in the ordinary course of his business; and
3. that he (the buyer) acted in good faith in buying the goods without notice of any lack of authority on the part of the factor, for example, *Folkes* v *King* [1923] 1 KB 282.

H, a mercantile agent, was instructed by a car owner, F, to sell it for at least £575. He sold it to K for £340 and misappropriated the money.

F was not entitled to recover the car from K. H had possession of the car in order to sell it with F's permission, and K acquired a good title by purchasing it in good faith and without notice of any fraud.

20

Sale of Goods, Consumer Credit and Supply of Goods and Services

20.22 Distance selling

20.23 Consumer guarantees

20.1 Sale of goods: definitions

'Contract of sale of goods' – a contract whereby the seller transfers, or agrees to transfer, the property in goods to the buyer, for a money consideration called the price: s2(1) Sale of Goods Act (SGA) 1979. All section references in this part of the book are to sections of this Act unless otherwise stated. 'Contract of sale' includes an agreement to sell as well as a sale: s61(1).

'Sale' – includes a bargain and sale as well as a sale and delivery: s61(1).

'Agreement to sell' – a contract of sale under which the transfer of the property is to take place at a future time or subject to a condition: s2(5).

'Property' – means the general property in goods, and not merely a special property: s61(1).

Other definitions to be found in s61(1), as amended, include:

'Bulk' means a mass or collection of goods of the same kind which –

1. is contained in a defined space or area; and
2. is such that any goods in the bulk are interchangeable with any other goods therein of the same number or quantity.

'Business' includes a profession and the activities of any government department or local and public authority.

'Buyer' means a person who buys or agrees to buy goods.

'Consumer contract' has the same meaning as in s25(1) of the Unfair Contract Terms Act 1977 and the onus of proving that a contract is not to be regarded as a consumer contract lies on the seller.

'Contract of sale' includes an agreement to sell as well as a sale.

'Delivery' means voluntary transfer of possession from one person to another except that in relation to ss20A and 20B it includes such appropriation of goods to the contract as results in property in the goods being transferred to the buyer.

'Fault' means wrongful act or default.

'Future goods' means goods to be manufactured or acquired by the seller after the making of the contract of sale.

'Goods' includes all personal chattels other than things in action and money; and in particular 'goods' includes emblements, industrial growing crops, and things attached to or forming part of the land which are agreed to be severed before sale or under the contract of sale and includes an undivided share in goods.

'Sale' includes a bargain and sale as well as a sale and delivery.

'Seller' means a person who sells or agrees to sell goods.

'Specific goods' means goods identified and agreed on at the time a contract of sale is made and includes an undivided share, specified as a fraction or percentage, of goods identified and agreed on as aforesaid.

'Warranty' means an agreement with reference to goods which are the subject of a contract of sale, but collateral to the main purpose of such contract, the breach of which gives rise to a claim for damages, but not to a right to reject the goods and treat the contract as repudiated.

In *St Albans City and District Council* v *International Computers Ltd* [1996] 4 All ER 481, the Court of Appeal held that a computer disk could properly be defined as 'goods' and as such would incorporate all the implied terms under the Sale of Goods Act 1979 (as amended) as well as the Supply of Goods and Services Act 1982.

20.2 Formation of the contract

The general rules of contract apply (see, for example, s3 as to capacity). No particular form is required: s4.

20.3 Perishing of the goods

In the case of a contract for the sale of *specific* goods:

1. if, without the knowledge of the seller, the goods have perished *at the time the contract is made*, the contract is void; s6;
2. if, without the fault of either party, the goods *subsequently* perish, the contract is void if the risk has not yet passed to the buyer; s7; if the risk has passed, the buyer bears the loss.

The risk passes with the property, except where otherwise agreed; or where delivery has been delayed through the fault of either party, in which case, the goods are at the risk of the party at fault in respect of any loss that might not have occurred but for such fault: s20. In *Sterns* v *Vickers* [1923] 1 KB 78, 120,000 gallons of spirit out of 200,000 in a tank was sold. A delivery warrant for the 120,000 gallons was given to the buyer who failed to act upon it, consequently the spirit deteriorated. The risk was held to lie with the buyer as the deterioration was his fault in that he had not collected the spirit as he should have done.

By virtue of the Sale and Supply of Goods to Consumers Regulations 2002, where the buyer deals as consumer the goods remain at the seller's risk until they are delivered to the consumer.

Goods have 'perished' if, through damage or deterioration, they have ceased to answer to the contract description, for example, *Asfar & Co* v *Blundell*, or if the goods have been stolen; even a partial loss is enough if the sale was of an indivisible parcel of specific goods, for example, *Barrow, Lane and Ballard Ltd* v *Phillip Phillips & Co Ltd*.

In *Asfar & Co* v *Blundell* [1896] 1 QB 123, a load of dates was impregnated with sewage unknown to the parties at the time of sale. The goods, though still technically in existence, were held to be 'perished' goods.

In *Barrow, Lane & Ballard Ltd* v *Phillip Phillips & Co Ltd* [1929] 1 KB 574 at the time of a contract to sell 700 bags of Chinese nuts, some 109 of the bags had been stolen.

It was held that the entire consignment had perished since the 700 bags were for the purpose of the contract indivisible.

20.4 The price

The price must be paid wholly or partly in money; it may be fixed in the contract or in an agreed manner, for example, by a third party; s9, or by the course of dealing between the parties; otherwise the buyer must pay a reasonable price; s8.

20.5 Time of payment

Stipulations as to the time of payment are not of the essence, unless otherwise agreed; s10(1). Failure to pay by the agreed date, if any, does not therefore release the seller from his own obligations under the contract.

20.6 Implied terms

Conditions and warranties

In addition to the *express* terms of the contract, certain terms relating to the goods are *implied* in the contract of sale by the SGA 1979. These terms may be either conditions or warranties. A *condition* is a term which goes to the root of the contract, breach of which entitles the buyer to reject the goods and treat the contract as repudiated, in addition to claiming damages.

A *warranty* is a collateral term, the breach of which gives rise to an action for damages, but does not release the buyer from his own obligations.

Whether a term is a condition or a warranty depends upon the construction of the contract. The buyer may elect to treat a breach of condition as a breach of warranty only, and he must do so if the contract is not severable and he has accepted any part of the goods: s1(4).

The implied terms are as follows.

As to title: s12

An implied term that the seller has a right to sell, for example, *Rowland* v *Divall*, and implied terms of quiet possession and freedom from encumbrances.

In *Rowland* v *Divall* [1923] 2 KB 500 the plaintiff 'bought' a car from the defendant who, it transpired, was not the owner. The true owner recovered the car. The court held that the plaintiff could recover the price he had paid from the defendant.

As to sales by description: s13

An implied term that the goods supplied shall correspond with the description; this section is applied very strictly in favour of the buyer. See *Re Moore and Landauer & Co* [1921] 2 KB 519. Where the buyer has not seen the goods, but relies on the description, it will be a sale by description (even if the goods are specific goods, for example, *Varley* v *Whipp*); but it may be a sale by description even where the buyer has seen the goods, for example, *Beale* v *Taylor*; and if the sale is by sample as well as by description there is a further implied condition that the bulk corresponds both with the sample and with the description.

In *Re Moore and Landauer & Co* a consignment of canned fruit was ordered to be delivered in boxes of 30 tins. Some of the boxes supplied contained only 24 tins. Consequently it was held that the consignment did not conform to the description.

In *Varley* v *Whipp* [1900] 1 QB 513, a reaping machine was ordered by a buyer, the machine having been described by the seller as new the previous year. In fact, it was much older. It was held that the machine did not comply with the description.

In *Beale* v *Taylor* [1967] 1 WLR 1193, the subject matter of this contract was described as a 1961 Triumph Herald convertible. The plaintiff saw the car and bought it. In fact, it turned out to be two different cars joined together. It was held that the car did not comply with the description.

As to quality: s14

The Sale and Supply of Goods Act 1994 made substantial amendments to s14 of the Sale of Goods Act 1979.

Section 14(3) as to fitness for a specific purpose remains substantially untouched. Otherwise the main changes are as follows. The new s14(2) SGA 1979 provides that where goods are sold in the course of a business there is an implied term that goods are 'of satisfactory quality'. Subsections (2A) and (2B) define 'satisfactory quality' as being of a standard that a reasonable person would regard as satisfactory having regard to description, price and all other relevant circumstances.

Subsection (2C) sets out exceptions to (A) and (B). In particular, if any defect making the goods unsatisfactory is drawn to the attention of the buyer, or if he examined the goods before purchase and the examination revealed or ought to have revealed the defect, then the terms implied by s14(2) do not apply.

The Sale and Supply of Goods to Consumers Regulations 2002 inserted subsections (2D)–(2F) and these new provisions apply to the seller's liability for public statements made by the seller or the producer, particularly in advertising or on labelling.

There is therefore an implied term that the goods are of satisfactory quality if the seller sells the goods in the course of a business. In *Jewson Ltd* v *Kelly* (2002) The Times 3 October the claimant sold 12 electric boilers to the defendant. When the claimant sued to recover the purchase price, the preliminary issue arose as to whether the claimant had been in breach of the term implied by s14(2) Sale of Goods Act 1979 that the goods supplied were of satisfactory quality. Mr David Foskett QC held that the boilers had not passed this test. Mr David Foskett QC explained that it was necessary to ask whether the reasonable person having considered the matters set out in s14(2A) and (2B) of the 1979 Act would have regarded the boilers as of satisfactory quality. The fact that the boilers intrinsically worked satisfactorily was not sufficient for them to be of satisfactory quality, since a reasonable person would have said that a new form of electric boiler, claiming to provide efficient low-cost heating in residential dwellings, ought to be capable of being shown to meet such a claim within the tests or procedures then prevailing. Furthermore, a reasonable person would say that without meeting such tests or procedures (or without an explanation as to why they were not satisfied), he or she would understand a proposed purchaser of a dwelling delaying, or even pulling out of the purchase. A reasonable person would therefore on balance have said that the boilers were not of satisfactory quality.

As mentioned above, this implied term does not apply to defects specifically drawn to the buyer's attention before the contract is made, nor does it apply if the buyer has examined the goods before the contract is made as regards defects which that examination ought to have revealed.

As to fitness for purpose

An implied term that goods sold in the course of a business are reasonably fit for the purpose expressly or by implication made known to the seller by the buyer: s14(3). Thus the buyer need not expressly state the purpose for which the goods are required if it is obvious, for example, *Frost* v *Aylesbury Dairy Co Ltd* [1905] 1 KB 608 where milk contained typhoid germs. It was held not fit for its purposes, for example, drinking – even though it had not been stated by the buyer that the milk would be drunk. But this condition will not be implied if the circumstances show that the buyer did not rely, or that it would have been unreasonable for him to rely, on the seller's skill or judgment.

Fitness for purpose is not necessarily a clearcut issue. In *Saphena Computing Ltd* v *Allied Collection Agencies Ltd* [1995] FSR 616, the 'goods' in question, computer software, had to be rendered fit for purpose over a period of time. A number of complicating factors, for example whether the contract was a true sale of goods contract or a contract for the supply of goods and services, tended to blur the main issue. Most goods are either fit or unfit, but in this case the software had to be programmed, re-programmed and systematically tested once in use, to reach a standard which could be described as fit for purpose.

As to sales by samples: s15

An implied term that the bulk will correspond with the sample in quality; and an implied term that the goods will be free from any defect, making their quality unsatisfactory, which would not be apparent on reasonable examination of the sample.

Exemption clauses

Normally, the implied terms may be varied or negatived by express agreement or by trade usage. But:

1. an express term does not negate an implied term unless it is inconsistent therewith;
2. any express term exempting the seller from all or any of the implied obligations as to title in s12 (see above) shall be void (s6(1) UCTA);
3. in a consumer sale, any term of the contract which purports to exclude or restrict the operation of ss13–15 SGA 1979, is void. A consumer sale is defined as:

   '... a sale of goods (other than a sale by auction or by competitive tender) by a seller in the course of a business where the goods are of a type ordinarily bought for private use or consumption and are sold to a person who does not buy or hold himself out as buying them in the course of business'.

   The onus is on the seller to prove that a particular sale is not a consumer sale (s6(2); s12 UCTA);
4. in the case of 'non-consumer sales', for example, where the buyer is in business to re-sell, an exemption clause is not enforceable to the extent that the buyer satisfies the court that it would not be fair and reasonable for the seller to rely on that term (s6(3); s11(2); s11(5) UCTA);
5. note also the relevance and utility of the Unfair Terms in Consumer Contracts Regulations 1999 (see Chapter 8).

New rights for consumers

The Sale and Supply of Goods to Consumers Regulations 2002 introduced a new Part 5A (ss48A–48F) into the 1979 Act in order to provide new rights for consumers. Where goods fail to conform to the contract of sale at the time of delivery, then under Part 5A the buyer firstly has the right to require the seller to repair or replace the goods within a reasonable time and without causing significant inconvenience to the buyer. If repair or replacement is impossible or disproportionate, or if the seller fails to repair or replace the goods within a reasonable time and without significant inconvenience to the buyer, then the buyer may require the seller to reduce the purchase price of the goods by an appropriate amount, or rescind the contract.

20.7 Passing of the property

The property passes at the time the parties intend it to pass, s17; but the property in *unascertained* goods cannot pass until they have been ascertained, s16.

In the absence of evidence to the contrary, the property is deemed to pass in accordance with the following rules: s18.

1. *Unconditional* contract for sale of *specific* goods in a *deliverable* state; the property passes when the contract is made, even though the time of payment or of delivery is postponed. In *Tarling* v *Baxter* [1827] 6 B & C 360, the buyer bought a haystack. Before he took it away it was destroyed by fire. Property had passed and so the loss fell on the buyer.

   Goods are in a 'deliverable state' when they are in such a state that the buyer would be bound to take delivery of them under the contract: s61.

2. Contract for sale of *specific* goods, still to be put in a deliverable state; the property does not pass until this has been done and the buyer has notice thereof.

3. Contract for sale of *specific* goods in a deliverable state, the price to be ascertained by the seller weighing, measuring, etc; the property does not pass until this is done and the buyer has notice thereof.

4. Goods delivered on *approval* or *sale or return* or similar terms; the property passes when the buyer:

   a) signifies his approval or acceptance to seller; or

   b) does any other act adopting the transaction; or

   c) retains the goods without giving notice of rejection within a fixed or reasonable time. A case which illustrates this point specifically is *Atari Corp (UK) Ltd* v *Electronics Boutique Stores (UK) Ltd* [1998] 1 All ER 1010 wherein the Court of Appeal addressed the point of a valid notice of rejection.

5. Contract for sale of *unascertained* or *future* goods sold by description; the property passes when goods of that description and in a deliverable state are *unconditionally appropriated* to the contract by one party with the consent of the other, for example, by the seller delivering the goods to the buyer or to a carrier on his behalf, without reserving the right of disposal. The buyer's assent to the appropriation may be given either before or after the appropriation, and may be implied. In *Pignatoro* v *Gilroy* [1919] 1 KB 459, a buyer ordered some bags of

rice which he was to collect when they were ready from the seller. The seller informed him the bags were ready. The buyer, however, did nothing for three weeks. The bags were stolen during this time. It was held that the buyer had by his action assented to the appropriation and thus the property in the goods and the risk of loss had passed to him.

Note that the Sale of Goods (Amendment) Act 1995 which became law on 19 September 1995, affects the sale of unascertained goods in certain cases. It relates to the sale of unascertained goods forming part of an identified bulk only (not to other forms of unascertained goods) and also to sales of undivided shares in goods.

Section 1 describes how property will pass in goods where there is a contract for a sale of a specified quantity of unascertained goods forming part of an identified bulk. This section allows a buyer of such unascertained goods to become an 'owner in common' of an identified bulk of goods. It gives effect to the concept of ascertainment by exhaustion. It defines the respective rights and duties of buyer and seller.

Section 2 defines the term 'bulk' and further clarifies the meaning of 'goods' and 'specific goods' in this context.

20.8 Transfer of title

The general rule is nemo dat quod non habet: no one can transfer title to goods except the true owner or his authorised agent. There are, however, some exceptions to this.

Estoppel

Where the owner is *estopped* by his conduct from denying the seller's authority to sell, for example, by 'holding out' a person as his agent; s21(1).

Sale by factor

Where goods are sold by a factor to a person taking in good faith without notice of any lack of authority; s21(2)(a); also see Chapter 19.

Sale under common law or statutory power

Where goods are sold under a common law or statutory power of sale or under a court order; s21(2)(b), for example, by a pawnbroker or sheriff.

Sale in market overt

The Sale of Goods (Amendment) Act 1994 abolished the concept of market overt as from 1 January 1995.

Sale under voidable title

Where goods held under a voidable contract are sold to a person taking in good faith without notice of the defect before the seller's title has been avoided; s23; this section applies, for instance, where the contract is voidable for fraud, for example, *Lewis* v *Averay* but not where it is void, or example, *Cundy* v *Lindsay*. For these cases, see Chapter 13.

Sale by buyer or seller in possession

Where the buyer or seller is, with the consent of the other party, in possession of the goods, or of the documents of title to the goods, and he sells the goods to a third person who takes them in good faith without notice of the claims of the other party, the third person will obtain a good title; s25; a change in the nature of the seller's possession, for instance, from possession as owner to possession as a bailee or even as a trespasser, does not affect the operation of the rule. See, eg, *Michael Gerson (Leasing) Ltd* v *Wilkinson* [2001] 1 All ER 148 where the Court of Appeal said that where a seller in possession of goods sold acknowledges that he is holding the goods on account of the buyer in circumstances where he recognises the purchaser's right to possess as owner and that his continuing possession is as a bailee with possession derived from that right, the transaction amounts to delivery to the buyer immediately followed by redelivery to the seller as bailee, whether the seller's custody is in the character of a bailee for reward or of a borrower.

Sale by hirer of motor vehicles

Where the hirer or buyer of a motor vehicle under a hire-purchase or condition sale agreement sells the vehicle to a *private* purchaser who takes it in good faith without notice of the agreement; similar protection is afforded to the first private purchaser from a trade or finance purchaser; ss27–29 Hire Purchase Act 1964. For example, in *Shogun Finance Ltd* v *Hudson* [2002] 4 All ER 572 the Court of Appeal heard that a rogue purchased a Mitsubishi Shogun SWB from a dealer, producing a genuine but stolen or unlawfully obtained licence in the name of Durlabh Patel. After the plaintiff finance company made a credit search which was acceptable, and having accepted the forged signature on the form of the agreement, the dealer accepted a 10 per cent deposit for the agreed price of £22,250 from the rogue, who subsequently sold the car to the defendant purchasing in good faith for £17,000. The plaintiff was awarded £18,374.52 in its claim for, inter alia, damages for conversion. The defendant appealed. Their Lordships decided (Sedley LJ dissenting) that the appeal would be dismissed. Dyson LJ said that only if the rogue was the 'debtor' within s27 of the Hire Purchase Act 1964 would the purported sale of the car to the defendant have been effective to pass title. Here, clearly, the rogue was not the debtor under the written hire purchase agreement. The plaintiff could not hold Mr Patel liable under the agreement because his signature had been forged, and he could claim the agreement was not his contract. The fact that his signature had been forged made all the difference. However, the Appeal Committee of the House of Lords gave permission to appeal.

Again in, *Hitchens* v *General Guarantee Corporation Ltd* (2001) The Times 13 March, another decision of the Court of Appeal, Mrs Rowley decided to purchase a Toyota Supra from a garage and arranged for the balance of the purchase price to be met under a lease purchase agreement with General Guarantee Group Ltd (the company). She signed the agreement on 22 February 1995: the company gave its oral approval of the agreement on that day but did not sign it until 28 February. On 22 February the garage released the car to Mrs Rowley who sold it that day to Mr Watts who immediately sold it to Mr Hitchens. He registered the vehicle with a new number. Mrs Rowley did not keep up the repayments and the company terminated the agreement. On 26 February 1997 the vehicle was repossessed by the company and Mr Hitchens brought proceedings to establish ownership. Their Lordships concluded that Mr Hitchens was indeed the owner. On ordinary contract principles there was a binding contract on 22 February under which ownership of the vehicle passed to the company and the vehicle was bailed by the dealer to Mrs Rowley who remained personally liable under the agreement, as was Mr Watts as undisclosed principal. When Mr Hitchens acquired the vehicle it 'had been bailed under a hire purchase agreement' under s27 of the Hire Purchase Act 1964 and the sale took effect.

Rix LJ said that *Hitchens* was even stronger than *Carlyle Finance Ltd* v *Pallas Industrial Finance Ltd* [1999] 1 All ER (Comm) 659 (see section 20.13) where the hire purchase agreement provided that property should not pass until a signature was obtained. In *Hitchens* the agreement did not contain such a provision.

20.9 Performance of the contract

The basic duties imposed by a contract of sale are *delivery* of possession of the goods by the seller, and *acceptance* and payment by the buyer; s27: unless otherwise agreed, delivery and payment are concurrent conditions: s28. Whether the buyer is to collect the goods or the seller is to send them to the buyer is to be determined by the terms, express or implied, of the contract between them: s29(1).

Delivery

Unless otherwise agreed, the place of delivery is the seller's place of business or residence. If the seller has agreed to send the goods to the buyer, he must do so within a reasonable time, at a reasonable hour, and at his own expense; s29; moreover, a seller who is required to deliver at the buyer's premises will be discharged if the goods are delivered to a person having apparent authority to receive them. In *Galbraith & Grant Ltd v Block* [1922] 2 KB 155, sellers were contractually bound to deliver a crate of champagne to the buyer's house. There it was received by a respectable looking and apparently authorised person. The champagne was never seen again. It was held that the sellers were entitled to the price from the buyers.

If the seller delivers more or less than the quantity contracted for, or delivers goods of the contract description mixed with other goods, the buyer may reject the whole of the goods or that part which does not conform with the terms of the contract; s30. The buyer cannot accept those goods that do not conform, unless the parties agree.

The buyer need not accept delivery by instalments, unless he has agreed to do so. In the latter event, if the goods are to be paid for separately, and there is a failure to make or take delivery of one or more instalments, the breach may constitute the repudiation of the whole contract, or a severable breach giving rise to a claim for damages only, depending upon the circumstances; s31. The test is the quantity of goods involved in relation to the contract as a whole and the likelihood of repetition of the breach. In *Maple Flock Co Ltd v Universal Furniture Products Ltd* [1934] 1 KB 148, a contract was made for the delivery of 100 tons of rag flock at a rate of three loads per week. The first 15 deliveries were satisfactory, the 16th was not, but the buyer nevertheless accepted a further four loads, all of which were satisfactory. The buyers then refused to take any further deliveries.

They were not entitled to do this. There was little likelihood of the breach being repeated.

Delivery of the goods to a carrier is prima facie a delivery of the goods to the buyer, but the buyer may decline to treat if the seller has failed to make a reasonable contract of carriage and the goods are lost or damaged in the course of transit: s32. An insertion in this section by the Sale and Supply of Goods to Consumers Regulations 2002 applies where a buyer deals as consumer.

Acceptance

The buyer is deemed to have accepted the goods when (s35) he intimates his acceptance to the seller; or the goods have been delivered to him and he does any act in relation to them inconsistent with the seller's ownership; or he retains the goods longer than is reasonable without intimating to the seller that he has rejected them.

But he is not deemed to have accepted them, where he has not previously examined them, until he has had a reasonable opportunity of examining them, and the seller must afford him this opportunity on tendering delivery if so requested; s34. Section 2 of the Sale and Supply of Goods Act 1994 amends ss34 and 35, giving a buyer, inter alia, the right to *partial* rejection of the goods. However, the full extent of this right is not yet known.

If the buyer properly refuses to accept the goods, he is not bound to return them to the seller; s36; an unjustified refusal renders him liable to the seller for any loss thereby caused; s37.

20.10 Remedies of the unpaid seller

In the event of non-payment, the seller has remedies against the goods and against the buyer.

Remedies against goods

An unpaid seller has the following rights over the goods.

1. A lien on the goods, if the property has passed and the seller is still in possession. If credit has been given, no lien can exist until the period of credit has expired, or the buyer is insolvent; s41.

    The right may be lost by waiver, for example, by assenting to a sub-sale, or loss of possession; s43.
2. A right to stop the goods in transit (stoppage in transit) and retake delivery while they are in the possession of a carrier if the buyer becomes insolvent, s44. The goods are still in transit if the buyer rejects them and the carrier continues in possession of them; but the goods cease to be in transit if the buyer takes delivery before they reach their destination, or where the carrier either acknowledges to the buyer that he holds the goods on his behalf, or where he wrongfully refuses to deliver the goods to the buyer; s45.
3. A right to *withhold delivery*, co-existent with the above rights, if the property has not passed to the buyer; s39(2). (Note, that this is not a lien – no one can have a lien over his own goods.)
4. An unpaid seller who has exercised his right of lien or stoppage in transit has a right of *resale* only if:

    a) the goods are of a perishable nature; or
    b) the seller gives notice of his intention to resell, and the buyer does not tender the price within a reasonable time thereof; or
    c) the right of resale is expressly reserved in the contract; s48.

The effect of resale is to rescind the original contract and the whole of the proceeds belong to the unpaid seller.

The unpaid seller's rights of lien or stoppage in transit against the goods are not affected by any sale or other disposition thereof by the buyer unless:

a) the seller has assented to it; or

b) a document of title to the goods has been transferred to the buyer, and the buyer has further transferred it to a person taking it in good faith and for value; s47.

Remedies against the buyer

Action for the price

The seller can sue the buyer for the price if the property has passed to the buyer; or a date for payment, irrespective of delivery, has been agreed, even though the property has not passed, s49. The Court of Appeal affirmed this point in *Bem Dis A Turk Ticaret S/A TR* v *International Agri Trade Co Ltd (The Selda)* [1999] 1 All ER (Comm) 619. Note also the provisions of s50 Sale of Goods Act 1979.

Action for damages for non-acceptance

If an action for the price is not available, the seller may claim damages if the buyer wrongfully refuses to accept and pay for the goods. The measure of damages is the estimated loss directly and naturally resulting in the ordinary course of events from the buyer's breach of contract. Where there is an available market for the goods in question, the measure of damages is prima facie to be ascertained by the difference between the contract price and the market price at the date of the breach, s50. However, if there is no available market, then the seller is entitled to damages for the loss of his bargain, and this depends on the state of demand for the goods. See *WL Thompson Ltd* v *Robinson (Gunmakers) Ltd*; contrast *Charter* v *Sullivan*.

In *WL Thompson Ltd* v *Robinson (Gunmakers) Ltd* [1955] Ch 177, the defendants contracted to buy a Standard Vanguard car from the plaintiffs. However, they refused to take delivery of the car. At the time there was no available market for this type of car. The measure of damages claimable by the plaintiffs was held to be the loss of profit on the sale.

In *Charter* v *Sullivan* [1957] 2 QB 117, a buyer failed to take delivery of a Hillman Minx car in circumstances where demand outstripped supply. It was held that the measure of damages was purely nominal since there was no difficulty in finding another buyer for the car.

20.11 Remedies of the buyer

The buyer may have one or more of the following remedies in the event of a breach of contract by the seller.

Remedies for damages for non-delivery

This is available if the seller wrongfully neglects or refuses to deliver the goods; s51. The damages are calculated in the same manner as in 'Action for damages for non-acceptance' (above).

Specific performance

Such an order may be made if the contract is for specific or ascertained goods, and the court thinks that this is an appropriate remedy; s52.

Action for breach of warranty

On a breach of warranty, or of a condition which the buyer chooses or is required to treat as a breach of warranty, the buyer may set off his claim for damages against the purchase price, or bring an action against the seller for damages for the breach, or both; s53.

A breach of condition, which can be treated as such, enables the buyer to reject the goods and to claim damages for the breach.

20.12 Cif and fob contracts

These terms relate to contracts for the sale of goods to be carried by sea. 'Cif' means 'costs, insurance and freight'; 'fob' means 'free on board'. In a cif contract, the seller pays insurance and freight, while in an fob contract, he delivers the goods to the vessel and the buyer is responsible for insurance and freight from that time on.

Cif contracts

Under a cif contract, the seller undertakes to ship the goods at his own expense to the port of destination and to insure them during the voyage; the property normally passes when the shipping documents are tendered to the buyer, though the risk passes when the goods have been lifted over the ship's rail; thus, if the goods are lost at sea, the buyer must still pay the price against tender of the documents.

Fob contracts

Under an fob contract, carriage and insurance are arranged by the buyer, the seller's duty being merely to delivery the goods on board an appointed ship; the seller must give the buyer sufficient information to enable him to insure the goods; s32(3). The risk and property usually pass to the buyer when the goods cross the ship's rail.

20.13 Hire-purchase, credit sale and conditional sale agreements

These types of agreement are governed by the Consumer Credit Act 1974, provided that they constitute what is known as a 'consumer credit agreement'. A consumer credit agreement for the purpose of the Act must be for an individual, and for credit not exceeding £5,000.

Hire-purchase agreements, conditional sale agreements and credit sale agreements may all qualify as 'consumer credit agreements'.

Hire-purchase agreements

A hire-purchase agreement is an agreement by an owner of goods to hire them out to a bailee, and to give the bailee an option to purchase conditional on his completing the necessary payments for the goods and complying with the terms of the agreement.

Conditional sale agreement

A conditional sale agreement is an agreement for the sale of goods under which the purchase price or part of it is payable by instalments, and the property in the goods or land is to remain in the seller (notwithstanding that the buyer is to be in possession of the goods) until such conditions as to the payment of instalments or otherwise, as may be specified in the agreement, are fulfilled. The issue of when a conditional sale materialises was addressed by the Court of Appeal in *Forthright Finance Ltd* v *Ingate (Carlyle Finance Ltd, third party)* [1997] 4 All ER 99 and subsequently in *Carlyle Finance Ltd* v *Pallas Industrial Finance Ltd* [1999] 1 All ER (Comm) 659 (CA). See also section 20.8, *Sale by hirer of motor vehicles.*

Credit sale agreements

A credit sale agreement is an agreement for the sale of goods, under which the purchase price or part of it is payable by instalments, but which is not a conditional sale agreement. The ownership in the goods therefore passes immediately to the buyer.

The Consumer Credit Act 1974

Under the Consumer Credit Act, a licence issued by the Director-General of Fair Trading must be obtained by a person wishing to carry on a consumer credit business. If a consumer credit agreement is entered into by an unlicensed creditor, the agreement is unenforceable against the debtor, unless the Director-General makes an order that agreements made during a certain period by the creditor are to be treated as though he had been licensed.

Powers are conferred on the Secretary of State to make regulations as to the form and content of the documents embodying consumer credit agreements. The object of the regulations is to ensure that the debtor is made aware of his rights and duties, the amount and rate of the total charge for credit, the protection and remedies available to him under the Act, and any other matters which in the opinion of the Secretary of State it is desirable for him to know about concerning the agreement. In every form of consumer credit agreement, the consumer must be left with a copy of the entire agreement for his own information.

Where the antecedent negotiations included oral representations made by the dealer or on his behalf in the presence of the debtor, then the debtor has the benefit of a 'cooling off' period, unless the agreement was signed by him at the creditor's or dealer's business premises. The right to cancel may be exercised by the debtor serving a notice of cancellation at any time between his signing the agreement and the fifth day following the day on which he received his copy of the executed agreement. The effect of cancellation is that the cancelled agreement is treated as if it had never existed. Any sum paid by the debtor under or in contemplation of the agreement is repayable. Subject to a lien for the repayment of any sums owing, the debtor must restore any goods he has in his possession to the person from whom he acquired possession, and take reasonable care of the goods. He need not return the goods to the owner, though he must allow the owner to collect them himself. If the owner has not collected them within 21 days, the buyer is under no further duty to take care of them.

The Supply of Goods (Implied Terms) Act 1973

By virtue of the Supply of Goods (Implied Terms) Act 1973, substantially the same terms are implied in the case of all hire-purchase agreement as are implied in contracts for the sale of goods (see section 20.6 with appropriate changes in terminology, for example, 'owner' is substituted for 'seller' and 'hirer' is substituted for 'buyer'). The Sale and Supply of Goods to Consumers Regulations 2002 amended s10 of the 1973 Act to provide additional implied terms in consumer cases.

Again, the implied terms can only be excluded in substantially the same circumstances as in a sale of goods (see section 20.6, 'Exemption Clauses').

The debtor under a hire-purchase or conditional sale agreement is entitled to terminate the agreement at any time before the final instalment. Unless the agreement provides for some smaller payment, the debtor is liable to pay to the creditor the amount (if any) by which one-half of the total price exceeds the aggregate of the sums paid and the sums due in respect of the total price immediately before the termination. The creditor cannot exercise any right of termination or repossession granted by the agreement unless he serves a 'default notice' upon the debtor. The default notice must specify the nature of the alleged breach; if the breach is capable of remedy, what action is required to remedy it and the date by which that action is to be taken; and if the breach is not capable of remedy, the sum (if any) required to be paid as compensation for the breach and the date by which it is to be paid. The date specified must be not less than seven days after the date of service of the default notice.

After one-third of the total price has been paid or tendered, the creditor cannot enforce any right to recover possession of the goods otherwise than by legal action. Contravention releases the hirer or buyer from all liability, and entitles him to recover all sums paid under the agreement. This provision does not apply if the hirer consents to repossession. The court on hearing the application for possession may order:

1. specific delivery of all the goods to the owner or seller; or
2. as in (1), but the operation of the order to be postponed on condition that the hirer or buyer or any guarantor pays the unpaid balance of the price at such times, and in such amounts, either as agreed by the parties or as the court thinks just; or
3. specific delivery of a part of the goods to the owner or seller, and for the transfer to the hirer or buyer of the title of the owner or seller to the remainder of the goods.

The limits on the creditor's right of termination or repossession do not apply to credit sale agreements because, under such an agreement, ownership in the goods has passed and the concept of termination or repossession does not arise.

20.14 Supply of goods and services

The Sale of Goods Act 1979 and the Supply of Goods (Implied Terms) Act 1973 cover, as we have seen, sale and hire-purchase agreements. Prior to 1982, the supply of services and some transfers of property in goods outside the then current statutory control were covered by the common law. To remedy the lacunae and embody the law as a code, the Supply of Goods and Services Act 1982 was enacted. The Act is divided into two major parts: Part I governing the supply of goods and, in particular, covering contracts for the transfer of property in goods and contracts for the hire of goods; Part II is exclusively concerned with the supply of services. All section references in this part of the book, unless otherwise stated, are to the Supply of Goods and Services Act 1982.

20.15 Contracts for the transfer of property in goods

Section 1 of the 1982 Act provides:

'(1) In this Act ... a "contract for the transfer of goods" means a contract under which one person transfers or agrees to transfer to another the property in goods, other than an excepted contract.
(2) For the purposes of this section an excepted contract means any of the following –

(a) a contract of sale of goods;

(b) a hire-purchase agreement;

(c) a contract under which the property in goods is (or is to be) transferred in exchange for trading stamps or their redemption;

(d) a transfer or agreement to transfer which is made by deed and for which there is no consideration other than presumed consideration imported by the deed;

(e) a contract intended to operate by way of mortgage, pledge, charge or other security.

(3) For the purposes of this Act a contract is a contract for the transfer of goods whether or not services are also provided or to be provided under the contract, and (subject to subsection (2) above) whatever is the nature of the consideration for the transfer or agreement to transfer.'

Section 1(1) includes contracts where property is transferred, or it is to be transferred, on the fulfilment of a condition.

'Property' is defined in s18(1) of the 1982 Act as 'the general property in "goods" ... and not merely a special property'. This reflects the definition in s61(1) Sale of Goods Act 1979; general property broadly meaning ownership.

By s1(2) of the 1982 Act, certain contracts are excepted from the operation of the Act, eg, contracts for the sale of goods and hire-purchase agreements.

20.16 Agreements within the 1982 Act

Section 1(3) of the 1982 Act is an important provision, stating that a contract which transfers property as defined in the Act remains within the Act, whether or not services are also provided or to be provided under the contract. The second limb of s1(3) brings within the ambit of the statute contracts regardless of whether the consideration is money consideration or otherwise. Accordingly, barter and exchange contracts, which fall outside the 1979 Act, are covered by the 1982 Act.

For example, the case of *Esso Petroleum Co Ltd* v *Commissioners of Customs and Excise* [1976] 1 All ER 117 where medallions were given to buyers of a certain quantity of petrol, although not sales of goods, would be transfers of property for the purposes of the 1982 Act.

More importantly, contracts for skill and labour or work and materials are within the 1982 Act if general property in goods passes.

In *Robinson* v *Graves* [1935] 1 KB 579, a contract for an artist to paint a portrait was a contract for skill and labour, not one of the supply of goods. The 1982 Act would now cover the contract.

Consequently, contracts under which goods and services are supplied, in so far as the essence of the contract is one for service and labour, will be subject to the 1982 Act. Contracts for the installation of central heating, plumbing and electrics will normally be within this part of the 1982 Act if property in goods passes.

Note: the essence of the contract must not be for the passing of property in goods (where the Sale of Goods Act 1979 will govern).

See and compare the following cases: *GH Myers and Co* v *Brent Cross Services Co* [1934] 1 KB 46, *Lee* v *Griffin* (1861) 30 LJ QB 252, *Cammell Laird & Co Ltd* v *Manganese Bronze and Brass* [1934] AC 402 and *Young & Marten Ltd* v *McManus Childs Ltd* [1969] 1 AC 454.

20.17 Implied conditions and warranties

All contracts within the scope of s1 of the Act have implied into them the conditions and warranties stipulated in ss2–5 of the 1982 Act. The distinction between condition and warranties has already been covered in depth, and students are referred back to the relevant parts of the course material.

Title

'2(1) In a contract for the transfer of goods, other than one to which subsection (3) below applies, there is an implied condition on the part of the transferor that in the case of a transfer of the property in the goods he has a right to transfer the property and in the case of an agreement to transfer the property in the goods he will have such a right at the time when the property is to be transferred.

(2) In a contract for the transfer of goods, other than one to which subsection (3) below applies, there is also an implied warranty that –

(a) the goods are free and will remain free until the time when the property is to be transferred, from any charge or encumbrance not disclosed or known to the transferee before the contract is made, and

(b) the transferee will enjoy quiet possession of the goods except so far as it may be disturbed by the owner or other person entitled to the benefit of any charge or encumbrance so disclosed or known.

(3) This subsection applies to a contract for the transfer of goods in the case of which there appears from the contract or is to be inferred from its circumstances an intention that the transferor should transfer only such title as he or a third person may have.

(4) In a contract to which subsection (3) above applies there is an implied warranty that all charges or encumbrances known to the transferor and not known to the transferee have been disclosed to the transferee before the contract is made.

(5) In a contract to which subsection (3) above applies there is also an implied warranty that none of the following will disturb the transferee's quiet possession of the goods, namely –

(a) the transferor;

(b) in a case where the parties to the contract intend that the transferor should transfer only such title as a third person may have, that person:

(c) anyone claiming through or under the transferor or that third person otherwise than under a charge or encumbrance disclosed or known to the transferee before the contract is made.'

Section 2 of the 1982 Act is identical to s12 of the 1979 Act save in so far as it applies to the transfer, rather than the sale, of goods. Both sections contain one condition and two warranties. See *Rowland* v *Divall*, Chapter 18, secton 18.2.

Correspondence with description

Section 3 of the 1982 Act provides:

'(1) This section applies where, under a contract for the transfer of goods, the transferor transfers or agrees to transfer the property in goods by description.

(2) In such a case there is an implied condition that the goods will correspond with the description.

(3) If the transferor transfers or agrees to transfer the property in the goods by sample as well as by description it is not sufficient that the bulk of the goods corresponds with the sample of the goods if the goods do not also correspond with the description.

(4) A contract is not prevented from falling within subsection (1) above by reason only that, being exposed for supply, the goods are selected by the transferee.'

Section 3 of the 1982 Act is adapted from s13 of the 1979 Act. The case law relevant to the development of that provision, and the decisions upon the old 1893 Sale of Goods Act, are applicable mutatis mutandis. See *Beale* v *Taylor* [1967] 3 All ER 253, *Grant* v *Australian Knitting Mills* [1936] AC 85, *Ashington Piggeries* v *Christopher Hill* [1972] AC 441 and *Arcos* v *Ronaasen* [1933] AC 470.

Quality or fitness for purpose

Section 4 of the 1982 Act provides:

'(1) Except as provided by this section and s5 below and subject to the provisions of any other enactment, there is no implied condition or warranty about the quality or fitness for any particular purpose of goods supplied under a contract for the transfer of goods.

(2) Where, under such a contract, the transferor transfers the property in goods in the course of a business, there is (subject to subsection (3) below) an implied condition that the goods supplied under the contract are of satisfactory quality.

(2A) For the purposes of this section and section 5 below, goods are of satisfactory quality if they meet the standard that a reasonable person would regard as satisfactory, taking account of any description of the goods, the price (if relevant) and all the other relevant circumstances.

(3) The condition implied by subsection (2) above does not extend to any matter making the quality of goods unsatisfactory –

(a) which is specifically drawn to the transferee's attention before the contract is made;

(b) where the transferee examines the goods before the contract is made, which that examination ought to reveal; or

(c) where the property in the goods is transferred by reference to a sample, which would have been apparent on a reasonable examination of the sample.

(4) Subsection (5) below applies where, under a contract for the transfer of goods, the transferor transfers the property in goods in the course of a business and the transferee, expressly or by implication, makes known –

(a) to the transferor, or

(b) where the consideration or part of the consideration for the transfer is a sum payable by instalments and the goods were previously sold by a credit-broker to the transferor, to that credit-broker,

any particular purpose for which the goods are being acquired.

(5) In that case there is (subject to subsection (6) below) an implied condition that the goods supplied under the contract are reasonably fit for that purpose, whether or not that is a purpose for which such goods are commonly supplied.

(6) Subsection (5) above does not apply where the circumstances show that the transferee does not rely, or that it is unreasonable for him to rely, on the skill or judgment of the transferor or credit-broker.

(7) An implied condition or warranty about quality or fitness for a particular purpose may be annexed by usage to a contract for the transfer of goods.

(8) The preceding provisions of this section apply to transfer by a person who in the course of a business is acting as agent for another as they apply to a transfer by a principal in the course of a business, except where that other is not transferring in the course of a business and either the transferee knows that fact or reasonable steps are taken to bring it to the transferee's notice before the contract concerned is made.'

Section 18(1) defines 'business' as including 'a profession and the activities of any government department or local or public authority'.

'Quality' as defined in s18(1) includes the 'state or condition' of goods.

In all respects, s4(2), (2A) and (3) mirror s14(2), (2A), (2B) and (3) of the Sale of Goods Act 1979. The cases discussed under s14 SGA should be referred to. Note:

1. for this condition to be implied in to the contract, the transferor *must* transfer property in the course of business;
2. as RG Lawson points out in his *Practical Guide to the Act*:

'The implied condition as to merchantable [satisfactory] quality refers to the goods supplied "under" the contract of transfer, thus encompassing more than just the goods, the property in which is to pass pursuant to the contract. For instance if a firm installs central heating fired by oil, any oil provided by the contractors will have to meet the requirement as to merchantable [satisfactory] quality even though it is not provided as part of the agreement but as part of an initial test to determine the satisfactory working of the equipment.'

Fitness for purpose

'4(4) Subsection (5) below applies where, under a contract for the transfer of goods, the transferor transfers the property in goods to the course of a business and the transferee, expressly or by implication, makes known –

(a) to the transferor, or

(b) where the consideration or part of the consideration for the transfer is a sum payable by instalment and the goods were previously sold by a credit-broker to the transferor, to that credit-broker,

any particular purpose for which the goods are being acquired.

(5) In that case there is (subject to subsection (6) below) an implied condition that the goods supplied under the contract are reasonably fit for that purpose, whether or not that is a purpose for which such goods are commonly supplied.

(6) Subsection (5) above does not apply where the circumstances show that the transferee does not rely, or that it is unreasonable for him to rely, on the skill or judgment of the transferor or creditbroker.

(7) An implied condition or warranty about quality or fitness for a particular purpose may be annexed by usage to a contract for the transfer of goods.

(8) The preceding provisions of this section apply to a transfer by a person who in the course of a business is acting as agent for another as they apply to a transfer by a principal in the course of a business, except where that other is not transferring in the course of a business and either the transferee knows that fact or reasonable steps are taken to bring it to the transferee's notice before the contract concerned is made.'

Again, the 1982 Act follows the provisions of s14(3) of the 1979 Act.

Section 4(8) corresponds with s14(5) of the 1979 Act; and s4(7) with s14(4) of the 1979 Act. See *Peter Darlington Partners Ltd* v *Gosho Co Ltd* [1964] 1 Lloyd's Rep 149.

An amendment to s4 made by the Sale and Supply of Goods to Consumers Regulations 2002 relates to the transferor's liability for public statements made by the transferor, the producer or his representative.

Transfer by sample

Section 15 Sale of Goods Act 1979 is the basis upon which s5 of the 1982 Act was drafted.

Section 5 provides:

'(1) This section applies where, under a contract for the transfer of goods, the transferor transfers or agrees to transfer the property in the goods by reference to a sample.

(2) In such a case there is an implied condition

(a) that the bulk will correspond with the sample in quality; and

(b) that the transferee will have a reasonable opportunity of comparing the bulk with the sample; and

(c) that the goods will be free from any defect, rendering them of unsatisfactory quality, which would not be apparent on reasonable examination of the sample.

(3) In subsection (2)(c) above "unsatisfactory" is to be construed in accordance with section 4(2A) above.

(4) For the purposes of this section a transferor transfers or agrees to transfer the property in goods by reference to a sample where there is an express or implied term to that effect in the contract concerned.'

20.18 Contracts for the hire of goods

Prior to the 1982 Act, simple hire or leasing agreements were outside the scope of the statutory implied terms appertaining to hire-purchase, conditional sale or ordinary sale contracts.

Sections 6 to 10 of the 1982 Act introduce the regime mutatis mutandi to hire agreements.

Section 6 defines the contracts concerned:

'(1) In this Act ... a "contract for the hire of goods" means a contract under which one person bails or agrees to bail goods to another by way of hire, other than an excepted contract.

(2) For the purposes of this section an excepted contract means any of the following –

(a) a hire-purchase agreement;

(b) a contract under which goods are (or are to be) bailed in exchange for trading stamps on their redemption.

(3) For the purposes of this Act ... a contract is a contract for the hire of goods whether or not services are also provided or to be provided under the contract, and (subject to subsection (2) above) whatever is the nature of the consideration for the bailment or agreement to bail by way of hire.'

Hire-purchase agreements are, of course, excluded from the operation of the 1982 Act, being governed already by the Supply of Goods (Implied Terms) Act 1973.

Note that although services may be provided under the hire contract as well as the goods, the provisions of this part of Part I of the 1982 Act still apply. For example, the contract for a hire of a car may include charges in respect of maintenance which the hirer is obliged to undertake with the owner.

A contract for the hire of goods encompasses contracts where goods are bailed by way of hire; viz the delivery of goods by one to another without title in the goods being transferred. The bailee, therefore, must have possession of the goods before the 1982 Act applies. Hire or leasing agreements are accordingly the main categories of agreement falling within s6 of the 1982 Act.

20.19 Implied conditions and warranties in hire contracts

The right to transfer possession

Section 7

'(1) In a contract for the hire of goods there is an implied condition on the part of the bailor that in the case of a bailment he has a right to transfer possession of the goods by way of hire for the period of the bailment and in the case of an agreement to bail he will have such a right at the time of the bailment.

(2) In a contract for the hire of goods there is also an implied warranty that the bailee will enjoy quiet possession of the goods for the period of the bailment except so far as the possession may be disturbed by the owner or other person entitled to the benefit or any charge or encumbrance disclosed or known to the bailee before the contract is made.

(3) The preceding provisions of this section do not affect the right of the bailor to repossess the goods under an express or implied term of the contract.'

Note:

1. section 7(1): the bailor must have a right to transfer possession (he need not be the owner of the goods);
2. section 7(2): the warranty follows the analogous provision in the 1979 Act.

However, there is no statutory warranty that goods are free from any undisclosed charge or encumbrance;

3. hire agreements may be regulated agreements within the Consumer Credit Act 1974 and, if so, either the free and voluntary consent of the bailee must be given at the time the bailor wishes to repossess or the order of the court is required.

By s8:

'(1) This section applies where, under a contract for the hire of goods, the bailor bails or agrees to bail the goods by description.

(2) In such a case there is an implied condition that the goods will correspond with the description.

(3) If under the contract the bailor bails or agrees to bail the goods by reference to a sample as well as a description it is not sufficient that the bulk of the goods corresponds with the sample if the goods do not also correspond with the description.

(4) A contract is not prevented from falling within subsection (1) above by reason only that, being exposed for supply, the goods are selected by the bailee.'

The section is analogous to the 1979 Act.

Quality or fitness

Section 9 of the 1982 Act provides:

'(1) Except as provided by this section and s10 below and subject to the provisions of any other enactment, there is no implied condition or warranty about the quality or fitness for any particular purpose of goods bailed under a contract for the hire of goods.

(2) Where, under such a contract, the bailor bails goods in the course of a business, there is (subject to subsection (3) below) an implied condition that the goods supplied under the contract are of satisfactory quality.

(2A) For the purposes of this section and section 10 below, goods are of satisfactory quality if they meet the standard that a reasonable person would regard as satisfactory, taking account of any description of the goods, the consideration for the bailment (if relevant) and all the other relevant circumstances.

(3) The condition implied by subsection (2) above does not extend to any matter making the goods unsatisfactory –

(a) which is specifically drawn to the bailee's attention before the contract is made,

(b) where the bailee examines the goods before the contract is made, which that examination ought to reveal, or

(c) where the goods are bailed by reference to a sample which would have been apparent on a reasonable examination of the sample.'

See discussion above.

Fitness for purpose

By s9:

'(4) Subsection (5) below applies where, under a contract for the hire of goods, the bailor bails goods in the course of a business and the bailee, expressly or by implication, makes known –

(a) to the bailor in the course of negotiations conducted by him in relation to the making of the contract, or

(b) to a credit-broker in the course of negotiations conducted by that broker in relation to the making of the contract, or any particular purpose for which the goods are being bailed.

(5) In that case there is (subject to subsection (6) below) an implied condition that the goods supplied under the contract are reasonably fit for that purpose, whether or not that is a purpose for which such goods are commonly supplied.

(6) Subsection (5) above does not apply where the circumstances show that the bailee does not rely, or that it is unreasonable for him to rely, on the skill or judgment of the transferor or creditbroker.

(7) An implied condition or warranty about quality or fitness for a particular purpose may be annexed by usage to a contract for the hire of goods.

(8) The preceding provisions of this section apply to a bailment by a person who in the course of a business is acting as agent for another as they apply to a bailment by a principal in the course of a business, except where the other is not bailing in the course of a business and either the bailee knows that fact or reasonable steps are taken to bring it to the bailee's notice before the contract concerned is made.'

These provisions again follow the Sale of Goods Act 1979 model. The only difference is the noticeable inclusion of the words 'in the course of negotiation'. It is doubted whether this adds anything to the interpretation of this section as compared to the previous statutory wording.

Section 9 of the 1982 Act was amended by the Sale and Supply of Goods to Consumers Regulations 2002 to cover public statements on the specific characteristics of the goods, particularly in advertising or on labelling.

Hire by sample

Section 10(1) applies where, under a contract for the hire of goods, the bailor bails or agrees to bail the goods by reference to a sample:

'(2) In such a case there is an implied condition –
(a) that the bulk will correspond with the sample in quality; and
(b) that the bailee will have a reasonable opportunity of comparing the bulk with the sample; and
(c) that the goods will be free from any defect, making their quality unsatisfactory, which would not be apparent on reasonable examination of the sample.
(4) For the purposes of this section a bailor bails or agrees to bail goods by reference to a sample where there is an express or implied term to that effect in the contract concerned.'

Exclusion of liability

The basic rule, which reflects s55 of the 1979 Act is confirmed in s11 of the 1982 Act.

By s11:

'(1) Where a right, duty or liability would arise under a contract for the transfer of goods or a contract for the hire of goods by implication of law, it may (subject to subsection (2) below and the 1977 Unfair Contract Terms Act) be negatived or varied by express agreement, or by the course of dealing between the parties, or by such usage as binds both parties to the contract.

(2) An express condition or warranty does not negative a condition or warranty implied by the preceding provisions of this Act unless inconsistent with it.

(3) Nothing in the preceding provisions of this Act prejudices the operation of any other enactment or any rule of law whereby any condition or warranty (other than one relating to quality or fitness) is to be implied in a contract for the transfer of goods or a contract for the hire of goods.'

The Unfair Contract Terms Act 1977 is expressly referred to in s11(1) of the 1982 Act, and the referment provision of that Act is s7.

Section 7 of the UCTA 1977 controls attempts to exclude liability where the possession or ownership of goods passed under or in pursuance of a contract not governed by the law of sale of goods and hire purchase.

To title

Unlike s6 of UCTA 1977, however, s7 permits the exclusion of terms (if any) as to title save in so far as the reasonableness test is satisfied. In Hire Purchase and Sale of Goods Act cases, s6 expressly forbids the exclusion of terms as to title.

Section 17(2) of Part III of the 1982 Act, however, adds a new s7(3A) to UCTA 1977, providing:

'(2) The following subsection shall be inserted after s7(3) of the 1977 Act:

(3A) Liability for breach of the obligations arising under s2 of the Supply of Goods and Services Act 1982 (implied terms about title etc in certain contracts for the transfer of the property in goods) cannot be excluded or restricted by reference to any such term.

(3) In consequence of subsection (2) above, in s7(4) of the 1977 Act, after "cannot" there shall be inserted "(in a case to which subsection (3A) above does not apply)".'

Although s2 of the 1982 Act is covered, the test of reasonableness must still be applied in relation to hire contracts under s7 of the 1982 Act.

Furthermore, the Consumer Transactions (Restrictions on Statements) Order 1976 (SI 1976 No 1813), which makes it unlawful to attempt to exclude terms implied by the Sale of Goods Act 1979, does not apply to s7 UCTA 1977 exclusions.

Correspondence with description, satisfactory quality and fitness for purpose

Section 7(2) of UCTA 1977 only deals with consumer contracts as defined in s12 of UCTA 1977 (see back to course materials). In respect of contracts falling within s7(2), and the implied terms as to correspondence with description or sample, satisfactory quality and fitness for purposes, terms cannot be excluded or restricted by contract.

In respect of non–consumer contracts, s7(3) of UCTA 1977 permits exclusion or restriction of the implied terms in so far as the clause is reasonable.

Note:

1. section 3 of UCTA 1977 which applies as is relevant to contracts within the 1982 Act;
2. for what is reasonable see s11 and Schedule 2 of UCTA 1977 and the previous discussion.

The Sale and Supply of Goods to Consumers Regulations 2002 inserted Part IB (ss11M–11S) of the 1982 Act. Where goods fail to conform to the contract of sale at the time of delivery, under Part 1B the transferee firstly has the right to require the transferor to repair or replace the goods within a reasonable time and without causing significant inconvenience to the transferee. If repair or replacement is impossible or disproportionate, or if the transferor fails to repair or replace the goods within a reasonable time and without significant inconvenience to the transferee, the transferee may require the transferor to reduce the purchase price of the goods by an appropriate amount, or rescind the contract.

20.20 Contracts for the supply of services

By s12:

'(1) In this Act a "contract for the supply of a service" means, subject to subsection (2) below, a contract under which a person ("the supplier") agrees to carry out a service.

(2) For the purposes of this Act, a contract of service or apprenticeship is not a contract for the supply of a service.

(3) Subject to subsection (2) above, a contract is a contract for the supply of a service for the purposes of this Act whether or not goods are also

(a) transferred or to be transferred, or

(b) bailed or to be bailed by way of hire,

under the contract, and whatever is the nature of the consideration for which the service is to be carried out.

(4) The Secretary of State may by order provide that one or more of ss13 to 15 below shall not apply to services of a description specified in the order, and such an order may make different provision for different circumstances.

(5) The power to make an order under subsection (4) above shall be exercisable by statutory instrument subject to annulment in pursuance of a resolution of either House of Parliament.'

Note that by subsection (3), contracts for the supply of a service are still governed by Part II of the Act notwithstanding that goods are transferred or to be transferred under the contract or that goods are bailed by way of hire. A hire-purchase agreement which involves the provision of a service, although unusual, would be governed by Part II of the 1982 Act.

Note that services provided by builders, architects, surveyors, estate agents, barbers, etc, are all within Part II, as are services provided by lawyers. The latter category may be exempted from the operation of the Act by the Secretary of State, who is empowered to do so by subsection (4) of s12.

Remember that a contract may come within s1(3) or s6(3) as well as s12(3) of the 1982 Act.

Section 12(2) of the 1982 Act expressly excludes a contract of service or apprenticeship from the provisions.

20.21 Implied terms in contracts for the supply of services

In this part of the Act, the reference is to implied terms as a general group; conditions and warranties are not distinguished.

Implied term about care and skill

Section 13:

> 'In a contract for the supply of a service where the supplier is acting in the course of a business, there is an implied term that the supplier will carry out the service with reasonable care and skill.'

Section 13 merely enacts the common law. The recent case of *Wong Mee Wan* v *Kwan Kin Travel Services Ltd and Others* [1996] 1 WLR 38, illustrated how, in the absence of statute, the common law will imply a duty to carry out the service concerned with reasonable care and skill. This case, referred to the Privy Council from Hong Kong where there is apparently no equivalent to the Supply of Goods and Services Act 1982, was nevertheless decided on exactly the same sort of implied common law terms as are provided for expressly by the statute.

In the important case of *Greaves & Co (Contractors) Ltd* v *Baynham Meikle and Partners* [1975] 3 All ER 99, Lord Denning in the Court of Appeal thought:

> 'The law does not usually imply a warranty that the professional man will achieve the desired result, but only a term that he will use reasonable care and skill. The surgeon does not warrant that he will cure the patient. Nor does the solicitor warrant that he will win the case. But, when a dentist agrees to make a set of false teeth for a patient, there is an implied warranty that they will fit his gums: see *Samuels* v *Davis* [1943] 2 All ER 3.'

See also the case of *Wilson* v *Best Travel Ltd* [1993] 1 All ER 353, in which it was made clear that s13 – that the supplier will carry out the service with reasonable care and skill – was – duty to do only what was reasonably practicable in the circumstances. In this case, when a tourist was injured abroad, the travel agents' duty extended only to checking that the hotel complied with all local safety standards. It could not be expected to insist on higher standards than that; it would be impractical to expect it.

Note that s13 of the 1982 Act only implies terms into a *contract*. Where no contract exists, reliance will have to be had on the tortious principles enunciated in *Hedley Byrne & Co Ltd* v *Heller & Partners Ltd* [1964] AC 465.

Implied term about time for performance

Section 14 of the 1982 Act provides:

'(1) Where, under a contract for the supply of a service by a supplier acting in the course of a business, the time for the service to be carried out is not fixed by the contract, left to be fixed in a manner agreed by the contract or determined by the course of dealing between the parties, there is an implied term that the supplier will carry out the service within a reasonable time.

(2) What is a reasonable time is a question of fact.'

This, again, is a codification of the common law. See *Rickards* v *Oppenheim* [1950] 1 KB 616.

Note, the section does not state whether the term is a condition or warranty. That must be inferred from whether the parties intend time to be of the essence. In most commercial contracts, time is of the essence and, therefore, a condition. If, however, a commercial contract did not stipulate dates, it could be argued that the parties could not have intended time to be of prime consideration.

Implied term about consideration

Section 15:

'(1) Where, under a contract for the supply of a service, the consideration for the service is not determined by the contract, left to be determined in a manner agreed by the contract or determined by the course of dealing between the parties, there is an implied term that the party contracting with the supplier will pay a reasonable charge.

(2) What is a reasonable charge is a question of fact.'

Note, that only if consideration is not agreed prior to or concurrent with the entering into the contract, does s15 apply. Quotations given by a tradesman are fixed price contracts, and are not variable upwards or downwards, s15 does not apply. Estimates, however, are just that and if the final charge exceeds the estimate, the receiver of the services is bound only to pay a reasonable price.

Exclusion of implied terms

Section 16:

'(1) Where a right, duty or liability would arise under a contract for the supply of a service by virtue of this part of this Act, it may (subject to subsection (2) below and the

1977 Act) be negatived or varied by express agreement, or by the course of dealing between the parties, or by such usage as bind both parties to the contract.

(2) An express term does not negative a term implied by this Part of this Act unless inconsistent with it.

(3) Nothing in this Part of this Act prejudices –

(a) any rule of law which imposes on the supplier a duty stricter than that imposed by section 13 or 14 above; or

(b) subject to paragraph (a) above, any rule of law whereby any term not inconsistent with this Part of this Act is to be implied in a contract for the supply of a service.

(4) This Part of this Act has effect subject to any other enactment which defines or restrict the rights, duties or liabilities arising in connection with a service of any description.'

Section 16 is self-explanatory. Note that s3 of UCTA 1977 is the provision which concerns Part II of the 1982 Act.

Stewart Gill Ltd v *Horatio Myer & Co Ltd* [1992] 2 WLR 721 shows that if a party seeks to rely on an exclusion clause in a contract for supply of goods and services, then the burden of proof is on that party to show the reasonableness of that exclusion.

20.22 Distance selling

The Consumer Protection (Distance Selling) Regulations 2000 came into force on 31 October 2000. They provide protection for a consumer ('a natural person who, in contracts to which these regulations apply, is acting for purposes which are outside his business') involved in a distance contract ('any contract concerning goods or services concluded between a supplier and a consumer under an organised distance sales or service provision scheme run by the supplier who for the purpose of the contract makes exclusive use of one or more means of distance communication up to and including the moment when the contract is concluded'). In other words, the Regulations apply, eg, where goods or services are purchased by mail order, by telephone or on the Internet.

Amongst other things, the Regulations:

1. require the supplier to give written confirmation of the transaction, including the right to cancel;
2. provide the consumer with a cooling-off period;
3. stipulate that the contract must be performed within 30 days, unless the parties agree otherwise;
4. prohibit the supply of unsolicited goods and services.

20.23 Consumer guarantees

By virtue of the Sale and Supply of Goods to Consumers Regulations 2002, where goods are sold or otherwise supplied to a consumer which are offered with a consumer guarantee, the consumer guarantee takes effect as a contractual obligation. The Regulations set out the requirements for the form and content of consumer guarantees and give powers to enforcement authorities to apply for an injunction against the guarantor in the event of non-compliance.

21

Assignment

21.1 Introduction

21.2 Methods of assignment

21.3 Limits of assignability

21.4 Assignment by operation of law

21.5 Negotiable instruments: a special case

21.1 Introduction

It is a general rule of common law that a contract between two persons cannot confer rights or duties on a stranger to that contract. However, it is possible for one of the parties to the contract to transfer the benefits of that contract to another person by the process of assignment. The question of validity, extent and effect of an assignment was examined by the House of Lords recently in *Investors Compensation Scheme Ltd* v *West Bromwich Building Society* [1998] 1 All ER 98. Interestingly, their Lordships held that a claimant's right to rescission could not be assigned.

For example, A agrees to sell a car to B for £5,000. A may then assign to X the right to receive the money from B. Once the assignment has been effected, X may sue B if he refuses to pay him. For examples of problems concerning assignment see the recent cases of *Linden Gardens Trust* v *Lenesta Sludge Disposals* [1993] 3 WLR 408 and *Pan Ocean Shipping Co Ltd* v *Creditcorp* [1993] 1 Lloyd's Rep 443.

Contractual rights belong to a category of property law known as choses in action:

  ' "Chose in action" is a known legal expression used to describe all personal rights of property which can only be claimed or enforced by action, and not by taking possession.'
  (*Torkington* v *Magee* [1902] 2 KB 427 at 430, per Channell J.)

Choses in action may be legal or equitable, dependent upon whether they were created by legal or equitable rules.

1. Legal choses in action include proprietary rights, such as debts and other contractual rights, policies of insurance, patents, copyrights and bills of lading.
2. Equitable choses in action include rights under a trust and legacies.

21.2 Methods of assignment

The historical evolution of the English law had a profound effect on the development of assignments. Thus it is important to examine the topic under three separate heads, which are common law; equity; statute law.

Common law

Although the common law recognised the right to transfer choses in possession, things that could be physically seized, it did not recognise assignments of choses in action.

At common law it was not possible for A to assign his contractual right against B to X. It was stated that such assignments would lead to 'officious intermeddling' in litigation, which used to constitute a wrong known as maintenance (not to be confused with the right of a divorced spouse to receive financial support from the other partner which also bears the same name).

There were a number of exceptions to this general common law prohibition, the most significant being negotiable instruments (see section 21.5).

There were also a number of alternative methods by which someone who is not a party to the original contract could obtain the right to sue the debtor under the contract.

Power of attorney
The original creditor could make the third party his agent for the purposes of suing the debtor on his behalf. However, this involved a complicated procedure that suffered a number of shortcomings.

Novation
If A wished to transfer his contractual right against B to X, all three of the parties could enter into a new contract, which entirely replaced the original contract, whereby it was agreed that the debt would no longer be owed to A but to X. X had to provide valuable consideration for this contract.

Note that novation requires the agreement of all three of the parties including the debtor, whereas an assignment does not require the agreement of the debtor.

Equity

The failure of common law to recognise assignments of choses in action, particularly contractual rights, was remedied by equity. Equity recognised such assignments and, furthermore, it did not require assignment to be carried out by formal methods – as long as there was a definite intention to carry out an assignment, equity could regard the transaction as valid.

Equity looks to intention rather than to form. However, there was one major exception to this equitable maxim: assignments of equitable interests, such as rights under trusts or legacies, had been in writing. This is now enshrined in s53(1)(c) Law of Property Act 1925.

It is important to determine whether the purported equitable assignment is of an absolute or non-absolute nature.

1. If an assignment is to be absolute, the assignor must transfer the totality of his interest in the chose in action.
2. A non-absolute assignment is where the assignor reserves aspects of the right in the property to himself after the transfer, such as:

    a) co-assignment of part, but not all, of the debt to the assignee. Thus the assignment of only £4,000 of the £5,000 debt will not be an absolute assignment;
    b) a conditional assignment of the debt, whereby it is agreed at the outset that if specified, but unpredictable, events occur, either the assignment will take place, or the assignment will cease, and the rights will be returned to the assignor;
    c) an assignment by way of charge, which does not transfer the whole of the specific fund to the assignee, but merely entitles him to a payment out of a fund.

Although notice of the equitable assignment need not be given to the debtor in order to secure the assignee's rights, it is expedient for the assignee to make certain that such notice has been given. The giving of notice is particularly important if there are a number of competing claims by several purported assignees since, under the rule in *Dearle* v *Hall* (1828), priorities are established according to the chronological order in which these assignees gave notice to the debtor. Thus failure or delay in giving notice may prejudice an assignee's claim.

Furthermore, the giving of consideration by the assignee to the assignor may have an important bearing on the assignment. If the assignor promises to transfer the chose in action to the assignee, but the assignee gives nothing in return this is, in common parlance, a promise to make a gift. Gifts are unenforceable unless they are complete or perfected. Thus until the gift is perfected the donor can change his mind and refuse to make the gift. If the assignee has provided consideration for the promise by the assignor, then the assignment will be as binding as any other contract.

An assignee takes 'subject to equities'. This means that the debtor may use the same defences, whether legal or equitable, against the assignee as would have been available against the assignor. Thus A, a garage owner, undertakes work on B's car; A subsequently assigns the right to collect the money to X. When B is sued for non-payment by X, he may successfully defer the action by pleading that the work performed by A was defective. A claim by a debtor for an unliquidated sum is a counter-claim, a claim by a debtor concerning a liquidated sum is a set-off. Other forms of defence, such as mistake, misrepresentation and defect of title, are also capable of being pleaded by the debtor.

From the above information several propositions may be made.

1. Equitable assignments of equitable choses in action: the assignee can sue in his own name, without joining the assignor. The assignment is subject to equities. Consideration is necessary unless the assignment is complete and perfect.
2. Equitable assignments of legal choses in action: intention to assign is the determining factor:

   a) the assignment is subject to equities;
   b) the assignee must joint the assignor in an action he takes against the debtor, either as co-plaintiff or, if he refuses to be co-plaintiff, as co-defendant;
   c) the assignee must have given consideration to the assignor.

Statute law

The Judicature Act of 1873 removed many of the conflicts between the old style Courts of Common Law and those of Equity. The new High Court administered both systems concurrently. Thus an assignee could sue in the High Court whether the chose was legal or equitable. A general method for assignments was created. This was re-enacted in s136(1) Law of Property Act 1925 which provides:

'Any absolute agreement by writing under the hand of the assignor (not purporting to be by way of charge only) of any debt or other legal thing in action, of which express notice in writing has been given to the debtor, trustee or other person from whom the assignor would have been entitled to claim such a debt or thing in action, is effectual in law (subject to equities having priority over the right of the assignee) to pass and transfer from the date of such notice:
(a) the legal right to such a debt or thing in action;
(b) the legal and other remedies for the same; and
(c) the power to give good discharge for the same without the concurrence of the assignor.'

Therefore, three conditions must be satisfied if the assignment is to be regarded as valid under statute law: it must be absolute; it must be written; and written notice must be given to the debtor.

However, great formality is not required, thus incorrect statements or omissions of the date of the assignment do not invalidate the transaction. Neither is the giving of consideration considered to be a vital essential of a statutory assignment.

It should be noted that equitable assignments may still be possible if the transaction fails to meet all the requirements of s136(1), for example, it is oral, or no written notice has been given to the debtor, or because it is a non-absolute assignment.

21.3 Limits of assignability

Rights cannot be assigned if they offend public policy or if they prejudice the debtor.

Public policy prevents valid assignments of certain contractual rights.

A wife cannot assign maintenance or other payments ordered pursuant to matrimonial proceedings if so doing would leave her without any means of support. See *Watkins* v *Watkins* [1896] P 222. A public officer cannot assign his salary. See *Liverpool Corporation* v *Wright* (1859) 28 LJ Ch 868. Other statutory provisions prevent assignment of payments, such as child benefit or social security payments.

Prejudice to the debtor may invalidate an assignment

Personal contracts

In many contracts, particularly involving simple debt, it makes little difference to the debtor whether he pays the original creditor or the creditor's assignee. However, certain contracts are considered to be 'personal' to the debtor insofar that he will only be required to perform them in favour of his creditor but to no one else, such as the purported assignee of the creditor. It is, for example, the right of the employee to decide who he wishes to work for. See *Noakes* v *Doncaster Amalgamated Collieries Ltd* [1940] AC 1014.

Even contracts for sale of goods may be considered personal since the supplier may carefully choose who he wishes to supply – due to reputation, financial standing or a wealth of similar reasons. Indeed, it is recognised that the contracting parties may even make it a term of their contract that the rights under that contract shall be unassignable.

Maintenance and champerty

Maintenance of a person, by giving them financial assistance to commence an action, and champerty, offering assistance in return for a percentage of any subsequent award of damages, were, until the Criminal Law Act 1967, crimes or torts. However, this Act removed tortious and criminal liability from such actions, but still preserved its contractual implication. Thus if an assignment will, in fact, lead to an 'officious intermeddling in litigation' by someone who should more correctly leave such issues to the original parties to the contract, then the courts may regard this as a bare right to sue, and will refuse to enforce the assignee's rights. The right will be 'bare' if it is not assigned along with some other property right to which it is connected. If, for example, A assigns the right to sue for damages for breach of covenant committed by a tenant to X, but retains the property and lease for himself, such an assignment would be void.

In relation to the assignment of rights under a contract, the law approaches questions of alleged champerty with an eye to the practical realities of the matter, not by way of theory: *Total Liban SA* v *Vitol Energy SA* [2000] 1 All ER 267. In that case a contention that the assignment of rights under a contract was void on the ground of champerty was rejected since, as a matter of practical reality, there was no real likelihood of the assignee achieving double recovery.

Criteria for assignment

The case of *Darlington Borough Council* v *Wiltshier Northern Ltd and Another* [1995] 1 WLR 68, makes it clear that the courts will look favourably on assignment if the parties to the original contract were aware that the contract was for the benefit of a third party and that rights would accrue to the third party. It would be illogical in such circumstances to deny a right of assignment to that third party.

21.4 Assignment by operation of law

The assignments that have been considered are all voluntary assignments of rights by the party's own volition. However, an involuntary assignment of the right to a chose in action may be brought about by operation of law on the death or bankruptcy of one of the contracting parties.

Assignment on death

As a general rule, all contractual rights and duties are transferred to the personal representatives of a deceased's estate. Those personal representatives may sue or be sued on any contract to which the deceased was a party. This rule does not apply to contracts for personal services.

Assignment as a bankruptcy/insolvency

When a debtor is adjudicated bankrupt, his property is vested in the trustee in bankruptcy who must endeavour to secure a fair distribution of the debtor's assets between the creditors of the bankrupt.

21.5 Negotiable instruments: a special case

The process of assignability can be a cumbersome and time-consuming process that is particularly unsuitable if a rapid succession of transactions is to be achieved by using the same chose in action to establish, for example, a long line of credit between, say, merchant bank, commercial bank, customer and subsequent users of the item in question. In order to allow speedy and reliable transactions, the negotiable instrument evolved primarily through the old Law Merchant, and this was readily accepted into the principles of common law and equity.

The more important types of negotiable instrument

A bill of exchange

A bill of exchange is an unconditional order in writing, addressed by one person to another, signed by the person giving it requiring the person to whom it is addressed to pay on demand a sum certain in money to, or to the order of, a specified person, or to bearer, s3(1) Bills of Exchange Act 1882. Bills of exchange are often used to fund international trade transactions.

A cheque

A cheque is a bill of exchange drawn on a banker payable on demand, s73 Bills of Exchange Act 1882.

Promissory notes

These are defined by s83 Bills of Exchange Act 1882, as an unconditional promise, in writing, made by one person to another, signed by the maker, engaging to pay on demand, or at a fixed time or determinable time in the future, a sum certain in money to or to the order of a specified person or to the bearer.

It differs from a bill of exchange in that the maker stands in place of the drawer.

Meaning of negotiability

Negotiable instruments possess special qualities not accorded to transactions that are regulated by the laws pertaining to assignments, namely the following.

Transfer of ownership

The rights of ownership of a negotiable instrument are transferred:

1. where the instrument is drawn payable to order, or is specially indorsed 'pay Smith or order', ownership is transferred by indorsement and delivery to the transferee; and
2. where the instrument is payable to bearer, a bank note, for example, or indorsed in blank by a mere signature on its reverse side, ownership is transferred by mere delivery.

Free from equities

When a negotiable instrument is negotiated, the transferee takes the rights of ownership freed from equities, as long as he is a holder in due course.

Holder may sue in his own name

In the event of the negotiable instrument being dishonoured through non-acceptance or non-payment, the holder may sue all previous parties to the instrument be they the drawer, acceptor or indorsers of the bills who transferred the indorsement and delivery.

It is surprising that although the common law refused to accept assignment due to the prospect of officious intermeddling in litigation, it readily accepted the speedier and more refined process of negotiability – largely due to the necessity of commercial practice.

Index

Law Update 2004 edition – due March 2004

An annual review of the most recent developments in specific legal subject areas, useful for law students at degree and professional levels, others with law elements in their courses and also practitioners seeking a quick update.

Published around March every year, the Law Update summarises the major legal developments during the course of the previous year. In conjunction with Old Bailey Press textbooks it gives the student a significant advantage when revising for examinations.

Contents
Administrative Law • Civil and Criminal Procedure • Commercial Law • Company Law • Conflict of Laws • Constitutional Law • Contract Law • Conveyancing • Criminal Law • Criminology • Employment Law • English and European Legal Systems • Equity and Trusts • European Union Law • Evidence • Family Law • Jurisprudence • Land Law • Law of International Trade • Public International Law • Revenue Law • Succession • Tort

For further information on contents or to place an order, please contact:

Mail Order
Old Bailey Press
at Holborn College
Woolwich Road
Charlton
London
SE7 8LN

Telephone No: 020 8317 6039
Fax No: 020 8317 6004
Website: www.oldbaileypress.co.uk

ISBN 1 85836 518 X
Soft cover 246 x 175 mm
400 pages approx
£10.95
Due March 2004

Unannotated Cracknell's Statutes for use in Examinations

New Editions of Cracknell's Statutes

£11.95 due 2003

Cracknell's Statutes provide a comprehensive series of essential statutory provisions for each subject. Amendments are consolidated, avoiding the need to cross-refer to amending legislation. Unannotated, they are suitable for use in examinations, and provide the precise wording of vital Acts of Parliament for the diligent student.

Constitutional and Administrative Law
ISBN: 1 85836 511 2

Equity and Trusts
ISBN: 1 85836 508 2

Contract, Tort and Remedies
ISBN: 1 85836 507 4

Land: The Law of Real Property
ISBN: 1 85836 509 0

English Legal System
ISBN: 1 85836 510 4

Law of International Trade
ISBN: 1 85836 512 0

For further information on contents or to place an order, please contact:

Mail Order
Old Bailey Press
at Holborn College
Woolwich Road
Charlton
London
SE7 8LN

Telephone No: 020 8317 6039
Fax No: 020 8317 6004
Website: www.oldbaileypress.co.uk

Suggested Solutions to Past Examination Questions 2001–2002

The Suggested Solutions series provides examples of full answers to the questions regularly set by examiners. Each suggested solution has been broken down into three stages: general comment, skeleton solution and suggested solution. The examination questions included within the text are taken from past examination papers set by the London University. The full opinion answers will undoubtedly assist you with your research and further your understanding and appreciation of the subject in question.

Only £6.95 due November 2003

Company Law
ISBN: 1 85836 519 8

Evidence
ISBN: 1 85836 521 X

Employment Law
ISBN: 1 85836 520 1

Family Law
ISBN: 1 85836 525 2

European Union Law
ISBN: 1 85836 524 4

For further information on contents or to place an order, please contact:

Mail Order
Old Bailey Press
at Holborn College
Woolwich Road
Charlton
London
SE7 8LN

Telephone No: 020 8317 6039
Fax No: 020 8317 6004
Website: www.oldbaileypress.co.uk

Old Bailey Press

The Old Bailey Press integrated student law library is tailor-made to help you at every stage of your studies from the preliminaries of each subject through to the final examination. The series of Textbooks, Revision WorkBooks, 150 Leading Cases and Cracknell's Statutes are interrelated to provide you with a comprehensive set of study materials.

You can buy Old Bailey Press books from your University Bookshop, your local Bookshop, direct using this form, or you can order a free catalogue of our titles from the address shown overleaf.

The following subjects each have a Textbook, 150 Leading Cases/Casebook, Revision WorkBook and Cracknell's Statutes unless otherwise stated.

Administrative Law
Commercial Law
Company Law
Conflict of Laws
Constitutional Law
Conveyancing (Textbook and 150 Leading Cases)
Criminal Law
Criminology (Textbook and Sourcebook)
Employment Law (Textbook and Cracknell's Statutes)
English and European Legal Systems
Equity and Trusts
Evidence
Family Law
Jurisprudence: The Philosophy of Law (Textbook, Sourcebook and
    Revision WorkBook)
Land: The Law of Real Property
Law of International Trade
Law of the European Union
Legal Skills and System
    (Textbook)
Obligations: Contract Law
Obligations: The Law of Tort
Public International Law
Revenue Law (Textbook,
    Revision WorkBook and
    Cracknell's Statutes)
Succession

Mail order prices:	
Textbook	£15.95
150 Leading Cases	£11.95
Revision WorkBook	£9.95
Cracknell's Statutes	£11.95
Suggested Solutions 1999–2000	£6.95
Suggested Solutions 2000–2001	£6.95
Suggested Solutions 2001–2002	£6.95
Law Update 2003	£10.95
Law Update 2004	£10.95

Please note details and prices are subject to alteration.

To complete your order, please fill in the form below:

Module	Books required	Quantity	Price	Cost
		Postage		
		TOTAL		

For Europe, add 15% postage and packing (£20 maximum).
For the rest of the world, add 40% for airmail.

ORDERING

By telephone to Mail Order at 020 8317 6039, with your credit card to hand.

By fax to 020 8317 6004 (giving your credit card details).

Website: www.oldbaileypress.co.uk

By post to: Mail Order, Old Bailey Press at Holborn College, Woolwich Road, Charlton, London, SE7 8LN.

When ordering by post, please enclose full payment by cheque or banker's draft, or complete the credit card details below. You may also order a free catalogue of our complete range of titles from this address.

We aim to despatch your books within 3 working days of receiving your order.

Name

Address

Postcode   Telephone

Total value of order, including postage: £

I enclose a cheque/banker's draft for the above sum, or

charge my   ☐ Access/Mastercard   ☐ Visa   ☐ American Express
Card number

☐☐☐☐ ☐☐☐☐ ☐☐☐☐ ☐☐☐☐

Expiry date   ☐☐☐☐

Signature: ....Date: ....